SECOND EDITION

HOMELAND SECURITY AND TERRORISM

Larry K. Gaines

California State University at San Bernardino

Janine Kremling

California State University at San Bernardino

Victor E. Kappeler

Eastern Kentucky University

330 Hudson Street, NY NY 10013

Vice President, Portfolio Management: Andrew Gilfillan
Portfolio Manager: Gary Bauer
Editorial Assistant: Lynda Cramer
Field Marketing Manager: Bob Nisbet
Product Marketing Manager: Heather Taylor
Director, Digital Studio and Content Production: Brian Hyland
Managing Producer: Jennifer Sargunar
Content Producer: Rinki Kaur
Manager, Rights Management: Johanna Burke
Operations Specialist: Deidra Smith
Creative Digital Lead: Mary Siener
Managing Producer, Digital Studio: Autumn Benson
Content Producer, Digital Studio: Maura Barclay
Full-Service Management and Composition: Integra Software Services Pvt. Ltd.
Full-Service Project Manager: Yohalakshmi Segar
Cover Design: Studio Montage
Cover Art (or Cover Photo): nirut123rf/123RF
Printer/Binder: LSC Communications, Inc.
Cover Printer: Phoenix Color/Hagerstown
Text Font: Times LT Pro

Library of Congress Cataloging-in-Publication Data

Names: Gaines, Larry K., author. | Kappeler, Victor E., author.
Title: Homeland security / Larry K. Gaines, California State University at San Bernardino, Victor E. Kappeler, Eastern Kentucky University.
Description: Second edition. | Boston : Prentice Hall, [2019]
Identifiers: LCCN 2017052302| ISBN 9780134549170 | ISBN 0134549171
Subjects: LCSH: United States. Office of Homeland Security. | Terrorism—United States—Prevention. | National security—United States. | Internal security—United States.
Classification: LCC HV6432.4 .G35 2019 | DDC 363.3250973–dc23 LC record available at https://lccn.loc.gov/2017052302

1 18

ISBN-10: 0-13-454917-1
ISBN-13: 978-0-13-454917-0

Dedication

This book is dedicated to the fine men and women in the military, federal agencies, state agencies, and local governments who protect us.

Contents

Preface

New to This Edition

Updated features and figures

- New Critical Infrastructure Protection Plan by the U.S. government
- Updated cybercrime and cybersecurity analysis
- Focus on ISIS terrorist activities and financial activities
- Updated analysis of disaster response system (Federal Emergency Management Agency)
- Analysis of current immigration and border security issues

On September 11, 2001, operatives of the terrorist group al Qaeda attacked the World Trade Center in New York City and the Pentagon in Arlington, Virginia, using hijacked passenger airliners. It was a wakeup call for America. It was the most significant terrorist attack on the United States, and it had a quashing impact on the country and the public psyche. Terrorism has existed throughout the world since there were nation-states, but the 9/11 attacks made Americans acutely aware of the problem and the United States' vulnerability. Although there had been numerous minor terrorist attacks in the United States, primarily by right-wing and left-wing radicals, no previous attacks came close to the magnitude of the 9/11 attacks.

President George W. Bush immediately took action. The United States invaded Afghanistan, the originating country of the attacks, closely examined our intelligence apparatus, and created the Department of Homeland Security. Although the U.S. government had long been involved in counterterrorism, the 9/11 attacks spawned a new era in which homeland security became a primary governmental objective. As with any new initiative, there were mistakes and much of what we did was trial and error. Nonetheless, we now are engaged in homeland security, and we are constantly making adjustments so that we can better deter attacks and respond to any attacks that might not be prevented. Thus, homeland security is a work in progress.

This text examines our efforts to secure our homeland, and it critically examines some of the problems that have occurred in the past. Since homeland security primarily is a response to the threat of terrorism, this threat is intertwined throughout the text. In order to understand homeland security, one must first understand the threat and operations of terrorist organizations. To a large extent, the organization and operation of homeland security are dictated by the terrorist threat. We therefore attempt to address both concerns so that the reader has a firm grasp of both terrorism and homeland security.

Both of these are complex issues with many facets to each. Homeland security includes a number of agencies within the Department of Homeland Security as well as agencies in other federal departments and state and local agencies. Homeland security has had an impact on every federal department as new initiatives and mandates have been developed. As an example, the creation of the Department of Homeland Security was the result of moving 22 agencies from other federal departments into the new department. The Department of Defense and the 16 agencies in our intelligence community are now more actively involved in counterterrorism. More federal agencies are involved in counterterrorism than in addressing America's crime problem. Homeland security is a monumental undertaking.

▶ Organization of the Text

The text contains 14 chapters organized into four major parts examining a variety of topics and issues that are important in understanding homeland security and terrorism. Each chapter begins with learning objectives that provide a roadmap for the chapter. Additionally, key terms are provided. The key terms represent important concepts or ideas that are critical to understanding the chapter material. Embedded in each chapter are HS Web Links and HS Analysis Boxes. The HS Web Links point to materials the reader can access in order to clarify points or obtain additional information about an area in the chapter. The HS Analysis Boxes are analytical situations that apply information in the chapter. They are designed to get the reader to analyze and critically think about important problems or issues in homeland security and terrorism. Discussion questions are also provided to assist the reader in identifying some of the key issues in each chapter. Finally, each chapter contains an extensive up-to-date reference list. These references serve to provide additional information about specific topics in the chapter.

▶ Part I: The Foundation for Homeland Security

Part I provides an in-depth foundation for understanding homeland security. Homeland security encompasses a wide range of agencies and activities. The chapters in Part I examine the various activities that constitute homeland security, the various agencies involved in securing our homeland, critical infrastructure or potential terrorist targets, and the laws that are used to counterterrorism.

Chapter 1: Introduction to Homeland Security

Chapter 1 provides a foundation for understanding the mechanics of homeland security. Essentially, homeland security was developed using two important documents. The first was the 9/11 Commission Report, which provided a great deal of information about our homeland security shortcomings. These shortcomings later evolved into objectives for government homeland security operations. For the most part, they focused on our intelligence establishment and our response to the 9/11 attacks. The second document was the *National Strategy for Homeland Security* developed by the Office of Homeland Security in 2002. The *National Strategy* was expansive in that it detailed a number of areas in need of development. The areas ranged from prevention to recovery. It resulted in a number of new programs and agency requirements.

Chapter 2: The Homeland Security Apparatus

Chapter 2 examines the various agencies involved in homeland security. When the Department of Homeland Security was organized, 22 agencies from other federal departments were transferred into the new department. This resulted in a great deal of confusion as agencies assumed new responsibilities in addition to old mandates. Also, a great deal of politics was involved in the creation of the department. Members of Congress and the administration in the White House had differing ideas about how homeland security should function. This led to a number of problems and a waste of energy and time. When we consider homeland security, we often focus exclusively on the federal government. However, if a terrorist attack occurs, it will directly affect a local jurisdiction and a state. Homeland security at the local and state levels is also examined in this chapter. It provides a comprehensive overview of agencies and their relationships.

Chapter 3: Overview of National Infrastructure Protection

Terrorists focus on targets. These targets are critical infrastructure and key assets. Critical infrastructure refers to industries, business, and activities that are of great importance to our economy and safety. Critical infrastructure includes mass transit, the Internet, banking, criminal justice agencies, businesses, and public gatherings such as the Super Bowl or college and high school sports events. Key assets refer to government monuments such as the Washington Monument or icons such as the Golden Gate Bridge. Their destruction might not result in a significant loss of lives or monetary loss, but it would certainly have a psychological impact on our country. The National Infrastructure Protection Plan was developed to provide guidance on protecting our infrastructure and key assets. This plan is examined in depth in Chapter 3.

Chapter 4: Legal Aspects of Homeland Security

The United States is a democracy that is guided by laws. This premise separates us from many other countries in the world. As such, the mechanics of combating terrorism must be grounded in law. A number of laws have been passed that assist us with counterterrorism. Additionally, presidents have signed presidential directives and presidential orders that are legally binding and are used to supplement laws. The directives and orders of Presidents George H. W. Bush, Bill Clinton, George W. Bush, Barack Obama, and Donald Trump are discussed. Additionally, important antiterrorism laws such as the USA PATRIOT Act are examined. This discussion demonstrates the complicated nature of counterterrorism. We have laws ranging in topics from terrorist finances to weapons of mass destruction to immigration policy. These laws and presidential directives and orders provide a comprehensive legal framework for protecting our country.

▶ Part II: Homeland Security and Terrorism

Part II focuses primarily on terrorism. Terrorism is the primary justification for homeland security—it drives this important governmental initiative. In order to develop an effective homeland security apparatus, it is important to understand the nature of terrorism. The chapters in Part II provide this foundation by defining terrorism and examining the various terrorist groups and their activities.

Chapter 5: Political and Social Foundations of Terrorism

If effective counterterrorism policies and operations are to be implemented, it is critical that we understand terrorism. First, this chapter defines terrorism and distinguishes it from other types of conflicts. The chapter provides a history of terrorism. Many people today think that terrorism is a new phenomenon; however, it has existed as long as there have been nation-states. It is used by countries and political or religious groups. Essentially, terrorism is used to undermine groups involved in a particular religion or countries that are seen as enemies as exemplified by al Qaeda's attacks on the United States. This chapter provides a political and social understanding of terrorist groups in terms of their formation and activities.

Chapter 6: The Nature and Geography of Terrorist Groups, State Sponsors of Terror, and Safe Havens

Today, many Americans focus exclusively on the terrorists who exist in the Middle East, since this is where several attacks on Americans have originated. Indeed, there are numerous terrorist groups in that part of the world. However, terrorism is not the exclusive domain of the Middle East. There are terrorist groups throughout the world. This chapter addresses the primary and active terrorist groups in terms of their activities and objectives. The discussion demonstrates that there are all sorts of groups and motivations. Additionally, several terrorist groups operate in the United States. These groups are identified and discussed in terms of their recent terrorist activities.

Chapter 7: Transnational Organized Crime and Terrorism

Transnational organized crime refers to organized criminal syndicates that operate across international borders. They represent large criminal organizations that are involved in a variety of criminal activities. They are a threat to countries since they depend on corruption and violence to achieve their illegal ends. We often think about terrorism and organized crime as two distinct problems. However, it should be noted that transnational organized crime groups exist in many of the same areas where terrorist groups exist. Terrorists often use organized crime groups to facilitate their attacks, and transnational organized crime groups sometimes use terrorist groups to accomplish their criminal ends. The relationship between transnational organized crime groups and terrorist groups is particularly problematic in that these relationships can facilitate more deadly attacks and more caustic criminal operations. We must focus on these relationships if we are to effectively deal with both groups. This chapter provides an understanding of them, their activities, and possible countermeasures to use against them.

▶ Part III: Defeating Terrorists and Their Activities

When considering counterterrorism, we too often focus exclusively on the battlefield. However, the battlefield is only one aspect or area of concern. Homeland security requires a full, direct attack on a variety of fronts. The chapters in this part examine several important issues, including intelligence, weapons of mass destruction, cyber terrorism, and terrorist finances. Each of these areas must be considered in developing effective counterterrorism measures.

Chapter 8: Intelligence and Counterintelligence and Terrorism

In the past, intelligence focused on countries and their activities. For example, during the Cold War, our intelligence community closely monitored the activities of the Soviet Union and the countries that were part of the Soviet bloc or were aligned with the Soviet Union. Today, we still collect intelligence about different countries' activities, but at the same time, we are also concerned with the activities of radical or terrorist groups that may reside in those countries. Moreover, since terrorists have likely infiltrated our borders, we must monitor activities in the United States. There are 16 agencies comprising the intelligence community. They have specific tasks and areas of responsibilities, but each now focuses on counterterrorism. Each agency's activities are addressed in this chapter.

Chapter 9: Homeland Security and Weapons of Mass Destruction

The most significant threat to our nation is weapons of mass destruction. The deployment of such a weapon could result in massive casualties and reverberating economic effects. This chapter provides a history of weapons of mass destruction. It also provides a discussion of each type: chemical, biological, and radiological or nuclear. Each type of weapon presents unique challenges in terms of prevention and response. The chapter examines the likelihood of their deployment in terms of constraints on terrorists. Some of the countermeasures are also discussed.

Chapter 10: Cybercrime and Terrorism

Cybercrime is the fastest-growing criminal activity in the United States and the world. It consists of cyber fraud and identity theft. A number of homeland security experts advise that cyber terrorism is second only to weapons of mass destruction in terms of threat. In this chapter, we distinguish among cybercrime, cyber terrorism, and cyber warfare. Although each is associated with cyber space, each is unique in presenting different challenges. There is sparse evidence that there has been extensive cyber terrorism. However, cyber warfare is increasingly being used by countries or governments against other countries and political groups. Finally, terrorists are extensively using the Internet to facilitate their activities. They use the web to espouse propaganda, recruit new members, solicit donations, and generate support for their activities. A number of terrorist groups have websites in a varicty of languages. Such websites must be monitored as they often provide intelligence about different groups' activities.

Chapter 11: Terrorist Financing

One of the issues examined by the 9/11 Commission was terrorist financing. The Islamic State, al Qaeda, and other terrorist operatives used a variety of mechanisms to funnel money to the 9/11 hijackers. Since then, our policy has been to attempt to cut off funding to terrorist groups whenever possible in an effort to starve them or restrict their activities. The United States and other countries have implemented laws and policies designed to prevent terrorist financing. This chapter examines the methods by which terrorist groups secure financing. Raising money, moving money, and banking money are discussed. It is interesting that terrorists use a variety of mechanisms. The chapter also examines countermeasures that have been implemented. Special attention is given to Saudi Arabia since a substantial amount of terrorist financing originates there. Finally, the financial needs of terrorist groups are discussed.

▶ Part IV: Homeland Security's Response to Terrorist Threats

Part IV examines the endgame in homeland security. It examines several topics, including immigration and border control, the response to homeland security incidents, and policing and homeland security. Border control and immigration are hotly contested political issues that have implications for homeland security in terms of preventing terrorists from entering the United States. This part also examines the framework for responding to terrorist attacks, including the role of the police and counterterrorism.

Chapter 12: Border Security and Immigration

Border security and immigration have become important political issues as a result of the threat of terrorism and the number of illegal aliens coming to our country. It is important to realize that these are two distinct issues that must be addressed. This chapter examines patterns of immigration in terms of the numbers of illegal immigrates and their points of origin. The methods by which we have attempted to seal our borders and their effectiveness are examined. It is noted that a number of people from a variety of countries have entered the United States illegally across our southern and northern borders. As such, border control policies are discussed in some detail. The United States has implemented a number of programs to better screen people, vehicles, and cargo entering our country. These programs are examined.

Chapter 13: The Response to Homeland Security Incidents

It is important that we have the capacity and organization to respond to any homeland security incident. The response to Hurricane Katrina is examined, since this event represents one of the largest disasters in our history, and lessons have been learned from the response. A delayed, inadequate response to a similar event likely would result in a larger number of casualties and more destruction. As such, the federal government has developed a number of plans that serve as a template for response. The plans integrate federal, state, and local resources. These plans are discussed in detail.

Chapter 14: Homeland Security and Policing

Chapter 14 examines the police in terms of their homeland security role. Any incident or terrorist attack will occur in a local community. As such, the police will be the first responders to the incident. The local police also play an important role in preventing terrorism by collecting information about activities and people in the community—police officers gather locally based intelligence. Fusion centers and intelligence-led policing are examined, as these are the primary programs used in policing to gather terror-related intelligence. Police organization is discussed since a number of police departments have developed homeland security units and made other alterations to their departments' structure. The importance of community policing relative to counterterrorism is examined. The special case of New York City is examined since that city has been attacked twice by terrorists and likely will be a target in the future.

▶ Instructor Supplements

Instructor's Manual with Test Bank. Includes content outlines for classroom discussion, teaching suggestions, and answers to selected end-of-chapter questions from the text. This also contains a Word document version of the test bank.

TestGen. This computerized test generation system gives you maximum flexibility in creating and administering tests on paper, electronically, or online. It provides state-of-the-art features for viewing and editing test bank questions, dragging a selected question into a test you are creating, and printing sleek, formatted tests in a variety of layouts. Select test items from test banks included with TestGen for quick test creation, or write your own questions from scratch. TestGen's random generator provides the option to display different text or calculated number values each time questions are used.

PowerPoint Presentations. Our presentations are clear and straightforward. Photos, illustrations, charts, and tables from the book are included in the presentations when applicable.

To access supplementary materials online, instructors need to request an instructor access code. Go to **www.pearsonhighered.com/irc**, where you can register for an instructor access code. Within 48 hours after registering, you will receive a confirming e-mail, including an instructor access code. Once you have received your code, go to the site and log on for full instructions on downloading the materials you wish to use.

Alternate Versions

eBooks. This text is also available in multiple eBook formats. These are an exciting new choice for students looking to save money. As an alternative to purchasing the printed textbook, students can purchase an electronic version of the same content. With an eTextbook, students can search the text, make notes online, print out reading assignments that incorporate lecture notes, and bookmark important passages for later review. For more information, visit your favorite online eBook reseller or visit **www.mypearsonstore.com.**

Acknowledgments

We thank the following individuals for reviewing the manuscript and making helpful comments:

Randal Davis, Santa Ana; David MacDonald, Eastfield College; Judith Matlin, Brown Mackie College; Carlos Parker, Cumberland County College; Russ Pomrenke, Gwinnett Technical College; Jennifer Estis-Sumerel, Itawamba Community College; Danny Davis, Keiser University; Vanessa Escalante, LA College International; Mohamad A. Khatibloo, Westwood College/AITA Colleges; John Brian Murphy, Goodwin College; Bobby B. Polk, Metropolitan Community College; Paul Scarborough, Sanford Brown College; Paul Scauzillo, Platt College; David Sexton, LA College International/State Center Community College District; Barbara J. Smith, Metropolitan Community College; and Joel Woods, ACR-Clawson.

About the Authors

Larry Gaines I am a professor of criminal justice at California State University, San Bernardino. Additionally, I am a former police officer and a former president of the Academy of Criminal Justice Sciences. During my academic career, I have taught a variety of courses in the areas of policing, drugs, gangs, and homeland security. I have authored a number of books in these areas. I am particularly interested in homeland security as the threats to our homeland are constantly evolving resulting in our having to closely monitor internal threats as well as threats and problems emanating across the globe. This results in the United States needing flexible homeland security policies and being able to act on a moment's notice. This book is our attempt to clarify the issues and provide information to the thousands of men and women who are involved in homeland security.

Janine Kremling I am an associate professor at California State University, San Bernardino, and have taught a wide variety of classes, such as transnational crime, which includes components on homeland security and terrorism. Students need a textbook that they can read and understand, one that helps them to organize the information, challenges them to think about the information, and assists them in studying. A well-written book can accomplish all of these goals and even help the students to think about their learning and studying skills and to improve them. I have published three textbooks: *Cyberspace, Cybersecurity, and Cybercrime* (2017) with Amanda Sharp-Parker, *Why Students Resist Learning* (2016) with Anton Tolman, and I have coauthored the book *Drugs, Crime, and Justice* (2014) with Larry Gaines.

Victor E. Kappeler is Dean and Foundation Professor of the College of Justice and Safety at Eastern Kentucky University. He is recognized as a leading scholar in such fields as policing, media, and the social construction of crime, and police civil liability, among other related fields. Dr. Kappeler continues to provide in-service training for police officers and is well published in professional areas of policing. Among many other honors, Kappeler received the 2006 Cabinet for Justice and Public Safety Award for Academic Excellence and the 2005 Outstanding Criminal Justice Alumnus Award from Sam Houston State University, where he earned his doctoral degree, and the Lifetime Achievement Award from the American Society of Criminology's Division on Critical Criminology.

1 Introduction to Homeland Security

LEARNING OBJECTIVES

1. *Discuss the impact of the 9/11 attacks on the United States and its citizens.*
2. *Know the mission and goals of homeland security.*
3. *Know the extent and meaning of homeland security, given that it has a number of definitions.*
4. *Understand the findings and implications of the 9/11 Commission Report.*
5. *Know the direction of homeland security as articulated in the National Strategy for Homeland Security.*

Key Terms

Fear of terrorism
Homeland security
Resilience
Disasters
Hazards
National Commission on Terrorist Attacks upon the United States
National Strategy for Homeland Security
Dual use analysis
Smart borders
Enhanced Border Security and Visa Entry Act
Counterterrorism
Joint Terrorism Task Forces
National Infrastructure Protection Plan
Select Agent Program
National incident management system
Radio inoperability
Push packs
Northern Command

▶ Introduction

The September 11, 2001, attacks on the World Trade Center in New York City and the Pentagon in northern Virginia altered the American political landscape. The attacks resulted in 3,030 deaths and 2,337 people were injured. Moreover, 343 firefighters and 75 police officers were killed while responding to the aftermath of the tragedy. The event had a significant impact on politics. National security and the threat of terrorism became the most prominent issues. The 9/11 attacks affected business. For example, several of the major airlines subsequently declared Chapter 11 bankruptcy. Restrictions were placed on international commerce, and foreign travel into the United States was restricted and became more difficult for many.

Crime Type	2014	2003
Being a Victim of Identity Theft	69	NA
Home Burglarized When Not at Home	45	48
Having Car Stolen or Burglarized	42	45
Home Burglarized When at Home	30	30
Have Child Physically Harmed while Attending School	31	35
Getting Mugged	31	28
Being a Victim of Terrorism	28	36
Being Attacked while Driving Your Car	20	26
Being Sexually Assaulted	18	23
Getting Murdered	18	18
Being a Victim of a Hate Crime	18	17
Being Assaulted or Killed by a Co-Worker or Other Employee Where You Work	7	9

FIGURE 1-1 Fear of Crime in the United States: Comparison between 2003 and 2014 (Percentages)

Source: Adopted from: University of Albany (2004) Sourcebook of Criminal Justice Statistics. www.albany.edu/sourcebook/pdf/t2392011.pdf (Accessed April 3, 2004)

Since the 9/11 attacks, the threat of terrorism has constantly been reinforced. In 2013, two brothers, Dzhokhar Tsarnaev and Tamerlan Tsarnaev, exploded two bombs at the finish line of the Boston Marathon, killing three people and injuring more than 180 others. Additionally, each year the Federal Bureau of Investigation (FBI) makes numerous arrests for terrorism-related offenses, thereby foiling attacks. For example, Inserra and Phillips (2015) identified 67 different plots that were uncovered and foiled by the FBI. The sporadic attacks and the constant discovery of plots keep terrorism in the forefront of homeland security measures.

The 9/11 attacks changed the American psyche. The United States became acutely aware that the world could be a dangerous place, and that the country was not immune from attacks originating on foreign soil; the United States was no different from many other countries that had experienced acts of terrorism. **Fear of terrorism** became a critical political and social issue. To some extent, the level of fear was stoked by the federal government's color-coded alert system, which was repeatedly broadcast and reported by the news media. Fear of a terrorist attack, however, took on new proportions. For example, in 2003, in a national crime survey, fear of being a victim of terrorism ranked third behind residential burglary and theft of one's auto, as displayed in Figure 1-1 ■.

The level of fear of being a victim of a terrorist attack diminished slightly between 2003 and 2014, but nonetheless, 28 percent of Americans polled stated that it created fear. It is interesting that in recent times there had been only a few terrorist attacks in the United States and only two perpetrated by terrorists from outside the country (both World Trade Center attacks), but the degree of fear relative to that of a common crime remains quite high. For example, although it varies from year to year, according to FBI UCR statistics, there are approximately 14,000 homicides a year (FBI, 2015), a crime significantly more prevalent than terrorism; but fear of terrorist victimization was rated much higher in 2003 and 2014. Realistically, the probability of a U.S. citizen being killed or injured as a result

HS ANALYSIS BOX 1-1

It is curious that fear of being a victim of a terrorist attack is quite high in comparison to the fear of other crimes that are more common. Many of these crimes are serious. Fear of crime and drugs has been a leading political and media phenomenon for several decades. Why do you think that fear of a terrorist attack is so high?

of a terrorist attack is quite low compared to all other crimes, and people are more likely to be killed in an automobile crash as compared to a terrorist attack. For instance, the Insurance Institute for Highway Safety reports that in 2015 there were a total of 32,166 fatal car accidents in which 35,092 people died (2017).

Sporadic and isolated terrorist events have occurred in the United States in the past, but they, for the most part, were homegrown. In the 1960s and 1970s, left-wing groups protesting the Vietnam War and various social issues were involved in a number of activities that today might be characterized as terrorist acts. These included bombings, kidnappings, bank robberies, and acts of sabotage. The most notable of these groups was the Symbionese Liberation Army, which, in addition to committing robberies and attacks on the police, kidnapped newspaper heiress Patty Hearst, who later became a part of the group and participated in several of their crimes. Most Americans viewed these acts as nothing more than common crimes. Terrorism was not part of the psychological equation.

Terrorism remained at the forefront of the nation's security agenda after the 9/11 attacks. The FBI and other law enforcement agencies have made numerous arrests of would-be terrorists who were plotting attacks or who were conspiring to aid terrorists. A number of attacks have been successful, including four where there were large number of casualties: the Fort Hood shooting where Nidal Malik Hassan, an army major, shot and

Alfred P. Murrah Federal Building after the bombing in 1995
FEMA Photo Library.

killed 13 people and wounded 32 others while shouting "Allahu Akbar" as he fired; the Boston Marathon attack in 2013 where two brothers, Dzhokhar and Tamerlan Tsarnaev, exploded two makeshift pressure cooker bombs at the finish line of the marathon, killing three people and injuring 260 others; in 2015, Mohammad Abdulazeez shot at a military recruiting center in a Chattanooga strip mall killing four marines and a sailor; and in San Bernardino, California, in 2015, a husband and wife team, Syed Rizman Farook and Tashfeen Malik, killed 14 people and wounded 21 others at a Christmas party given by one of Farook's co-workers. There have been no other attacks of the magnitude of the 9/11 attacks, but the specter of terrorism is ever present.

► The United States and Terrorist Attacks

HS Web link: To learn more about the Oklahoma City Bombing and Timothy McVeigh, go to http://www.law.umkc.edu/faculty/projects/ftrials/mcveigh/mcveightrial.html.

The most significant terrorist attack in the United States prior to the 9/11 attacks was the 1995 Oklahoma City bombing. Timothy McVeigh and Terry Nichols, using a truckload of fertilizer blew up the Alfred P. Murrah Federal Building, killing 168 and injuring 674 people (Michel and Herbeck, 2001). This attack was perpetrated by U.S. right-wing extremists, and although most people were appalled by the act, it did not have a lasting impact on American perceptions of safety or on the political landscape. It was viewed as an anomaly or common crime. There was no rush to increase the levels of homeland security. There was little or no public discourse about targeting or monitoring extremist groups to prevent future attacks.

Prior to 9/11, the only terrorist attack on American soil perpetrated by offenders from another country was the first World Trade Center attack on February 26, 1993. Ramzi Yousef and several coconspirators detonated a bomb made from 500 pounds of urea nitrate-hydrogen. The bomb was planted in the North Tower parking garage with the intent of destroying the North Tower and causing it to collapse or topple onto the South Tower, knocking it down (Wright, 2006). The plan did not succeed, but the explosion resulted in the deaths of 6 people and 1,042 were injured. Even though the 1993 attack was significant in terms of loss of life, injuries, and destruction, it had little impact on the American people or U.S. policy. Again, the terrorist act was treated as an anomaly and a crime. It was not seen as a wakeup call.

Previously, Middle Eastern terrorists had staged attacks against American interests in other parts of the world. In October 2000, al Qaeda terrorists attacked the USS *Cole* in Aden Harbor, Yemen, while the ship made a routine fuel stop. The terrorists approached the ship in a small boat and exploded a large bomb once they were in close proximity to the ship. The explosion resulted in 17 sailors being killed and 39 others being injured. Al Qaeda had previously perpetrated two other attacks. On August 7, 1998, al Qaeda operatives used car bombs to attack the U.S. embassies in Dar es Salaam, Tanzania, and Nairobi, Kenya. The bombings were coordinated and exploded almost simultaneously. In Dar es Salaam, 11 people were killed and 85 injured, and in Nairobi, 212 people, including 12 Americans, were killed and an estimated 4,000 people were injured. Osama bin Laden took credit for the bombings, stating that they were a response to the U.S. invasion of Somalia (Wright, 2006).

HS Web Link: To learn more about the Pan Am Flight 103 bombing, go to http://history1900s.about.com/od/1980s/a/flight103.htm.

The deadliest terrorist attack on Americans prior to the 9/11 attacks occurred in 1988 when terrorists planted explosives on a Pan Am flight 103 leaving London's Heathrow International Airport destined for New York. The Boeing 747 exploded and crashed in Lockerbie, Scotland. All 243 passengers and 16 crewmembers were killed. One hundred and eighty-nine of the victims were American (Emerson and Duffy, 1990). Several years later, Abdel Basset Ali al-Megrahi, a Libyan intelligence officer, was convicted of the crime. Suffering from terminal cancer, he was released from a Scottish prison and returned to Libya in August 2009. The release and his homecoming were extensively covered by the American media and caused outrage in the United States.

Historically, small, isolated groups with the wherewithal to engineer a few isolated events or attacks have initiated terrorist activities. Many of the attacks were overseas, such as the embassy bombings and the attack on the USS *Cole*; therefore, they raised little interest among the American people. Many Americans saw these events as isolated "foreign problems" and not constant threats. The 9/11 attacks, however, were prosecuted by an outside terrorist group that had international standing, support, funding, and a history of attacking Americans. As one politician summed it up, historically, the United States was protected by friendly neighbors to the north and south and by oceans on the east and west (see Clarke, 2008). Until the two World Trade Center attacks and the attack on the Pentagon, Americans had not experienced an attack from an outside enemy since Pearl Harbor at the beginning of World War II. Previous to that, the last attack on American soil by another country occurred during the War of 1812.

The 9/11 attacks resulted in new thinking at all levels of government. President George W. Bush immediately went to war. He declared a "war on terrorism." As part of

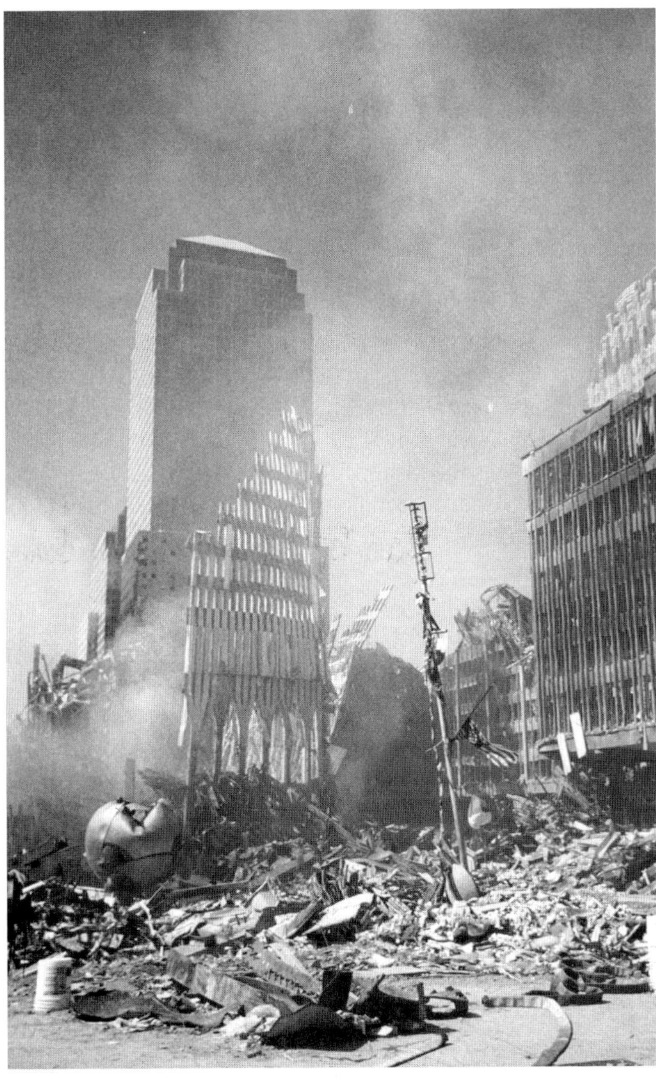

World Trade Center after the 9/11 attack
FEMA Photo Library.

that war, he ordered American troops to invade Afghanistan and Iraq. The 9/11 attacks were said to have originated from Afghanistan, and the Bush administration advanced the idea that Saddam Hussein, the leader of Iraq, was amassing weapons of mass destruction (WMDs) and would provide them to terrorists to attack the United States. While engaged in overseas military operations, the public was told it faced the possibility of a "shadow enemy" within the United States. The nation had to be prepared to thwart an enemy attack on American soil and, if not successful in this endeavor, preparation needed to be made to adequately respond to the consequences of an attack. This is the essence of homeland security: preparation for an attack that could come at any time, affect any number of targets, and result in untold casualties and damage to people and national infrastructure. A climate of fear was promoted that portrayed an unprecedented level of danger coming from both external and internal enemies who could mount an attack at any time and in any place in the country.

When the 9/11 attacks occurred, America was not only vulnerable to attack, but the country was also woefully unprepared to prevent it. There previously had been a number of terrorist attacks throughout the world, including a few in the United States, but guarding against attack had been a low priority (Clarke, 2008). The 9/11 attacks and the fear in their aftermath significantly changed the national philosophy and ushered in a new strategy and American defense system. Nonetheless, the country had little foundation from which to build a national prevention strategy. The country essentially started at zero, or near zero, and was told it needed to build defenses to the possibility of asymmetric terrorist attacks.

▶ What Is Homeland Security?

There is substantial confusion over the phrase **homeland security**. Much that has been written about homeland security focuses singularly on potential terrorist attacks. Some of the discourse, however, also examines responses to natural disasters and other catastrophes. When natural disasters and catastrophes are included within the homeland security purview, it obviously broadens the mission. While recognizing that there are definitional issues relating to homeland security operations, the focus of this text is primarily on homeland security and terrorist attacks.

Homeland Security Missions and Goals

The Office of Homeland Security (2007a) defined homeland security as "a concerted national effort to prevent terrorist attacks within the United States, reduce America's vulnerability to terrorism and minimize the damage, and recover from attacks that do occur" (p. 3). The *Quadrennial Homeland Security Review Report* (DHS, 2010, 2014) later defined homeland security as "a concerted national effort to ensure a homeland that is safe, secure, and resilient against terrorism and other hazards where American interests, aspirations and way of life can thrive" (p. 13). There are two primary differences between these two Department of Homeland Security (DHS) definitions. First, the *Quadrennial Review* provides a new focus on **resilience**. Although there are varying definitions of resilience, it can be defined as mitigating any attacks and ensuring a rapid recovery. Second, the new DHS definition specifically includes hazards, which encompasses all sorts of natural and manmade disasters or catastrophes. This definition firmly includes Federal Emergency Management Agency (FEMA) within the homeland security rubric.

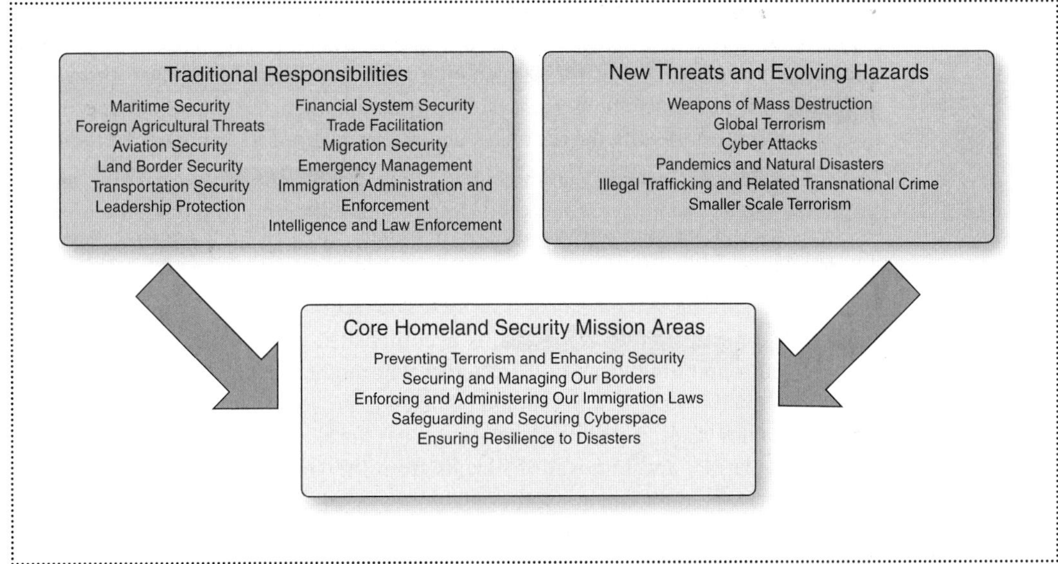

FIGURE 1-2 Evolution of Homeland Security
Source: Department of Homeland Security. (2010). *Quadrennial Homeland Security Review Report: A Strategic Framework for a Secure Homeland.* Washington, D.C.: Author, p. 14.

Homeland security's mission and responsibilities have quickly evolved. Figure 1-2 ■ displays traditional responsibilities and new threats and evolving hazards. The traditional responsibilities encompass many of the federal government's responsibilities prior to the 9/11 attacks and the creation of the DHS. These responsibilities were assigned to a variety of federal agencies. The new threats and evolving hazards recognize the importance of dealing with terrorism and their modes of attack, pandemics and natural disasters, and transnational crime. In essence, the role of homeland security has been substantially expanded.

The *Quadrennial Review* identifies five overarching missions for homeland security:

1. **Preventing terrorism and enhancing security.** As noted in the preceding text, terrorist attacks are of grave concern to the American people, and preventing such attacks is an important homeland security mission. Three primary goals are encased in this mission. First, is to prevent terrorist attacks. This is accomplished by gathering data on any threats through intelligence, deterring and disrupting potential terrorist operations, protecting potential targets from terrorism, stopping the spread of violent extremism, and engaging communities. The second primary goal is to prevent the unauthorized acquisition or use of WMDs and WMD materials. The underlying objectives within this goal include anticipating emerging threats, controlling access and movement of materials and technology, and protect against hostile use of WMDs. The third goal is to manage risks to critical infrastructure, key leadership, and events. To do this we must understand and prioritize risks to these assets, provide protection, make these assets resilient to attacks, and protect government leaders, facilities, and special events.
2. **Securing and managing our borders.** Many threats to the United States occur when terrorists illegally enter our country, and securing our borders is an important homeland security mission. This mission has three goals. First is to effectively control U.S. air, land, and sea borders. This is accomplished by preventing the illegal entry of people, weapons, dangerous goods, and contraband. The second goal is to safeguard lawful

trade and travel by securing the global supply chain, securing conveyances in transportation networks, and managing the risk posed by people and goods in transit. The third goal is to disrupt and dismantle transnational organized crime and terrorist organizations. These organizations must be identified and their leaders apprehended, and governments must identify the pathways and modes of operation and disrupt them.

3. **Enforcing and administering our immigration laws.** Immigration has become an important homeland security issue as the United States attempts to protect the borders. The security of the country's borders can be accomplished by pursuing two goals. The first goal is to strengthen the immigration system by promoting lawful immigration and expediting the administration of immigration services. The second goal, prevention of unlawful immigration, is accomplished partially by reducing illegal employment opportunities and other factors that might attract illegal immigrants to enter the United States. Actions should be taken to prevent illegal entry or admission of undesirables such as criminals or dangerous foreign nationals. Arrests, detainment, prosecution, and removal of illegals from the United States will curb illegal immigration to a significant extent.
4. **Safeguarding and securing cyberspace.** Cyberspace is becoming more vulnerable and important to American society. A primary goal here is to create a safe, secure, and resilient cyber environment by prioritizing threats, managing the risks to cyberspace, preventing crime and other malicious uses of cyberspace, and developing a private–public partnership to better respond to threats. A secondary goal is to promote cybersecurity knowledge and innovation. There needs to be an investment in innovative technology and procedures and in fostering a well-trained workforce with the capacity to respond to cyber threats, and enhance public awareness about the potential cyber threats.
5. **Ensuring resilience to disasters or hazards.** Responding to all hazards remains an important homeland security mission. To accomplish this mission, four goals have been identified by the DHS. First, hazards must be mitigated by reducing vulnerability to disasters. The second goal is to enhance preparedness through community planning, and to strengthen capabilities such as law enforcement, evacuation, public health, mass care, and public works so as to respond more effectively to hazards. The third goal is to ensure effective emergency response. This is accomplished by providing information to the public on a timely basis, conducting disaster response drills, and providing timely and effective disaster relief. The fourth goal within this mission is rapid recovery. Here, response capabilities must be enhanced to ensure that essential services can be continued when there is a disaster or hazard.

HS Web Link: To read the *National Strategy for Homeland Security*, go to http://www.dhs.gov/xlibrary/assets/nat_strat_homelandsecurity_2007.pdf.

These five missions and their corresponding goals are addressed in depth throughout this text. They provide a framework for action. They describe how the United States can prevent and be prepared for a disaster, terrorist attack, or any other hazard. Moreover, in 2012, the DHS (2012) issued its strategic plan for 2012–2016 and provided a roadmap for accomplishing these objectives.

Definitional Issues and Homeland Security

Terrorism has been around as long as there have been tribes and nation-states. Homeland security is a relatively new concept or government function in the United States. Many other countries, however, have long been concerned with homeland security. For example, it has been a national imperative and a matter of survival in Israel throughout its more than 60 years of existence; and England dealt with terrorism for decades. In the past, the U.S. government attempted to protect its borders, but the motivation was not to keep terrorists out of the country. For the most part, border security focused on illegal drug trafficking and importation, preventing undocumented people from entering the country, ensuring that tariffs were collected on imported goods from other countries, and preventing illegal goods such as counterfeit name-brand clothing and prescription drugs from entering the United States. Little thought was given to intercepting terrorists or WMDs. Consequently, few homeland security mechanisms were in place prior to the 9/11 attacks.

Homeland security has evolved over time and has several operational definitions, but there is little consistency among constituent groups. Most definitions are formed by the duties and responsibilities of those charged with performing homeland security functions. They tend to define it based on organizational purposes. Obviously, if it is not well defined operationally, efforts may be off target, creating excessive expenditures, cracks or creases in coverage, and overall inefficiency. This is not only wasteful, but it also results in a more vulnerable America. A uniform definition should guide the government's efforts to make the nation more secure.

Bellavita (2008) examined the homeland security literature and noted that a number of definitions have evolved. These definitions vary based on events that are targeted by homeland security programming:

1. Terrorism—the prevention and response by federal, state, and local governments and by the private sector to terrorist acts and to mitigate their impact on American society.
2. All Hazards—concerted efforts to prevent and disrupt attacks, protect against natural and human-made hazards, and respond to and recover from such incidents.
3. Terrorism and Catastrophes—efforts by the DHS and other governmental agencies to respond to and recover from terrorist and catastrophic events that affect security.
4. Jurisdictional Hazards—each political jurisdiction in the United States may have different perceptions as to what constitutes homeland security. A mayor in a small city in Kansas likely will view it differently as compared to the mayor of New York City.
5. Meta Hazards—efforts to mitigate or prevent any social trend or threat that disrupts the American way of life, for example, climate change or shortages of petroleum.
6. National Security—governmental efforts to protect the sovereignty, territory, domestic population, and critical infrastructure in the United States.
7. Security Uber Alles—used by governmental officials to justify the curtailment of American civil liberties and personal freedom; emphasis of process over outcomes.

Although there is substantial overlap across several of these views of homeland security, a number of subtle and not so subtle differences do exist. First, many of the definitions focus on terrorism, whereas others also include **disasters** and **hazards**; a disaster is an event that has occurred, whereas hazards are conditions that may lead to a disaster. With the FEMA being part of the DHS, it would appear that homeland security would de facto include disasters or catastrophes and hazards. Yet, a majority of government pronouncements focus solely on terrorism, whereas others include natural and human-made hazards such as industrial accidents, tornados, earthquakes, floods, and hurricanes. There are differences in the structure of homeland security if it is intended to respond to disasters and hazards.

The use of the terms hazards and disasters raises another issue. To what extent or magnitude does an event fit within the scope of homeland security? For example, in 2008, a bridge across the Mississippi River on Interstate 35W in Minneapolis, Minnesota, collapsed, resulting in 13 deaths and approximately 100 people being injured. The bridge collapse certainly resulted in significant economic damage to the area's economy. Was a disaster of this magnitude to be included within the rubric of homeland security? A terrorist attack of the same magnitude certainly would receive the attention of the homeland security apparatus. The inclusion of disasters and hazards in the definition of homeland security at this point is nebulous at best, and it clouds the organization of the homeland security apparatus and its operation. Even so, events such as these are routinely included within homeland security's scope, but it remains unanswered as to which criterion or demarcation should result in an event becoming a homeland security issue. Local officials obviously will have a more inclusive view of these terms as compared to federal officials.

Second, the scope of homeland security, according to some authorities, has been expanded to include social trends (meta hazards) thought to affect national security. For example, in 2008 a National Intelligence Estimate (NIE) was released that detailed the impact of climate change on national security. It was forcefully argued that ultimately climate change would negatively affect national security as many unstable countries experience flooding, famine, and population migration. These changes could result in terrorist attacks and the overthrow of governments in a number of nation-states. This position was reinforced in the 2014 *Quadrennial Homeland Security Review*. If meta hazards are included in the definition of homeland security, what resources should be devoted to them, and which meta hazards should receive attention.

Third, to a great extent, homeland security has become operationalized as preventing and mitigating the possible use of WMDs with little regard for disasters or hazards. Although the homeland security rhetoric includes discussions of responses to hazards and catastrophes, the primary focus remains on WMDs. This is particularly problematic for the DHS since FEMA is located under its organizational umbrella, and there are far more natural disasters than terrorist attacks. In 2015, there were 77 FEMA-declared disasters (FEMA, 2015). The sheer number of natural disasters and declarations per year, on the average over 100 (FEMA, 2015), will impact homeland security's organization and operational imperatives.

Finally, homeland security has come to be defined as a limitation on and a tool to adversely affect personal freedoms and rights. Those focusing on the expansion of government powers tend to emphasize processes over outcomes. It is reasoned that if homeland security operatives have the proper authority, then they will be able to establish security for the country. The USA PATRIOT Act gave expansive powers to the federal government in terms of spying on suspected terrorists. Foreigners suspected of terrorist ties and their family members are routinely prohibited from coming to the United States, and American travelers are routinely subjected to intrusive inspections and restrictions. Until 2015, the National Security Agency monitored and collected e-mails and telephone numbers, including those belonging to American citizens. Perhaps such measures can be justified should they result in America being safer. The average citizen seems oblivious to or unconcerned with these limitations on their freedoms. Opponents of these procedures see them as attacks on civil liberties, while supporters deem them as additional protection for the country. Regardless, Americans' rights have been affected, and only time will tell if these security measures have contributed to safety or just resulted in intrusions into the daily lives of citizens.

Homeland security definitional issues abound, making it questionable whether workable policies can be promulgated at the federal, state, or local level. The inability to properly or accurately define the scope of homeland security is creating a social and political abyss. The lack of workable policies results in incomplete or deficient homeland security actions, and it likely increases the nation's vulnerability to attacks, disasters, and hazards. The following sections examine homeland security in terms of terrorist attacks while realizing that natural and human-made disasters play a key role in homeland security.

HS ANALYSIS BOX 1-2

Given that there are numerous definitions of homeland security and that the department is expected to respond to a wide spectrum of events, the idea of homeland security itself becomes somewhat confusing. The inclusion of diverse events changes the direction and perspective of homeland security. Does the inclusion of all the different events strengthen or weaken homeland security and why? Second, which of these definitions should dominate national policy making?

Collateral Benefits from Homeland Security

The enhancement of homeland security and response capabilities provides other benefits. The experience with Hurricane Katrina in 2005 demonstrated that the United States lacked the ability to respond to a variety of natural disasters. In addition to hurricanes, there are earthquakes, tornados, fires, and floods. Enhanced homeland security allows the nation to more effectively respond to these events. The same response channels are utilized in both terrorist attacks and disasters.

Ghamari-Tabrizi (2006) notes that to some extent political leaders and government officials may be overemphasizing responses to terrorist attacks and should give greater consideration to responding to natural and human-made disasters, especially in terms of FEMA's response. Currently, planning emphasizes terrorist attacks with the belief that such planning will better enable the federal and state governments to respond to natural disasters. As noted earlier, natural disasters are more likely to occur and do occur more frequently. Ghamari-Tabrizi suggests that perhaps homeland security should be approached from the other direction. That is, plan for natural disasters and use the resultant mechanisms to respond to terrorist attacks should they occur. This, to some extent, would result in a change in priorities and affect some agencies' roles. Such a reversal of roles likely would increase agencies' ability to respond to natural disasters, and it is questionable if it would detract from the ability to respond to terrorist attacks. This shift in policy, however, is not politically acceptable since homeland security and defense against terrorism are two of today's primary political mantras.

▶ The Scope of Homeland Security

Many people, when contemplating homeland security, focus on governmental efforts and programs implemented to protect the country from terrorists. However, referring to the goals enumerated in the *Quadrennial Homeland Security Review* (DHS, 2010, 2014) and the *National Strategy for Homeland Security* (Office of Homeland Security, 2007a), it becomes obvious that homeland security is much more encompassing and is international in scope. For example, the goals discuss activities such as the international interdiction of terrorists and weapons and the prevention of the emergence of violent radicalization around the world. Homeland security for America is seen as an international prerogative involving American agencies and a number of foreign government agencies. The United States has developed working and cooperative relationships with many countries. An example of such cooperation was the arrest by British authorities of alleged terrorists who had plotted to blow up several transatlantic flights to the United States. On August 9, 2006, authorities arrested 24 suspects who allegedly planned to use a peroxide-based explosive to destroy the planes while they were over the Atlantic Ocean. Several American

Primary Agency	Relationship Agency	Activities
American Intelligence Agencies, for example, CIA, NSA, State Dept.	Foreign Intelligence and Police Agencies	Identify international terrorist groups Identify individual terrorists in other countries Uncover and investigate possible terror plots Track terrorists as they move from one country to another Compile databases of terrorists and activities
Federal Bureau of Investigation	Foreign Intelligence and Police Agencies	Work with American intelligence agencies and foreign intelligence and police agencies in monitoring foreign terrorists that may be attempting to enter the United States Maintain case files on possible terrorists and activities in the United States Investigate terrorist acts at home and abroad Monitor suspicious persons and activities Coordinate activities with state and local police agencies
Department of Homeland Security	Foreign Governments Other Federal, State, and Local Agencies	Monitor persons entering and leaving the United States Reduce passport, visa, and other document fraud Monitor shipments of material into and out of the United States Respond to acts of terrorism to mitigate impact Coordinate with the states on protecting national infrastructure assets Secure our borders from illegal entry Coordinate port, airline, and transportation security Respond to and investigate terrorist events
State Governments (state police, civil defense, national guard, and disaster)	Department of Homeland Security	Develop and implement state homeland security plans Respond to terrorist events
Local Governments (police, fire, civil defense, para-medics, and hospitals)	State Governments and Federal Agencies	First responder to terrorist events Collect intelligence in conjunction with state agencies and FBI

FIGURE 1-3 National and International Homeland Security Activities

governmental agencies worked with British authorities during the investigation and subsequent arrests. Several U.S. agencies worked with French authorities in the aftermath of the attacks in France. These efforts focus not only on responding to terrorist acts but also on gathering intelligence about terrorists and their activities that can be used to thwart attacks on American soil and apprehend terrorists.

Homeland security is an international, multilayered effort. Figure 1-3 ■ provides a breakdown of the umbrella of homeland security activities.

As can be seen in Figure 1-3 ■, homeland security involves a variety of agencies from across the world. It also involves numerous federal, state, and local agencies. Moreover, they are involved in a variety of activities ranging from intelligence to law enforcement to responding to terrorist events. These activities result in the task of homeland security being extremely complicated and require a substantial amount of coordination across various governments and numerous levels of government.

Today all levels of government are immersed in homeland security. As noted earlier, numerous definitional issues surround homeland security. Nonetheless, strategies and tactics need to be developed to institute greater levels of safety for people, and a number of these efforts are underway. The *9/11 Commission Report* (National Commission on Terrorist Attacks upon the United States, 2004) and the *National Strategy for Homeland Security* provide the foundation for these activities. The 9/11 Commission document critiqued national security efforts and established milestones or benchmarks for progress, whereas the *National Strategy for Homeland Security* provided detailed program direction. These two documents essentially provided a roadmap for future developments in homeland security. However, there were efforts and cautionary reports that attempted to spur homeland security efforts prior to 9/11. They are briefly addressed here.

▶ Pre-9/11 Efforts to Improve Homeland Security

Although the United States was unprepared for the 9/11 attacks (see the 9/11 Commission Report), previously efforts had been made to improve national security. In 1998, Secretary of Defense William Cohen chartered the Commission on National Security/21st Century. The Commission (1999) produced a multi-volume report that examined the international security environment, developed a national strategy to meet environmental needs, and evaluated current security agencies and arrangements and made recommendations for improvement. Although a number of the recommendations were aimed at improving the military, several important homeland security recommendations were contained in the report, including the establishment of a national homeland security agency, creation of an assistant secretary for homeland security to coordinate department of defense efforts to serve the homeland, giving the national guard the primary responsibility of homeland security, and creating a select committee to provide congressional support for homeland security.

In 1998, Congress directed the U.S. attorney general and the Department of Justice to develop a plan to "serve as a baseline strategy for coordination of a national policy and operational capabilities to combat terrorism in the United States and against American interests overseas" (Attorney General, 1999, p. 1). The plan addressed several issues, including deterring terrorism, crisis management, cyber issues, infrastructure, and coordination of government entities should there be an attack.

Essentially the U.S. Commission on National Security/21st Century and the U.S. attorney general's report were foundational for the development of the national strategy for homeland security as they made a number of recommendations. These reports demonstrate that the threat to the security of the nation was beginning to be a national priority and concern, but unfortunately the 9/11 attacks occurred before many of the recommendations could be implemented.

▶ The 9/11 Commission Report

The 9/11 attacks resulted in substantial turmoil in the nation's capital with the two primary political parties, interest groups, and political factions blaming each other for the security failure. It became clear that there was a need to evaluate the country's vulnerability to terrorist attacks and to determine the mistakes that had been made in the past that contributed to the security agencies being unprepared for such an eventuality. Consequently, the **National Commission on Terrorist Attacks upon the United States** (9/11 Commission) was created to examine past policies and make recommendation for establishing security. The bipartisan commission interviewed government officials to gauge our nation's readiness. The report provided a comprehensive and detailed account of the 9/11 attacks and a fairly unbiased review of the failings of the existing national security apparatus. The *9/11 Commission Report* is especially telling since the 9/11 Commission found that several intelligence agencies had information concerning possible attacks and the attackers, but not one agency put the pieces together. These mistakes occurred at the highest level of government. For example, George Tenet, director of the CIA, stated that he briefed a number of high-level officials in the Bush White House, including Secretary of State Condoleezza Rice, but no action was taken and the possible impending attacks were given little consideration (Eggen and Wright, 2006). Essentially, not only were intelligence agencies unprepared or inadequately briefed, there were "vast caverns" between each of the agencies and the executive branch whereby information was seldom shared or properly vetted. Indeed, the agencies tended to compete with one another as opposed to cooperating toward a shared goal—safeguarding America.

HS Web Link: To view the 9/11 Commission Report, go to http://www.911commission.gov/report/911Report.pdf.

As a result of its work, the 9/11 Commission made 41 recommendations that can be found in Chapters 12 and 13 of the report (summarized in Figure 1-4 ■). The recommendations were divided into three broad areas: (1) homeland security and emergency response, (2) intelligence and congressional reform, and (3) foreign policy and nonproliferation (9/11 Commission, 2004).

A number of recommendations concerned homeland security. The 9/11 Commission recommended that Congress create one committee to oversee homeland security. It noted that emergency response agencies should adopt FEMA's incident command system resulting in uniformity when responding to terrorist events. Homeland security funding to the states and local governments should be based on potential targets as opposed to some other formula. It noted that the Transportation Security Administration (TSA) should make screening of passengers, cargo, and luggage for explosives a priority. Screening should be improved at the borders and at sites of critical infrastructure.

The 9/11 Commission was extremely critical of the government's intelligence apparatus. It noted that the intelligence community needed reorganization. It recommended the position of national intelligence director be created to oversee and manage national intelligence operations. Most important, the national intelligence director would ensure that the various intelligence agencies cooperated and shared information. It recommended that the director of the CIA rebuild that organization, incorporating more human intelligence capabilities and ensuring that information from all sources is analyzed more effectively, and take steps to ensure that intelligence is shared with other consumers of the information. It recommended the creation of a National Counterterrorism Center staffed by personnel from the intelligence agencies. The center would facilitate counterterrorism planning and operations as well as facilitate the flow of information among agencies. The Commission also noted that congressional oversight of intelligence was dysfunctional, which contributed to a number of problems.

Homeland Security and Emergency Response
Radio spectrum for first responders
Incident command system
Risk-based homeland security funds
Critical infrastructure assessment
Private sector preparedness
National strategy for transportation security
Airline passenger prescreening
Airline passenger explosive screening
Checked bag and cargo screening
Terrorist travel strategy
Comprehensive screening system
Biometric entry-exist screening system
International collaboration on borders & document security
Standardize secure identification
Intelligence and Congressional Reform
Director of national intelligence
National Counterterrorism Center
FBI national security workforce
New missions for CIA director
Incentives for information sharing
Government-wide information sharing
Northern Command planning for homeland defense
Full debate on PATRIOT Act
Privacy and civil liberties oversight board
Guidelines for government sharing of personal information
Intelligence oversight reform
Homeland security committees
Unclassified top-line intelligence budget
Security clearance reform
Foreign Policy and Nonproliferation
Maximum effort to prevent terrorist from acquiring WMD
Afghanistan
Pakistan
Saudi Arabia
Terrorist sanctuaries
Coalition strategy against Islamist terrorism
Coalition detention standards
Economic policies
Terrorist financing
Clear U.S. message abroad
International broadcasting
Scholarship, exchange, and library programs
Secular education in Muslim countries

FIGURE 1-4 9/11 Commission Recommendations.

The 9/11 Commission.
National Archives and Records Administration.

The Commission made recommendations about foreign policy and nuclear nonproliferation. An examination of the recommendations regarding U.S. relationships with other countries made it obvious that the United States had to develop a new foreign policy that considered terrorism. Many pre-9/11 international relationships were predicated on cold war thinking, and economic relationships, primarily the acquisition of petroleum, drove a great deal of foreign policy. For example, the Commission recommended a reconsideration of the relationship with Saudi Arabia, noting the need for political and economic reform in that country. Several recommendations centered on economic development in those countries perceived as breeding grounds for terrorists. The Commission recommended creating alliances with other countries to fight global terrorism. In other words, America needed to confront the conditions that spawned terrorists.

HS ANALYSIS BOX 1-3

The 9/11 Commission examined a number of areas relating to the 9/11 attacks on New York City and Washington, D.C., and found many deficiencies. The federal government has continually moved to make improvements across the board. Of the areas identified by the Commission, in your opinion, which ones are the most critical to homeland security? Which of the areas should receive the highest priority in terms of completion?

▶ The National Strategy for Homeland Security

The 9/11 Commission was not the sole governmental body examining homeland security. The Office of Homeland Security in the White House was also examining the nation's security and plotting a roadmap for the future. In 2002, the office issued the ***National Strategy for Homeland Security***. This report was subsequently updated in 2007, but the original document provided a comprehensive, detailed roadmap with many of its recommendations mirroring those of the 9/11 Commission. Today, the *National Strategy for Homeland Security* provides primary guidance for homeland security strategies and tactics.

The Office of Homeland Security (2007a) identified a number of critical mission areas: (1) intelligence and warning, (2) border and transportation security, (3) domestic counterterrorism, (4) protecting critical infrastructure, (5) defending against catastrophic terrorism, and (6) emergency preparedness and response. In addition, several foundational areas were identified. These areas represented supportive changes needed to facilitate homeland security. They included (1) law, (2) science and technology, (3) information sharing and systems, and (4) international cooperation.

Intelligence and Warning

Terrorists are often successful when they conduct a surprise attack. Therefore, the discovery of information about an impending attack could lead to preventative action. Alternatively, if the attack did occur, its consequences could be mitigated. Thus, it would seem imperative that the U.S. government create the capacity to gather intelligence on terrorists and terrorist organizations and use that information to prevent attacks. The *National Strategy for Homeland Security* identified a number of initiatives that should be pursued, including the following:

- ***Enhance the Analytic Capabilities of the FBI.*** This included hiring more agents to enhance the collection and analysis of terror-related intelligence.
- ***Build New Capabilities Through Information Analysis and Infrastructure Protection.*** The DHS was tapped to increase the ability to collect information and provide guidelines to better protect critical infrastructure.
- ***Implement a Homeland Security Advisory System.*** A color-coded system was developed to advise citizens of potential terrorist-related dangers.
- ***Dual Use Analysis to Prevent Attacks.*** **Dual use analysis** refers to monitoring the purchase and use of material, equipment, and chemicals that have legitimate social purposes, but that can also be used by terrorists to mount an attack. Such materials should be identified and their sale and transfer, especially in large quantities, should be monitored and, in some cases, investigated to prevent their importation to terrorist groups.
- ***Employ Red Team Techniques.*** Red teams are used to conduct mock attacks on facilities to test their security systems and measure their preparedness.

HS Web Link: To read more about the Homeland Security Advisory System, go to https://www.dhs.gov/national-terrorism-advisory-system.

Border and Transportation Security

The *National Strategy* identified several objectives to enhance border and transportation security. The United States is part of a global community with which it carries on substantial international commerce, imports, and exports. For example, the North American Free Trade Agreement (NAFTA) essentially opened the northern and southern borders to uncountable traffic. A global economy demands the efficient flow of people and goods, but at the same time, security measures need to be implemented to ensure safety, particularly regarding terrorists and WMD materials. Measures identified in the strategy included the following:

- ***Ensure Accountability in Border and Transportation Security.*** In the past, numerous federal and state agencies were involved in border and transportation inspection, regulation, and control, resulting in little accountability. A number of federal agencies have been transferred to the DHS, resulting in all border security and inspection agencies being located in one department.
- ***Create Smart Borders.*** Smart borders enhance our capacity to keep illegal aliens from entering our country and consist of a multilayered composition of land, sea, and air surveillance, supplemented with electronic surveillance such as radar capable of identifying people attempting to cross the border illegally.
- ***Increase Security for International Shipping Containers.*** Nearly half of the imports arrive by container, with approximately 5.7 million containers entering the country each year. More effective efforts should be made to screen them for WMDs and WMD materials.

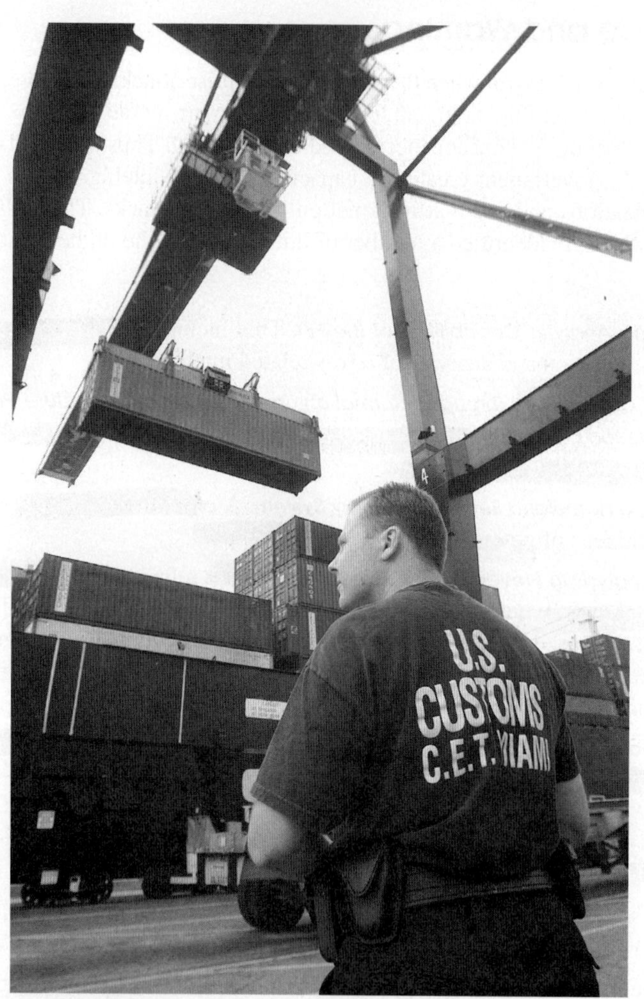

Customs officers inspect seaport containers.
James Tourtellotte/CBP.

- ***Implement the Aviation and Transportation Act of 2001.*** This law emphasizes security in a number of transportation areas, including commercial airlines, interstate transportation of hazardous materials, shipping container security, critical infrastructure security, and information sharing across agencies involved in the enhancement of security.
- ***Expand the Role of the U.S. Coast Guard.*** The U.S. Coast Guard plays a key role in national defense, maritime safety, flow of shipping and vessels, and protection of natural resources. The Coast Guard now has an expanded role of intercepting ships to inspect them for undocumented people, contraband, or WMDs.
- ***Reform Immigration Services.*** These services were reorganized in the DHS to make them more efficient when processing the more than 7 million immigration and visa applications each year. It also allows for more focused enforcement of immigration laws. As a part of this reform, the DHS implemented the **Enhanced Border Security and Visa Entry Act**. One of the requirements of this act was that foreign visitors possess travel documents that contain biometric information such as fingerprints. This requirement helps reduce the use of forged documents by visitors and possible terrorists. Reforms have also concentrated on deporting undocumented people.

Domestic Counterterrorism

Counterterrorism is now a critical component of government action at all levels—federal, state, and local. Heretofore, local and state governments did not play much of a role in counterterrorism; these activities were seen as falling under the purview of the federal government. Today, there is a need for new programs and better coordination with federal agencies in the DHS and the FBI in the area of counterterrorism. Along these lines, federal agencies must enhance cooperation, information sharing, and tactical operations:

- ***Improving Intergovernmental Law Enforcement Coordination.*** A primary initiative endorsed in the *Strategy* was the expansion of the FBI's **Joint Terrorism Task Forces** (JTTFs). The JTTFs represent a coordinating body at the federal level to integrate law enforcement counterterrorism efforts. They consist of representatives from federal law enforcement, international law enforcement, and state and local police. Serving as an overarching mechanism to coordinate enforcement and intelligence activities, the JTTFs represent a systematic continuous coordination of efforts and a flow of counterterrorism information at all levels of government.
- ***Facilitating the Apprehension of Potential Terrorists.*** The FBI extended its efforts to provide information to local law enforcement agencies to facilitate the capture of "potential" terrorists and to enhance these investigations. The National Crime Information Center (NCIC) database was expanded to include information about terrorists and possible terrorist activities. The FBI works with the State Department to add information about suspected terrorists and make the database available to immigration and consular officers. It has developed a consolidated terrorist watch list used by all agencies that is more useful when screening people coming into the country. The FBI works with foreign governments to collect information on terrorists in those countries.
- ***Enhancing Investigations and Prosecutions.*** Counterterrorism, the investigation of terrorists and their activities, represents one of the most complicated operations that can be conducted. These investigations attempt to discover terrorists before they are able to perpetrate their crimes. A greater emphasis must be placed on these investigations if national security is to be achieved. This will entail closer working relationships among a variety of federal, state, and local agencies.

- ***Restructuring the FBI to Emphasize the Prevention of Terrorist Attacks.*** In the past, the FBI's effort to combat terrorism or foreign espionage was one of several offenses investigated by the agency. Today, the FBI has been reorganized to make these offenses a higher priority. It has created a number of new counterterrorism positions and has shifted hundreds of agents from criminal investigation to anti-terror investigations. It is also deploying squads of anti-terrorist experts who can assist field offices in investigations. The National Joint Terrorism Task Force headquartered at the FBI serves as the primary investigative terrorism countermeasure on American soil.
- ***Targeting and Attacking Terrorist Financing.*** Targeting terrorist financing and money laundering remains a high priority at the federal level. The FBI and the U.S. Department of the Treasury now work together to combat terrorist financing.

Protecting Critical Infrastructure

When most people think of homeland security, they think of protective measures implemented to keep them safe when they travel, when they are in their homes or at work, and when they shop or are involved in recreational or entertainment activities. They see the baseline of homeland security as preventing an attack in the United States. As such, the *National Strategy for Homeland Security* has identified a number of initiatives designed to provide Americans better levels of physical protection:

- ***Unify Responsibility for Infrastructure Protection in the DHS.*** The creation of the DHS consolidated responsibility for protecting national critical infrastructure. Even though a number of federal agencies remain involved in protecting critical physical and human assets, the efforts are coordinated by the DHS.
- ***Build and Maintain a Complete and Accurate Assessment of Critical Infrastructure and Key Assets.*** The United States of America has numerous critical infrastructure and key assets. These assets are thought to be the targets of future terrorist attacks. The DHS must identify and assess vulnerabilities (as discussed in more detail in Chapter 3). This assessment consists of identifying protection levels required for various assets and key targets.
- ***Develop Partnerships with State and Local Governments and the Private Sector.*** Effective protection of critical infrastructure depends on the federal government working closely with the private sector as well as with state and local governments. The private sector controls approximately 85 percent of America's critical infrastructure (Office of Homeland Security, 2007b). The firms controlling this infrastructure have the technical expertise to target harden the infrastructure, and they must initiate protective measures such as barriers, fencing, access controls, and so on to make it more difficult for possible terrorists to infiltrate infrastructure. State and local police departments are responsible for providing security to local communities, and as such, they are not only first responders to terrorist attacks, but they also deter attacks through effective policing measures. The federal government, private sector, and state and local governments provide layered protection for infrastructure.
- ***Develop a National Infrastructure Protection Plan.*** In 2006, the DHS released the National Infrastructure Protection Plan (NIPP), which is discussed in detail in Chapter 3. The NIPP provides a model to provide critical infrastructure protection. Nonetheless, there is a need to constantly review how well assets are being protected and how protective levels can be improved.
- ***Secure Cyberspace.*** The use of electronic data powers the American economy. It is the foundation for commerce. Efforts must be made to ensure the security of these systems. In addition to the DHS and the FBI, a number of other federal agencies are currently working to improve cyber security.

- ***Develop Models for Effective Protective Solutions.*** Protective measures must be prioritized by focusing first on those infrastructure assets that are critical to the economy and the safety of citizens. Destruction of some of these assets would have a greater negative effect as compared to the destruction of others. First, analytical models can be developed to show which assets are most critical. This assists in identifying priorities. Second, these analytical models can identify shortfalls in security systems and possibly identify points of attacks on various assets.
- ***Guard Critical Infrastructure from Inside Threats.*** Past history demonstrates that insiders, including current or former disgruntled employees, have participated in acts that can cripple or negatively affect parts of critical infrastructure. The Office of Homeland Security (2002) advises that in the food-processing industry, these insiders have been responsible for nearly all the previous incidents of food tampering. The DHS is now establishing protocols or standards for conducting background investigations of potential employees. Facilities should establish security zones where key operations are conducted. These security zones would be controlled areas with limited access to employees. Only those employees who have security clearances would be allowed to enter.
- ***Partner with the International Community to Protect Transnational Infrastructure.*** We now live in a global economy and critical infrastructure is tied to and connected with that of other countries. NAFTA has opened up the northern and southern borders of the United States. The nation receives a substantial amount of electricity from Canada and natural gas and petroleum products from Mexico and South America. These resources are vital to keep commerce operating. It is advisable for the American government to work with these nations in protecting international resources and assets. Dependency on international markets results in homeland security reaching well beyond the nation's borders.

Defend Against Catastrophic Events

Homeland security involves defense against catastrophic events such as radiological, biological, chemical, and nuclear attacks. Additionally, such defenses better enable a response to natural catastrophes such as earthquakes, floods, tornados, or hurricanes. The *National Strategy for Homeland Security* has identified several initiatives in this area:

- ***Prevent Terrorist Use of Nuclear Weapons Through Better Sensors and Procedures.*** Effective homeland security involves the development and deployment of more effective sensors that detect nuclear or radiological materials that could enter the country or be transported within the borders. The DHS is charged with not only the development of these sensors but also the development of procedures to strategically deploy them to ensure maximum protection from attacks. The DHS is working with the Department of Transportation to deploy sensor systems throughout the national transportation infrastructure.
- ***Detect Chemical and Biological Materials and Attacks.*** Security demands the ability to detect the use of biological and chemical weapons. The Environmental Protection Agency is currently upgrading air-monitoring stations to detect biological, chemical, and radiological substances. It is also important for officials to recognize and report any suspicious diseases that may be the result of the release of WMDs. The Centers for Disease Control and Prevention (CDC) is expanding its efforts to detect and diagnose bioterrorism threats. The CDC is also working with state and local health departments to ensure early detection and notification. The DHS is working with the Department of Agriculture to establish monitoring systems for livestock. There are a number of diseases that could cripple farming industries.

- ***Develop a Broad Spectrum of Vaccines, Antimicrobials, and Antidotes.*** Preparation for a biological or chemical attack requires stockpiling medicines necessary to treat those who might come into contact with a biological or chemical agent. Although the country possesses the medicines needed to deal with some of the chemical or biological agents that could be used in a terrorist attack, new and more effective agents must be developed. The inventory of these agents must also be expanded. Development abilities must also be enhanced within the biotech field to increase the production of agents and to develop new more effective agents. Ample supplies must also be kept on hand should there be an attack that affects large numbers of people.
- ***Implement the Select Agent Program.*** Numerous civilian medical, pharmaceutical, and medical research laboratories across the country house dangerous viruses and bacteria. These private and governmental installations work with a number of biological agents that could be used in a terrorist attack. These laboratories are working to develop antidotes to the associated diseases and to learn how these various bacteria and viruses attack human and animal hosts. These biological agents could be accidentally released or someone working in one of the labs could purposively release them. The **Select Agent Program** attempts to regulate the shipment of biological organisms and toxins. Many of the laboratories have only minimum security. It is obvious that there must be a measure of control to prevent their release.

Emergency Preparedness and Response

One of the primary objectives of homeland security is to mitigate the consequences of any terrorist attack. This requires adequate preparation to effectively respond to an incident. FEMA is the lead federal agency in responding to terrorist attacks and natural disasters and catastrophes. Other agencies, however, can be involved, including the military and various federal homeland security agencies. Since any attack would occur at the local level, state and local agencies must be prepared to respond. The *National Strategy for Homeland Security* outlines a number of initiatives designed to better prepare for possible catastrophes:

- ***Integrate Federal Response Plans.*** The DHS is charged with developing a master plan that includes all disciplines or agencies in an all-hazards response plan (discussed in more detail in Chapter 13). The plan would guide federal action in any type of terrorist attack, natural disaster, or catastrophe. In the past, each agency had its own plan, and in totality, these plans constituted a patchwork response.
- ***Create a National Incident Management System.*** As noted earlier, state and local governments and agencies are involved in any response to a catastrophe. A number of private entities, such as the Red Cross, Salvation Army, and churches, also become involved in responding to catastrophes. The DHS developed a **national incident management system** that coordinates activities not only of federal agencies but also those of state and local agencies as well as private organizations. This is discussed in more detail in Chapter 13.
- ***Improve Tactical Counterterrorism Capabilities.*** There are federal, state, and local law enforcement assets that are available to intercede in possible terrorist attacks. These assets include local SWAT teams, emergency response medical teams, and hostage negotiators. Several federal agencies also have first responders who can be dispatched to a scene. A national incident management plan developed deployment protocols and incident management strategies.
- ***Seamless Communications Among All Responders.*** A critical problem area identified as a result of the response to the 9/11 attacks was that first responders often could not communicate with one another because they used different radio frequencies. This

resulted in a lack of coordination in their responses. Nationally, first responders must be able to communicate with one another in these situations. This radio inoperability, due to inconsistent radio frequencies among first responders, must be eliminated.

- ***Prepare Health-Care Providers for Catastrophic Terrorism.*** A WMD attack would certainly overwhelm local hospital and health-care facilities. Various federal agencies are now preparing surge capabilities to assist local assets in the event of an incident. Elements include disaster medical assistance teams and national medical response teams.
- ***Augment America's Pharmaceutical and Vaccine Stockpiles.*** A surge in casualties as a result of a biological, chemical, or radiological attack would result in an explosive demand for medications. The DHS in conjunction with the Department of Health and Human Services will maintain 12 strategically located sites that will contain push packs containing 600 tons of antibiotics, vaccines, and medical supplies. The push packs can be deployed to a site in less than 12 hours. Additionally, critical vaccines and antibiotics will continue to be stockpiled.
- ***Prepare for Chemical, Biological, and Radiological Decontamination.*** The DHS will require annual certification of first responder preparedness to ensure that first responders will be able to work safely in contaminated areas. A number of government grants have become available for local and state agencies to train, equip, and conduct exercises or simulations for first responders.
- ***Plan for Military Support of Civil Authorities.*** The military has extensive personnel, equipment, and expertise that can be utilized in a catastrophe. Additionally, the National Guard is a significant force that can be fairly quickly deployed in an emergency. The military's Northern Command coordinates National Guard and Reserve responses to catastrophes. This represents a unified command that can coordinate resources and respond quickly to situations.

Legal Initiatives

The new environment of homeland security assumes that there is a constant threat. In addition to program changes and the realignment of government agencies and services, the legal system is being altered to respond to these newly perceived threats. The Office of Homeland Security has identified a number of legal measures that could be incorporated as a response to terrorism:

- ***Enable Critical Infrastructure Information Sharing.*** The *National Strategy for Homeland Security* contains numerous recommendations advocating that governmental agencies and the private sector be able to quickly share vital information with other units of government. This is particularly important when establishing protocols for the protection of critical infrastructure. Many businesses and industries have been unwilling to share information for fear that public knowledge could provide proprietary information to competitors or could be used by the public to attack their integrity or operating processes. Some advocate that laws must allow for the communication of information to appropriate governmental agencies, but at the same time, protect its integrity and limit its dissemination. This information could be used to evaluate levels of protection and vulnerability and the location of materials that could be used as WMDs.
- ***Streamline Information Sharing Among Intelligence and Law Enforcement.*** The 9/11 Commission (2004), in the wake of the 9/11 attacks, found that intelligence information sharing and cooperation were major problem areas. In the past, numerous legal requirements forbade government law enforcement and intelligence agencies from sharing information. The USA PATRIOT Act addressed a number of these problems, but legal guidelines in conjunction with operational procedures must be constantly evaluated to

ensure that they allow agencies to share important information. The director of national intelligence has the primary responsibility for ensuring cooperation.

- ***Review the Authority for Military Assistance in Domestic Security.*** Federal law prohibits the military from becoming involved in civil law enforcement except when authorized by the Constitution or by Congress. For example, federal laws were changed to allow the military to become involved in drug interdiction. Should there be a terrorist attack, the military could play a key role in the response in terms of mitigation. Federal laws should be reviewed and revised when appropriate to ensure that the military can be quickly dispatched and its services utilized.

HS Web Link: To learn more about the proposed standards for state drivers' licenses, go to https:// www.dhs.gov/real-id.

- ***Coordinate Minimum Standards for State Driver's Licenses.*** The minimum requirements to obtain a driver's license and the information contained on it vary across the 50 states; there is no standard format. Terrorists, including members of al Qaeda involved in the 9/11 attacks, have exploited these inconsistencies. The United States should have a uniform driver's license.
- ***Suppress Money Laundering.*** The Money Laundering Suppression Act (P.L 103-325) urges the states to adopt uniform laws to license and regulate financial institutions. The USA PATRIOT Act encourages the states to adopt laws to control or prevent money laundering. The adoption of these laws will make it more difficult for terrorist organizations to launder their money, and it will protect law-abiding citizens engaging in legitimate financial transactions
- ***Review Quarantine Authority.*** Many state quarantine laws are well over 100 years old and do not adequately address the possibility of biological attacks. The state laws should be reviewed and evaluated in terms of their ability to adequately deal with a biological attack and prevent the spread of diseases.

Science and Technology

There is a need to increase the ability to respond to the deployment of WMDs. These WMDs remain a real threat to the populace and more effective technology needs to be developed in a number of areas. The Office of Homeland Security has identified several areas that require technological and scientific advances:

- ***Develop Chemical, Biological, and Radiological Countermeasures.*** Mechanisms need to be developed that prevent terrorists from using WMD. This includes developing sensors for detecting radioactive, chemical, and biological materials. There is also a need to develop more effective antivirals to treat citizens who might become exposed to biological weapons. Finally, more effective tracking systems must be implemented to ensure that these materials are not stolen or otherwise lost or unaccounted for in laboratories or during transportation.
- ***Develop Systems for Detecting Hostile Intent.*** Behavioral science must be applied more quickly to the war on terrorism. Law enforcement must have the tools to predict terrorist behavior. Perhaps there are behavioral precursors or activities that can identify those potentially involved in terrorism. Such systems would be most useful to augment airport security. Similar systems could be implemented at borders to screen people as they enter the United States.
- ***Apply Biometric Technology to Identification Devices.*** Fingerprints have been used as the primary means of identification for more than a century. Today, law enforcement uses DNA to investigate crimes. More effective and efficient identity devices such as retinal scanning need to be developed. Terrorists or other persons of interest who are on the FBI's watch list may obtain false documents, but an effective biometric system would result in their identification.

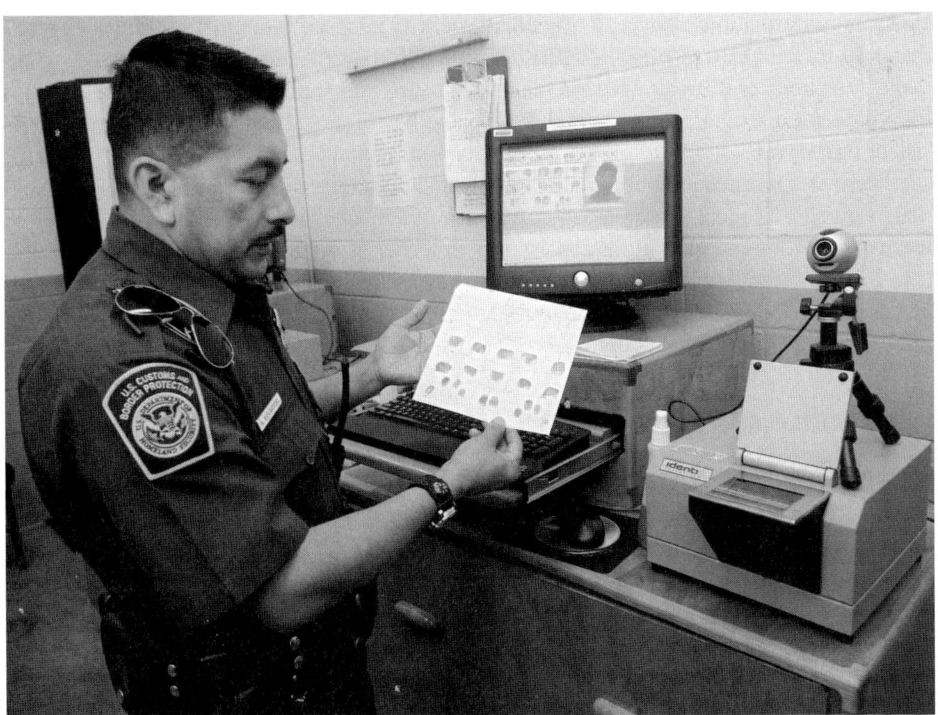

FBI agent using an automated fingerprint identification system.
Denis Poroy/AP Images.

- ***Improve the Technical Capabilities of First Responders.*** Police, fire, and emergency medical personnel are the first to respond to an attack, and some future attack could involve WMDs. Systems must be developed that ensure first responders' safety. More effective sensing devices are needed to alert first responders to potential radiological, biological, or chemical hazards. There is a need for more effective protective gear so that first responders are not injured when responding to a WMD catastrophe. Effective decontamination equipment and treatment procedures are needed to ensure their safety. There is a need for substantial technology innovation in this area.
- ***Technological Research in Homeland Security.*** The DHS needs to develop a research capacity to usher in greater innovations. As a start, there is a need to coordinate this research. The DHS must establish a bureaucracy that facilitates the timely development of innovative technology. A national laboratory should be established with the mission to facilitate research in this area, and simultaneously, the DHS should work with the national laboratories and private contractors to develop new technology.

Information Sharing and Systems

The preceding sections identified a need for substantial new programming. The DHS has approximately 230,000 employees and coordinates its operations with other federal, state, and local agencies as well as with the private sector. This massive structure requires command, control, and coordination. A number of informational needs have been identified. In the "Information Sharing and Systems" section of the *National Strategy for Homeland Security*, the Office of Homeland Security (2002) reiterates a number of these needs, including the integration of information sharing across state and local governments and within the federal government, as well as the need to improve public safety communications. Additionally, the *Strategy* suggests the adoption of common meta-data standards for electronic information relative to homeland security. One problem that currently exists is that data are kept by a number of agencies using different data management systems. This makes it extremely difficult to merge data sets to perform sophisticated analyses. It makes it difficult for one agency to pass raw data to another agency. If data are stored using consistent frameworks, it will allow for more data mining and better analyses.

There also is a need to improve the quality and dissemination of public health information. Some health records are on paper, whereas others are stored electronically. Even with electronic records, there is little consistency in terms of systems and systems integration across health-care providers. There is a need to be able to analyze large numbers of records across large geographical areas to identify any trends or problems that might suggest that a biological weapon has been deployed.

International Cooperation

Terrorism does not know any boundaries. Countries on every continent have been attacked by terrorists, some struggles having been waged for decades. Indeed, it is a global war on terrorism, and success requires international cooperation. Additionally, shared borders with Mexico and Canada make it likely that terrorists will attempt to enter the United States by crossing a border. A number of initiatives have previously been examined, including the need for smart borders, combating fraudulent travel documents, and inspection and control of international shipping containers. There are other international issues that must be pursued:

- ***Intensify International Law Enforcement Cooperation.*** There have been terrorist attacks in Europe and elsewhere committed by the same groups that could attack the United States. U.S. law enforcement officials must cooperate with police officials in foreign countries. This includes sharing intelligence information, information about terrorist attacks and investigations, and information about terrorist groups. This cooperation can provide a wealth of information beneficial to all countries. The sum of this information is greater than what comes from examining only the various parts or pieces of intelligence. When the United States works with other nations that have been attacked, it not only provides mitigation assistance, but intelligence information is also gained about groups with the capacity and wherewithal to mount an attack in the country.
- ***Help Foreign Nations Fight Terrorism.*** The United States must assist foreign countries fighting terrorism, especially countries in the Middle East and Europe. The United States can provide foreign governments with training, military assistance, and equipment to help secure their borders. Government officials must identify programs that can be applied internationally and assist in their implementation.
- ***Review Obligations and Limitations Associated with Treaties and International Law.*** The overwhelming majority of international treaties and laws limiting U.S. law enforcement and intelligence operations in foreign countries were approved under the Cold War paradigm. This new era of terrorism has substantially altered the world and international relations. This means that new methods are required to combat this new enemy. The federal government must examine existing international relationships and limitations posed by treaties and international laws. These must be changed to ensure maximum cooperation with other counties in the war on terrorism. The United States must implement mutual legal assistance treaties with other countries and work with the United Nations to enact proposals that hinder terrorist activities and facilitate international cooperation.

The previous sections provide a detailed examination of the *National Strategy for Homeland Security*. Although issued in 2002, it represents one of the most comprehensive roadmaps to homeland security, and it serves as the foundation for decisions and policy making today. It details a number of needs across the complete spectrum of homeland security requirements.

HS ANALYSIS BOX 1-4

The *9/11 Commission Report* and the *National Strategy for Homeland Security* provide a roadmap for implementing homeland security. The federal government has expended a great deal of resources in implementing the various recommendations. What are the areas of overlap between these two documents? The *National Strategy* is comprehensive in addressing issues across a wide range of deficiencies. Are there any areas that you recognize that are not addressed in the *National Strategy*, but should be?

▶ Costs of Homeland Security

With increased homeland security activity comes increased costs. The DHS is one of the largest departments in the federal government with over 230,000 employees. In 2016, DHS's budget was $64,858,484,000. Of course, this budget is for a large number of different agencies that are involved in a wide variety of activities.

Figure 1-5 ■ shows where these expenditures have occurred and also, to some degree, federal priorities. FEMA receives a large amount of funding. This is the result of the agency responding to a large number of emergency disasters each year. Of the law enforcement

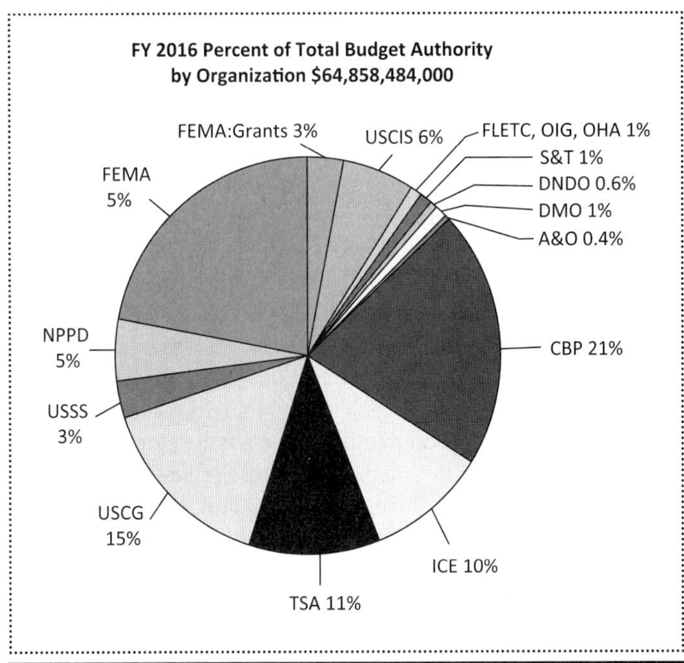

FIGURE 1-5 How about "Funding Priorities 2016"

Agencies in Figure 1-5: FEMA-Federal Emergency Agency; DMO-Departmental Management and Operations; A&O-Analysis and Operations; OIG-Office of the Inspector General; CBP-Customs and Border Protection; ICE-Immigration and Customs Enforcement; TSA-Transportation Security Administration; USCG-U.S. Coast Guard; USSS-U.S. Secret Service; NPPD-National Protection Program and Protection Directorate; OHA-Office of Health Affairs; U.S. Citizenship & Immigration Services; FLETC-Federal Law Enforcement Training Center; S&T-Science & Technology Directorate; and DNDO-Domestic Nuclear Detection Office.

Source: DHS (2016). *Budget-in-Brief: Fiscal Year* 2016. Author, p. 9.

agencies (ICE, CBP, TSA, USSS, and USCG), Customs and Border Protection (CBP) receives the largest percentage of funds. A number of the agencies like the Departmental Management and Operations (DMO) or Analysis and Operations (A&O) support the management of DHS, while other agencies such as the Domestic Nuclear Detection Office (DNDO) and Science & Technology Directorate (S&T) provide research capability for the DHS. Considering all the agencies housed within the DHS, it is apparent that the DHS is involved in a wide range of activities.

Kahan (2013) has been critical of the DHS organization, noting that the department has two primary functions: non-homeland security responsibilities and homeland security. He notes that the DHS has a "smorgasbord" of non-homeland security activities that may interfere with the DHS's ability to carry out some of its homeland security responsibilities. Within the various agencies, the programs and budgets for these two responsibilities are intermingled. The most obvious is FEMA's responsibility for responding to disasters. Other agencies have similar dilemmas; the U.S. Coast Guard interdicts drug smugglers and protects shipping lanes and the CBP collects tariffs on goods coming through our ports of entry. Kahan cautions that the non-homeland security responsibilities may consume larger portions of agencies' budgets, thus reducing the agencies' ability to perform the many non-routine homeland security responsibilities. Kahan advises that the agencies should clearly enumerate homeland responsibilities and ensure that they are properly conducted. The DHS should re-examine its organization structure to see if changes can insure that the homeland security responsibilities are not neglected.

There has been criticism of homeland security expenditures in Congress, and a 2012 study commissioned by Senator Tom Colburn of Oklahoma was highly critical of the DHS, the urban Areas Security Initiative Program, in particular. Since 2003, the DHS spent $7 billion on the program, which was designed to provide units of state and local government and first responders grants so that they would be better prepared in the event of a terrorist attack. The report found numerous examples of financial excess. Columbus, Ohio, spent $98,000 for an underwater robot to patrol its rivers; Peoria, Arizona, spent $90,000 to install cameras and car barriers at the spring training field for the San Diego Padres and Seattle Mariners; Clovis, California, police used a $200,000 armored personnel carrier to patrol an annual Easter egg hunt; and police in Oxnard, California, spent $75,000 to outfit a cultural center with surveillance equipment and alarms (Coburn, 2012). These are just a few of the many questionable expenditures made as a result of the program. Governments and agencies are purchasing all sorts of equipment that may or may not be related to improving homeland security.

The problem is that many local communities have not developed a comprehensive plan detailing their vulnerabilities and the methods by which to reduce those vulnerabilities, and the DHS has not been holding them to any standard; expenditures should be used to specifically attend to homeland security. It also infers that the DHS needs to have an operational plan at the local level to make these funding decisions. This is especially critical since it is impossible to secure all communities across the country. There, perhaps, are numerous DHS programs that are wasteful, absorbing resources that could be used to attend to real homeland security needs.

Regardless, the United States is not the only country that has substantially increased homeland security expenditures. European nations have been reorganizing their homeland security apparatuses and devoting more resources to them, especially in light of the attacks that have occurred there. Lipowicz (2008) reports that Saudi Arabia is drastically increasing its homeland security and antiterrorism allocations. Lipowicz notes that the Saudis will spend $115 billion during the next decade and will be second only to the United States in homeland security expenditures. Today, Saudi Arabia has 24 agencies devoted to homeland security with an estimated 250,000 employees. Costs will continue to rise as countries attempt to protect themselves from terrorist attacks.

Harvey (2007) notes that these expenditures are paradoxical in that higher levels of expenditures often beget ever-increasing levels of government investment. First, such expenditures represent a substantial amount of costs, public sacrifice, and political capital. He suggests that as expenditures increase there will be an increase in people's expectation of safety. When failures or attacks occur, public outrage could increase. This results in greater political commitment to higher levels of protection and substantial increases in spending. In other words, failure drives expenditures. Success seldom enters the picture in terms of funding. More substantial costs can be anticipated in the future.

Indirect Costs

In addition to the direct costs associated with homeland security, there are indirect costs that are not considered when calculating the total cost of homeland security. One significant indirect cost is the increase in government spending outside the rubric of homeland security. The Northern Command, a major military command, was created to provide homeland defense on American soil, so a significant amount of its budget can be attributed to homeland security. The Department of Defense, especially the Defense Intelligence Agency, is involved in countering terrorism. Homeland security functions have been enhanced in many federal governmental departments, CIA, FBI, NSA, and so on, and it is likely that their costs are not included in any calculations of homeland security costs.

Other indirect costs should be considered. First, security costs at airports have increased because of TSA operations. It has also resulted in numerous passenger delays and additional costs. People likely are spending thousands, if not millions, of hours at airports, which results in a loss of productivity. Second, the government has increased restrictions on international travel, making it difficult for many businesspeople to travel to the United States, and in some cases, some of these people are not allowed to enter. For example, President Trump enacted a policy temporarily restricting travel to the United States from six Islamic countries. Given the global economy, these restrictions negatively affect business arrangements and productivity. Third, the government is more closely screening imports for WMDs that may be coming into the United States. This results in delays and substantially increased transportation costs. The cost of security produces numerous indirect costs that affect the economy.

Summary

Homeland security is now a critical political and practical part of the American landscape. The 9/11 attacks resulted in substantial changes in a number of areas. Homeland security has become a way of life, and this is unlikely to change anytime in the foreseeable future.

This chapter provides an introduction to homeland security and the definitional issues surrounding it. Although most people see homeland security as a defense against terrorist attacks, the homeland security apparatus is concerned with disasters and future hazards as well as terrorist attacks. Homeland security requires a response to a host of disasters, including terrorist attacks. The fact that disasters such as hurricanes and earthquakes are included in the response protocols complicates the direction and organization of homeland security. The all-hazards approach may complicate effective responses to terrorism.

After the 9/11 attacks, the United States had little in terms of government organization or enterprise to counter future attacks. The formation of homeland security essentially started at zero, and bureaucracies were developed that could effectively respond to threats. Essentially, the DHS was created and became the lead agency in preparing for terrorist events. However, since this was a relatively new phenomenon, there was no foundation for organizing homeland security efforts. Two documents have served as roadmaps for homeland security, the *9/11 Commission Report* and the *National Strategy for Homeland Security*. The *9/11 Commission Report* basically provided an assessment of the problems with security arrangements at the time and made a number of suggestions for improvement. The *National Strategy for Homeland Security*, on the other hand, provided a detailed map on how to proceed with establishing security. It was comprehensive and detailed a number of critical areas requiring immediate and long-term development. Today, the *National Strategy* has been updated with the *Quadrennial Homeland Security Review Reports*, and they serve as the primary policy guide for homeland security. Numerous federal agencies are engaged in fulfilling the recommendations outlined by these documents.

Discussion Questions

1. An examination of fear of crime studies shows that fear of being a victim of a terrorist attack is much higher than that of more common crimes and homicide. Given the limited number of terrorist attacks on American soil and the limited number of deaths and injuries, why does fear of a terrorist attack rank so high?
2. There is a debate over what problems should be covered or addressed by homeland security. How does this debate affect the organization and operations of homeland security?
3. The *9/11 Commission Report* and the *National Strategy for Homeland Security* form the foundation for homeland security. Compare and contrast these two documents in terms of scope and direction.
4. The Homeland Security Advisory System has been used to alert Americans about terrorist activities and impending attacks. How effective is this system and why?
5. The *National Strategy for Homeland Security* addresses an expansive array of homeland security activities and objectives. Which three areas do you believe are the most critical? Why?
6. In 2009, the world was threatened by a swine flu (H1N1) pandemic. Did homeland security efforts improve our capacity to deal with the threat? How?
7. Describe why it is important for state and local officials to be involved in homeland security.

References

Attorney General. (1999). *Five-Year Interagency Counterterrorism and Technology Crime Plan.* Washington, D.C.: Author.

Bellavita, C. (2008). "Changing homeland security: What is homeland security?" *Homeland Security Affairs*, 4(2): 1–30.

Carrell, S. (2007). "Lybian jailed over Lockerbie wins right to appeal." *The Guardian* (June 29). www.guardian.co.uk/uk/2007/jun/29/lockerbie.scotland (Accessed August 7, 2008).

Clarke, R. (2008). *Your Government Failed You: Breaking the Cycle of National Security Disasters: Breaking the Cycle of National Security Disasters.* New York: HarperCollins.

Coburn, T. (2012). *Safety at Any Price: Assessing the Impact of Homeland Security Spending in U.S. Cities.* Washington, D.C.: U.S. Senate.

Department of Homeland Security. (2016). *Budget-in-Brief: Fiscal Year 2016.*

Department of Homeland Security. (2014). *Quadrennial Homeland Security Review Report: A Strategic Framework for a Secure Homeland.* Washington, D.C.: Author.

Department of Homeland Security. (2012). *Strategic Plan: Fiscal Years 2012–2016.* Washington, D.C.: Author.

Department of Homeland Security. (2010). *Quadrennial Homeland Security Review Report: A Strategic Framework for a Secure Homeland.* Washington, D.C.: Author.

Eggen, D. and R. Wright. (2006). "Tenet told 9/11 panel that he warned Rice of Al Qaeda: Former CIA head said she took threat seriously." *The Boston Globe,* http://www.boston.com/news/nation/washington/articles/2006/10/03/tenet_told_9/11_panel_that_he_warned_rice_of_al_qaeda/ (Accessed July 15, 2008).

Emerson, S. and B. Duffy. (1990). *The Fall of Pan Am 103: Inside the Lockerbie Investigation.* New York: Putnum.

FBI (2015). *Crime in the United States, 2013.* http://www.fbi.gov/about-us/cjis/ucr/crime-in-the-u.s/2013/crime-in-the-u.s.-2013/tables/1tabledatadecoverviewpdf/table_1_crime_in_the_united_states_by_volume_and_rate_per_100000_inhabitants_1994-2013.xls (Accessed May 6, 2015).

FEMA. (2015). *Disaster declarations by year.* http://www.fema.gov/disasters/grid/year (Accessed May 7, 2015).

Ghamari-Tabrizi, S. (2006). "Lethal fantasies: With its eye on the 'universal adversary,' homeland security catastrophes." *Bulletin of the Atomic Scientists*, 62(1): 20–22.

Harvey, F. (2007) "The homeland security dilemma: Imagination, failure, and the escalating costs of perfecting security." *Canadian Journal of Political Science*, 40: 283–316.

Highway Institute for Highway Safety Highway Loss Data Institute. (2017). General Statistics. http://www.iihs.org/iihs/topics/t/general-statistics/fatalityfacts/state-by-state-overview.

Inserra, D. and J. Phillips (2015). "67 Islamist terrorist plots since 9/11: Spike in plots inspired by terrorist groups, unrest in Middle East." *The Heritage Foundation.* http://www.heritage.org/terrorism/report/67-islamist-terrorist-plots-911-spike-plots-inspired-terrorist-groups-unrest.(Accessed May 6, 2015).

Kahan, J. (2013). "The two faces of DHS: Balancing the department's responsibilities." *Homeland Security Affairs*, 9.

Lipowicz, A. (2008). "Saudi homeland security costs spike." *WashingtonTechnology*. https://washingtontechnology.com/articles/2008/05/29/saudi-homeland-security-costs-spike.aspx (Accessed August 6, 2008).

Michel, L. and D. Herbeck. (2001). *American Terrorist: Timothy McVeigh and the Oklahoma City Bombing*. New York: Harper Books.

National Commission on Terrorist Attacks upon the United States. (2004). *The 9/11 Commission Report*. New York: W.W. Norton.

Office of Homeland Security. (2007a). *National Strategy for Homeland Security*. Washington, D.C.: Author.

Office of Homeland Security. (2007b). *National Infrastructure Protection Plan*. Washington, D.C.: Author.

Office of Homeland Security. (2002). *National Strategy for Homeland Security*. Washington, D.C.: Author.

University of Albany. (2007). *Sourcebook of Criminal Justice Statistics*. Washington, D.C.: Bureau of Justice Statistics. www.albany.edu/sourcebook/pdf/t239.pdf (Accessed September 19, 2008).

U.S. Commission on National Security/21st Century. (1999). *New World Century: American Security in the 21st Century*. Washington, D.C.: GPO.

Wright, L. (2006). *The Looming Tower: Al-Qaeda and the Road to 9/11*. New York: Knopf.

2 The Homeland Security Apparatus

LEARNING OBJECTIVES

1. *Analyze the development of homeland security in the United States.*
2. *Describe the Department of Homeland Security's organization.*
3. *Describe the various agencies within the Department of Homeland Security.*
4. *Explain the roles of agencies outside the Department of Homeland Security.*
5. *Explain the role of the Department of Defense in homeland security and defense.*
6. *Discuss the role of state governments in homeland security.*

Key Terms

Chemical and Biological Rapid Response Team
Child Exploitation Investigations Unit
Computer Forensics Unit
Container Security Initiative
Counter-Proliferation Investigations Program
Customs and Border Protection
Customs-Trade Partnership against Terrorism
Department of Defense
Department of Homeland Security
Domestic Nuclear Detection Office
Federal Air Marshal Program
Federal Emergency Management Agency
Federal Law Enforcement Training Center
Fugitive Operations Program
Homeland defense
Immigration and Customs Enforcement
Known Shippers Program
Mission diffusion
National Gang Unit
National Guard Weapons of Mass Destruction–Civil Support Teams
NORTHCOM
Office of Homeland Security in the White House
Operation SOAR
Priority Enforcement Program
Transportation Security Administration
U.S. Citizenship and Immigration Services
U.S. Coast Guard
U.S. Secret Service
Uniform Division

▶ Introduction

Since 2001, homeland security has become a significant governmental and private sector enterprise. New governmental bureaucracies were created with the primary mission of providing homeland security. The **Department of Homeland Security** (DHS) is the primary federal agency charged with providing security, although other federal departments are involved, and states have developed agencies charged with implementing homeland security programs. This chapter examines the homeland security apparatus. It discusses the federal agencies and some of the state initiatives designed to effectuate homeland security. The DHS serves as the hub of operations or the primary point organization for homeland security.

Department of Homeland Security

Before the creation of the DHS, homeland security was coordinated by the **Office of Homeland Security in the White House**. It was headed by Tom Ridge, whose title was assistant to the president for homeland security. When the DHS was created, Ridge transitioned into the newly created cabinet position. The DHS was created as a result of the Homeland Security Act of 2002 (Public Law 107-296) and was officially inaugurated on March 1, 2003 (DHS, 2008). The DHS was given the responsibility to be the lead federal agency in securing the country. Although at first glance this appears to have been a simple, straightforward task, it was in reality very complicated, involving a matrix of programs and agencies. The creation of DHS was accomplished by reorganizing a number of departments in the federal government. More than 100 units and bureaus from other departments were transferred to the new DHS. After its creation, the DHS became the third largest department in the federal government with more than 230,000 employees (DHS, 2008). Only the Departments of Defense and Veterans Affairs are larger. It represented the largest federal government reorganization since President Harry Truman merged the various branches of the military into the Department of Defense. Figure 2-1 ■ provides a listing of the units and agencies that were shifted to the newly organized DHS.

HS Web Link: To learn more about the Department of Homeland Security, go to http://www.dhs.gov/index.shtm.

As noted in Figure 2-1 ■, a number of agencies and sub-agencies were reorganized in the DHS. Independent agencies such as the U.S. Coast Guard and the U.S. Secret Service were placed under the DHS umbrella. Several agencies from the Departments of Energy, Justice, and Treasury were moved to the DHS. The Federal Emergency Management Agency (FEMA), which had been independent, was consumed within the DHS. A review of the agencies moved to the DHS demonstrates the complexity and comprehensiveness of the consolidation.

Political Considerations in the Creation of the Department of Homeland Security

The Department of Homeland Security was created in 2003 with much fanfare from Congress and the White House. Its creation indicated to the American populace that the federal government was making a substantial effort to increase security. After the 9/11 attacks, fear of terrorist attacks dominated public opinion. People visually and emotionally witnessed the destruction of the World Trade Center Towers and part of the Pentagon. This moved national security to the forefront of people's thinking and fears. The dramatic nature of the event and the devastation of the attacks ensured that there would be a response.

However, the creation of the DHS was, in the minds of many politicians and bureaucrats, not an effective solution to the problem of homeland security. Many believed that adequate governmental apparatuses were in place, but they lacked proper coordination (Clarke, 2008). Coordination would provide better results as compared to developing a new bureaucracy. Indeed, coordination had existed across various departments when dealing with a number of significant problems in the past. For example, the National Security Council has been responsible for coordinating national security efforts across a variety of agencies and across federal government departments for approximately 50 years.

Original Agency (Department)	Current Agency/Office
The U.S. Customs Service (Treasury)	U.S. Customs and Border Protection-inspection, border and ports of entry responsibilities U.S. Immigration and Customs Enforcement—customs law enforcement responsibilities
The Immigration and Naturalization Service (Justice)	U.S. Customs and Border Protection—inspection functions and the U.S. Border Patrol U.S. Immigration and Customs Enforcement—immigration law enforcement: detention and removal, intelligence, and investigations U.S. Citizenship and Immigration Services—adjudications and benefits programs
The Federal Protective Service	U.S. Immigration and Customs Enforcement
The Transportation Security Administration (Transportation)	Transportation Security Administration
Federal Law Enforcement Training Center (Treasury)	Federal Law Enforcement Training Center
Animal and Plant Health Inspection Service (part) (Agriculture)	U.S. Customs and Border Protection—agricultural imports and entry inspections
Office for Domestic Preparedness (Justice)	Responsibilities distributed within FEMA
The Federal Emergency Management Agency (FEMA)	Federal Emergency Management Agency
Strategic National Stockpile and the National Disaster Medical System (HHS)	Returned to Health and Human Services, July 2004
Nuclear Incident Response Team (Energy)	Responsibilities distributed within FEMA
Domestic Emergency Support Teams (Justice)	Responsibilities distributed within FEMA
National Domestic Preparedness Office (FBI)	Responsibilities distributed within FEMA
CBRN Countermeasures Programs (Energy)	Science & Technology Directorate
Environmental Measurements Laboratory (Energy)	Science & Technology Directorate
National BW Defense Analysis Center (Defense)	Science & Technology Directorate
Plum Island Animal Disease Center (Agriculture)	Science & Technology Directorate
Federal Computer Incident Response Center (GSA)	US-CERT, Office of Cybersecurity and Communications in the National Programs and Preparedness Directorate
National Communications System (Defense)	Office of Cybersecurity and Communications in the National Programs and Preparedness Directorate
National Infrastructure Protection Center (FBI)	Dispersed throughout the department, including Office of Operations Coordination and Office of Infrastructure Protection
Energy Security and Assurance Program (Energy)	Integrated into the Office of Infrastructure Protection
U.S. Coast Guard	U.S. Coast Guard
U.S. Secret Service	U.S. Secret Service

FIGURE 2-1 Agencies Transferred to the DHS

In actuality, the DHS's creation had its impetus from Connecticut Senator Joe Lieberman. Initially, President George W. Bush's administration was opposed to the creation of such a department. Lieberman, a Democrat at the time, proposed the department's creation in the U.S. Senate. When the proposal began to get widespread support and traction from Democrats and Republicans alike, the White House offered its own version to prevent the Democrats from gaining political mileage or advantage in the homeland security political arena (Clarke, 2008). The creation of the DHS was initially problematic, as it required substantial time, energy, and resources being spent on developing a bureaucracy as opposed to dealing directly with homeland security problems. Moreover, the reorganization did not completely deal with the coordination problem. Even though a number of agencies were moved to the DHS, numerous agencies outside it retained homeland security responsibilities, for example, the Federal Bureau of Investigation (FBI) or the Central Intelligence Agency (CIA), but were not merged into the new department. Further, the DHS included a number of agencies with dissimilar missions, for example, FEMA, Customs, and the Coast Guard, complicating coordination and contributing to mission distortion within the DHS.

Richard Clarke (2008), who held a number of high-level positions in intelligence in the State and Defense Departments, advised that the DHS was a product of politics and fear, not careful analysis. The DHS was set up without adequate resources or regulatory powers and without strong leadership. Clarke is not alone in his criticism. Shapiro (2007) noted that politics played a key role in the department's organization, resulting in numerous problems in the various agencies within the DHS.

Kamarck (2007) had identified a number of issues that questioned the effectiveness of the DHS. She advised that the bureaucracy was too cumbersome and expansive and that some functions of the department should be moved to other departments. For example, should FEMA be a part of the DHS? Perrow (2002) argues that homeland security has resulted in FEMA's budget being diverted from its original mission, making the agency less responsive and effective. Prior to the creation of the DHS, FEMA was a cabinet-level department. Kahan (2015) noted that FEMA has always been a political issue with different presidents moving the agency in and out of the cabinet. The merging of border protection agencies with emergency response agencies has resulted in coordination and mission diffusion problems and perhaps has weakened both agencies. The DHS should focus on border protection and as a conduit for integrating and sharing homeland security intelligence with state and local governments and the private sector. Although well intended, the merging of many agencies into an expansive DHS certainly has resulted in many control, coordination, and management problems.

Since its inception, a number of problems have plagued the DHS, which is typical when new agencies are created or when there is a massive reorganization. It is also noteworthy that terrorism and homeland security are constantly evolving and with that comes a level of uncertainty. The following sections discuss some of those problems.

White House and Congressional Oversight

Homeland security remains a prominent political issue, and as such, it draws the interest of politicians. Oftentimes, political interests override organizational imperative. Politicians are all too often more interested in managing appearances as opposed to solving real problems. It would seem that the secretary of the Department of Homeland Security would have exclusive domain over its operation and long-term objectives. However, the White House and Congress have substantial oversight responsibilities and exert substantial influence and control over the department. The White House is responsible for promulgating a national strategy regarding homeland security. This responsibility resides with the White House since a coherent strategy would include numerous other federal departments as well as the DHS. Obviously, the DHS would be involved in policy development, but final authority rests with the White House.

Congress has fared no better in terms of providing guidance to the DHS. Some 100 committees and subcommittees in the House and Senate have some degree of oversight of homeland security (Yager, 2013). This diffusion results in inconsistency and a general lack of cohesiveness in terms of congressional oversight, appropriations, and the submission and passage of important homeland security–related legislation. Given the number of congressional committees the secretary reports to, it is surprising that the secretary has time to manage the department. Yager reported that in 2009, Janet Napolitano, the DHS Secretary, estimated that the DHS spent 33,000 hours preparing reports for Congress, 41,000 hours were spent preparing and delivering briefings to Congress, and 58,000 hours were spent responding to letters to Congress. It would make more sense for one committee in the House and Senate to have this oversight responsibility, but too often committee chairs and members are unwilling to defer their authority adding a cumbersome workload to the department. Authority over some aspect of homeland security always plays well with their electorates.

In some cases, the overlapping congressional oversight has led to conflict among committees. Laing (2011) reported that Representative John Mica, chair of the House Transportation and Infrastructure Committee, and Pete King, chair of the Homeland Security Committee, wrangled over control of the Transportation Security Agency (TSA). At one point, Mica put forth an amendment cutting $270 million from the TSA budget. The result of the amendment would have required the TSA to hire civilian contractors to conduct screening. This conflict has continued. In 2012, the Aviation Subcommittee held hearings on TSA-related investigations and complaints, but TSA officials did not attend the meeting stating the committee did not have any jurisdiction over the TSA (Gauthier, 2012).

This problem has been recognized by a number of authorities. For example, the *National Strategy for Homeland Security* (Office of Homeland Security, 2002) recommended that the secretary have more latitude in reorganizing the DHS, and Kamarck (2007) recommended that congressional oversight be consolidated into one committee in the House of Representatives and one committee in the Senate. Given the fluid nature of terrorism and the department's many and varied range of responsibilities, it is obvious that the DHS, as the primary response mechanism, should have increased flexibility. However, the political tethers binding the department have not been loosened. This remains a formidable problem.

Agency Confusion and Mission Distortion

The manner in which the DHS was created led to a number of problems not only for the department but also for the individual agencies subsumed within it. In terms of the DHS, its rapid organization and deployment resulted in substantial confusion. At first glance, it would appear that the DHS has proprietary responsibility for homeland security. However, a number of agencies outside the DHS have significant security roles and responsibilities, for example, agencies within the Department of Defense, the FBI, the Treasury Department, and the Energy Department to name a few. The diffusion of interests has ultimately resulted in coordination and command issues (Hambridge, Howitt, and Giles, 2017) (see Wermuth, 2005).

At the same time, the reorganization resulted in agencies acquiring new responsibilities generally without a reduction in old mandates. This resulted in **mission distortion** or confusion regarding individual agencies' missions and priorities. For example, the U.S. Customs and Border Protection (CBP) is charged with interdicting terrorists entering the United States. Additionally, the agency is responsible for protecting American agriculture from harmful pests and agricultural diseases, stemming the flow of drugs and other contraband, and collecting import duties. These duties are wide ranging and asymmetric. How should

HS ANALYSIS BOX 2-1

The previous discussion shows that politics were heavily involved in the creation of the Department of Homeland Security. It also shows that during its inception, there were numerous organizational and operational problems. Of course, this is consistent with many governmental endeavors. Given the political history of the DHS and the current political atmosphere in the United States, do you believe that we have improved homeland security? Why?

the CBP's duties be prioritized? How do the antiterrorism duties fit within its organizational structure and operations? These became critical questions and resulted in substantial bureaucratic confusion within many of the agencies in the DHS. Homeland security duties, for the most part, were simply added to the agencies' original or traditional responsibilities. The creation of the DHS did not result in clear and tight operational procedures to guide lower-level managers and supervisors.

Kahan (2013) has referred to this situation as the "two faces" of the DHS where agencies have both homeland and non-homeland security responsibilities. He advises that non-homeland security responsibilities may consume larger portions of agencies' resources, resulting in inadequate resources for homeland security. Day-to-day operations in DHS agencies generally center on non-homeland security activities, not homeland security.

The initial development of the DHS resulted in numerous problems, which occur when a new agency is developed or undergoes significant changes. The DHS has made progress with regard to a number of these problems, but the executive branch should continue to focus on improving the DHS's overall operating effectiveness, especially when balancing traditional responsibilities with homeland security.

▶ The Structure of the Department of Homeland Security

As discussed earlier in the chapter, the DHS was created by hobbling together a number of agencies from throughout the federal government into the new department. Additionally, a number of other agencies were added as new responsibilities were identified. Complex organizations are constantly evolving. Working relationships among agencies must be constantly refined, and in some cases, agencies must be reorganized as the homeland security terrain evolves. As an example, the FBI today has many more agents devoted to counterterrorism and the bureau has increased the number of foreign-language interpreters. Change is a natural part of organizational evolution, and if it does not occur, most likely the DHS will in some regard become less effective in pursuing its various missions.

Figure 2-2 ■ provides an organizational chart depicting those agencies in the DHS and their reporting chain of command. As noted, the DHS has approximately 230,000 employees dispersed across a number of agencies.

The DHS is a cabinet-level agency within the executive branch. It is headed by a secretary, who reports to the president. The department contains a number of administrative and support units as well as operational units that generally are headed by an assistant secretary or a director.

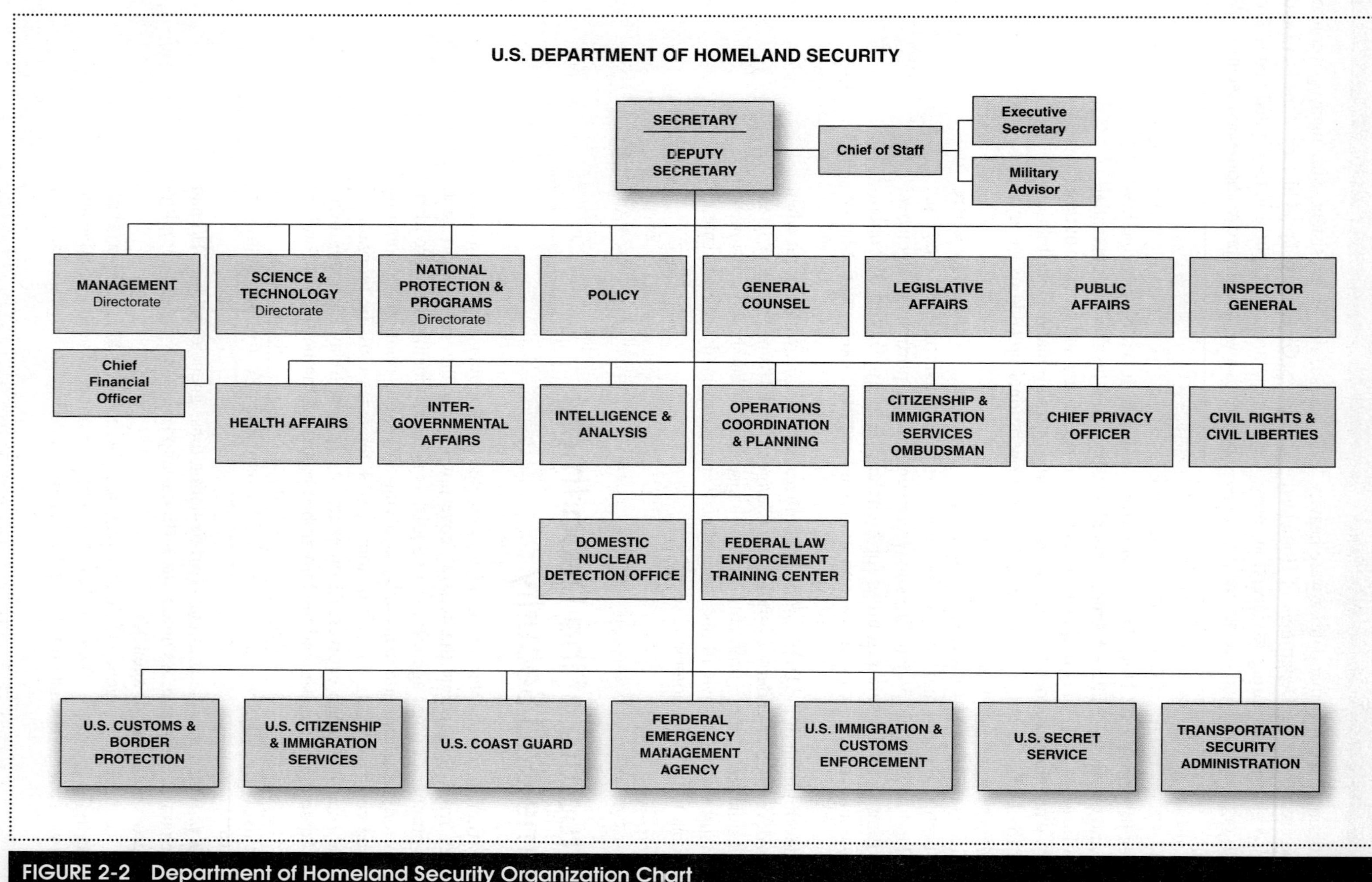

FIGURE 2-2 Department of Homeland Security Organization Chart

Source: DHS. (2016). Organizational Chart. https://www.dhs.gov/sites/default/files/publications/Public%20Org%20Charts%202017.04.12.pdf (Accessed July 21, 2017).

DHS Administrative and Support Agencies

As noted there are several administrative and support offices within the DHS. Several key agencies are briefly described here:

- **Management Directorate** ensures that employees have well-defined responsibilities, provides accounting services for the department, oversees the hiring of employees, engages in property management, and tracks performance.
- **Science and Technology Directorate** is responsible for developing and procuring technology that facilitates the DHS's mission. For example, its scientists and engineers develop sensors to detect materials used for weapons of mass destruction (WMD), facial recognition software, and robots to disarm bombs. Figure 2-3 ■ lists some of the areas in which the directorate develops technology.
- **National Protection & Programs Directorate** leads in the effort to protect the nation's physical and cyber infrastructure. Its offices include the Federal Protective Service, Office of Biometric Identity Management, Office of Cybersecurity and Communications, Office of Cyber & Infrastructure Analysis, and the Office of Infrastructure Protection.
- **Legislative Affairs** works with and communicates with members of Congress and congressional committees about department policies and programs and keeps senior members of the DHS informed about congressional issues.
- **Public Affairs** coordinates public affairs activities of all the component agencies within the DHS and serves as the lead information office when there is a national emergency or disaster.
- **Office of the Inspector General** conducts and supervises audits, investigations, and inspections of DHS activities to uncover or deter fraud, abuse, and mismanagement.
- **Office of Health Affairs** advises DHS leadership on public health problems and issues and works with public health agencies across the country to better respond to a public health crisis.
- **Office of Intergovernmental Affairs** works with state, local, territorial, and tribal governments to achieve an integrated approach to homeland security.
- **Office of Intelligence and Analysis** provides the department with intelligence and information on homeland security. It provides intelligence analysis, collects and manages information pertinent to homeland security, and shares information so that the department can take action.

- Chemical, biological, radiological, nuclear, and enhanced explosives sensors and detection equipment standards
- X-ray and gamma-ray technical performance standards, including detection standards for bulk explosives, weapons, and contraband
- Interagency standards for decontamination technologies, protocols, and training
- Standards supporting first responders; incident management standards; communications standards; and chemical, biological, radiological, and nuclear (CBRN) protective equipment and urban search-and-rescue robots standards
- Standards for biometrics including latent fingerprint analysis standards, rapid biometric evaluation standards, and biometric image and physical feature quality standards for identity cards and travel documents
- Test and evaluation policies and processes

FIGURE 2-3 DHS Science and Technology Accomplishments

- **Office of Operations Coordination** monitors the security of the United States and coordinates departmental activities with governors, homeland security advisors, law enforcement personnel, and infrastructure operators across the country.
- **Citizenship & Immigration Services Ombudsman** works with individuals and employers to resolve problems with U.S. Citizenship and Immigration Services. It also makes recommendations to fix problems and improve the quality of services.
- **Office for Civil Rights and Civil Liberties** supports the department's mission and activities while safeguarding civil rights and civil liberties.

The following sections provide an overview of some of the operational units within the DHS. Notice that there are a number of agencies that in their aggregate have a wide range of responsibilities and activities.

Transportation Security Administration

HS Web Link: To learn more about the TSA, visit http://www.tsa.gov/.

The **Transportation Security Administration** (TSA) was moved to the DHS from the Department of Transportation. When most people think of the TSA, they focus on airport security. However, the TSA's mandate is much broader. The primary responsibilities of the TSA are to protect the nation's entire transportation system, including aviation, waterways, rail, highways, public transportation, and pipelines. Thus, the agency has a substantial responsibility, with aviation being only a small portion of the overall mandate.

The TSA attempts to ensure freedom of movement for people and commerce. The most visible members of the TSA are in airports. There are 450 airports from Guam to Alaska employing about 50,000 screeners. TSA air travel responsibilities include the screening of luggage and passengers for destructive devices. In a typical year, TSA agents will screen 650 million passengers, and 2 million carry-on and checked bags. The TSA deploys several systems to accomplish this monumental task. First, it uses explosive detection machines when screening checked luggage. These machines determine if there are trace explosives in the luggage or on the luggage. Second, carry-on baggage is screened in a similar manner. TSA officers collect samples of residue and analyze them for trace explosive materials. The agency deploys machines that blow air onto passengers and the air is collected and analyzed for explosive materials. TSA officers also use bomb-sniffing dogs. There are about 1,047 dog-sniffing teams stationed in 82 airports, along with 33 bus, rail, and transit systems (Janson, 2017). The TSA also checks passenger profiles against terrorist databases.

The TSA is in the process of upgrading its technology for screening passengers. The agency is experimenting with backscatter technology that projects X-ray beams over the body to create a reflection of the body displayed on the monitor, as well as millimeter wave technology that bounces harmless electromagnetic waves off the body to create a black-and-white three-dimensional image (TSA, 2010a). This technology has been installed in many U.S. airports. The use of such technology is controversial since they display a passenger's body without their consent.

TSA officials are having an impact on airline security. In 2015, TSA agents discovered a record 2,653 firearms in baggage or in people's possession, and most of the weapons were loaded. This was a 20 percent increase over 2014. The top five airports where firearms were discovered were Dallas/Fort Worth, Atlanta, Phoenix, Houston, and Denver. Most people reported that they forgot they had the weapons. In addition to the firearms, TSA agents confiscated additional dangerous objects such as knives, razors, stun guns, ammunition, and firearm components (TSA, 2016). However, there are problems with TSAs programs. In a security test, a TSA undercover operation found that TSA screeners failed to find 67 out of 70 weapons that passed through screening (Sasse, 2015). Even though screeners detect and confiscate many weapons, it appears that many weapons go undiscovered by TSA agents at our nation's airports.

Some of the guns confiscated by TSA officers.
Transportation Security Administration.

The TSA has concentrated on air travel security, but the technology is beginning to be deployed in other travel sectors. For example, the TSA is using some of its bomb-sniffing dogs in subways. This is a critical move given the number of people who travel using mass transit systems and because in other countries terrorists have detonated bombs in subways and on buses and trains (e.g., in Great Britain and Spain). The TSA has teamed with the New York City Transit Authority to test passive millimeter wave technology. The system screens for explosives as passengers enter the Staten Island ferry.

After the 9/11 attacks, new regulations allowed pilots to carry firearms in the cockpit of their aircraft. The TSA is responsible for training pilots on how to use firearms. All flight crew members are provided with self-defense training to improve their ability to control situations on aircraft. A substantial amount of cargo is transported by air, much of which is on passenger planes. The TSA monitors and regulates cargo that is being shipped by air, and the agency audits shippers to ensure that only approved cargo is transported. The **Known Shippers Program** ensures that only cargo from approved or known shippers can be transported in certain instances. Cargo is also x-rayed to identify possible explosive devices. The TSA has made efforts to secure hazardous materials and explosives that are transported on the nation's highways. Drivers who transport such materials now must obtain a hazardous materials endorsement (HME) for their commercial driver's license. The TSA conducts background investigations prior to the issuing of the HMEs. In 2006, the TSA began to require similar background checks for drivers from Canada and Mexico who transported dangerous materials into the United States.

Federal Air Marshal Program

One of the law enforcement components within the TSA is the **Federal Air Marshal Program**, which deploys armed officers on civilian aircraft whose purpose is to intervene in possible hijackings or other terrorist activities. When the 9/11 attacks occurred, there were only 50 air marshals, and they were assigned primarily to international flights. Even though the

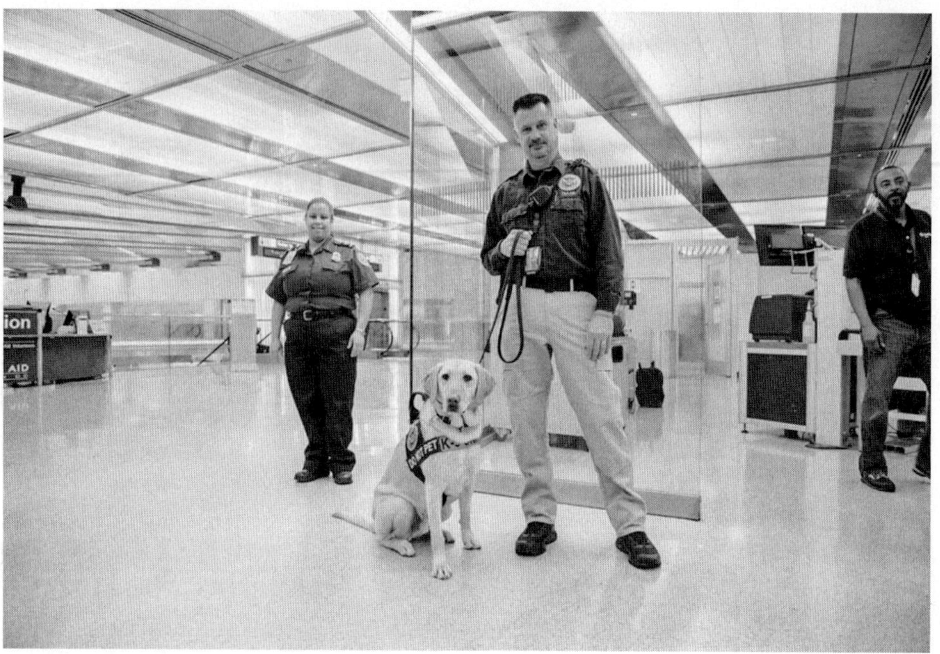

TSA agents are using dogs to check for explosive materials at U.S. transportation hubs.
Transportation Security Administration.

program has been expanded, most of the daily 28,000 flights do not have an air marshal onboard. The air marshals also work with local law enforcement, the FBI, and other federal agencies coordinating antiterrorism activities.

U.S. Customs and Border Protection

HS Web Link: To learn more about the Customs and Border Protection, go to http://www.cbp.gov/.

Customs was created in 1789 to collect tariffs on goods imported into the United States. The tariffs collected by Customs essentially supported the federal government for more than 125 years and funded a substantial amount of the country's early infrastructure. **Customs and Border Protection** (CBP) was organized by merging inspectors from the Agriculture Quarantine Inspection Program, Immigration and Naturalization Services, Inspection Services, Border Patrol, and the Customs Service. According to the CBP, the primary law enforcement responsibilities for the agency are (1) apprehending criminals and others who illegally attempt to enter the United States, (2) seizing illegal drugs and other contraband, and (3) protecting U.S. agriculture from harmful pests and diseases. On a typical day CBP agents will welcome 1 million visitors to the United States, inspect 67,000 cargo containers, arrest 1,000 individuals, and seize nearly six tons of illicit drugs (CBP, 2016). CBP has expansive responsibilities.

The national debate over undocumented immigration has resulted in additional personnel and the development of new technology to help secure the country's borders. A primary homeland security mission of the CBP is to prevent terrorists and terrorist weapons, including weapons of mass destruction, from entering the United States. Included in this mission is the apprehension of undocumented immigrants and smugglers. The agency arrests over 300,000 people a year coming across the border illegally.

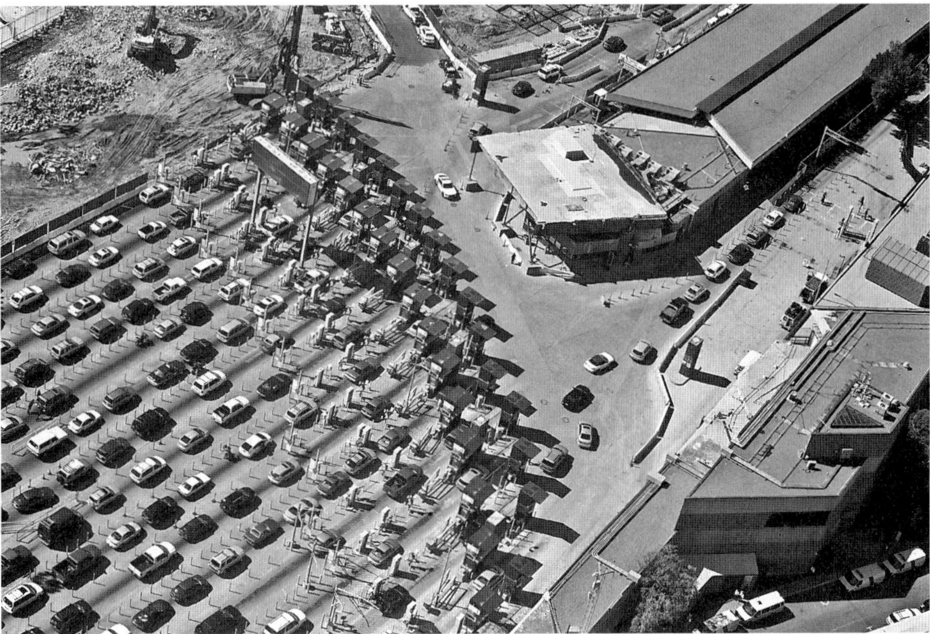

Cars line up at the San Ysidro inspection station, the busiest land port in the United States.
U.S. Customs and Border Protection.

Border Crossings and Ports of Entry

The CBP has checkpoints at ports of entry including border crossings, sea ports, and airports where international flights enter the United States. People entering the United States are stopped to ensure that they have proper documentation, passports, and visas, and that they are not smuggling contraband. Automobiles, buses, freight trains, and marine craft entering the United States are checked. In addition to checking people, cargo is inspected for contraband, WMD or WMD materials, and agriculture products that may contain disease or harmful pests.

On a typical day, CBP agents will

- Process 1,026,234 passengers and pedestrians; 70,334 truck, rail, and sea containers; and 307,680 incoming privately owned vehicles
- Conduct 1,333 apprehensions between U.S. ports of entry
- Arrest 21 wanted criminals at U.S. ports of entry
- Refuse entry to 241 inadmissible persons at U.S. ports of entry
- Discover 425 pests at U.S. ports of entry and 4,447 materials for quarantine—plant, meat, animal byproduct, and soil
- Seize 10,327 pounds of drugs and $650,117 in undeclared or illicit currency
- Identify 548 individuals with suspected national security concerns
- Intercept 76 fraudulent documents

Cargo Inspection

The CBP is primarily involved in protecting America's supply chain by adopting the tenets of the president's *National Strategy for Global Supply Chain Security*. This protection entails an international layered response whereby CBP monitors cargo from its emanation point until it reaches the United States. The United States depends on this supply chain for all sorts of foodstuffs, medicines, machinery, and so on. By monitoring and safeguarding the supply chain, CBP officers help ensure that contraband or WMD materials are not smuggled into the United States. The CBP uses its **Container Security Initiative** (CSI) to accomplish this. The CSI is a program where CBP officers are stationed in foreign locations and work with host foreign government counterparts to identify and inspect suspect containers. The **Customs-Trade Partnership against Terrorism** is a similar program where safe shippers in other countries are identified as being safe. They are vetted and their containers are expedited through the shipping process. By working with trusted foreign governments and other partners, the CBP expedites the flow of goods in the United States.

The CBP uses a variety of methods to inspect cargo containers. Traditionally, they were inspected manually by officers and dogs. These methods now are supplemented with radiation detection devices and container imaging equipment. They are used at our seaports as well as on our land borders to inspect cargo transported by trucks. The CBP has also installed these devices in foreign ports to inspect cargo that is being shipped to the United States.

Agriculture Inspection

As noted earlier, CBP works with agents from the U.S. Department of Agriculture to inspect certain agriculture products to prevent harmful pests from coming into the United States. American agriculture is a multi-billion dollar industry. Should these pests enter, they could have a devastating impact on American crops. CBP agents routinely intercept prohibited meat, plant materials, and other animal products at the various ports of entry into the United States.

Border Patrol

The Border Patrol agents of the CBP are responsible for patrolling more than 7,000 miles of the Canadian and 2,000 miles of the Mexican borders. Additionally, Border Patrol marine

CBP officers X-ray food coming into New York.
U.S. Customs and Border Protection.

HS ANALYSIS BOX 2-2

Looking at the activities performed by the CBP, it is evident that the agency is involved in a wide range of activities that do not relate to homeland security. Based on the agency's performance, as reviewed, which of these activities do you believe are the most important? Are there activities that should be assigned to another agency? Do you think these activities take away from the agency's ability to perform homeland security duties?

units patrol the coastal waters around Florida. The most substantial obstacle when patrolling our land borders is the terrain, especially along the Mexican border, which is where the largest number of smuggling and illegal immigrant activities occurs. The border is primarily desert and mountains, which makes patrolling and observation extremely difficult.

Border Patrol uses air and vehicular patrols. In some cases, all-terrain vehicles and horses are used. The patrols look for illegal immigrants or evidence that they are using a particular route. In some cases, fences have been constructed in areas that have high traffic. The fences alter illegal immigrants' routes and reduce the amount of area that must be constantly patrolled. For example, fences in San Diego, California, substantially reduced illegal entries in the area. In some areas, drones are used to look for illegal immigrants or smuggling operations. Video cameras have been installed in some areas.

The CBP is involved in a substantial number of activities across a broad spectrum of security areas. They demonstrate that the agency is involved in a variety of measures that are critical to national security, particularly screening terrorists who may attempt to enter the United States. The CBP is responsible for points of entry, the border, and ports, be they marine or airports. Once undocumented people have entered the United States or traveled beyond points of entry, U.S. Immigration and Customs Enforcement assumes jurisdiction (this agency is discussed in the following text).

U.S. Immigration and Customs Enforcement

Immigration and Customs Enforcement (ICE) was created by combining the law enforcement arm of the Naturalization Service, the intelligence and investigative sections of the former Customs Service, and the U.S. Federal Protective Services. It is headed by an assistant secretary, and it is the largest investigative branch within the DHS. The inclusion of the U.S. Federal Protective Services resulted in ICE being responsible for the protection of 8,800 federal properties. ICE has three primary areas of concentration to achieve its mission: (1) immigration enforcement, (2) investigating illegal movement of people and goods, and (3) preventing terrorism (ICE, 2016). Whereas Customs and Border Protection secures our borders, ICE has immigration and other responsibilities beyond the borders or in the interior of the United States. Consequently, ICE has a range of investigative responsibilities:

HS Web Link: To learn more about ICE, go to http://www.ice.gov/.

Dismantling gang organizations by targeting their members, seizing their financial assets, and disrupting their criminal operations.

Investigating employers and targeting undocumented workers who have gained access to critical infrastructure worksites (such as nuclear and chemical plants, military installations, seaports, and airports).

Investigating fraudulent immigration benefit applications and fraudulent illegal document manufacturing.

Investigating the illegal export of U.S. ammunitions and sensitive technology.

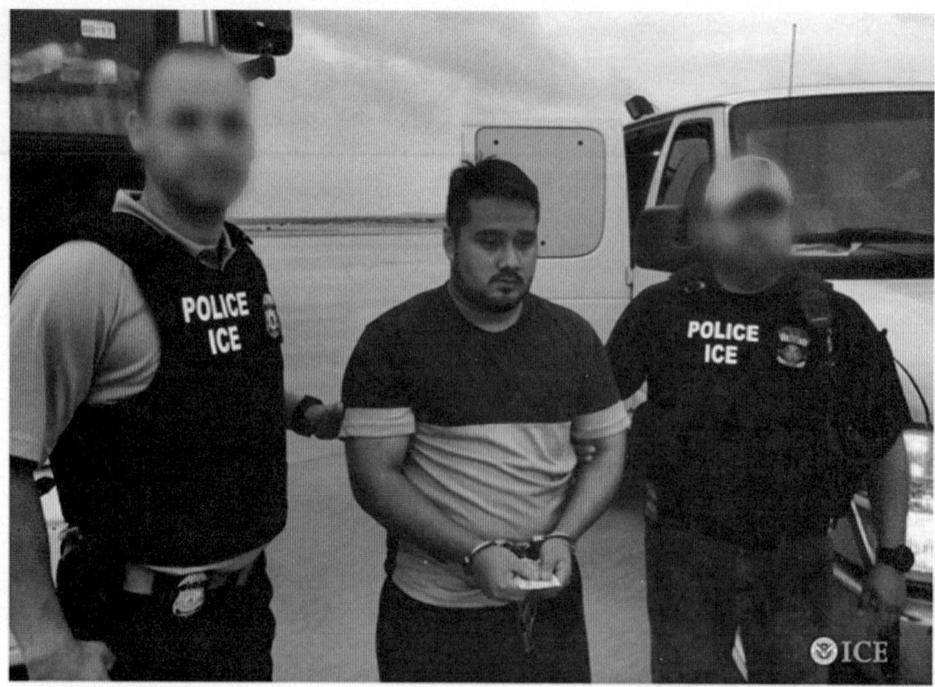

ICE agents remove Salvadorian man wanted for aggravated homicide.
U.S. Immigration and Customs Enforcement.

1. Investigating criminal organizations that smuggle and traffic in humans across our borders.
2. Ensuring that people ordered removed by the courts depart the United States as quickly as possible.
3. Destroying the financial infrastructure that criminal organizations use to earn, move, and store illicit funds.
4. Targeting and intercepting counterfeit products smuggled into the United States.
5. Providing support to state and local law enforcement communities in the areas of forensic documents and cyber crimes (ICE, 2009).

Immigration Enforcement

Apprehending and Removal of Criminal Illegal Immigrants ICE has a number of programs that focus on immigration enforcement. The **Criminal Alien Program** targets priority illegal immigrants who are incarcerated in jails or prisons and at-large criminal illegal immigrants who have circumvented arrest or identification. If an illegal immigrant is convicted of a crime, ICE agents will proceed with legal procedures to remove him or her from the United States. The program is designed to remove as many criminals from the United States as possible. The **Fugitive Operations Program** has similar responsibilities. Agents assigned to this program attempt to locate and arrest fugitive illegal immigrants, illegal immigrants who previously were removed from the United States, criminal illegal immigrants, and those who have violated our immigration laws. For example, **Operation SOAR**, one of the program's operations, focused on removing foreign-born sex offenders. A third enforcement program is the **Priority Enforcement Program**. Once an illegal immigrant is arrested by local or state law enforcement, his or her fingerprints are sent to the FBI and ICE. If the individual is considered high priority as a result of criminal activities, ICE agents will issue a detainer to have the person turned over to ICE for removal once the local or state charges have been resolved. Finally, ICE's **National Gang Unit** fights transnational criminal gangs. The unit collects intelligence on these gangs, members, and activities and works with state and local authorities to disrupt them through arrest or deportation and the seizure of assets and contraband.

Detention Operations ICE's Enforcement and Removal Operations (ERO) oversees immigration detention facilities. Any noncitizen who is apprehended and needs custodial supervision is placed in one of the detention centers. The ERO processes cases, detained and non-detained, as they progress through the immigration court proceedings. Once a judge issues an order, the ERO executes the order. When a case involves an unaccompanied minor, he or she is supervised by the Department of Health and Human Services, Office of Refugee Resettlement.

ICE Workplace Enforcement A major problem has been the employment of illegal immigrants. This practice has served as a magnet for illegal immigrants to come to the United States. Today, ICE agents check many workplaces to determine if illegal immigrants are employed in an effort to reduce the practice. When inspecting a worksite, agents will look for evidence of worker mistreatment, trafficking, smuggling, harboring, visa fraud, identification document fraud, and criminal conduct. When such problems are identified, ICE obtains search warrants, makes arrests, and pursues indictments with the U.S. Attorney. Inspection priority is given to critical infrastructures such as chemical plants, dams, emergency services communications, and critical manufacturing. ICE agents also focus on employers who have been caught previously hiring illegal immigrants.

Investigating Illegal Movement of People and Goods

ICE has several units devoted to investigating a wide range of criminal problems.

Cyber Crimes The Cyber Crimes Center provides technical support to domestic and international investigations where the criminal activity crosses our borders. The Center consists of three units: the Cyber Crimes Unit, the Child Exploitation Investigation Unit, and the Computer Forensics Unit. The Cyber Crimes Unit investigates computer-related crimes such as identity theft, money laundering, financial fraud, narcotics trafficking, and illegal exports. For example, in 2012, ICE in conjunction with Europol and several European law enforcement agencies seized 132 Internet domain names. The websites were being used to sell knockoff or counterfeit goods (Associated Press, 2012). The Child Exploitation Investigations Unit targets crimes that involve the sexual exploitation of children including child pornography and child sex tourism. The unit works with other national and international agencies when conducting investigations. The unit also participates in programs designed to identify child victims and rescue them when possible. The **Computer Forensics Unit** perform digital analyses on computers to assist in investigations.

Human Trafficking ICE recognizes that human trafficking is a global problem and that many victims are transported across our borders. ICE works with CBP to identify and disrupt human trafficking operations. ICE also works with the U.S. Citizenship and Immigration Services to protect victims by procuring visas. Human trafficking is targeted by identifying large-scale smuggling operations. ICE agents attempt to collect intelligence about these operations to guide investigations. Also, agents try to investigate and prosecute everyone along the smuggling chain, not just the smugglers who transport the victims.

Contraband Interdiction An important activity with regard to contraband interdiction is drug interdiction. ICE agents have substantial knowledge about drug trafficking operations as a result of working on U.S. borders. They are familiar with routes, smuggling

ICE agents seize one ton of marijuana at the Port of Long Beach.
US Immigration and Customs Enforcement.

techniques, and persons involved in the transportation of drugs. Agents observe behaviors and activities to identify possible smugglers. Also, agents conduct undercover operations and use informants to identify suspects. Finally, they work with other federal, state, and local agencies to collect intelligence and interdict drugs.

ICE agents are involved in the investigation of money laundering. Once drugs and other contraband are sold in the United States, organized crime groups like the drug cartels must move the money back to their home country. Consequently, substantial amounts of money move across the borders, especially the southern border, and ICE agents attempt to interdict it. ICE agents work with other agencies to identify criminal networks in the financial, trade and transportation industries that may be engaging in money laundering. In one case, Arthur Budovsky of the Liberty Reserve was convicted of money laundering. He operated a worldwide Internet bank with more than 600,000 accounts. He admitted to laundering more than $250 million with much of the funds derived from investment fraud, credit card fraud, identity theft, and computer hacking (ICE, 2016b).

ICE interdicts firearms, ammunition, and explosives leaving and coming into the U.S. Many of the drug cartels attempt to purchase weapons in the United States. These weapons are vital to Mexico's drug wars. ICE agents attempt to stop the flow of weapons. In one case, Eyad Farah of Barrington, Texas, was convicted for his part in a smuggling operation where firearms were concealed in vehicles that were purchased at auction and shipped to the Middle East.

Preventing Terrorism

The Counter-Proliferation Investigations Program is a program designed to protect the homeland by preventing the export of technology and sensitive commodities to foreign countries. The United States manufactures components that can be used to construct sophisticated weapons and other machinery that can be a threat to our national security. The program combats the trafficking of

- WMD and associated delivery systems
- Conventional military weapons, equipment, and technology

- Controlled dual-use commodities and technology
- Firearms and ammunition
- Financial and business transactions with sanctioned or embargoed countries and terrorist groups

ICE is a member of the Joint Terrorism Task Force (JTTF). The JTTF investigates, detects, and arrests terrorists as well as dismantling terrorist organizations. In a two-year period, ICE agents were involved in over 1,100 terrorist investigations resulting in over 500 arrests. In one investigation, ICE agents arrested 31 people including a procurement officer for a terrorist organization who were smuggling weapons (ICE, 2016b).

ICE is the largest investigative agency within the DHS and is involved in a number of wide-ranging investigations. It is responsible for the security in the interior United States and enforces a large number of federal statutes. The agency apprehends large numbers of illegal immigrants each year. For example, in one year,

- ICE conducted 235,413 removals of illegal immigrants.
- ICE conducted 69,478 removals of individuals apprehended by ICE officers (i.e., interior removals). Of these, 63,539 (91%) were previously convicted of a crime.
- ICE conducted 165,935 removals of individuals apprehended at or near the border or ports of entry.
- The leading countries of origin for removals were Mexico, Guatemala, Honduras, and El Salvador.
- 1,040 individuals removed by ICE were classified as suspected or confirmed gang members.

U.S. Citizenship and Immigration Services (USCIS)

In 2003, the services and functions of the U.S. Immigration and Naturalization Service (INS) were transferred to the Department of Homeland Security as the **U.S. Citizenship and Immigration Services** (USCIS). The enforcement and inspection functions within the INS were transferred to the Customs and Border Protection Agency. The USCIS is responsible for the administration of immigration and naturalization adjudication functions and establishing immigration services policies and priorities. This agency essentially is the court where immigration cases are heard. These functions include the following:

HS Web Link: To learn more about the USCIS, go to http://www.uscis.gov/portal/site/uscis.

1. Adjudication of immigrant visa petitions
2. Adjudication of naturalization petitions
3. Adjudication of asylum and refugee applications
4. Adjudications performed at the service centers
5. All other adjudications performed by the INS

As a result of the 9/11 terrorist attacks, governmental agencies have more closely examined the legality of numerous people's status. Many people have overstayed their visas and otherwise entered the United States illegally. The USCIS is responsible for hearing appeals when deportation proceedings begin. On a typical day, the USCIS will

- Welcome 3,200 new citizens; typically, 35 of them are already serving their adopted country in the United States armed forces.
- Grant permanent residence to 4,000 people and issue 6,500 Permanent Resident Cards.

- Process 183 refugee applications around the world and grant asylum to 55 people already in the United States.
- Provide immigration services, engage in fraud prevention and detection, and serve as government liaisons in 25 international field offices in 22 countries.
- Process 2,040 petitions filed by employers to bring workers to the United States.
- Conduct 148,000 national security background checks.
- Ensure the employment eligibility of more than 58,000 new hires in the United States.
- Fingerprint and photograph 15,000 applicants.

These activities demonstrate that the USCIS is involved in a number of investigations. These activities have become much more critical since 9/11. For example, Customs and Border Protection agents are apprehending larger numbers of undocumented people as they cross the border and are employed in the United States. USCIS must adjudicate all those who fight deportation. They sometimes must adjudicate suspected terrorists or those who may have ties to terrorists who are being deported. They also are involved in cases in which undocumented criminals are being deported from the United States. Thus, they play a key role in keeping the country safe.

U.S. Secret Service

HS Web Link: To learn more about the U.S. Secret Service, go to http://www.secretservice.gov/.

The **U.S. Secret Service** was established in 1865, and its primary mission at the time was to capture counterfeiters and reduce counterfeiting. During the Civil War, approximately one-third of all the money in circulation was counterfeit. Today, countries such as North Korea are counterfeiting American money to raise hard currency (Berlinger and Cohen, 2017). Counterfeiting undermines our economic system and national security.

In 1901, after President McKinley was assassinated, Congress directed the Secret Service to provide protection for the president. Prior to that time, there was no federal agency responsible for presidential protection. This remains the primary responsibility of the Secret Service. In 1922, during the administration of President Warren G. Harding, the Secret Service created the **Uniform Division**, which provides protection for the White House, the Treasury Building, presidential offices, the vice president's residence, and foreign diplomatic missions. In 2003, when President George W. Bush reorganized federal law enforcement, the Secret Service was moved from the Treasury Department to the Department of Homeland Security.

The USA PATRIOT Act increased the Secret Service's role in investigating fraud and related activity in connection with computers. The act also authorizes the director of the Secret Service to establish nationwide electronic crimes task forces to assist the law enforcement and private sectors and academia in detecting and suppressing computer-based crime. The act increased the statutory penalties for the manufacturing, possessing, dealing, and passing of counterfeit U.S. or foreign obligations. It also allows enforcement action to be taken to protect financial payment systems while combating transnational financial crimes perpetrated by terrorists or other criminals.

The Secret Service provides protection to the president, vice president, their immediate families, former presidents and their wives and children (up to the age of 16), visiting heads of foreign states and other distinguished visitors, and presidential and vice presidential candidates within 120 days of the general presidential election.

The U.S. Secret Service has the National Threat Assessment Center, which reports on a variety of threats. In 2015, the center examined all the attacks on the federal government between 2001 and 2013. The center studied 43 different attacks and provided an analysis of the incidents and the suspects.

Agents guarding Pope Francis during his visit in 2015.
Jin Lee-Pool/Getty Images.

U.S. Coast Guard

Historically, the primary responsibility of the **U.S. Coast Guard** was the enforcement of maritime laws. This responsibility included ensuring the safe flow of maritime traffic, maritime security including the interdiction of drugs coming into the United States, protection of natural resources including fish and protected environmental areas, and maritime safety by ensuring that craft abided by laws and regulations. As an example, in 2010, the U.S. Coast Guard was given the responsibility of coordinating the mitigation of the oil platform explosion and oil spill in the Gulf of Mexico near Louisiana. Today, the mission of the U.S. Coast Guard has been expanded to watch for threats to national security. The agency is responsible for protecting more than 361 ports and 12,383 miles of coastline, America's longest border. In fact, port and waterway security consume more than half of the Coast Guard's budget (O'Rourke, 2006).

In one year, the U.S. Coast Guard,

- Responded to over 17,000 search-and-rescue cases, saved 3,430 lives and more than $47 million in property.
- Removed 90,997 kilograms of cocaine and 108,535 pounds of marijuana bound toward the United States.

HS ANALYSIS BOX 2-3

In terms of homeland security, it appears that the U.S. Secret Service has three primary objectives: (1) executive protection, (2) stop counterfeiting, and (3) stop the counterfeiting of financial documents and credit card fraud. How do these three objectives relate to homeland security?

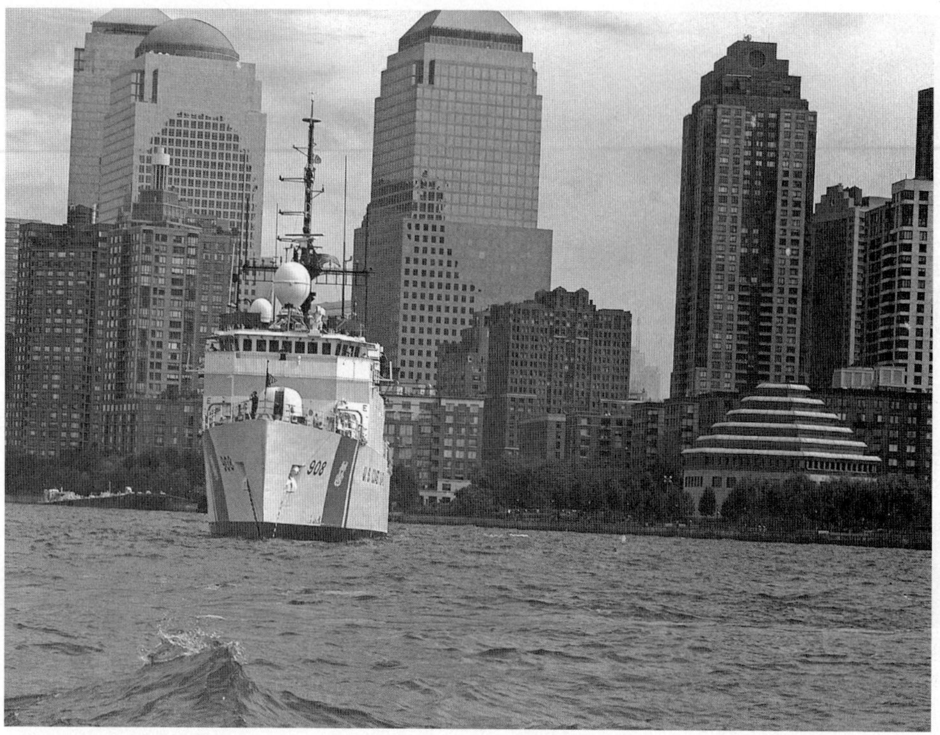
U.S. Coast Guard cutter guarding the Hudson River after the 9/11 attacks.
United States Coast Guard.

- Continued the deployment of six Patrol Boats and 400 personnel to protect Iraqi critical maritime oil infrastructure and train Iraqi naval forces.
- Conducted 189 escorts and patrols to support 67 domestic U.S. military cargo out loads.
- Conducted 25,393 container inspections.
- Conducted 623 boardings of high-interest vessels designated as posing a greater than normal risk to the United States.
- Interdicted more than 7,747 undocumented migrants attempting to illegally enter the United States.
- Screened over 212,000 vessels, including over 126,000 commercial vessels and 30 million crewmembers and passengers prior to arrival in U.S. ports (U.S. Coast Guard, 2016).

The U.S. Coast Guard coordinates its activities with civilian law enforcement and the U.S. military. Whereas the U.S. Customs and Border Protection protects points of entry, the U.S. Coast Guard provides a parameter defense. This is accomplished by interdicting and investigating suspicious vessels prior to their entering maritime ports. As such, the U.S. Coast Guard investigates people and activities especially as they relate to terrorism, narcotics smuggling, undocumented immigrants attempting to enter the United States, and transnational crime.

The previous sections detailed the activities of the enforcement and security units within the DHS. In addition to enforcement and security, the DHS has a number of units that provide support and mitigation should there be a terrorist attack or some type of catastrophe. The following sections describe some of these units.

Flooding in Cape Girardeau, MO. In 2016.
FEMA Photo Library.

Federal Emergency Management Agency

In 2001, the **Federal Emergency Management Agency** (FEMA) became part of the DHS. It is the federal agency responsible for responding to and mitigating disasters and catastrophes in the United States. The agency derives its authority from the Robert T. Stafford Relief and Disaster Act (1988) and has about 14,000 employees. FEMA is activated once the president declares an area a disaster. Historically, the agency has responded to numerous natural disasters such as hurricanes, floods, tornados, and earthquakes. FEMA is responsible for a quick and long-term response. In terms of an immediate response, FEMA is a first responder that attempts to meet disaster victims' water, food, and shelter needs. FEMA personnel coordinate activities with state and local personnel and largely depend on contractors to provide immediate services and supplies. In the long term, FEMA is responsible for providing support during the rebuilding of a disaster area. This is accomplished through the provision of grants and low-interest loans to affected people.

HS Web Link: To learn more about FEMA, go to http://www.fema.gov/.

FEMA has a significant homeland security role. When there is an event, natural disaster, or terrorist attack, FEMA is called to help mitigate damage and problems. It adds resilience to our communities and infrastructure by helping normalize the situation. FEMA also provides communities and local and state agencies with grants to purchase equipment so they are better prepared to respond to any events. FEMA also funds or provides training so that first responders have the required skills and knowledge.

Many consider moving FEMA to the DHS was ill advised. Although FEMA responds to terrorist attacks, its principle responsibility remains to respond to disaster declarations. The agency responds to a variety of disasters including severe storms, floods, tornados,

Year	Number of Disaster Declarations
2015	79
2014	84
2013	95
2012	112
2011	242
2010	108
2009	115
2008	143
2007	136
2006	143

FIGURE 2-4 FEMA Disaster Declarations
Source: Data obtained from FEMA, http://www.fema.gov/disasters/grid/year

wildfires, mudslides, and landslides. Figure2-4 shows the number of disaster declarations by year for a 10-year period. These data show that FEMA primarily responds to non-terrorist events. Nonetheless, the procedures used to respond to disasters are the same as those used to respond to terrorist events.

Federal Law Enforcement Training Center

The **Federal Law Enforcement Training Center** (FLETC) is responsible for training law enforcement officers from about 90 federal agencies as well as officers from state and local departments. FLETC's primary training center is located in Brunswick, Georgia, but it also has facilities in Charleston, South Carolina; Artesia, New Mexico; and Cheltenham, Maryland. The addition of FLETC to the DHS enabled the DHS to rapidly increase terrorist-related training. Moreover, it allowed a number of federal agencies to receive integrated and coordinated training. That is, there is terrorist-related curriculum that is consistent across all agencies in addition to specialized training for individual agencies. For example, FLETC provides intelligence analysis and counterterrorism operations, which is now an integral part of all federal law enforcement operations. Having all the training housed in a limited number of locations results in a more efficient training program across the board.

Domestic Nuclear Detection Office

The use of radiological or nuclear materials poses the greatest threat to our population. The **Domestic Nuclear Detection Office** (DNDO) is responsible for implementing domestic nuclear and radiological detection and coordinating responses to these types of threats. Detection is accomplished through technological and non-technological means. Technological detection consists of the strategic placement of radiological sensors to detect radiation, while non-technological detection includes the reporting of materials. The DNDO uses a layered response to accomplish this mission. Radiation monitors are used to scan people, materials, and transport vehicles including cargo containers for radiological and nuclear materials at international border crossings. Law enforcement deploy detectors at special events or terrorist target areas. U.S. Coast Guard officers carry scanners when boarding vessels. The DNDO has placed detection sensors in an increasing number of cities. For example, sensors have been deployed in New York City because it is likely to be attacked again.

Department of Defense and Homeland Security

Today, the Department of Defense (DoD) is extensively involved in security efforts. Given that the DoD is responsible for protecting the nation from attacks by other nations and the magnitude of possible terrorist attacks, it is natural that the resources from the DoD be enlisted in homeland security or defense efforts. The DoD is familiar with terrorist tactics, has the organizational capacity to deal with such problems, and has a wealth of personnel and technology to devote to mitigating a terrorist attack or assisting the DHS in preventing such an attack.

The DoD sees its role as homeland defense. The DoD has two interrelated roles in homeland security. First, Homeland defense is defending against threats such as terrorism, weapons of mass destruction, and cyber incidents. Second, the DoD provides civil support. Here, the DoD supports other federal agencies in responding to a major domestic event or disaster (GAO, 2012). For example, the Army was sent to New Orleans after Hurricane Katrina. These limited roles allow the DoD to avoid becoming involved in missions that are under the purview of the DHS and other agencies. Instead, the DoD provides support to the DHS and other agencies involved in homeland security. Therefore, the DoD's involvement is limited to specific types of situations. Former Secretary of Defense Donald Rumsfeld identified three such situations: (1) extraordinary situations or circumstances that require traditional military action or missions, (2) emergency situations or catastrophes as a result of terrorist attacks or some natural disaster, and (3) provision of security assistance at National Security Special Events such as the Olympics (see Bowman, 2003; Goss, 2006). For the most part, the DHS and other agencies are primarily involved in homeland security, and DoD personnel become involved only in limited situations.

HS Web Link: To learn more about the DoD's homeland defense role, go to http://www.fas.org/man/crs/RL31615.pdf.

Because of potential terrorist attacks and a need for the military to become involved in some homeland security situations, the DoD created a new command, the Northern Command (NORTHCOM). NORTHCOM's area of responsibility includes the continental United States, Alaska, Canada, Puerto Rico, and the Virgin Islands. Hawaii and the U.S. territories remain under the control of the Pacific Command. Additionally, NORTHCOM's authority includes a 500-mile sea and air approach to the United States. NORTHCOM has subsumed the North American Aerospace Defense Command (NORAD) since the 9/11 attacks involved aircraft. NORAD would be involved in intercepting and neutralizing any attack involving aircraft. Here, NORAD would coordinate activities with the Federal Aviation Administration. NORTHCOM's Joint Task Force North is stationed in Texas and is responsible for supporting federal law enforcement agencies in the interdiction of suspected transnational threats including terrorists, narco-trafficking, alien smuggling, and weapons of mass destruction. NORTHCOM would also command any National Guard units that are federally activated for homeland security purposes. NORTHCOM does not have a large contingent of personnel but depends on other military units that have designated terrorist prevention or response missions.

The military has a number of assets that are indispensable in homeland security. First, it has units that can respond to a chemical, biological, radiological, or nuclear (CBRN) incident. The DoD has a joint service Chemical and Biological Rapid Response Team (CB-RRT) that is designed to support civilian authorities in the event of a chemical or biological attack or catastrophe. This unit is activated once such an incident has occurred. The DoD has also authorized 55 **National Guard Weapons of Mass Destruction–Civil Support Teams** that can be federally activated should there be a CBRN incident. The CB-RRT and other military units can advise civilians on how to respond to attacks, diagnose attacks to determine the types of agents used, measure the scope and dangers associated with an attack, and assist in mitigating the impact of an attack. The DoD plays an important role if WMDs are used.

An important military asset is the National Guard. Normally, the National Guard is under the control of state governments. However, the National Guard can be federalized and called upon to provide homeland defense or civil support. The National Guard fills in the gap between homeland security and homeland defense. Homeland security is primarily concerned with protecting U.S. territory while homeland defense primarily guards against external threats. The National Guard is a military force that can provide assistance to homeland security forces when there is a significant need. One problem exists, however, Governors may activate the National Guard for matters or situations where they are inadequately trained or equipped (Goss, 2006). There are new tactical needs as a result of the National Guard's civil support role within the context of homeland security. We need to clearly identify these roles and ensure that the Guard is adequately prepared.

▶ State-Level Homeland Security

HS Web Link: To learn more about New York's homeland security program, go to http://www.dhses.ny.gov/media/documents/NYS-Homeland-Security-Strategy.pdf.

Most if not all states now have a state-level office or department devoted to homeland security. Most states have housed these functions or departments within a larger emergency management department. These offices have four primary responsibilities: (1) coordinate state efforts with the DHS, (2) coordinate the homeland security efforts within the state, (3) coordinate state and federal homeland security grants and expenditures, and (4) provide education and training to people involved in homeland security activities. Larger states tend to have more sophisticated homeland security apparatuses as compared to smaller states. Nonetheless, these state agencies play a key role in prevention, mitigation, and response should a terrorist attack or other catastrophe occur.

For example, the state of New York has a fairly comprehensive homeland security apparatus. The state's primary agency is the Division of Homeland Security and Emergency Services. The division has four primary offices: emergency management (OEM), fire prevention and control (OFPC), counter terrorism (OCT), and interoperable and emergency communications (OIEC) (New York State Division of Homeland Security, 2016). The OEM is responsible for coordinating the state's response to any emergencies. Here, state emergency management personnel will work with first responders at the scene of a disaster or terrorist attack. They also will obtain additional resources as required and coordinate with federal agencies if necessary. The OEM also provides technical support to agencies as well as training, hazard identification, and planning. The OEM essentially is New York's frontline agency for mitigation of disasters.

The OFPC provides fire services, training and technical assistance to fire services throughout the state. Fires, whether they are fires of structures or large areas, pose a hazard to people and infrastructure. Moreover, a terrorist attack can result in large scale fires. The OFPC attempts to ensure that these first responders are prepared in terms of equipment and training. The OCT's mission is to support local, state, federal, and private concerns in the prevention, protection, and preparation for acts of terrorism. It is not a law enforcement agency, but provides support activities in the areas of coordination and communication. Finally, the OIEC is the state agency that deals with any inoperable communications problems. One of the primary problems when first responders responded to the 9/11 attacks was radio inoperability. That is, the responders from different agencies communicated on different radio frequencies and therefore could not communicate with each other. This resulted in many problems during the response. The OEIC attempts to ensure communications operability so that these problems do not occur in the future.

In addition to state agencies, a number of cities and counties have homeland security bureaus or offices. Orange County, California, has a homeland security unit in the sheriff's department consisting of five bureaus. The Special Enforcement Bureau consists of SWAT, Air-Support Unit, Hazardous Devices Unit, and Tactical Arrest Team. The Mass Transit Bureau contains the Transit Authority, Explosive Detection Unit and Module Rail Section. The Marine Operations Bureau consists of three sheriff's stations along Orange County's beaches. The Mutual Aid Bureau contains a Counter Terrorism Section and works with the Joint Terrorism Task Force. Finally, the unit has the Orange County Intelligence and Assessment Center. Orange County's organization demonstrates that units of local government have developed fairly sophisticated homeland security operations.

In addition to the prevention of terror activities, the office works with criminal justice agencies to collect and share counterterrorism information. It also works with a variety of other state agencies to develop a database of critical infrastructure and associated threats. It provides agencies with intelligence advisories and works with law enforcement to develop better public awareness in reporting potential terrorist activities. In conjunction with the DHS and the New York City, the agency equips police officers with radiological detection devices. Finally, New York officials work with Canadian officials in securing border crossings into and out of the United States (Office of Homeland Security of New York, 2007).

These activities demonstrate that state agencies are actively involved in homeland security operations. Even though the federal government has primary responsibility for safeguarding the nation, it falls on the states to develop plans and apparatuses for responding to terrorist threats. The states are actually on the frontline for many of these threats. Activities in each state represent another layer that terrorists must penetrate before successfully committing an attack.

HS ANALYSIS BOX 2-4

All states are now involved in homeland security, and some states have progressed at a more rapid rate as compared to others. New York, since it has been attacked twice, is likely to be more advanced in homeland security measures than other states. Locate your state's homeland security website. How does your home state compare to New York? If you are a resident of New York, compare New York to another state. Can you identify any deficiencies?

Summary

This chapter presented an overview of the apparatus that is involved in providing homeland security. The primary federal agency is the DHS, which was created in reaction to the 9/11 attacks on our country. The attacks resulted in substantial changes at the federal and state government levels. The DHS was created by combining a number of agencies from throughout the federal government into one department that could coordinate homeland security efforts. The creation of the DHS was not without problems, including all sorts of issues with regard to command and control, and a number of problems existed in terms of coordinating the agencies within the new department. White House and congressional politics also provided a number of obstacles. Nonetheless, the DHS continues to mature and evolve, continuously improving in terms of affording the American people protection from terrorist attacks.

The various agencies housed in the DHS were discussed. These agencies and their missions demonstrate the complexity of homeland security. The TSA is not only responsible for airline safety, but it also is involved in all other transportation safety initiatives. The customs agencies, ICE, CBP, and USCIS, essentially are charged with protecting our nation from terrorists who try to enter the United States. Additionally, these agencies safeguard the nation by attempting to intercept any WMD or WMD materials before they can be imported into the country.

The DoD is also involved in homeland security. If there is a biological, chemical, or radiological attack, the DoD has the resources that can best deal with the situation. These resources are under the command of NORTHCOM, which coordinates all DoD homeland security efforts. Additionally, the DoD has several intelligence agencies that, as a part of their mission, collect intelligence information on terrorists and their potential activities. The DoD coordinates its activities with those of the DHS.

Finally, the individual states have homeland security offices or agencies. These entities coordinate all homeland security efforts in the state. These activities range from public education and governmental employee training to assisting with the implementation of homeland security programming. The New York Office of Homeland Security has been discussed in some detail. New York City has been attacked twice by terrorists, and it is likely that the state will be targeted in the future. The New York state agency must successfully coordinate the state's activities with those of local governments and the federal government. Although the primary responsibility of safeguarding the nation rests with the federal government, individual states do have to develop plans and apparatuses for responding to terrorist threats.

Discussion Questions

1. Politics played a key role in the formation of the Department of Homeland Security. What impact did this have in terms of the department's overall effectiveness in the short and long term?
2. There are 22 agencies in the Department of Homeland Security. How well do you think they work together, given their diverse roles and responsibilities?
3. Of the 22 agencies that comprise the Department of Homeland Security, which ones are you familiar with based on your consumption of news and current events?
4. What role does the Department of Defense play in homeland security?
5. Do you believe that immigration and border security are major homeland security issues? Why?
6. Since FEMA is the only agency that responds to natural disasters, do you believe it should be placed in another federal department? Why?

References

Associated Press. (2012). "Feds seize 132 domain names to stop knockoff sales." *Wall Street Journal* (November 28). http://online.wsj.com/article/AP23542355cd744cc3a9d3a6aa66301f16.html (Accessed November 26, 2012).

Bowman, S. (2003). "Homeland security: The Department of Defense's role." *Report for Congress*. Washington, D.C.: Congressional Research Service.

CBP. (2008). CBP website. (Accessed July 12, 2008).

CBP. (2010). *Snapshot: A Summary of CBP Facts and Figures*. (Accessed June 21, 2010).

CBP. (2016). About CBP. http://www.cbp.gov/about# (Accessed February 2, 2016).

Clarke, R. (2008). *Your Government Failed You: Breaking the Cycle of National Security Disasters*. New York: HarperCollins.

Department of Homeland Security. (2008). *Homepage*. http://www.dhs.gov/index.shtm (Accessed July 7, 2008).

Department of Homeland Security. (2012). *Department of Homeland Security Strategic Plan, Fiscal Years 2012-2016*. Washington, D.C.: Author.

Gauthier, A. (2012). "Who holds jurisdiction over TSA?" (December 2): *IVN*. http://ivn.us/2012/12/02/who-holds-jurisdiction-over-the-tsa/ (Accessed December 2, 2012).

Goss, T. (2006). "Who's in charge?" *Homeland Security Affairs*. https://www.hsaj.org/articles/173 (Accessed February 12, 2016).

Government Accounting Office. (2003). *Airport Passenger Screening: Preliminary Observations on Progress Made and Challenges Remaining*. Washington, D.C.: Author.

Government Accounting Office. (2012). *Homeland Defense: DOD Needs to Address Gaps in Homeland Defense and Civil Support Guidance*. Washington, D.C.: Author.

Hambridge, N. B., Howitt, A. M., and Giles, D. W. (2017). Coordination in Crises: Implementation of the National Incident Management System by Surface Transportation Agencies." Homeland Security Affairs 13, Article 2 (April 2017). https://www.hsaj.org/articles/13773

Immigration and Customs Enforcement. (2009). *Homepage*. http://www.ice.gov/ (Accessed January 10, 2009).

Immigration and Customs Enforcement. (2016). *Overview*. https://www.ice.gov/ (Accessed February 3, 2016).

Immigration and Customs Enforcement. (2016a). *Liberty Reserve Founder Pleads Guilty to Money Laundering*. https://www.ice.gov/news/releases/liberty-reserve-founder-pleads-guilty-money-laundering (Accessed February 3, 2016).

Immigration and Customs Enforcement. (2016b). *Joint Terrorism Task Force*. https://www.ice.gov/jttf (Accessed February 3, 2016).

Janson, B. (2017). TSA dog teams hunt for explosives, boost security and speed travelers along. USA Today, Sept. 21 at https://www.usatoday.com/story/news/2017/09/21/tsa-dog-teams-hunt-explosives-game-boosts-security/669316001/

Kahan, J. H. (2013). What's in the name? The meaning of homeland security. *Journal of Homeland Security Education*, 2: 1–18.

Kahan, J. (2015). "Failure of FEMA—Preparedness or politics?" *Journal of Homeland Security and Emergency*, 12: 1–21.

Kamarck, E. (2007, November). "Fixing the Department of Homeland Security." *Progressive Policy Institute*. http://www.ppionline.org/documents/FixingDHS11142007.pdf (Accessed August 10, 2008).

Laing, K. (2011). "GOP chairmen joust for TSA jurisdiction." *The Hill* (June 7). (Accessed December 3, 2012).

New York State Homeland Security Strategy 2017–2020. New York State Homeland Security and Emergency Services. 2016. http://www.dhses.ny.gov/media/documents/NYS-Homeland-Security-Strategy.pdf

Office of Homeland Security. (2002). *National Strategy for Homeland Security*. Washington, D.C.: Author.

Office of Homeland Security State of New York. (2007). *Annual Report, 2007*. Albany, NY: Author.

O'Rourke, R. (2006). *Homeland Security: Coast Guard Operations—Background and Issues for Congress*. Washington, D.C.: Congressional Research Service.

Perrow, C. (2002). "Using organizations: The case of FEMA. *Homeland Security Affairs*, 1(2): 1–8.

Richard A. Clarke (2008). Memorandum for Condoleezza Rice, January 25, 2001, (https://nsarchive2.gwu.edu//NSAEBB/NSAEBB147/clarke%20memo.pdf).

Robert T. Stafford Disaster Relief and Emergency Assistance Act (1988), PL 100-707.

Sasse, B. (2015). "There are TSA secrets worse than a 96% fail rate." *USA Today*. http://www.usatoday.com/story/opinion/2015/06/08/tsa-investigation-security-sen-ben-sasse-column/28643213/ (Accessed July 9, 2015).

Shapiro, J. (2007). *Managing Homeland Security: Develop a Threat-Based Strategy*. (Opportunity 08 Paper). Washington, D.C.: Brookings Institution.

TSA. (2010a). *Imaging Technology: Innovation & Technology*. http://www.tsa.gov/approach/tech/imaging_technology.shtm (Accessed May 20, 2010).

TSA. (2016). *TSA 2015 Year in Review*. http://blog.tsa.gov/2016/01/tsa-2015-year-in-review.html (Accessed February 2, 2016).

USA Patriot Act (PL 107-56).

U.S. Citizenship and Customs Service. (2008). Website. http://www.uscis.gov/portal/site/uscis (Accessed August 11, 2008).

U.S. Coast Guard. (2016). *U.S. Coast Guard Snapshot, 2014*. http://www.uscg.mil/top/about/doc/uscg_snapshot.pdf (Accessed February 8, 2016).

U.S. Secret Service. (2016). *Website*. https://www.secretservice.gov/about/history/ (Accessed August 12, 2014).

Wermuth, M. (2005). "The Department of Homeland Security: The road ahead." *Testimony Presented to the Senate Committee on Homeland Security and Governmental Affairs*. Santa Monica, CA: Rand Corp.

Yager, J. (2013). "DHS consolidation hopes dim." *The Hill* (January 13). http://thehill.com/homenews/administration/276753-dhs-consolidation-hopes-dim (Accessed January 14, 2013).

3 Overview of National Infrastructure Protection

LEARNING OBJECTIVES

1. *Understand the meaning of critical infrastructure.*
2. *Know the three categories of critical infrastructure.*
3. *Be able to critique the National Critical Infrastructure Database.*
4. *Know the National Infrastructure Protection Plan framework.*
5. *Describe the problems associated with different types of critical infrastructure assets.*
6. *Understand how terrorists view and possibly target various critical infrastructure assets.*

Key Terms

Big bang theory of asset protection
Bottom-up approach
Buffer zone plan
Consequences assessment
Critical infrastructure assets
Critical infrastructure sectors
Cyber infrastructure
Descriptive measures
Effectiveness
Hard targets
Human assets
Infrastructure survey tool
Mitigation
National Asset Database
National Critical Infrastructure Prioritization Program
Outcome measures
Physical infrastructure
Process evaluations
Protective security advisors
Risk management activities
Security goals and objectives
Soft targets
Strategic National Risk Assessment
Target hardening
Threats
Vulnerability

▶ Introduction

Homeland security is a governmental effort to protect national **critical infrastructure assets**. According to the Department of Homeland Security (2006), there are three primary categories of critical infrastructure: (1) human, (2) physical, and (3) cyber. **Human assets** refer to the large numbers of people who congregate because of living situations, working conditions, or social events and who need to be protected. Homeland security efforts focus on protecting groups of people to prevent a large number of casualties. Thus, numbers of people drive protection decisions. Although people can be the targets of terrorist attacks, infrastructure is also important. **Physical infrastructure** refers to transportation (air, rail, waterway, and roadway infrastructure); manufacturing facilities, especially petrochemical facilities; large employers; and nuclear facilities, such as reactors, storage devices, and materials being transported regionally or nationally. In essence, an attack on a physical infrastructure facility may not result in a large number of deaths, but it could have a significant economic impact in the region or country. Finally, **cyber infrastructure** refers to information networks used to transfer vast amounts of information and to coordinate business, industry, banking, and, to a large degree, people's daily lives. It also refers to keeping information secure from those who would access and steal it for illegal or illegitimate uses.

HS Web Link: To learn more about our national infrastructure protection, go to http://www.dhs.gov/files/programs/editorial_0827.shtm.

The protection of people may include individuals such as government officials at the federal, state, or local level or high-profile individuals such as Hollywood actors, business or corporate leaders, or politicians. These people are potential targets as their deaths would create a great deal of publicity for the terrorist act, or the deaths could result in governmental or private sector inefficiency at some level, resulting in economic loss. Groups of people are also possible targets. A sporting event or entertainment venue may be targeted. A busy shopping area or mall is another potential target as are schools, churches, government assemblies, or rallies. For example, the majority of bombs targeting civilians detonated during the Iraq War were usually in shopping venues. In 2013, gunmen from the Somali terrorist group Al-Shabaab attacked the Westgate mall in Nairobi, Kenya, killing at least 67 people and wounding scores of others (BBC, 2014). In 2015, terrorists conducted coordinated attacks on multiple venues, including a theater during a concert, a soccer match, and restaurants using bombs and AK-47 automatic weapons. Over 120 people were killed as a result of the attacks (Almasy, Melhan, and Bitterman, 2015). These types of attacks result in publicity and tend to have a greater impact on the population by affecting travel, personal freedom, and commerce.

In terms of physical infrastructure, there are literally millions of potential targets. A given city, of nearly any size, may have hundreds of potential targets. Every city and town in the United States at least periodically has substantial population gatherings, whether they are town meetings, high school sporting events, or local celebrations such as parades or festivals. Many cities have manufacturing facilities associated with the petrochemical industry, which if attacked could result in the release of dangerous chemicals. The destruction of roadways or bridges in metropolitan areas could have an economic impact since it would impede work and commerce. Dangerous chemicals and petroleum products are often transported by rail or the trucking industry, which are potential targets. Communications, banking centers, and postal or shipping facilities are also viable targets.

Other areas of concern that have not been given adequate attention by homeland security policy makers are food and water supply chains. For example, in 2015, customers at Chipotle restaurants in several states became ill from *Escherichia coli* infection, resulting in an extensive investigation by the Centers for Disease Control and Prevention (Mohney, 2016). In the past, criminals have used biological weapons on food. In 1984, the biotoxin *Salmonella typhimurium* was deposited in several restaurant salad bars in Dalles, Oregon. Although no deaths were reported, there were 715 cases of poisoning and another 117 people exhibited symptoms (Weaver, 1985). The possibility also exists that someone could introduce toxins into water sources, potentially causing deaths, illness, and a loss of public confidence in government. The point is that numerous critical infrastructure assets are potential targets, and homeland security necessitates that they be considered when planning for attacks and taking preventive measures. This results in a vast and complex endeavor.

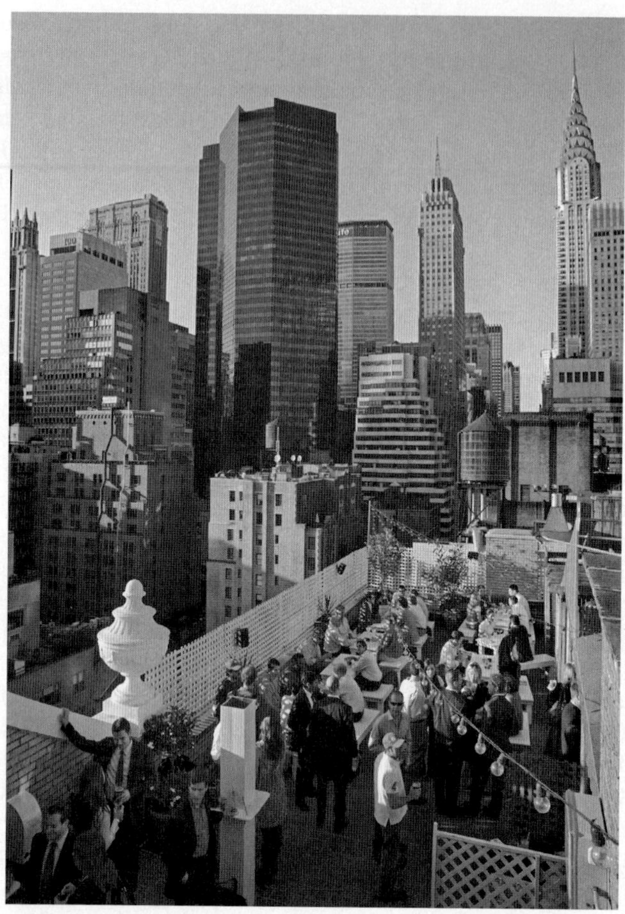

Every city has numerous potential physical infrastructure targets.
Katja Heinemann/Aurora Photos/Alamy Stock Photo.

▶ Threats to Critical Infrastructure

As discussed in Chapter 1, homeland security, although initially envisioned to respond to terrorist attacks, became much broader addressing a range of hazards. This was primarily the result of FEMA being included in the DHS. Figure 3-1 ■ demonstrates the different and varied threats to critical infrastructure. Moreover, the United States has had relatively few terrorist attacks on our critical infrastructure, but other threats have had numerous impacts. Regardless, making individual infrastructures more resilient from terrorist attacks will to some extent increase their protection from other threats such as natural disasters. We therefore must be diligent in identifying and taking measures to increase security and resilience.

The **Strategic National Risk Assessment** (SNRA) was conducted by the DHS as part of the department's efforts to develop a national preparedness system. When considering the threats that are displayed in Figure 3-1 ■, there is no specification in terms of extent or magnitude. The SNRA was developed to provide some guidance or thresholds to be considered when classifying a hazard as constituting a national event. Fatalities and injuries and economic loss were used to establish the thresholds (see DHS, 2011). Figure 3-2 ■ shows the thresholds for various events.

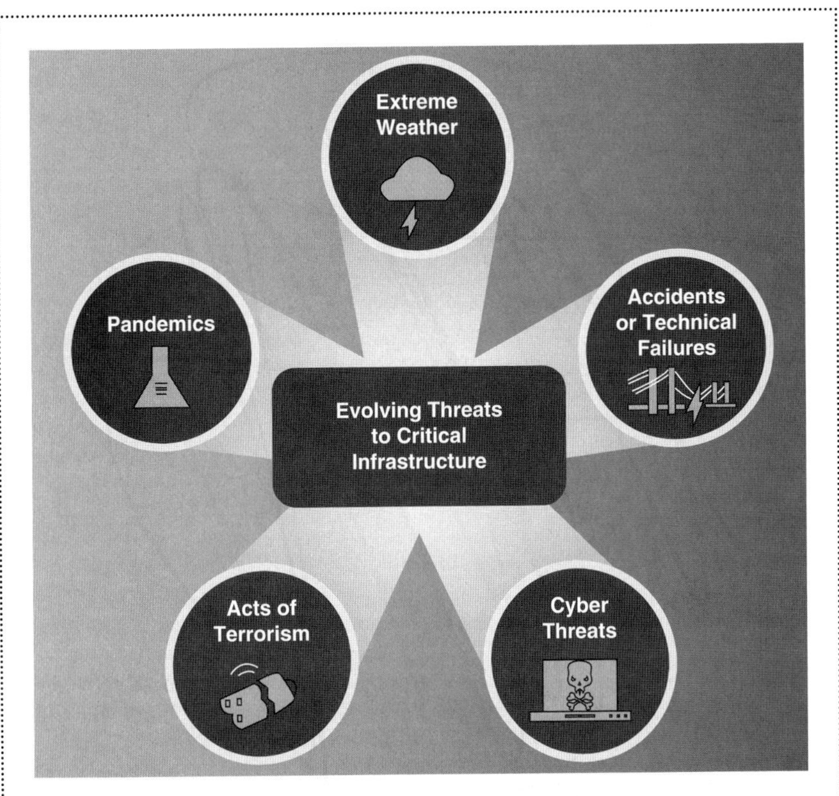

FIGURE 3-1 Threats to Critical Infrastructure

Source: DHS (2013). *NIPP 2013 Partnering for Critical Infrastructure Security and Resilience*. Washington, D.C.: DHS, p. 8.

Threat/Hazard Group	Threat/Hazard Type	National-Level Event Description
Natural	Animal Disease Outbreak	An unintentional introduction of the foot-and-mouth disease virus into the domestic livestock population in a U.S. state
	Earthquake	An earthquake occurs within the U.S. resulting in direct economic losses greater than $100 million
	Flood	A flood occurs within the U.S. resulting in direct economic losses greater than $100 million
	Human Pandemic Outbreak	A severe outbreak of pandemic influenza with a 25% gross clinical attack rate spreads across the U.S. populace
	Hurricane	A tropical storm or hurricane impacts the U.S. resulting in direct economic losses of greater than $100 million
	Space Weather	The sun emits bursts of electromagnetic radiation and energetic particles causing utility outages and damage to infrastructure
	Tsunami	A tsunami with a wave of approximately 50 feet impacts the Pacific Coast of the U.S.
	Volcanic Eruption	A volcano in the Pacific Northwest erupts impacting the surrounding areas with lava flows and ash and areas east with smoke and ash
	Wildfire	A wildfire occurs within the U.S. resulting in direct economic losses greater than $100 million

(Continued)

Threat/Hazard Group	Threat/Hazard Type	National-Level Event Description
Technological/ Accidental	Biological Food Contamination	Accidental conditions where introduction of a biological agent (e.g., *Salmonella, E. coli,* botulinum toxin) into the food supply results in 100 hospitalizations or greater and a multi-state response
	Chemical Substance Spill or Release	Accidental conditions where a release of a large volume of a chemical acutely toxic to human beings (a toxic inhalation hazard, or TIE) from a chemical plant, storage facility, or transportation mode results in either one or more offsite fatalities, or one or more fatalities (either on- or offsite) with offsite evacuations/shelter-in-place
	Dam Failure	Accidental conditions where dam failure and inundation results in one fatality or greater
	Radiological Substance Release	Accidental conditions where reactor core damage causes release of radiation
Adversarial/ Human-Caused	Aircraft as a Weapon	A hostile non-state actor(s) crashes a commercial or general aviation aircraft into a physical target within the U.S.
	Armed Assault	A hostile non-state actor(s) uses assault tactics to conduct strikes on vulnerable target(s) within the U.S. resulting in at least one fatality or injury
	Biological Terrorism Attack (non-food)	A hostile non-state actor(s) acquires, weaponizes, and releases a biological agent against an outdoor, indoor, or water target, directed at a concentration of people within the U.S.
	Chemical/Biological Food Contamination Terrorism Attack	A hostile non-state actor(s) acquires, weaponizes, and disperses a biological or chemical agent into food supplies within the U.S. supply chain
	Chemical Terrorism Attack (non-food)	A hostile non-state actor(s) acquires, weaponizes, and releases a chemical agent against an outdoor, indoor, or water target directed at a concentration of people using an aerosol, ingestion, or dermal route of exposure
	Cyber Attack against Data	A cyber attack which seriously compromises the integrity or availability of data (the information contained in a computer system) or data processes resulting in economic losses of a billion dollars or greater
	Cyber Attack against Physical Infrastructure	An incident in which a cyber attack is used as a vector to achieve effects which are "beyond the compute" (i.e., kinetic or other effects) resulting in one fatality or greater or economic losses of $100 million or greater
	Explosives Terrorism Attack	A hostile non-state actor(s) deploys a man-portable improvised explosive device (LED), vehicle-borne IED, or vessel LED in the U.S. against a concentration of people, and/or structures such as critical commercial or government facilities, transportation targets, or critical infrastructure sites, etc., resulting in at least one fatality or injury
	Nuclear Terrorism Attack	A hostile non-state actor(s) acquires an improvised nuclear weapon through manufacture from fissile material, purchase, or theft and detonates it within a major U.S. population center
	Radiological Terrorism Attack	A hostile non-state actor(s) acquires radiological materials and disperses them through explosive or other means (e.g., a radiological dispersal device or RDD) or creates a radiation exposure device (RED)

FIGURE 3-2 Thresholds for Different Threats or Events

Source: Department of Homeland Security. (2011). *The Strategic National Risk Assessment in Support of PPD8: A Comprehensive Risk-Based Approach toward a Secure and Resilient Nation.* Washington, D.C.: DHS, pp. 2–5. https://www.dhs.gov/xlibrary/assets/rma-strategic-national-risk-assessment-ppd8.pdf (Accessed February 25, 2016).

▶ Federal Agencies Involved in the Protection of U.S. Assets

A number of federal agencies are involved in the protection of critical infrastructure. Departments and agencies within the federal government are charged with specific sector responsibilities. These departments and agencies have some level of homeland security protective responsibility for those assets that fall within their purview. Figure 3-3 ■ provides a breakdown of these agencies and their areas of responsibilities.

As shown in Figure 3-3 ■, a number of department-level federal agencies are involved in homeland security. Many are cabinet-level departments; thus, numerous lower-level agencies within each of these departments play a role in security. The task of homeland security is divided among the agencies according to industries that are regulated or controlled by the various departments and by general governmental responsibilities. Homeland security is an encompassing task requiring a coordinated effort not only within the federal government

Sector-Specific Agency	Critical Infrastructure/Key Resources Sector
Department of Agriculture[1] Department of Health and Human Services[2]	Agriculture and Food
Department of Defense[3]	Defense Industrial Base
Department of Energy	Energy[4]
Department of Health and Human Services	Public Health and Healthcare
Department of the Interior	National Monuments and Icons
Department of the Treasury	Banking and Finance
Environmental Protection Agency	Drinking Water and Water Treatment Systems
Department of Homeland Security	
Office of Infrastructure Protection	Chemical Commercial Facilities Dams Emergency Services Commercial Nuclear Reactors, Materials, and Waste
Office of Cyber Security and Telecommunications	Information Technology Telecommunications
Transportation Security Administration	Postal and Shipping
Transportation Security Administration, United States Coast Guard[5]	Transportation Systems[6]
Immigration and Customs Enforcement, Federal Protective Service	Government Facilities

FIGURE 3-3 Federal Agencies and Their Critical Infrastructure Resources Sector
Source: DHS. (2006). *National Infrastructure Protection Plan*, Washington, D.C.: Author.
[1]The Department of Agriculture is responsible for agriculture and food (meat, poultry, and egg products). [2] The Department of Health and Human Services is responsible for food other than meat, poultry, and egg products.
[3] Nothing in this plan impairs or otherwise affects the authority of the Secretary of Defense over the Department of Defense (DoD), including the chain of command for military forces from the President as Commander in Chief, to the Secretary of Defense, to the commander of military forces, or military command and control procedures.
[4] The Energy Sector includes the production, refining, storage, and distribution of oil, gas, and electric power, except for commercial nuclear power facilities.
[5] The U.S. Coast Guard is the SSA for the maritime transportation mode.
[6] As stated in HSPD-7, the Department of Transportation and the Department of Homeland Security will collaborate on all matters relating to transportation security and transportation infrastructure protection.

HS ANALYSIS 3-1

Numerous federal agencies are involved in homeland security. Each of these agencies has specific responsibilities or areas that it attempts to control or prevent terrorist activities. Many are outside the Department of Homeland Security. Do you believe that there are other federal agencies that should have such responsibilities? Do you believe there will be coordination problems? Coordination is important to ensure that all possible targets are protected.

but also among state and local agencies that are involved in the security framework. Thus, the central questions are, "How well will these agencies cooperate and provide an optimal response or solution to a homeland security event?" and "Are there gaps in security as a result of the decentralization of some security responsibilities?" Response to security events becomes complicated and bureaucratic, since so many agencies are involved.

Nonetheless, primary responsibility for securing specific infrastructure assets or potential terrorist targets has been assigned to specific federal departments. For example, the Transportation Security Administration (TSA) is responsible for the security of transportation systems. This includes not only airports but also other transportation systems, including trucking and rail. The TSA is also charged with protecting U.S. shipping and postal services. The Coast Guard protects water transportation lanes and ports in the Atlantic and Pacific Oceans and the Gulf of Mexico. The Department of the Treasury secures banking and finance systems. One of the duties here is to stop terrorist financing. The Department of the Interior plays a homeland security role by protecting national monuments and icons such as the Lincoln Memorial or Grant's Tomb. The Department of Energy has an expansive role in homeland security, as it is responsible for acquiring energy and protecting energy sources. Since terrorists may attempt to acquire nuclear materials from a U.S. facility or attack such a facility to create a radiological catastrophe, the Department of Energy is on the front line of homeland security. These examples demonstrate how homeland security responsibilities are dispersed throughout the federal government.

▶ Scope of U.S. Critical Infrastructure Assets

Given that a primary task of homeland security is the protection of critical infrastructure assets, it becomes important to identify those assets. This is a monumental task as there are thousands of potential assets spread across the United States. The first task in identifying them is to define critical infrastructure assets. For the purposes of compiling a list of such assets and providing guidance to the DHS, **critical infrastructure assets** were defined in the USA PATRIOT Act (P.L. 107-56) as follows:

> Systems and assets ... so vital to the United States that the incapacity or destruction of such systems and assets would have a debilitating impact on security, national economy security, national public health and safety, or any combination of those matters.

Collection of critical infrastructure assets for a national database began in 2003, and there was a great deal of criticism leveled at the project. It appears that the DHS used unclear or inconsistent standards when compiling the list. For example, Moteff (2007) noted that the database not only included duly recognized assets consistent with the definition enumerated in the USA PATRIOT Act and the *National Strategy for the Physical Protection of Critical Infrastructure and Key Assets*, but it also included assets that should not have been in the listing. There were events and locations that were included, such as petting zoos, parades, and local festivals, which are of dubious value in terms of national security priorities.

The criteria for inclusion in a database have been refined on several occasions. Currently, four criteria are used: potential fatalities, economic loss, mass evacuation length,

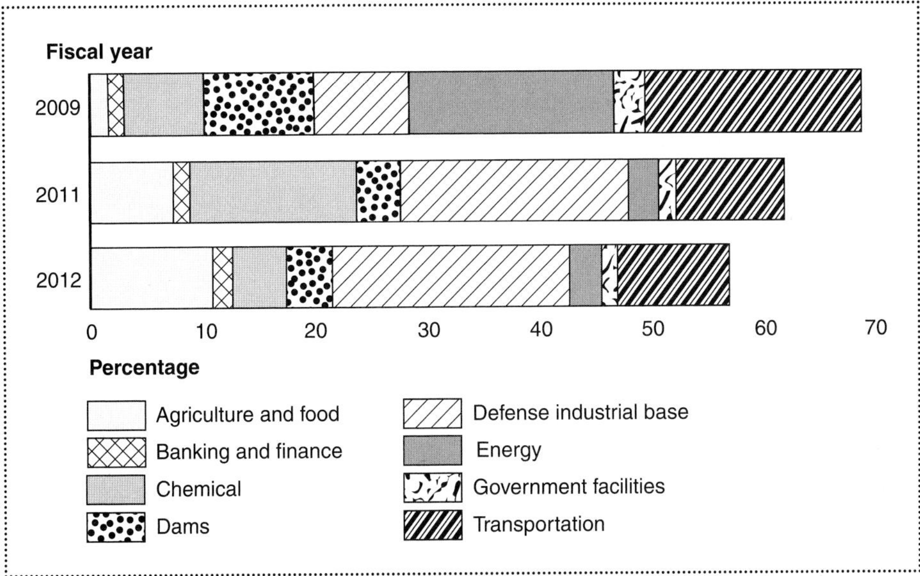

FIGURE 3-4 Distribution of Critical Assets on the National Critical Infrastructure Prioritization Program List by Select Sectors

Source: Government Accounting Office. (2013). *Critical Infrastructure Protection: DHS List of Priority Assets Needs to be Validated and Reported to Congress.* Washington, D.C.: GAO, p. 21.

and national security impacts (GAO, 2013). In essence, they should be of national importance, and their destruction or disablement should have a significant negative impact on the country. The DHS collects information on assets as part of its **National Critical Infrastructure Prioritization Program**. Criteria for inclusion have changed several times. Figure 3-4 ■ provides the distribution of critical assets on the National Critical Infrastructure Prioritization Program List by select sectors for 2009, 2011, and 2012.

The assets referenced in Figure 3-4 ■ consist of the assets identified from eight core areas and constitute about 70 percent of all identified assets. There are 16 core asset areas, so these eight contain the majority of all the assets (the following section discusses the core asset areas). The distribution of assets has changed over the years as the DHS has attempted to refine the definition of asset inclusion. Defense industrial base and agriculture contain the largest number of assets.

▶ Critical Infrastructure Sectors

The DHS attempted to clarify the identification and classification of assets by identifying **critical infrastructure sectors**. This not only simplified asset identification and classification, it also established a framework whereby government officials and officials associated with the enterprise in each sector could more easily work together to identify critical infrastructure and methods by which to afford them the necessary level of protection.

HS ANALYSIS 3-2

A number of problems have been associated with building the National Asset Database. It appears that criteria in some cases are hard to apply. Based on the criteria discussed above, what assets in your community should be included in the database? How would the assets that you identify compare with some of the assets in other cities?

The DHS identified 16 critical infrastructure sectors:

- Chemical sector
- Commercial facilities sector
- Communications sector
- Critical manufacturing sector
- Dams sector
- Defense industrial base sector
- Emergency services sector
- Energy sector
- Financial services sector
- Food and agriculture sector
- Government facilities sector
- Health care and public health sector
- Information technology sector
- Nuclear reactors, materials, and waste sector
- Transportation systems sector
- Water and wastewater systems

National Critical Infrastructure Prioritization Program

The **National Critical Infrastructure Prioritization Program** established a schema to categorize critical infrastructure for federal agencies, states, and various infrastructure sector operators to develop lists of the critical infrastructure for their sector. The various assets are then classified

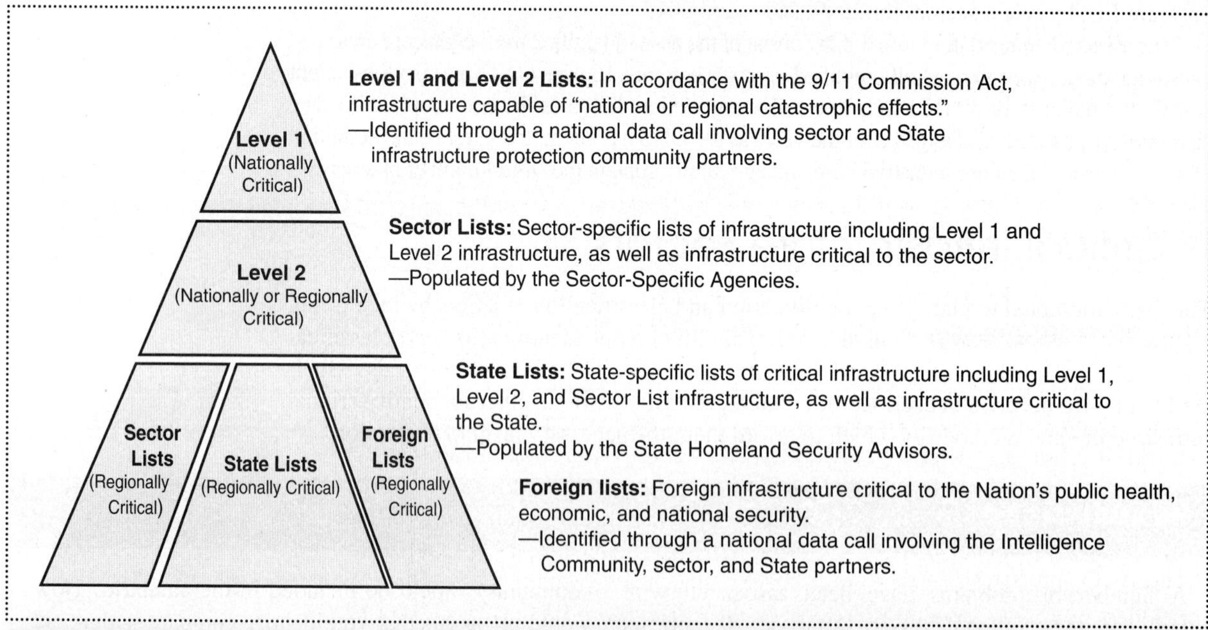

Level 1 (Nationally Critical)
Level 2 (Nationally or Regionally Critical)
Sector Lists (Regionally Critical)
State Lists (Regionally Critical)
Foreign Lists (Regionally Critical)
Level 1 and Level 2 Lists: In accordance with the 9/11 Commission Act, infrastructure capable of "national or regional catastrophic effects."
—Identified through a national data call involving sector and State infrastructure protection community partners.
Sector Lists: Sector-specific lists of infrastructure including Level 1 and Level 2 infrastructure, as well as infrastructure critical to the sector.
—Populated by the Sector-Specific Agencies.
State Lists: State-specific lists of critical infrastructure including Level 1, Level 2, and Sector List infrastructure, as well as infrastructure critical to the State.
—Populated by the State Homeland Security Advisors.
Foreign lists: Foreign infrastructure critical to the Nation's public health, economic, and national security.
—Identified through a national data call involving the Intelligence Community, sector, and State partners.

FIGURE 3-5 Priority Scheme for Critical Infrastructure
Source: DHS. (2010). *Communications Sector-Specific Plan*, Washington, D.C. Author, p. 39

NCIPP Level 1	NCIPP Level 2
Those CIKR that, if disrupted, could result in at least two of the following consequences: 1. Greater than 5,000 prompt fatalities. 2. Greater than $75 billion in first-year economic consequences. 3. Mass evacuations with a prolonged absence of greater than 3 months. 4. Severe degradation of the country's national security capabilities, including intelligence and defense functions, but excluding military facilities.	Those CIKR that, if disrupted, could result in at least two of the following consequences: 1. Greater than 2,500 prompt fatalities. 2. Greater than $25 billion in first-year economic consequences. 3. Mass evacuations with a prolonged absence of greater than 1 month. 4. Severe degradation of the country's national security capabilities, including intelligence and defense functions, but excluding military facilities.

FIGURE 3-6 Criteria Used to Categorize Level of Criticality for the Chemical Sector
Source: DHS. (2010). *Chemical Sector-Specific Plan.* https://www.dhs.gov/xlibrary/assets/nipp-ssp-chemical-2010.pdf (Accessed March 4, 2016).

using the scheme in Figure 3-5 ■: level 1 (nationally critical) or level 2 (nationally or regionally critical) (GAO, 2013). Sector lists include assets that were submitted within the various sectors such as banking, agriculture, and chemical but were not deemed to meet level 1 or level 2. Similarly, the state lists and foreign lists are important critical infrastructures within the sector, but they do not meet the criteria for inclusion in level 1 or level 2. They are added to a catalog of important assets. The advantage of the National Critical Infrastructure Prioritization Program is that it is rather comprehensive, but at the same time it sets priorities.

Some of the critical infrastructure sectors developed criteria by which to classify different assets as level 1 or level 2 or added assets to a list. Figure 3-6 ■ contains the criteria developed by the chemical sector.

▶ The National Infrastructure Protection Plan: Conceptual Operation of Homeland Security Protection

Thus far, this chapter has examined efforts to identify those critical infrastructure assets that should receive a high priority in terms of deploying protective measures. Once assets are identified, measures must be taken to ensure their safety. Woodbury (2005) advises that a system needs to be developed that maximally protects infrastructure assets; it is the *raison d'etre* for homeland security. Furthermore, he advises that these efforts should be measured and evaluated, which would result in several benefits. First, measurement allows for accountability. Today, billions of dollars are being spent on homeland security, and evaluation will provide information on whether these expenditures have resulted in enhanced safety. Second, measurement should guide future expenditures. Investments should be made in security activities and processes that are proven to be successful. Finally, measurement provides an estimate of success—knowledge of the level of safety afforded as a result of expenditures and efforts.

The DHS has devised a conceptual model for affording some assets appropriate levels of protection and security. The national infrastructure plan was developed in 2006 and modified in 2013. The *National Infrastructure Protection Plan (2013): Partnering for Critical Infrastructure Security and Resilience* (DHS, 2013) represents a national model for implementing homeland security for infrastructure assets. The model is flexible and can be applied to an individual asset, system, or industrial sector.

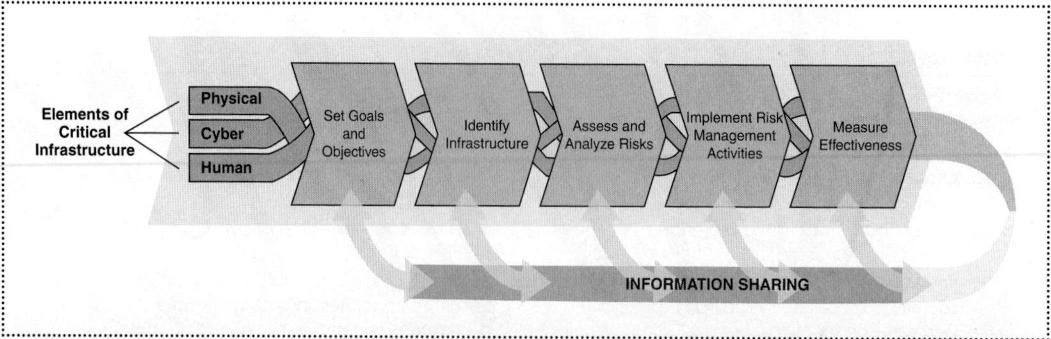

FIGURE 3-7 Critical Infrastructure Risk Management Framework
Source: DHS. (2013). NIPP 2013: *Partnering for Critical Infrastructure Security and Resilience.* Washington, D.C.: DHS, p. 15.

Figure 3-7 ■ provides a conceptual or policy view of homeland security as it is implemented in the United States. The model is constructed to ensure continuous evaluation in an effort to identify deficiencies and to constantly enhance effectiveness.

The model is grounded in risk management and program evaluation. It requires that risks or threats to critical infrastructure are considered in decision making. It is a highly structured approach that attempts to reduce uncertainty related to a threat. It recognizes that owners of critical infrastructure have valuable information to contribute to risk management, and the federal government must partner with the private sector to maximally reduce risks. The model consists of five distinct actions that lead to the security of human, physical, and cyber assets. Each action is dependent on the others to implement an effective security system. Moreover, the model has a continuous feedback loop so that evaluation and adjustments can be made at each level to enhance protection. The following sections examine each of the five actions.

Set Goals and Objectives

The establishment of **security goals and objectives** refers to determining a level of security and resilience for the human, physical, and cyber assets. The DHS (2006) advises that security goals "define specific outcomes, conditions, endpoints, or performance targets that collectively constitute an effective protective posture" (p. 30).

The process of setting goals includes identifying and assessing threats, vulnerabilities, and the consequences to critical infrastructure should there be an attack or any other disaster. Once accomplished, the asset should be secured and protective measures enacted. An important part of this process is to also ensure that rapid recovery measures are in place, thereby enhancing resilience. The information obtained should be shared with asset administrators to help safeguard other assets. The sharing of information can help safeguard complete industries (DHS, n.d.).

Goal and objective setting is a process that occurs across all critical infrastructure sectors. For example, the chemical and petroleum industries will have one set of goals and objectives while the agriculture or banking industries will have other goals and objectives. This ensures that goals and objectives meet the needs of each sector.

Identify Infrastructures

The DHS has developed an inventory of critical infrastructure assets. The lists of assets are provided by sector industries and the states. Additionally, a number of assets have been identified by federal agencies. The inventory catalogs the assets that are regionally and locally significant as well as infrastructure that is nationally important.

Cyber infrastructure is of particular interest, especially those systems that are business systems, control systems, access control systems, and warning or alert systems. Many of these systems could have a catastrophic impact if they were neutralized. Efforts have been made to identify the cyber systems that are critical to sectors (national implications) and that are at the greatest risk.

It is important to note that the list of critical infrastructures remains fairly fluid. That is, it is a judgment call as to whether a particular asset is critical or has national implications. It is obvious that some are critical, while others are not. However, this is not true for all assets. This makes the process of identifying infrastructures more difficult.

Assess and Analyze Risks

A complicated formula for analyzing risk to infrastructures was developed in the *2006 National Infrastructure Protection Plan.* The formula considered risk, consequences of attack, infrastructure vulnerability, and level of threat. The formula required that each of the factors be quantified. However, this was extremely difficult and often consisted of gross estimates. For instance, we do not know the level of threat to a specific infrastructure, such as the probability of an attack. The *2013 Partnering for Critical Infrastructure Security and Resilience* uses a similar threat identification formula, but it is less complicated and does not depend on trying to quantify all the variables. The 2013 model is discussed here and consists of three factors: threat, vulnerability, and consequence. When risk assessment is conducted, it is important that each assessment is documented so that results can be verified and are reproducible. Moreover, the assessment must be logical and consider all possible threats and consequences. This allows the application of the model to other similar assets.

Threats can be natural or man-made and a variety of threats exist. The federal government identifies and analyzes terrorist threats. Historical data can be used to assess natural

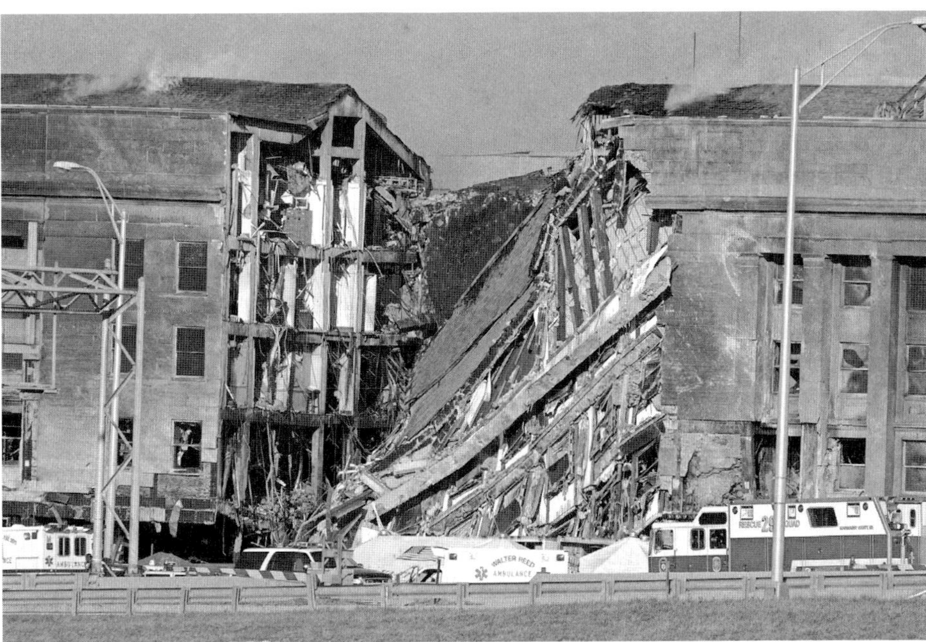

Aftermath of the 9/11 terrorist attack on the Pentagon.
US Navy Photo/Alamy Stock Photo.

threats such as floods or tornados. Infrastructure managers can shed light on the possibility of theft, vandalism, sabotage, cyberattacks, and other deliberate acts.

Vulnerability refers to assessment of the ease or difficulty with which an attack can be successfully carried out on the asset. Some infrastructures have protective measures such as fences, limited access, restricted employee restrictions to specific areas, and surveillance systems. Critical infrastructures require additional protective measures. Also, different critical infrastructure sectors will require a different array of protective measures.

A **consequences assessment** should comprehensively consider various consequences in case of an attack or a disaster. The consequences may be related to public health, economic activity, psychological distress, or government's ability to provide services. Indirect consequences such as the impact of the destruction of one asset on the other assets or systems should be considered. This is especially true when cyber systems are affected.

Implement Risk Management Activities

The implementation of effective **risk management activities** can have a number of benefits to industry. The DHS (2006) lists the following benefits:

1. Deter attacks—activities may result in attackers believing the risk is greater than the potential effects of a planned attack.
2. Devalue—levels of security may result in less damage from a possible attack; another disincentive to possible terrorists.
3. Detection—implementation of risk management activities not only hardens targets, they also enhance protectors' ability to detect attacks. Most likely, facility administrators will deploy some intelligence operations as well as target-hardening tactics, which may assist in uncovering potential attackers. For example, video cameras not only serve to deter, but they also allow for the collection of information about people in the immediate area.
4. Defend—as the homeland security processes mature, they will include more defensive measures. For example, primary security measures will be supplemented with perimeter hardening, fencing, and access control to expand security concentrically around possible targets.

For the most part, the discussion in this section has focused on hardware and target hardening. **Target hardening** refers to the implementation of access control, video cameras, fencing and buffer zones around targets, and structural changes that enhance security. There are also human elements in an effective security plan: First, training programs must be developed and provided to employees. These training programs should indoctrinate employees on the need for security. Too often employees are not committed to the importance of security issues. Annual or biannual training can reinforce their importance. Second, organizational policies and procedures that enforce security should be developed. Security policies and procedures would help ensure that security is a part of the organizational culture. Third, middle management and supervisors should be given greater authority and responsibilities in security matters. Security should become an important part of their jobs. Finally, security measures, both human and physical, can be reinforced through periodic inspections. Regular inspections should be conducted by supervisors, managers, and risk management personnel to ensure that policies and procedures are being followed and to examine physical security measures to determine their effectiveness.

Mitigation as well as security should be considered. Mitigation here refers to actions that allow a critical infrastructure to quickly return to normal operations, if there is a terrorist attack or other disaster. This may include the installation of backup systems or the ability to temporarily move operations to another facility. Facility managers should maintain stores of spare parts in the event of a major disruption. In some cases, mitigation is just as important as security.

Measure Effectiveness

The final action in the homeland security risk management framework is the measurement of **effectiveness**. Woodbury (2005) notes that there must be accountability in protective measures and systems to ensure that they function as envisioned. The DHS (2006) advises that three types of measures can be taken: (1) descriptive measures, (2) process or output measures, and (3) outcome measures. In terms of **descriptive measures**, system operators will develop an inventory of risk management activities that can be compared to the lists from similar facilities so that operators can be informed of the effective actions that can be taken.

Process evaluations focus on security efficacy. The various security measures are examined to ensure that they achieve desired results. These evaluations attempt to determine if security measures are implemented as envisioned by policy makers. A process evaluation will ensure that security measures meet standards or requirements and necessary adjustments are made when there are inconsistencies. To a large extent, process evaluations ensure that programs are operating as expected.

Finally, **outcome measures** attempt to measure whether the facility has the desired level of security. As discussed earlier in the chapter, the first step in the homeland security process is the development and articulation of security goals or standards: Is the potential target or critical infrastructure sufficiently safe from an attack? This is usually accomplished by applying standard attack scenarios. Deficiencies in the security level, noted during evaluation, may be the result of two factors. First, the security plan that was implemented at the facility was deficient—it did not result in adequate levels of security. Second, it may be the result of the plan not being implemented correctly—process evaluation issues. The outcome measures are the key indicators of a facility's readiness and ability to withstand an attempted breach; when outcomes are less than satisfactory, remedial action must be taken.

When evaluations are conducted across all critical infrastructure assets, the resulting database can provide an overview of the country's security. Moreover, individual industry evaluations can be aggregated to determine an industry's relative safety from attack. Such a database can be used to rank various industries in terms of their ability to withstand or thwart an attack. The process of evaluation also results in core metrics. That is, there will be security measures that can be applied to all assets; however, certain protective measures may be applicable to a particular group of assets. Once these core metrics are identified, they can be applied to a particular industry or set of assets, facilitating security implementation and evaluation. Planning, implementation, and evaluation are expedited as a result of this process.

▶ Critique of the National Infrastructure Protection Plan Model

The five-phased model of the homeland security risk management framework as outlined in the *National Infrastructure Protection Plan* is a comprehensive model that is based on data collection at a number of levels. It is based on rational comprehensive planning and decision making that assumes that the planner or decision maker has all the necessary information and is able to process all the information before making a decision. However, a substantial amount of information is unavailable to decision makers when using risk management. Problems are not clearly enumerated, and officials do not have complete information by which to make decisions. First, there are no firmly established security goals. An examination of many security goals demonstrates that they are general statements and global in nature, for example, "provide security," "prevent attack," or "mitigate problems." But realistically, they are not useful when attempting to understand the level of security that is required for critical infrastructure assets; for instance, what level of security should exist for a petrochemical facility, electric transmission line, or a federal reserve bank? Precise security standards have not been established across all industries. Realistically, we cannot have security without security goals or performance standards.

Second, in terms of identifying assets, the DHS has been working on a National Asset Database for a number of years. However, it remains questionable if the database is accurate—how many nonessential assets are included in the database and how many essential assets are excluded? Moteff (2007) found a number of such inconsistencies. Nonetheless, the database does provide a starting point and, perhaps, is the strongest link in the protection chain. Further efforts are needed to ensure the accuracy of the database. This involves the development of clear criteria for the inclusion of assets in the database.

It may be possible to provide adequate security for the most important assets, but many others of less importance will remain viable targets. Attacking a shopping mall or exploding a car bomb may not have as profound an impact as attacking a petrochemical plant; nonetheless, it would significantly affect the U.S. population at a number of levels. Protection levels for some assets may lead to displacement whereby terrorists simply attack targets that are more vulnerable.

Ellig, Guiora, and McKenzie (2006) examined data on suicide bombers in Israel and found that they often detonated their bombs on busy streets because shopping malls had more security. Mueller (2008) recommends that officials abandon compiling critical infrastructure asset lists altogether or at least identify only the most important or most critical economic assets and concentrate efforts on those assets. He also advises that the probability of any given asset being attacked is zero and rather than spending billions on asset protection, it may be more economical to rebuild any assets that are destroyed by terrorists.

Third, and likely the most problematic, is assessing risks. To perform this function, one must have accurate information about (1) consequences of an attack or destruction of a particular asset, (2) vulnerability of an asset, and (3) the level of threat. Officials have not adequately determined the consequences of attacks on specific assets. Currently, security standards do not exist for much of the critical infrastructure, and without such standards, it is somewhat difficult to determine a potential target's or a group of targets' vulnerability. Even with standards, a determination of vulnerability is quite subjective with a degree of inherent error. The threat level is even more complicated. There have been relatively few terrorist attacks, but there are multiple terrorist organizations that would harm the country. In essence, it cannot be known which of the thousands of possible targets could be the focus of terrorists' plans.

The fourth step in the model is to implement security measures. As noted earlier in the text, there are numerous security measures that can be implemented. How will it be determined which of the standards should be applied to a particular industry? Should all the assets in a particular industry be required to implement the same security measures? This assumes that there are few differences across assets in an industry and core measures can be used throughout. In many industries, there are newer and older facilities that in terms of security and construction are very different. There may be so many differences within particular industries that so-called core standards will be of little use.

The fifth step in the model is measure effectiveness. Governments in general do not comprehend the idea of evaluation. An examination of programs across all sectors of the economy and society would show that government focuses on "output" or "effort." Members of Congress, the president, and other members of the executive branch often discuss new programs, how much is being spent on a given problem, or the number of citizens being served. Much of this programming is guided by "pork barrel" politics, interest groups, or the need to appear to be doing something that is important. The point is that

HS ANALYSIS 3-3

The *National Infrastructure Protection Plan* outlines a comprehensive model to safeguard the critical infrastructure assets of the United States. However, the model appears to be extremely complicated, requiring a great deal of data and information. Conversely, the bottom-up approach appears to be less complicated and depends, to some extent, on current industry standards. What are the differences between these two approaches? Which approach do you believe would result in the highest levels of security? Why?

politicians and government in general seldom examine a program or activity to evaluate whether it accomplishes what it is supposed to: Does the program solve the problem (outcomes)? Cost-effectiveness is often discussed in government, but seldom implemented.

The *National Infrastructure Protection Plan* as detailed in this chapter represents a comprehensive strategy to protect the people and the critical assets of the United States. It is a rational and comprehensive model that examines protective standards, infrastructure assets, threats, protection, and feedback to determine how well assets individually and collectively are protected from terrorist attacks. However, it is questionable as how effective the plan is. At this juncture, it appears to be a more conceptual than realistic model. At best, it has been applied piecemeal across some of the U.S. industries. Many of these protective measures were mandated prior to the plan, so it is questionable if the model has had much effect in protecting the United States. It appears to be a theoretical or conceptual plan that presents an "ideal" benchmark for the future (Parfomak, 2016).

▶ A Bottom-Up Approach

As noted, numerous problems are associated with the *National Infrastructure Protection Plan*. It represents a comprehensive, top-down approach to developing protection for infrastructure. It seems that actual protection mechanics are lost in its complexity and comprehensiveness. The process is unwieldy. Woodbury (2005) suggests that perhaps the first step in infrastructure protection is to identify the protective measures that are in place. This **bottom-up approach** would allow us to determine which security measures are in place across various industries. It would lead to the identification of core security systems across the various industries. Second, once systems or measures have been identified, they should be evaluated in terms of their costs and effectiveness. What levels of security do they provide? This could lead to the development of an inventory of best practices that can be shared with various industries. It would also provide information about the protective levels of assets and industries, which is a necessary next step in future policy formulation. A simpler bottom-up approach could very well lead to higher levels of security, at least in terms of asset protection.

There has been some movement toward a bottom-up approach. In 2009, the Federal Emergency Management Agency issued a draft copy of the *Target Capabilities List: User Guide*. The stated goal of the *Target Capabilities List* is to "provide more user-friendly, accessible, and credible capacity targets with which to link all preparedness cycle activities to strengthen preparedness across prevention, protection, response, and hazard mitigation capabilities" (Department of Homeland Security, 2009, p. 3). It requires that government and private entities identify "credible targets" and link them to homeland security processes—a bottom-up approach. It is interesting that the document discusses potential targets in terms of classes or industries. Each class is then directly linked to stated capabilities and responsible parties. In other words, protection and response goals are established for each class of potential target or critical infrastructure asset. This appears to be a more efficient method or approach to critical infrastructure protection.

▶ The Buffer Zone Protection Plan

In 2012, the DHS implemented a new program to assist local agencies in securing critical infrastructure. The program, the **Buffer Zone Plan**, attempts to assist local agencies in securing critical infrastructure by providing grants to local agencies to enhance protection (DHS, 2012b). Essentially, the program requires that critical infrastructure be identified and funding is provided to extend security measures outward and identify and mitigate vulnerabilities. In essence, local agencies can apply for grants to purchase license plate reader equipment, video surveillance equipment, and other equipment that may be used to secure a critical infrastructure. Owners of the critical infrastructure can request assistance from the Office of Infrastructure Protection to provide on-site assistance in determining additional security needs. The DHS has identified 1,849 sites to monitor in all 50 states and in 2010 made $48 million in grants (Patberg, 2012).

Patberg examined how the program was being implemented in several northern New Jersey towns. He found grants had been used to purchase infrared technology, high-tech cameras, and automatic license plate readers to observe people in several locations, including reservoirs, financial hubs, and malls. The license plate readers collect information and compare it to watch lists. The program can collect a substantial amount of intelligence around high-risk critical infrastructure.

▶ The Reality of Critical Infrastructure Protection: States' Responsibilities

Most of this chapter has examined the federal framework for protecting the nation's critical infrastructure assets. Conspicuously absent from this discussion has been state and local governments' collective responsibilities. However, when a disaster or terrorist attack occurs, the target of the attack will be an asset located in a local jurisdiction within a state. Therefore, the states and local governments have substantial responsibility for the protection of infrastructure assets. The *National Infrastructure Protection Plan* discusses the importance of state and local governments' involvement in homeland security. Their responsibilities mirror the federal government in that they should organize and plan for homeland security events, be involved in infrastructure risk management, share information with the private sector and other government bodies, and coordinate activities with agencies involved in homeland security.

A few of the states have developed critical infrastructure protection plans, and they range in terms of coverage and sophistication. Rhode Island (2016) has a plan that describes the state's goals, which mirror those of the federal government. Some cities have critical infrastructure plans. San Diego (2016) has a sophisticated plan that outlines an organizational structure, roles and responsibilities, critical assets, and assessment methodologies. Unfortunately, many states and municipalities have not developed plans, and worse, they have not given due consideration to infrastructure protection.

One of the problems with the approach to critical infrastructure protection is the adherence to the **big bang theory of asset protection** (Lewis and Darken, 2005). Here, the most attention, efforts, and resources have been assigned to high-value targets, but in most cases, these are targets that are the least likely to be attacked. For example, a nuclear reactor is a high-value, but well-protected target, but a chemical plant is of lesser value as a target, but also less secure. There are thousands of targets geographically dispersed across the United States, and their protection falls squarely on state and local officials. Over the past several years, there have been small but devastating attacks in places like Boston, San Bernardino, and Chattanooga.

> **HS Web Link:** To learn how the DHS is providing grants to the states to improve homeland security, go to http://www.dhs.gov/ynews/releases/pr_1260283102665.shtm.

Key Critical Infrastructure Sectors

A discussion of potential targets of terrorist attacks generally distinguishes between soft and hard targets. **Hard targets** are generally but not always military in nature and are hardened with a variety of security measures. **Soft targets**, on the other hand, generally refer to civilian targets that have little protection and are vulnerable to attack. The primary purpose of the *National Infrastructure Protection Plan* (DHS, 2006, 2013) is to enhance security around soft targets. Unfortunately, there are numerous such targets that are vulnerable to attack.

When most U.S. citizens think of terrorists, they focus almost exclusively on Middle Eastern terrorist groups such as al-Qaeda, Hamas, Hezbollah, or ISIS. There certainly are a number of global jihadist groups that desire to attack U.S. infrastructure. However, they are not alone. For example, Ackerman, Bale, and Moran (2006) identify U.S. radical right-wing groups and ecology or "eco-terrorist" groups as also having the motive to attack infrastructure. In some ways, members of these groups see some infrastructures as epitomizing their perceived injustices in the United States, and their destruction would make an important political statement. Thus, there are many threats to infrastructure assets.

The following sections examine some of the critical infrastructure sectors and their vulnerabilities. DHS managers of the 16 critical infrastructure sectors listed above have been charged with developing a sector-specific plan. These plans use the Critical Infrastructure Risk Management Framework as enumerated above.

Water and Wastewater Systems

There are approximately 160,000 public drinking water systems and 16,000 wastewater treatment systems in the United States (DHS, 2010b). Water systems consist of water source, conveyance, storage, treatment, and distribution systems. Moreover, these water supply systems are concentrated in specific geographical areas. Zimmerman (2006) advises that 45 percent of the U.S. population is served by 6.8 percent of the water systems. Terrorists can disrupt water supplies in three ways. The computer networks that control water systems could be hacked or fall prey to a cyberattack. Such an attack could cause the release of water out of reservoirs or other containment facilities or contaminate the water through faulty or inadequate treatment.

Water could be contaminated with the release of toxins, bacteria, or other contagion. Although there have been no documented terrorist attacks on the nation's water supplies to date, there have been documented cases of sabotage. In one case, a water tower in Spokane, Washington, was broken into and the water was contaminated with bacteria; at the same time, a water reservoir in nearby Idaho was contaminated with the same bacteria. Two other water supplies were contaminated, one with bacteria and the other with toxic chemicals (Forest, 2006).

Chemical and petroleum storage units dot the United States, with many of them close to waterways. One of these facilities could be destroyed or otherwise compromised, resulting in water contamination. In 2014, a chemical storage facility near Charleston, West Virginia, leaked about 40,000 gallons of 4-methylcyclohexane methanol (MCHM), a chemical used in processing coal, into the Elk River in close proximity to the city's primary water treatment plant. The leak resulted in water being shut off to 300,000 residents. Many residents had consumed the contaminated water before the leak was announced (CBS News, 2014). Fortunately, the chemical is not a major threat to human health, but it causes skin and eye irritation (Biello, 2014). A breach of more toxic chemical facilities close to municipal water intake facilities could result in numerous deaths or injuries.

Chemical and petroleum facilities can be attacked by terrorists and such attacks can be destructive to community and the economy.
Jordi clave garsot/Alamy Stock Photo.

Chemical Sector

A chemical sector security summit is held each year to educate key players and to develop homeland security plans for the chemical industry. Participants include the DHS and the Chemical Sector Coordinating Council, which consists of representatives from the various chemical industries. Since the chemical sector produces many toxic and dangerous substances it is important that facilities and chemicals be secured. The Chemical Facility Anti-Terrorism Standards program identifies and regulates high-risk chemical facilities to ensure that they have adequate security measures in place. Any facility that has a chemical on the DHS list must complete a Chemical Security Assessment Tool (CSAT). This allows the DHS to monitor the quantity of chemicals at specific locations as well as assess facilities' security measures. The program attempts to ensure that hazardous chemicals are securely housed.

Commercial Facilities Sector

This sector includes a diverse number of facilities that draw large numbers of people for business, shopping, entertainment, or lodging. It includes facilities such as casinos, hotels, amusement parks, stadiums, shopping centers or malls, and sports facilities and activities. Figure 3-8 ■ provides a summary of commercial facilities assets.

The DHS (2015a) advises that the commercial facilities sector is coming under increased risk. Commercial facilities are **soft targets**. Soft targets can be defined as

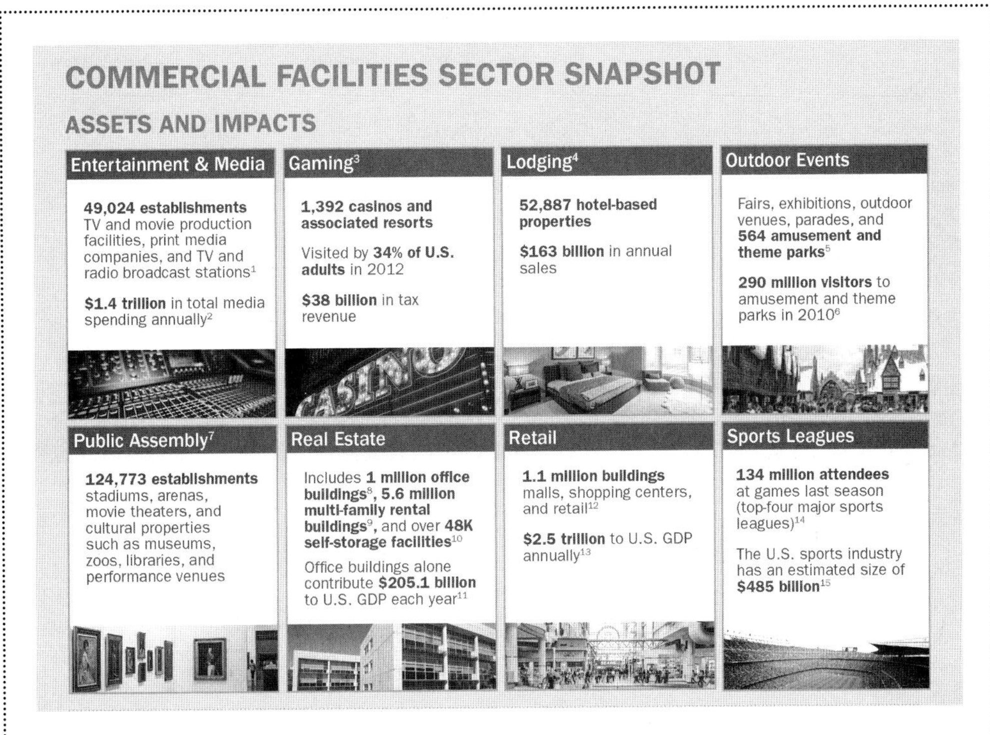

FIGURE 3-8 Commercial Facilities Assets
Source: DHS. (2015). *Commercial Facilities Sector-Specific Plan*. Washington, D.C.: Author.

targets with low levels of security and are vulnerable to attack. Terrorists often attack soft targets such as hotels, restaurants, schools, and hospitals. Robbins (2006) found that between 1968 and 2005, 73 percent of terrorists' targets were soft targets. These risks include terrorist threats from both domestic and international groups and increased cyberattacks.

Soft target managers are encouraged to use the critical infrastructure risk management format discussed above to secure their facilities. The DHS provides facilities managers with an online **infrastructure survey tool** to assist them in assessing their facilities. Also, **protective security advisors** are available for consultation and conduct on-site assessments. The DHS also provides training programs for specific industries to assist in improving security.

Hotel Security

Hotels are one of the most common targets of terrorist attacks. They are prime targets because the terrorists often are able to inflict large numbers of casualties, invoke panic and other psychological consequences, and adversely affect a community and possibly a country's economy. Hotels are potential targets because there generally are large numbers of hotels in large urban areas, allowing the terrorists to choose a high-value soft target that is readily accessible and allows for escape. Hotels generally have little security, which also facilitates attack. They have a constant flow of people, making it possible for terrorists to

City	Year	Type of Attack	Casualities	Group Responsible
Bamako, Mali	2015	Mass Shooting	20	Al-Mourabitoun
Ouaqadouqou, West Africa	2016	Mass Shooting	28	AQAIM
Sousse, Tunisia	2015	Mass Shooting	37	Unknown
Stockholm, Sweden	2015	Bombing	0	Unknown
Mogadishu	2015	Suicide Bomber	12	Al Shabaab
El-Arish, Egypt	2015	Car Bomb	4	ISIS

FIGURE 3-9 Sample of Terrorist Attacks on Hotels
Source: Information collected from a variety of news outlets.

mingle and fit in with the clientele. Figure 3-9 ■ provides a partial listing of recent major hotel bombings across the globe.

An examination of hotel bombings shows a number of trends. First, the attackers generally concentrate on luxury hotels (Jenkins, 2009). Many of the hotels were owned by Hilton and Marriott. Hotel attacks seem to be a tactic that is used by a variety of terrorist groups. Hotels are often frequented by government, international, and military leaders. In some cases, terrorists have struck when such dignitaries were in the hotel, scheduled to be at the hotel, or had recently stayed in the hotel. It appears that mass shootings are the most common mode of attack. This seems to indicate that many hotels have security measures to prevent vehicle bombings or terrorists from planting bombs. An overwhelming majority of the bombings occur in areas wrought with political strife and terrorist activities(Jenkins, 2009; Bergen, 2015).

Communications Sector

The communications sector is one of the most critical infrastructure sectors since all other sectors to some degree depend on it for their operations. The communications infrastructure consists of a vast network of satellites, communication lines, cable, broadcast facilities, and various networks that transmit Internet traffic. In addition to physical attacks, communications infrastructure is vulnerable to cyberattacks. The vast majority of the communications sector is privately owned, which limits what the federal government can do directly to improve security.

The federal government has taken some steps to ensure communications resilience. The federal government, in conjunction with the private sectors, plans for communications duplication. If one system or section of a communications network becomes inoperable, other systems can immediately compensate and handle the additional workload. This makes communications resilient to any type of incident. Infrastructure assets are categorized using the scheme in Figure 3-5 ■ above. DHS works with owners of level 1 and level 2 infrastructure to ensure that these assets meet security standards.

A major problem identified as a result of the response to the 9/11 attacks was communications inoperability; first responders from different agencies could not communicate with each other. Today, the DHS Office of Emergency Communications works with agencies at all levels to ensure effective communications during emergencies.

Critical Manufacturing Sector

Critical manufacturing is an important part of our economic engine. Attacks on some segments of this sector could have disastrous effects on a variety of critical infrastructures across other sectors. There are five primary industries within this sector: metal

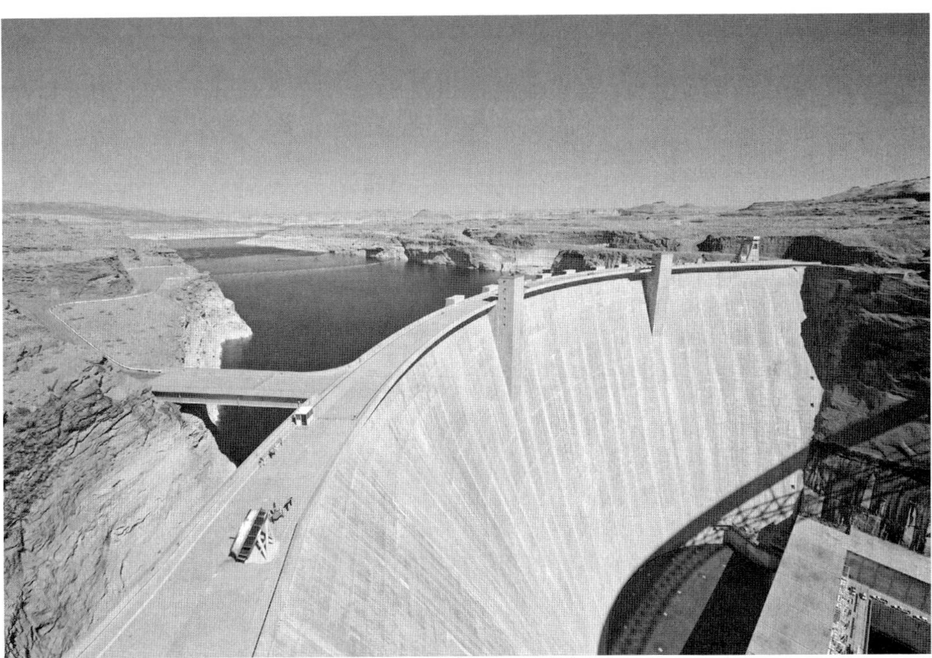

Glen Canyon Dam, Lake Powell, Page Arizona. Dams can be high-value targets for terrorists.
Neale Clark/robertharding/Alamy Stock Photo.

manufacturing, machinery manufacturing, electrical equipment, appliance and component manufacturing, and transportation equipment manufacturing. Most manufacturing consists of multiple locations connected via supply chains where various parts are transported to a final location for final assembly. Thus, supply chains are as critical as some of the manufacturing facilities. The Critical Manufacturing Government Coordinating Council consisting of government and sector representatives develop security standards. Essentially, manufacturing facilities are identified and then prioritized based on the importance of their products. Higher priority facilities are examined more closely in terms of their security and the existence of redundant operations to fill any void should there be a disrupting incident. Protection efforts can include target hardening, security systems, personnel security programs, and cybersecurity measures.

Dams Sector

Dams are critical to water retention and control, and serve numerous uses, including water supplies, agricultural irrigation, flood control, river navigation for shipping, electricity generation, waste management, and recreation. There are approximately 87,000 dams in the United States, and it is estimated that 4,000 are structurally deficient (DHS, 2015b). Many dams are vulnerable to explosive attacks by terrorists, but the most common threat is cyberattacks. Many of these dams are controlled by computer monitoring and control systems, which can be hacked. It does not appear that many of these deficient dams will be structurally improved in the near future. Thus, the primary homeland security objectives are to monitor the dams and develop effective emergency notification systems for citizens who would be affected by a breach and safeguard against cyberattacks. High-hazard dams have been identified and emergency action plans are being developed for each of them. Additionally, the states have been developing dam safety programs.

Defense Industrial Base Sector

The defense industrial base sector consists of industries involved in research and development and the design and production of military weapons systems and their component parts. The sector includes large manufacturers such as Boeing who assemble aircraft to small manufacturers who make individual components for the aircraft, and there are thousands of these facilities worldwide. Given the nature of this sector, it is critical that assets be prioritized. The Department of Defense (DoD) establishes priorities based on national defense mission. Facilities that make products that are a high priority for the country's defense are given a higher priority in terms of security. In addition, the DoD collects consequence, threat, and vulnerability data for sites. The data are used to prioritize infrastructure and to develop protective measures. Asset owners are responsible for the first level of protection.

The greatest threat to the defense industrial base is cyberattacks and cyber espionage. Cyberattacks to control systems can result in faulty products or a breakdown of weapons systems construction. Moreover, these facilities are constantly attacked by hackers, many from countries such as Russia, China, Iran, or North Korea. These countries attempt to learn U.S. military secrets to reduce their defense development costs or to develop countermeasures to U.S. systems (Alexander, 2011). Physical and cyber security are of equal importance.

Emergency Services Sector

The emergency service sector consists of a number of functions, including law enforcement, fire and emergency services, emergency management, emergency medical services, and public works. Essentially, this sector is composed of first responders. There is a range of risks, including terrorist attacks, extreme weather, and cyberattacks. In general, emergency services facilities are vulnerable to threats since they are numerous, geographically dispersed, and accessible to the public. They are highly dependent on communications, including radio, telephone, and the Internet. For example, if a cyberattack would overwhelm the 911 emergency call center with fake phone calls, police and medical teams would not be able to respond to actual emergencies. Such a cyberattack coupled with a physical terrorist attack would greatly increase the negative consequences of such a terrorist act. Imagine, terrorists were attacking a hotel and no emergency calls would reach the police department. The terrorists would have much more time to kill people in the hotel.

Resilience and mitigation are the two primary objectives in securing emergency services operations. These objectives are accomplished through effective communications and partnerships. In terms of communications, emergency services agencies must be able to communicate with each other within the same county or area and also with agencies from other areas so that responses to large events can be coordinated. These agencies need to develop partnerships with agencies in surrounding communities so that adequate resources can be garnered when there is a significant event. Communications inoperability has been a problem in the past, so a high priority is to ensure that regional and statewide communications are readily available. Emergency services agencies should conduct exercises to test their ability to coordinate and respond to different types of events.

Energy

The energy sector—oil, natural gas, and electricity—has a massive infrastructure footprint. The electric industry serves 140 million households and the nation consumes approximately 3.6 trillion kilowatt hours of electricity annually. The electricity is distributed through an extensive power grid that touches every corner of the country and consists of over 6,000 miles of high-voltage transmission lines. Additionally, there are over 6,000 power plants in the United States. There are more than a half million oil-producing wells in the United States and 153 refineries and more than 1,400 petroleum storage facilities. There are about 1.5 million miles of natural gas lines, about 500,000 natural gas wells and about 500 gas processing wells serving the people of the United States (Bullock et al., 2005; DHS, 2010).

The energy infrastructure is geographically dispersed, and for the most part, it is unguarded. This makes the energy infrastructure vulnerable to terrorist attacks. Although there have not been any terrorist attacks on these assets to date, there have been acts of vandalism and sabotage (see Forest, 2006). Industrial accidents and natural disaster events also have destroyed facilities, causing supply disruptions. In 2008, there was a severe gasoline shortage in the southeastern United States as a result of a hurricane that destroyed a primary refinery in Louisiana. There have been numerous blackouts and brownouts, some severe and lasting for long periods of time. When hurricane Sandy hit the northeast in 2012, many sections of New York and New Jersey were without power for weeks. The lack of electricity hampered rescue and rebuilding efforts. The most common problem is deteriorating or overburdened infrastructure. Potential terrorist attacks, realistically, would have little impact on this infrastructure, as witnessed by the effects of the industrial accidents and natural disasters. This infrastructure is fairly redundant, and when there is a disruption, facilities are quickly repaired or resources are rerouted to the affected area.

However, some of these facilities should receive special consideration. Since most of the energy supply movement is controlled by computer systems, it must be ensured that these automated control systems are secure from hacking and other cyberattacks—security software and hardware should be constantly evaluated and updated. Some of the facilities store or contain large amounts of natural gas or petroleum products, and their destruction could result in a shortage of supplies for consumers and environmental and economic problems for those residing in the immediate area.

Special consideration should be given to the fact that U.S. military and intelligence installations receive electrical power from the nation's energy grid, and this grid is controlled by the private sector. Military and intelligence operations could be hampered in

U.S. energy grid is vast and open and may become a target for terrorists.
Gareth Fuller/AP Images.

the event of loss of electrical power. It would have a cascading affect since many overseas operations are controlled and coordinated at facilities in the United States. Therefore, it is critical that the electrical grid be safeguarded and these facilities have backup generators.

Transportation Security

The transportation sector consists of seven subsectors: aviation, freight, rail, highway, maritime, mass transit and passenger rail, and pipelines. The 9/11 attacks pointed to a significant security problem within the national aviation network. Airplanes were commandeered and used as bombs, resulting in the loss of 3,000 lives and billions of dollars in damage. The Aviation and Transportation Act was passed, in the wake of the 9/11attacks. The act accomplished three security tasks: (1) it established the TSA and charged it with the security of the national transportation system, (2) mandated that TSA employees screen passenger luggage and air freight, and (3) by December 2002 screen all passenger baggage using X-ray equipment. Today, passengers are screened using electromagnetic devices that detect metal (possible weapons). The TSA uses millimeter-wave passenger-screening technology. This machine transmits radio waves that are reflected off the passenger, producing a detailed image to identify any possible weapons or explosives. The new technology is more effective compared to electromagnetic screening. Even though the TSA is responsible for security screening, the individual airport authorities and the airlines are ultimately responsible for overall security, which often is coordinated by the Federal Aviation Administration.

Other precautions are also being taken. In 2007, the Department of State embedded a computer chip in all newly issued U.S. passports (also known as e-passports). The chip stores the photo as well as other biometric data. The U.S. Customs and Border Protection has been studying facial recognition software whereby photos of the passport holder is compared to the data contained on the chip (Cushin, 2015). This program will help prevent terrorists and others from using stolen passports.

Another threat to air travel security is physical attacks on airports. In 1999, Ahmed Ressam was arrested as he entered the United States from Canada with the intent to set off a bomb at the Los Angeles Airport (PBS, 2017). In 1997, four Muslim men were arrested in New Jersey for planning to attack JFK International Airport. They had planned to bomb jet fuel supply tanks and a major fuel pipeline (Buckley and Rashbaum, 2007). In 2002, Hesham Mohamed Hadayet, an Egyptian, killed two people and wounded several others at an El Al ticketing station in Los Angeles before being killed by security personnel (Weiss and Landsberg, 2002). These incidents bring attention to the fact that airport security must go beyond screening passengers, baggage, and cargo. A number of parameter issues must be considered.

In 2017, the United States banned passengers from carrying laptops and notebook computers on flights from several countries. Intelligence revealed that terrorist bomb makers were attempting to construct bombs for insertion in the devices while allowing the devices to boot-up when checking in at the airport. A total ban on the devices is being considered (Noack, Lazo, and Barret, 2017).

Ground Transportation

The United States has an extensive ground transportation system that includes roadways and rail. Both of these conduits carry massive numbers of passengers and cargo, including hazardous materials. They are concentrated in large urban areas and present challenges to homeland security. Numerous transportation disasters have killed and injured people, and a number of incidents have involved hazardous materials. Although there have not been terrorist attacks on these sectors, past experience points to such as possibility. For example,

Rail transportation is vital in U.S. metropolitan areas.
NTSB/Alamy Stock Photo.

a number of terrorist attacks on Israeli citizens have been by suicide bombers detonating bombs on buses (BBC, 2016). The subway attacks in Madrid in 2004 (Sciolino, 2004), Moscow in 2013 (Taylor, 2017), and London in 2017 (Said-Moorehouse, 2017) provide credence to transportation being a likely target for terrorists. These incidents resulted in large numbers of casualties.

People and hazardous materials are the two primary considerations in ground transportation systems. Regarding the safeguarding of people, some precautions have been implemented in the United States (see Forest, 2006). A number of transportation authorities have installed cameras to detect suspicious persons and activities. Trash cans or trash receptacles have been removed from transit stations as terrorists have planted bombs in these receptacles in other countries. In some cities, such as New York City, passengers and their belongings are subject to random searches to deter terrorists from carrying bombs onto buses and subways. The DHS is working to develop explosive detection sensors for installation in mass transit facilities. The TSA has been training explosive detection canines that are being deployed in airports and mass transit terminals. In the wake of the 2005 London bombings, British authorities have deployed millimeter-wave passenger-screening technology to screen passengers at mass transit terminals. In 2015, passengers on a train from Amsterdam to Paris subdued a suspected terrorist carrying an AK-47, pistol, knife, and ammunition. If he had not been subdued, he may have shot numerous passengers. This incident resulted in a number of U.S. legislators calling for more security on U.S. passenger trains (Alcorn and Rivoli, 2015). Thus, it appears that there is a need to ramp up mass transit security. The major problem facing transit authority officials is a lack of funding. Many of these systems are bankrupt or their budgets are at a breakeven point. Nonetheless, attacks on these soft targets could have a devastating effect.

The transportation of hazardous chemicals and material presents different problems. All sorts of hazardous materials are transported by rail and trucks throughout the United States. The U.S. Department of Transportation advises that there are 1.2 million daily

HS ANALYSIS 3-4

Numerous types of physical infrastructure are considered when establishing a homeland security program. Of the various industries or types of infrastructure discussed in this section, which ones should receive the highest priority? How did you arrive at your decision?

shipments of hazardous materials by truck, rail, and air. These shipments range in size from several ounces to several tons (McGuire, 2005). Moreover, unlike mass transit, the shipment of hazardous materials occurs literally everywhere throughout the country. Hitherto, little consideration had been given to the transportation of hazardous materials unless there was some accident or incident involving them, and there are numerous major incidents each year occurring in rural and urban areas. For the most part, the DHS has initiated programs with haulers and shippers to better track hazardous materials while in transit. This will add a measure of accountability in the shipping of hazardous materials. Nonetheless, these materials present a significant hazard. Trucks or railcars containing hazardous materials can be blown up or tampered with to cause leakage in highly populated areas. At this point, monitoring seems to be the primary strategy to prevent terrorist attacks.

▶ Infrastructure from the Terrorists' Viewpoint

The preceding sections outlined the many issues surrounding the protection of critical infrastructure of the United States. This section examines critical infrastructure from the terrorist's perspective. Even though there are literally thousands of potential targets in the United States, not all are equally inviting to the terrorist as a potential target. Indeed, some critical infrastructures are secured or located in such a manner that their attack would be quite difficult. Others may be located in geographical areas that make their attack difficult because of potential logistical problems for terrorists. Theoretically, some critical infrastructures are not potential targets because terrorists do not have the opportunity to mount a successful attack. If we better understand the limitations or constrictions placed on terrorists, we may be better able to identify those targets that are at greater risk.

Clarke and Newman (2006) have examined the opportunity for terrorist attacks in detail. They note that the commission of a terrorist act, like a criminal act, requires that terrorists have the opportunity to carry it out. As such, there are conditions that must exist for terrorists to be able to attack a specific target. They identified four factors or conditions that must exist for an attack to occur, as shown in Figure 3–10 ■.

As can be seen in Figure 3-10 ■, there are limitations on terrorists' target choices. Not all targets are created equal—some have natural inhibitors that cause them to be disregarded by potential terrorists. This information allows the examination of critical infrastructure from the terrorists' perspective and provides two important advantages when attempting to secure the country's infrastructure. By applying the four conditions to critical infrastructure, a rough determination about the infrastructure's vulnerability or its potential as a target can be obtained. For example, a high-value target located in mid-America has a lower level of risk since it may be more difficult for terrorists to travel there undetected and acquire the tools and weapons to mount an attack. The number of potential targets that may be considered by terrorists can be limited. Terrorists are more likely to attack a target in urban areas, especially those that have larger Middle Eastern populations—they must

Conditions	
1. Targets	Although there are multiple targets, many are not worthy or suitable for a variety of reasons: (a) destruction of target does not achieve terrorists' objectives; (b) located in an area where strangers, especially Middle Easterners, would be observed; (c) target is too well guarded; and (d) the size or nature of the target makes total destruction difficult.
2. Weapons	Not all weapons are appropriate for a given target. Weapons required to attack a specific target may not be available. For example, some targets are more suitable for attack with biological weapons, but if these are not available, an attack cannot be effectively mounted. Today, it is difficult to obtain large amounts of explosives to attack a large target. The attack on a potential target can be mounted only with the appropriate weapons.
3. Tools	Terrorists must acquire a number of tools, including vehicles, pilot's license, proper identity papers, identification allowing access to a target, and so on. These tools are necessary to conduct an attack. If they cannot be obtained, an attack cannot occur.
4. Facilitating Conditions	Terrorists often exploit security lapses, loopholes, and so on when choosing a target. If these do not exist, it is inherently more difficult to mount an attack. The degree of security often is not known until immediately prior to an attack, which serves to dissuade an attack.

FIGURE 3-10 Conditions Necessary to Facilitate a Terrorist Attack

be able to blend in with the population to avoid suspicion. Second, it advises us on how to deploy additional security measures for high-value targets. We can apply the four conditions to a location and make an estimate of the probability of attack. The steps or criteria outlined in Figure 3-5 ■ likely will produce better estimates as compared to the formula outlined in the *National Strategy for Homeland Security*. Moreover, they likely will provide more information about how to safeguard some high-value targets.

It is informative to apply Clarke and Newman's conditions to an actual situation. An examination of Gaza in Palestine shows that Hamas has been conducting a war with the Israelis for a number of years. Its primary modes of attacks have been suicide bombers and rocket attacks. The Israelis have attempted to thwart suicide bombers by walling off Gaza and searching Palestinians who leave the area and enter Israel. This essentially affects potential terrorists' tools and weapons. Because the movements of Palestinians are restricted, some of the facilitating conditions are also limited. The walling off of Gaza has prevented most weapons from entering the area, although some weapons are smuggled into Gaza through tunnels from Egypt. Moreover, the Israelis frequently target and attack suspected rocket launching locations and storage facilities, making such attacks difficult. Even though Hamas has launched hundreds of rockets into Israel, they have been crude and have produced few casualties. The bottom line is that there are conditions that limit Hamas's modes and methods of attack. Limitations should be a part of the calculus as we decide on infrastructure protection.

HS ANALYSIS 3-5

Clarke and Newman examine the selection of targets from the terrorists' perspective. They recognize that terrorists have limitations, especially logistical issues. Based on their analysis, do you reside in an area that is more or less susceptible to terrorist attacks? How should this affect homeland security planning in your area?

► Complacency: The Threat to Homeland Security

This chapter has examined a number of issues relative to infrastructure protection. Given the turmoil throughout the world, the United States must be ever vigilant as an attack can occur at any time. Over time, the country has become complacent and to some extent let its guard down. Complacency is the most formidable foe of homeland security. In other words, we must work to maintain vigilance. Failure to do so only enhances the probability of future attacks.

There are several factors that contribute to complacency. The 9/11 attacks occurred years ago, and the Boston Marathon attack is slowly slipping into history. The absence of attacks removes people's fear and resolve. Moreover, since new attacks have not occurred it must be that homeland security is functioning properly and effectively. The world continuously provides the United States with problems whether it's Russia invading another country, the Taliban in Afghanistan or Pakistan, or the Islamic State of Iraq and Syria because such world events often overshadow and minimize programs like homeland security. The United States spends billions of dollars each year on homeland security; more so than on many other programs or problems. Some people therefore reason that homeland security must be adequate. Finally, homeland security is a complex endeavor not only in theory but also in application. The search is for simple solutions for complex questions so that it results in avoidance behaviors.

Essentially, complacency must be constantly battled; it is a disease that can lay the country open to attack. The world and its threats are constantly evolving, necessitating that homeland security be examined and improved constantly. Moreover, it must be remembered that one weak link or mistake in homeland security can result in dire consequences.

Summary

Homeland security has been a governmental initiative for generations, but the 9/11 attacks in New York City and Washington, D.C., made it a national prerogative. U.S. citizens became acutely aware that they could be attacked and were in danger from foreign extremists. Currently, there is no clear definition of homeland security. It includes a number of problems or conditions centering on terrorist attacks, catastrophes, and hazards. The lack of definition leads to operational problems and an unclear path for implementation. Upon examining the literature, it appears that homeland security essentially consists of three primary objectives: (1) prevention of terrorist attacks, (2) protection of U.S. citizens and infrastructural resources, and (3) response and recovery from incidents that do occur. It is all encompassing in that numerous federal, state, and local agencies are involved in implementing homeland security. The primary concern, however, is the protection of people and infrastructure.

The framework for implementing homeland security is enumerated in the *National Infrastructure Protection Plan*. It is a national imperative that is applicable to all infrastructure and human resources. It represents the foundation for planning and security implementation. It consists of five steps or phases:

1. Establishment of security or protection goals
2. Identification of critical infrastructure assets
3. Assess risks to various assets and industries
4. Implement protection programs
5. Measure the effectiveness of measures that have been implemented

Numerous issues are associated with the model. For the most part, it is too comprehensive and complicated. It is questionable as to what degree the model has been implemented. That is, it may remain as a theoretical perspective or concept that is unachievable across many infrastructure sectors. The relative responsibilities of the local, state, and federal governments have not been solidified. Nonetheless, a national strategy must be developed for protecting people and infrastructure, one that can be implemented clearly and comprehensively. It seems a first step should be an inventory of current modes of protection and an evaluation of their effectiveness. This would provide a solid foundation from which to build in the future.

Discussion Questions

1. What is critical infrastructure?
2. How is the federal government organized in terms of responsibility for safeguarding critical infrastructure assets?
3. Discuss the National Asset Database and its effectiveness in contributing to homeland security.
4. What are the elements in the *National Infrastructure Protection Plan and Risk Management Framework* and how do they function?
5. What is the bottom-up approach to infrastructure protection and how does it compare to the *National Infrastructure Protection Plan and Risk Management Framework*?
6. Water is an important critical infrastructure asset. How can water systems be attacked?
7. From a terrorist's standpoint, what conditions must exist for an attack to be successful?
8. What is the big bang theory of asset protection?

References

Ackerman, G., J. Bale, and K. Moran. (2006). "Assessing the threat to critical infrastructure." In *Homeland Security: Protecting America's Targets,* Vol. 3, pp. 33–60. Westport, CT: Praeger Security International.

Alcorn, C. and D. Rivoli (2015). "Pols urge TSA to ramp up anti-terrorism technology at railroads—especially Penn Station." http://www.nydailynews.com/new-york/polls-anti-terrorism-tech-penn-station-article-1.2337320 (Accessed August 31, 2015).

Alexander, D. (2011). *U.S. defense forms face relentless cyber-attacks*. Reuters, Sept. 7. https://www.reuters.com/article/us-aero-arms-summit-cybersecurity/u-s-defense-firms-face-relentless-cyberattacks-idUSTRE7867F120110907.

Almasy, S., P. Melihan, and J. Bittermann (2015). "Paris massacre: At least 128 killed in gunfire and blasts, French officials say." *CNN,* http://www.cnn.com/2015/11/13/world/paris-shooting/index.html (Accessed July 21, 2017).

BBC (2014). "Westgate mall attack in 60 seconds." http://www.bbc.com/news/world-africa-29247163 (Accessed February 14, 2016).

BBC (2016). "Israel says Jerusalem bus bombing was Hamas suicide attack." April, 21. http://www.bbc.com/news/world-middle-east-36100485.

Bergen, P. (2015). Why terrorists target hotels. CNN, Nov. 20. http://www.cnn.com/2015/11/20/opinions/bergen-hotels-targeted-terrorists/index.html

Biello, D. (2014). How dangerous is the coal-washing chemical spilled in West Virginia. *Scientific American.* January, 10. https://www.scientificamerican.com/article/how-dangerous-is-the-chemical-spilled-in-west-virginia/.

Buckley, C. and Rashbaum, W. K. (2007). *4 men accused of plot to blow up Kennedy airport terminals and fuel lines*. June, 3. *New York Times*. http://www.nytimes.com/2007/06/03/nyregion/03plot.html.

Bullock, J., G. Haddow, D. Coppola, E. Ergin, L. Westerman, and S. Yeletaysi. (2005). *Introduction to Homeland Security.* Burlington, MA: Elsevier.

CBS News. (2014). "Chemical spill shuts off water to 330K in West Virginia." http://www.cbsnews.com/news/some-people-treated-for-water-related-issues-in-w-va/ (Accessed January 29, 2014).

Clarke, R. (2008). *Your Government Failed You: Breaking the Cycle of National Security Disasters*. New York: HarperCollins.

Clarke, R. G. V. and Newman, G. R. (2006). *Outsmarting the Terrorists*. Greenwood Publishing Group.

Department of Homeland Security. (2015a). *Commercial Facilities Sector-Specific Plan: An Annex to the NIPP 2013*. Washington, D.C.: Author.

Department of Homeland Security. (2015b). *Dams Sector-Specific Plan: An Annex to the NIPP 2013.* Washington, D.C.: Author.

Department of Homeland Security. (2013). *NIPP 2013: Partnering for Critical Infrastructure Security and Resilience.* Washington, D.C.: Author. https://www.dhs.gov/sites/default/files/publications/National-Infrastructure-Protection-Plan-2013-508.pdf

Department of Homeland Security. (2012a). *National Terrorism Advisory System.* http://www.dhs.gov/files/publications/ntas-public-guide.shtm (Accessed March 28, 2012).

Department of Homeland Security. (2012b). *Buffer Zone Protection Program.* https://www.fema.gov/media-library/assets/documents/20601. (Accessed November 26, 2012).

Department of Homeland Security. (2011). *The Strategic National Risk Assessment in Support of PPD8: A Comprehensive Risk-Based Approach toward a Secure and Resilient Nation.* Washington, D.C.: Author. https://www.dhs.gov/xlibrary/assets/rma-strategic-national-risk-assessment-ppd8.pdf (Accessed February 25, 2016).

Department of Homeland Security. (2010a). *Energy Sector-Specific Plan, 2010.* http://www.dhs.gov/xlibrary/assets/nipp-ssp-energy-2010.pdf (Accessed March, 2016).

Department of Homeland Security. (2010b). *Water and Wastewater Systems Sector-Specific Plan, 2010.* https://www.dhs.gov/xlibrary/assets/nipp-ssp-water-2010.pdf (Accessed March 4, 2016).

Department of Homeland Security. (2006). *National Infrastructure Protection Plan.* Washington, D.C.: Author.

Department of Homeland Security. (n.d.) *Supplemental Tool: Executing a Critical Infrastructure Risk Management Approach.* Washington, D.C.: Author.

Department of Homeland Security. (2009). *Target Capabilities List: User Guide.* Federal Emergency Management Agency (FEMA). https://info.publicintelligence.net/TargetCapabilities UserGuide_17February2009.pdf.

Ellig, J., A. Guiora, and K. McKenzie. (2006). *A Framework for Evaluating Counterterrorism Regulations.* Washington, D.C.: Mercatus Center, George Mason University.

Forest, J. (2006). "Protecting America's critical infrastructure: An introduction." In *Homeland Security: Protecting America's Targets, Volume III: Critical Infrastructure*, ed. J. Forest, pp. 1–29. Westport, CT: Praeger Security International.

Government Accounting Office. (2013). *Critical Infrastructure Protection: DHS List of Priority Assets Needs to be Validated and Reported to Congress.* Washington, D.C.: GAO.

Jenkins, B. (2009). *Terrorists Can Think Strategically: Lessons Learned from the Mumbai Attacks.* Santa Monica, CA: RAND Corp.

Lewis, T. and R. Darken. (2005). "Potholes and detours in the road to critical infrastructure protection policy." *Homeland Security Affairs*, 1(2): 1–15.

McGuire, R. (2005). Statement before the Committee on Homeland Security, Subcommittee on Economic Security, Infrastructure Protection, and Cybersecurity, U.S. House of Representatives (November 1). (Accessed December 9, 2008).

Mohney, G. (2016). "Chipotle restaurants to temporarily close for safety meeting. *ABC News*, http://abcnews.go.com/Health/chipotle-restaurants-temporarily-close-safety-meeting/story?id=36311235 (Accessed February 23, 2016).

Moteff, J. (2007). *Critical Infrastructure: The National Asset Database.* CRS Report for Congress. Washington, D.C.: Congressional Research Service.

Mueller, J. (2008, March). "The quixotic quest for invulnerability: Assessing the costs, benefits, and probabilities of protecting the homeland." Paper presented at the National Convention of the International Studies Association, San Francisco.

Noack, R., Lazo, L., and Barret, D. 2017). Britain. and U.S. ban most electronic devices in cabins on flights from several Muslim-majority countries. *The Washington Post*, March 21. https://www.washingtonpost.com/local/trafficandcommuting/us-unveils-new-restrictions-on-travelers-from-eight-muslim-majority-countries/2017/03/21/d4efd080-0dcb-11e7-9d5a-a83e627dc120_story.html?utm_term=.8ec975e8a61e.

Office of the President. (2003). *The National Strategy for the Physical Protection of Critical Infrastructure and Key Assets.* Washington D.C.: Author.

Patberg, Z. (2012). "North Jersey towns acquiring high-tech surveillance gear." *The Record*, (Nov. 22), http://www.northjersey.com/news/North_Jersey_cops_enlisted_in_anti-terrorism_surveillance.html?page=all (Accessed November 26, 2012).

Parfomark, P. W. (2016). *Pipelines: Securing the Veins of the American Economy.* Committee on Homeland Security Subcommittee on Transportation Security. U.S. House of Representatives. Congressional Research Service. http://docs.house.gov/meetings/HM/HM07/20160419/104773/HHRG-114-HM07-Bio-ParfomakP-20160419.pdf.

PBS. (2017). *Ahmed Ressam's Millenium Plot.* https://www.pbs.org/wgbh/pages/frontline/shows/trail/inside/cron.html.

Rhode Island. (2015). *Rhode Island Critical Infrastructure Program Overview.* http://www.riema.ri.gov/resources/emergencymanager/prepare/preparednessconference/files/Session_4_Critical%20Infrastructure%20Brief%20for%20August%20Conference.pdf (Accessed March 4, 2016).

Robbins, J. (2006). "Soft targets, hard choices." In *Homeland Security: Protecting America's Targets,* Vol. 2, pp. 37–50. Westport, CT: Praeger Security International.

Said-Moorehouse, L. (2017). London terror attack latest: Second man arrested in Tube bombing, September 17. http://www.cnn.com/2017/09/17/europe/london-tube-terror-incident/index.html.

San Diego. (2008). *San Diego Operational Area Critical Infrastructure Protection Plan,* http://www.sandiegocounty.gov/oes/WebEOC/Documents/San_Diego_OA_CIP_Plan.pdf (Accessed March 4, 2016).

Sciolino, E. (2004). Bombings in Madrid: The attack; 10 bombs shatter trains in Madrid, killing 192, March 12. *New York Times.* http://www.nytimes.com/2004/03/12/world/bombings-in-madrid-the-attack-10-bombs-shatter-trains-in-madrid-killing-192.html.

Taylor, A. (2017). The recent history of suicide attacks in Russia. *The Washington Post*, April 3. https://www.washingtonpost.com/news/worldviews/wp/2017/04/03/the-recent-history-of-terrorist-attacks-in-russia/?utm_term=.fc95bbeb5683.

Weaver, J. (1985). "Statement." *Congressional Record (Procedures and Debates, 99th Congress)*, 131(3–4) (February 28): 4185–89.

Weiss, K. R. and Landsberg, M. (2002). *Gunman kills two at LAX*, July 5. *LA Times.* http://articles.latimes.com/2002/jul/05/local/me-laxshoot5.

Woodbury, G. (2005). "Measuring prevention." *Homeland Security Affairs*, 1(1): 1–9.

Zimmerman, R. (2006). "Critical infrastructure and interdependency." In *The McGraw-Hill Homeland Security Handbook*, ed. G. Kamien, pp. 523–45. New York: McGraw-Hill.

4 Legal Aspects of Homeland Security

LEARNING OBJECTIVES

1. *Explain the legality and role of presidential orders.*
2. *Outline the progression of executive orders as they relate to homeland security and counterterrorism.*
3. *Discuss the Foreign Intelligence Surveillance Act Court.*
4. *Discuss the USA PATRIOT Act and its scope.*

Key Terms

Executive orders
Proliferation of Weapons of Mass Destruction
Blocking Property of Weapons of Mass Destruction Proliferators and Their Supporters
Prohibiting Transactions with Terrorists Who Threaten to Disrupt the Middle East Peace Process
Blocking Property and Prohibiting Transactions with Persons Who Commit, Threaten to Commit, or Support Terrorism
National Counterterrorism Center
Interpretation of the Geneva Conventions Common Article 3 as Applied to a Program of Detention and Interrogation Operated by the Central Intelligence Agency
Homeland Security Information Sharing
Strengthening the Sharing of Terrorism Information to Protect Americans
Establishing the President's Homeland Security Advisory Council and Senior Advisory Committees for Homeland Security
Public Alert and Warning System
Review and Disposition of Individuals Detained at the Guantánamo Bay Naval Base and Closure of Detention Facilities
Special Interagency Task Force on Detainee Disposition
Antiterrorism and Effective Death Penalty Act of 1996
USA PATRIOT Act
Foreign Intelligence Surveillance Act of 1978

▶ Introduction

In the aftermath of the terrorist attacks on September 11, 2001, the U.S. Congress enacted a series of laws designed to curb the possibility of another attack on American soil. These laws were passed with great speed and much public and media attention. The speed at which these laws were enacted is evidenced by the fact that the most well-known legislation, the USA PATRIOT Act, was passed by the U.S. House of

Representatives with only one representative having read the bill before it was voted into law (Abourezk, 2008). Although well intended, many of the provisions of the new federal antiterrorist legislation were so sweeping, unclear, and susceptible to abuse by government officials that corrective orders, new legislation, or judicial action was taken to address some of their many shortcomings.

Concern with terrorism and terrorist groups was not merely the product of the attacks of September 11, nor was it limited to the legislative branch of government. Long before the attacks on Washington, D.C., and New York City, U.S. presidents have been issuing executive orders and directives designed to address the threat of terrorism. President Bill Clinton, for example, issued numerous executive orders that either directly or indirectly dealt with many of the issues surrounding terrorism. President George H. W. Bush was perhaps the most prolific issuer of orders addressing terrorism. President Barack Obama has also issued executive orders providing new directions in homeland security and terrorism. In all, a growing body of executive orders needs to be considered along with legislation passed by the Congress of the United States.

This chapter considers some of the most essential presidential executive orders, congressional legislation, and law enforcement authorizations and practices that have been crafted to combat terrorism and create a safe homeland. As can be seen, they provide a legal foundation for strengthening our ability to fight terrorism and respond to terrorist acts.

▶ Presidential Executive Orders and Directives

Presidents of the United States have the authority to issue a variety of executive orders, directives, and military orders (Relyea, 2008). Perhaps the oldest and best known of these presidential instructions are **executive orders**. Executive orders are instructions to federal officials and agencies and are designed to govern the execution of public policy. When exercising presidential authority under emergency conditions, however, executive orders can take on a much more serious quality: "For example, President Roosevelt used an executive order on February 19, 1942, to require the internment of American citizens of Japanese ancestry who were living in certain designated Pacific coast defense areas" (citation omitted, Relyea, 2008: 8–9). Following the terrorist attacks of September 11, 2001, President George W. Bush began issuing executive orders and a new series of presidential directives called *Homeland Security Presidential Directives* (HSPDs). During his presidency, Bush issued at least 24 of these directives (Relyea, 2008) and numerous executive orders. Executive orders and directives can have far-reaching consequences. For example, HSPD-6 issued by President Bush created an elaborate terrorist identification and watch system as illustrated in Figure 4-1 ■.

Executive orders and directives, although not legislation, have the force of law depending on their substantive effect. The contents of an executive order link policy statements and judgments of the executive branch of government to existing legislation. In essence, unlike a law enacted by Congress, a presidential order or directive itself does not carry the force of law, but rather the contents of the order and its relationship to existing authorities are determinative of its legal effect. Executive orders and directives are policy statements that link governmental policy to existing legislation by drawing upon existing statutes for their authority or by providing direction for the application of the statutes they draw upon for their authority. An executive order remains in effect until a president changes it.

HS Web Link: To learn more about presidential executive orders, go to http://www.thisnation.com/question/040.html.

In the following section of this chapter, we review the provisions of several executive orders and directives issued by U.S. presidents that were designed to combat terrorism or provide a legal basis for developing homeland security measures.

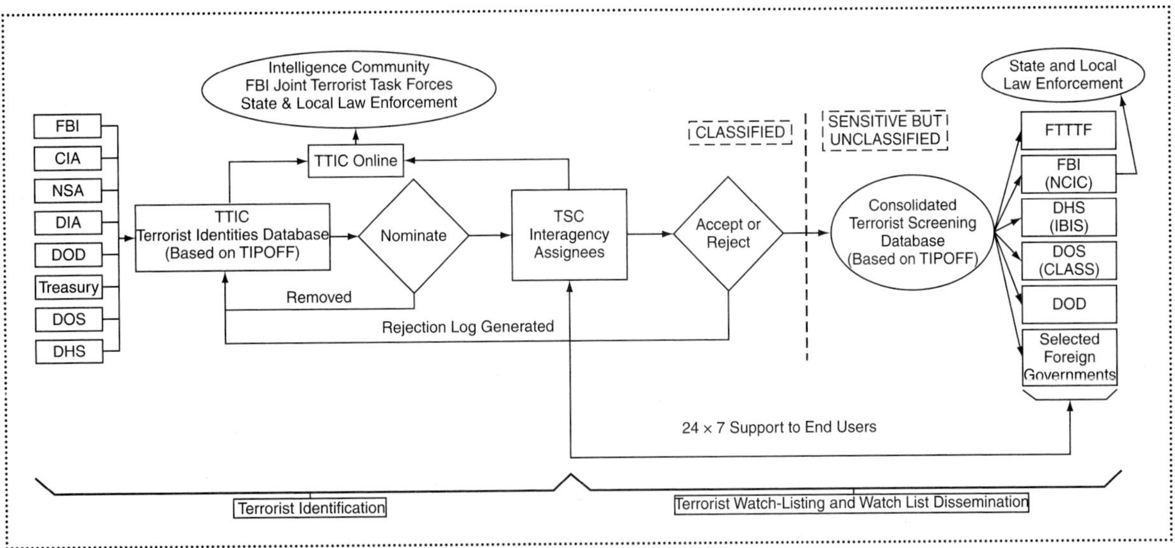

FIGURE 4-1 Terrorist Identification, Watch-Listing, and Watch List Dissemination under HSPD-6
Source: Krouse, W. J. (2004). Terrorist Identification, Screening, and Tracking under Homeland Security Presidential Directive 6. CRS Report for Congress, April 21, 2004, p. 16.

Executive Orders of President Clinton

Although the public generally does not associate President Clinton with the "war on terrorism" or even the development of homeland security, he issued a number of executive orders that laid much of the policy foundation for the prevention of terrorism. President Clinton's orders evidence concern with four broad areas of government policy relating to homeland security: (1) control over the proliferation of weapons of mass destruction (WMDs), (2) control of financial transactions that could be used to support terrorism, (3) collection of intelligence information, and (4) protection of the nation's critical infrastructure. We consider each of these areas in the following sections that review executive orders.

Proliferation of Weapons of Mass Destruction

President Clinton issued Executive Order #12938, **Proliferation of Weapons of Mass Destruction**, on November 14, 1994, under the International Emergency Economic Powers Act (50 U.S.C. 1701) and the National Emergencies Act (50 U.S.C. 1601), which enabled him to enact orders and directives during emergency situations. Declaring that the proliferation of nuclear, biological, and chemical weapons (WMDs) and their delivery systems constituted "an unusual and extraordinary threat to the national security," the president issued an executive order against their proliferation. The order (1) established multilateral international coordination to control the proliferation of WMDs and their delivery systems; (2) established a system for controlling exports of WMDs and any goods, technology, or services that could be used to "develop, produce, stockpile, deliver, or use weapons of mass destruction or their means of delivery"; (3) imposed sanctions on foreign persons and any foreign country that "use, develop, produce, stockpile, or otherwise acquire chemical or biological weapons" in violation of international law; and (4) prohibited any government agency from procuring or entering into "any contract for the procurement of" WMD materials.

On June 28, 2005, President George H. Bush issued Executive Order #13382, **Blocking Property of Weapons of Mass Destruction Proliferators and Their Supporters**, designed to take

National security cases often are adjudicated in the U.S. Supreme Court.
The Supreme Court of the United States.

additional steps to control the proliferation of WMDs by expanding the orders issued by President Clinton. The new order allowed blocking of the property and financial assets of any person or group thought to have given support for or engaged, or attempted to engage, in activities or transactions that have materially contributed to, or pose a risk of materially contributing to, the proliferation of WMDs or their means of delivery (including missiles capable of delivering such weapons), including any efforts to manufacture, acquire, possess, develop, transport, transfer, or use such items, by any person or foreign country of proliferation concern. These orders provided operating agencies with guidance on how to prevent the proliferation of WMD materials. Since the threat posed by WMDs was so great, Presidents Bush and Clinton issued orders not only to prevent them from entering the United States but also to prevent other countries from facilitating terrorists' acquisition of WMDs and WMD materials. They also enabled the federal government to take action against anyone who violated these orders.

HS ANALYSIS BOX 4-1

WMDs are the greatest danger to homeland security. Executive Order #13382 attempts to prevent WMDs from falling in the hands of terrorists. It is an effort by the United States to prevent other countries from sharing technology. Do you believe that financial punishment as proscribed in the executive order has the ability to stop nations from sharing technology? Does the executive order have any effect on terrorist groups or rogue nations?

Prohibiting Transactions with Terrorists Who Threaten to Disrupt the Middle East Peace Process

President Clinton issued Executive Order #12947, Prohibiting Transactions with Terrorists Who Threaten to Disrupt the Middle East Peace Process, on January 23, 1995, to control acts of violence by certain Middle Eastern groups. The president was concerned that "foreign terrorists that disrupt the Middle East peace process constitute an unusual and extraordinary threat to the national security, foreign policy, and economy of the United States." The executive order prohibited financial transactions between U.S. citizens and any group of foreign persons designated by the secretary of state, the secretary of the treasury, or the attorney general (AG) as constituting a "significant risk of committing acts of violence that have the purpose or effect of disrupting the Middle East peace process, or to assist in, sponsor, or provide financial, material, or technological support for, or services in support of, such acts of violence." The order prohibited donations to groups that engage in acts of violence and specifically prohibits "the making or receiving of any contribution of funds, goods, or services to or for the benefit of" people designated under the order. The order charged the FBI with investigating violations of its prohibitions.

The order was modified on August 20, 1998, by Executive Order #13099, which purposefully broadened its scope and directed its provisions against terrorist groups and specifically named Osama bin Laden and al Qaeda among other groups and individuals as terrorists. Later, on September 23, 2001, President Bush further bolstered the provisions of these orders by issuing Executive Order #13224, Blocking Property and Prohibiting Transactions with Persons Who Commit, Threaten to Commit, or Support Terrorism, which expanded the number of people designated as posing a significant risk of committing acts of terrorism that threaten the security of the United States.

The United States and other countries have been attempting to broker Middle East peace for decades. For example, President Clinton held the Wye River Talks in 1998, resulting in minor concessions on both sides, and he coordinated additional talks in 2000 (Migdalovitz, 2005). The Israeli-Palestinian issue has long served as a flashpoint for terrorism. There are numerous groups that are opposed to any peace settlement. Presidents Clinton and Bush provided a legal foundation by which to deal with individuals, countries, and groups that interfere with the peace process.

Blocking Property and Prohibiting Transactions with the Taliban

On July 4, 1999, President Clinton issued an executive order prohibiting transactions with the Taliban in Afghanistan and blocking the movement of their financial assets. The order stemmed from the president's concern that territory under Taliban control was being used as a safe haven and base of operations for Osama bin Laden and the al Qaeda organization and that their continued threats of violence "against the United States and its nationals constitute an unusual and extraordinary threat to the national security." The president ordered that all assets of the Taliban or of people who controlled or provided "financial, material, or technological support for" the Taliban be frozen. The order also prohibited any transaction, including the exporting or importing, of "any contribution of funds, goods, or services to or for the benefit of the Taliban" or "the exportation, re-exportation, sale, or supply, directly or indirectly, from the United States ... of any goods, software, technology (including technical data), or services to the territory of Afghanistan controlled by the Taliban."

President Bush later terminated this executive order on July 2, 2002, commenting that the ability of the Taliban, al Qaeda, and Osama bin Laden to use Afghanistan as a safe haven and base of operation had been "significantly altered given the success of the military campaign in Afghanistan" (Executive Order #13268). Ironically, during the first year of President Barak Obama's term, the Taliban and al Qaeda's ability to use Afghanistan as a safe haven became a national security issue, demonstrating how rapidly conditions can change.

Foreign Intelligence Physical Searches

On February 9, 1995, President Clinton issued an executive order authorizing the AG "to approve physical searches, without a court order, to acquire foreign intelligence information for periods of up to one year" and "to approve applications to the Foreign Intelligence Surveillance Court ... to obtain orders for physical searches for the purpose of collecting foreign intelligence information." The order, based on the Foreign Intelligence Surveillance Act of 1978 (50 U.S.C. 1801 et seq., as amended by Public Law 103-359), also authorized select government officials heading national security or defense agencies "to make the certifications required by ... the Act in support of applications to conduct physical searches." The order was twice modified by President Bush following creation of the Office of Director of National Intelligence and after amendment of the Foreign Intelligence Surveillance Act of 1978 (50 U.S.C. 1801 et seq.).

The original order and its modifications set the stage for controversy surrounding our domestic surveillance program during the Bush administration. Civil libertarians attacked wiretaps that were conducted as a result of the order. Later, it was mandated that such searches be reviewed by the court that was established to consider wiretaps. Little public information is available on the extent to which the Clinton administration used the provisions of the order.

Critical Infrastructure Protection

Recognizing that national infrastructure is vital to the safe and efficient operation of the nation and "that their incapacity or destruction would have a debilitating impact on the defense or economic security of the United States," President Clinton issued an executive order on July 15,1996, to protect and ensure their operation. Critical infrastructures included "telecommunications, electrical power systems, gas and oil storage and transportation, banking and finance, transportation, water supply systems, emergency services (including medical, police, fire, and rescue), and continuity of government." The order recognized that critical infrastructure threats included both physical threats to real material property and electronic threats to radio frequencies, information systems, and communications systems. The order also acknowledged that much of the nation's infrastructure was under the control of the private sector.

The order established the *President's Commission on Critical Infrastructure Protection*, which was changed with (1) identifying and consulting with members of the public and private sectors having interests in critical infrastructure assurance, (2) assessing the scope and nature of threats to critical infrastructure, (3) determining legal and policy issues arising from efforts to secure critical infrastructure, and (4) making recommendations for a "comprehensive national policy and implementation strategy to protect critical infrastructures from physical and cyber threats."

To ensure the protection of critical infrastructure while the commission was carrying out its work, the president established an *Infrastructure Protection Task Force* (IPTF) in the Department of Justice. The IPTF's function was to

(i) provide, or facilitate and coordinate the provision of, expert guidance to critical infrastructures to detect, prevent, halt, or confine an attack and to recover and restore service;

(ii) issue threat and warning notices in the event advance information is obtained about a threat;

(iii) provide training and education on methods of reducing vulnerabilities and responding to attacks on critical infrastructures;

(iv) conduct after-action analysis to determine possible future threats, targets, or methods of attack; and

(v) coordinate with the pertinent law enforcement authorities during or after an attack to facilitate any resulting criminal investigation (see also Executive Order #13025, 1996; Executive Order #13041, 1997).

This executive order and the work done by the commission and task force provided a foundation for much of the work that went into the development of the National Infrastructure Protection Plan that was discussed in Chapter 3. The plan now serves as the foundation for protecting our critical infrastructure assets.

In all, President Clinton issued several executive orders that laid the foundation for developing executive policy on combating the threat of terrorism. Many of these orders provided the basis for subsequent decisions made by the executive branch. Key among this policy foundation were concerns with WMDs, intelligence collection, financial transactions, and protection of infrastructure.

Executive Orders of President George W. Bush

The 9/11 attacks occurred early in President Bush's administration. After the attacks, he issued a number of executive orders to strengthen our ability to combat possible terrorist attacks and to strengthen homeland security.

Establishing the Office of Homeland Security and the Homeland Security Council

Perhaps the most important executive order issued by President George W. Bush was that of October 8, 2001, establishing an *Office of Homeland Security* (OHS) and the Homeland Security Council. The Homeland Security Council consisted of representatives from several executive branch departments and was charged with making policy and advising the president on homeland security matters.

The mission of the OHS was to "develop and coordinate the implementation of a comprehensive national strategy to secure the United States from terrorist threats or attacks." The OHS was to work with federal, state, and local agencies to "coordinate the executive branch's efforts to detect, prepare for, prevent, protect against, respond to, and recover from terrorist attacks within the United States." The order charged the newly created OHS with at least five basic responsibilities: (1) work with federal, state, and local agencies; (2) prepare for and mitigate the consequences of terrorist threats and attacks; (3) coordinate efforts to prevent terrorist attacks within the United States; (4) protect critical infrastructure from the consequences of terrorist attacks; and (5) respond to and promote recovery from any terrorist threats or attacks on the United States. In addition to these major responsibilities, the OHS was charged with providing incident management, continuity of government, and the development of programs for educating the public about terrorism. This order established the foundation for the development of the Department of Homeland Security.

The development of the Department of Homeland Security proved to be an important step in developing our homeland security apparatus. The OHS later evolved into the Department of Homeland Security (Scardaville and Spencer, 2002). Prior to this change, the OHS developed a number of reports that remain crucial to homeland security operations—for example, the *National Strategy for Homeland Security*, which outlined the plan for homeland security (as discussed in Chapter 1).

National Counterterrorism Center

On August 27, 2004, President Bush issued an Executive Order #13354, creating the National Counterterrorism Center to

(a) serve as the primary organization in the United States Government for analyzing and integrating all intelligence possessed or acquired by the United States Government pertaining to terrorism and counterterrorism, excepting purely domestic counterterrorism information . . .;

(b) conduct strategic operational planning for counterterrorism activities, integrating all instruments of national power, including diplomatic, financial, military, intelligence, homeland security, and law enforcement activities within and among agencies;

(c) assign operational responsibilities to lead agencies for counterterrorism activities that are consistent with applicable law and that support strategic plans to counter terrorism . . .;

(d) serve as the central and shared knowledge bank on known and suspected terrorists and international terror groups, as well as their goals, strategies, capabilities, and networks of contacts and support; and

(e) ensure that agencies, as appropriate, have access to and receive all-source intelligence support needed to execute their counterterrorism plans or perform independent, alternative analysis.

HS Web Link: To learn more about the executive order establishing the NCTC, go to http://www.fas.org/irp/offdocs/eo/eo-13354.htm.

The National Counterterrorism Center (NCTC) served as an important step in coordinating our intelligence operations. The 9/11 Commission (2004) found that a significant intelligence problem was the lack of communications and sharing of intelligence information across U.S. domestic intelligence agencies. The NCTC is composed of representatives of all the intelligence agencies, helping ensure better coordination. The body coordinates all counterterrorism activities on U.S. soil.

Interrogation of Terrorist Suspects

Perhaps the most controversial order issued by President Bush was the one directing the manner of detention and methods of interrogation to be used against detainees in the "war on terror," Executive Order #13440, Interpretation of the Geneva Conventions Common Article 3 as Applied to a Program of Detention and Interrogation Operated by the Central Intelligence Agency. Because the country was engaged in an armed conflict with al Qaeda and that group was responsible for the attacks on the United States on September 11, 2001, President Bush issued an executive order specially designating members of al Qaeda, the Taliban, and associated forces as "unlawful enemy combatants" and stripping them of the protections afforded under the Third Geneva Convention. The Geneva Conventions provide prisoners of war with certain protections and prohibits abuse and torture.

Under the provisions of the order, the Central Intelligence Agency (CIA) was allowed to carry out a program of detention and interrogation outside of the rules of the Third Geneva Convention. This included "enhanced interrogation" practices. These interrogations and detentions were to be applied to any "alien detainee who is determined by the Director of the Central Intelligence Agency"

> (A) to be a member or part of or supporting al Qaeda, the Taliban, or associated organizations; and (B) likely to be in possession of information that:
>
> **(1)** could assist in detecting, mitigating, or preventing terrorist attacks, such as attacks within the United States or against its Armed Forces or other personnel, citizens, or facilities, or

against allies or other countries cooperating in the war on terror with the United States, or their armed forces or other personnel, citizens, or facilities; or

(2) could assist in locating the senior leadership of al Qaeda, the Taliban, or associated forces.

The order allowed the director of the CIA to determine interrogation practices as long as he viewed them as "safe for use with each detainee" and that detainees received "the basic necessities of life, including adequate food and water, shelter from the elements, necessary clothing, protection from extremes of heat and cold, and essential medical care." The CIA director was also given the authority to develop and approve a "plan of interrogation tailored for each detainee in the program ..., train all interrogators and personnel in the program, monitor the program, and, determine the program's compliance with applicable law." In essence, the CIA director was given total control over the detention and interrogation of any person he designated as an "unlawful enemy combatant," including the determination of the legality of interrogation practices.

Controversy surrounding the order, including allegations of detainee abuse and torture as well as national and international outrage, led President Obama to revoke Executive Order #13440 by issuing Executive Order #13491; in 2009, President Obama argued that the practices undermined national security and justice.

Presidential Directives Enhancing Homeland Security

Over the course of his presidency, George W. Bush issued a series of executive orders designed to enhance homeland security and protect against the threat of terrorism. These included Executive Order #13311, 2003, Homeland Security Information Sharing, and Executive Order # 13356, Strengthening the Sharing of Terrorism Information to Protect Americans. These executive orders allowed various federal agencies to share information about potential terrorists and terrorist activities. Prior to the issuance of these executive orders, federal laws prohibited some intelligence agencies from sharing this information. President Bush issued Executive Order #13260, 2002, Establishing the President's Homeland Security Advisory Council and Senior Advisory Committees for Homeland Security. These bodies provided the initial planning for our homeland security organization. Executive Order #13407, 2006, Public Alert and Warning System, created the color-coded warning system to advise the public of terrorist threat levels.

In addition to these executive orders, President Bush issued at least 24 "Homeland Security Directives," which are presented in Figure 4-2 ■.

Radvanovsky (2006) notes that the Department of Homeland Security was directed to immediately implement these HSPDs. Essentially, they provide an organization or framework for implementing homeland security, with each directive focusing on a specific content area. They provide direction to each of the departments that are involved in an area. They assist in ensuring that there are no gaps in coverage or protection.

HS Web Link: To learn more about the Homeland Security Presidential Directives, go to https://www.dhs.gov/presidential-directives.

HS ANALYSIS BOX 4-2

There has been substantial controversy over the handling of noncombatant terrorists. The CIA and other entities performed rendition whereby suspected terrorists were taken against their will to other countries and interrogated and sometimes tortured. Civil libertarians decried such policies for violating prisoners' rights. On the other hand, the United States was attacked and the threat of additional attacks remains. How do we balance the rule of law with national security?

Number	Title	Date
HSPD 1	Organization and Operation of the Homeland Security Council	29 Oct 01
HSPD 2	Combating Terrorism through Immigration Policies	29 Oct 01
HSPD 3	Homeland Security Advisory System	11 March 02
HSPD 4	National Strategy to Combat Weapons of Mass Destruction	11 December 02
HSPD 5	Management of Domestic Incidents	30 September 03
HSPD 6	Integration of Screening Information to Protect Against Terrorism	16 September 03
HSPD 7	Critical Infrastructure Identification, Prioritization, and Protection	17 December 03
HSPD 8	National Preparedness	17 December 03
HSPD 9	Defense of United States Agriculture and Food	30 January 04
HSPD 10	Biodefense for the 21st Century	28 April 04
HSPD 11	Comprehensive Terrorist-Related Screening Procedures	27 August 04
HSPD 12	Identification Standard for Federal Employees and Contractors	27 August 04
HSPD 13	Maritime Security Policy	21 December 2004
HSPD 14	Domestic Nuclear Detection	15 April 2005
HSPD 15	U.S. Strategy and Policy in the War on Terror (classified)	6 March 2006
HSPD 16	National Strategy for Aviation Security	22 June 2006
HSPD 17	Nuclear Materials Information Program	28 August 2006
HSPD 18	Medical Countermeasures Against Weapons of Mass Destruction	31 January 2007
HSPD 19	Combating Terrorist Use of Explosives in the United States	12 February 2007
HSPD 20	National Continuity Policy	4 April 2007
HSPD 21	Public Health and Medical Preparedness	18 October 2007
HSPD 22	Domestic Chemical Defense	Classified
HSPD 23	Cyber Security and Monitoring	8 January 2008
HSPD 24	Biometrics for Identification and Screening to Enhance National Security	5 June 2008

FIGURE 4-2 Homeland Security Presidential Directives

Source: DHS. (2010). Homeland Security Directives. http://www.dhs.gov/xabout/laws/editorial_0607.shtm (Accessed October 4, 2010).

Executive Orders of President Barack Obama

National Defense

On March 16, 2012, President Obama signed Executive Order National Defense Resources Preparedness, which states that the U.S. industrial and technology base is the foundation for national defense preparedness. This executive order is meant to strengthen the U.S. industrial and technology base to be prepared to respond to National

Defense needs. Being prepared for a crisis means having sufficient resources available to respond quickly and efficiently. For instance, if there was an attack on the U.S. power grid, it would be imperative to have backup resources and personnel and technology to get power back up quickly.

Guantanamo Bay Review

President Barack Obama issued Executive Order #13492, Review and Disposition of Individuals Detained at the Guantánamo Bay Naval Base and Closure of Detention Facilities, on January 22, 2009, requiring review and disposition of all pending cases against prisoners held by the Department of Defense at the Guantanamo Bay Naval Base. The order required closure of that detention facility. Approximately 800 individuals had been detained in the facility for more than seven years. Controversy over these detentions and the circumstances and conditions in which detainees were confined led the president to determine that the disposition of these cases and the closure of the facility would "further the national security and foreign policy interests of the United States and the interests of justice."

The order required an immediate review of all Guantanamo detentions and the disposition of their cases by (1) a determination of transfer, (2) a determination of prosecution, or (3) an alternative determination. The order also required that during the review period all U.S. government officials act in conformity with all applicable laws governing conditions of confinement, including the Geneva Conventions.

On the same day that President Obama issued the Guantanamo executive order, he issued another executive order establishing a Special Interagency Task Force on Detainee Disposition

> to conduct a comprehensive review of the lawful options available to the Federal Government with respect to the apprehension, detention, trial, transfer, release, or other disposition of individuals captured or apprehended in connection with armed conflicts and counterterrorism operations, and to identify such options as are consistent with the national security and foreign policy interests of the United States and the interests of justice.

Although President Obama issued the order in 2009, a year later Guantanamo was still in operation. It could not be determined legally or practically how to deal with the remaining prisoners in the facility.

Ensuring Lawful Interrogations

On January 22, 2009, President Obama issued an executive order revoking President Bush's Executive Order #13440 of July 20, 2007. The order countermanded "All executive directives, orders, and regulations inconsistent with this order, including but not

HS ANALYSIS BOX 4-3

The detention facility at Guantanamo Bay has proven to be extremely controversial over the years. President Bush created the facility to keep terrorists out of the United States and to try them using military tribunals. Regardless of intent, the facility created worldwide controversy and presidential candidate Obama pledged to close it once elected president. After taking office, President Obama released 242 inmates but was not able to close the facility. By March 2017, there were still 41 prisoners held at Guantanamo. The annual cost to operate the prison is $445 million and each inmate costs $10 million (Human Rights First, 2017). Should the United States maintain Guantanamo Bay? Are there other options to maintain national security?

limited to those issued to or by the Central Intelligence Agency (CIA) from September 11, 2001, to January 20, 2009, concerning detention or the interrogation of detained individuals." The order essentially required federal agencies to follow the interrogation techniques outlined in the Army Field Manual (2 22.3). The order directed the CIA to "close as expeditiously as possible any detention facilities that it currently operates" and prohibited it from operating detention facilities in the future. The order also directed federal officials to

> provide the International Committee of the Red Cross with notification of, and timely access to, any individual detained in any armed conflict in the custody or under the effective control of an officer, employee, or other agent of the United States Government or detained within a facility owned, operated, or controlled by a department or agency of the United States Government.

This order was controversial in that there had been a significant public debate on how the United States should treat enemy combatants and others suspected of being involved in terrorist activities. It established new guidelines for agencies.

On March 7, 2011 President Obama issued Executive Order #13567 establishing a Periodic Review of Individuals Detained at Guantanamo Bay Naval Station Pursuant to the Authorization for Use of Military Force. This order implements a mandatory review of each detainee as soon as possible but no later than one year from the date of the order. This periodic review also includes detainees who were or are being moved from Guantanamo Bay to a faculty in the United States. In addition, there must be a file review of each detainee every six months and a full review every three years to determine whether the detainee should continue to be held.

Presidents Clinton, Bush, and Obama have issued a number of executive orders pertaining to homeland security. In total, they outline a number of policy decisions and programs that strengthen our ability to combat terrorism and enhance safeguarding our homeland.

Executive Orders of President Donald Trump

Early in his presidency, President Trump issued a number of executive orders focusing primarily on border security, immigration, and public safety.

Sanctuary Cities and Public Safety from Illegal Immigrants

On January 25, 2017, President Trump issued his first Executive Order #13768 with regard to national security: Enhancing Public Safety in the Interior of the United States. The executive order outlines some changes to immigration policies and also seeks to strip "sanctuary cities" from federal funding. Stripping federal funding from "sanctuary cities" is proving to be a more difficult task than expected by President Trump. The order also calls for the hiring of 10,000 additional immigration officers. This goal is difficult to accomplish, as will be discussed in Chapter 12. Finally, the order establishes an office for victims of crimes committed by illegal immigrants and tasks police with the increased arrest of illegal immigrants.

Construction of a Border Wall

On the same day, President Trump signed a Executive Order #13767 Border Security and Immigration Enforcement Improvements, which aims to increase border security by directing federal funding toward the building of a border wall to Mexico and the hiring of an additional 5,000 border patrol agents. Both of these goals face substantial problems which will be discussed in detail in Chapter 12. Finally, the order ends the "catch and release" practice of illegal immigrants and calls for the detention and return of illegal immigrants to their home countries.

HS ANALYSIS BOX 4-4

President Trump, during his election campaign, promised the American people that he would restrict travel from Muslim countries until the government could examine vetting policies and procedures for people coming to our country. Given the number of terrorist plots that had occurred, he wanted to ensure that we were properly vetting visitors to the United States. Do you believe that restricting visitors coming from some countries makes us safer? What are the negative consequences of restricting people coming to the United States?

Restricting Travel to the United States from Seven Muslim Countries

On January 27, 2017, President Trump signed Executive Order #13769 Protecting the Nation from Foreign Terrorist Entry into the United States, also referred to as the "travel ban" or "travel restriction." The order bans immigrants from seven countries—Syria, Iran, Iraq, Lybia, Sudan, Yemen, and Somalia—for 90 days. The order also prevents refugees from entering the United States for 120 days. Refugees from Syria are not allowed to enter the United States at all. President Trump's executive orders have been met by much criticism and protest. Especially, the so-called travel ban has brought about protests at U.S. airports and within cities and has also been adjudicated in several courts. A series of lawsuits were filed against the travel ban and a judge in Washington stopped its implementation.

On March 6, 2017, President Trump issued a revised Executive Order Protecting the Nation from Foreign Terrorist Entry into the United States. This revised order prevents citizens from six countries from entering the United States. Iraq was removed from the revised order and it allowed for case-by-case exceptions. However, the revised order was immediately blocked by a federal judge and the U.S. Court of Appeals for the Ninth Circuit upheld the decision. The U.S. Supreme Court heard the case and allowed portions of the executive order to go into effect. The Court essentially advised that the government had to allow close relatives from the restricted countries to travel to the United States. Otherwise, the government could control travel from the six listed countries.

▶ Federal Antiterrorism Statutes

In addition to the executive orders, Congress has passed a number of federal statutes relating to terrorism and homeland security. Several of the key statutes are addressed here.

Antiterrorism and Effective Death Penalty Act of 1996

On April 24, 1996, following the bombing of the Alfred P. Murrah Federal Building in Oklahoma City, Congress enacted the Antiterrorism and Effective Death Penalty Act of 1996 (AEDPA; Pub. L. No. 104-132, 110 Stat. 1214) with broad-based bipartisan political support. The AEDPA, signed into law by President Clinton, was intended to prevent terrorism by (1) streamlining the implementation of the death penalty, (2) modifying the law on restitution to the victims of terrorism, (3) making it more difficult for terrorists to secure sources of financial and material support, (4) making it easier to exclude and remove foreign terrorists from the United States, and (5) placing greater restrictions on the possession and use of materials capable of producing catastrophic damage by terrorists (Doyle, 1996).

One of the main provisions of the law is the reduction of the power of federal judges to grant relief for habeas corpus abuses. Habeas corpus is the legal procedure by which, under the U.S. Constitution, detainees may seek relief from unlawful imprisonment through judicial review. Article 1, Section 9, of the Constitution states: "The privilege of the writ of habeas corpus shall not be suspended, unless when in cases of rebellion or invasion the public safety may require it." Under Title I of AEDPA, federal courts are restricted from granting detainees relief from violations of habeas corpus unless a state court makes a decision that is "(1) contrary to, or involved an unreasonable application of, clearly established Federal law, as determined by the Supreme Court of the United States; or (2) resulted in a decision that was based on an unreasonable determination of the facts in light of the evidence presented in the State court proceeding" (Pub. L. No. 104-132, 110 Stat. 1214). A second provision of the act is a reduction in the number of subsequent habeas petitions a detainee can present to the courts. The law created an absolute bar on second or successive petitions by a detainee once a judicial determination is made. The act also prevents the U.S. Supreme Court from reviewing a denial of a habeas petition by a federal court of appeals.

The AEDPA was an effort to deal more effectively with terrorists. Although the act was passed as a result of an attack by a right-wing domestic terrorist, it became useful in the wake of the 9/11 attacks.

The USA PATRIOT Act

Perhaps the most well-known and controversial law enacted by the U.S. Congress in the aftermath of the terrorist attacks of September 11, 2001, is the **USA PATRIOT Act**. The legislation was passed by the Senate on October 11, 2001, and subsequently passed by the House on October 24, 2001. President George W. Bush signed the bill into law on October 26, 2001. The act was based on a Department of Justice proposal that was modified by the Congress before it was enacted into law. The purpose of the act was to grant greater powers and authority to federal enforcement officials to investigate and prosecute those responsible for the September 11, 2001, attacks and to protect the country from future attacks like those carried out in New York and Washington, D.C. The act, whose full title is "Uniting and Strengthening America by Providing Appropriate Tools Required to Intercept and Obstruct Terrorism" (USA PATRIOT Act), was a sweeping law that modified or amended more than a dozen other federal statutes and greatly expanded the powers of members of the federal executive branch of government and federal law enforcement officials. The breadth of changes made by the act is illustrated in Figure 4-3 ■, which shows selected federal statutes modified by the law.

Bank Holding Company Act of 1956, 12 U.S.C. 1841
Communications Act of 1934, 47 U.S.C. 151
Controlled Substance Import and Export Act, 21 U.S.C. 951
Controlled Substances Act, 21 U.S.C. 826
Electronic Communications Privacy Act of 1986 (ECPA), 18 U.S.C. 2510
Fair Credit Reporting Act (FCRA), 15 U.S.C. 1681
Federal Deposit Insurance Act, 12 U.S.C. 1811
Federal Wiretap Statute, 18 USC 119
Foreign Assistance Act of 1961, 22 U.S.C. 2291
Foreign Intelligence Surveillance Act (FISA) 50 U.S.C. 1805
Intelligence Reform and Terrorism Prevention Act of 2004, Public Law 108–458; 118 Stat. 3742
National Security Act, 50 U.S.C. 401
Omnibus Crime Control and Safe Streets Act of 1968, 42 U.S.C. 3797
Right to Financial Privacy Act of 1978, 12 U.S.C. 3401
Title III of the Omnibus Crime Control and Safe Streets Act of 1968, 18 U.S.C. 2510
Violent Crime Control and Law Enforcement Act of 1994, Public Law 103–322; 49 USC 46502

FIGURE 4-3 Selected Federal Statutes and Sections Modified by the USA PATRIOT Act and Its Reauthorization

The act contains some 10 titles and more than 1,000 sections. An examination of the statutes that were modified as listed in Figure 4-3 ■ shows how sweeping the act was. It addressed a number of areas, including intelligence, investigations, controlled substances, crime, privacy, and financial transactions. It modified a number of governmental functions to enhance terrorism investigations and to prevent terrorist attacks.

A comprehensive treatment of the legislation would require a book-length work that is well beyond the scope of this chapter. There are, however, several key areas that require some individual attention and should be of interest to students of homeland security. The act addresses four key areas of concern for homeland security: (1) the collection of communication information and data, (2) conducting foreign intelligence investigations, (3) controlling money laundering, and (4) funding and enhancing national border security (Doyle, 2002). We will consider each of these areas in the sections that follow.

HS Web Link: To learn more about the USA PATRIOT Act, go to http://www.fas.org/irp/crs/RS21203.pdf.

Collection of Communications

To understand how the act changed the ability of federal officials to collect communications information used in criminal investigations, especially those involving suspected terrorism and terror-related activities, it is necessary to look back at the provisions of Title III of the Omnibus Crime Control and Safe Streets Act of 1968, 18 U.S.C. 2510-2522 (Title III). Title III was substantially altered by the passage of the act. As a result of Supreme Court decisions restricting the government's ability to conduct investigations based on electronic surveillance, Congress enacted Title III to generally restrict eavesdropping on telephone, face-to-face, and computer forms of communication.

Title III created a three-tier system of protection from governmental surveillance. Under the first and most protective tier of the schema, federal law enforcement officers needed permission of senior members of the Justice Department to seek a court order authorizing the collection of private communications. Under the law, these permissions could be granted only when investigating a selected number of crimes listed in the statute. The law carefully restricted the process of the surveillance by law enforcement officers, limited the communication that could be seized, and controlled the duration and breadth of surveillance activities. Additionally, the statute required courts to notify the parties involved in the communications that the activities had occurred following the collection of the communications.

At the second and next lower level of protection, federal law enforcement officials could seek a court order for telephone records and e-mails for any crime without Justice Department approval.

At the third and lowest tier of protection, federal law enforcement officials could themselves certify the need for surveillance, rather than getting a court order approving the use of pen registers and trap and trace devices that capture the identity and source of communications rather than their actual content. Government intrusion at the lowest tier of protection did not need to be reported to the parties involved in the communication.

Passage of the USA PATRIOT Act in 2002 substantially altered each of these three tiers of protection. Provisions of the act

- permit pen register and trap and trace orders for electronic communications (e.g., e-mail);
- authorize nationwide execution of court orders for pen registers, trap and trace devices, and access to stored e-mail or communication records;
- treat stored voice mail like stored e-mail (rather than like telephone conversations);
- permit authorities to intercept communications to and from a trespasser within a computer system (with the permission of the system's owner);
- add terrorist and computer crimes to Title III's predicate offense list;

- reinforce protection for those who help execute Title III, ch. 121, and ch. 206 orders;
- encourage cooperation between law enforcement and foreign intelligence investigators;
- establish a claim against the United States for certain communications privacy violations by government personnel; and
- terminate the authority found in many of these provisions and several of the foreign intelligence amendments with a sunset provision (Doyle, 2002: 2–3).

In essence, the act, under certain circumstances, allows law enforcement officials greater liberty to collect and review communications records and stored e-mails, treats voice mail as if it were e-mail, reduces the requirement of probable cause necessary to secure a warrant, and in some cases allows federal officials to bypass the judiciary entirely. The act also expands the types of information federal officials can collect from communication service providers, including credit card and banking records. The act also adds to an already expansive list of crimes, outlined under Title II, which do not require a warrant or court order for monitoring. Cyber crimes, terrorist-related crimes, the activities of hackers, and crimes involving interstate and foreign commerce were added to the list of crimes.

U.S. Freedom Act

The governments' ability to collect communications in bulk from Americans changed on June 2, 2015, when President Obama signed the U.S. Freedom Act. Prior to the Act, the National Security Agency (NSA) had collected phone call information from millions of Americans. The U.S. Freedom Act is meant to strengthen national security, and it also protects civil liberties. The government can no longer collect bulk communications of American's telephone records and Internet communications. It also controls government overreach by limiting data collection to the "greatest extent reasonably practical." The new law basically means that the government cannot collect bulk data from a service provider or a specific geographic region, such as a city. Data collection has to be more specific, that

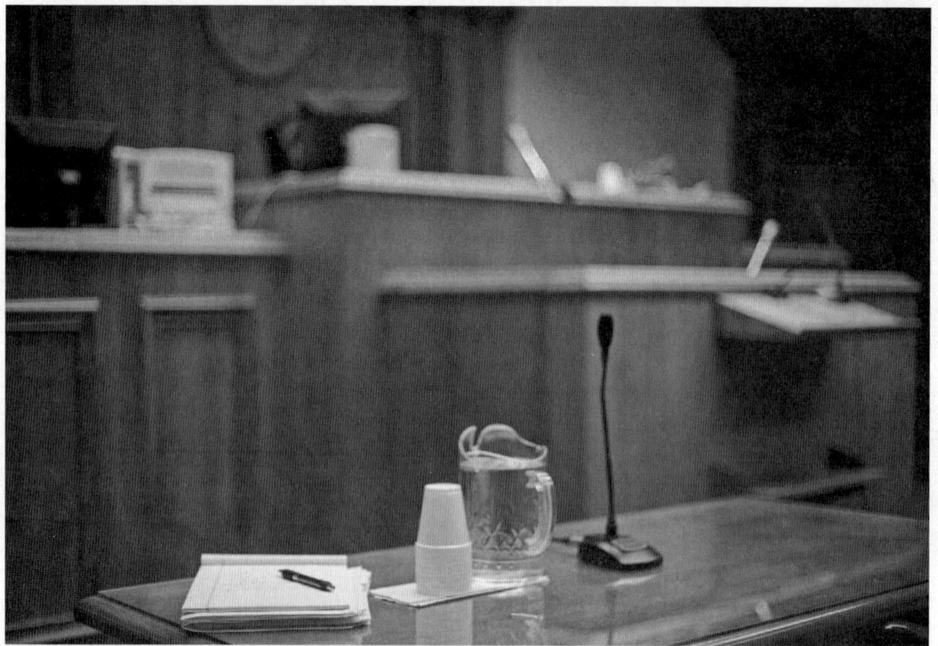

A number of foreign intelligence cases have been presented in the courts.
Mark Strozier/Alamy Stock Photo.

is, the government must show that there is "reasonable suspicion that the suspect is linked to a terrorist organization." But the U.S. Freedom Act also extended the expiration date of three PATRIOT Act provisions to December 2019. These provisions cover wiretaps and the lone wolf surveillance authority.

The U.S. Freedom Act also has consequences for the Foreign Intelligence Surveillance Act (FISA). There are three main provisions: First, it creates a panel of amicus curie at the FISA court to provide guidance on matters of privacy and civil liberties, communications technology, and other technical or legal matters. Second, it declassifies FISA court opinions, which makes the interpretations of law given by the Court public. It's no longer a "secret court." Third, tech companies will have a range of options for describing how they respond to national security orders.

Communications and Terrorist Organizations

There are also two executive orders that relate to the communication and terrorist organizations. Just as the government collects information from people with suspected terrorist ties, the United States also actively attempts to limit the communications published by terrorist organization. On March 14, 2016, President Obama signed Executive Order #13721, Developing an Integrated Global Engagement Center to Support Government-wide Counterterrorism Communications Activities Directed Abroad. The purpose was to diminish the influence of terrorist organizations by reducing their ability to communicate and message to people, including social media messages. The Islamic State (ISIS) and other terrorist organizations spread their messages and recruit heavily via social media outlets, such as Facebook and Twitter. The Counterterrorism Communication Initiative was tasked to coordinate, integrate, and synchronize all communications to foreign audiences abroad. The order also called for developing collaboration between governmental and non-governmental partners to disseminate messages consistent with U.S. policy.

The Obama administration was also concerned about the ability to communicate during national security and emergency situations. Executive Order #13618, Assignment of National Security and Emergency Preparedness Communications Functions, issued on July 6, 2012, dissolved the National Communication System and replaced it with an executive committee with three main functions. First, the committee would oversee federal national security and emergency preparedness communications functions. Second, the committee was tasked to establish a programs office within the Department of Homeland Security to assist the executive committee. Third, the committee would assign specific responsibilities to federal government entities. The purpose of the order is to ensure that the federal government has the ability to communicate at all times and under all circumstances.

Foreign Intelligence Investigations

The USA PATRIOT Act amended the FISA. FISA originally required that federal law enforcement officials certify for special courts that "the purpose for the surveillance is to obtain foreign intelligence information." Under this provision, although evidence of a crime might be uncovered during a foreign intelligence investigation, the legislation was to be used for intelligence gathering and not for "fishing" for evidence of a crime or as a way of getting around the offenses listed in Title III. The act also allowed for physical searches based on lower standards.

The act expanded the authority of federal officials to collect information on foreign intelligence within the United States when conducting investigations. It also allowed the sharing of intelligence information among federal agencies. Sauter and Carafano (2005) noted that this provision tore down the wall that hampered investigations prior to the 9/11 attacks. Prior to the act, several federal agencies involved in intelligence and counterterrorism were not allowed to share information. The act also lowered the consequence for officials who abuse privacy and third parties who assist authorities in collecting information. According to Doyle (2002), the act

- permits "roving" surveillance (court orders omitting the identification of the particular instrument, facilities, or places where the surveillance is to occur when the court finds the target is likely to thwart identification);
- increases the number of judges on the Foreign Intelligence Surveillance Act (FISA) court from 7 to 11;
- allows application for a FISA surveillance or search order when gathering foreign intelligence is *a significant* reason for the application rather than *the* reason;
- authorizes pen register and trap and trace device orders for e-mail as well as telephone conversations;
- sanctions court-ordered access to any tangible item rather than only business records held by lodging, car rental, and locker rental businesses;
- carries a sunset provision;
- establishes a claim against the United States for certain communications privacy violations by government personnel; and
- expands the prohibition against FISA orders based solely on an American's exercise of his or her First Amendment rights (p. 3).

Money Laundering

Money laundering is the illegal movement of cash or items of value that are derived from the commission of a crime or valuables that are intended to assist in the commission of a crime (discussed in more detail in Chapter 11). Money laundering involves the movement or concealment of the movement of valuables in a manner as to elude detection or cover up a crime. These practices can range from structuring financial transactions in certain ways to limiting the amount of money that is transferred as well as moving valuables through multiple institutions to conceal sources. Money laundering can be used in association with traditional crimes or used to support or fund terrorist activities. Money laundering has been historically controlled through the creation of a complex array of regulations, reporting requirements, and criminal laws.

Passage of the USA PATRIOT Act addressed the problem of money laundering in three basic areas. First, it expanded the authority of the secretary of the treasury to regulate U.S. financial institutions. Under the regulatory provisions of the act, the secretary of the treasury was to propagate rules

- under which securities brokers and dealers as well as commodity merchants, and advisors must file suspicious activity reports (SARs);
- requiring businesses, which were only to report cash transactions involving more than $10,000 to the IRS, to file SARs as well;
- imposing additional "special measures" and "due diligence" requirements to combat foreign money laundering;
- prohibiting U.S. financial institutions from maintaining correspondent accounts for foreign shell banks;
- preventing financial institutions from allowing their customers to conceal their financial activities;

- establishing minimum new customer identification standards and recordkeeping and recommending an effective means to verify the identity of foreign customers;
- encouraging financial institutions and law enforcement agencies to share information concerning suspected money laundering and terrorist activities; and
- requiring financial institutions to maintain anti–money laundering programs which must include at least a compliance officer; an employee training program; the development of internal policies, procedures and controls; and an independent audit feature (Doyle, 2002: 3–4).

Second, the act created new crimes to control money laundering and enhanced punishment for this crime. The act

- outlaws laundering (in the United States) any of the proceeds from foreign crimes of violence or political corruption;
- prohibits laundering the proceeds from cybercrime or supporting a terrorist organization;
- increases the penalties for counterfeiting;
- seeks to overcome a Supreme Court decision finding that the confiscation of over $300,000 (or attempt to leave the country without reporting it to customs) constituted an unconstitutionally excessive fine;
- provides explicit authority to prosecute overseas fraud involving American credit cards; and
- endeavors to permit prosecution of money laundering in the place where the predicate offense occurs (Doyle, 2002: 4).

Third, the act modified the ways forfeitures could be carried out and granted the government greater power to confiscate the property of anyone thought to support, plan, aid, authorize, or participate in an act of domestic or international terrorism. Under the provisions of the act, the government can present its evidence for forfeiture in secret and the person having his or her property confiscated bears the burden of proving his or her innocence. No criminal conviction for terrorism is required for the confiscation of property, and in some cases, all of a person's or organization's assets can be seized regardless of whether or not the individual's assets can be linked to an act associated with terrorism. The act

- establishes a mechanism to acquire extended jurisdiction, for purposes of forfeiture proceedings, over individuals and entities;
- allows confiscation of property located in this country for a wider range of crimes committed in violation of foreign law;
- permits U.S. enforcement of foreign forfeiture orders;
- calls for the seizure of correspondent accounts held in U.S. financial institutions for foreign banks [that] are in turn holding forfeitable assets overseas; and
- denies corporate entities the right to contest a confiscation if their principal shareholder is a fugitive (Doyle, 2002: 4–5).

In July 24, 2011, Executive Order #13581, Blocking Property of Transnational Crime Organizations, was issued. The purpose of this order is to restrict the money flow to transnational crime organizations. Many terrorist organizations, especially ISIS, engage in drug and human trafficking and other transnational crimes to raise money for their terrorist activities. Cutting of money is maybe the most effective strategy to weaken terrorist organizations.

Funding and Enhancing National Border Security

The USA PATRIOT Act provides for changes in the ways in which foreign nationals can be treated under the laws of the United States and the amount of funding and types of security used to control the national borders, and it creates new crimes and procedures for dealing with the potential for terrorism. Provisions of the act designed to enhance funding of border security do the following:

- authorize the appropriations necessary to triple the number of Border Patrol, Customs Service, and Immigration and Naturalization Service (INS) personnel stationed along the Northern Border, section 401;
- authorize appropriations of an additional $50 million for both INS and the Customers Service to upgrade their border surveillance equipment, section 402;
- remove the $30,000 ceiling on INS overtime pay for border duty, section 404;
- authorize appropriations of $2 million for a report to be prepared by the Attorney General on the feasibility of enhancing the FBI's Integrated Automated Fingerprint Identification System (IAFIS) and similar systems to improve the reliability of visa applicant screening, section 405;
- authorize the appropriations necessary to provide the State Department and INS with criminal record identification information relating to visa applicants and other applicants for admission to the United States, section 403; and
- authorize appropriations of $250,000 for the FBI to determine the feasibility of providing airlines with computer access to the names of suspected terrorists, section 1009 (Doyle, 2002: 40–50).

Enhanced monitoring along the nation's borders is provided for by the act with these provisions:

- instruct the Attorney General to report on the feasibility of the use of a biometric identifier scanning system with access to IAFIS for overseas consular posts and points of entry into the United States, section 1007;
- express the sense of the Congress that the Administration should implement the integrated entry and exit data system called for by the Illegal Immigration Reform and Immigrant Responsibility Act of 1996 (8 U.S.C. 1365a), section 414;
- add the White House Office of Homeland Security to the Integrated Entry and Exit Data System Task Force (8 U.S.C. 1365a note), section 415;
- call for the implementation and expansion of the foreign student visa monitoring program (8 U.S.C. 1372), section 416;
- limit countries eligible to participate in the visa waiver program to those with machine-readable passports as of October 1, 2003 (8 U.S.C. 1187(c)), section 417;
- instruct the Attorney General to report on the feasibility of using biometric scanners to help prevent terrorists and other foreign criminals from entering the country, section 1008; and
- authorize reciprocal sharing of the State Department's visa lookout data and related information with other nations in order to prevent terrorism, drug trafficking, slave marketing, and gun running, section 413 (Doyle, 2002: 49–50).

▶ U.S. Foreign Intelligence Surveillance Court

As a result of domestic spying by federal law enforcement officials during the Vietnam era, Congress passed the **Foreign Intelligence Surveillance Act of 1978** (FISA; 50 U.S.C. §1803). The act was designed to control foreign agents involved in espionage within the United

States and also to protect U.S. citizens from governmental abuses. The law authorized the creation of the U.S. Foreign Intelligence Surveillance Court (FISC). The basic function of the FISC is to monitor and control the surveillance activities of federal law enforcement officials who are investigating suspected foreign intelligence operatives in the United States. Passage of the USA PATRIOT Act, however, extended the surveillance to U.S. citizens under certain circumstances and expanded provision of the law to include the collection of intelligence on terrorism and terrorist activities.

HS Web Link: To learn more about the FISA court, go to http://usgovinfo.about.com/od/uscourtsystem/a/fiscourt.htm.

One of the primary functions of the court is to review requests for electronic surveillance warrants. Because the work of the court involves national security issues, the FISC is basically a "secret" court that operates outside public observation and review. Although the court keeps records of its activities, these records are not available to the public and the court does not operate in a public forum. According to Lee Tien (2001) of the Electronic Frontier Foundation,

> The records and files of the cases are sealed and may not be revealed even to persons whose prosecutions are based on evidence obtained under FISA warrants, except to a limited degree set by district judges' rulings on motions to suppress. There is no provision for the return of each executed warrant to the FISC, much less with an inventory of items taken, nor for certification that the surveillance was conducted according to the warrant and its 'minimization' requirements. (p. 1)

The court can meet any time of day or night and any day of the week. Also, there is always at least one judge available to review warrant requests. The only parties involved in the court's processes are government officials.

Although the FISA legislation and the FISC were born out of a concern over privacy abuses by federal law enforcement officials, both are clearly designed to favor the government and the issuance of investigative warrants, not to protect citizens' privacy and liberty interests. If the AG decides that an emergency situation exists, he or she is authorized to begin a program of surveillance without an FISC warrant. The AG must, however, inform the court of the operation within 72 hours. If a member of the FISC rejects a search application, the decision can be appealed to U.S. Foreign Intelligence Surveillance Court of Review. Based on existing information, the rejection of a warrant application by the FISC is a rare happening and more often than not warrant applications are modified and issued by the court rather than being rejected. According to a report from the Director of the Office of the U.S. Courts on Activities of the Foreign Intelligence Surveillance Courts for 2016, the FISC received 1,752 applications for surveillance. The court granted 1,378 applications, 339 were modified, 26 orders were denied in part, and 9 applications were rejected in full.

Controversy arose when it was learned that:

> Under a presidential order signed in 2002, the intelligence agency [NSA] has monitored the international telephone calls and international e-mail messages of hundreds, perhaps thousands, of people inside the United States without warrants over the past three years in an effort to track possible "dirty numbers" linked to Al Qaeda. (Risen, Lichtblau, and Walsh, 2005)

It is possible that the program, conducted by the National Security Agency (NSA), was designed to collect information that was later used to seek warrants from the FISA court. The practice was sufficiently serious to cause one FISA Court judge to resign his position (Leonning and Linzer, 2005). Although controversial, the FISC, as a result of the act, has expanded electronic intelligence gathering. It is seen as a method by which to identify possible terrorists and terrorist plots.

Civil libertarians and others have been critical of the FISA courts and the intelligence agencies' activities. Many believe that it is a violation of the Fourth Amendment. There have been numerous lawsuits attempting to stop intelligence agencies from "snooping" on foreign and American citizens. However, the courts consistently have ruled that such activities are lawful or unchallengeable. For example, in 2012, the U.S. Supreme Court ruled on a case brought before the court by the American Civil Liberties Union. The Court in *Clapper, Director of National Intelligence et al v. Amnesty International USA et al.* held that the plaintiffs did not have standing. In order for someone to bring such a case, they must be the subject of some injury. Since the names of the subjects being scrutinized is not public, there is no one who has standing; no one can attest that he or she was the subject of eavesdropping. FISA activities will continue and remain lawful regardless of perceived invasions of privacy.

HS ANALYSIS BOX 4-5

The FISA court, like a number of antiterrorism laws and procedures, has been controversial. Essentially, the court hears requests for government surveillance secretly and none of the courts findings is made public. Do you believe the U.S. government should have the power to secretly conduct electronic surveillance on American citizens when there is probable cause to believe the citizen is involved in terrorist activities? Do you believe government agencies may spy on Americans using the FISA procedure for other purposes?

Summary

This chapter reviewed some of the many sweeping legal changes that have taken place since the terrorist attacks of September 11, 2001. These changes were not merely limited to new legislation but included changes in executive orders and the operations of the courts. Most of these changes were directed at giving law enforcement and intelligence officials greater power to combat the possibility of terrorism.

The chapter considered executive orders issued beginning with President Clinton's and through President Trump's administration. Executive orders are presidential instructions to federal officials and agencies that are written to govern the execution of public policy. Many of the executive orders issued by Presidents Clinton, Bush, Obama, and Trump have been implemented either to prevent the possibility of a terrorist attack or to correct overreaches of the executive branch of government. Most of these orders were designed to assist in establishing a higher level of homeland security. Controlling WMDs, limiting transactions that could be used to facilitate terrorist activities, enhancing the collection of intelligence, and providing protection to the nation's infrastructure were the main areas in which policy changes have been developed.

Since the terrorist attacks of 9/11, Congress has enacted or modified a substantial number of laws designed to prevent terrorism and establish homeland security. Perhaps the most well-known and controversial law enacted by the U.S. Congress in the aftermath of the terrorist attacks of September 11, 2001, is the USA PATRIOT Act. The act addressed four key areas of concern: (1) collecting communication information and data, (2) conducting foreign intelligence investigations, (3) controlling money laundering, and (4) funding and enhancing national border security.

Finally, the chapter addressed the U.S. FISC, which was designed to control foreign agents involved in espionage within the United States and also to protect U.S. citizens from governmental abuses. Passage of the USA PATRIOT Act, however, extended the surveillance to U.S. citizens under certain circumstances and expanded provision of the law to include the collection of intelligence on terrorism and terrorist activities. Although the FISA legislation and the FISC were born out of a concern over privacy abuses by federal law enforcement officials, both are clearly designed to favor the government and the issuance of investigative warrants, not to protect citizens' privacy and liberty interests. Most of the legal changes that have taken place since 9/11 have been controversial because they upset the historic balance between security and law enforcement needs on the one hand and privacy and liberty interests on the other.

Discussion Questions

1. What is the legal standing of presidential executive orders and directives and how do presidents use them?
2. Given the executive orders issued by Presidents Clinton, Bush, and Obama, what issues were paramount for each president? Were there any trends?
3. What are the primary initiatives implemented as a result of the USA PATRIOT Act?
4. What are FISA courts? What are the legal controversies surrounding them?
5. What actions have been taken affecting terrorist financing?

References

Abourezk, J. G. (2008). "Another 'surge' is needed—This time, of common sense." Washington Report on Middle East Affairs, 27(1): 35–37.

Clapper, Director of National Intelligence, et al. v. Amnesty International USA et al. (2012). Slip Opinion. http://www.supremecourt.gov/opinions/12pdf/11-1025_ihdj.pdf (Accessed February 26, 2013).

Doyle, C. (1996). Antiterrorism and Effective Death Penalty Act of 1996: A Summary. American Law Division, Federation of American Scientists. http://www.fas.org/irp/crs/96-499.htm (Accessed February 2, 2011).

Doyle, C. (2002). CRS Report for Congress: The USA PATRIOT Act: A Sketch. Washington, D.C.: Congressional Research Service.

Executive Order #13025 Amendment to Executive Order 13010, The President's Commission on Critical Infrastructure Protection, November 13, 1995.

Executive Order #13041 Further Amendment to Executive Order 13010, as Amended, April 3, 1997.

Executive Order #12947 Prohibiting Transactions with Terrorists Who Threaten to Disrupt the Middle East Peace Process, January 23, 1995.

Executive Order #13099 Prohibiting Transactions with Terrorists Who Threaten to Disrupt the Middle East Peace Process, August 22, 1998.

Executive Order #13224 Blocking Property and Prohibiting Transactions with Persons Who Commit, Threaten to Commit, or Support Terrorism, September 23, 2001.

Executive Order #13260 Establishing the President's Homeland Security Advisory Council and Senior Advisory Committees for Homeland Security, March 19, 2002.

Executive Order #13268 Termination of Emergency with Respect to the Taliban and Amendment of Executive Order 13224 of September 23, 2001, July 2, 2002.

Executive Order #13311 Homeland Security Information Sharing, July 29, 2003.

Executive Order #13354 of August 27, 2004 National Counterterrorism Center, September 23, 2001.

Executive Order #13382 Blocking Property of Weapons of Mass Destruction Proliferators and Their Supporters, June 28, 2005.

Executive Order #13407 Public Alert and Warning System, June 26, 2006.

Executive Order #13440 Interpretation of the Geneva Conventions Common Article 3 as Applied to a Program of Detention and Interrogation Operated by the Central Intelligence Agency, July 20, 2007.

Executive Order #13491 Ensuring Lawful Interrogations, January 22, 2009.

Executive Order #13492 Review and Disposition of Individuals Detained at the Guantánamo Bay Naval Base and Closure of Detention Facilities, January 22, 2009.

Executive Order #13618 Assignment of National Security and Emergency Preparedness Communications Functions, July 6, 2012.

Executive Order #13721 Developing an Integrated Global Engagement Center to Support Government-Wide Counterterrorism Communications Activities Directed Abroad and Revoking, March 14, 2016.

Hosenball, M., and M. Isikoff. (2008). "Unintended consequences." *Newsweek* (March 24): 47.

House of Representatives. (2015). USA Freedom Act. https://judiciary.house.gov/issue/usa-freedom-act/ (Accessed June 5, 2017).

Human Rights First. (2017). Guantanamo by the Numbers. Fact Sheet. https://www.humanrightsfirst.org/sites/default/files/gtmo-by-the-numbers.pdf (Accessed June 14, 2017).

Leonning, C. D., and D. Linzer. (2005). "Spy court judge quits in protest: Jurist concerned Bush order tainted work of secret panel." *Washington Post* (December 21).

Migdalovitz, C. (2005). The Middle East Peace Talks. Washington, D.C.: Congressional Research Service.

Military Order Detention, Treatment, and Trial of Certain Non-Citizens in the War against Terrorism. (2001). *Federal Register*, 66 (222): 57831–57836.

Moschella, W. (2004). Memo from Assistant Attorney General. Washington, D.C.: U.S. Department of Justice, April 30. http://www.fas.org/irp/agency/doj/fisa/2003rept.pdf (Accessed April 29, 2010).

Moss, R. D. (2000). Memorandum for the Counsel to the President. Washington, D.C.: Office of Legal Counsel, Department of Justice.

National Commission on Terrorist Attacks upon the United States. (2004). The 911 Commission Report. New York: W.W. Norton.

Olsen, K. (2007). "Patriot Act's wide net." Nation (September 24): 8.

Radvanovsky, R. (2006). *Critical Infrastructure*. Boca Raton, FL: Taylor and Francis.

Relyea, H. C. (2008). Presidential Directives: Background and Overview, Updated November 26, 2008. CRS Report for Congress, Order Code 98-611 GOV.

Risen, J., E. Lichtblau, and B. Walsh. (2005). "Bush lets U.S. spy on callers without courts. *New York Times* (December 16). http://www.nytimes.com/2005/12/16/politics/16program.html?pagewanted=all (Accessed January 6, 2011).

Sauter, M., and J. Carafano. (2005). *Homeland Security*. New York: McGraw-Hill.

Scardaville, M., and J. Spencer. (2002). "Federal homeland security policy." The Heritage Foundation. http://www.heritage.org/Research/Reports/2002/06/Federal-Homeland-Security-Policy (Accessed April 26, 2010).

Tien, L. (2001). Foreign Intelligence Surveillance Act: Frequently Asked Questions (and Answers). Electronic Frontier Foundation (September 27).

Uniting and Strengthening America by Providing Appropriate Tools Required to Intercept and Obstruct Terrorism (USA PATRIOT Act). P.L. 107-56, 115 Stat. 272 (2001).

Volz, D. (2016). U.S. Spy Court Rejected Zero Surveillance Order in 2015: Memo. http://www.reuters.com/article/us-usa-cybersecurity-surveillance-idUSKCN0XR009 (Accessed May 5, 2016).

Yeh, B. T., and C. Doyle. (2006). USA PATRIOT Improvement and Reauthorization Act of 2005: A Legal Analysis. CRS Report for Congress, Updated December 21, 2006.

5 Political and Social Foundations of Terrorism

LEARNING OBJECTIVES

1. *Describe the continuum of social conflict.*
2. *State the definition of terrorism.*
3. *Discuss the history of terrorism.*
4. *Explain the causes of terrorism.*
5. *Describe the types of terrorism.*
6. *Discuss the strategies for dealing with terrorism.*

Key Terms

Normative social conflict
Civil disorder and riots
Terrorist activities
Guerilla warfare
Civil War
Social construct
Terrorism
Premeditation
Political agenda
Noncombatants or civilians
Sub national or clandestine groups
Sicari and Zeolots
Anarchists and socialists
State-sponsored terrorism
Caliphate
Propaganda of the deed
Globalization
Almost states
Black spots
Failed States
Social movements
Frustration-aggression theory
Relative deprivation
Identity crisis
Narcissistic rage
Moral disengagement
Dissent Terrorism
Left-wing and Right-wing terrorism
Religious motivated terrorism
Criminal terrorism
Crush terrorist groups unilaterally
Crushing terrorist groups multilaterally
Containment
Defensive actions
Diversion
Deligitimation
Transforming terrorist breeding grounds

▶ Introduction

Over the course of its short history, a substantial amount of confusion as to the primary objective for the U.S. system of homeland security has existed. For example, Bellavita (2008) examined the homeland security literature and noted that a number of definitions have evolved.

Mass prayer outside Al-Aqsa Mosque in Jerusalem that led to clashes with Israeli security forces.
Ziv Koren/Polaris/Newscom.

He advised that the need for homeland security has been associated with terrorism and all types of hazards, including catastrophes, jurisdictional hazards, and meta-hazards (large-scale or multiple hazards); national security; and government's desire to curb civil liberties. The outbreaks of Swine flu or N1H1 flu in 2009 and the Zika virus in the beginning of 2016 were considered by many to be a homeland security threat as they were viruses that potentially could have infected large numbers of Americans. Nonetheless, the primary motivation for homeland security is the threat of terrorist attacks on American soil or on American interests abroad.

This chapter examines terrorism in terms of its roots, history, motivation, and political and social implications. It primarily focuses on terrorism that has developed and spread from the Middle East, since this form of terrorism poses the greatest threat to our homeland security today. In essence, we must understand and specify the problem before acting. Without doing so, our countermeasures may be unproductive or ineffective and a waste of valuable resources. This task is complicated by the numerous types or forms of terrorism and their different motivations. For example, terrorist acts in Latin America have different forms and motivations as compared to terrorism that occurs in the Middle East. American response to terrorism must be tailored to the underlying nature of the terrorists and their acts. However, before examining these issues, it is important to define terrorism. We must distinguish terrorism from war, insurgency, and other conflicts, even though these other forms of aggressions sometimes intersect and overlap with terrorism. We must also distinguish terrorism from other forms of criminality. Terrorism indeed is a criminal act, and terrorists often resort to criminal acts to raise the funds required to perpetrate their acts, but terrorism is distinguishable from crime in that it represents a distinct type of activity requiring specific governmental and societal responses.

Continuum of Social Conflict

All societies, regardless of their level of civility, experience some conflict generally evolving around political, social, economic, or religious issues. Figure 5-1 ■ shows the continuum of social conflict. The lowest level is normative social conflict, whereas the most

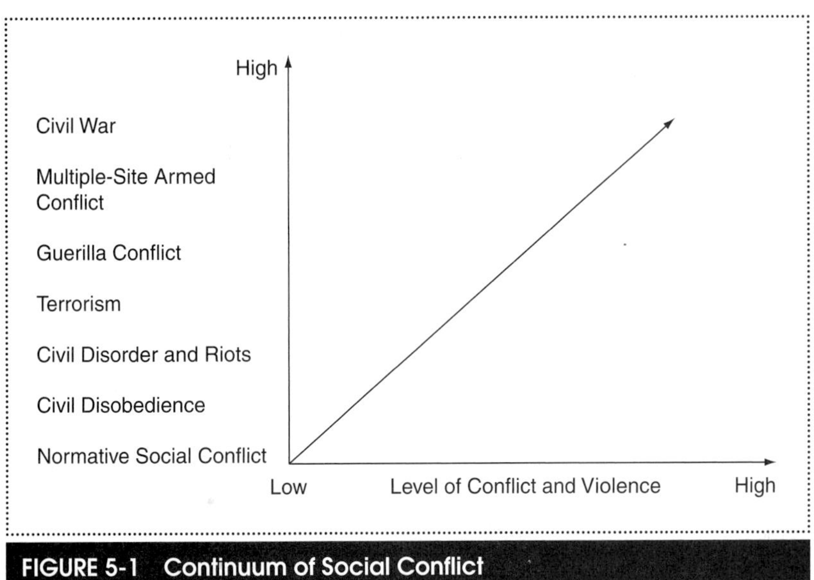

FIGURE 5-1 Continuum of Social Conflict

extreme cases lead to civil war. For example, America has limited violence, but there is substantial conflict or consternation over a number of political and social issues. Americans are constantly experiencing **normative social conflict**, that is, conflict about the norms and expectations in society. This level of conflict is also inherent to many Muslim countries in which Shiites and Sunnis vie for power. In some cases, this normative conflict will result in **civil disobedience**, such as work stoppages, protests, or strikes. A higher level of discontent results in **civil disorder and riots**, such as those that have occurred throughout the Middle East in recent years. **Terrorist activities** occur when a sufficient number of people are discontent with the social or government structure. They generally are highly committed to some cause and have a measure of support from the general population. If conditions persist and an increasing level of support is exhibited by the population, the terrorist activities may evolve into **guerilla warfare**. If conditions continue to worsen, the country or area may become embroiled in armed conflict or even a **civil war** such as that which occurred in Iraq and Syria when the Islamic State (ISIS) was formed. ISIS is a Sunni jihadist group that claims to have religious authority over all Muslims and seek to assert their claim using violent methods (Rand, 2017). Terrorism is an expression of social discontent and is one type of conflict that can occur.

▶ Defining Terrorism

To some extent, **terrorism** is a **social construct** in that different people have various definitions of the term. It is a pejorative term in that it has extremely negative associations and always connotes death and destruction. Society is constantly exposed to the term by the news media, politicians, and popular entertainment venues, and it is applied to a wide variety of actors, conditions, activities, and situations. As a social construct, the term is used to demonize people, societies, and actions. Its use solicits highly emotional responses. Politicians are able to garner support by attacking terrorists and anything remotely associated with them, regardless of guilt or involvement. For example, American Muslims have been demonized as a result of Islamic terrorism, and crimes against them have increased only because of their religion.

Labeling an act or a person a terrorist has a partisan dimension. For example, Israelis label Palestinian suicide bombers as terrorists, whereas the Palestinians see such behavior as an act of defiance or retribution for acts perpetrated on the Palestinian people by the Israelis. The Palestinians see themselves as freedom fighters, not terrorists. The Israelis see their actions as a defense against attacks by the Palestinians. Right-wing extremists in the United States, such as Timothy McVeigh, who blew up the federal building in Oklahoma City in 1995, do not see themselves or their organizations as terrorists. They see themselves as fighting government oppression. Thus, the terrorist label largely is dependent upon political perspective or whether one is the aggressor or the victim.

It is important to note that perspectives change over time. For example, Ahmad (2003) noted that members of the Jewish underground in Palestine in the 1930s and 1940s were described as terrorists, but by 1944, these terrorists were characterized as freedom fighters by the Western press. The change was largely due to the events of the Holocaust and Western liberal thinking. The reclassification of the members of the Jewish underground as freedom fighters helped gain support for a Jewish state among the Western press and population, irrespective of previous terrorist activities or labels. In 1979, the Soviet Union invaded Afghanistan. The mujahedeen who fought the Soviets were characterized by President Reagan as "freedom fighters." Today, many of these same freedom fighters are aligned with or a part of ISIS, al Qaeda, or the Taliban, and we now characterize them as terrorists. Thus, at one point in history, a group may be seen as terrorists and at another point in time, freedom fighters. Perspective, like politics, can change. To some extent, activities only partially help define terrorism; whether a group is a friend or foe also contributes to the characterization.

Terrorism can originate from a variety of sources or directions. First, the state can sponsor or perpetrate it. There is a long history of states in Africa, Asia, and South America using terrorist tactics on their own people. The government of Sudan used terrorist activities to kill, starve, and create political refugees by attacking its citizens in the Darfur region. Several countries have launched terrorist campaigns in the Congo in the fight for that country's mineral resources. Right-wing and left-wing political groups in a variety of countries have created paramilitary groups that use terrorist activities to further their political agendas. Transnational organized crime groups such as the drug cartels in Mexico have used terror to undermine the rule of law and the legitimate government. A number of religious groups have resorted to terrorism, including radical Muslims in the Middle East who have terrorized legitimate governments and citizens who belong to other religious faiths or who are otherwise opposed to them. In the United States, radical Christians have bombed abortion clinics and murdered abortion doctors, and animal rights groups have burned university research centers and the personal property of researchers. All sorts of groups have been involved in promoting terrorism for their various objectives.

Some would argue that there is no such thing as terrorism; they argue that the term is so nebulous and fraught with political insinuations that it is of little use. They would argue that terrorists are involved in a variety of crimes: bombings, homicide, kidnapping, extortion, narcotics trafficking, tax evasion, and so forth. Terrorists who are involved in these activities actually are little more than organized criminals with a political agenda that is supported by criminal activity. Perhaps our focus should not be on the politics but on the crime and criminal organizations. For example, Hoffman (2009a) advises that terrorists should be identified by their acts, not by their ideology or politics. Indeed, numerous politicians commit crimes to further their personal wealth and political agenda, and these activities may not have a direct effect on people, but they certainly almost always have an indirect impact. For example, the government of Afghanistan is ripe with corruption. To some extent, these politicians are no less criminal than some terrorists.

Nonetheless, given that terrorism is a socially constructed term with multiple meanings and dimensions, it is important to develop an operational definition—what does it mean within the context of governmental operations and responses? Whittacker (2001) compiled a listing of governmental definitions:

> The unlawful use of force or violence against persons or property to intimidate or coerce government, a civilian population, or any segment thereof, in furtherance of political or social objectives (FBI).
>
> The calculated use of violence or threat of violence to inculcate fear, intended to coerce or intimidate governments or societies as to the pursuit of goals that are generally political, religious or ideological (U.S. Department of Defense).
>
> Premeditated, politically motivated violence perpetuated against noncombatant targets by sub-national groups or clandestine agents, usually intended to influence an audience (U.S. Department of State).

These institutional definitions demonstrate that there is no consistent definition of terrorism. This condition of course can contribute to inconsistent or hazy policy. However, the various definitions do have some common threads. Pillar (2003) examined a number of terrorism definitions and identified four consistent themes. First, terrorism involves **premeditation**. Terrorism generally is perpetrated through violent acts, but it can also involve other criminal acts. Regardless, these acts are planned and perpetrated with the intention of having some impact on victims or enemies. Second, terrorists and their acts are motivated by some **political agenda**. Terrorists' political agendas range from the religious to the cultural or social. Terrorists commit many of the same crimes as do ordinary criminals, but terrorists have a political agenda, whereas ordinary criminals commit their acts for financial gain. For example, a number of politicians and the media have referred to the Central American gang Mara Salvatrucha 13, or MS-13, as a terrorist group. Its members certainly are violent and are involved in a wide variety of crimes, including numerous homicides, but their motive is financial gain, not the overthrow of any government. So, are they terrorists? Third, generally the terrorists' targets

Woman looking for belongings in bombed-out rubble, a common occurrence in the war-torn Middle East.
Images by Itani/Alamy Stock Photo.

Afghan police searching for terrorists in Kunduz.
Ton koene/Alamy Stock Photo.

are **noncombatants or civilians**. Attacks on civilians have a substantial psychological impact on terrorists' perceived enemies. Such attacks also demonstrate their power among supporters or potential supporters. Attacks on civilians help undermine or weaken governments, which, ultimately, is the terrorists' primary objective. When terrorists believe they have the capacity, they will attack military targets as a way of demonstrating that the government is ineffectual or inept. A final thread running through definitions of terrorism is that terrorists are generally **subnational or clandestine groups**. They are identified by their political cause, which is opposed to the government under attack.

Perhaps an example is illustrative. On June 10, 2009, James W. Von Brunn walked into the Holocaust Memorial Museum in Washington, D.C., and began firing a rifle at museum patrons, killing a security guard before he was seriously wounded. Von Brunn, according to the Anti-Defamation League, was a Holocaust denier. He was a notorious racist and anti-Semitic. In a previous publication, he praised Adolf Hitler (Hall, Bello, and Heath, 2009). Many viewed the shooting as another hate crime, whereas a few in the media viewed it as an act of terrorism. How would the reaction have been different if the shooting were performed by a Muslim as opposed to a neo-Nazi? Most likely, the media would uniformly have handled the incident as an act of terrorism, touting the increase in terrorist incidents and fueling public fear even though the incident was isolated. Fear as a result of terrorist activities has had a substantial impact on public opinion.

In a more recent example, in 2016, Omar Mateen went to a gay bar in Orlando, Florida, and using an assault rifle killed 49 people and wounded 53 others. It was the worst mass killing since 9/11. Many labeled the shooting as an act of terrorism since Mateen, although born in America, was of Afghanistan descent. He called the police during the shooting three times, each time swearing allegiance to different Middle Eastern terrorist groups, Hezbollah, ISIS, and al Qaeda. Interestingly, all three groups are sworn enemies, insinuating that Mateen knew little about them. Some immediately called the shooting an act of terrorism, while others saw it as a hate crime. Still others saw it as the result of mental illness. These examples demonstrate that it sometimes is difficult to conclusively identify acts of terrorism.

Finally, it should be noted that there are different types of terrorism. For the most part, the configuration of a particular terrorist group is dependent upon environment,

HS ANALYSIS BOX 5-1

Forst (2009) identifies several dimensions associated with terrorist groups. Given what you know about ISIS, how well does ISIS meet or fit these dimensions? Identify other terrorist groups and compare them to Forst's dimensions. Forst's dimensions show that there are different kinds of terrorist groups operating throughout the world.

relationship with the state, motivation, and goals. There can be a variety of terrorist organization configurations. Forst (2009) noted that the categories can be understood by examining the following dimensions:

- Political motivation involving attempts to topple governments
- State-sponsored terrorism such as in the 1970s when the Khmer Rouge killed nearly 2 million Cambodians
- The group is affiliated with other terrorist organizations or networks (smaller groups associated with other terrorist organizations such as al Qaeda)
- Planning and organization
- Religious or ethnic motivation
- The group's targets, people, or symbols of the state or perceived oppressors (terrorist groups generally have specific types of targets and focus on that type)
- Types of people targeted (civilians or civilian groups or governmental officials) (see p. 8)

Examining the various terrorist groups using these criteria can provide a better understanding of the group's motivations, activities, and operations. It can also result in more effective countermeasures.

A Brief History of Terrorism

Given that it is difficult to define terrorism because it is socially constructed and the meaning one associates with the term is subjective and dependent upon perspective, it is illuminating to provide a brief history of the subject. A history of terrorism provides perspective and a better understanding of its origins. The history enables one to develop a more concrete understanding of terrorism and its implications. Since the term terrorism is socially constructed, it is largely defined by past terrorist acts.

Early Forms of Terrorism

Terrorism is not a new phenomenon. It likely has existed since people began to combine into political collectives and states. Burgess (2003) advised that some of the earliest examples include the **Sicari** and **Zeolots**, Jewish groups that were active during the Roman occupation of the Middle East during the first century. The Sicari attacked and primarily killed Jews they deemed to have abandoned their faith, whereas the Zeolots killed Romans and Greeks. Many of the killings occurred in daylight in front of witnesses. These highly visual killings were meant to send messages to the Romans and the Jews who collaborated with them. Highly visual and public attacks remain one of terrorists' primary weapons today. Later, other groups began to use the tactics of the Sicari and Zeolots. For example, in the eleventh century, a Shiite Muslim sect killed politicians and other religious persons who did not subscribe to their version of Islam. They became known as *assassins*, a term that is still in use today.

HS Web Link: To learn more about early terrorism, go to http://www.terrorism-research.com/history/early.php.

The French Revolution

The term *terrorist* or *terrorism* comes from the French Revolution or the *regime de la terreur* (reign of terror) that prevailed in France from 1793 to 1794. The Revolution leader, Maximilien Robespierre set out to rid France of the enemies of the Revolution and killed large numbers of Frenchmen. Burgess (2003) noted that the revolution was an orgy of bloodletting (p. 3). Robespierre believed the ends justified the means. He saw mass killings as a way to not only change government but also cleanse the country so that the new government would be free of its enemies and it could be sustained. This was the justification provided for killing 40,000 of his countrymen. It represented a mentality that is prevalent among terrorists today—human life is less important as compared to the collective cause.

Late Nineteenth- and Early Twentieth-Century Terrorism

Beginning in the 1800s and extending into the early 1900s, political ideology contributed to terrorism and unrest. A substantial amount of terrorism was conducted by **anarchists** and **socialists** who were interested in social justice and were anti-capitalist and anti-government. The anarchists wanted to destroy government, while the socialists desired to redistribute wealth. This movement to a large extent was rooted in Karl Marx's works and ideology. The overwhelming majority of their acts were aimed at government officials and others who were seen as supporters of a social order that oppressed the poor. Their aim was to destroy the ruling governments and replace them with a new social order.

The Russian Revolution occurred in 1917. The revolutionaries or Bolsheviks (communists) overthrew the Tsarist government, killing Tsar Alexander II. Russia had been in upheaval for a number of years prior to the revolution as Bolsheviks killed government officials, military leaders, and supporters of the Tsar (Ternon, 2007). World War I had depleted the Russian Army and Russia had experienced numerous defeats on the battlefield. The Tsar was forced to abdicate the throne. The Bolsheviks ultimately were able to seize control of the country. The French and Russian Revolutions showed the world how terrorism could weaken and lead to the overthrow of governments. Terrorism entered the world stage.

Nationalist groups in Ireland, India, Japan, the Ottoman Empire, and the Balkans also attacked government officials (Burgess, 2003). In 1894, French President Carnot was killed by an Italian anarchist. In 1897, the Austrian empress and the Spanish prime minister were killed. The United States was not immune from these anti-government forces as two U.S. presidents (Garfield and McKinley) were assassinated during this period. Laqueur (1996) points out that if world leaders had assembled in 1900, their primary concern would have been terrorism.

During this period, **state-sponsored terrorism** emerged, whereby governments assisted terrorist groups in attacking political opponents or other countries. For example, Serbia armed and trained a number of terrorists, one of whom killed Archduke Franz Ferdinand, heir to the Austrian throne on June 28, 1914. This assassination resulted in the start of World War I. Bulgaria used terrorists to try to undermine the government of Yugoslavia. Immediately prior to World War II, Nazi Germany, Fascist Italy, and Stalinist Russia used terror tactics somewhat similar to those used by Robespierre to control their own populations. Governments quickly learned that terrorism was a useful tool to undermine other governments and to control their own populations.

After World War II, a number of conflicts broke out throughout the Middle East, Europe, Asia, and Africa in countries such as Kenya, Malaysia, Cyprus, Palestine, Ireland, and Algeria. These conflicts were in reaction to colonization, mainly by the French and English, and a variety of groups in a number of countries fought to gain their independence. They primarily used terrorist tactics to fight the colonialists. For example, the State of Israel grew out of such a conflict. In many cases, these conflicts consisted of guerilla warfare. Although these guerillas often used terrorist tactics against their enemies, they differed from terrorists in that the conflicts often involved irregular paramilitary groups fighting colonial powers. These groups fully understood the power of terrorism and tended to use it when it served their needs.

Terrorism in the Late Twentieth Century

In the 1960s and 1970s, the nature of terrorism changed direction in that terrorist groups included not only nationalists but also a number of left-wing groups that emerged across the globe. For example, the Red Brigades in Italy; the Red Army Faction in West Germany; and a number of groups in the United States, such as the Black Panthers, the Weather Underground or Weathermen, and the Symbionese Liberation Army. These left-wing groups essentially reacted to capitalism and the perceived injustices perpetrated on the poor. They became notorious as a result of their bombings, gun battles with police officers, and bank robberies. At the same time, a number of nationalist groups came to the forefront, including the Provisional Irish Republican Army, the Basque ETA in Spain, and the Palestinian Liberation Organization (PLO), which were fighting for nationalistic interests or independence. One group, the Black September conducted one of the most notorious terrorist attacks at the time when its members kidnapped and killed 11 Israeli athletes at the 1972 Olympic Games in Germany.

Patty Hearst was kidnapped and became part of the Symbionese Liberation Army.
AF archive/Alamy Stock Photo.

State-sponsored terrorism became prevalent. The Soviet Union, its eastern bloc allies, and China supported terrorist groups in countries throughout the world, and countries such as Iran, Syria, and Libya began to sponsor terrorist groups to support the Palestinians. For example, Hezbollah and Hamas have received substantial resources from Syria and Iran. Cuba, a client state of the Soviet Union, tried to export communism through terror to South and Central America.

Terrorism in Early America

There have been incidents of terrorism throughout America's history. In fact, the American Revolutionary War was touched by the Boston Tea Party in 1773, where Americans dressed as Indians dumped British tea in the Boston Harbor (Walker, 2010). In 1865, the Ku Klux Klan was formed in Tennessee by former Confederate General Nathan Bedford Forest. The Klan has terrorized and intimidated blacks and other minority groups since its inception (Trelease, 1995). In 1856, John Brown and his followers killed several pro-slavery supporters in Kansas. Later in 1859, Brown attempted to start an insurrection at Harpers Ferry, Virginia, when he attempted to take over the federal armory. He planned to arm slaves who would fight to abolish slavery in America (Horwitz, 2012). In 1954, four Puerto Rican nationalists shot 30 rounds from a balcony in the House of Representatives injuring five representatives. They wanted to maintain Puerto Rican independence (Roig-Franzia, 2004). These are examples of individuals or groups committing terrorism.

In the late 1800s, anarchy or an anti-state philosophy spread across America and Europe. In 1886, there was a bombing in Chicago known as the Haymarket Affair, where an anarchist threw a bomb that killed several police officers who were present at a demonstration by striking workers. In 1910, the *Lost Angeles Times* was bombed, killing 21 people. The bombing was a result of the paper's anti-union stand. During this period up to the 1920s, there were multiple bombings and attacks by the anarchists against the government and corporate leaders. For example, in 1892, an anarchist attempted to assassinate Henry Clay Frick, chairman of the Carnegie Steel Company, and Leon Czolgosz assassinated President William McKinley in 1901 (Hubac-Occhipinti, 2007). The anarchists primarily were concerned with unemployment and the government's support for the conditions that workers were facing. These examples show that terrorism has a long history in the United States and that it is not a new phenomenon.

▶ Terrorism Today

Today, American counterterrorism strategies focus on weakening the operations by ISIS, the Taliban, and al Qaeda, although numerous other groups are also a threat to American interests. Al Qaeda perpetrated the 9/11 attacks on New York and Washington and essentially has declared war on the United States. Al Qaeda, housed primarily in Afghanistan and Pakistan, has a worldwide network that is sophisticated and resilient relative to other terrorist groups. It is able to raise millions of dollars annually and has made political inroads in a number of countries including Yemen, Libya, and Somalia. Relative to earlier terrorist groups or organizations, it is a "super power" because of its financing and influence. Its stated objective is to rid Muslim lands of American and Western influences. The organization also wants to install theocratic governments to promote the Islamic religion, especially in the Middle East.

Another terrorist superpower was ISIS. ISIS was born out of the Iraqi War and the Civil War in Syria. ISIS declared a **caliphate** establishing an Islamic State. The group took control of territory in Syria and Iraq. ISIS primarily consisted of Sunni tribal paramilitary groups and Sunni military officers who were displaced by the Shiites after the Iraqi War.

Hundreds of foreign fighters joined ISIS, resulting in a formable army. In addition to fighting the governments of Iraq and Syria, ISIS fought a coalition of western countries, countries from the Middle East, and Eastern Europe led by the United States. They had been on a brutal killing binge that resulted in the deaths of thousands of civilians, even producing videos of the beheading of their prisoners, including Americans and Europeans. They differed from many other terrorist groups by controlling territory and establishing a government. By 2017, ISIS was essentially defeated by Iraqi and American troops.

There is one distinct difference between today's terrorists and those from the past. Today, terrorists seldom attack government officials; they attack civilian targets and attempt to create as many deaths and injuries as possible. These attacks have been referred to as the **propaganda of the deed** and they deliver strong messages to a larger audience. Although such attacks have a profound and direct impact on the victims, they also have a psychological impact on non-victims. Such attacks show populations that their government is weak and cannot protect them. This often results in people supporting the terrorists out of fear. For example, in Chapter 1, we discussed fear of crime surveys in the United States. Even though there have been relatively few major attacks occurring in only three cities (New York, Washington, and Oklahoma City) and several minor attacks, fear of being a victim of a terrorist attack is ranked high relative to all other forms of victimization. Realistically, the probability for a given American to be a victim of such an attack is almost nonexistent.

A review of the history of terrorism shows a number of similarities with the "new" terrorism of today. Contemporary politicians, security experts, and the media treat today's threats as a new phenomenon. However, as Field (2009) pointed out, the actual behavior of terrorists has not changed to any degree over time. The tactics and motivations of today's terrorists are quite consistent with those of terrorists throughout history. Perhaps the only difference is that terrorists' weapons have become more deadly and destructive.

▶ The Roots and Causes of Terrorism

In this section, we examine the etiology of terrorism. There are multiple causes that individually and in combination result in terrorist groups being formed and attacking their perceived or actual enemies. Moreover, some causes affect particular groups or individuals, whereas other causes result in conflict and terrorism for other groups. Some of these causes are macro level, such as the clashes between civilizations or cultures and globalization, whereas others such as religious, ethnic, or tribal clashes are at a more micro level. On an individual level, a person may perceive that a group has wronged him or her and react by committing a terrorist act as a personal vendetta. Therefore, we examine the major causes or contributors to terrorism, especially Middle Eastern terrorism.

Globalization

Globalization is an ever-increasing social phenomenon affecting nations and peoples across the globe. It is rapidly changing and transforming our world. Nassar (2005) noted that globalization is a global reality, resulting in a shared destiny and interdependence. The interconnectedness cannot be disputed, stopped, or discounted. It is a fact of life. It will continue and have a significant impact on countries and people. It results in winners and losers, and the losers often become xenophobic and are more prone to become involved in conflicts.

To some extent, globalization is seen as a force that is homogenizing the world—providing consistency and uniformity in a world composed of differences, inconsistencies, and conflicts. It is reasoned that increased globalization will result in a global social and economic network, with adherents from across many countries. This is not a new concept. After World War I, the League of Nations was formed, and later, its successor, the United Nations, was seen as a vehicle to resolve world conflict. In essence, creation, of these bodies was viewed by many as the foundation for a world government and a new world order. Other organizations embodying this unifying objective have been created, including the World Trade Organization, the International Monetary Fund, and the World Bank. Globalization has come to mean many things, including interdependence, liberalization, secularization, consumerism, democratization, universalism, Westernization, and capitalism (see Nassar, 2005; Cronin, 2004). To some extent, some in third-world countries see it as a sophisticated effort to reestablish colonization. They see globalization as infringing upon their culture and way of life.

Today, however, one of the most commonly mentioned reasons for the growth of terrorism is globalization. It has contributed to terrorism in two ways. First, as noted, globalization has been an effort to homogenize the social and economic fabrics of countries. In essence, it has to a degree been an assault on long-standing, accepted cultures that have existed for hundreds of years in many countries, particularly the Middle East. To this end, Kay (2004) noted that globalization is a mechanism by which countries exert power and control. As a consequence, many of those who are the recipients or who are on the blunt end of globalization have objected to the "Westernization" of their cultures. Some see Westernization as demonic and as a crusade against their way of life. They also see globalization as a method by which Western industrialized nations can control their country and other nondeveloped countries. Western cultures assume that other cultures long for change and that this change is beneficial, an assumption not accepted by many of those who are the subject of Westernization.

HS Web Link: To learn more about globalization, go to http://www.globalization101.org/what-is-globalization/ http://blogs.worldbank.org/youthink/globalization-values.

Second, globalization has resulted in a more interconnected world. Today, borders do not inhibit communication, business transactions, or the transfer of money and commodities. Terrorists have seized these new opportunities or tools to facilitate their objectives and attacks. Terrorists now can more easily communicate with one another. They can quickly transfer funds from one country to another to finance operations. Modern technology has made it increasingly more difficult for governments to unearth and thwart such activities. To some extent, global terrorist groups now operate similarly to multinational corporations and governments in terms of their interconnectivity.

Religion

Religion, perhaps, has the deepest roots in terms of playing a role in terrorism. Religion is a primary component of many cultures and civilizations—in some cases, religion defines a culture or society. For example, government and everyday life in some Islamic countries are dictated by the Koran. Many Muslims long for theocracy to replace secular governments. Many Americans see themselves as Christians and believe that government should be operated consistent with Christian principles. Israel is a Jewish state and many others such as Muslims are afforded second-class status. The decades-long conflict in Northern Ireland primarily was between Irish Catholics and Irish Protestants. Thus, we see religion playing a role in conflicts and terrorism. Religion plays a more important and dominant role in some people's lives than does their association with a country or nationalism. Hoffman (1995) advises that religion plays a much larger role in terrorism today than in the past. Religiously oriented terrorists of all sorts use religious precepts to legitimize violence. Hoffman (2006) advises that religious-based terrorism has increased substantially, and it now represents about one-half of the terrorist groups in the world.

Terrorism predicated on religion often leads to more violence as compared to terrorism that emerges for secular reasons. Martin (2003) noted that religious terrorists participate in unrestrained violence and are willing to use the most deadly weapons possible. Secular terrorists tend to be more restrained. Religious terrorists have an unrestricted choice of targets—anything or anyone who is not of their religious persuasion. Secular terrorists attack only those who are perceived as enemies, usually the government or government officials. Religious terrorist groups are confined to zealots or "true believers" who are more willing to attack perceived enemies with impunity. For example, al Qaeda has indiscriminately attacked citizens in numerous countries with the intent of inflicting as many casualties as possible.

Israeli-Palestinian Conflict

An important underlying factor contributing to global terrorism is that the Israeli-Palestinian conflict has gone unresolved for so many years. As Nassar (2005) noted, "The Israeli-Palestinian conflict has been characterized by terrorist atrocities committed by both sides. The terror attacks demonstrate the full viciousness that accompanies the migration of nightmares between nations" (p. 59). Not only is it a long-standing conflict, it is one that has gained the world's attention, particularly in Arab and Muslim countries. The Israelis took Palestinians' land and forced thousands to flee to neighboring countries. Palestinians essentially are a people without a country. The conflict serves as a backdrop for much of the angst that currently exists in the Middle East.

To a large extent, the plight of the Palestinian people has become a rallying call for Muslims. It is a prism through which many Arabs and Muslims see the world and make judgments. Numerous Muslim terrorist groups use this conflict as a tool for recruitment, raising funds, and justifications for jihadist activities. The conflict is not so much a cause as it is a rationale for involvement. As long as the conditions in Palestine remain unresolved, it is much easier for numerous Muslim terrorist groups to obtain funding and recruit new fighters.

Russian Invasion of Afghanistan

In 1979, the Soviet Union invaded Afghanistan with the purpose of overthrowing the government and installing a Soviet-aligned government in the country. The Russian invasion was rather ruthless with the Russians killing scores of civilians, particularly women and children. Muslims throughout the region immediately began to garner support for the Afghans. Fighters arrived from other countries, Muslim charities began collecting large amounts of money to be used in the fight, and Afghan tribes were united in the effort to expel the Russians. Later, the United States and Saudi Arabia provided billions of dollars in military aid to the Afghans to facilitate their war efforts. The Russians were eventually defeated and left the country.

This war has a number of implications for terrorism today. First, it unified many of the radical Muslim groups in the country, and today, a number of these groups comprise the al Qaeda, ISIS, and Taliban organizations that are fighting the United States. Second, the war resulted in the establishment of a fairly complex and comprehensive system of charities to raise funding for mujahedeen and jihadists. This fairly efficient charity system is used today by several terrorist groups, including al Qaeda. Finally, the defeat of the Russians

HS ANALYSIS BOX 5-2

Although there are several causes of terrorism, it seems that the Israeli-Palestinian conflict is directly or indirectly a part of the conflict. If there were a peace settlement, do you believe that it would have an impact on Muslim-based terrorism? How do you think it would affect terrorism?

showed the Muslim and Arab world that it could defeat large world powers. The war emboldened terrorists to take on the United States. Thus, the Russian invasion of Afghanistan did not necessarily cause terrorism, but its outcome has facilitated it.

Wahhabism

Saudi Arabia's largest export is oil. Its second-largest export is Wahhabism, a particularly radical or conservative form of the Sunni Muslim religion. Many of its proponents believe that people and governments should adhere to Sharia Law. Sharia Law is derived from a literal interpretation of some of the passages espoused in the Koran. Saudi Arabia has financed mosques and madrassas (Islamic religious schools) in Pakistan and a number of other countries. This conservative form of Islam has sown the seeds for modern jihad (Allen, 2009; Venkatraman, 2007).

Authoritarian Governments

Many of the governments in the Middle East, Africa, and Asia can be characterized as authoritarian. These governments oppress their citizens politically, economically, and socially in order to maintain control. For example, in 2013, General el-Sisi led a coalition to overthrow Egypt's only elected president, Mohamed Morsi. Morsi had been elected after the Arab Spring when several Middle Eastern countries attempted to install democratically elected governments, and President Hosni Mubarak was forced to resign from office. Mubarak, a general at the time, had previously used the military to assume power. Morsi was a member of the Muslim Brotherhood, a radical religious/political party that exists in a

Egyptian President Abdel Fattah el-Sisi, who took control of Egypt by force.

ITAR-TASS Photo Agency/Alamy Stock Photo.

number of Middle Eastern countries. Upon taking power, el-Sisi suppressed public demonstrations, imprisoned thousands, and controlled the press. He again outlawed the Muslim Brotherhood in a similar fashion as Mubarak had done. Although underground, the Muslim Brotherhood and other Muslim groups continue to try to wrestle control of Egypt from the military including the commission of terrorist acts. Egypt has had a number of problems with terrorists in the Sinai Peninsula.

Some of the Gulf States in the Middle East, Bahrain, Qatar, and the United Arab Emirates also have problems with the Muslim Brotherhood. Saudi Arabia's monarchy routinely executes critics of the government. Despot Middle Eastern governments routinely suppress their populations, which leads to homegrown radicalization and, in some cases, terrorism. Authoritarian governments must oppress their citizens in order to maintain control. This is a pattern in a number of countries and creates breeding grounds for terrorists.

The United States supports a number of these authoritarian governments in the Middle East, North Africa, and Asia for a variety of reasons, including oil, to fight terrorism, and to counter Iran and Russia. This support has in some cases resulted in various groups labeling the United States as an enemy. One of the several reasons, Osama bin Laden targeted the United States was its support for the Saudi and Israeli governments. A number of terrorist and radical groups see the United States as an enemy for this reason. It is a case where your friends' enemies become your enemies.

Failed States and Terrorism

Non-functioning governments or weak governments are breeding grounds for terrorists and terrorist organizations. Before examining failed states in more depth, it should be noted that the term failed state is rather amorphous; it does not have clear delineation as there are degrees of failed states. Stanislawski (2008) has identified gradations of failed states or degrees of stateness. Some states are more effective at governing than others in terms of their territorial control and performance of government functions. There are quasi-states where there are boundaries, but the government is weak and has little control over the territory. Afghanistan could be characterized as quasi-state since the government has little control outside Kabul. **Almost states** are regions or areas within another country that function as their own state. The Kurdish area in Iraq is an almost state. It has its own government and military and effectively governs its lands. It is likely that this will lead to conflicts with the Iraqi central government in the future much like the conflict between the Turkish Kurds and the Turkish government. Finally, there are **black spots**. Black spots are areas within a state that are ungoverned. A prime example of a black spot is the tribal region in Pakistan. This region is home to al Qaeda and the Taliban. Finally, there are **failed states**. The best example is Somalia. It has had no working central government since 1991 and currently is ruled by war lords. Today, the terrorist group al-Shabab, which is affiliated with al Qaeda, is fighting to create a fundamentalist Islamic state in Somalia. The country is also home to a number of pirates who operate in the Gulf of Aden.

Plummer (2012) argued that focusing on failed statehood as the cause for the development of terrorism is simplistic. The attributes of the failed state as well as the failure of the state must also be examined as many of these attributes contribute to the formation of terrorist groups. He noted that countries that place less effort into social welfare have more connections to terrorism and incidents (also see Burgoon, 2006; Schneider et al., 2010). Burgoon advised that social welfare reduces poverty, inequality, insecurity, and religious extremism. These conditions often contribute to the growth of terrorism. For example, Hamas in Gaza and Hezbollah in Lebanon have wide public support because of their social welfare programs. The presence of an ethnic or religious community with a history of being persecuted or repression will create a black spot from which terrorism can emerge and operate. ISIS, which primarily consists of Sunnis, evolved in Syria as a result of their oppression by the Bashar al Assad regime. Economic underdevelopment results in poverty, which in turn contributes to terrorism. Economic disparity within or among countries can create rage and terrorism. For example, the Shiites in Iraq repressed the Sunnis after the American withdrawal, which resulted in the Iraqi Sunnis sympathizing with ISIS.

Failed states of one sort or another exist on every continent. They are ripe for the formation of terrorism. President George W. Bush's foreign policy agenda included nation building. If we had been more successful, we likely would have had an impact on terrorism. Nonetheless, failed states will continue to be breeding grounds for crime and terrorism, which means that we will continue to be involved in countering terrorism. The only solution is more effective governance in these countries or a strong law enforcement and defensive posture.

This section identifies a number of causes that have resulted in terrorism. There is no one cause that can adequately explain it. It likely is a combination of causes that affects an individual or group. Conditions conducive to terrorism may exist for a period of time. The onset or triggering of terrorist activities generally is explained by social movements or dramatic events affecting large portions of the population.

▶ Individual Explanations of Terrorism

The causes of terrorism just discussed focus primarily on macro-level variables that have been used to explain the phenomenon. In addition to macro-level conditions, other factors also make some people more susceptible to becoming a terrorist as compared to others. Even though some members of a culture, area, or religious group become terrorists, others do not. There are individual factors that contribute to people joining terrorist causes. Several theories attempt to explain why an individual would be a terrorist.

Borgeson and Valeri (2009) identify five primary psychological theories or conditions that might explain people's involvement in terrorism: (1) frustration-aggression, (2) relative deprivation, (3) negative identity, (4) narcissistic rage, and (5) moral disengagement.

The **frustration-aggression theory** posits that stress often leads to frustration, and in turn, frustration that remains unabated can result in aggression. The lower classes in many countries, which are considerable in size, have large numbers of young people who are frustrated over their social conditions or livelihoods. Indeed, an examination of the nationalities of terrorists shows that many come from countries that are economically, socially, or politically oppressed. These societies have remained stagnant for generations, resulting in people who perceive that they have few if any opportunities to better themselves. This frustration sometimes leads to individuals striking out at those who they perceive as their oppressors.

Second, Borgson and Valeri identify **relative deprivation** as a contributor to terrorism. Relative deprivation occurs when individuals compare their station in life and opportunities with those of others and find a negative disparity and become frustrated as a result. In some cases, when they compare their station in life with that of others, they develop unrealistic expectations about what they can achieve or what they deserve. Of course, one of the contributing factors to these unrealistic expectations has been globalization, which has made many people aware of others' higher standards of living—the vast differences between Western societies and many third-world societies. The expansion of media outlets in many of these countries has made such differences blatantly apparent (Ahmed, 2007). The perceived inequity has resulted in resentment, anger, and aggression. For example, today many living in Muslim or Arab countries believe that Western nations are stealing or at a minimum not paying market value for scarce resources such as oil. They perceive that they are being deceived and disadvantaged by Western oil-consuming nations.

A third possible factor is a negative **identity crisis**. Here, individuals do not have a sense of belonging and come to identify with population subgroups or tribes rather than the country in which they reside. In some cases, these groups are radical or involved in criminal activities. Terrorist groups such as al Qaeda, ISIS, Hamas, and Hezbollah become attractive to people with negative identity crises—adherents are easily recruited, especially when they also feel that they have been deprived. Belonging to a radical group that accepts them gives them identity and a sense of belonging.

Fourth, **narcissistic rage** refers to a personality complex with which individuals become egotistical, selfish, and conceited. They have little regard for others, and they generally become this way during their formative years. When they become offended or cannot have their way, they tend to lash out at those whom they perceive to have harmed them. Terrorist organizations are particularly attractive to the narcissistic personality. They provide a forum to express their grievances and anger. Membership serves as a vehicle for them to feel important. It also provides a mode by which to punish or hurt those people or groups that they dislike. Belonging to a terrorist organization or being a terrorist essentially allows, to some extent, unrestrained behavior.

Finally, **moral disengagement** occurs when people move to a fantasy world—their worldview becomes distorted and unrealistic. They may see themselves as a hero with a cause. They believe their actions, although harmful to some, are overwhelmingly beneficial and appreciated by others—the ends justify the means. A prime example is Robespierre's slaughtering of several thousand French citizens during the French Revolution as discussed earlier. People who are morally disengaged are able to neutralize their negative actions by demonizing their victims. For example, today many jihadists see the American government as being evil, perpetrating crimes on Muslim people. Since the Koran prohibits the killing of innocent people, the jihadists advise that the American people elect their government, therefore, the American people are evil, thus allowing Americans to be killed indiscriminately. This thinking allows the jihadists to morally disengage from the evil acts that they commit.

Omar Mateen who conducted the terror attack on the Orlando nightclub in 2016. Was he a terrorist or mentally ill?

Handout/Alamy Stock Photo.

This discussion demonstrates that there are numerous psychological and individual factors that might contribute to a person becoming a terrorist. Many terrorists come from a background or society that exemplifies strain, political and social repression, and deprivation. These social factors have a significant impact on people's psyche. Nonetheless, a psychological condition is just one of many factors (cultural, economic, political, religious, and sociological) that contribute to terrorism. Indeed, there is no single psychological profile for terrorists (Long, 1990); they come from a wide range of backgrounds and possess a variety of perspectives and rationales for their involvement. Terrorist groups are able to attract large numbers of adherents who are uniquely dangerous and deadly.

▶ Types of Terrorism

It is important to understand that there are a variety of terrorist organizations and terrorist activities across the globe. Martin (2003) examined worldwide terrorism and developed a typology of terrorist groups. This typology perhaps more effectively allows for a more comprehensive understanding of terrorism. Martin identified five types of terrorism based on motivation: (1) state-sponsored terrorism, (2) dissident terrorism, (3) terrorists from the left and right, (4) religious terrorism, and (5) criminal terrorism.

State-Sponsored Terrorism

Terrorist activities that occur as a result of state-sponsored terrorism are similar to those perpetrated by other groups. The primary difference lies in their motivation. **State-sponsored terrorism**, as its name implies, consists of terrorist acts that occur at the direction, directly or indirectly, of the state or government. The targets of this type of terrorism can be politicians and political parties or groups within the host country, government leaders or politicians and groups in other countries, or other countries in general. For example, political regimes often use paramilitary terrorist groups to attack competing political opponents. Leaders in one country may use terrorism against another country that is seen as a political rival. Figure 5-2 ■ provides the types of support that a state can provide to the terrorists.

Currently, the U.S. Department of State has listed three countries that are state sponsors of terrorism: Iran, Syria, and Sudan (U.S. Department of State, 2016). Cuba had been listed as a state sponsor of terrorism, but in 2016, President Obama resumed relations with Cuba and

Category	Type of Support
Political	The state campaigns for the terrorist group or cause in an attempt to undermine the group's enemies
Logistics	The state provides financing, weapons, or other supplies to assist the terrorist group in defeating its enemy
Episodic	The state assists the group in a particular incident or situation whose outcome is beneficial to the state
Combined operational	The state sends soldiers or fighters to join the terrorist group in a battle

FIGURE 5-2 Types of Support for Terrorist Organizations by Nation States
Source: Adapted from Martin, G. (2013). *Understanding Terrorism: Challenges, Perspectives, and Issues,* Thousand Oaks, CA: Sage.

removed Cuba from the list. The U.S. State Department designation results in withholding U.S. foreign aid assistance, a ban on defense exports and sales, control over some dual-use items (items that can be used for defense and nondefense purposes), and financial restrictions.

The fact that the U.S. Department of State only lists three countries for states sponsoring terrorism is not intended to imply that other countries do not sponsor terrorism to further their objectives. In the case of Sudan, Syria, and Iran, their actions are so grievous that they rise above those of other states. There are numerous instances when countries have meddled in other countries' business via terrorism or attempted to control some dissent group or population.

Dissent Terrorism

Dissent terrorism refers to a dissent group using terrorist activities against its government. Prime examples include the Sri Lanka Tamil Tigers, who fought the government for independence; the Irish Republican Army, which fought the British government over control of Northern Ireland; and the Basque Separatists in Spain, who had an on-going terrorist campaign for independence. Additionally, dissent terrorism is quite common on the continent of Africa where different dissent groups are constantly fighting governments for control. In some cases, these terrorist campaigns are waged for independence; in others, the fight is over power, wealth, and control.

Terrorists on the Left and Right

Left-wing and right-wing terrorism is rooted in political ideology, and it generally occurs in countries where one political philosophy dominates, generally in a repressive fashion, and ideological opponents juxtaposed to the rulers fight to overthrow the government. There are ample examples. Fidel Castro overthrew the Batista government in 1959, installing a communist government in the island state. The governments of Peru and Columbia fought communist-inspired terrorist groups for a number of years. Many right-wing authoritarian rulers use right-wing paramilitary organizations or groups to attack and terrorize their political opponents, usually socialists. In most cases, this form of terrorism pits capitalism against socialism.

Religious Terrorism

Today, **religious motivated terrorism** dominates the world stage, and it has been the primary motivational factor for world terrorism for the past several decades. This form of terrorism dominates the Middle East (Hoffman, 2006). The number of religious motivated terror groups outnumbers all other forms of terrorist groups. Even though many associate religious motivated terrorism with the Muslim religion, there are other religious groups that are engaged in terrorism. What makes this problem more difficult is that they are far more lethal or deadly as compared to secular groups. In many cases, they see or regard violence as a divine duty or sacramental act conveyed by sacred text and imparted by clerical authority (Hoffman, 1995). Consequently, there are no moral constraints on their activities. They kill innocent citizens including women and children with impunity.

As noted, this form of terrorism is not restricted to the Muslim faith. Some of the same attributes, violence legitimized by religious precepts, a preoccupation with perceived nonbeliever or sinner enemies, and isolation from mainstream society, drive other religious groups. For example, American Christian white supremacists have committed all sorts of crimes as a result of their faith and hatred for other groups such as African Americans and Jews. Christian extremists have murdered doctors who perform abortions and have blown up abortion clinics. Radical Jewish messianic groups have used terrorism to further their religious tenants, which include the safeguarding of Israeli territory and preventing the government from relinquishing it to Palestinians.

Criminal Terrorism

Whereas the forms of terrorism just discussed are motivated by politics or religion, **criminal terrorism** refers to terrorist acts that are used to facilitate crime and criminal profits. Perhaps the most cogent example of criminal terrorism today is the drug cartels in Mexico. The majority of drugs coming into the United States today come through Mexico. The Mexican cartels produce large quantities of marijuana, black tar heroin, and methamphetamine. The immense size of the drug trade has resulted in the cartels amassing large amounts of money by which to raise large and sophisticated paramilitary groups; bribe police, military, judicial, and government officials; and essentially bring the state to its knees. As discussed earlier, terrorism is associated with political and religious motives, and crime normally does not fall within the scope of the definition of terrorism. However, the case of the Mexican drug cartels demonstrates that there is a fine line that separates criminal organizations from terrorist organizations. In Mexico, the drug cartels' criminal actions now threaten to undermine the government, and indeed, many of the violent actions perpetrated by these cartels are aimed at making the government less effective in dealing with crime. In the case of Mexico, we can accurately classify the cartels as terrorist organizations because they are involved in political objectives, undermining the government, as well as profits. Chapter 7 examines transnational organized crime. As noted there, criminal terrorism exists throughout the world, weakens legitimate governments, and results in anarchy.

▶ Level of Terrorist Activities

Terrorism is an ongoing, worldwide problem with attacks occurring in numerous countries. Of course, a large number of attacks are occurring in Iraq and Afghanistan as a result of the wars. Even so, there are numerous attacks in other countries. The U.S. Department of State attempts to maintain a count of terrorist attacks and the level of deaths associated with them. Figure 5-3 ■ provides a breakdown of worldwide attacks for the year 2015.

Month	Total Attacks	Total Deaths*	Total Injured*	Total Kidnapped/ Hostages
January	1270	2340	2781	1726
February	1078	2127	2713	894
March	903	2378	2829	1214
April	928	2919	2650	1155
May	1017	2676	2705	1725
June	929	2727	3407	535
July	986	2946	3645	1204
August	993	2400	3349	1260
September	881	2266	3491	543
October	1040	2300	2722	877
November	928	1610	2581	769
December	821	1639	2447	287
Total	**11774**	**28328**	**35320**	**12189**

FIGURE 5-3 Terrorist Attacks and Casualties Worldwide by Month, 2015
Source: U.S. State Department. (2015). *Country Reports on Terrorism 2015.* http://www.state.gov/j/ct/rls/crt/2015/257526.htm.

	Total Attacks		Total Deaths*		Deaths per Attack*		Total Injured*		Injured per Attack*		Total Kidnapped/ Hostages	
	2015	2014	2015	2014	2015	2014	2015	2014	2015	2014	2015	2014
Iraq	**2418**	3370	6932	9926	2.99	3.07	**11856**	15137	5.23	4.79	**3982**	2658
Afghanistan	**1708**	1594	5292	4507	3.24	2.91	**6246**	4700	4.00	3.15	**1112**	719
Pakistan	**1009**	1823	1081	1761	1.10	0.99	**1325**	2836	1.36	1.61	**269**	879
India	**791**	764	289	418	0.38	0.57	**508**	639	0.68	0.89	**862**	305
Nigeria	**589**	663	4886	7531	9.29	12.81	**2777**	2251	7.67	6.31	**1341**	1298
Egypt	**494**	292	656	184	1.34	0.63	**844**	452	1.73	1.55	**24**	29
Philippines	**485**	378	258	240	0.54	0.65	**548**	367	1.16	1.00	**119**	145
Bangladesh	**459**	124	75	30	0.16	0.24	**691**	107	1.52	0.87	**4**	7
Libya	**428**	554	462	435	1.24	0.90	**657**	567	1.85	1.21	**764**	336
Syria	**382**	232	2748	1698	7.99	8.24	**2818**	1473	9.78	9.32	**1453**	872
Worldwide	**11774**	**13482**	**28328**	**32763**	**2.53**	**2.57**	**35320**	**34785**	**3.30**	**2.86**	**12189**	**9461**

FIGURE 5-4 Ten Countries with the Most Terrorist Attacks in 2015
Source: U.S. State Department. (2015). *Country Reports on Terrorism 2015.* http://www.state.gov/j/ct/rls/crt/2015/257526.htm.

As noted in Figure 5-3 ■, there is an average of about 1,000 attacks per month with about 2,000 deaths and scores injured as a result of these attacks per month. Also note that there are hundreds of kidnappings per month. Kidnapping is just one of the many crimes that terrorists commit to obtain money for their operations.

It is also worthwhile to examine where terrorist attacks occur. Figure 5-4 ■ provides a breakdown of the 10 countries with the most terrorist attacks in 2015.

There were 11,774 terrorist attacks in 2015, with 9,222 occurring in these 10 countries. It is also noteworthy that all 10 of these countries have significant Muslim populations with a majority of the attacks perpetrated by jihadist groups. Radical Muslims are the driving force behind most of the terrorism today. It is also centered in one part of the world.

Finally, it is informative to examine who is perpetrating terrorist attacks. Figure 5-5 ■ provides a listing of the five terrorist groups that has conducted the most attacks.

	Total Attacks		Total Deaths*		Total Injured*		Total Kidnapped/ Hostages	
	2015	2014	2015	2014	2015	2014	2015	2014
Taliban	1093	895	4512	3492	4746	3313	954	649
Islamic State of Iraq and the Levant (ISIL)	931	1090	6050	6328	6010	5859	4759	3180
Boko Haram	491	454	5450	6663	3318	1747	1549	1217
Maoists/Communist Party of India-Maoist	343	307	176	191	163	165	707	163
Kurdistan Workers' Party (PKK)	238	47	287	12	580	19	136	68

FIGURE 5-5 Five Terrorist Groups Conducting the Largest Number of Terrorist Attacks in 2015
Source: U.S. State Department. (2015). *Country Reports on Terrorism 2015.* http://www.state.gov/j/ct/rls/crt/2015/257526.htm.

Only the Maoists/Communist Party of India is a non-Islamic terrorist group. The Islamic State of Iraq is located in Iraq, Syria, and Libya and is spreading to some other countries. Boko Haram is a terrorist group based in Nigeria and is active in Chad, Niger, and Cameroon. It has pledged allegiance to ISIS. The Kurdistan Workers' Party is based in Turkey and Iraq. Since the mid-1980s, the group has waged an armed struggle with Turkey over self-determination. The group wants to create its own state.

► Strategies for Dealing with Terrorism

In years past, the United States has deployed a variety of strategies to combat worldwide terrorism. These have ranged from all-out military intervention such as in Iraq and Afghanistan to military and humanitarian aid in countries such as Pakistan. Some of these efforts have achieved moderate success, whereas others have been less fruitful. Byman (2009) upon examining the terrorism landscape and government responses has identified seven strategies that cover the range of possible strategies. They include (1) crushing terrorist groups unilaterally, (2) crushing terrorist groups multilaterally, (3) containment, (4) defense, (5) diversion, (6) delegitimation, and (7) transforming terrorist breeding grounds. Obviously, we should carefully consider strategies, and we should select the strategies that produce the optimum outcomes for a given situation.

Crushing Terrorist Groups Unilaterally

The instinct of the United States is to attack and **crush terrorist groups unilaterally**, which means that one country or group battles a terrorist group by itself and destroys it. After the 9/11 attacks, the United States sent armed forces into Afghanistan and later into Iraq. Initially, the U.S. strategy was to take out the al Qaeda and Taliban fighters—a strategy that was supported by a large number of politicians and citizens. This strategy results in high body counts and much destruction. The idea is that if you annihilate the enemy, his will to fight will be diminished.

Several examples of crushing terrorists' strategies are available. Since 1983, the Tamil Liberation Tigers of Sri Lanka fought the government to create their own independent state on the island. The insurrection claimed tens of thousands of lives over the years. In 2002, a peace was brokered, but shortly thereafter the conflict began again in earnest. In 2009, the government applied maximum military force including large-scale attacks on rebel strongholds to root out the separatists (CIA, 2009). Fighting resulted in large numbers of casualties and the displacement of thousands of citizens. The government was able to defeat the rebels in the end, however.

Similarly, in 2006, Israeli troops invaded Lebanon with the intent of destroying Hezbollah military positions. The fighting killed well over 1,000 people and as many as 1 million people were displaced during the fighting. After over a month of fighting, the Israelis withdrew. Although the Israeli army inflicted substantial damage to Hezbollah positions, it had little effect on its operations in Lebanon. Similarly, the Israelis launched an attack on Hamas in the Gaza Strip in 2009. Hamas had fired hundreds of rockets from Gaza into Israel, and the invasion was intended to destroy Hamas's military capability. The attack resulted in several thousand Palestinian casualties, but in the end, it did not eliminate Hamas's capability to conduct terrorist attacks on Israel. Therefore, it is questionable if this strategy is effective.

Crushing Terrorist Groups Multilaterally

The **crushing terrorist groups multilaterally** strategy is similar to the previous strategy, but it includes efforts to solicit political and military support from other countries. The intent is to crush the terrorist group, but it involves a shared effort. For example, when the United States invaded Afghanistan after the 9/11 attacks and Iraq shortly thereafter, the United States attempted to build a coalition of countries. Multilaterally attacking a terrorist group has a number of advantages. First, it allows for sharing of the military operations. For example, the presence of a multinational force in Afghanistan and Iraq allowed the United States to send fewer troops to those countries. Second, it results in the sharing of expenses. Wars and conflicts are expensive. The involvement of several countries spreads the expense across several countries, thus reducing the expenses for a given country. Third, it provides a strategic advantage. When multiple countries are involved, facilities, ports, bases, intelligence services, and so on can be shared, providing substantial strategic flexibility. Finally, when several countries are involved in a conflict, it is much easier to sway world public opinion.

Containment

Containment is an alternative whereby nations do not attempt to defeat a particular terrorist group, but the idea is to restrict its movements and operations to confined areas. Here, antiterrorist forces concentrate on terrorist activities occurring outside their domain of control. For example, for years Philippine authorities have been fighting the Abu Sayyaf, an Islamic group fighting for an independent province in the Philippines. For the most part, the government contained them to the southern portion of the country. Government countermeasures focus primarily on the perimeter, thus to some extent controlling the terrorist activities. Israel uses the containment strategy to control Hamas, which is located in the Gaza Strip.

Byman (2009) notes that this was the American strategy for decades. It is impossible to find every terrorist, making crushing a particular group difficult. On the other hand, efforts can be made to limit its operations, and these efforts often result in positive outcomes. Containment is a much less expensive alternative to attempting to crush or destroy a terrorist group in that it requires fewer resources. Containment also results in fewer political and public relations problems since the antiterrorist forces focus on safeguarding and helping potential victims. Containment also results in terrorist organization stagnation—limiting their ability and successes—which can over time negatively affect recruitment, resources, and ability to operate. For example, since the 9/11 attacks, only a handful of Americans have been killed by al Qaeda outside Iraq and Afghanistan. The United States and other countries have been successful in destroying and containing many of its operations by killing its leaders and attacking cells of al Qaeda operatives.

Defense

The first three alternatives discussed here are offensive in nature. In some cases, strong **defensive actions** have a significant impact on terrorist groups. In other words, if they are not able to wage successful attacks against their enemies, they become impotent or appear to be so, which makes it more difficult to recruit new fighters and raise money. A prime example of a defensive strategy is Israel's security barrier. The barrier separates most of the West Bank from Israel. After construction of the barrier, the number of suicide bombings in Israel diminished significantly. In Chapter 3, we discussed critical infrastructure protection, a primary initiative in homeland security. The primary purpose of critical infrastructure protection is to prevent terrorist attacks or make them much more difficult.

A primary problem with defense, as discussed in Chapter 3, is that it is difficult to identify what must be defended or protected. The United States literally has thousands of potential targets of varying value to the American public and to potential terrorists. It is questionable if homeland security experts have adequately identified or even made decisions about protection priorities. Even when protection measures are implemented, they may result only in displacement, whereby terrorists select new tactics or targets. Effective defense is questionable and perhaps elusive.

Diversion

Diversion is a process whereby a victim or potential victim of terrorists attempts to divert terrorists' attention to another terrorist target or victim. It is somewhat of a "bait and switch" tactic. Byman (2009) noted that this is a fairly common tactic. For example, the United States criticized Russia for its handling of rebel groups in Chechnya. This criticism, at least to some extent, diverted terrorists' attention from the United States. Pakistan for decades used the Kashmir dispute with India to channel Pakistani terrorists' actions. In the 1980s, a number of Middle Eastern countries sent their radicals or jihadists to Afghanistan to fight the Russians, thus relieving pressure in their own countries. The United States repeatedly speaks of human rights in a number of countries. The motivation of such statements comes into question. Are the statements a genuine effort to improve conditions in a targeted country, or are they more useful in helping focus terrorists' attention on a target other than the United States? Many terrorists and jihadists have come to despise the repressive governments of their own countries. When taken too far, a diversion policy likely will anger the government that is the target of the diversion. In some cases, it may result in the fall of a government that is friendly with the United States and its replacement with one that facilitates terrorism against our country.

Delegitimation

A long-range strategy for dealing with a terrorist group is **delegitimation**. In this case, the government attacks the terrorist group along a number of fronts in an effort to cause citizens and potential supporters to question the group's motives, tactics, and ability to genuinely improve people's life conditions. In many cases, the government will employ moderate clerics, preachers, political leaders, media, and other groups to condemn the terrorists and their activities. The government will highlight its own programs and efforts that appeal to the citizenry. Of particular importance is the government's ability to highlight the innocent citizens who are the casualties of terrorist attacks. For example, after attacks in the kingdom in 2003, Saudi Arabia began to portray the gruesome impact of the attacks in the media. It damaged the credibility of the terrorists and lessened support for them (Byman, 2009). America and its allies have demonized ISIS as a result of their killing thousands of Muslims in an effort to reduce support. Of course, it should be realized that the terrorists are engaged in a similar campaign, using every opportunity to criticize their enemy and delegitimize it. For example, terrorist groups across the globe used the photos and American actions at the Abu Ghraib prison in Iraq to incite support and anti-Americanism. The Taliban in Pakistan and Afghanistan blame numerous civilian casualties on the United States in an effort to delegitimize America and the Pakistani and Afghan governments. In the end, the government or enemy must be able to show that it offers a better life and more opportunities as compared to the terrorist group. It becomes a battle for minds and hearts.

Transforming Terrorist Breeding Grounds

Transforming terrorist breeding grounds is a strategy that is similar to delegitimation except that it is more long term and comprehensive in nature. An examination of terrorist groups and organizations shows that they predominately, but not always, exist in countries or areas that are poor and repressed. For example, France, Belgium, and England have had Islamic terrorist problems, and these problems to some extent have been the result of these groups not being able to assimilate into the middle classes in those countries. Nevertheless, today most terrorist groups are located in third-world countries or areas where social and economic problems are endemic. The terrorists and those who affiliate with them often perceive that they have no choice but to wage war with those who oppress them.

As Gurr (1990) noted, democratic reforms can substantially reduce the support for terrorists and win over those who otherwise might be recruited by them. Inclusion is a far better tactic than exclusion. Li (2005) found that democratic reform tended to reduce the incidence of terrorist events, whereas government constraints tended to increase them. The RAND Corporation (Jones and Libicki, 2008) examined 648 terrorist groups between 1968 and 2006 and found that only 7 percent of the terrorist campaigns ended as a result of military force, whereas 43 percent of them ended as result of political transition. Political, social, and economic reform can be effective countermeasures to terrorism.

It must be remembered that the transformation of a terrorist breeding ground is difficult, wrought with pitfalls, and expensive. To transform an area, political institutions, economies, and social systems must be addressed successfully. Politically, those who are disenfranchised must become part of the government structure and their grievances must be addressed. The oppressed must be provided economic opportunities. Too often the economic and political elite within a country see any social or economic changes as threatening their way of life, particularly their relative power and wealth. They tend to fight such reforms even though the reforms likely will create a safer and more peaceful environment. Nonetheless, systemic changes in some cases are the only way to deal with growing terrorism problems.

Transformation is a lesson that has been learned well by numerous terrorist organizations. For example, Hamas and Hezbollah, although labeled terrorist organizations, have considerable influence not only because of their military capabilities but also because both of these organizations conduct considerable charitable campaigns. Many Arab and Muslim countries do not possess social safety nets for their citizens. Organizations such as Hamas and Hezbollah, however, fill these gaps in places such as Lebanon and Palestine. For example, after the 2006 Israeli invasion of Lebanon, Hezbollah immediately assisted the populace in rebuilding destroyed portions of the country. Hezbollah was more effective than the Lebanese government in providing assistance to the Lebanese people. Helping citizens has a lasting impact, and it produces long-lasting loyalty. The terrorists have been successful in a number of areas in transforming citizens to support the terrorists and their objectives.

There are several alternative strategies by which to combat terrorism. Selection of a strategy must be based on the nature of the problem and intervention capabilities. Obviously, those strategies that assist people in affected areas tend to have the greatest potential for success.

HS ANALYSIS BOX 5-3

As discussed earlier, several strategies can be used to defeat terrorists. Which of the strategies presented do you think would be most effective in dealing with the Taliban in Afghanistan and Pakistan? Which strategy do you believe would be the most ineffective? Why?

Female PKK Kurdish fighters drill in Iraqi Kurdistan.
Eddie Gerald/Alamy Stock Photo.

▶ Women Terrorists

Women terrorists are not a new phenomenon. Women were substantially involved in right-wing and left-wing terrorist organizations throughout the latter part of the last century (Herschinger, 2014) and remain so today. Indeed, the large number of women terrorists involved in the Chechen conflicts, especially as suicide bombers, resulted in them being termed "Black Widows." It should not be surprising that women act as terrorists. They often become involved in armed conflicts or uprisings, and many countries now have women serving in the military. Historically, women were viewed as victims and little consideration was given to their involvement in terrorist activities. Over the past several decades, there has been a general recognition of their perpetrator roles, resulting in the need to examine women terrorists more closely.

Women within the context of terrorism have two primary roles. First, they support the male fighters. Terrorist organizations often have access to a number of women who have family members who are part of the terrorist group. In other cases, women are somehow recruited into the group. Therefore, terrorism is closely aligned with the trafficking of women. These two venal activities go hand-in-hand within the terrorist community. Once recruited, females often become enslaved objects. The acquisition of females by terrorist organizations through either volunteering or kidnapping facilitates the recruitment and retention of male foreign fighters. Moreover, women can serve as a reward structure for these fighters when they are successful in battle. Many of the fighters have experienced deficient social reward systems and the provision of women especially as sex objects provides a strong, pervasive reward system. In some cases, the women are sold or traded to increase the wealth of the terrorist group. Binetti (2015) has referred to this process as the three Rs: recruit, reward, and retain.

A number of these trafficked females come from the West. Berlinger (2015) estimated that over 3,400 foreign fighters from the West have joined ISIS in Iraq and Syria. Hoyle, Bradford, and Frenett (2015) estimated that as many as 550 of these fighters or terrorist participants are women. Binetti (2015) discussed how ISIS and other terrorist groups use the Internet and social media to recruit women. She advised that they use the process of grooming, a process that is also used by pedophiles to recruit victims. The girls are befriended online. Ultimately they are told that they are loved. They are praised and flattered, which often occurs in secretive chat rooms. These girls often fantasize that they are going to be with men who love them. They are told they have a higher purpose in life. This process is especially powerful with young girls with low esteem and who have experienced conflict with their parents or peers. Once they travel to meet their terrorist recruiters, they find an alternative reality. They may be forced to marry a jihadist fighter. Many are gang raped or traded among multiple men. When not fulfilling their sexual roles, they are made to care for the various fighters.

A second role for women is that of suicide bomber. Women are increasingly used as suicide bombers. Here, women can be motivated in several ways. First, they may have a religious motivation. They see martyrdom as a way to reach paradise in the afterlife. They also see it as resulting in Allah protecting their families. Second, they may be motivated by political beliefs. They perceive that they are being oppressed by the West or a political despot. A suicide bombing can constitute part of the fight for freedom (Kruglanski et al., 2009). A third motivation is the quest for personal significance. Many women, depending on their country of residence, tend to be treated and viewed as second-class citizens. Over time this can result in strain to the point that the woman seeks escape and recognition within the larger community. Thus, the motivation to become a suicide bomber can come from a variety of sources.

Terrorists have found that women suicide bombers are advantageous. Cunningham (2003) noted that they represent a low investment on the part of the terrorist group because many women volunteer for the assignment. Second, since women generally are viewed as nonviolent, they raise little suspicion on the part of their targets, helping ensure success. Finally, women suicide bombers result in a psychological effect. Since women are seen as being more peaceful, their acts are more shocking to the victims. O'Rourke (2009) studied suicide bombings and found that women bombers often killed larger numbers of victims.

Summary

This chapter examined the political and social foundations for terrorism. When examining homeland security, it is important to have an understanding of the primary threat to the homeland—terrorist acts committed against and in the United States. As noted, terrorism is not the only threat or problem that is subsumed within homeland security—for example, natural disasters, pandemic flu outbreaks, and other catastrophes—but it is without question the most threatening, given the possibility that terrorists will use some form of weapons of mass destruction when attacking America. In essence, homeland security necessitates that we prepare for all sorts of major problems.

Regarding terrorism, we noted that it is difficult to define it. Definitions abound; even different departments and agencies within the federal government have different definitions. What makes it difficult to define is that it is embodied in politics or perspective. For example, one person's terrorist is another person's freedom fighter. To some extent, terrorism can be viewed as the commission of crime, usually a horrific crime, to achieve political, social, or religious objectives as opposed to having a financial motive. Moreover, the majority of victims of terrorism are innocents, and oftentimes, the victim count includes large numbers of women and children. It is a premeditated act that attacks legitimate governments or competing groups.

Terrorism is not a new phenomenon; it has a long history, and there have been all sorts of groups involved in terrorist activities throughout the ages. A host of causes contribute to terrorism. Today, we have a particular mix of worldwide terrorist organizations and groups, and we can identify some of the causes. These include culture, globalization, religion, the Israeli-Palestine conflict, the Russian invasion of Afghanistan, and individual social psychological factors that affect individuals' decision to become terrorists. We cannot definitively point to any single factor or root cause.

There are also different types of terrorism. These types are distinguished by motivation. Essentially, there are state-sponsored terrorism, whereby the state or state actors attempt to use terrorism against their enemies; dissent terrorism, whereby groups within a country, usually ethnocentric, are disgruntled with the political arrangements and attempt to use terrorism to change the political landscape; left-wing and right-wing terrorists, who are politically motivated to change government arrangements; religious terrorists, who attempt to change the government into a theocratic state; and finally, terrorist activities by criminal organizations attempting to affect a government in order to facilitate their criminal enterprises. These forms of terrorism crop up periodically and can be present in any country.

The U.S. Department of State and the National Counterterrorism Center attempt to monitor the levels of terrorist activities. A large portion of the terrorist acts today are committed in Iraq and Afghanistan as a result of the wars being conducted there. We are also witnessing an increase in attacks in other countries. Even though weapons of mass destruction remain a frightening consideration, most terrorist attacks are conducted using conventional weapons and explosives, and a large percentage of attacks are performed via suicide bombers.

Finally, we addressed the various strategies for countering terrorism. They range in scope from military action to humanitarian aid. Militarily, a country can attempt to use force to destroy a terrorist threat by itself or in conjunction with a consortium of allies. Rather than destroying the terrorist group or organization, which is quite difficult, a country can attempt to use various tactics to contain it. Another strategy focuses on homeland security, whereby a country attempts to protect its borders and critical infrastructure from attack. A strategy that has been used with great frequency by a variety of governments has been to divert the wrath of the terrorists toward another enemy or target, which is generally accomplished by highlighting the injustices perpetrated by other countries. **Deligitimation** is a process whereby the victims of terrorism and other countries attempt to implement programs that provide citizens with greater benefits as opposed to any provided by the terrorists. They also point out the atrocities committed by the terrorists, especially on innocent civilians. The goal is to move public opinion away from the terrorists and gain support for the government. A final strategy is transforming terrorist breeding grounds. We can identify areas that produce large numbers of terrorists. If we can improve the social and economic conditions in these areas, we likely can reduce the appeal of terrorism and reduce the number of converts.

This chapter examined the political and social aspects of terrorism. It is important to understand the dynamics of terrorism if we are to construct effective homeland security programming. It is important that homeland security is achieved by a mix of programs that addresses every aspect of threats to the homeland.

Discussion Questions

1. What is the continuum of social conflict? Provide examples of current conflicts in the world that fit each of the categories within the continuum.
2. There are numerous definitions of terrorism. What are the various elements contained in these definitions?
3. Discuss the various causes of terrorism.
4. Which countries are involved in state-sponsored terrorism? Which groups or activities do they support?
5. Discuss the types of terrorism. Which types are the greatest threat to the United States?
6. Discuss the various ways of defeating terrorism. In your opinion, which method would be most effective in defeating terrorism in the Middle East?

References

Ahmad, E. (2003). "Terrorism: Theirs and ours." *Terrorism and Counterterrorism: Understanding the New Security Environment*, ed. R. Howard and R. Sawyer, pp. 47–53. New York: McGraw-Hill.

Ahmed, A. (2007). *Journey into Islam: The Crisis of Globalization.* Washington, D.C.: Brookings Institution.

Allen, C. (2009). *God's Terrorists: The Wahhabi Cult and the Hidden Roots of Modern Jihad.* Philadelphia, PA: Da Capo Press.

Bellavita, C. (2008). "Changing homeland security: What is homeland security?" *Homeland Security Affairs*, 4(2): 1–30.

Berlinger, J. (2015). "The names: Who has been recruited to ISIS from the West." *CNN*. February 26. http://www.cnn.com/2015/02/25/world/isis-western-reecruits/ (Accessed March 24, 2016).

Binetti, A. (2015). "A new frontier: Human trafficking and ISIS's recruitment of women from the west." *Information2Action: A Publication of the Georgetown Institute for Women, Peach & Security*. Washington, D.C.: Georgetown Institute for Women, Peach & Security.

Borgeson, K., and R. Valeri. (2009). *Terrorism in America*. Sudbury, MA: Jones and Bartlett.

Burgess, M. (2003). "A brief history of terrorism." CDI: Center for Defense Information. http://www.cdi.org/friendlyversion/printversion.cfm?documentID=1502 (Accessed April 14, 2009).

Burgoon, B. (2006). "On welfare and terror: Social welfare policies and political-economic roots of terrorism." *Journal of Conflict Resolution*, 50: 176–203.

Byman, D. (2009). "US counter-terrorism options: A taxonomy." *Terrorism and Counterterrorism: Understanding the New Security Environment*, 3rd ed., ed. R. Howard, R. Sawyer, and N. Bajema, pp. 460–482. New York: McGraw-Hill.

Central Intelligence Agency. (2009). *The World Fact Book*. https://www.cia.gov/library/publications/the-world-factbook/geos/ce.html (Accessed May 14, 2009).

Cronin, A. (2004). "Behind the curve: Globalization and international terrorism." *Defeating Terrorism: Shaping the New Security Environment*, ed. R. Howard and R. Sawyer, pp. 29–50. New York: McGraw-Hill.

Cunningham, K. (2003). "Cross-regional trends in female terrorism." *Studies in Conflict & Terrorism*, 26: 171–195.

Field, A. (2009). "The 'new terrorism': Revolution or evolution." *Political Science Review*, 7(2): 195–207.

Forst, B. (2009). *Terrorism, Crime, and Public Policy*. New York: Cambridge University Press.

Gurr, T. (1990). "Terrorism in democracies: Its social and political bases." *Origins of Terrorism: Psychologies, Ideologies, Theologies, and States of Mind,* ed. W. Reich, pp. 87–98. New York: Cambridge University Press.

Hall, M., M. Bell, and B. Heath. (2009). "Shooting suspect was on anti-hate groups' radar." *USA Today*. http://www.usatoday.com/news/nation/2009-06-10-shooter_N.htm (Accessed August 18, 2009).

Herschinger, E. (2014). "Political science, terrorism and gender." *Historical Social Research*, 39: 46–66.

Hoffman, B. (1995). "Holy terror: The implications of terrorism motivated by a religious imperative." *Studies in Conflict and Terrorism*, 18(4): 271–284.

Hoffman, B. (2009a). "Defining terrorism." *Terrorism and Counterterrorism: Understanding the New Security Environment*, ed. R. Howard and R. Sawyer, pp. 4–33. New York: McGraw-Hill.

Hoffman Martin, B. (2006). *Inside Terrorism*. New York: Columbia University Press.

Hoyle, C., A. Bradford, and R. Frenett. (2015) *Becoming Mulan? Female Western Migrants to ISIS*. London: Institute for Strategic Dialogue. www.strategicdialogue.org/ISDJ2969_Becoming_Mulan_01.15_WEB.PDF (Accessed March 24, 2016).

Horwitz, T. (2012). *Midnight Rising: John Brown and the Raid that Sparked the Civil War.* New York: Henry Holt and Company.

Hubac-Occhipinti, O. (2007). "Anarchist terrorists of the nineteenth century." *The History of Terrorism: From Antiquity to Al Qaeda*, ed. G. Chaliand and A. Blin, pp. 113–131. Berkeley, CA: University of California Press.

Jones, S., and M. Libicki. (2008). *How Terrorist Groups End: Lessons for Countering of Qa'ida*. Santa Monica, CA: RAND.

Kay, S. (2004). "Globalization, power, and security." *Security Dialogue*, 35(1): 9–25.

Kruglanski, A., X. Chen, M. Dechesne, S. Fishman, and E. Oreheck (2009). "Fully committed: Suicide bombers' motivation and quest for personal significance." *Political Psychology*, 30: 331–357.

Laqueur, W. (1996). "Postmodern terrorism." *Foreign Affairs*, 75(5): 24–36.

Li, Q. (2005). "Does democracy promote or reduce transnational terrorism incidents?" *Journal of Conflict Resolution*, 49(2): 278–297.

Long, D. (1990). *The Anatomy of Terrorism*. New York: Free Press.

Martin, G. (2003). *Understanding Terrorism: Challenges, Perspectives, and Issues*. Thousand Oaks, CA: Sage.

Nassar, J. (2005). *Globalization & Terrorism: The Migration of Dreams and Nightmares*. New York: Rowman & Littlefield.

O'Rourke, L. (2009). "What's special about female suicide terrorists?" *Security Studies*, 18: 681–718.

Pillar, P. (2003). "The dimensions of terrorism and counterterrorism." *Terrorism and Counterterrorism: Understanding the New Security Environment*, ed. R. Howard and R. Sawyer, pp. 24–46. New York: McGraw-Hill.

Plummer, C. (2012). "Failed states and connections to terrorist activity. *International Criminal Justice Review*, 22: 416–449.

Rand. (2017). *The Islamic State (Terrorist Organization)*. https://www.rand.org/topics/the-islamic-state-terrorist-organization.html.

Roig-Franzia, M. (2004). "A terrorist in the house." *Washington Post Magazine*. February 22: W12.

Schneider, F., T. Bruck, and D. Meierrieks. (2010). The economics of terrorism and counter-terrorism: A survey (CESIFO Working Paper No. 3011). http://papers.ssrn.com/sol3/papers.cfm?abstract_id¼1590148 (Accessed 12, 2010).

Stanislawski, B. H. (2008). Para-States, Quasi-States, and Black Spots: Perhaps not states, but not "ungoverned territory," either. *International Studies Review*, 10(2): 366-396.

Ternon, Y. (2007). Russian Terrorism, 1878–1908. G. Challand & A. Blin (eds.) *The History of Terrorism: From Antiquity to Al Qaeda*, Berkley, CA. University of California Press. 147–150.

Trelease, A. (1995). *White Terror: The Ku Klux Klan Conspiracy and Southern Reconstruction.* Baton Rouge, LA: LSU Press.

U.S. Department of State. (2016). *State Sponsors of Terrorism.* http://www.state.gov/j/ct/list/c14151.htm (Accessed April 12, 2017)

Venkatraman, A. (2007). "Religious basis for Islamic terrorism: The Quran and its interpretations." *Studies in Conflict & Terrorism*, 30: 229–248.

Walker, I. (2010). *Tea Party*. Boston, MA: ABDP Publishing.

Whittacker, D. (2001). *The Terrorism Reader*. London: Routledge.

6 The Nature and Geography of Terrorist Groups, State Sponsors of Terror, and Safe Havens

LEARNING OBJECTIVES

1. *Describe the various terrorist groups in the world.*
2. *Identify the most dangerous terrorist groups.*
3. *Describe the terrorist groups operating in the United States.*
4. *Explain the radicalization process.*

Key Terms

Hamas
ISIS of the Sinai Province
Hezbollah
Muslim Brotherhood
Islamic State of the Levant
Kurdistan Workers' Party
Al Qaeda
Al Qaeda in Iraq
Islamic Courts Union
Haqqani Network
Boko Haram
Al-Shabaab
Al Qaeda in the Islamic Maghreb
Pakistani Taliban
Lashkar-e-Tayyiba
Taliban
Abu Sayyaf Group
National Liberation Army
Revolutionary Armed Forces of Columbia
Shining Path
Political extremism
Single-issue terrorism
Lone wolf
Radicalization
Radicalization process
Earth Liberation Front
Animal Liberation Front

Introduction

As with the very definition of terrorism, foreign terrorist groups, the state sponsors of terror, and safe havens are all phrases fraught with conceptual difficulty (LaFree and Dugan, 2009; Symeonidou-Kastanidou, 2004). Whether a group of individuals is seen as a terrorist organization, an extremist group, or a band of radical freedom fighters is often a matter of perception and ideology. Although it may be trite to say, what one person may see as a terrorist organization, others may see as a group of freedom fighters, protectors, or guerilla resistors. One way of determining the status of a group is to look at a country's designation of the group. Several countries, including the United States, can formally designate a group a "foreign terrorist organization."

Likewise, nation states have the ability to designate other countries as "state sponsors of terror" and consider regions of the world as safe haven for terrorism. Although these designations provide some clarity in determining the differences among groups that are considered terrorist organizations, nations do not always agree on which groups they view as terrorists. In this chapter, we discuss the nature of terrorist groups, describing many of these groups, their principal mission, and their location of operation. We consider only the major and most active groups that are generally seen by Western governments as terrorist organizations. Many organizations designated by various governments as terrorist groups go under various names that often differ by the country describing them as well as by the groups themselves. Many of these groups merge over time with other groups, abandon their struggle, or become inactive for a variety of reasons. Figure 6-1 ■ shows the various organizations that have been designated as terrorist by the governments of the United States, the European Union, Australia, and Canada.

Abdallah Azzam Brigades (AAB)
Abu Nidal Organization (ANO)
Abu Sayyaf Group (ASG)
Al-Aqsa Martyrs Brigade (AAMB)
Ansar al-Dine (AAD)
Ansar al-Islam (AAI)
Ansar al-Shari'a in Benghazi (AAS-B)
Ansar al-Shari'a in Darnah (AAS-D)
Ansar al-Shari'a in Tunisia (AAS-T)
Army of Islam (AOI)
Asbat al-Ansar (AAA)
Aum Shinrikyo (AUM)
Basque Fatherland and Liberty (ETA)
Boko Haram (BH)
Communist Party of Philippines/New People's Army (CPP/NPA)
Continuity Irish Republican Army (CIRA)
Gama'a al-Islamiyya (IC)
Hamas
Haqqani Network (HQN)
Harakat ul-Jihad-i-Islami (HUJI)
Harakat ul-Jihad-i-Islami/Bangladesh (HUJI-B)
Harakat ul-Mujahideen (HUM)
Hizballah
Indian Mujahedeen (IM)
Islamic Jihad Union (IJU)

FIGURE 6-1 *(Continued)*

Islamic Movement of Uzbekistan (IMU)
Islamic State of Iraq and the Levant (ISIL)
ISIL Sinai Province (ISIL-SP)
Jama'atu Ansarul Muslimina Fi Biladis-Sudan (Ansaru)
Jaish-e-Mohammed (JEM)
Jaysh Rijal Al-Tariq Al-Naqshabandi (JRTN)
Jemaah Ansharut Tauhid (JAT)
Jemaah Islamiya (JI)
Jundallah
Kahane Chai
Kata'ib Hizballah (KH)
Kurdistan Workers' Party (PKK)
Lashkar e-Tayyiba (LeT)
Lashkar i Jhangvi (LJ)
Liberation Tigers of Tamil Eelam (LTTE)
Mujahidin Shura Council in the Environs ofJerusalem (MSC)
Al-Mulathamun Battalion (AMB)
National Liberation Army (ELN)
Al-Nusrah Front (ANF)
Palestine Islamic Jihad (PIJ)
Palestine Liberation Front—Abu Abbas Faction (PLF)
Popular Front for the Liberation of Palestine (PFLP)
Popular Front for the Liberation of Palestine-General Command (PFLP-GC)
Al-Qa'ida (AQ)
Al-Qa'ida in the Arabian Peninsula (AQAP)
Al-Qa'ida in the Islamic Maghreb (AQIM)
Real IRA (RIRA)
Revolutionary Armed Forces of Colombia (FARC)
Revolutionary People's Liberation Party/Front (DHKP/C)
Revolutionary Struggle (RS)
Al-Shabaab (AS)
Shining Path (SL)
Tehrik-e Taliban Pakistan (TTP)

FIGURE 6-1 U.S. Government-Designated Foreign Terrorist Organizations
Source: U.S. Department of State (2016). *Country Reports on Terrorism, 2015.* Washington, D.C.: Author.

There are a number of active terrorist organizations around the globe. In 2015, there were a reported 11,774 terrorist attacks worldwide resulting in 28,328 deaths (Jones, 2016). The National Consortium for the Study of Terrorism and Responses to Terrorism (START) located at the University of Maryland maintains a database of terrorist groups and attacks. There have been more than 600 groups engaged in terrorism since 1998, with more than 21,000 terrorist attacks (see Zenko, 2012). START tracked terrorist attacks in 2011 and ranked the groups with the most attacks.

HS ANALYSIS BOX 6-1

Based on the above information, there are dozens of terrorist groups in the world. As a consumer of international news and information, which ones have you heard about? Which ones do you think are the most dangerous?

The top 10 groups were:

Group	Attacks
Communist Party of India-Maoists	371
Taliban	254
Al-Shabaab	163
Boko Haram	124
Fuerzas Armadas Revolucionarias de Colombia (FARC)	83
Tehrik-i-Taliban Pakistan	80
Al Qaeda in the Arabian Peninsula	75
New People's Army	48
Kurdistan Workers' Party (PKK)	35
Baloch Republican Army	22

Interestingly, although the Taliban and al Qaeda receive the most government and media coverage, they are ranked second and seventh in terms of the number of terrorist attacks, and a communist terrorist group in India was responsible for the most attacks. The START data demonstrate that there are a variety of groups with different motives involved in terrorism.

In the first section of the chapter, we attempt to familiarize the reader with some of the basic information about prominent terrorist groups by their geographic area of operation. We then turn our attention to states that have been designated by the U.S. government as "state sponsors of terror." Following a discussion of these states and the problems associated with making this designation, we explore the concept of terrorist safe havens, looking at parts of the world that are said to be inviting for terrorism or extremist activities. Finally, we examine terrorism in the United States.

▶ Foreign Terrorist Organizations

Although terrorist groups exist throughout the world, a large number are located in the Middle East. This area has the highest concentration of groups and state sponsors of terror. Recently, these groups have become the most problematic and most active as a result of their attacks and violence. This section examines some of these terrorist organizations.

Middle East and North Africa Groups

Several groups are located in the Middle East and North Africa residing in various countries.

There are several causes for this concentration of terrorist groups in the region. First, there are a number of countries such as Syria, Libya, Yemen, and Somalia where the governments have collapsed (failed states). Second, there are areas in countries with stable governments that have large areas that are ungoverned, including Egypt, Pakistan, Mali, Afghanistan, Iraq, and South Sudan (black holes). Finally, the conflict between Sunni and

Shite Muslims pitting Saudi Arabia and Iran and their various allies against each other has contributed to terrorism. Religion is the rationale many of these terrorist groups use to justify their radicalism, but simply, their actions violate the tenants of Islam as spelled out in the Koran. Control, power, and money play a key role in many of the conflicts and terrorist actions. Here, we examine the most notable groups.

Israel, the West Bank and Gaza, and Jerusalem

Israel and the Palestine territories are one of the epicenters of conflict in the Middle East, and this has contributed to the creation of a number of terrorist groups that operate in the area. Hamas is a Sunni group that operates in the Gaza Strip. In 2006, Hamas won the legislative elections and installed a government in Gaza. Hamas has launched numerous rocket attacks against Israel, which resulted in the Israeli military conducting major offensives causing large numbers of deaths and destruction. For example, in 2008, Hamas fought a 28-day war with Israel in an effort to stop an international blockade of Gaza (State Department, 2009). Hamas has two wings. A military wing that coordinates attacks on Israel and a political wing that provides social services to the people of Gaza. Hamas continues to build a terrorist infrastructure in the West Bank (U.S. State Department, 2016).

Islamic State-Sinai Province (ISIL-SP), which is affiliated with ISIS, is located in the Golan Heights and has conducted attacks on Israel. The Yamouk Martys Brigade, another terrorist group located in the Gaza Strip, has launched numerous rocket attacks on Israel. The Palestinian Islamic Jihad is located in the Gaza Strip and the West Bank and continues to battle the Israelis. Hezbollah located in Lebanon on occasion has launched full-scale attacks resulting in the Israeli military entering Lebanon to battle the group. Most of the attacks on Israel have been rocket attacks, but recently there has been an increase in lone wolf attacks where the attackers used knifes and other similar weapons to attack individuals or small groups in Israel.

HS Web Link: To learn more about the various terrorist groups, go to https://www.state.gov/j/ct/rls/crt/.

Egypt

Ansar Beit al-Maqdis is one of Egypt's most violent groups and has pledged allegiance to ISIS. It operates in the Sinai where the Egyptian government has little control. It has conducted numerous armed attacks on Egyptian police, military, and civilians. In one attack in 2014, the group killed 31 Egyptian soldiers. The group also uses drive-by

ISIS threatens to behead two Japanese captives.
Handout/Alamy Stock Photo.

shootings and roadside bombs. The group has also blown up gas lines in Sinai that deliver gas to Israel. The Egyptian government has not been able to exert control over the group or the Sinai region.

Al Jihad is also known as the Egyptian Islamic Jihad and was founded in the 1970s in Egypt. The organization is a splitter group of the Muslim Brotherhood and seeks to convert the state of Egypt into an Islamic nation. Al Jihad merged with al Qaeda in 2001. The group has attacked both U.S. and Israeli interests and is responsible for the 1981 assassination of Egyptian President Anwar Sadat. The group was also responsible for the Egyptian Embassy bombing in Islamabad in 1995 and a disrupted plot against the U.S. Embassy in Albania in 1998. The group has not committed independent acts of terrorism since its merger with al Qaeda in 2001 (U.S. State Department, 2009).

The **Muslim Brotherhood** has a significant following in Egypt and is politically active, attracting large numbers of Egyptians. Its goal is to overthrow the authoritarian Egyptian government. Egyptian presidents have jailed thousands of members of the Muslim Brotherhood because of their political activities. In 2011, Hosni Mubarak resigned as president, and in 2012, Mohamed Morsi was elected president. Morsi was a member and supporter of the Muslim Brotherhood. He was deposed a year later by the military and Abdel Fattah e-Sisi was installed as president. Sisi immediately outlawed the brotherhood, jailing many of its members. The group is active in several of the Gulf States.

Today, the most potent terrorist group in Egypt is the Sanai Province located primarily in the Sinai Peninsula, which is affiliated with ISIS. In one month, the group launched 130 attacks primarily against the military and police officials. These attacks have resulted in hundreds of deaths. The group attempted to seize a part of the Sinai Peninsula. The group is problematic since the area is sparsely populated and there is support for the group and few Egyptian military and police are stationed in the area. It is also problematic since oil pipelines that provide fuel to Israel run through the area (Malsin, 2015).

Iraq

The **Islamic State of the Levant** or ISIS has been the dominant terrorist group in Iraq. ISIS began in Syria and then took over a large part of Iraq with the intention of creating an Islamic state. By 2017, Iraqi and coalition troops had retaken most of the territory back with the intention of totally defeating ISIS. Additionally, Hezbollah and Iran sent fighters to help defeat ISIS. ISIS was able to gain substantial ground in Iraq because the Iraqi government was dominated by Shiites and had oppressed the Sunni minority. Many Sunni warlords and tribes jointed ISIS as well as many former military leaders from Saddam Hussein's government. ISIS has been brutal, killing large numbers of civilians, police officers, and military personnel. The group attracted large numbers of foreign fighters even from Western Europe and the United States and was able to finance their operations from captured oil fields, extortion, and kidnapping. The group also had substantial military armaments that were captured from the Iraqi military. ISIS was able to recruit a number of Sunni warlords and their fighters, but their brutality resulted in other warlords aligning with the Iraqi government. It was not until the Iraqi army became more organized that progress was made in defeating the group. In December 2017, the Iraqi Prime Minister Haider al-Abadi announced that ISIS has been defeated and the war is over.

Turkey

Turkey bordering Syria, Iraq, and Iran, has aligned itself against Syria's president Bashar al-Assad, and has supported rebels who have been fighting to defeat him. At the same time, Turkey has been fighting ISIS, which has conducted attacks on Turkey's southern border. In some cases, Turkey sent troops into its Syrian border region to attack ISIS and prevent the group from targeting Turkish cities. These skirmishes have been minor compared to the military operations in Iraq.

In the recent past, the Kurdistan Workers' Party (PKK), a Turkish political party that was founded in 1974, has increased its terrorist activities. An estimated 12 million Kurds live in Turkey. The primary goal of the group is the establishment of an independent Kurdish state in southeast Turkey and northern Iraq and to fight the Turkish government to establish an autonomous region within Turkey. Since 1984, it is estimated that the group has killed at least 37,000 people (Spindlove and Simonsen, 2010). The PKK raises large amounts of money through the heroin trade. It transports heroin from Afghanistan and Turkey to other countries.

Most recently, however, the Kurds have concentrated on fighting ISIS, and the Kurds have been America's most reliable ally in the fight against ISIS. This has been problematic for the United States since Turkey and Iraq see the Kurds as a threat because the group wants to establish its own country on Turkish and Iraqi soil. The dynamics will certainly change once ISIS is defeated as neither Turkey nor Iraq want to give up control of their lands.

Lebanon

Lebanon has a fractured central government with a large number of minority groups residing in the country. Syria has a strong influence in the country and frequently attempts to control the country's politics, and terrorist groups operating in Syria often commit terrorist attacks in Lebanon. There are several terrorist groups located in Lebanon such as Hamas, the Popular Front for the Liberation of Palestine, Asbal al-Ansar, Palestinian Islamic Jihad, and several other groups. However, the dominant terrorist group is Hezbollah or the "Party of God." Hezbollah is a radical Islamic organization that was formed in 1982, as a result of the Israeli invasion of Lebanon. It takes its ideological inspiration from the Iranian revolution and the teachings of the late Ayatollah Khomeini (U.S. State Department, 2009). The group seeks to eradicate Western influence in Lebanon and the Middle East and is dedicated to the destruction of the State of Israel, resistance to Israeli occupation of Palestine, and the liberation of the Palestinian people. The U.S. State Department advises that the group is the most sophisticated in providing television shows and distributing content via the Internet. It has strong influence on Lebanon's Shiite community as a result of its

Bin Jbell, Southern Lebanon after fighting between Hezbollah and Israel.
Alan Gignoux/Alamy Stock Photo.

connections to Iran. The Lebanese government as well as many others in the Arab world recognize Hezbollah as a legitimate "resistance group" and political party. Hezbollah plays a key role in the Lebanese government.

The group has been active in Europe, North and South America, and Africa and has been involved in numerous anti-U.S. and anti-Israeli terrorist attacks. Prior to September 11, 2001, it was responsible for more American deaths than any other terrorist group (U.S. State Department, 2009). The Council of Foreign Relations (2009) notes that the group's most significant terrorist activities included the 1983 suicide truck bombing of marines in Lebanon that killed more than 200 people, the 1992 bombing of the Israeli Embassy in Argentina, and a 2006 raid into Israel during which the group kidnapped two Israeli soldiers.

Today, Hezbollah has sent a large number of fighters to Syria in support of President Bashar al-Assad and to fight ISIS.

Syria

Syria is engaged in a civil war that has been raging since 2011. It has resulted in the displacement of millions of Syrians and about 220,000 people have been killed (Gilsinan, 2015). The conflict is the result of Sunnis attempting to remove the Assad government, which is pro-Shiite. The civil war left a vacuum, allowing ISIS to form and control parts of Syria and invade parts of Iraq. Iraqi forces defeated ISIS in 2017, and continued into Syria in an effort to completely dismantle the organization by attacking its capitol in Raqqa. A number of terrorist groups have been affiliated with Syria in the past, but the civil war has placed the focus on ISIS and the rebels fighting the Assad regime.

Osama bin Laden, founder of al Qaeda, was killed by Navy Seal Team Six in 2011.
FBI Headquarters.

International

Al Qeada, "the Base," is a network of Sunni extremist groups that was founded in 1988 by Osama bin Laden. Originally, the group was made up of members who fought in Afghanistan against the Soviet Union. The organization was based primarily in Afghanistan and Pakistan and had close working relationships with the Taliban, who provided protection and sanctuary. After the American invasion of Afghanistan, al Qaeda moved its operations into the Taliban region of Pakistan. **Al Qaeda** acts as an organizer of associated groups that operate in the Middle East, Africa, and Central Asia. The group's primary mission is the overthrow of secular governments in Islamic countries and the eradication of Western influences in Islamic states.

Al Qaeda has widespread appeal. Whereas many terrorist groups justify their terrorist acts and angst on a particular group, government, country, or condition, al Qaeda focuses on creating a theocracy. Its members believe that government should emanate from God, not man. The Koran provides dictates for a theocracy and thus undermines democracies and other forms of government. As such, it is able to appeal to all Muslims to some degree, and given the economic, social, and political conditions in many Muslim countries, it becomes very attractive.

Al Qaeda remains a threat to the United States and is committed to attacking American interests across the globe. It is believed to focus its planning on targets that would produce mass casualties, dramatic destruction, and economic problems (U.S. State Department, 2009). The group is responsible for suicide attacks, bombings, kidnappings, and hijackings. The networks or their associates were responsible for the bombings of U.S. embassies, the bombing of the USS *Cole*, and the 9/11 attacks on the World Trade Center and the Pentagon. The United States has stepped up its operations in Afghanistan and the Pakistani government has taken a more active role in combating al Qaeda and the Taliban. There also has been an increase in al Qaeda activity in Yemen as a result of instability in the country.

During much of the war in Iraq, **al Qaeda in Iraq** (AQI) was active. It was composed of Sunni Arabs who lost control of the country after the American invasion. It primarily attacked Shiites and coalition forces using guerilla tactics such as car bombs, suicide bombings, and roadside explosives. In 2006, Abu Musab al Zarqawi, the group's leader, was killed after American warplanes dropped a 500-pound bomb on the house where he was meeting with other insurgents (Knickmeyer and Finer, 2006). The death of al Zarqawi proved to be a major setback for the group. According to the U.S. State Department (2009), by 2008, much of AQI had been neutralized by coalition and Iraqi forces. Nonetheless, AQI continues to have a presence and continues its attacks and may become more active again in the future.

The central command of al Qaeda has been decimated as a result of coalition ground activities in Iraq and Afghanistan, drone attacks on al Qaeda leadership in Pakistan, and enhanced and multination cooperative intelligence operations across the world. Osama bin Laden founded al Qaeda and controlled its terrorist activities. In 2011, navy seals entered bin Laden's compound in Abbottabad, Pakistan, and killed him. These activities have resulted in a decentralized structure consisting of cells located throughout the world. Today, al Qaeda remains a problem, but it cannot mount actions similar to the 9/11 attacks. Nonetheless, there are several affiliated groups that continue to support al Qaeda, including al Qaeda in the Arabian Peninsula (primarily in Yemen), al Qaeda in the Islamic Maghreb (primarily in North Africa), al-Shabab (primarily in Somalia), and al-Nusra Front (primarily in Syria). Although these groups are affiliated with al Qaeda, they operate independently and the affiliation for the most part is in name only; that is, the groups use the name al Qaeda, but do not work together with the actual al Qaeda members.

ISIS has had a profound impact on al Qaeda. Berger (2014) described how the two groups have been competing to be the world's jihadi superpower. ISIS has drained many of the resources that previously had been devoted to al Qaeda, including money, personnel, and support. In some cases, the two groups have tried to outdo the other by demonstrating its strength though attacks. ISIS's ability to declare an Islamic caliphate and take and hold territory resulted in substantial support. It will be interesting to see what happens when ISIS is defeated.

As noted in Figure 6-1 ■, numerous groups are involved in terrorist activities in the Middle East, and only the most active groups are discussed here. It is important to realize that many of these groups are cooperating with one another, but others are competing and in some cases engaged in open conflict. There are constant power struggles as groups attempt to become more powerful militarily and politically. They all have one thing in common: their support for the Palestinians and their hatred for Israel and the United States. The Israeli-Palestinian problem continues to be a flashpoint, resulting in numerous acts of terrorism.

The following section examines some of the terrorist groups that exist on the continent of Africa. A number of these conflicts involve Muslims, but some involve other groups with different agendas.

African Groups

Of particular interest to the United States is the Horn of Africa. This area is composed of Ethiopia, Somalia, Eritrea, and Kenya. A great deal of its instability is the result of Ethiopia and Somalia fighting over the Ogaden region of Ethiopia (Spindlove and Simonsen, 2010). In 1991, the government of Somalia was overthrown by clan warlords. Somalia has not had a functioning government since then. It has deteriorated with constant clan fighting and lawlessness. The conditions in the Horn are ripe for the creation of terrorist organizations.

Kenya

Al Qaeda has had a number of cells in Kenya. Members of al Qaeda have blended in with the population and are relatively safe from Kenya's weak government. Al Qaeda launched attacks on the U.S. embassy in Nairobi in 1998. A major problem with Kenya has been that it does not have any counterterrorism laws (U.S. State Department, 2009). This condition has made it difficult to deal with al Qaeda. Additionally, numerous Muslim groups openly support al Qaeda. For the most part, operatives have slipped out of Kenya to participate in operations in neighboring countries.

Today, al-Shabaab is the primary terrorist group attacking Kenya. In 2015, the group attacked Garissa University killing 147 students. Although located primarily in Somalia, it conducts attacks in surrounding countries.

Somalia

Islamic Courts Union (ICU) controlled most of southern Somalia. It came into power after the government collapsed in 1991. The ICU essentially filled a void as a result of the anarchy and lack of organization in the country. It installed Sharia or Islamic law. The ICU consisted of Islamic clans that had aims similar to the goals of the Taliban in Afghanistan—it essentially forbid anything Western. The populace supported the ICU as it brought order and reduced the amount of lawlessness. In 2006, a transitional government was established in Somalia. With the support of the American Central Intelligence Agency (CIA), Ethiopian troops invaded Somalia and fighting with Somali Transitional Federal Government troops defeated the ICU. Although defeated and having lost power, the ICU remains a force in the country.

Al-Shabaab ("the youth") is a radical group that broke away from the ICU. The leader of the ICU was a moderate, and al-Shabaab leaders believed in more violent measures. The group has used terrorist tactics such as suicide bombings, shootings, and assassinations against the Somalia government and Ethiopians. It has been suggested that the group has ties with al Qaeda. In 2008, one of the group's leaders pledged allegiance to Osama bin Laden on a video. The group has forced young men to join as fighters, and there has been an influx of foreigners, including Americans, joining the group's ranks. In 2008, several young Somali men disappeared from Minneapolis. According to the Federal Bureau of Investigation (FBI), one of the men was later involved in a suicide bombing in Somalia (Hanson, 2009). It is estimated that the group has several thousand fighters.

HS Web Link: To learn more about al-Shabab, go to https://www.counterextremism.com/threat/al-shabab.

To counter al-Shabaab and other terrorist groups in the Horn, the United States created the Combined Joint Task Force, Horn of Africa (CJTF-HOA). The CJTF-HOA is a military operation that focuses on terrorists in the region. West (2005) and Feickert (2005) advised that the CJTF-HOA has been extremely successful. The task force has targeted several terrorist organizations and a number of terrorist leaders. The task force has killed a number of these high-value terrorists and essentially destroyed a considerable number of these groups' leaders. Feickert noted that the program has been so successful that it should be a model for fighting terrorists in other regions.

Nigeria

Boko Haram is located primarily in Nigeria, has conducted a number of terrorist attacks in Nigeria, and is also active in Chad, Niger, and Cameroon. Boko Haram means "western education is sin." The group has increasingly targeted schools with girls and in 2014 kidnapped about 276 girls from a secondary school in Chibok. Many of the girls, who were mostly Christians, were forced to marry their captors and have children. Other were used as suicide bombers. Some girls were able to escape and some were released or rescued since 2014, but by 2017, 113 girls were still unaccounted for. Despite much effort by the Nigerian government and the announcement in December 2016 that Boko Haram has been crushed, the group continues to be a great threat. In 2015, its leaders announced that the group was supporting ISIS. Also, in 2015, the group killed over 1,000 people in Nigeria alone (U.S.

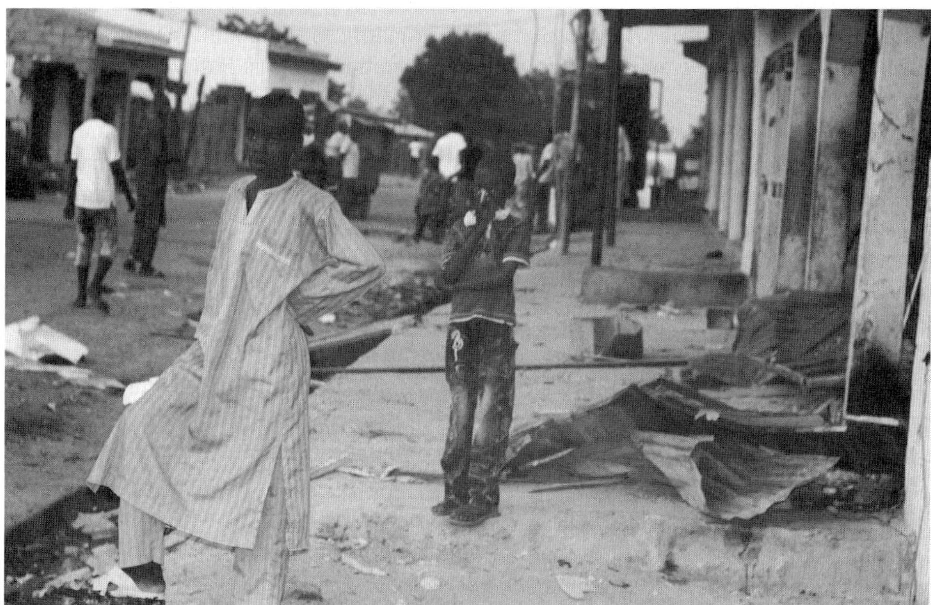

A Boko Haram bomb destroyed several buildings and killed several people as they were watching a football match.
Sombo sombo/Alamy Stock Photo.

State Department, 2016). The Institute for Economics and Peace (2015) advised that Boko Haram is the world's deadliest terrorist organization. The group is indiscriminate in terms of whom it attacks and uses all methods to attack: bombs, Improvised Explosive Devices (IEDs), and conventional firearms. In 2015, Nigeria began working with other counties in the region forming the Multi-National Joint Task Force to combat Boko Haram.

As in the Middle East, there are numerous other groups in Africa. The **al Qaeda in the Islamic Maghreb** operates in Algeria along with several other smaller groups. This group's objective is to overthrow the government and install an Islamic government. It has attacked government officials and tourists. In 2007, the group detonated a car bomb near government officials killing 28, and in the same year, a suicide bomber attempted to kill the president. The blast killed 22 and injured 107 people (ADL, 2010). In 2015, the group ambushed an Algerian army patrol, killing nine people (U.S. State Department, 2016). Another Algerian group, the Armed Islamic Group, is also attempting to overthrow the Algerian government and has conducted numerous attacks in France, which had assisted the Algerian government in clamping down on terrorist organizations.

There are numerous conflicts elsewhere in Africa. The sub-Saharan region for decades has been in the throes of civil wars, with terrorist tactics being one of the primary tools. The region is rich in minerals, including diamonds and oil, with fighting centering on control of those resources. Child armies, slavery, and starvation contribute to the problems. There is also tribal and ethnic fighting as different groups vie for political power and control. Many parts of Africa are in constant conflict and turmoil.

Asian Groups

There are several terrorist groups operating in Asia and are spread across the region. Here, some of the most notable groups are discussed.

Pakistan

Pakistan is a hotbed of terrorist groups and activities. After the coalition invasion of Afghanistan, Osama bin Laden and his al Qaeda forces moved to northern Pakistan. Now al Qaeda coordinates its worldwide activities from the area. There are numerous tribes that support or are a part of the Taliban that reside primarily in the South Waziristan region. Additionally, there are groups conducting terror operations against India as a result of the dispute over Kashmir.

The **Pakistani Taliban** consists of a group of tribes that are predominately Pashtun. In addition to having a large presence in northwest Pakistan, Pashtunis are the largest ethnic group in Afghanistan, constituting approximately 40 percent of the population. The Pashtunis also constitute the largest majority of Taliban. Although the Pakistani and Afghani Taliban are differentiated by command structure, they have close tribal relations and common goals. The goal of the Taliban is to install Sharia law; defeat the government, which it claims is ineffective; and remove Western influence from Pakistan and Afghanistan. It is believed that the Pakistani Taliban have 30,000 to 35,000 fighters, a considerable force to confront the Pakistani Army. Most recently, the group has increased its use of car bombings and suicide bombings. The most prominent was the bombing of the Marriott Hotel in Islamabad where 60 people were killed. The group primarily focuses on government and military targets (U.S. State Department, 2009). The Pakistani government has been taking a more active role in combating the Pakistani Taliban, and the United States has used drone missile attacks on suspected Taliban leaders. These attacks have resulted in the deaths of a number of high-ranking Taliban leaders.

Lashkar-e-Tayyiba or the Righteous Army is a Pakistani group that developed in the 1980s. It operates in the Indian states of Kashmir and Jammu as well as in Pakistan. The main goal of the group is to end India's control of these states. The group has used suicide bombings and attacks against government officials and Indian security forces. The group received international attention in 2008, when it conducted a coordinated multi-target attack in Mumbai, India. The attack targeted a Jewish center, hotels, a cinema, and the port area. In the wake of the attack, 164 people were killed and scores were injured (Sahba, 2008). Only one attacker was captured alive. Pakistan has investigated the incident and made a number of arrests. Lashkar-e-Tayyiba is one of the largest of the traditionally Kashmir-focused militant groups (U.S. State Department, 2009). The group has links with the Taliban and al Qaeda as well as extremist groups in Chechnya and the Philippines.

Numerous other groups are operating in Pakistan. For example, the Tehrik-e-Pakistan attacked an army school in Peshawar killing 150 children and staff (U.S. State Department, 2016). Jaish-e-Mohammed is a Pakistan-based Kashmiri Islamic group that seeks Pakistani rule in the Indian territory of Kashmir. Jaish-e-Mohammed is thought to be responsible for an attack on the Indian Parliament that killed 9 and injured 18 people. In July 2004, Pakistani authorities arrested a Jaish-e-Mohammed member wanted in connection with the 2002 abduction and murder of U.S. journalist Daniel Pearl. In 2006, the Jaish-e-Mohammed claimed responsibility for a number of attacks, including the killing of several Indian police officials in the Indian-administered Kashmir capital of Srinagar (U.S. State Department, 2009).

Afghanistan

The United States has been fighting the Taliban in Afghanistan for over 16 years. The **Taliban** is located in Pakistan and Afghanistan and is currently was led by Mullah Muhammad Omar. American and coalition forces invaded Afghanistan in 2011 after the 9/11 attacks. At the time, the Taliban ruled Afghanistan and refused to turn over Osama bin Laden to the United States. Since the invasion, the United States has focused its efforts on defeating the Taliban and installing a functional government in the country. The Taliban consists of several groups and warlords, but the primary faction is the **Haqqani Network**. This group continues to launch high-profile attacks and occupy or control large parts of Afghanistan with the aim of installing Sharia Law in Afghanistan. In 2015, Omar was declared dead. The new leader is Mullah Haibatullah Akhundzada. He has demanded that NATO and United States troops leave Afghanistan. Akhundzada is highly critical of the current president of Afghanistan, Ashraf Ghani.

HS Web Link: To learn more about the Taliban, go to https://www.infoplease.com/who-are-taliban.

The group has conducted attacks throughout the country, including the capital, Kabul. The group has two primary tactics, gain control in rural areas, especially areas close to the Pakistani border, and conduct terror attacks in cities and villages that are not under their control. They believe they will win by attrition; American and coalition forces will tire of fighting and ultimately withdraw. This is evidenced by the long war and the fact that the Taliban refuses to negotiate with the Afghanistan government and the United States, although efforts have been made to negotiate with the group.

In 2015, ISIS announced that it had created an affiliate in Afghanistan and Pakistan, ISIL-Khorasan. In 2015, ISIL-K initiated a radio station, "Voice of the Caliphate," broadcasting in the Pashto language (U.S. State Department, 2016). Given ISIS's defeats in Iraq and Syria, the ISIS leadership may ultimately move its operations to Afghanistan since the country remains in turmoil.

The leadership of al Qaeda has been decimated; a branch al Qaeda in the Indian Subcontinent (AQIS) remains in Afghanistan. AQIS remains a potent problem. Al Qaeda exists in a number of countries and has a resilient organizational structure. The group can expand its influence, especially if the Taliban and ISIL-K recede in power and control.

Central Asia

Another area of concern are the central Asian countries of Turkmenistan, Uzbekistan, Tajikistan, Kyrgyzstan, and Kazakhstan. These countries once were part of the Soviet Union and are now independent. Many of these newly formed governments are corrupt and weak. They are impoverished countries and serve as transshipment routes for drugs. Their authoritarian governments have resulted in citizen unrest and disaffection. Several Islamic groups have formed in the area, and their close proximity to Iran, Afghanistan, and Pakistan likely will facilitate additional radical groups moving into the area. For example, the Islamic Movement of Uzbekistan is a radical organization that seeks to replace the government with one based on Islamic law. It conducted some of the first suicide bombings in central Asia (U.S. State Department, 2009). Also, in the Xinjiang province in China to the east, the Uighars are attempting to create an Islamic state. The Hizb ul Tahrir is a Palestinian organization that is growing in the area. The group initially came to the region to preach and convert the region's residents to Islam (White, 2009). Many of its members believe that a Muslim country or region can be formed in the area. The region has the beginnings of a new terrorism front.

India

India has a significant terrorism problem. In 2016, the Indian government released a report documenting that since 2005, more than 700 people had been killed and over 3,200 were injured as a result of terrorist attacks (Mahapatral, 2016). There are numerous terrorist groups operating in India, including al Qaeda and ISIS. Moreover, groups from Pakistan periodically attack Indian targets. The motivation for the attacks is the conflict with Pakistan over Kashmir. Additionally, India has a significant Muslim population that remains at odds with the country's Hindu majority. There have been atrocities on both sides, with Hindus attacking Muslims and vice versa.

Pacific Rim Area

The Pacific Rim countries of the Philippines, Indonesia, and Malaysia have experienced an upswing in terrorism activities. One group, the Jemaah Islamiyyah, is intent on establishing an Islamic state incorporating Indonesia, Malaysia, the southern Philippines, Singapore, and Brunei. The group is considered one of the largest transnational groups in Southeast Asia and has links with al Qaeda. The group has staged a number of high-profile attacks, including the 2004 bombing outside the Australian Embassy in Jakarta, the 2003 bombing of the J.W. Marriott Hotel in Jakarta, and the 2002 Bali bombing that killed more than 200 people. The Bali bombing was one of the deadliest terrorist attacks since 9/11. In 2001, Singapore authorities uncovered a plot by the group to attack the U.S. and Israeli embassies and British and Australian diplomatic buildings in Singapore. The group has provided operational support and training for Philippine Muslim violent extremists (U.S. State Department, 2009).

The **Abu Sayyaf Group** is an extremist group that operates in the Southern Philippines. The group supports a separate Islamic state in the southern part of the country. A substantial portion of the country's Muslim population resides there, and many have the same aspirations as those of members of al Qaeda. The group has engaged in bombings, kidnappings, and assassinations primarily directed against security forces, businesses, and religious leaders (Public Safety Canada, 2009).

In 2017, the Maute group, a splinter group of the Abu Sayyaf Group, took the city of Marawi and held off the Philippine army. ISIS began to move fighters into the area to support the Mautes. Fighters from Saudi Arabia, Chechnya, Indonesia, Yemeni, and other countries joined the terrorist group (Abuza, 2017). The United States has sent advisors and aircraft to the area. It is feared that if ISIS takes hold in the southern Philippines, it can export terrorism to a number of Muslim countries in the region. Indonesia with the world's largest Muslim population is a potential target.

Latin American Groups

Numerous terrorist groups are operating in Latin America. Their motivations are quite different as compared to the groups in Asia, Africa, and the Middle East. First, terrorism south of the United States is driven by politics. A number of countries historically have

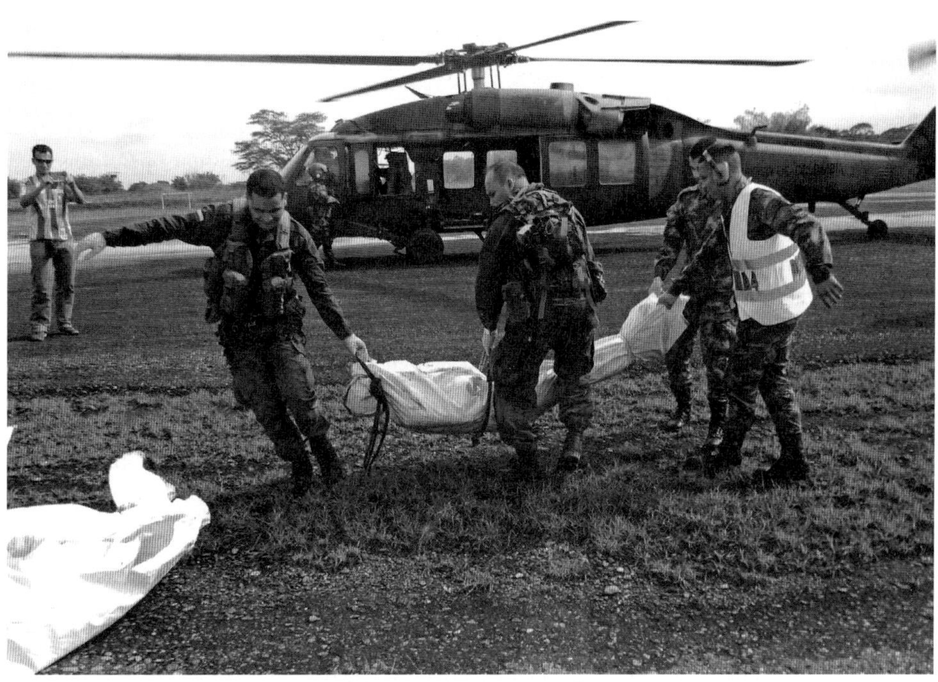

Columbian troops in counterterrorism operation against FARC.
Luis Alfredo Zapata/COLPRENSA/Xinhua/Alamy Stock Photo.

had inefficient, authoritarian governments, which has resulted in the formation of left-wing and right-wing groups that have used terrorism to advance their agendas. Second, several countries in the region have large oil reserves, and wealth from these operations has not been distributed equitably across the population. In many cases, conflicts have erupted between the rich and the poor. Finally, the transnational narcotics trade has resulted in substantial political corruption, violence, and organized criminal groups amassing substantial wealth. These groups have been destabilizing governments. A number of terrorist groups have become involved in the narcotics trade to finance their activities, and in some cases, to accumulate wealth. It is difficult to distinguish if some of these groups are organized crime groups or terrorist groups.

Colombia

Two significant left-wing groups are operating in Colombia. The **National Liberation Army** has the primary mission of establishing a people's revolutionary government. Because of the exploitation of Colombia's natural oil resources, the group has targeted many of its attacks on the foreign-controlled oil industry. It is also involved in the narcotics trade and has been involved in a number of kidnappings and political assassinations. The **Revolutionary Armed Forces of Colombia** (FARC) is an armed rebel group that operates in Colombia. The group was established in the 1960s and is the largest left-wing group operating in that country. FARC's mission is to overthrow the Colombian government and replace it with a leftist government that would promote the interests of the people of the country and those of Latin America. As a rebel group, the organization has engaged in bombings, hijackings, assassinations, and the kidnapping of Colombian officials. It is extensively involved in the drug trade, working with some of Colombia's drug cartels. At this point, it is difficult to distinguish these two groups from drug trafficking or criminal organizations even though they are recognized as terrorist organizations.

The Colombian government has had a number of successes countering these groups in recent years with financial and military assistance from the United States. In 2015, the

HS ANALYSIS BOX 6-2

Several potent terrorist groups are operating in South and Central America. Some are narco-terrorists, whereas others have a political agenda. Moreover, they have a long history of demonstrating that governments have not been able to effectively defeat them. Their operations have remained south of U.S. border. Do you believe that it is possible for their operations to creep northward into the United States? Should we be as concerned with the southern terrorist groups as we are with the Middle Eastern groups?

number of attacks by the two groups declined, which was the result of more effective coordinated military actions and the Columbian government engaging in peace talks with the groups on land reform, political participation, drug trafficking, and victim's rights (U.S. State Department, 2016). The potential exists for the government to negotiate a lasting peace with the two groups.

Peru

The **Shining Path** operates in Peru and was founded in 1980 as a breakaway group from the Communist Party of Peru. The group's main objective was to overthrow the Peruvian government and replace it with a communist government. The group has been responsible for bombings, political assassinations, and attacks throughout Peru. The Peruvian government, over the past several years, has successfully killed or captured a number of the group's leaders, substantially weakening it (U.S. State Department, 2016). The group appears to use the drug trade to support itself, and drugs have supplanted a number of its political activities. The Peruvian government essentially has killed or defeated most of the group's members.

European Groups

Historically, a number of terrorist groups have operated in Europe, especially during the Cold War. Most of these groups were left-wing or socialist and communist. Examples include the Red Brigade in Italy, the Red Army Faction in Germany, and the Communist Combat Cells of Belgium. During the Cold War, these groups were actively pursuing a socialist agenda through violence, including kidnappings, bombings, and other attacks. Essentially, left-wing terrorism in Western Europe has all but vanished. The departure of European left-wing radical and terrorist groups is attributable to the fall of the Soviet Union. The Soviets provided these groups with substantial support and funding. The fall of the Soviet Union also resulted in interest in socialism as a viable political framework to wane. The creation of the European Union also reduced terrorism by removing government boundaries and creating a more unified view of the world.

Few terrorist organizations are still operating in Western Europe, but the most substantial terrorist-related problem now is Islamic terrorists who are attacking Western ideas and Western countries. Muslim terrorists have initiated attacks in Madrid, London, Nice, Paris, Brussels, Copenhagen, Berlin, Marseilles, and Istanbul, to name a few cities. Several thousand Muslims have left Europe to join jihad movements in countries that are marked with ongoing terrorist fighting, and many have returned to their European homes radicalized. There also is a considerable Muslim population in many Western European countries who might become more involved in terrorist activities in the future. This is a continuing threat.

As Figure 6-2 ■ demonstrates, there have been multiple attacks across Europe. None of these attacks can be attributed to any non-jihadi groups. The frequency of attacks shows that Europe is facing a significant jihadi terrorism problem.

Year	Location	Attack Details
2015	Paris	Multiple shooting attacks, including attack, on the magazine *Charlie Hebdo*. Seventeen were killed in the attacks.
	Nice, France	Man attacked soldiers guarding a Jewish community center. The attacker was arrested.
	Copenhagen	Man opened fire at an event held by Lars Vilks. He had drawn a picture of the prophet Muhammad. The assailant later killed a man at a Synagogue.
	Villejuif, France	Algerian man attempted to steal a car and accidently shot himself. He was a Syrian jihadist and planned attacks on a church.
	Saint-Wuentin-Fallavier, France	Man beheaded his employer and caused an explosion at a factory.
	Olgnies, France	Man threatened passengers on a train shooting one passenger. He was subdued by two U.S. military personnel.
	Berlin	An Iraqi citizen stabbed a police officer. He was killed by another officer.
	Paris	Multiple attacks on a restaurant, the Bataclan theater, and outside a football stadium. Overall, 89 people were killed.
2016	Marseilles	A boy attempted to behead a teacher claiming to act in the name of ISIS.
	Istanbul	Bomber blew himself up near a Mosque killing 13 people. Turkish authorities believed ISIS was involved.
	Hanover, Germany	Girl stabbed a police officer. Her brother attempted to fire bomb a shopping mall. Brother had fought in Syria.
	Istanbul	Suicide bombing near a shopping street.
	Brussels	Three coordinated suicide bombings at the Brussels airport and at a metro station killing 32 people and 340 people were injured.
	Essen, Germany	Three teens connected to Islamic extremists exploded a bomb at a Sikh wedding injuring three people.
	Magnanville, France	Man shouting Islamic slogans killed a police officer and the officer's wife. Police killed the attacker.
	Istanbul	Coordinated attacks at the Istanbul airport killing 45 people and more than 230 were injured.
	Nice, France	A cargo truck was driven into crowds killing 86 and injuring 434. ISIS claimed responsibility.
	Wurzburg, Germany	Afghan teen attacked passengers on a train and was killed by police.
	Ansbach, Germany	Syrian refugee detonated a bomb in a wine bar killing himself and wounding 15. He had pledged allegiance to ISIS.
	Saint-Etienne-du-Rouvray, France	Two men took hostages at church killing a priest and wounding another man. Attackers were killed by police. ISIS took credit for the attack.
	Charleroi, Belgium	An assailant shouting Allahu Akbar attacked two police officers with a machete. He was killed by a third officer.
	Moscow	Two Chechen men attacked police officers at a police station with a knife and axe seriously wounding one. ISIS took credit for the attack.
	Brussels	Three officers were attacked by a man wielding a machete. Two officers received stab wounds.
	Berlin	A man drove a truck into a crowd at a Christmas market killing 12 and injuring 56. ISIS took credit for the attack.
2017	Istanbul	Man opened fire at a nightclub killing about 40 people and injuring 70. ISIS claimed credit for the attack.
	Paris	A soldier was attacked by a man wielding a machete injuring the soldier. Man had posted ISIS support material before the attack.

FIGURE 6-2 *(Continued)*

Year	Location	Attack Details
	Orly Airport, Paris	Man attempted to take a woman officer's gun and was shot by officers. He shouted "I am ready to die for Allah."
	London	Man drove a car into pedestrians on bridge killing four and injuring 46. He was killed by police officers.
	St. Petersburg	A suicide bomber exploded a bomb on the metro killing 16 and 64 others were injured. An al Qaeda affiliate claimed responsibility.
	Stockholm	Man drove a hijacked truck into a crowd in a shopping area killing five and injuring 14. Suspect had shown sympathies for ISIS.
	Paris	Man shot three police officers and a bystander in a shopping area and was killed by police. He had a note defending ISIS.
	Manchester	A suicide bombing after a concert killed 22 civilians.
	London	Van ran over multiple pedestrians on a London bridge and then stabbed multiple people. They were killed by police officers.
	Paris	Man attacked police officer at the Notre Dame de Paris with a hammer. He had pledged allegiance to ISISL.
	Paris	Man driving a car containing guns and explosives rammed a police car causing a fire that killed the terrorist. He had expressed support for ISIS.
	Brussels	Terrorist ran into Brussels Central Station where he detonated a bomb and continued to run carrying a suicide vest. He was killed by soldiers.
	Hambury	Islamist stabbed seven people in a supermarket killing one while shouting "Allahu Akbar."

FIGURE 6-2 Listing of European Terrorist Attacks
Source: Adapted from various news media reporting.

Terrorism in America

The previous section primarily addressed Muslim terrorists. These terrorists reside in a number of countries in the Middle East, Africa, and Asia. Islamic-inspired terrorism is a problem for the United States. LaFree, Yang, and Crenshaw (2009) examined international terrorist groups from 1970 to 2004 and identified 53 terrorist groups that were anti-American, of which 31 were radicalized Islamic groups. The remaining 22 groups were communist or socialist inspired or drug trafficking groups that engaged in terrorism. Only al Qaeda has successfully launched an attack on American soil. Nonetheless, in addition to radical Muslim terrorism, there are other terrorist groups including right-wing terrorists or militias and eco-terrorists operating in the United States that could mount attacks.

The FBI (2002) has developed a classification for domestic terrorism. First is **political extremism**, whereby groups are using terrorism to affect political change. Second, **single-issue** terrorism refers to groups focusing on a particular issue such as animal rights activists or anti-abortion activists who resort to violence and other terrorist activities. Finally, the **lone wolf** is an individual who uses terrorist activities to attack people as a result of an issue or perceived injustice or political ideology.

Radical Muslim-Inspired Terrorism

Al Qaeda perpetrated the most significant terrorist attack on the United States with the 9/11 attacks on New York City and the Pentagon. Since the 9/11 attacks, there have not been any attacks by Muslim extremists like the 9/11 attacks, but there has been significant terrorist activity, including lesser attacks in San Bernardino, Orlando, and Chattanooga.

Year	Number Charged or Deceased Prior to Charges Filed	Year	Number Charged or Deceased Prior to Charges Filed
2001	2	2009	45
2002	21	2010	35
2003	15	2011	25
2004	14	2012	15
2005	17	2013	17
2006	18	2014	29
2007	15	2015	79
2008	5	2016	44

FIGURE 6-3 Terror-Related Arrests by Year

Source: Bergen, P., A. Ford, A. Sims, and D. Sterman (2017). *Terrorism in America after 9/11*, Washington, D.C.: New America. https://www.newamerica.org/in-depth/terrorism-in-america/ (Accessed August 5, 2017).

There are numerous examples of Islamic-inspired terrorists being arrested in the United States after 9/11. Bergen and his colleagues (2017) found that over 400 people have been charged with terrorism-related crimes including terrorism, providing material support, plotting to travel to join a jihadi group, and so on. Figure 6-3 ■ provides a breakdown of the yearly terror-related arrests.

As shown in Figure 6-3 ■, the number of arrests has been fairly consistent since 2009 and greater than previous years. The increase is likely due to the FBI having more resources to devote to terror-related investigations. It should also be noted that the FBI likely has hundreds of ongoing investigations and terror suspects under surveillance.

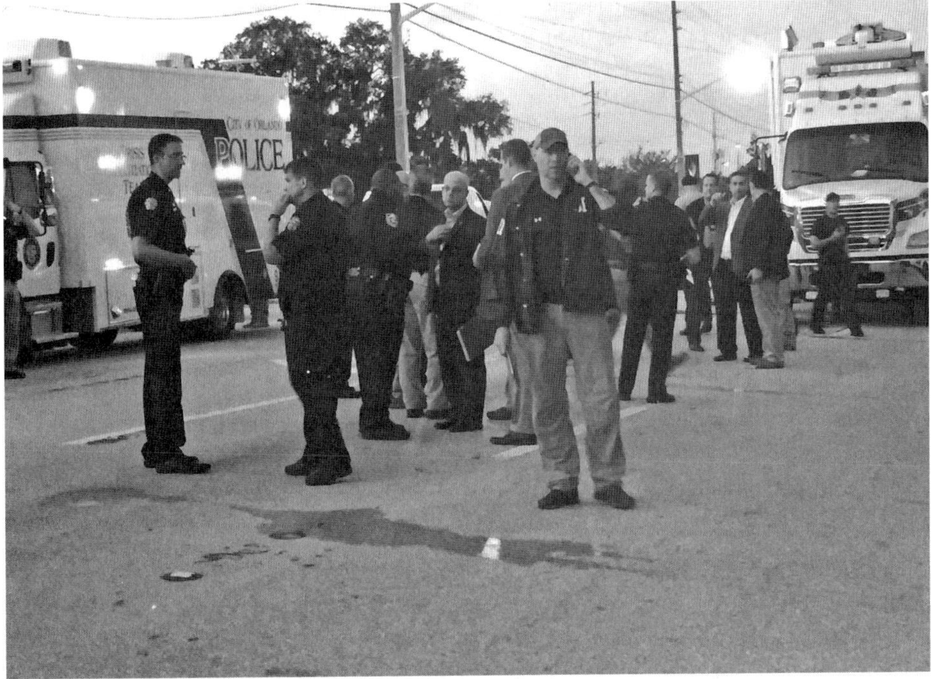

Police officers outside the Orlando nightclub after Omar Mateen killed 49 people.
Orlando Police Department/Xinhua/Alamy Stock Photo.

There is some concern over people coming to the United States from Muslim majority counties or who are Muslim. However, Bergen and his colleagues examined over 400 cases and found that 85 percent charged with a terrorism-related offense were U.S. citizens or permanent residents. Only 15 percent were non-residents or unknown. The overwhelming majority of arrests were of people who were American residents.

The Relationship between Jihadi Terrorist Groups and Terrorist Events

ISIS or some other group almost immediately takes credit for any terrorist attack regardless of the magnitude or its location in the world. For example, ISIS took credit for the Orlando nightclub shooting where Omar Mateen killed 49 people and wounded 58 others. But, to what extent did ISIS affect Mateen's actions? Did ISIS in actuality have any effect on Mateen?

Bergen (2017) examined ISIS and "credit taking" and identified five relationships between terrorist organizations and terrorist events. First are attacks that are directed by the core terrorist group. An example of this type of relationship is the 9/11 attacks that were planned, funded, and carried out at the direction of bin Laden. Second are attacks that are conducted by an affiliate of the terrorist organization. The ISIS-Khorasan, a splinter group of the Taliban and associated with ISIS, conducted attacks in Afghanistan. Third are the attacks conducted by groups affiliated with the central terror group but have little or no real connection to the group. An example here is Boko Haram, which has pledged support of ISIS and has conducted numerous attacks but ISIS has no input into these attacks. Boko Haram's attacks are independent of ISIS. Fourth are attacks that are enabled by the central terrorist organization. This means that the organization assists the attacker financially or logistically. Given the ferocity in the FBI's investigations of possible terrorists, it is difficult for any foreign group to provide this type of support. The final type is where individuals latch onto a group's ideology and commit a terrorist act such as the case with Omar Mateen.

An examination of terrorist attacks in the United States likely shows that people latching on to a particular terrorist ideology occurs in the vast majority of cases. The other four types seldom if ever are present for American terrorists. The relationship between American terrorists and foreign terrorist organizations is minimal at best and more likely to be non-existent.

Radicalization: The Greatest Threat to America

Radicalization is the greatest threat to the United States (Stern, 2016). There have been a number of Americans who have gone to the Middle East to engage in jihadi wars. There have been several thousand would-be jihadists who have similarly traveled from Europe; since they are Europeans, they can easily travel to the United States. Such actions demonstrate that they have the psychological or political background to engage in terrorist acts in the United States and Europe. Many of these individuals were radicalized before going to the Middle East, while others likely were radicalized while there.

Essentially, the **radicalization process** is where someone accepts an extremist belief system, generally jihadist, and consequently has the wherewithal to support or carry out violence to effect changes in society. Jihadists have as their primary goals to bring down the United States and to establish a caliphate in the Middle East.

Radicalization is a process (Horgan, 2003). Horgan notes that it generally starts when people become frustrated with their lives. The risk factors discussed in Chapter 5 contribute to this frustration, demonstrating that there are numerous ways for someone to begin the radicalization process. Generally, the radicalization process consists of four phases: (1) pre-radicalization, (2) indoctrination and increased group bonding, (3) conversion and identification, and (4) acts of terrorism or planned attacks. **Pre-radicalization** is where the subject becomes disenchanted or frustrated. The indoctrination and increased group bonding phase is where the subject becomes increasingly exposed to radical information. This may occur when the subject begins to concentrate on radical material on the Internet, associates with a radical group of friends, or attends a mosque that has a radical imam. This phase essentially involves inculturalizaton, where radical ideas are integrated into the subject's belief system. Phase three, conversion and identification, is where the subject joins or accepts the ideas of the radical movement. He or she becomes a total believer. The last stage is **radicalization**, where the subject becomes so radicalized that he or she plans or perpetrates terrorist acts.

Europe has had a more substantial problem with radicalized terrorists as compared to the United States (e.g., see Figure 6-1 ■). Muslims who have come to America have had an easier time integrating in our society as compared to France, Great Briton, and other European countries. Nonetheless, there have been several cases where people have become radicalized and committed terrorist acts—the San Bernardino shootings, the Chattanooga navy reserve center, and the Orlando nightclub shooting, to name a few.

A primary tool used by radical extremists to recruit members is social media. Stern advises that the United States has not done enough to counter the extremist information on social media (Stern, 2016). Bergen and his colleagues (2017) investigated the role of media in radicalization. Figure 6-4 ■ provides the percentage of American jihadis who maintained a social media profile with jihadist material.

Since 2011, the percentage of American jihadis who used jihadi social media ranged from 40 to 90 percent. These high percentages demonstrate that social media plays an important role in radicalization. Many experts advise that the United States should put more effort into taking jihadi websites off the Internet and increase the number of websites that counter jihadi messaging.

Jenkins (2010) advised that it is costly and dangerous to attempt to arrest jihadists after they have committed a terrorist attack; we should intervene before an attack occurs. Currently, our primary strategy is intelligence and law enforcement. He advised that we should expend considerably more effort on prevention by reaching out to the Muslim

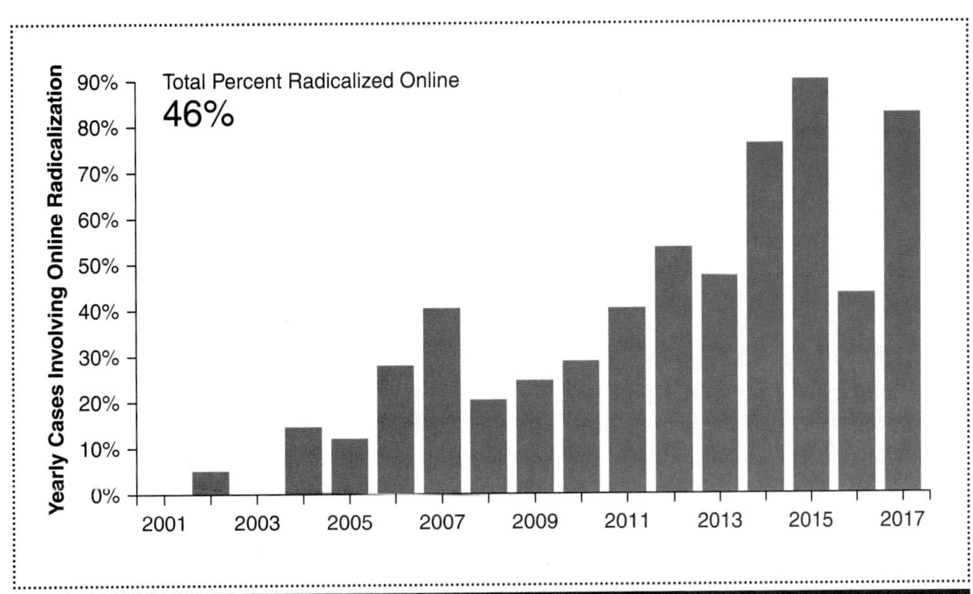

FIGURE 6-4 American Jihandis Radicalized Online

Source: Bergen, P., A. Ford, A. Sims, and D. Sterman (2017). *Terrorism in America after 9/11* Washington, D.C.: New America. https://www.newamerica.org/in-depth/terrorism-in-america/ (Accessed August 5, 2017).

Cross burning at Ku Klux Klan rally.
Ken Hawkins/Alamy Stock Photo.

communities. Recently, an advisory commission headed by William Webster, former CIA and FBI director, recommended to the secretary of homeland security that community policing and other outreach programs likely would have a positive influence on disenfranchised Muslims (Dilanian, 2010). Today, a number of police departments are attempting to develop better relations with these communities by creating advisory boards, citizen-police forums, and so on. Some departments have employed Muslim chaplains. Outreach may result in the identification of community problems that can be resolved before there is radicalization. Such programs may result in Muslim Americans reporting suspicious activities or individuals in their communities.

Right-Wing Terrorists and Militias

In 2016, three men belonging to a group called "the Crusaders" were arrested for conspiring to bomb a Somali immigrant community in Garden City, Kansas, and in 2015, Dylann Roof, a self-avowed white supremacist, entered a Charleston, South Carolina, church and killed nine black church members. In 2016, about a dozen people occupied the Malheur National Wildlife Refuge in Oregon. They were protesting federal land policies. Robert Dear attacked a Planned Parenthood clinic in Colorado Springs, killing three people and injuring nine others (Hamilton and Owen, 2017).

In 2017, right-wing groups organized to protest the removal of a statue of Robert E. Lee in Charlottesville, Virginia. The event attracted members of the Ku Klux Klan, right-wing militias, skinheads, neo-Nazis, white nationalists, and a host of other such groups. It was the first time that so many right-wing groups coalesced together around an issue. At one point, a car slammed into a crowd of counterdemonstrators, killing one and injuring over a dozen people. It was similar to terrorist attacks in France and Great Britain and was an example of a brazen terrorist attack on American soil. There are numerous examples of right-wing terrorism. They are over-shadowed by jihadi terrorism, but right-wing terrorism in the United States is just as dangerous. Right-wing extremist groups consist of a number of extreme religious, racist, and anti-government groups.

Mark Potak (2010) of the Southern Poverty Law Center advises that the number of American hate groups has remained at record levels, approximately 1,000. The variety of right-wing hate groups includes militias, Ku Klux Klan, neo-Nazis, patriot groups, and skinhead groups. There are common threads running through all these groups. First, they often evoke the name of "God." To some extent, they believe that the "white man" is the chosen one and attack, verbally and physically, immigrants, Jews, Catholics, and minorities. Second, they believe that there is a government conspiracy to take our freedoms and guns and install a socialist government in the United States. They essentially want to arm themselves and be prepared for a holy war to be waged against the government and others who they see as threatening their values.

David Carter and his colleagues (2014) calculated the potential threat posed by right-wing groups in the United States. Their findings are provided in Figure 6-5 ■.

Carter and his colleagues identify a number of right-wing groups that potentially can commit or conspire to commit terrorist acts. Many of these groups have a long history of violence. They, like jihadi groups, have a significant presence on the Internet and potentially can radicalize numerous people, especially considering that there are large numbers of Americans that subscribe to radical right-wing philosophies.

Although right-wing extremism initially diminished after the Oklahoma City bombing, there has been a significant increase over the past several years. They are anti-American in that they fail to accept the inclusive democratic values that are prevalent today. These groups have a history of attacking public officials and infrastructure targets. The potential attacks on public officials and critical infrastructures make these groups a primary concern in homeland security. This concern is legitimate. Bergen and his colleagues (2017) found that deadly attacks by jihadist-inspired attackers had killed 95 people in the United

Type of Group	Potential Threat (2013–14)	Potential Threat (2006–07)
Sovereign Citizens	3.20 (1)	2.49 (7)
Islamic Extremists/Jihadists	2.89 (2)	3.13 (1)
Militia/Patriot	2.67 (3)	2.61 (6)
Racist Skinheads	2.58 (4)	2.82 (3)
Neo-Nazis	2.56 (5)	2.94 (2)
Extreme Animal Rightists	2.54 (6)	2.79 (4)
Extreme Environmentalists	2.51 (7)	2.74 (5)
Klux Klux Klan	2.38 (8)	2.47 (8)
Left-Wing Revolutionaries	2.36 (9)	2.04 (13)
Extreme Anti-Abortion	2.36 (9)	2.30 (11)
Black Nationalists	2.34 (11)	2.35 (10)
Extreme Anti-Tax	2.33 (12)	2.47 (8)
Extreme Anti-Immigration	2.33 (12)	2.41 (9)
Christian Identity	2.19 (13)	2.59 (8)
Idiosyncratic Sectarians	2.19 (13)	2.13 (12)
Millennial/Doomsday Cults	2.17 (15)	1.93 (14)
Reconstructed Traditions	2.13 (16)	2.04 (13)

FIGURE 6-5 Relative Danger Posed by Various Right-Wing Groups in America
Source: Carter, David, and Steve Chermak, Jeremy Carter, Jack Drew. *Understanding Law Enforcement Intelligence Processes.* Report to the Office of University Programs, Science and Technology Directorate, U.S. Department of Homeland Security College Park, MD: START, 2014.

HS Web Link: To learn more about right-wing militias, go to http://www.pbs.org/newshour/bb/armed-militia-groups-surging-across-nation/.

States between 2000 and 2016 while right-wing extremists had killed 67. To a great extent, our attention is focused exclusively on jihadis while neglecting right-wing conspiracies.

Eco-Terrorism and Animal Rights Groups

Today, a few left-wing terrorist groups are operating in the United States. One such group is the **Earth Liberation Front** (ELF). ELF formed in England in 1992 when eco-terrorists from Earth First and animal rights extremists associated with the **Animal Liberation Front** joined together. The FBI has declared ELF as a terrorist organization since its members have used arson, bombings, and other violent acts to accomplish their ends (Jarboe, 2002). The Anti-Defamation League (ADL) (n.d.) has estimated that these groups have caused over $100 million in damage. ELF is one of the most active terrorist groups operating in the United States.

ELF has been most active in the western United States. Its members have attacked universities, professors, government facilities, and private businesses and corporations they see as being destructive to the environment or harming people or animals. Their primary mode of operation is arson or incendiary devices. They have attacked animal research laboratories at the ExpUniversity of California at Davis and Michigan State University. Other significant attacks include those on a Bureau of Land Management wild horse facility near Burns, Oregon; a U.S. Department of Agriculture animal damage control building near Olympia, Washington; and the destruction of a Vail, Colorado, ski facility. ELF and other such groups normally attack property, not people. In a more recent case, two individuals were arrested for freeing 5,740 minks across the country, causing hundreds of thousands of dollars in damages. They were arrested by the FBI's Joint Terrorism Task Force for conspiracy to violate the Animal Enterprise Terrorism Act (Associated Press of Oakland, California, 2015). However, they are capable of violence (Jarboe, 2002).

HS ANALYSIS BOX 6-3

A variety of terrorists reside in the United States. There are different groups with different motives. At this point, which types of groups are the most dangerous? Should homeland security officials be as concerned with right-wing groups as they are with Muslim extremists?

Summary

In this chapter, we reviewed some of the concepts involved in the geography of terrorism. First, we examined a number of terrorist groups and their bases of operations. Numerous such groups with different agendas are spread across the globe. However, there are concentrations, especially in the Middle East. These predominately consist of Muslim extremists and groups. A number of these groups have contributed to terrorism in the United States.

We also looked at jihadi terrorism in the United States. Authorities make a number of jihadi arrests each year. Most of the attacks and plots have little to do with foreign terrorist organizations. Nonetheless, we see that ISIS, al Qaeda, and Boko Haram perhaps are the most active foreign terrorist organizations since their activities span across several countries.

Finally, we examine right-wing and eco-terrorism. Statistically, right-wing terrorism has resulted in large numbers of attacks on American soil and may be as dangerous as jihadi terrorism. We tend to not give adequate consideration to right-wing terrorist activities. Eco and animal rights terrorism occurs less frequently, but these forms of terrorism have resulted in substantial costs to society.

Discussion Questions

1. Terrorist groups are located throughout the world. Which of these groups poses the greatest danger to the United States?
2. There are right-wing and eco-terrorist groups located in the United States. Which type of group poses the greater danger to our country? Why?
3. The Middle East contains the largest number of terrorist groups. What distinguishes these groups from other terrorist groups in the world?
4. How are individuals radicalized?
5. Based on the information provided in this chapter, which terrorist groups should the United States target? Why?

References

Abuza, Z. (2017). "Why another Philippines terrorist attack is coming." *The Diplomat*. http://thediplomat.com/2017/07/why-another-philippines-terrorist-attack-is-coming/ (Accessed August 9, 2017).

ADL. (2010). *Al Qaeda in the Islamic Maghreb (AQIM)*. http://www.adl.org/terrorism/symbols/al_qaeda_maghreb.asp (Accessed May 7, 2010).

ADL. (n.d.). Ecoterrorism: Extremism in the Animal Rights and Environmentalist Movements. https://www.adl.org/education/resources/reports/ecoterrorism.

Associated Press of Oakland, California. *Animal Activists Face Domestic Terrorism Charge in Freeing 5,740 Mink*. http://www.theguardian.com/us-news/2015/jul/25/animal-activists-minks-domestic-terrorism-charges (Accessed August 6, 2015).

Bergen, P. (2017). *Jihadist Terrorism 15 Years after 9/11: A Threat Assessment.* Washington, D.C.: New America. https://na-production.s3.amazonaws.com/documents/jihadist_terrorism_after_911_FINAL.pdf (Accessed August 4, 2017).

Bergen, P., A. Ford, A. Sims, and D. Sterman. (2017). *Terrorism in America after 9/11*. Washington, D.C.: New America. https://www.newamerica.org/in-depth/terrorism-in-america/ (Accessed August 5, 2017).

Berger, J. M. (2014). "The Islamic state vs. al Qaeda." *Foreign Policy*. http://foreignpolicy.com/2014/09/02/the-islamic-state-vs-al-qaeda/ (Accessed November 3, 2016).

Carter, D., S. Chermak, J. Carter, and J. Drew. (2014). *Understanding Law Enforcement Intelligence Processes*. Report to the Office of University Programs, Science and Technology Directorate, U.S. Department of Homeland Security. College Park, MD: START.

Council on Foreign Relations. (2009). *Hezbollah*. http://www.cfr.org/publication/9155/ (Accessed May 5, 2010).

Dilanian, K. (2010). "Fighting threats from within." *Los Angeles Times* (May 27), A1, A14.

FBI. (2002). *Terrorism 2000/2001*. Washington, D.C.: Author.

Feickert, A. (2005). *U.S. Military Operations in the Global War on Terrorism: Afghanistan, Africa, the Philippines, and Columbia*. Washington, D.C.: Congressional Research Service.

Gilsinan, K. (2015). "The confused person's guide to the Syrian civil war." *The Atlantic*. http://www.theatlantic.com/international/archive/2015/10/syrian-civil-war-guide-isis/410746/ (Accessed November 9, 2016).

Hamilton, K., and T. Owen (2017). *Whitelisted: 10 Plots and Attacks by White People Trump Left Off His Terrorism List*. https://news.vice.com/story/10-plots-and-attacks-by-white-people-the-white-house-left-off-its-terrorism-list (Accessed August 5, 2017).

Hanson, S. (2009a). "Al-Shabaab." *Council on Foreign Relations*. http://www.cfr.org/publication/18650/ (Accessed May 6, 2010).

Horgan, J. (2003). "Leaving terrorism behind: An individual perspective." *Terrorists, Victims and Society: Psychological Perspectives on Terrorism and Its Consequences*, ed. Andrew Silke. New York: Wiley.

Institute for Economics and Peace. (2015). *Global Terrorism Index, 2015*. New York: Author.

Jarboe, T. (2002). "The threat of eco-terrorism." *Testimony before the House Resources Committee, Subcommittee on Forests and Forest Health*. http://www.fbi.gov/congress/congress02/jarboe021202.htm (Accessed June 2, 2010).

Jenkins, M. (2010). *Would-be Warriors: Incidents of Jihadist Terrorist Radicalization in the United States since September 11, 2001*. Santa Monica, CA: RAND.

Jones, S. (2016). "11,774 terror attacks worldwide n 2015; 28,328 deaths due to terror attacks." *CNSNews.com*. http://www.cnsnews.com/news/article/susan-jones/11774-number-terror-attacks-worldwide-dropped-13-2015 (Accessed October 27, 2016).

Knickmeyer, E., and J. Finer. (2006). "Insurgent leader al Zarqawi killed in Iraq." *Washington Post* (June 8). http://www.washingtonpost.com/wp-dyn/content/article/2006/06/08/AR2006060800114.html (Accessed May 2, 2010).

LaFree, G., and L. Dugan. (2009). "Research on terrorism and countering terrorism." *Crime and Justice: A Review of Research*, ed. M. Tonry, pp. 413–477. Chicago: University of Chicago Press.

LaFree, G., S. Yang, and M. Crenshaw. (2009). "Trajectories of terrorism: Attack patterns of foreign groups that have targeted the United States." *Criminology & Public Policy*, 8: 445–474.

Mahapatral, D. (2016). "Since 2005, terror has claimed lives of 707 Indians." *The Times of India*. http://timesofindia.indiatimes.com/india/Since-2005-terror-has-claimed-lives-of-707-Indians/articleshow/53234226.cms (Accessed August 4, 2017).

Malsin, J. (2015). "Egypt is struggling to cope with its ISIS insurgency." *Time* (July 23). http://time.com/3969596/egypt-isis-sinai/ (Accessed June 1, 2017).

Potak, M. (2010). *Rage on the Right, the Year in Hate and Extremism.* http://www.splcenter.org/get-informed/intelligence-report/browse-all-issues/2010/spring/rage-on-the-right (Accessed June 2, 2010).

Public Safety Canada. (2009). *Public Safety Canada.* http://www.publicsafety.gc.ca/prg/ns/le/cle-eng.aspx (Accessed June 20, 2010).

Sahba, L. (2008). "HM announces measure to increase security." Indian Press Information Bureau. http://pib.nic.in/release/release.asp?relid=45446 (Accessed May 7, 2010).

Spindlove, J., and C. Simonsen. (2010). *Terrorism Today.* Upper Saddle River, NJ: Prentice Hall.

Stern, J. (2016). "Radicalization to extremism and mobilization to violence: What have we learned and what can we do about it?" *Annals, AAPSS*, 668 (2016): 102–117.

Symeonidou-Kastanidou, E. (2004). "Defining terrorism." *European Journal of Crime, Criminal Law, and Criminal Justice*, 12: 14–35.

U.S. Department of State. (2009). *Country Reports on Terrorism.* Washington, D.C.: Author.

U.S. Department of State. (2016). *Country Reports on Terrorism, 2008.* Washington, D.C.: Author. http://www.state.gov/s/ct/rls/crt/2008/index.htm (Accessed May 3, 2016).

West, D. (2005). *Combating Terrorism in the Horn of Africa.* Boston: Harvard University, Belfer Center for Science and International Relations.

White, J. (2009). *Terrorism and Homeland Security.* Belmont, CA: Cengage.

Zenko, M. (2012). "The latest in tracking global terrorism data." *Council on Foreign Relations* (November 19). http://blogs.cfr.org/zenko/2012/11/19/the-latest-in-tracking-global-terrorism-data/ (Accessed November 27, 2012).

Islamic state and the crisis in Iraq and Syria in maps. BBC News. http://www.bbc.com/news/world-middle-east-27838034. Retrieved Jan 1, 2018.

Boko Haram releases dozens of Chibok schoolgirls, say Nigerian officials. The Guardian, 05/06/17 https://www.theguardian.com/world/2017/may/06/boko-haram-releases-dozens-of-kidnapped-chibok-schoolgirls Retrieved Jan 1, 2018

Afghanistan: Taliban leader wants US and NATO troops out. Deutsche Welle, 06/23/2017. http://www.dw.com/en/afghanistan-taliban-leader-wants-us-and-nato-troops-out/a-39387625

7 Transnational Organized Crime and Terrorism

LEARNING OBJECTIVES

1. *Explain the different kinds or types of crime.*
2. *Define transnational organized crime.*
3. *Describe the different models of transnational organized crime.*
4. *Describe how the various transnational organized crime groups are structured.*
5. *Discuss the different crimes and activities associated with transnational organized crime.*

Key Terms

Transnational organized crime
Supply-side economics
Illegal goods and services
Hierarchal, organized entities
Street crime
Organized crime
White-collar crime
Globalization of the economy
Increased numbers and heterogeneity of immigrants
Improved communications technology
Proliferation of transportation technology
Weak governments
Political models
Economic models
Market model
Social models
Cultural model
Ethnic network model
Social network model
Standard hierarchies
Regional hierarchies
Clustered hierarchy
Core group configuration
Criminal networks
Drug trafficking
Human smuggling
Human trafficking
Smuggling of technology and WMD materials
Arms trafficking
Gray market
Piracy
Non-drug contraband smuggling
Financial fraud
Environmental crimes
Quasi-states
Almost states
Black spots
Failed states
Partnership Motivations and Disincentives
Appropriation of Tactics
Organizational Evolution and Variation

▶ Introduction

This chapter examines **transnational organized crime** (TOC), which loosely defined refers to organized criminal groups that operate multinationally. TOC is examined in terms of criminal activities, focusing on key players or TOC groups, extent of the problem, structure, and operational activities. This chapter also examines the relationship between transnational crime and other forms of crime, particularly terrorism. It is important to examine TOC within the context of homeland security since there are numerous similarities between TOC and terrorism.

When examining terrorism, many people consider it to be an assault on people, society, or government. Government officials and political commentators often use the most negative terms possible to elicit maximum drama. Realistically, however, terrorism generally is the commission of a crime by a group of organized individuals. Their crimes often center on violence, but these violent acts nonetheless are criminal acts. Terrorists are also involved in other types of crime that are instrumental to their terrorist objectives. They are involved in accumulating wealth for the furtherance of their terrorist political objectives. Moreover, TOC and terrorist groups have parallel organizations that are sometimes cooperating or even integrated (Wagley, 2006; Rollins and Wyler, 2013; Decker and Pyrooz, 2015). TOC groups often are used to strategically facilitate terrorism. As Mueller (1998) notes, terrorism is a form of TOC.

▶ Defining Transnational Organized Crime

It is difficult to define TOC or organized crime precisely because there are numerous TOC groups or organizations spread across the globe involved in a variety of criminal and sometimes noncriminal activities. For this reason, some researchers argue that there is not a commonly accepted definition for organized crime or TOC (Small and Taylor, 2005). A description of organized crime likely serves to provide a better understanding of the phenomenon than attempting to develop a definition. Kenney and Finckenauer (1995) have identified several characteristics associated with organized crime groups, and these characteristics are applicable to TOC. They are listed in Figure 7-1 ■.

Organized criminal organizations are nonideological in that they do not have a political or religious agenda; they pursue economic gain through criminal enterprises (Glenny, 2005). They have organization since they often are engaged in several criminal activities that can cross multiple political jurisdictions. Van Dijk (2008) studied 40 organized crime

- Are nonideological
- Have an organized hierarchy
- Are perpetual over time
- Use force or the threat of force
- Restrict membership
- Obtain profits through illegal enterprises or means
- Provide illegal goods and services that are desired by the public
- Use corruption to neutralize politicians
- Seek a monopoly or control over specific criminal enterprises
- Have job specialization or differentiation
- Adhere to a code of secrecy
- Utilize extensive planning to achieve long-term goals

FIGURE 7-1 Characteristics of Organized Crime Groups

groups and found that 70 percent were involved in activities in three or more countries and 58 percent were involved in multiple activities, which requires a well-organized network. They are perpetual in that they are organized and operated to conduct criminal activities (e.g., narcotics trafficking, extortion, money laundering, economic crimes) for long periods of time. They rely on force to gain compliance from competitors, government officials, and, in some cases, client-citizens. They have restricted membership. These organized crime groups, such as the Russian Mafia or the Yakuza, a Japanese criminal group, are similar to legitimate enterprises and terrorist organizations. They select or employ people who are competent or possess necessary skills or who can manage a criminal activity, and these employees must be trustworthy. They provide illegal goods and services to the public. Organized crime uses **supply-side economics**, as does a legitimate business or enterprise (see Rengert, 2003). It provides illegal goods and services (drugs, prostitution, gambling, human subjects, etc.) that are desired by the public. Organized crime attempts to neutralize law enforcement and political systems through corruption, bribery, and coercion (see Van Dijk, 2008).

HS Web Link: To learn more about how TOC is a threat, go to https://www.fbi.gov/investigate/organized-crime.

Organized crime groups operate more effectively with the tacit or overt approval of political systems, which is why they generally are more prevalent in countries or areas that have weak governments. They often seek to monopolize a criminal enterprise in a geographic area, which may be a local community, region, or country. This monopoly is established through violence or intimidation and, to some extent, by allying with the political system and law enforcement officials. A prime example is Mexico, where many police, justice, and other governmental officials have been co-opted or corrupted by the drug cartels. In a number of cases, when the cartels were unable to co-opt officials, they simply killed them; this often results in a higher level of compliance by other officials. Monopolies result in larger profit margins for the organized crime group.

Organized crime organizations have some level of specialization. That is, the soldiers or associates have specific duties, often working in groups and coordinated by managers or leaders. There is a strict code of secrecy. Members who violate this code are often killed or their families are killed. The code of secrecy reduces the possibility of law enforcement

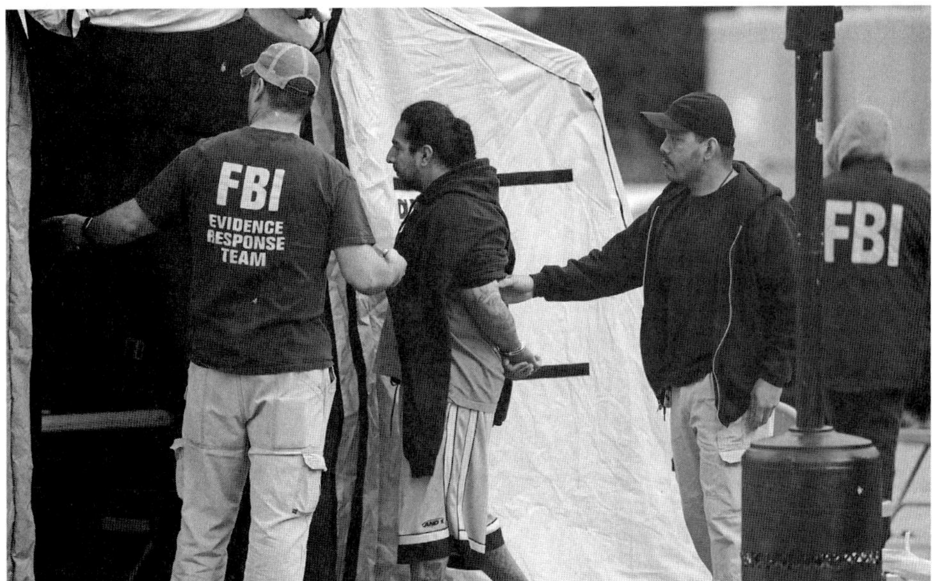

FBI agents arrest suspected members of the MS-gang.
Jae C. Hong/AP Images.

penetration into the organization, and it helps prevent competing organized crime groups from attacking the organization or making inroads into the criminal monopoly. Finally, organized crime groups plan extensively. They have long-term goals and are involved in complicated networks when conducting their activities. Planning is essential to perpetual successes.

Rather than defining TOC, Cockayne (2007) identified two perspectives associated with TOC. First, he noted that TOC can be a set of activities that supply **illegal goods and services** to meet a demand. Simple TOC organizations often focus on a few illegal operations, whereas more complex TOC organizations will be involved in a host of interrelated criminal and legitimate activities. As TOC organizations grow, they tend to become more complex organizationally and involved in more activities to further their illicit economic agenda.

Second, TOC groups consist of **hierarchal, organized entities**, as discussed later in this chapter. They essentially are business-like organizations that operate in the shadows and outside government oversight. Like the private sector, they develop relationships with other TOC organizations, legitimate business entities, governments, and sometimes terrorist organizations to facilitate their criminal enterprises. Cockayne questions whether TOC is a set of activities or an entity or organization. He argues that perhaps this is irrelevant. Actions should be taken when criminal enterprises assume an international or transnational posture. When a group or organization achieves international status, it has the potential to negatively affect large numbers of people and even governments. It creates significant harm across multiple geographical boundaries. Finally, the United Nations has defined TOC as "offenses whose inception, prevention and/or direct or indirect effects involved more than one country" (United Nations, 1995: 4).

These definitions and descriptions demonstrate that TOC is a series of sophisticated and sometimes complicated crimes involving multiple actors across international boundaries. When an organized crime group stretches across several countries or large areas, it demonstrates the power, influence, and negative effects it may have on individual countries.

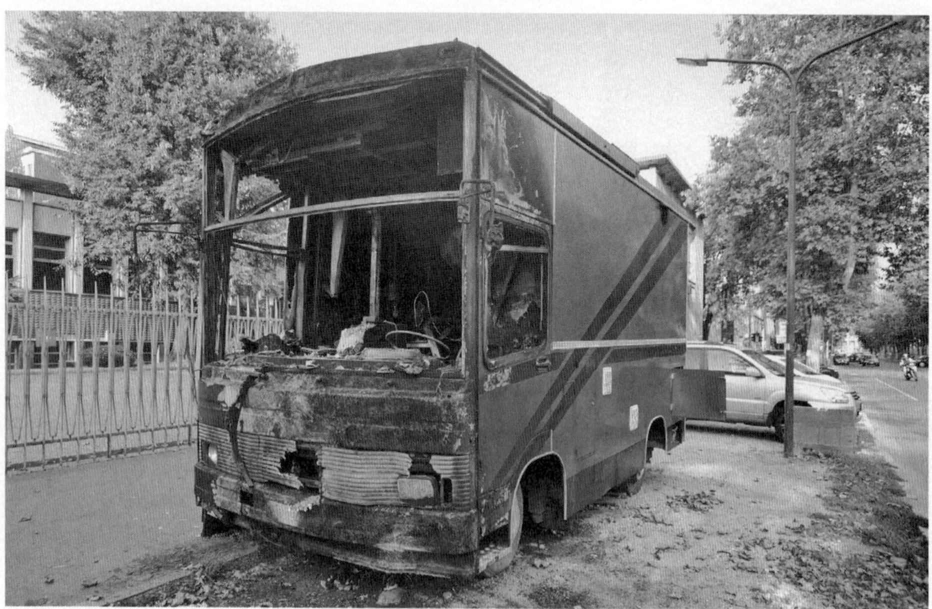

A van destroyed by a Mafia family because the owner refused to pay protection money.

Dino Fracchia/Alamy Stock Photo.

HS ANALYSIS BOX 7-1

We discuss organized crime as an economic enterprise. To some extent, it is similar to any other enterprise whether it be McDonalds, Ford, Wal-Mart, or some other business. What are the similarities between organized crime and these legitimate businesses? What are the differences? Can you analyze a criminal enterprise using economic terms and activities?

It goes well beyond street thugs, local gangs, or localized criminal groups. In addition to criminal problems, TOC has a negative impact on government and social institutions as well as the daily lives of those who reside near its places of operation.

The Federal Bureau of Investigation (FBI) (2017) has identified problem areas with the largest number of TOC groups. They include Africa, the Balkans, Asia, Eurasia, and the Middle East. Many of the countries in these areas have weak governments, making them conducive to TOC. Moreover, as demonstrated by the FBI's report, significant TOC groups exist across the globe.

Distinguishing Types or Categories of Crime

One way to better understand TOC is to examine it in relation to other kinds of crime. Historically, government officials, policy makers, and crime researchers have attempted to distinguish among street crime, white-collar crime, and organized crime (Edwards and Gill, 2002). Vice crimes generally have been subsumed within the organized crime category since vice was these criminals' primary modus operandi.

Society, especially American society, traditionally has viewed street crime as being more problematic and intrusive on people's lives relative to other forms of crime. **Street crime** results in visible deaths, injuries, and economic losses that are vividly portrayed in the news and popular media—there are observable victims. White-collar crime and organized crime generally have not had high visibility, and as such, most people have been unconcerned with these categories of crime. **Organized crime** is involved primarily in victimless crimes such as gambling, loan sharking, narcotics trafficking, and prostitution and the provision of desired illegal goods and services to the general public. **White-collar crime**, which includes numerous forms of fraud, for the most part, has been invisible to the public unless the government has made a case against some corporate entity. However, the 2008 recession that resulted in home foreclosures, high unemployment, and the bailout of large financial institutions resulted in the American people becoming more aware of white-collar crime and its impact on society.

An examination of these three general categories of crime shows that their differences are a matter of degree. For example, organized criminal syndicates often infiltrate legitimate businesses and, using white-collar crime techniques, destroy the business, absconding with its resources and capital or using them as a front for illegitimate enterprises such as money laundering. Organized crime figures and white-collar criminals have on occasion resorted to homicide, embezzlement, and other forms of street crime to further their criminal ends. White-collar criminals sometimes conspire with organized crime operatives, for example, in the illegal disposal of toxic waste and other environmental crimes. White-collar criminals frequently are involved in manipulating the costs of goods and services to increase profit. They circumvent work safety standards and produce substandard products. Some suggest that white-collar crime results in more deaths, injuries, and economic loss than do street crimes (Friedrichs, 1996). There is substantial participative overlap across these three forms of crime, and differentiating them sometimes can be difficult. For the most part, TOC participants generally are involved in all forms of crime, depending on the situation, environment, and criminal enterprise.

As noted earlier, terrorism represents a new category of crime that morally and politically is distinct from other types of crime. Actually, it is not new, but it has received substantial public attention as a result of the 9/11 attacks and the subsequent concern with homeland security. Like other forms of crime, terrorism includes street crimes, white-collar crimes, and TOCs that terrorists will use to accomplish their goals. Although there is a measure of overlap between "other criminals" and terrorists, there are some fundamental differences between these criminal types. Clarke and Newman (2006) enumerate several differences:

1. The motivations for crime and terrorism are vastly different—the former being committed for self-gratification, the latter for a higher cause.
2. Terrorists are much more determined than criminals.
3. Terrorism requires much more planning and is much less opportunistic than most crime.
4. Terrorism depends on external funding.
5. Terrorism usually involves much larger-scale acts.
6. Terrorism can only be committed by organized groups, whereas crime is more often a solitary undertaking (p. 5).

This chapter examines TOC because it is a tool used by terrorists to further their objectives. A number of terrorist organizations mirror TOC organizations in terms of structure and some of their activities. They use criminal activities to raise capital for their maintenance and attacks. They sometimes use TOC groups to facilitate their various activities. TOC groups have extensive networks that can be used in partnership to facilitate attacks or raise funding. It is sometimes difficult to categorize crime by types and perpetrators since different groups will use all sorts of criminal activities depending on needs and opportunities. Nonetheless, there appear to be a number of connections between TOC and terrorist activities.

▶ Impact of Transnational Organized Crime

TOC can have an impact on nation-states and large numbers of citizens, especially when criminal activities dominate an area. Felbab-Brown (2008) examined TOC and found that it can result in several critical problems, especially for countries that are underdeveloped or have weak governments. Criminal organizations attempt to corrupt governments. They bribe the government officials, police, customs officials, judges, and financial institutions. Such activities further politically weaken governments, reduce legitimate economic opportunities for citizens, and result in the loss of tax and other revenues for the government.

When bribery does not work, criminal organizations often resort to violence and intimidation. Van Dijk (2008) found that 81 percent of the TOC groups he studied used violence extensively. Many police and military units in Mexico have been compromised or intimidated by the Mexican drug cartels. In some cases, officials have become directly involved with the drug cartels, participating in drug and other illegal activities as a result of intimidation or corruption; in other cases, they do not enforce laws or attempt to counter these unlawful activities. In some areas, there is almost a total absence of a justice system. This has led to anarchy and lawlessness.

Felbab-Brown (2008) noted that in the 2007 Guatemala elections, TOC members murdered 50 political candidates and their supporters. They undertook a concerted effort to take control of Guatemala's political institutions. The same conditions exist in Mexico. In 2008, Mexican drug traffickers assassinated the country's highest ranking law enforcement official (Rollins and Wyler, 2013). Essentially, TOC groups penetrated the governments with the intention of controlling certain governmental activities to promote their illicit activities. The situation is not limited to Guatemala and Mexico; there are numerous countries across the world where this is occurring with different degrees of success.

TOC intrusions into legitimate government and business activities become a slippery slope as state actors co-opt criminals and actively solicit direct involvement in criminal activities. As such intrusions become successful, they result in officials reciprocating and seeking to establish informal and sometimes formal relations with TOC to share the wealth so to speak. Guatemalan military officials, for example, used profits derived from TOC relations to support their budgets and provide income for senior military officials (Felbab-Brown, 2008). In some cases, TOC soldiers organized into government-approved militias. These militias then protect corrupted officials, stamp out political opposition, and closely guard their illicit criminal operations. The TOC network becomes enmeshed in the political and social fabric of the country (U.S. Government Working Group, 2000). In some cases, the military and police are used to attack other competing cartels, further solidifying TOC's hold on the country.

HS Web Link: To learn more about the TOC and globalized economy, go to https://www.unodc.org/toc/en/crimes/organized-crime.html.

Third, TOC undermines and threatens the state not only in terms of justice and social order but also in terms of economic viability. Large-scale criminal activities in a state or area can have a number of negative macroeconomic effects. Van Dijk (2008) discovered that 75 percent of the TOC groups he studied had penetrated the legitimate economy. Felbab-Brown (2008) noted that such activities can contribute to inflation, real estate speculation, currency instability, and the displacement of legal production. When large-scale TOC activities are present, the government frequently is less likely to invest in economic development and there generally is less foreign investment.

Finally, TOC and illicit criminal economies threaten the security of the state. In the 1980s, the Shining Path in Peru and the Revolutionary Army Forces of Columbia (FARC) in Colombia controlled large swaths of those countries and essentially attempted to overthrow the legitimate governments. In the early 2000s, the Islamic State (ISIS) controlled large parts of Syria and Iraq with the intent of establishing a caliphate state. It took years of fighting to regain control.

The White House (2011) advised that drug kingpin Jose Americo Bubo Na Tchuto was appointed as Naval Chief of Staff in the West African country of Guinea-Bissau, demonstrating the extent to which governments can be infiltrated by TOC figures.

Even though the United States has a strong government and efficient law enforcement, TOC poses a real threat. It can undermine American enterprise worldwide. The White House (2011) summarizes the issue:

> TOC threatens U.S. economic interests and can cause significant damage to the world financial system through its subversion, exploitation, and distortion of legitimate markets and economic activity. U.S. business leaders worry that U.S. firms are being put at a competitive disadvantage by TOC and corruption, particularly in emerging markets where many perceive that the rule of law is less reliable. The World Bank estimates about $1 trillion is spent each year to bribe public officials, causing an array of economic distortions and damage to legitimate economic activity. The price of doing business in countries affected by TOC is also rising as companies budget for additional security costs, adversely impacting foreign direct investment in many parts of the world. TOC activities can lead to disruption of the global supply chain, which in turn diminishes economic competitiveness and impact the ability of the U.S. industry and transportation sectors to be resilient in the face of such

disruption. Further, transnational criminal organizations, leveraging their relationship with state-owned entities, or industrial actors, could gain influence over key commodities markets such as gas, oil, aluminum, and precious metals, along with potential exploitation of the transportation sector. (pp. 5–6)

▶ Conditions Facilitating Transnational Organized Crime

Although TOC has existed for decades, it has become more problematic recently, especially in light of the threat of terrorist attacks. TOC is ever-present, existing throughout the world. As Shelley (1999) noted, criminal organizations are present in every region in the world. They are in obscure places such as remote islands because many of these places provide the safe havens and offshore banking systems that facilitate organized crime. Today, there are more TOC organizations, and they are much larger than in the past, span greater geographical areas often operating in several different countries, and are involved in larger amounts of crime both in terms of the number of criminal activities and the magnitude of their criminal activities (Van Dijk, 2008). These changes have resulted in new challenges for law enforcement. As complex international organizations, they have become more difficult to counter, requiring international law enforcement cooperation and coordination.

Finckenauer (2000) and Reuter and Petrie (1999) have identified three factors that have contributed to this phenomenal growth: globalization, increased numbers and heterogeneity of immigrants, and improved communications technology. First, **globalization of the economy** has provided TOC new avenues by which to commit its criminal conspiracies. As the U.S. Government Interagency Working Group on International Crime Threat Assessment (2000) noted,

> The dynamics of globalization, however, particularly the reduction of barriers to movement of people, goods, and financial transactions across borders, have enabled international organized crime groups to expand both their global reach and criminal business interests. International organized crime groups are able to operate increasingly outside the traditional parameters, take quick advantage of new opportunities, and move more readily into new geographic areas. The major international organized crime groups have become more global in their operations, while many smaller and more local crime groups have expanded beyond their country's borders to become regional crime threats. (p. 4)

As the Working Group noted, the removal of borders resulting in the free flow of people, commodities, and information eliminated a number of barriers to TOC. Now, TOC groups can operate across a number of borders with impunity. It has also resulted in TOC groups aligning with other TOC groups to launder money; smuggle drugs, other contraband, and people; engage in criminal conspiracies; and become involved in financial fraud and other schemes. The removal of border restrictions has reduced TOC groups' risks and costs when conducting these criminal activities and enabled them to become engaged in larger numbers of criminal enterprises.

There is little official examination of TOC activities unless their criminal actions are discovered by law enforcement. When law enforcement does discover TOC involvement, it often is difficult for officials to take effective actions, especially when the TOC group is housed in another country that does not cooperate with international law enforcement or has been corrupted. Complicating this problem is that countries have different laws and criminal procedures, sometimes making it difficult for a country to take action against TOC groups in other countries. TOC groups oftentimes use borders to hide from or evade law enforcement officials.

Increased numbers and heterogeneity of immigrants refers to the fact that today there are larger numbers of cohesive immigrant populations in a number of countries. Globalization has resulted in the removal of borders, allowing groups to migrate, and this migration often results in the importation of criminal activities that are culturally based. This has resulted in ethnic and religious enclaves in cities and countries.

The migration and concentration often result in the importation of a new class of criminals and victims. Crime that was common in their old countries becomes an accepted practice in the new country. The criminals often maintain contacts and relations with criminals in their old country, and these relationships often result in transnational criminal operations. There are numerous examples, including Russian and Eastern European organized crime groups, Asian triads (underground societies) operating out of Taiwan and China, Japanese Yakuja, and street gangs such as the MS-13 from Central America. Finckenauer and Waring (1998) observed that there are 200 large Russian organized crime groups operating in 58 countries. Crime at this point becomes entrepreneurial and multinational.

Improved communications technology has played a key role in the growth of TOC. Internationally dispersed TOC groups can now communicate more easily, facilitating the development and operation of criminal conspiracies and enhancing command and control across borders. The era of enhanced communications also facilitates crime by reducing technical restrictions on the transfer of monies and the shipment of goods from one country to another. For example, cocaine shipments can be coordinated more effectively, and payments can be more easily transferred among individuals and across countries. It allows TOC to react to changing conditions more rapidly and become more efficient.

Additionally, Reyes and Dinar (2015) advised that the **proliferation of transportation technology** has significantly contributed to TOC. The world's vast networks of highways, airline travel, and container shipping have made it much easier for TOC groups to move illegal goods anywhere in the world. The system is so vast, it is virtually impossible for a country to effectively monitor goods and people entering or leaving a country.

Finally, it should be noted that **weak governments** play a key role in the formation of TOC organizations; these governments do not have the wherewithal or the tools to combat large and sophisticated TOC groups. Weak governments not only are unable to muster the resources to tackle TOC groups, but they are also susceptible to corruption that results in its facilitation. A prime example is Somalia. There essentially is no functioning central government in that country; the government is failed. It is ruled by warlords who function by engaging in a wide range of criminal activities. Somalia's coast has one of the largest concentrations of pirates in the world. Al-Shabaab, a large terrorist group, is also housed in Somali. Saul (2017) noted that it is sometimes difficult to differentiate between TOC and terrorism as they are involved in similar activities.

HS ANALYSIS BOX 7-2

Over the past decade, gangs have become a major problem in cities in the United States and other countries. In many cases, these gangs form along ethnic and racial lines. Given your knowledge about gangs from the news media and other sources, can you identify some ethnically based gangs? Can you identify gangs that are not ethnically based? Where do the gangs you have identified reside and commit their crimes?

Another example is the Ciudad del Este area, or the tri-border area (Brazil, Argentina, and Paraguay), which is lawless with dozens of criminal organizations from across the world operating there including Middle Eastern terrorist groups. Hezbollah, al Qaeda, Egypt's Al-Gama'a al-Islamiyya, al-Jihad, and al-Muqawamah have been known to operate in the region (Hudson, 2002).

▶ Networking: The Etiology of Transnational Organized Crime Groups

Criminal organizations, like everything else, have a beginning. There are conditions that facilitate the creation of TOC groups. Not all TOC groups have the same initiation. They form in a myriad of social milieus as a result of different social, political, and economic conditions. Some form as a result of familial ties, whereas others are constituted as a result of tribal connections and alliances. Business relationships often lead to criminal cabals; such relationships may result in opportunities for participants to acquire larger amounts of money. It is informative to examine the environmental conditions that result in the creation of TOC groups. An understanding of the conditions may lead to preventive or enforcement efforts when dealing with them.

Williams and Godson (2002) advised that the etiology of TOC groups can be explained using three models: (1) political models, (2) economic models, and (3) social models. The models identified by Williams and Godson do not necessarily represent distinct paths to the creation of TOC. Indeed, some TOC groups may originate as a result of factors that can be found in one or more models; however, Williams and Godson's models provide an understanding of TOC's origin in various locales.

Political Models

Political models refer to TOC groups forming as a result of weak nation-states. Weak nation-states generally are characterized by ethnic conflict or terrorist activity. This conflict often is due to different groups vying for power or control over the government and criminal and legitimate enterprises. These states have ineffective central governments that cannot cope with the conflict or terrorism. These states frequently are unable to meet consumer demand even for basic staples, creating a market for TOC groups. The state becomes a petri dish in which organized crime groups grow and spread like a bacterial culture. Democratic states have high acceptance levels of government control and the rule of law and tend to be more resistant to organized crime activities. They have the social and law enforcement institutions that are better able to deal with the criminal threat.

Economic Models

Economic models explain TOC groups' creation as a result of becoming involved in various enterprises. Two economic models help explain the emergence of TOC groups (Williams and Godson, 2002). First is the **market model**, whereby TOC groups focus on criminal or illegal markets.

When there is sufficient demand for illegal goods and services, illicit enterprises will evolve to fulfill the demand. The rapidity and extent of this evolution is often dependent upon the capacity of the nation-state to control such activities as well as the levels of demand. Initially, small groups emerge to fill the demand. When these groups are left alone, they continue to evolve. They form alliances with other groups, attempt to acquire more territory, co-opt governmental intervention via corruption, and often grow into larger criminal enterprises.

Social Models

Social models postulate that the growth of TOC groups is predicated on environmental factors. Williams and Godson (2002) have identified three social models that can be used to explain the emergence of TOC groups: (1) the cultural model, (2) the ethnic network model, and (3) the social network model. The **cultural model** refers to culturally based TOC groups. Some cultures are closed in that they have little regard for government; have strong communal, religious, and family ties; and generally are suspicious of outsiders, choosing to have little contact with them. The culture often exerts more control over its populace than the formal government or the rule of law. Loyalty to the culture is more important than loyalty to the country or state. The isolation, combative relationship with the larger society, and cultural dominance allow criminal-based norms to impregnate the culture over time. Examples of cultural-based TOC groups include the Sicilian Mafia and the Chinese Triads.

The **ethnic network model** is similar to the cultural model except that it refers to members of a tribe, culture, or ethnic group that is multinational. Members of the Sicilian Mafia and Chinese Triads migrated to the United States and other countries. Nigerian immigration to South Africa, the United States, Russia, Italy, and Brazil resulted in Nigerian criminal organizations in those countries. Once relocated, they maintain contact with the criminal groups in their previous homelands. In many cases, ethnic loyalties form the basis for recruiting new members into the criminal cabal, which facilitates the growth of criminal activities and enterprises in the countries where members of the network are located and spawns a large multinational TOC network.

The third social model explaining the emergence of TOC groups is the **social network model**. A number of organized crime scholars characterize organized crime organizations as being social networks regardless of culture or ethnicity (Potter, 1993). They observe that organized crime is fragmented, does not have sophisticated organizations, but is based on opportunity and patron-client relationships (Albini, 1971). Under the social network model criminal organizations emerge as members develop contacts with other criminals and clients through social networking. Criminals who are proficient in their trade are able to avoid arrest and increase the number of participants within their social network and increase the amount of criminal activity that occurs across the network. Associations may be family based, clients, other criminals, members of ethnic groups, and so on. Membership within the network is the result of new members being able to contribute to the criminal enterprises. They are not geographically limited and often extend across borders. Involvement is based on convenience, facilitation, and acquaintanceship.

Finally, it should be noted that the conditions that give rise to organized crime also can be used to explain the formation of a number of terrorist organizations. Terrorist organizations often are centered on religion or a political cause, but political, economic, and social conditions often contribute to their initial formation and growth.

▶ How Transnational Crime Is Organized

Crime committed by large-scale criminal operations is not a simple matter. Large-scale operations are analogous to similarly sized business operations. As noted earlier, large-scale criminal enterprises are complex organizations and have some level of hierarchy and specialization. For example, Rush (1999) examined the Cali drug cartel in Colombia and found specialized positions such as financial advisors, cell or regional managers, bookkeepers, stash house sitters or guardians, cocaine handlers, money handlers, motor pool personnel, and others. TOC groups must organize and attract people with various skills or expertise; businesses and terrorist organizations face a similar task. Like legitimate businesses, they must develop working relationships with outside groups. These groups may be other TOC groups, legitimate businesses or individuals, and in some cases terrorist organizations. Cocaine cartels must work with growers, transportation personnel, and wholesale or retail sellers. Some terrorist groups raise money by committing a variety of crimes including drug dealing, thus intersecting with TOC groups. Arms dealers must work with arms manufacturers, transportation, and governments and other consumers. As the TOC organization expands its operations, its organizational structure becomes more complex.

Wagley (2006) differentiates traditional organized crime from what he terms "more modern networks." Traditional organized crime was hierarchical, used a family structure, and operated for an extended period, whereas the newer organizations are more decentralized, often using a cell structure. Shelly (1999) and Williams (1998) advised that criminal organizations of the new millennium can be characterized as flexible and somewhat fluid in structure. First, they must be able to pursue ever-changing environmental conditions and economic opportunities. The primary objective of TOC is financial gain; flexibility allows organizations to rapidly change and pursue new opportunities. Second, greater awareness of the dangers posed by TOC has increased law enforcement scrutiny and enforcement actions. TOC groups must be flexible enough to avoid police interventions. Third, there is the constant threat of competition. These competitors often exert pressure through violent action and political associations to attack competitors. TOC groups must be able to adapt and change rapidly as a result of these threats.

In 2000, the United Nations Centre for International Crime Prevention examined 40 organized crime groups in 16 countries in terms of organization. The study found the following characteristics:

1. Two-thirds of the groups were organized around a hierarchy, while the remaining one-third were loosely organized.
2. Most of the groups studied were medium-sized with 20 to 50 members.
3. Most of the groups studied relied on violence to further their objectives.
4. Only about one-third of the groups were ethnically based and about one-half of the groups did not have any ethnic or social identity.
5. Many of the groups were involved in only one primary crime activity. Other research, however, shows that many are involved in multiple criminal enterprises (Van Dijk, 2008).
6. Most of the groups were involved in transnational criminal activities.
7. The majority of the groups used corruption to further their economic objectives. Here, Van Dijk found that 75 percent of the TOC groups he studied were involved in corruptive activities.
8. About one-third of the groups had developed political influence within the area or region.

HS Web Link: To learn more about Russian organized crime, go to http://www.globalsecurity.org/military/world/para/russian-organized-crime.htm.

The UN study demonstrates variability in TOC organization. It also shows that these organizations are involved in a variety of activities, and it is difficult to classify or make generalizations about the structure and functioning of TOC groups. Nevertheless, the UN developed a typology of TOC organizations or networks. The UN study identified five unique organizational structures used by TOC. An examination of these structures is informative since the organization of terrorist groups likely is similar.

Standard Hierarchy

Standard hierarchies mirror those found in many legitimate organizations and are generally found in the more sophisticated or developed TOC organizations. They generally have a single leader with subordinate managers who have clear operational responsibilities and control. There is some level of specialization whereby members are delegated different responsibilities and tasks. Leaders and managers maintain strict discipline and generally membership is ethnically homogeneous. In terms of size, the membership generally ranges from about 10 to several hundred members, but there are a number of drug trafficking organizations using the standard hierarchy that are much larger.

A number of TOC organizations are organized using the standard hierarchical format. Organized crime groups from China use this format. These groups center on a single individual and members are absolutely loyal. Most of the members are recruited from the criminal class. They enforce obedience by using violence and are involved in a variety of crimes and often invest in legitimate businesses. Many of the TOC groups from Eastern Europe and Russia also use this form of organization. These groups are involved in a blend of legitimate business and crime. A number of Mexican and Colombian drug cartels are also structured in this fashion. Some terrorist organizations, for example, ISIS and Hamas, use the hierarchical structure.

Regional Hierarchy

The second type of structure identified by the UN study was **regional hierarchies**. They are similar in structure to standard hierarchies except they have branches or structured groups in multiple locations. There is a centralized authority, and this authority exerts some level of control over the branches. Nonetheless, the branch leaders have a degree of autonomy in terms of controlling the branch and making decisions in terms of criminal and legitimate enterprises. A prime example of the regional hierarchy organization is outlaw motorcycle gangs. For example, the Hell's Angels are organized by chapters, but the chapter leaders maintain contact and coordination with the main chapter. The UN study noted that the Italian mafia is organized similarly. These groups have a number of families. Within each family are middle-level managers who are responsible for controlling an area, but each manager reports to the head of the family. A number of Japanese-based organized crime groups, including Fuk Ching, Yamaguchi-Gumi, and the Yakuza, operate similarly. A number of prison gangs in the United States operate using this structure.

Clustered Hierarchy

The third type of organization identified in the UN study was the clustered hierarchy. The **clustered hierarchy** is similar to the regional hierarchy except that in the clustered hierarchy the various criminal groups have a larger measure of independence. Each group may have a different structure, but they all operate within an umbrella that is coordinated to some degree by a central authority. The overall organization may form to divide markets or areas to reduce conflict, or the arrangements may be forged in order to facilitate criminal activities. Clustered hierarchies are engaged in a wide range of criminal activities since the clusters are composed of groups spread over a large geographical area. Many American organized crime groups fit this model. Each family has its territory and is independent, but each one often coordinates some of its activities with other families. A number of American youth gangs also fit this category. Also, given that al Qaeda has been attacked on a number of fronts, it appears that today it utilizes this format.

Core Group

The fourth type of TOC structure is the **core group configuration**. Here, a small core group of individuals control the activities. The core membership is involved in all the organization's enterprise from management to conducting the criminal activities. The core is surrounded by a number of associates who may be called upon as needed. These groups are relatively small with about 20 members. There are two such groups in the Netherlands that specialize in human trafficking. They often focus on a limited number of criminal activities.

Criminal Network

The final type of criminal organization is the criminal network. **Criminal networks** consist of a group of individuals who are loosely connected as a result of a criminal activity. The criminal activity and personal loyalty tie the individuals together. The associations facilitate the criminal activity. They typically are involved in financial crimes such as forgery or large-scale fraud. Individuals or small groups within the network are chosen because of their abilities, connections, or expertise. Some of the members may be involved in money laundering, forging documents, and disposing of the financial instruments. The associations are constantly changing since new or different expertise may be needed as the crimes and scams morph into new areas.

This section has discussed five types of networks that are used by TOC groups. Since the 9/11 attacks, law enforcement organizations worldwide have been focusing on terrorist and TOC groups. TOC groups have been targeted because of the scope of their criminal activities and because terrorist groups often participate in TOC activities or work closely with TOC groups, especially at the cell level. This intensified enforcement in some cases has resulted in the destruction of standard and regionalized TOC organizations, forcing them to become decentralized. Moreover, the age of Internet communications and globalization has made decentralized operations more efficient.

Decentralization of some terrorist organizations has occurred as a result of governments' efforts to combat them, for example, al Qaeda. Decentralization often results in the broader organization not having the resources to fund each cell or core group at adequate levels, which results in greater decentralization, as the individual cells independently pursue economic opportunities. Additionally, even though terrorists are often religiously or politically motivated, they also have a desire to be financially successful or independent. In some cases, greed dominates or circumvents philosophy, which sometimes results in terrorists replacing or substituting their terrorist desires with criminal activities. Crime and the accumulation of wealth become more important than "the cause." We see terrorists involved in TOC for personal gain and to fund their terrorist activities. For example, Hezbollah has been involved in cocaine trafficking and al Qaeda and the Taliban have been involved in opium and heroin trafficking. It becomes difficult to differentiate terrorist organizations from TOC organizations.

▶ Transnational Organized Crime Activities

There are numerous TOC groups across the world. Indeed, they exist in every country; some countries have larger numbers of these groups as compared to other countries. A number of studies have identified a wide range of criminal activities in which TOC groups are involved (U.S. Interagency Working Group, 2000; Wagley, 2006). Rabasa et al. (2006) and Sanderson (2004) examined the criminal activities of terrorist organizations, and they found that the two groups' activities were very similar and overlapped. The following provides an overview of the crimes committed by TOC groups and terrorist groups.

Drug Trafficking

Drug trafficking is the largest and most extensive illegal activity for TOC groups. It is carried out worldwide and affects every country. TOC groups are involved in drug trafficking at several levels: (1) production, (2) smuggling and transportation, and

Mexican authorities begin an inspection of a body dump near Tijuana, Mexico.
Guillermo Arias/Xinhua/Alamy stock photo.

(3) wholesale and retail operations. Some TOC groups are involved at all three levels; others are involved in only one or two levels of activities.

Afghanistan is the largest supplier of opium with a large portion of production being carried out or supervised by the Taliban and al Qaeda terrorist groups. In 2014, the United National Office on Drugs and Crime estimated that Afghanistan's opium crop was valued at $853 million. The country produced an estimated 6,400 tons of opium. Most of the opium is grown in areas controlled by the Taliban. In addition to being involved in growing and production, the Taliban taxes farmers for each kilo of opium they produce. Opium is a substantial revenue source for the Taliban. Here, the Taliban are both a terrorist organization and a TOC group.

TOC smuggling and transshipment operations are extensive. The Colombian drug cartels transship drugs to other countries where they are sold at the retail and wholesale levels by TOC groups. Much of the cocaine, marijuana, and methamphetamine coming into the United States is smuggled in by Mexican drug cartels. Other TOC groups wholesale cocaine in other parts of the world. The Italian mafia based in southern Italy distributes a large amount of the drug to parts of Europe, and numerous other TOC groups based in Europe, Asia, and Africa distribute cocaine and other illegal drugs. The transportation of drugs in Europe has become fairly easy with the advent of the European Union. There no longer are borders or border inspections to inhibit drugs from moving from one country to another.

Drug trafficking is a growing TOC problem. The White House (2011) reported that Mexican drug cartels are escalating the level of violence to protect their operations in Mexico and expand them in the United States. Latin American cartels are working with local criminal organizations in West Africa to move cocaine to Western Europe and the Middle East, and Afghan groups are working with West African organized crime groups to smuggle heroin to Europe and the United States. TOC groups throughout the world are now interconnected, making investigation more difficult and increasing illicit drug supplies.

Another issue is micro-drug trafficking. Clarke (2016) noted that we too often concentrate on the large drug operations and neglect the small ones. He noted that many terrorist groups are decentralized into small cells and that many of these cells derive a significant amount of income to fund their activities through small-scale drug sales. TOC groups and terrorist organizations are involved in all aspects of drug trafficking.

Human Trafficking

The movement of people who do not possess proper documentation (visas or passports) across international borders has become a major problem. This problem assumes two forms. First, there are large numbers of people who essentially decide to move from one country to another (migrate) and do so without documentation. In some cases, they simply avoid border restrictions and "sneak" into the new country. In other cases, **human smuggling** is involved. Here, they may hire someone to take them or to facilitate their journey and entry (these facilitators often are referred to as "mules"). The United Nations Office on Drugs and Crime estimated that human smuggling from Latin America to the United States generated approximately $6.6 billion, demonstrating that human smuggling is a significant organized crime activity (see White House, 2011). Many use forged documentation or remain in a country after their visas have expired. These people voluntarily move from one country to another. The majority of illegal immigrants in the United States fit this category. (This issue is discussed in more detail in Chapter 13.)

Human trafficking, on the other hand, refers to the forced migration of people. Article 3 of the UN Protocol to Prevent, Suppress and Punish Trafficking in Persons, Especially Women and Children, Supplementing the UN Convention against Transnational Organized Crime, defines human trafficking as

> The recruitment, transportation, transfer, harboring or receipt of persons, by means of threat, use of force or other means of coercion, of abduction, of fraud, of deception, of the abuse of power or of a position of vulnerability or of the receiving or giving of payment ... to a person having control over another person, for the purpose of exploitation.

The U.S. Working Group (2000) further illuminates the problem:

> Traffickers of women and children, much like narcotics traffickers, operate boldly across sovereign borders. They prey on women from countries where economic and employment prospects are bleak, organized crime is rampant, and females have a subordinate role in society. Often these women are tricked into leaving their countries by false promises of a better economic life abroad; traffickers lure victims with false advertisements and promises of jobs as models, dancers, waitresses, and maids. Once the women are abroad, traffickers use a variety of means to sell and enslave them. In other instances, traffickers buy young girls from their relatives. (p. 9)

Figure 7-2 ■ helps distinguish regular migration from human trafficking.

Human trafficking has become a significant TOC activity. The U.S. State Department (2015) identified the purposes of human trafficking: (1) sex trafficking, (2) child sex trafficking, (3) forced labor, (4) bonded labor or debt bondage, (5) domestic servitude, (6) forced child labor, and (7) unlawful recruitment and use of child soldiers. The *Federal Action Plan on Services for Victims of Human Trafficking in the United States 2013–2017* estimated that there are 20 million people worldwide who have been trafficked (Department of Justice, Department of Health and Human Services, and Department of Homeland Security, n.d.). Of this number, it is estimated that 14,550 to 17,500 people are trafficked in the United States annually.

There are organizations that specialize in the trafficking of women and children. In these cases, the women and children are sold for forced labor or sexual activities. The

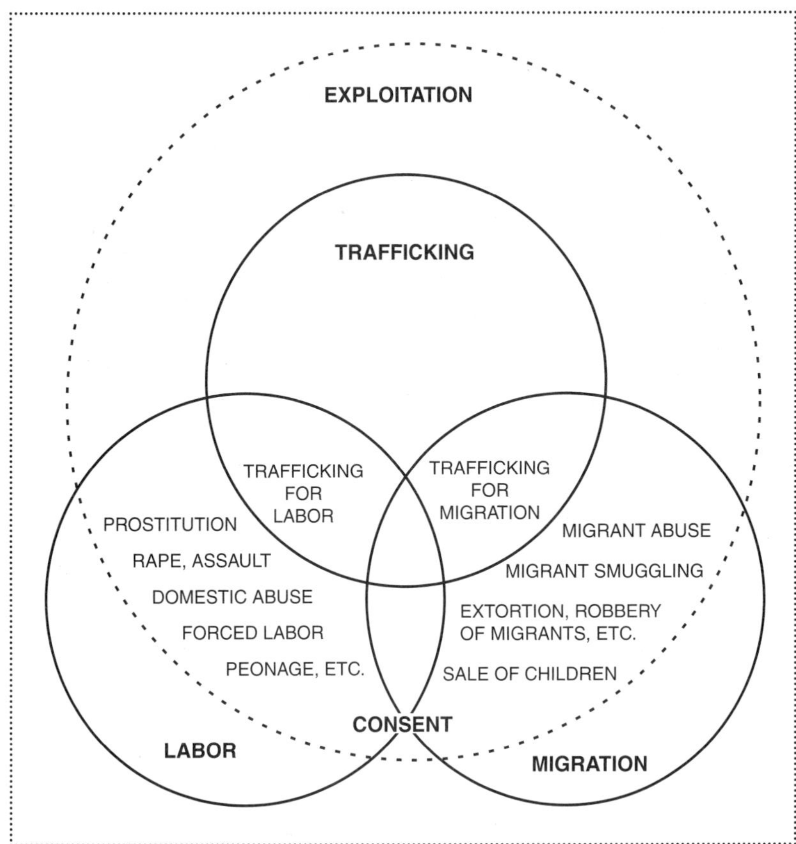

FIGURE 7-2 Schematic Representation of Relationships among Exploitation, Trafficking, Migration, Smuggling, Labor, and Consent

Source: Newman, G. (2006). *The Exploitation of Trafficked Women.* Problem-Solving Guides Series No. 38. Washington, D.C.: Office of Community Oriented Policing Services.

International Labor Organization (2005) estimated that at any given time, 2.5 million people are working as forced laborers, of whom 42 percent are in prostitution. A few organizations participate in both activities. The type of human trafficking engaged in by a TOC largely depends on its location and its connections or demand.

Of great concern from a homeland security standpoint is that these smuggling and human trafficking networks may bring terrorists into the United States. These networks are constantly moving people; thus, the ability to do so is present. As noted, a number of these networks are involved in other crimes such as narcotics smuggling. It is reasonable to assume that they would have no compulsion to smuggle terrorists into the United States or other countries. Terrorist organizations certainly have the resources to pay for their passage. It is extremely dangerous when human smuggling rings and terrorist organizations intersect.

Smuggling of Technology and WMD Materials

Smuggling of technology and WMD materials refers to illegally transferring weapons technology from one country to another. In Chapter 9, we examine weapons of mass destruction. It is notable that there is a market for smuggling materials and technology for weapons of mass destruction (WMDs), and the smuggling of these materials

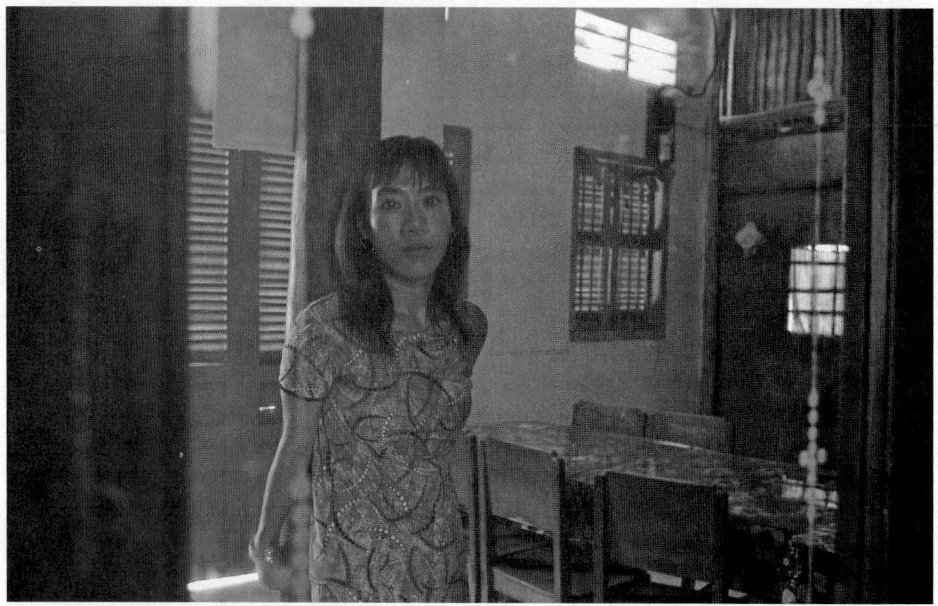

Dang Thi Nai 25 was bought for $250 from her mother and trafficked to Taiwan.
Jack Picone/Alamy Stock Photo.

appears to be increasing. Indeed, an international smuggling ring involved in the sale of nuclear technology and information was uncovered in Pakistan. A. C. Khan, the head of Pakistan's nuclear program, had sold technology to countries such as North Korea, Iran, and Libya (Frantz and Collins, 2007; MacCalman, 2016). MacCalman found that Khan was able to raise hundreds of millions of dollars for Pakistan's nuclear program by selling technology.

The U.S. Interagency Working Group (2000) noted that there have been 14 confirmed seizures of smuggled fissile materials totaling 15.3 kilograms of weapons-usable uranium and 368.8 grams of plutonium. These seizures demonstrate the existence of smuggling operations, and these groups likely will continue to attempt to smuggle uranium and plutonium since there likely is a lucrative market for radiological materials.

HS Web Link: To learn more about how TOC groups and terrorists smuggle WMDs, go to http://edocs.nps.edu/npspubs/institutional/newsletters/strategic%20insight/2007/williamsAug07.pdf.

More recently, a European Parliament report advised that ISIS was recruiting scientists to wage war with WMDs. The report also speculated that the terror group had already smuggled WMD materials into Europe (Paganini, 2015). The number of Europeans returning from Syria and Iraq substantially increase the probability that WMD materials will be smuggled into Europe.

Arms Trafficking

The end of the Cold War and several smaller wars throughout the world has resulted in an overabundance of weapons in circulation. When these weapons are not needed by governments, they become a commodity that can be sold on the black market. They represent a resource to their owners that can be converted into cash. Platt (2015) noted that arms trafficking is second only to drug trafficking in terms of financial benefits. **Arms trafficking** is the illegal selling of weapons to prohibited groups or countries, usually those in which conflicts are occurring. It is a multi-billion-dollar industry. It is estimated that approximately $1 billion is spent each year in the illicit weapons trade (Small Arms Survey, 2002). There are also a number of black marketeers who are constantly selling weapons around the world.

A substantial portion of illegal arms are sold on the gray market. The **gray market** consists of individual arms dealers who subvert the legitimate arms licensing processes and requirements. They illegally ship or smuggle arms to sanctioned countries by disguising the shipments as something other than arms. For example, they may ship arms under the guise of humanitarian aid or as farm equipment or other machinery. In some cases, the arms pass through several brokers and other handlers before they reach their final destination. The brokers who smuggle weapons sometimes develop intricate mazes of shipment points in an attempt to ensure that authorities do not discover the arms.

An array of weapons is sold on the black market. They include parts for larger and sophisticated weapons systems, assault rifles, portable anti-tank and anti-aircraft weapons, light artillery and mortars, military-grade explosives, and munitions. It is estimated that several million dollars' worth of weapons are sold annually to countries and groups that are under United Nations embargos (U.S. Interagency Working Group, 2000). Many of these weapons fall into the hands of terrorists, insurgents, and organized crime groups such as drug cartels. Many terrorist groups obtain their weapons from state sponsors. For example, many of the weapons used by insurgents and terrorists in Iraq and Afghanistan came from Iran and other countries opposed to the United States.

Although our primary concern is for WMDs, it appears that small arms are the real weapons of mass destruction because they result in the greatest number of deaths. For example, small arms were used in the Charlie Hebdo Paris attack and the San Bernardino and Chattanooga attacks, and small arms and explosives were used in the Paris terrorist attack. Small arms pose a threat to state sovereignty, especially in underdeveloped nations with ongoing insurgencies or conflicts. Whereas countries vigorously police chemical, biological, and radiological weapons, only minimal effort is exerted to control small weapons.

In some corners of the world, illegal arms dealing intermingles with other TOC activities. Rabasa and her colleagues (2006) identified several instances in which guns were traded for drugs. FARC insurgents from Colombia traded cocaine for guns with Paraguayan gunrunners. Hezbollah has been found to be active in Paraguay, obtaining drugs that ultimately would be used to fund some of its operations in the Middle East and possibly elsewhere. TOC and terrorist groups devise economic models that oftentimes use the barter system to obtain money for their various purposes. They identify markets and work to obtain the goods that are needed in those markets. In some cases, they may acquire or trade goods several times before obtaining their objective.

Cukier (2008) advised that there are a number of reasons why the illegal arms trade has not been controlled. First, there is a strong demand for arms, especially in countries that are rife with political or religious conflict. Second, arms embargos are ineffective in that they often do not apply to states that are involved in the weapons trade. Third, there are inadequate controls, including recordkeeping and verification over manufacturers, brokers, and shippers who are involved in the gun trade. Fourth, border control is inadequate in many of the countries that sell and purchase weapons. Finally, although some countries are very interested and committed to controlling illegal arms, most are not resulting in limited scope enforcement.

Trafficking in Precious Gems

There is a large world market for precious gems and metals. Their opulence is valued by the rich and elite throughout the world, resulting in a substantial demand. The smuggling of precious gems has become a source of significant revenue for organized crime, warlords, insurgents, and terrorists especially in Africa, which is home to a number of armed conflicts and insurgencies. For example, the National Union for the Total Independence of Angola (UNITA) insurgent group in Angola, rebels in the Democratic

Naval personnel from the USS *Truxtun* conduct anti-piracy operations.
The U.S. Navy.

Republic of the Congo, and the Revolutionary United Front in Sierra Leone use black market gems to finance their wars. Al Qaeda uses diamonds to raise funds and launder money (Le Billon, 2006).

Approximately three-quarters of the world's diamonds are mined in Africa, and in 1998, it was estimated that the value of the diamonds mined was $5.2 billion, and approximately 13 percent were mined illegally, primarily by insurgent groups. In some gem-producing countries, insurgents control and mine larger quantities of diamonds than do the governments. The sale of diamonds by insurgent groups not only results in the availability of funds to fuel wars and conflicts, but it also results in substantial revenue losses for these governments, generally weak nation-states, making it more difficult for them to respond to insurgencies and economic problems plaguing the country (U.S. Government Interagency Working Group, 2000). These diamonds and other gems have come to be called "blood diamonds" or "conflict diamonds" as they often are mined by slaves or captives and sold by warlords and insurgents to finance armed conflicts. The African diamond trade has made it intrinsically more difficult to solve these African conflicts.

Africa is not the only source of the black-market gem and precious metal trade; Russian, Chinese, and Italian organized crime groups are extensively involved in this activity. Russian officials estimate that between $100 and $300 million worth of diamonds are smuggled out of Russia each year (U.S. Government Interagency Working Group, 2000). In many cases, the organized crime groups infiltrate legitimate mines and businesses, procure the commodities, smuggle them out of the country, and sell them on the black market. The high demand for gems and precious metals creates a substantial market and high profits for the groups.

Piracy

Piracy is an attack on ships by intruders who intend to steal cargo or ransom the ship, its contents, or crew and passengers. Most people have the impression that maritime piracy was abolished long ago. However, it remains a significant problem, especially off the coasts of Africa and Asia and in some cases South America and the Caribbean. There are approximately 50,000 ships carrying about 80 percent of the world's traded cargo. This number does not include pleasure and other private non-cargo ships on the high seas. The large number of ships at sea at any given time represents multiple targets for pirates who see piracy as a lucrative business.

Piracy is a growing TOC activity. The frequency of piracy and the level of violence remain quite high even though several governments, including the United States, are making a concerted effort to reduce the problem. In one year, there were 406 incidents reported with 153 vessels boarded, 49 vessels hijacked, and 84 attempted attacks. A total of 1,052 crewmembers were taken hostage with 68 injured and 8 killed (International Chamber of Commerce, 2010). *The Journal of Commerce* (Zhongming Fan, and Xu, 2017) reported that bulk carriers and container ships are the most frequently attacked. Chemical tankers, product tankers, and general cargo ships are also attacked. Large ships are the primary targets of pirates. As an example, in 2008, pirates based in Somalia intercepted a Ukrainian freighter carrying Russian tanks, rocket-propelled grenades, and other munitions. The pirates demanded a $20 million ransom for the ship, its contents, and its 11-member crew (Gettleman and Ibrahim, 2009). A few months later, pirates attacked and ransomed a Saudi Arabian oil tanker containing $100 million worth of oil (McKenzie, 2009). These attacks demonstrate that pirates are capable of attacking even the largest nonmilitary ships and their attacks are becoming more brazen.

Most of the maritime piracy is conducted by organized crime groups with terrorist or insurgent groups possibly nominally involved in such activities. However, terrorists have plotted the destruction of ships at sea. In 2000, al Qaeda terrorists from Yemen attempted to ram the USS *The Sullivan* with a boat laden with explosives. The attack failed, but later in the year, they were successful in their attack on the USS *Cole*. That attack resulted in the deaths of 17 sailors and considerable damage to the *Cole*. In 2004, the same tactic was used to attack a French oil tanker, the *Limberg*, off the coast of Yemen, and in 2004, Abu Sayyaf, a terrorist group based in the Philippines, claimed responsibility for an explosion on a large ferry that killed at least 100 people. In 2002, the Moroccan government arrested a group of al Qaeda operatives suspected of plotting raids on British and U.S. tankers passing through the Strait of Gibraltar.

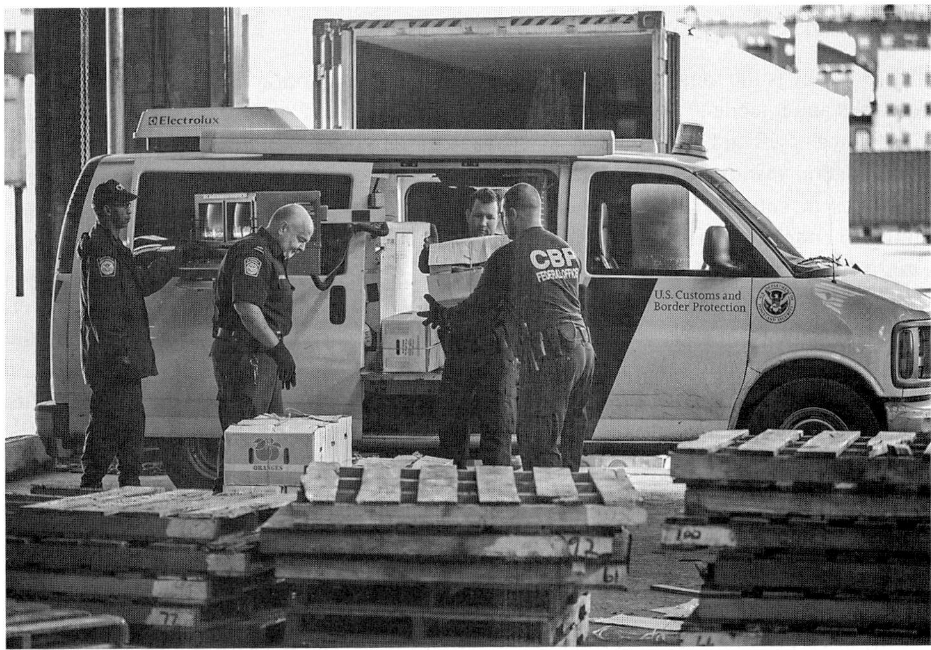

Customs and border protection agents confiscate counterfeit goods coming into the United States.
614 Collection/Alamy Stock Photo.

Non-Drug Contraband Smuggling

Non-drug contraband smuggling refers to smuggling legitimate goods such as alcohol, cigarettes, textiles, and various luxury goods to evade taxes and tariffs. Smuggling these goods is safer as compared to drug smuggling since the penalties are much less severe. For example, Russia and China have the highest tariffs on luxury goods and the newly created economic elite craves the nuances and trappings of wealth. When smugglers are able to import goods without the tariffs, especially if they are obtained from the originating country where they are less costly or stolen, they are able to realize a substantial profit on the black market. Colombian drug traffickers used money from drug operations to purchase cigarettes and smuggle them into Colombia, avoiding tariffs resulting in lost revenue to that country.

The United States is not immune from such activities. In 2000, FBI agents made several raids in North Carolina and arrested members of a Hezbollah cell who were smuggling cigarettes from North Carolina to Michigan. They made weekly trips, and each trip netted them $3,000 to $10,000. Hezbollah members were able to raise several million dollars with their cigarette smuggling operation. Mohammed Yousef and Chawki Hammound used the proceeds to purchase and ship night vision goggles, mine detection equipment, laser range finders, blasting caps, and other military hardware to Hezbollah operatives (Horwitz, 2004; Mutschke, 2000). According to an FBI investigation, terrorists financed the 1993 World Trade Center Bombing with counterfeit textile sales from a store in New York City, and in 1996, the FBI arrested Sheik Omar Abdel Rahman on terrorism charges. Agents confiscated 100,000 counterfeit items there were to be sold to raise money for Rahman's terrorist organization. And, INTERPOL found that Chechen rebels funded some of their operations through the sale of DVDs (Pollinger, n.d.).

Terrorists are extensively involved in counterfeit goods. It represents a way to raise large amounts of money, depending on the goods being sold. The crime often is not on law enforcement's radar, resulting in a fairly safe way to make money.

Counterfeiting

U.S. currency is the most commonly counterfeited currency because it is accepted in most countries and it tends to hold its value relative to other currencies. Essentially, it is the universal currency. The U.S. Treasury estimates that there is $570 billion in genuine currency in circulation worldwide, with about two-thirds of the currency outside the United States. Advances in computer and print technology have substantially increased TOC groups' ability to counterfeit currency and other financial instruments such as fictitious securities. Drug traffickers, terrorist groups, and other TOC groups are involved in counterfeiting. Some Russian and Italian organized crime groups are principally involved. Moreover, some countries such as North Korea have counterfeited American currency. The White House (2011) suggested that North Korea may have collaborated with TOC groups when producing counterfeit American currency. The greatest problem is that these groups are using counterfeit currency to finance other criminal or terrorist operations.

HS Web Link: To learn more about counterfeit American money, go to http://www.frbsf.org/federalreserve/money/funfacts.html.

Theft

The FBI (2017) now has a TOC program dedicated to dismantling TOC groups. The bureau has identified a number of TOC groups and noted that they are involved in a wide variety of criminal activities, including the crimes listed in this section. Additionally, they are involved in a number of high-end theft activities, including art theft, cargo theft, organized retail theft, jewelry and gem theft, and vehicle theft. These commodities when stolen in bulk provide TOC groups with large amounts of income. As an example, ISIS looted a number of archeological sites in Syria and Iraq and sold artifacts to raise money.

Financial Fraud

Financial fraud refers to activities that illegally or improperly obtain money and other valuables from citizens and businesses via some financial scam. Common scams include insurance fraud, lottery fraud, scam business propositions, tax avoidance, offshore investment scams, pyramid schemes, credit fraud, and so on. Schemes by TOC groups are responsible for stealing billions of dollars annually from citizens, businesses, and government entitlement programs. It has grown because of our dependence on the Internet for financial transactions and because more substantial information about people and their finances is available via the Internet. Also, we continue to move toward a cashless society in which credit, debit, and bank cards are the primary instruments of commerce. Van Dijk (2008) reports that globally, 1 percent of people with credit cards have been victimized by credit card fraud, and more than one-quarter of Internet fraud is perpetrated via credit card fraud. Russian, Nigerian, and Asian TOC groups are principally involved in these activities.

The U.S. Government Interagency Working Group (2000) noted that Russian organized crime groups have penetrated the international banking community, oftentimes using funds derived from criminal enterprises to purchase banks and other financial institutions. This allows them to obtain financial information on individuals and other corporations, launder money, and become involved in insider trading and other financial crimes. They have become involved in Russia's expanding gas and oil industries. Here, they use extortion, steal gas, and oil and sell it on the black market, and bribe public officials to facilitate these activities. Some have estimated that $12 billion annually is moved out of Russia by Russian organized crime groups.

American citizens are the target of a number of fraudsters from countries across the globe. They generally use e-mails, faxes, or letters soliciting donations to charities, invitations to invest in a new highly profitable company, assist in accessing fictitious financial accounts, or advise the e-mail recipient that he or she has won or inherited a large amount of money in a foreign country. Generally, the victim is required to pay upfront fees, taxes, or tariffs for the money to be released to the victim. The fraudster merely keeps the money and the victim receives nothing in return except perhaps a bitter lesson. Victims report losing several million dollars each year as a result of these schemes. Businesses are similarly targeted through stolen credit card numbers and forged identities. A number of Russian TOC groups have been hacking into bank and other financial institutions to steal credit card and personal information.

Environmental Crimes

Environmental crimes consist of the improper or illegal disposal of trash and hazardous waste. Countries across the globe have passed progressive laws controlling the disposal of trash and hazardous waste materials. In many cases, there are not ample legitimate outlets for disposal, or in most cases, the cost of proper disposal is substantial. These conditions provide new opportunities for TOC groups. The U.S. Government Interagency Working Group (2000) estimated that the illegal dumping of trash and hazardous materials is a $10 to $12 billion industry. Organized crime groups in Russia, China, and Japan are principally

HS ANALYSIS BOX 7-3

Financial fraud, particularly identity theft and the theft of credit card information, is the fastest-growing crime in the United States and the world. There literally are thousands of victims losing millions of dollars each year. Have you been a victim of financial fraud? What have you done to reduce the probability that you will become a victim?

Illegal dumping of garbage in a river.
Lenz/Alamy Stock Photo.

involved, but other groups are also involved to a lesser extent. Oftentimes, the hazardous materials will be combined with scrap metal or other commodities and shipped out of country. The waste is sometimes shipped to countries with lax laws; in other cases, the waste will be dumped in waterways or buried in desolate areas. Of particular concern is the illegal disposal of radioactive waste. This material could be used by terrorists to build a "dirty bomb."

Failed States and Transnational Organized Crime and Terrorism

We have noted that TOC flourishes in failed states. It is also true for terrorism. Nonfunctioning governments or weak governments are breeding grounds for terrorists and terrorist organizations. Before examining failed states in more depth, it should be noted that the term failed state is rather amorphous; it does not have clear delineation as there are degrees of failed states. Stanislawski (2008) has identified gradations of failed states or degrees of stateness. Some states are more effective at governing than others in terms of their territorial control and performance of government functions. There are **quasi-states** where there are boundaries, but the government is weak and has little control over the territory. Afghanistan could be characterized as a quasi-state since the government has little control outside Kabul. **Almost states** are regions or areas within another country that functions as its own state. The Kurdish area in Iraq is an almost state. It has its own government and military and effectively governs its lands. It is likely that this will lead to conflicts with the Iraqi central government in the future much like the conflict between the Turkish Kurds and the Turkish government. Finally, there are **black spots**. Black spots are areas within a state that is ungoverned. A prime example of a black spot is the tribal region in Pakistan. This region is home to al Qaeda and the Taliban. Finally, there are **failed states**. The best example is Somalia. It has had no working central government since 1991 and currently is ruled by war lords. Today, the terrorist group al-Shabab, which is affiliated with al Qaeda,

HS ANALYSIS BOX 7-4

Here, we discuss failed states, quasi-states, black spots, and almost states. A number of terrorist groups are located in these types of geographical areas. Identify five different terrorist groups (see Figure 6-1 ■ in Chapter 6 for a listing) and try to determine if they are located in one of the above types of geographical areas. Can you identify a terrorist group that is in a stable nation-state?

is fighting to create a fundamentalist Islamic state in Somalia. The country is also home to a number of pirates who operate in the Gulf of Aden.

Plummer (2012) argued that focusing on failed statehood as the cause for the development of terrorism is simplistic. The attributes of the failed state as well as the failure of the state must also be examined as many of these attributes contribute to the formation of terrorist groups and TOC. He noted that countries that place less effort into social welfare have more connections to terrorism and incidents (also see Burgoon, 2006; Schneider et al., 2010). Burgoon advised that social welfare reduces poverty, inequality, insecurity, and religious extremism. These conditions often contribute to the growth of terrorism. For example, Hamas in Gaza and Hezbollah in Lebanon have wide public support because of their social welfare programs. The presence of an ethnic or religious community with a history of being persecuted or repression will create a black spot from which terrorists can emerge and operate. ISIS, which primarily consists of Sunnis, evolved in Syria as a result of oppression by the Bashar al-Assad regime. Economic underdevelopment results in poverty, which in turn contributes to terrorism. Economic disparity within or among countries can create rage and terrorism. For example, the Shiites in Iraq repressed the Sunnis politically, socially, and economically after the American withdrawal. The repression of the Sunni's resulted in the Iraqi Sunnis sympathizing with ISIS.

Failed states of one sort or another exist on every continent. They are ripe for the formation of TOC and terrorism. President George W. Bush's foreign policy agenda included nation building. If we had been more successful, we likely would have had an impact on TOC and terrorism. Nonetheless, failed states will continue to be breeding grounds for crime and terrorism, which means that we will continue to be involved in countering TOC and terrorism. The only solution is more effective governance in these countries or a strong law enforcement and defensive posture.

Links between Transnational Organized Crime and Terrorist Organizations

As noted earlier, in numerous instances, there is a convergence between TOC groups and terrorist organizations, and in some cases, it is difficult to discern differences between these two types of organizations (Picarelli, 2012). A prime example is narco-terrorism, in which terrorists are trafficking drugs to support their activities, and the terrorists are used by drug traffickers for protection, money laundering, and transportation. This point is amplified by the fact that about one-third of the organizations on the State Department's list of foreign terrorist organizations are also on the list of targeted U.S. drug suppliers (see Schmid, 2003), and 29 of the 63 organizations of the Department of Justice's FY2010 Consolidated Priority Organization Targets list, which includes the most significant drug trafficking organizations, were associated with terrorist groups (White House, 2011). This section more fully explores the relationships between TOC and terrorist organizations. It is important to understand these relationships when developing enforcement and prevention priorities. Neglecting TOC organizations may allow openings for terrorist groups. On the other hand, if law enforcement agencies can dismantle a TOC group, that may negatively affect affiliated terrorist groups.

There are a number of similarities between TOC groups and terrorist organizations. For example, Schmid (1996) identified the following:

- Both operate secretly and usually from an underground.
- Both use muscle and ruthlessness and produce mainly civilian victims.
- Intimidation is characteristic of both groups.
- Both use similar (although no entirely overlapping) tactics: kidnappings, assassinations, and extortion.
- Both exert control over individuals within the group.
- Both use front organizations such as legitimate businesses or charities.

Later, in a 2003 paper, Schmid identified areas of dissimilarity between TOC and terrorist organizations:

- Terrorist groups are usually ideologically or politically motivated, whereas organized crime groups are profit oriented.
- Terrorist groups often wish to compete with governments for legitimacy; organized crime groups do not. Organized crime desires to circumvent the legal system so that the legal system does not impede the maximizing of profits.
- Terrorist groups relish media attention and oftentimes exert efforts to receive it; organized crime groups attempt to remain in the shadows receiving as little notoriety as possible.
- Terrorist victimization and violence are generally less discriminate than those of organized crime groups.

There is substantial overlap between TOC and terrorist groups, and at the same time, a number of differences exist. The similarities result in the two types of criminals (based on motivation) having similar modus operandi to the point that sometimes these groups are hard to distinguish from each other. Although organized criminal groups often resort to crimes that produce a monetary reward, they sometimes use violence as a means to this end. Some organized crime groups are more violent than others. For example, violence or the threat of violence is a central part of extortion, which is commonly practiced by a number of TOC groups. Terrorists have political objectives, but TOC groups often have their own quasi-political objectives. They often attempt to corrupt government officials and governments to facilitate their criminal ends. Well-established governments, especially open democracies, tend to be more resistant to intrusion by criminal organizations. Thus, the activities of TOC groups and terrorist groups often parallel, and to some extent their objectives sometimes overlap.

It should be recognized that there are impediments to TOC groups cooperating with terrorist organizations. The Canadian Centre for Intelligence and Security (2006) has identified several such impediments. First, in some cases, terrorist groups and TOC groups that are co-located come into conflict as a result of competition for criminal activities or territories; multiple organizations conducting the same criminal enterprise reduce each organization's margin of profit. Second, both terrorist and TOC organizations demand high levels of loyalty from their members. Alliances with other groups may jeopardize member loyalty, and they increase the probability of government detection or infiltration. Third, a number of terrorist organizations are ephemeral-sporadic—they have the wherewithal, motivation, or resources to conduct only one or a few attacks and do not need outside assistance. Fourth, TOC groups are organized around profits, not politics. They shun the media and any other attention. TOC groups may be unwilling to enter into a cooperative relationship with a terrorist organization because of the potential public exposure. In the long term, it likely would be bad for business. Finally, many traditional crime groups are intensely nationalistic. Even though they commit large numbers of crime, they are loyal to their homeland. Indeed, it is the homeland and its legal and socioeconomic system that provide the TOC group with the opportunities for its profitable criminal activities. Therefore, it likely will be opposed to terrorist organizations that desire to change the status quo. Even though such impediments exist, there still are instances when TOC groups are cooperating and working with terrorist organizations.

In some areas, the connection between TOC and terrorist organizations is blatantly clear. A prime example is the tri-border area of Paraguay, Brazil, and Argentina—an area that is rife with drug trafficking, money laundering, arms smuggling, and other illegal activities. In 1992, Hezbollah detonated a bomb outside the Israeli embassy in Buenos Aires, killing 29 people, and in 1994, it detonated a car bomb attack in the same city, targeting a Jewish-Argentine community center and killing 87. In both cases, evidence pointed to Ciudad del Este, or the tri-border area, as the staging point for the attacks (Shelly and Picarelli, 2005). Sanderson (2004) noted that Hezbollah is not the only Middle Eastern terrorist organization in the area. Hamas and Gamaa al Islamiyah have elements there committing crimes and raising money for terrorist activities. South American terrorist organizations such as the Colombian terrorist group FARC are also present.

Another such area is the border between Pakistan and Afghanistan where al Qaeda is involved in opium production to finance its terrorist operations. Indeed, al Qaeda has developed criminal syndicates throughout Central Asia and North Africa to augment its terrorist campaigns (Sanderson, 2004). A substantial amount of the opium produced in this area is processed by the Kurdistan Workers' Party (PPK) and Turkish TOC groups (Canadian Centre for Intelligence and Security, 2006). Given that approximately 90 percent of the world's illegal opium production is in Afghanistan and is largely controlled by al Qaeda and the Taliban, these terrorist organizations must develop links with other terrorist and TOC groups to market the drugs.

In these examples, terrorists work closely with TOC organizations to facilitate criminal activities and raise funds for their worldwide attacks. The intersection of the numerous and varied terrorist groups with TOC groups results in a dangerous cocktail of violence and criminal efficiency. It not only means that TOC groups are jointly working with terrorist organizations, it also means that terrorist organizations are cooperating with other terrorist groups. Such symbiotic relationships can result in more proficient criminal and terrorist organizations.

▶ The Continuum of Terrorism and Transnational Organized Crime

There are alliances between TOC and terrorist groups, and in some cases, they overlap. Makarenko (2004) examined the relationship between the two groups and developed a continuum of their cooperation as shown in Figure 7-3 ■.

Terrorism

Alliances and cooperation between TOC and terrorist groups for mutual gain and goal accomplishment

Terrorists use criminal activities for financing and other operational purposes

No relationships or coexistence in a geographical area

TOC groups use terror tactics to facilitate financial gains

Alliances and cooperation between TOC and terrorist groups for mutual gain and goal accomplishment TOC Groups

FIGURE 7-3 Continuum of TOC and Terrorist Cooperation
Source: Adopted from Makarenko, T. (2004). "The Crime-terror continuum: Tracing the interplay between transnational organized crime and terrorism." *Global Crime*, 6: 129–145.

As depicted in Figure 7-3 ■, both groups can initiate contact and negotiate relationships with the other group. When this occurs, the terrorists and the TOC group are co-joined in extreme cases. There are all sorts of alliances that can be formed: money laundering, smuggling, drug trafficking, and so on. Shelly (1999) identified that whenever TOC groups or terrorist groups destabilize governments, it is beneficial to both groups. In some cases, alliances can be based on the provision of services between groups. For example, al Qaeda developed a relationship with Bosnian criminal groups to establish a drug transportation route for Afghan heroin into Europe through the Balkans (Makarenko, 2004).

▶ Incentives for TOC and Terrorist Organizations to Cooperate

Even though terrorist groups are primarily motivated by religion, they require large sums of money to finance their operations; they also are motivated by greed and opportunity. The financial greed results in pursuing relationships that facilitate resource acquisition. Rollins and Wyler (2013) have identified three primary reasons for TOC and terrorist organizations to cooperate. First, there is **Partnership Motivations and Disincentives**. Here, partnership can be a force multiplier as well as a strategic weakness. Conditions may exist that cooperation results in a TOC group and a terrorist group achieves the benefits. TOC or terrorist groups may have skills or contacts that the other group needs. Terrorist groups in North Africa and Asia assist TOC groups transport drugs; both groups profit. On the other hand, a terrorist organization and a TOC group may coexist in an area and compete for profit-making opportunities causing conflict. In 2011, a plot to assassinate the Saudi ambassador to the United States was uncovered. Iranians paid members of the Los Zetas drug cartel $1.5 million to conduct the assassination (Rollins and Wyler, 2013). There are many opportunities for these organizations to partner.

Second, **Appropriation of Tactics** is where TOC and terrorist groups acquire tactics from each other in order to achieve their goals. Both groups are involved in criminal activity, money laundering, illegal weapons acquisitions, smuggling, and corrupting government officials. In some cases, TOC groups and terrorist groups have learned from each other, while in other cases they have cooperated.

Finally, **Organizational Evolution and Variation** is where environmental influences over time necessitate that the organization move in other directions or change operations to acquire resources or achieve goals. In some cases, TOC groups have become more politically motivated to combat government intervention, while terrorist groups have focused more on crime as a result of greed. For example, al Qaeda affiliates, PPK, Revolutionary Armed Forces of Columbia, Haqqani Network, and Hezbollah are involved in criminal activities. These groups learn from each other and sometimes share tactics.

Summary

This chapter examined TOC. It is important to understand this form of criminality because of its relationships, affiliations, and intersections with terrorist organizations. In many cases, terrorist organizations are using transnational crime to raise funds for their terrorist attacks, buy arms and explosives, and maintain their networks. As noted in Chapter 12, it is important that governments reduce funding to terrorist organizations using any means possible. Reduced funding not only will reduce attacks, but it will also make it difficult for these organizations to maintain themselves or expand. Moreover, TOC constitutes a growing and dangerous form of crime. It corrupts governments, leads to governmental ineffectiveness, and results in a socioeconomic structure in many countries that has dire consequences for their populations. It should receive governments' attention because of the harm it does to many societies.

Researchers have found that TOC groups use a variety of organizational structures. Some are classically organized using a pyramid structure with strict command and control, rules, specialization whereby different members are assigned specific tasks, and a strict recruitment system. Other TOC groups are more decentralized, with some of them quite large and encompassing a number of TOC operations across several countries. It is interesting that TOC organizations mirror terrorist organizations in their organizational structures, and in some cases, TOC organizations are integrated with terrorist organizations on some levels. The exact organizational structure often is the result of the environment, criminal opportunities, and the amount of governmental and law enforcement pressure. TOC organizations, as well as terrorist organizations, often become more decentralized when there is substantial law enforcement pressure.

TOC groups are involved in a variety of criminal enterprises. These activities include counterfeiting, trafficking drugs and narcotics, exportation of counterfeit clothing and luxury goods, international transportation of stolen luxury items such as stolen high-value automobiles, money laundering, trading in gems and precious metals, piracy, and environmental crimes. It should be noted that violence and governmental corruption are activities that are commonly associated with these TOC activities. A TOC group's involvement is largely dependent upon opportunities—involvement in some of these crimes is the result of the TOC's location near the resources or a viable market.

It is informative to consider the relationships between TOC groups and terrorism. As noted, they often use similarly constructed organizational frameworks and share a number of other similarities. These similarities represent "pulls" that make it conducive for these two types of organizations to develop alliances for their mutual benefit. At the same time, there are "pushes" that prevent TOC groups and terrorist organizations from developing cooperative relationships. Thus, these relationships remain tenuous and sometimes are forged temporarily; in other cases, they may have a measure of permanence. Regardless, these relationships can facilitate an increase in crime and terrorism. It is vital that governments focus on TOC groups.

Discussion Questions

1. What is the interplay of street crime, white-collar crime, organized crime, and terrorism?
2. What are the characteristics of organized crime groups?
3. How does TOC interact with or otherwise affect governments?
4. What factors have facilitated the growth of TOC? How?
5. There are two economic models explaining the emergence of TOC. Explain their operation and differences.
6. Compare the various TOC structures.
7. How do drugs contribute to TOC and terrorism?
8. How are terrorist groups and TOC groups similar? Different?
9. What are the factors that contribute to TOC and terrorist groups cooperating?

References

Albini, J. (1971). *The American Mafia: Genesis of a Legend*. New York: Appleton Crofts.

Burgoon, B. (2006). "On welfare and terror: Social welfare policies and political-economic roots of terrorism." *Journal of Conflict Resolution*, 50: 176–203.

Canadian Centre for Intelligence and Security. (2006). "Actual and potential links between terrorism and criminality." *Trends in Terrorism Series*. http://www.carleton.ca/cciss/res_docs/itac/omalley_e.pdf (Accessed October, 31, 2008).

Clarke, P. (2016). "Drugs & thugs: Funding terrorism through narcotics trafficking." *Journal of Strategic Security*, 9: 1–15.

Clarke, R., and G. Newman. (2006). *Outsmarting the Terrorists*. Westport, CN: Praeger.

Cockayne, J. (2007). *Transnational Organized Crime: Multilateral Responses to a Rising Threat*. Washington, D.C.: International Peace Academy.

Cukier, W. (2008). *The Illicit Trade in Small Arms: Addressing the Problem of Diversion*. Ottawa: Peacebuild Small Arms Working Group.

Decker, S. H., and D. Pyrooz. (2015). "Street gangs, terrorists, drug smugglers, and organized crime." *The Handbook of Gangs*, Oxford University Press: 294–308.

Department of Justice, Department of Health and Human Services, and Department of Homeland Security. (n.d.). *Federal Action Plan on Services for Victims of Human Trafficking in the United States 2013-2017*. http://www.ovc.gov/pubs/FederalHumanTraffickingStrategicPlan.pdf (Accessed May 18, 2016).

Edwards, A., and P. Gill. (2002). "Crime as enterprise? The case of transnational organized crime." *Crime, Law & Social Change*, 37: 203–223.

FBI. (2017). *Transnational Organized Crime*. https://www.fbi.gov/investigate/organized-crime (Accessed August 10, 2017).

Felbab-Brown, V. (2008). *Tackling Transnational Crime: Adapting U.S. National Security Policy*. Washington, D.C.: Brookings Institution.

Finckenauer, J. (2000). *Meeting the Challenge of Transnational Crime*. Washington, D.C.: National Institute of Justice.

Finckenauer, J., and E. Waring. (1998). *Russian Mafia in America*. Boston, MA: Northeastern University Press.

Frantz, D., and C. Collins (2007). "Those nuclear flashpoints are made in Pakistan." *Washington Post* (November 11). http://www.washingtonpost.com/wp-dyn/content/article/2007/11/07/AR2007110702280.html (Accessed August 28, 2017).

Friedrichs, D. (1996). *Trusted Criminals in Contemporary Society*. Belmont, CA: Wadsworth.

Gettleman, J. and Ibrahim, M. (2009). Somali pirates get ransom and leave arms freighter. *The New York Times* (February 5), http://www.nytimes.com/2009/02/06/world/africa/06pirates.html.

Glenny, M. (2005). "The lost war." *Washington Post* (August 19): B1, 5.

Horwitz, S. (2004). "Cigarette smuggling linked to terrorism." *Washington Post* (June 8): A1.

Hudson, R. (2002). *A Global Overview of Narcotics-Funded Terrorists and Other Extremist Groups*. A Report Prepared by the Federal Research Division, Library of Congress.

International Chamber of Commerce. (2010). *2009 Worldwide Piracy Figures Surpass 400*. http://www.icc-ccs.org/news/385-2009-worldwide-piracy-figures-surpass-400 (Accessed January 17, 2011).

International Labor Organization. (2005). *A Global Alliance against Forced Labor*. Geneva: ILO.

Kenney, D., and J. Finckenauer. (1995). *Organized Crime in America*. Belmont, CA: Wadsworth.

Le Billon, P. (2006). "Fatal transactions: Conflict diamonds and the (anti)terrorism consumer." *Antipode*, 38: 778–801.

MacCalman, M. (2016). "A.Q. Khan nuclear smuggling network." *Journal of Strategic Security*, 1: 104–118.

Makarenko, T. (2004). "The Crime-terror continuum: Tracing the interplay between transnational organized crime and terrorism." *Global Crime*, 6: 129–145.

McKenzie, D. (2009). *Exclusive: Pirate tells how comrades drowned*. CNN (January 14). http://www.cnn.com/2009/WORLD/africa/01/12/somalia.pirates/index.html.

Mueller, G. (1998). "Transnational crime: Definitions and concepts." *Transnational Organized Crime*, 4: 13–21.

Mutschke, R. (2000). "Threats posed by the convergence of organized crime, drug traffickers, and terrorism." Testimony of the Assistant Director, Criminal Intelligence Directorate, International Criminal Police Organization-Interpol, before the U.S. Judiciary Committee, Sub-Committee on Crime (December 13).

Paganini, P. (2015). ISIS recruited experts set to wage chemical and biological attacks, Dec. 6, Security Affairs. http://securityaffairs.co/wordpress/42572/intelligence/isis-wmd-attacks.html

Picarelli, J. (2012). "Osama bin Corleone? Vito the jackal? Framing threat convergence through an examination of transnational organized crime and international terrorism." *Terrorism and Political Violence*, 24: 180–198.

Platt, S. (2015). "Trafficking of human beings and smuggling of migrants." *Criminal Capital*, pp. 121–137. UK: Palgrave Macmillan.

Plummer, C. (2012). "Failed states and connections to terrorist activity." *International Criminal Justice Review*, 22: 416–449.

Pollinger, Z. (n.d.). *Counterfeit Goods and Their Potential Financing of International Terrorism*. http://michiganjb.org/issues/1/article4.pdf (Accessed August 17, 2017).

Potter, G. (1993). *Criminal Organizations: Vice Racketeering and Politics in an American City*. Prospect Heights, IL: Waveland Press.

Rabasa, A., P. Chalk, K. Cragin, S. Daly, H. Gregg, T. Karasik, K. O'Brien, and W. Rosenau. (2006). *Beyond al-Qaeda: The Outer Rings of the Terrorist Universe*. Santa Monica, CA: Rand.

Rengert, G. (2003). "The distribution of illegal drugs at the retail level: The street dealers." *Drugs, Crime, and Justice*, ed. L. Gaines and P. Kraska, pp. 175–192. Prospect Heights, IL: Waveland Press.

Reuter, P., and C. Petrie. (1999). *Transnational Organized Crime: Summary of a Workshop*. Washington, D.C.: National Academy Press.

Reyes, L., and S. Dinar (2015). "The convergence of terrorism and transnational crime in central Asia." *Studies in Conflict & Terrorism*, 38: 380–393.

Rollins, J., and L. Wyler (2013). *Terrorism and Transnational Crime: Foreign Policy and National Security*. Washington, D.C.: Congressional Research Service.

Rush, G. (1999). *Organized Crime, Drugs and Street Crime*. San Clemente, CA: Law Tech Publishing.

Sanderson, T. (2004). "Transnational terror and organized crime: Blurring the lines." *SAIS Review*, 24(1): 49–61.

Saul, B. (2017). "The legal relationship between terrorism and transnational crime." *International Criminal Law Review*, 17: 417–452.

Schmid, A. (1996). "The links between transnational organized crime and terrorist crimes." *Transnational Organized Crime*, 2(4): 40–82.

Schmid, A. (2003). "Links between terrorist and organized crime networks: Emerging patterns and trends." Terrorism Prevention Branch Office on Drugs and Crime, United Nations, Vienna.

Schneider, F., Bruck, T., and Meierrieks, D. (2010). The economics of terrorism and counter-terrorism: A survey (CESIFO Working Paper No. 3011). http://papers.ssrn.com/sol3/papers.cfm?abstract_id¼1590148 (Accessed 12, 2010).

Shelly, L. (1999). "Identifying, counting and categorizing transnational criminal organizations." *Transnational Organized Crime* (Spring): 1–18.

Shelly, L., and J. Picarelli. (2005). "Methods and motives: Exploring the links between transnational organized crime and international terrorism." *Trends in Organized Crime*, 9(2): 52–67.

Small, K., and B. Taylor. (2005). "State and local law enforcement response to transnational crime." *Trends in Organized Crime*, 10(2): 5–16.

Small Arms Survey. (2002). *Small Arms Survey 2002: Counting the Human Cost*. Oxford: Oxford University Press.

Stanislawski, B. (2008). "Para-states, quasi-states, and black spots: Perhaps not states, but not ungoverned territories either." *International Studies Review*, 10: 366–396.

United Nations. (1995). *Results of the Supplement to the Fourth United Nations Survey of Crime Trends and Operations of Criminal Justice Systems on Transnational Crime, Interim Report by the Secretariat*. New York: Author.

U.S. Government Interagency Working Group. (2000). *International Crime Threat Assessment*. http://www.fas.org/irp/threat/pub45270intro.html (Accessed September 24, 2008).

Van Dijk, J. (2008). *The World of Crime: Breaking the Silence on Problems of Security, Justice, and Development across the World*. Los Angeles, CA: Sage.

Wagley, J. (2006). *Transnational Organized Crime: Principal Threats and U.S. Responses*. Washington, D.C.: Congressional Research Service.

White House. (2011). *Strategy to Combat Transnational Organized Crime*. Washington, D.C.: Author.

Williams, P. (1998). "Organizing transnational crime: Networks, markets and hierarchies." *Transnational Organized Crime*, 57–58.

Williams, P., and R. Godson. (2002). "Anticipating organized and transnational crime." *Crime, Law & Social Justice*, 37: 311–355.

8 Intelligence and Counterintelligence and Terrorism

LEARNING OBJECTIVES

1. *Discuss the importance of intelligence and problems associated with its collection.*
2. *Describe the role and functions of the director of national intelligence.*
3. *Describe the kinds of intelligence that are collected.*
4. *Distinguish the various methods of intelligence collection.*
5. *Identify the members of the intelligence community and explain their responsibilities.*

Key Terms

Director of National Intelligence
Human Intelligence or HUMINT
National Clandestine Service
Signals Intelligence or SIGINT
Measures and Signatures Intelligence or MASINT
Imagery Analysis or IMINT
Open Source Intelligence or OSINT
Central Intelligence Agency
Directorate of Operations
Intelligence Directorate
Science and Technology Directorate
Directorate of Digital Innovation
Defense Intelligence Agency
Defense Clandestine Service
Department of Energy
Office of Intelligence and Counterintelligence
Department of Homeland Security
Office of Intelligence and Analysis
State Department
Bureau of Intelligence and Research
Bureau of Counterterrorism and Countering Violent Extremism
International Security and Nonproliferation
Conflict and Stabilization Office
Office to Monitor and Combat Trafficking in Persons
Treasury Department
Office of Foreign Assets Control
Office of Terrorist Financing and Financial Crime
Financial Crimes Network
Drug Enforcement Administration
Intelligence Division
Federal Bureau of Investigation
National Security Branch
Counterintelligence division
Counterterrorism division
Joint terrorism task force
High Value Detainee Investigation Group
Weapons of Mass Destruction Directorate
National Geospatial-Intelligence Agency
National Reconnaissance Office
National Security Agency
Edward Snowden
Coastwatch Program
Intelligence Cycle
U.S. Northern Command
U.S. Special Operations Command
Joint Special Operations Command
Counterintelligence
Domestic industrial espionage

Introduction

Throughout the early years of the war in Iraq, President George W. Bush and representatives in his administration repeatedly advised that, "We had to get them [the terrorists] over there before they attacked us over here." Although this philosophic musing was used to justify the Iraqi war, with questionable effectiveness, it did signify or at least recognize a need for U.S. intelligence operations to extend well beyond U.S. borders to collect information about those who would attack us or otherwise do our country harm. The 9/11 attacks vividly identified that U.S. intelligence apparatus was sorely lacking as enumerated by the 9/11 Commission (National Commission on Terrorist Attacks, 2004). We needed our intelligence agencies to more effectively identify those individuals and groups who intended to attack us or otherwise do us harm; determine if they had the capability to attack us; and find out about their activities, especially if they were a prelude to an attack. We now are engaged in a global conflict with terrorism as our enemy; it is an asymmetric or unconventional conflict resulting in the need for effective strategies and tactics. It is unlike any other conflict or war that our country has fought.

The end of the cold war resulted in a paradigm shift in terms of intelligence. During the cold war, we were interested in politicians, governments, armies, and other state activities. Our intelligence apparatus primarily focused on China and the Soviet bloc—they were our enemies. We were interested in learning about their actions so that we could be prepared and able to counter any attacks or other threats. With the fall of the Soviet Union, everything changed. The American military-industrial complex was deemphasized. Congress allocated fewer funds to defense as we attempted to realize a "peace dividend" or savings to fund more domestic programs. The military shrunk in size and fewer resources were allocated to intelligence. We, to some extent, became involved in a number of smaller wars and conflicts across the globe. We exerted few efforts or resources to uncover information about new enemies. Nonetheless, we had to shift from a global security perspective to one that considered small wars and non-state actors (Baldwin, 1995).

The American embassy bombings in Africa, the attack on the USS *Cole* in Yemen, and the first World Trade Center bombing were the first major attacks on the United States by al Qaeda, but it was the later and more devastating 9/11 attacks that resulted in immediate and massive changes in government and the public psyche. Terrorism immediately became the primary, if not the only, government concern, and within the realm of terrorism, intelligence, or the lack thereof, was jolted to the forefront. Politicians, political pundits, and the mainstream media severely criticized perceived intelligence failures and inadequacies. Indeed, there were pieces and snippets of information about the impending 9/11 attacks that had been collected by a number of intelligence organizations, but they had not been collated and analyzed so that we could successfully identify the impending attack. The National Commission on Terrorist Attacks (2004) documented the many lapses in intelligence gathering and analysis. The primary criticism was that the various intelligence agencies failed to cooperate, share information, and communicate with one another. The intelligence community consisted of a number of intelligence fiefdoms and operated as such. There was no mechanism putting the pieces together and looking at the "big picture."

The 9/11 attacks spurred Congress and the president into action. Enforcement and intelligence agencies were given more powers primarily through the USA PATRIOT Act. Executive orders and laws were passed that authorized and facilitated the sharing of information across intelligence agencies. Enhanced surveillance activities were authorized. Most important, the intelligence community was reorganized with the creation of the position of director of national intelligence (DNI) with the passage of the Intelligence

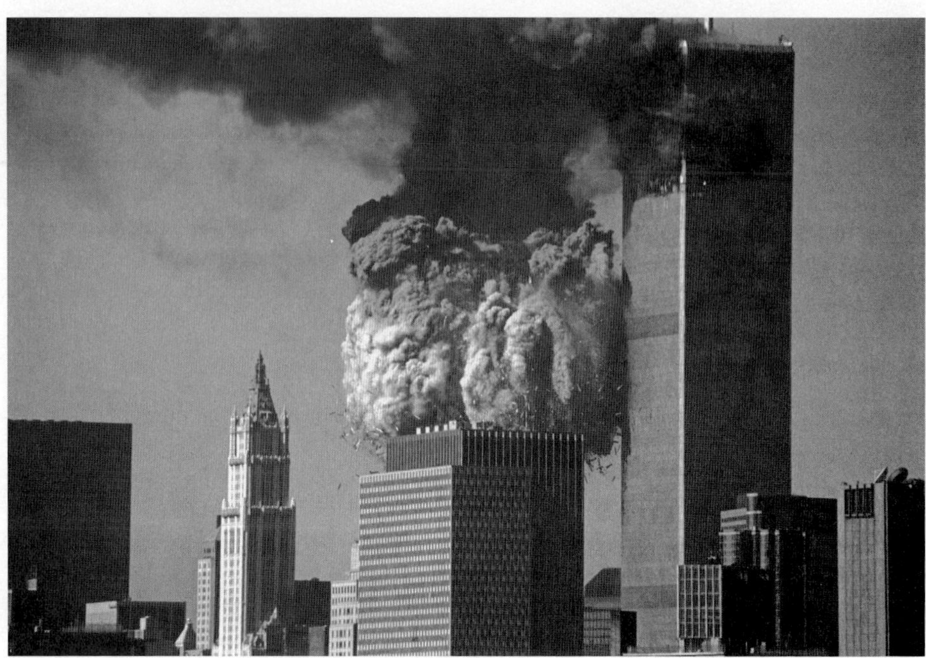

The devastating 9/11 attacks on the World Trade Center.
Beth Dixson/Alamy Stock Photo.

Reform and Terrorist Prevention Act of 2004. The act was legislated to improve the cooperation and coordination of the American intelligence community. Prior to the passage of the act, the director of the Central Intelligence Agency (CIA) supposedly served as coordinator of the intelligence apparatus in addition to his or her duties as director of the CIA. However, the director of the CIA historically had little oversight authority or capability over other intelligence agencies and largely concentrated on managing the CIA. The creation of the DNI supposedly improved our intelligence operations.

Intelligence Failure—What Does It Mean?

As noted, the 9/11 attacks and the 9/11 Commission Report (2004) squarely identified intelligence failures as a significant national security problem. However, this is a broad statement that provides little guidance in repairing the problem. Hypothetically, intelligence failures can occur at multiple levels (Clarke, 2017). First, starting at the lowest level of the intelligence chain, we can fail to collect critical or applicable intelligence information. This problem is discussed in more detail later in this chapter. Second, once it is collected, intelligence agencies fail to recognize its importance, link it with other pertinent information, or otherwise interpret it in a useable policy format. The analysis has shortcomings. Third, intelligence agencies fail to share information, resulting in many incomplete pieces of the same puzzles. The passage of the Intelligence Reform and Terrorist Prevention Act of 2004 was intended to solve this problem and progress has been made. Fourth and perhaps most damning, politicians and policy makers cherry pick intelligence to meet their needs. Several behavioral modes occur here. Policy makers and politicians disregard intelligence that is counter to their beliefs or political positions. The politics of policy formulation trump common good and effective responses. It also results in politicians and policy makers pressuring intelligence agencies' analysts to find the right answers for the wrong questions, often leaving gaps in what we should know about a national security issue.

Although in the post–cold war period we have had gaps in our intelligence-gathering capabilities, particularly human intelligence—field operatives collecting information at ground level, our intelligence agencies have done a reasonably good job of collecting needed information. Further, our intelligence agencies perhaps possess the most skilled analytical capabilities of any country in the world. Our failure has been in the areas of sharing and cherry picking information.

Our intelligence failure was not at the collection and analysis end but at the consumption end. Politics and careers overshadowed correct intelligence answers and correct, effective responses.

HS Web Link: To learn more about intelligence failures and causes, go to https://govinfo.library.unt.edu/911/report/911Report_Exec.htm.

The Director of National Intelligence

The **director of national intelligence** is the titular head of the intelligence community. The DNI advises the president on national security intelligence matters. Additional duties vested with the DNI include the following:

- Ensure that timely and objective national intelligence is provided to the President, the heads of departments and agencies of the executive branch; the Chairman of the Joint Chiefs of Staff and senior military commanders; and the Congress
- Establish objectives and priorities for collection, analysis, production, and dissemination of national intelligence
- Ensure maximum availability of and access to intelligence information within the Intelligence Community
- Develop and ensure the execution of an annual budget for the National Intelligence program (NIP) based on budget proposals provided by IC [intelligence community] component organizations
- Oversee coordination of relationships with the intelligence or security services of foreign governments and international organizations
- Ensure the most accurate analysis of intelligence is derived from all sources to support national security needs
- Develop personnel policies and programs to enhance the capacity for joint operations and to facilitate staffing of community management functions
- Oversee the development and implementation of a program management plan for acquisition of major systems, doing so jointly with the Secretary of Defense for Department of Defense programs, that includes cost, schedule, and performance goals and program milestone criteria (Office of the Director of National Intelligence, 2016).

These duties squarely place responsibility for managing and coordinating intelligence activities with the DNI. Prior to the creation of the DNI, the intelligence agencies were to a large extent uncoordinated. There remain some questions relative to the DNI's effectiveness. The DNI submits the budgets for the intelligence agencies. In 2016, the intelligence community had a budget of $50.3 billion (Office of the Director of National Intelligence, 2016). The DNI currently has little control over the agencies' budget formulation or objectives. The agencies

HS ANALYSIS BOX 8-1

Establishing the DNI was seen as a way to better coordinate our intelligence services. Do you think the diversity of agencies complicates this task? Do you think that there are too many agencies reporting to the DNI, thus affecting the office's effectiveness?

TABLE 8-1 Intelligence Agencies under the DNI

Air Force Intelligence	National Geospatial-Intelligence Agency
Department of the Treasury	Department of Energy
National Reconnaissance Office	Department of Homeland Security
National Security Agency	Defense Intelligence Agency
Department of State	Marine Corps Intelligence
Navy Intelligence	Coast Guard Intelligence
Army Intelligence	Federal Bureau of Investigation
Drug Enforcement Administration	Central Intelligence Agency

HS Web Link: To learn more about the DNI, go to https://www.dni.gov/index.php.

submit them to the DNI, which presents them to Congress. For example, the largest portion of the intelligence budget is contained in the Department of Defense. Since the secretary of defense is a cabinet-level position and the DNI is not, it begs the question as to how much control the DNI will have on the overall intelligence budget and its associated objectives.

The DNI coordinates 16 different intelligence organizations as noted in Table 8-1 ■.

▶ Conceptual Overview of Homeland Security Intelligence

In the past, intelligence focused on foreign enemies, and our intelligence activities often centered on foreign lands and activities. Homeland security, on the other hand, is the defense of the American homeland, which substantially expands our collective view of intelligence. This new intelligence perspective is depicted in Figure 8-1 ■.

As shown in Figure 8-1 ■, there basically are four spheres or dimensions relative to intelligence: foreign, domestic, military, and homeland security. In terms of homeland security, the various law enforcement and homeland security agencies are interested in

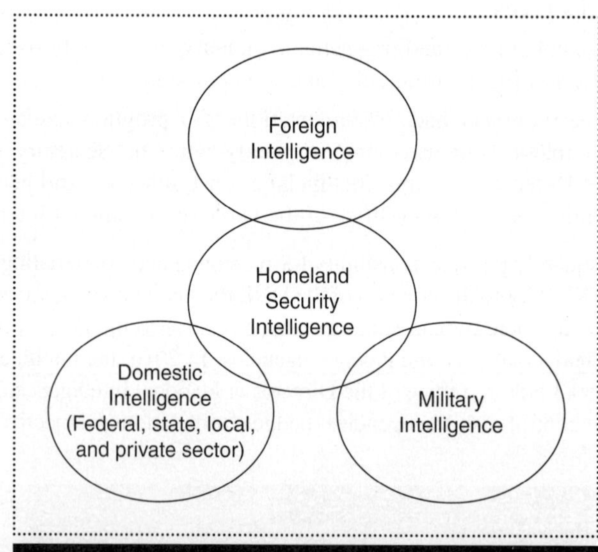

FIGURE 8-1 Dimensions of Intelligence
Source: Masse, T. (2006). *Homeland Security Intelligence: Perceptions, Statutory Definitions, and Approaches.* Washington, D.C.: Congressional Research Service, p. 5.

collecting domestic intelligence about impending attacks, terrorists, and terrorist activities. The increase in lone wolf attacks and the possibility of terrorist cells in our country (Worth, 2016) have become an ever-increasing homeland security priority. However, since terrorism is substantially international in character, it requires that we look well beyond our borders. Thus, several intelligence agencies within the intelligence community collect foreign intelligence—intelligence about what is transpiring in other countries relative to terrorists and state actions. Military intelligence, on the other hand, has the same view but centers on strategic and tactical military operations. Nonetheless, military perspectives sometimes overlap with terrorist activities, and the military intelligence apparatus obtains information about possible attacks on the United States by terrorists. Finally, as a result of the 9/11 attacks and the need to protect our homeland, local and state police agencies, the first-line homeland defense, have become more actively involved in collecting information about possible terrorists and terrorist plots (Fisher, 2016). Each of these spheres contributes to homeland security intelligence. Part of the intelligence process is to merge or aggregate the information originating from these spheres into coherent information that can be used by policy makers to respond to threats.

Types of Intelligence Collection Activities

Before examining the various intelligence agencies that comprise our intelligence community, it is important to examine the types of intelligence collection activities that agencies use. Many people, when contemplating intelligence, think about James Bond and other similar characters in the entertainment genre. Although governments have spies, they seldom, if ever, are involved in the activities that are displayed on television or in the movies. Indeed, most intelligence activities are mundane; analysts pour over information and attempt to discover answers, trends, and so on. Former Department of Homeland Security (DHS) Secretary Michael Chertoff (2006) noted,

> Intelligence as you know, is not only about spies and satellites. Intelligence is about the thousands and thousands of routine, everyday observations and activities. Surveillance, interactions—each of which may be taken in isolation as not a particularly meaningful piece of information, but when fused together, gives us a sense of the patterns and the flow that really [are] at the core of what intelligence analysis is all about.... We [DHS] actually generate a lot of intelligence...we have many interactions every day, every hour at the border, on airplanes, and with the Coast Guard. (p. 1)

As Chertoff indicated, intelligence is the aggregate of volumes of information. It is the sum of the many parts. This sum is achieved only when the necessary information is collected by a variety of agencies and individuals and from a variety of sources. In essence, more comprehensive collection efforts generally result in a more complete intelligence picture. As such, intelligence collection consists of five different types of collection activities (Clarke, 2008; OPSEC, 1996; Richelson, 2008), which will be discussed next.

Human Intelligence

First, **human intelligence or HUMINT** is the collection of intelligence by field agents and other individuals, or human sources. Basically, there are two types of HUMINT. One is clandestine HUMINT, the secret relationships forged between American intelligence personnel and foreign sources. It closely resembles what many perceive as espionage. The other is overt HUMINT, open-source intelligence whereby intelligence personnel contact foreign government personnel, read governmental reports, and obtain information that is

HS ANALYSIS BOX 8-2

As noted, human intelligence was neglected for many years. There are numerous examples of human intelligence in movies, television, and fictional books. Essentially, spies are numerous and involve in all sorts of activities. Thinking of the last spy movie you watched, what types of activities were involved? Were they effective? Do you think human intelligence is similar to the way intelligence operations are portrayed in the movies?

openly available to the public. Overt HUMINT is most often performed by state department personnel and military attaches and is discussed in more detail later.

Up until the mid-twentieth century, HUMINT was the primary mode of intelligence gathering. Countries did not have spy satellites or other sophisticated electronics with which to spy on adversaries. Beginning in the 1950s, HUMINT was deemphasized when intelligence agencies began to use technology beginning with spy planes (the U2) and later satellite imaging. The 9/11 attacks demonstrated a significant weakness in our intelligence collection. We had few HUMINT resources, which in large part resulted in our not being able to anticipate the 9/11 attacks, and we had too little information about al Qaeda and other terrorist organizations that desired to attack our homeland (MacGaffin, 2005). Technological spying could not provide us with enough information about terrorist groups since to a large extent, they remain hidden from electronic surveillance. We were overly dependent on electronic spying (Margolis, 2013). Subsequently, we have increased our HUMINT efforts, and without question, they are the most effective method of obtaining intelligence about terrorist groups. As Betts (2003) noted, "Human intelligence is key because the essence of the terrorist threat is the capacity to conspire. The best way to intercept attacks is to penetrate the organizations, learn their plans, and identify perpetrators so they can be taken out of action" (p. 475). Terrorist organizations or groups evolve or change rapidly. HUMINT, when in place, allows us to collect better and more timely information about their threats.

Today, most HUMINT is performed by the CIA's **National Clandestine Service**. It operates from our embassies and consulates, which provide it with cover. As embassy or consulate employees, agents of the National Clandestine Service have diplomatic immunity if they are discovered. A number of clandestine officers work under nonofficial cover. They pose as business persons, scientists, and so on. However, most spying is performed by foreign nationals. American diplomats and other intelligence personnel often recruit these foreign nationals to spy or collect information. They may be opposed to the government or in many cases are attracted by significant payments. Once recruited, they are managed or handled by American intelligence personnel. Most countries rely on this method of collecting intelligence. As an example, foreign governments likely collect substantial intelligence about the United States by infiltrating our government, defense contractors, corporations, and universities.

Signals Intelligence

Signals intelligence or SIGINT includes the interception of electronic communications and deriving intelligence from those communications. These electronic communications are of different types, including telephone, Internet, facsimile, radio, and radar. The interception of radar allows us to determine the locations of ships, aircraft, and previously unknown military facilities. We monitor telephone and Internet communications in an effort to obtain information about impending attacks and about enemies and organizations. For example, there have been several occasions on which the terrorist threat level has been elevated because of Internet "chatter" among suspected terrorists and terrorist organizations (e.g., see Lumpkin, 2002). We also track high-value terrorist targets such as Taliban and ISIS leaders using SIGINT. SIGINT is often used to identify targets for drone strikes.

All governments and terrorist organizations must communicate for command and control purposes, and these communications potentially can be intercepted. Our SIGINT capabilities have resulted in our killing of a number of terrorist leaders, and it has reduced terrorist organizations' command and control functions by eliminating communications channels. SIGINT has not prevented the terrorists from communicating among themselves, but it has substantially inhibited them. SIGINT is primarily performed by the National Security Agency (NSA).

Measures and Signatures Intelligence

The third form of intelligence collection is **measures and signatures intelligence or MASINT**, which falls under the Defense Intelligence Agency (DIA). Our government has deployed a variety of electronic sensors throughout the world to gather information. They include radar, infrared, seismic, and radiological detection devices. These sensors are constantly monitored in an effort to collect intelligence on military and nuclear activities. This allows us, for example, to collect information about nuclear programs and nuclear-powered vessels. A spectrographic analysis of a rocket can provide information about the propellant that the rocket is using, which in turn advises of the sophistication of the rocket program. Generally, MASINT is targeted or focused on a location or particular activity. MASINT is extremely important in determining other countries' military capabilities and movements. For example, MASINT is a primary source of information about North Korea's nuclear program.

Imagery Intelligence

Imagery analysis or IMINT is housed with the National Geospatial-Intelligence Agency (NGA). The forerunner of IMINT was the U2 spy plane program, which began in the mid-1950s. The planes flew at 70,000 feet and provided surveillance of the Soviet Union, other Soviet bloc countries, and other countries of interest. For example, it was a U2 plane that provided evidence that the Russians had moved nuclear missiles into Cuba in 1962.

Today, our image intelligence has become more sophisticated through satellite imagery. We have deployed satellites that provide significant detail. They are used to monitor government activities in countries such as Russia and China, and they are used to monitor terrorist activities in numerous Middle Eastern, Asian, and African countries. For example, we attempt to monitor terrorist movements and training camps in countries such as Afghanistan and Pakistan through imagery. IMINT has been steadily improving with advances in technology, and we are now better able to capture more detailed information through imagery.

Open Source Intelligence

Open-source intelligence or OSINT is collected from public or open data for the purpose of intelligence gathering. Today, vast quantities of information are available through public or open records, and much of that information is available through the Internet. Intelligence analysts are increasingly using the Internet to collect information. In some cases, it can provide hard intelligence about a specific activity; in other cases, it can be used to collect background information about a problem. Numerous online technical journals provide an abundance of information about conventional weapons, nuclear energy and weapons, and other technology that is useful. For example, some analysts have estimated that Russia derives approximately 90 percent of its intelligence from open sources (OPSEC, 1996). Most, if not all, terrorist organizations have websites. They are monitored and analysts sometimes find information that is useful in the war on terrorism.

This discussion provides an overview of the various types of intelligence collection modes. Intelligence is a discipline that uses a number of methodologies and collects vast amounts of information from numerous sources. Once collected, the information must be collated and analyzed. That is, all the pieces must come together at one point so that analysts and policy makers can see the overall or total picture. One of the primary responsibilities of the DNI is to ensure that this occurs.

Agencies within the American Intelligence Community

The DNI is now responsible for coordinating our intelligence efforts. Sixteen agencies currently comprise the intelligence community. Each of the primary agencies will be briefly examined in terms of its role in homeland security.

Central Intelligence Agency

The **Central Intelligence Agency** was created in 1947 with the passage of the National Security Act. The act also created the position of director of central intelligence, a position held by the director of the CIA. The director of central intelligence was tasked with coordinating our intelligence functions. As such, the CIA became the lead intelligence agency (CIA, 2016). However, this was changed in 2004 when the DNI position was created with the passage of the Intelligence Reform and Terrorist Prevention Act.

Today, the CIA uses a variety of methods to collect intelligence, with an emphasis on HUMINT. It has operatives stationed throughout the world, making contacts and collecting HUMINT. Once intelligence is collected, the agency is responsible for collating the information and providing answers to questions posed by policy makers in the White House, Congress, State Department, and other executive offices. Essentially, analysts pour through volumes of information looking for relationships and, more or less, connecting the dots. It collects intelligence in foreign countries, whereas the Federal Bureau of Investigation (FBI) is responsible for collecting domestic intelligence.

Perhaps the best way to understand the CIA is to examine its primary operational components. The agency is divided into four directorates: Operations, Intelligence, Science and Technology, and Support. The **Directorate of Operations** is the agency's clandestine arm. It coordinates and evaluates clandestine HUMINT operations across the intelligence community. It conducts clandestine activities to collect information that is not obtainable through other means, and it conducts counterintelligence and special activities as authorized by the president. The **Intelligence Directorate** provides timely, accurate, and objective all-source intelligence analysis on the full range of national security and foreign policy issues to the president, cabinet, and senior policy makers in the U.S. government. For example, this directorate until recently provided the PDB and World Intelligence Review; now there is shared responsibility for these reports, but the directorate still provides substantial input.

The **Science and Technology Directorate** is responsible for the technical support of clandestine officers in the field. It advises the clandestine officers on technical operations and matters that are involved in activities such as audio and video surveillance. This directorate also provides secure communications for CIA personnel and assets (CIA, 2016)

The **Directorate of Digital Innovation's** primary task is to conduct cyber espionage. It would use some of the same tactics as being used by the NSA. It would gather information on foreign spies' digital footprints. These activities would enable the agency to better hid the activities of its operatives and locate foreign nationals who may be prone to work with the agency. The directorate is organized into 10 centers with each center focused on a region such as Africa or Middle East. The centers will also monitor cyberspace for attacks on the United States (Bennett, 2015).

The CIA works with a number of local paramilitary and other groups that are aligned with the United States. The CIA worked with the Northern Alliance in Iraq in the early years of the Iraqi War (House Select Committee on Intelligence, 1996; Weisman, 2002). Most recently, the CIA has worked with Kurdish forces fighting ISIS and armed anti-Assad rebels in Syria (McKirdy and Smith-Spark, 2017). The agency has also worked with a number of groups in Northern Africa to combat al Qaeda and other terrorist groups.

HS Web Link: To learn more about the CIA, go to https://www.cia.gov/.

Defense Intelligence Agency

The **Defense Intelligence Agency** is housed in the Pentagon and is the agency primarily responsible for military intelligence. As such, it focuses on strategic and tactical military operations. It is responsible for providing military-related intelligence and counterintelligence information to the secretary and deputy secretary of defense, chairman of the Joint Chiefs of Staff, and the DNI. The DIA is the military's equivalent of the CIA. The DIA is concerned with all sources of intelligence, whereby information is collected through a variety of means and then collated and analyzed to provide answers to policy, strategic, and tactical questions.

Although the DIA is primarily concerned with defense-related intelligence, as a result of the terrorism threat and the level of terrorist activities across the globe, the DIA is actively involved in counterterrorism. The DIA plays a key role in collecting terrorism intelligence, especially in those instances when insurgency operations will affect national security and U.S. military operations (DIA, 2009).

The DIA is concerned with a broad array of security and intelligence initiatives.

- The agency is concerned with the international terrorist hot spots in Africa, Asia, and the Middle East. Additionally, the DIA monitors Russian and Chinese activities in terms of their impact on the United States.

It is noteworthy that our national security concerns involve problems or conflicts that are dispersed throughout the world. Even though these problems are located on continents far from our shores, they ultimately will have some national security impact on the United States.

In 2012, it was announced that the Pentagon had established a new **Defense Clandestine Service** (Miller, 2012). The new service is designed to enhance the DIA's espionage operations and to develop closer working relations with the CIA. Creation of the service was the result of a study completed by the DNI that concluded the military's spying focus should go beyond tactical considerations in Iraq and Afghanistan. It will result in the DIA becoming more involved in terrorism intelligence. It is expected that the unit will grow by several hundred operatives and result in an increase in human intelligence operations.

Department of Energy

The **Department of Energy** (DOE) is responsible for maintaining U.S. energy supplies, promoting energy research, and procuring additional sources of energy. As such, nuclear energy is one of the DOE's primary responsibilities. This responsibility includes securing nuclear plants, materials, and by-products, since these materials can be used to construct a weapon of mass destruction (WMD). Additionally, the DOE ensures the integrity and safety of the country's nuclear weapons; promotes international nuclear safety; advances nuclear nonproliferation; and provides safe, efficient nuclear power plants for

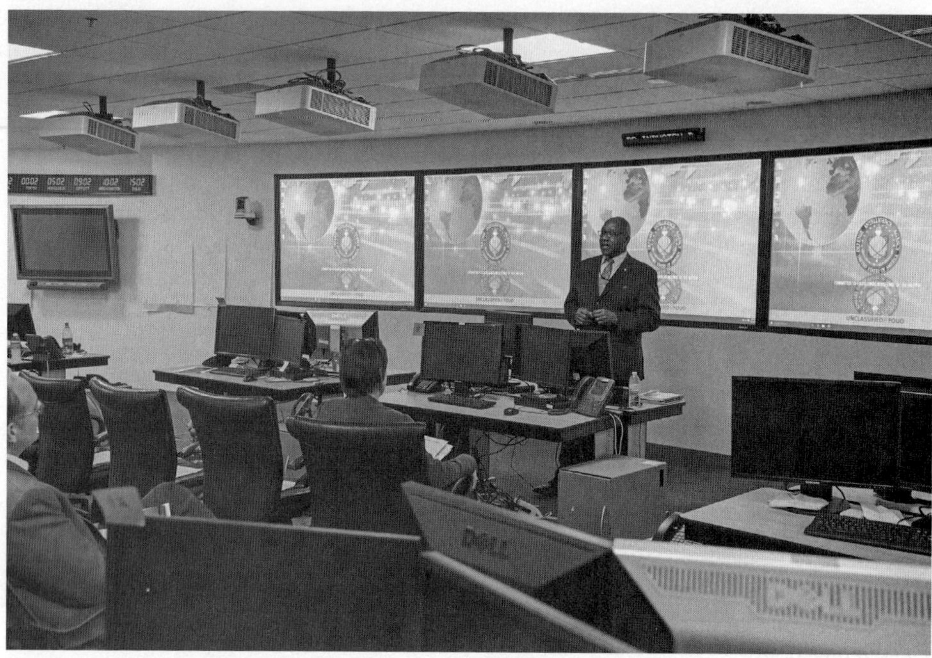

DIA official holds a briefing on artificial intelligence and big data.
Defense Intelligence Agency.

the U.S. Navy (DOE, 2009). Naval nuclear power plants are regulated by the DOE since many of the navy's ships are nuclear powered.

The DOE has several intelligence and security programs to fulfill this mandate housed under the department's **Office of Intelligence and Counterintelligence**. First, it has a cyber security program. Since the DOE has a substantial amount of information relative to nuclear energy and weapons, the DOE has a cyber security program to protect this information. Cyber security is important since nuclear facilities and other energy supply systems are operated via computer controls and systems. Second, the DOE promulgates security regulations for the nuclear energy industry. These regulations ensure that nuclear materials receive the utmost security. Third, the DOE is involved in preventing the spread of WMDs by providing expertise and technical analysis of foreign programs to determine if such weapons can be developed. For example, DOE personnel have been involved in analyzing Iran's nuclear programs. The DOE also attempts to detect nuclear-related activities such as those that have been conducted in North Korea. The DOE plays a key role in the collection and analysis of nuclear-related intelligence. The department's counterintelligence program is designed to collect information about these activities and prevent foreign governments or groups from obtaining materials and information.

Department of Homeland Security

The **Department of Homeland Security** maintains a sizable intelligence function as part of its operations to provide national homeland security. The DHS's **Office of Intelligence and Analysis** is responsible for coordinating the department's intelligence efforts. In addition to analyzing intelligence information, the office coordinates the intelligence received from DHS agencies, including

- U.S. Citizenship and Immigration Services
- U.S. Coast Guard

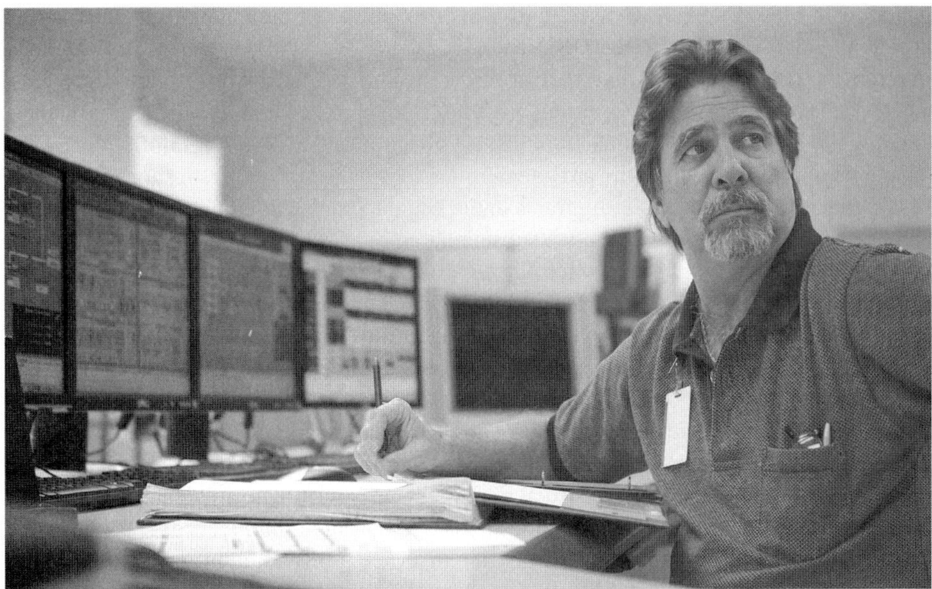

The DOE provides timely technical intelligence analysis on all aspects of foreign nuclear weapons, nuclear materials, and energy issues.
DenGuy/E+/Getty Images.

- U.S. Customs and Border Protection (CBP)
- U.S. Immigration and Customs Enforcement (ICE)
- U.S. Secret Service
- Transportation Security Administration (TSA) (DHS, 2017)

As noted in Chapters 2 and 3, the DHS is responsible for protecting the homeland, which is an expansive responsibility. Of particular interest to the department is the protection of our critical infrastructure, as discussed in Chapter 3. The DHS is involved in collecting and using intelligence to achieve this mission. In order to accomplish this mission, the DHS has identified five intelligence priorities:

- Threats to border security, including human trafficking, narcotics smuggling, money laundering, and transnational threats
- Threats of radicalization and extremism, particularly from Sunni and Shiite groups, whereby the department attempts to monitor the processes that attract and indoctrinate potential members
- Threats from particular groups that may attempt to import materials for WMDs and people entering or traveling to the United States who may be terrorists or potential terrorists
- Protection of the nation's critical infrastructure, including working with local and state governments and the private sector in developing plans and operational guidelines that safeguard these assets
- Safeguarding against WMD attacks, including the identification of individuals and groups that may become involved in such attacks (DHS, 2017).

Given these five priorities, it becomes obvious that the DHS has a considerable obligation to collect intelligence. For the most part, the operational DHS agencies have extensive intelligence operations. For example, the U.S. Coast Guard has port and waterways security responsibilities, which is an immense responsibility for preventing all sorts of smuggling, including WMDs. The U.S. Coast Guard is also a member of the intelligence community, providing direct feedback to the DNI. The USCIS interacts with large numbers of illegal immigrants, some of whom may be involved in terrorist or criminal activities. The U.S. CBP has the responsibility for securing our borders and preventing potential terrorists from entering the United States, which requires the collection and analysis of information about people who have entered or who are attempting to enter the U.S. ICE is responsible for investigating all sorts of illegal immigrants in the United States, including potential terrorists and criminals. This agency collects a substantial amount of information on these people. Finally, the TSA provides security for our airports and flights, and historically, the airlines have been prime targets for terrorists, resulting in a significant intelligence responsibility. The DHS's Office of Intelligence and Analysis coordinates these intelligence activities.

Complicating the DHS's intelligence mission is its need to work with state and local governments as well as other federal agencies. In the past, intelligence information was shared with other agencies on a "need to know" basis, which resulted in federal agencies being unwilling to work with state and local agencies. Since the DHS has responsibility for securing our national critical infrastructure, it must work with state and local agencies. An important part of this cooperative relationship is the sharing of intelligence. Local and state law enforcement, essentially, are the front line in terms of providing infrastructure protection. One method of sharing intelligence has been the development of fusion centers where local, state, and federal agencies in a geographical area receive and analyze localized intelligence (fusion centers are discussed in more detail in Chapter 14). Moreover, state and local agencies, since they are on the front lines, potentially have numerous opportunities to gather information of local and sometimes national importance regarding terrorist threats.

Department of State

The **State Department** is responsible for American foreign relations. The department maintains embassies and consulates across the world. These embassies and consulates interact with foreign governmental officials on a daily basis, attempting to solve problems and to ensure that we have the best relations possible with the various countries. As such, the State Department is very much interested in the political, social, and economic problems confronting these countries; in many cases, the State Department works to help maintain governments' stability. Stable governments are in our best interests. Within this mix of concerns are terrorist activities, since they may undermine legitimate governments or result in attacks on our country. The State Department actively collects intelligence within these countries relative to political, social, and economic issues. Our embassies and consulates often are the headquarters or operational points for CIA and other intelligence operatives working in these countries.

The State Department's primary unit for intelligence is the **Bureau of Intelligence and Research**. The bureau is a member of the intelligence community and thus shares information with the other 15 intelligence agencies. This provides the bureau with a substantial amount of information on countries. The focal point of the bureau's work is to ensure that intelligence activities support foreign policy and national security purposes. In other words, the bureau is interested in intelligence that advises of activities and changes in a country that could result in shifts in American foreign policy or alert our policy makers on impending international problems. For example, the State Department monitors the political activities in countries such as Pakistan. If the government of Pakistan becomes unstable, it would substantially increase the likelihood that terrorists would obtain nuclear weapons. The State Department must monitor the governments of other countries so that our foreign policies are consistent with prevailing conditions.

In some cases, the State Department is involved in counterintelligence. The **Bureau of Counterterrorism and Countering Violent Extremism** develops coordinated strategies and approaches to defeat terrorism abroad and secure counterterrorism cooperation of international partners (State Department, 2017). The bureau publishes the *Country Reports on Terrorism*, which identifies terrorist threats throughout the world. The State Department monitors terrorist activities within countries, using a range of sources. This information is used by our diplomats to negotiate with governments to enact policies that will reduce terrorist activities and other threats to American national security. The State Department negotiates with foreign governments in an effort to reduce the spread of nuclear weapons and other WMDs, which is handled by the International Security and Nonproliferation Unit.

Finally, the State Department's Conflict and Stabilization Office monitors conditions in other countries that lead to destabilization. Destabilization can lead to an increase in terrorism. The office also provides assistance to other countries to improve their efforts to counter terrorism. The State Department attempts to improve the antiterrorism infrastructure in these countries. The International Narcotics and Law Enforcement Office assists other countries in countering their drug trafficking problems, and the Office to Monitor and Combat Trafficking in Persons works with other countries to counter human trafficking. The state department is involved in a variety of intelligence operations.

HS Web Link: To learn more about State Department intelligence operations, go to http://www.state.gov/s/inr/.

Department of the Treasury

The Treasury Department plays a key role in homeland security. As discussed later in Chapter 11, terrorist financing and money laundering are primary concerns in the war on terrorism. We must make every effort to cut off or reduce the funding available to terrorist organizations and their supporters, and the Treasury Department is the lead agency in the attempt to accomplish this objective (2017).

The Office of Intelligence and Analysis is responsible for obtaining intelligence about questionable financial activities including threats and vulnerabilities. The office must examine extensive financial data and trouble spots to identify problems. The intelligence gathered by the office is then used by the Office of Terrorist Financing and Financial Crimes to develop counter strategies.

The Office of Foreign Assets Control enforces economic and trade sanctions against targeted foreign countries, terrorists, and international narcotics traffickers. Additionally, the office enforces trade sanctions against countries that engage in the proliferation of WMDs. For example, this office enforces the trade sanctions against North Korea as a result of its nuclear proliferation.

The Office of Terrorist Financing and Financial Crimes develops a variety of programs to control money laundering, terrorist financing, and criminal activities both domestically and internationally. When threats or problems are identified, this office develops and implements solutions. For example, the primary weapon used by the Treasury Department is to deny access to the American banking system by foreign governments, groups, and individuals. This weapon has a crippling effect since the American banking system is integrated throughout the world. Individual banks and financial systems can be targeted. The office works with other intelligence and law enforcement agencies to inhibit terrorists from obtaining money for their terrorist acts and catching terrorists who are engaging in financial crimes.

The Financial Crimes Enforcement Network (FinCEN) is operated by the Treasury Department and is a network connecting local, state, and federal law enforcement in financial crimes investigations. FinCEN focuses on a number of financial crimes such as money laundering, drug assets, and fraud. In some cases, these financial crimes are used to facilitate terrorist activities or groups. FinCEN accomplishes this mission by working with banks to ensure that Department of Treasury policies are implemented and by working with law enforcement to facilitate investigations.

Drug Enforcement Administration

The **Drug Enforcement Administration** (DEA) is the central agency in the United States for combating the worldwide drug problem. One of its primary missions is to interdict drugs coming into the United States from foreign countries. To this end, the DEA has agents stationed in 56 countries (DEA, 2016). These agents monitor drug activities in the host countries and work with local police agencies to eliminate or reduce the production of drugs and their flow from the host country.

The DEA is involved in the collection of homeland security intelligence for two primary reasons. First, the drug problem is international in scope and in some cases threatens to topple legitimate governments. For example, the lawlessness in Mexico and Central America as a result of the drug cartels is a threat to the United States. Narco-terrorism is a threat to many governments in the area. Second, a number of terrorist groups are now using narcotics trafficking as a way to raise money. For example, a number of terrorist groups including the Taliban are involved in the heroin trade in Afghanistan. In 2016, the DEA announced that it had uncovered a major Hezbollah drug trafficking organization, where the group was using funds derived from drug trafficking to buy weapons and to fund its other activities (Perper, 2016). Drug enforcement is an important part of the war on terrorism and requires a substantial intelligence effort.

The DEA organization contains an **Intelligence Division**. The intelligence division has three responsibilities. First, collect intelligence to support the DEA and other American law enforcement agencies. Second, work with other law enforcement agencies to produce narcotics intelligence, and finally, effectively report, analyze, and exchange drug intelligence with other law enforcement and intelligence agencies. As noted, there is overlap between drug trafficking and terrorist activities, and in some cases, it is difficult to separate

U.S. Coast Guard seized over 17 metric tons of cocaine acting on intelligence provided by the DEA.

U.S Drug Enforcement Administration.

or distinguish the two criminal activities. The inclusion of the DEA in the intelligence community allows the United States to more effectively respond to terrorism by identifying narco-terrorist organizations and money laundering schemes. Other intelligence organizations likely can provide the DEA with information that will assist the agency in attacking large-scale drug trafficking operations, and the reverse is true whereby the DEA may develop intelligence information on drug trafficking that may assist other agencies in identifying terrorist activities.

Federal Bureau of Investigation

The **Federal Bureau of Investigation** is responsible for criminal law enforcement, domestic counterintelligence, domestic counterterrorism, and cybercrime investigation. Essentially, the FBI is responsible for rooting out, identifying, and thwarting terrorist plots that occur on American soil. It is the primary agency in dealing with domestic terrorism.

The FBI's **National Security Branch** contains five divisions, counterintelligence division, counterterrorism division, high-value detainee investigation group, WMD directorate, and cyber division. The **counterintelligence division** collects intelligence and works to keep advanced weapons including WMDs from being compromised, protects intelligence community secrets, protects our nation's critical infrastructure assets, and counters the activities of foreign spies. The division focuses on foreign intelligence activities.

The **counterterrorism division** is responsible for investigating and responding to terrorist attacks. The counterterrorism fly team, which is housed in the division, is charged with responding to and investigating any attacks. The division also has a terrorist financing operations section that tracks down terrorist financing and uses the information to gather more in-depth information on terrorists or terrorist groups. The **joint terrorism task forces** (JTTFs) are also located in this division. The JTTFs include state and local law enforcement as well as federal intelligence and enforcement agencies. This comprehensive

FBI agents involved in a hostage rescue training mission.
Marmaduke St. John/Alamy Stock Photo.

FBI
U.S. Marshals Service
Bureau of Alcohol, Tobacco and Firearms
U.S. Secret Service
U.S. State Department/Diplomatic Security Service
Immigration and Customs Enforcement
U.S. Border Patrol
Postal Inspection Service
Treasury Inspector General for Tax Administration
Internal Revenue Service
U.S. Park Police
Federal Protective Services
Air Force Office of Special Investigations
U.S. Army
Naval Criminal Investigative Services
Central Intelligence Agency
State and Local Law Enforcement

FIGURE 8-2 Members of the JTTFs

membership helps ensure that critical intelligence information is shared with agencies that may become involved in a terrorist threat. It also results in all domestic terrorism intelligence being assembled and analyzed in one organization, which results in a more comprehensive and complete examination of information. Members of the JTTFs are listed in Figure 8-2 ■.

Finally, the FBI is involved in establishing fusion centers at the local level (discussed in more detail in Chapter 14). The fusion centers are composed of FBI agents, other federal law enforcement personnel, state and local police officials, and other public safety officials such as fire and medical emergency. The fusion centers operate in similar fashion as the JTTFs. Personnel associated with the fusion centers provide intelligence information to the group that is disseminated and examined. They focus on possible terrorists and terrorist activities and serve as an early warning system. Information collected at the fusion center level is directed to the FBI and the JTTFs. The fusion centers represent a concerted and coordinated intelligence effort at the lowest level.

The **high-value detainee investigation group** interrogates terrorist suspects and other criminals who have been arrested or incarcerated. When terrorists are arrested, they often have information about other terrorists or possible terrorist activities. It is important that they be interviewed in order to foil other terrorist plots. Considerable intelligence can be obtained through these interviews.

WMD is the greatest threat to homeland security. The **weapons of mass destruction directorate** is responsible for responding to WMD threats. A great deal of intelligence is obtained through the JTTFs and other FBI units about possible WMD attacks. The directorate uses this intelligence as well as information obtained by the unit to plan responses.

The FBI is responsible for the investigation of terrorism on American soil. The agency has made over 500 terrorism cases in the United States. These cases evolve around providing material support for terrorists, plotting terrorist activities and attacks, and conspiring to join terrorist organizations. The number of arrests demonstrates a considerable amount of terrorist activity in the homeland and a high degree of success by the FBI. A casual

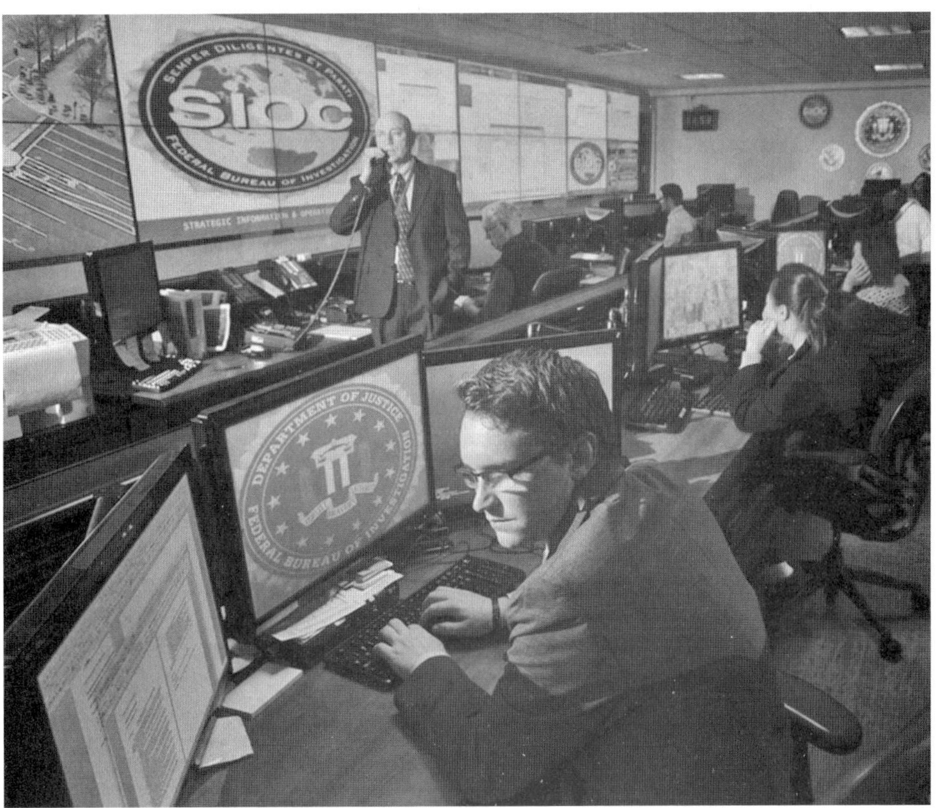

The Strategic Information and Operations Center, the FBI's global command and communications center.
FBI Headquarters.

examination of the numbers indicates that our counterintelligence has been successful. However, Aaronson (2013) shined a different light on these arrests. He maintained that many of the arrests are the result of collusion, whereby the FBI through informants brings potential terrorists into a plot and arrests them. Aaronson advised that the problem is that many of the suspects caught up in these sting operations are mentally deficient, incompetent, and otherwise incapable of conducting any kind of an attack. He maintains the FBI fundamentally is more interested in giving the appearance of counterterrorism effectiveness through arrests than ensuring our country is safe. Even if his supposition is partially correct, it would seem that the magnitude of arrests may serve as a deterrent to more capable potential terrorists.

Finally, the FBI maintains a list of criminals and terrorists who have committed extraordinary crimes. The list contains high-value terrorists from across the globe. The FBI works with domestic and international law enforcement agencies to apprehend these criminals and terrorists.

National Geospatial-Intelligence Agency

The **National Geospatial-Intelligence Agency** is housed in the Department of Defense. It is a combat support agency, meaning that its primary function is to support military operations. However, it now plays a dominant role in counterterrorism and homeland

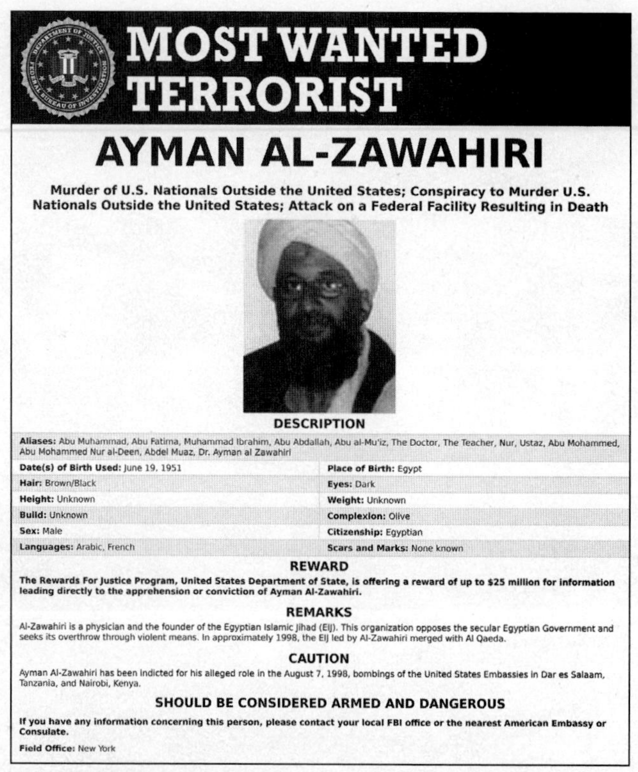

MOST WANTED
TERRORIST

AYMAN AL-ZAWAHIRI

Murder of U.S. Nationals Outside the United States; Conspiracy to Murder U.S. Nationals Outside the United States; Attack on a Federal Facility Resulting in Death

DESCRIPTION

Aliases: Abu Muhammad, Abu Fatima, Muhammad Ibrahim, Abu Abdallah, Abu al-Mu'iz, The Doctor, The Teacher, Nur, Ustaz, Abu Mohammed, Abu Mohammed Nur al-Deen, Abdel Muaz, Dr. Ayman al Zawahiri

Date(s) of Birth Used: June 19, 1951	**Place of Birth:** Egypt
Hair: Brown/Black	**Eyes:** Dark
Height: Unknown	**Weight:** Unknown
Build: Unknown	**Complexion:** Olive
Sex: Male	**Citizenship:** Egyptian
Languages: Arabic, French	**Scars and Marks:** None known

REWARD

The Rewards For Justice Program, United States Department of State, is offering a reward of up to $25 million for information leading directly to the apprehension or conviction of Ayman Al-Zawahiri.

REMARKS

Al-Zawahiri is a physician and the founder of the Egyptian Islamic Jihad (EIJ). This organization opposes the secular Egyptian Government and seeks its overthrow through violent means. In approximately 1998, the EIJ led by Al-Zawahiri merged with Al Qaeda.

CAUTION

Ayman Al-Zawahiri has been indicted for his alleged role in the August 7, 1998, bombings of the United States Embassies in Dar es Salaam, Tanzania, and Nairobi, Kenya.

SHOULD BE CONSIDERED ARMED AND DANGEROUS

If you have any information concerning this person, please contact your local FBI office or the nearest American Embassy or Consulate.

Field Office: New York

FBI wanted poster for Ayman Al-Zawahiri, founder of the Egyptian Islamic jihad.

Source: FBI- Most Wanted Terrorist. Screenshot taken from https://www.fbi.gov/wanted/wanted_terrorists/ayman-al-zawahiri/@@download.pdf

security. Essentially, the NGA acquires and produces imagery and map-based intelligence information in support of national defense, homeland security, and navigation safety. The term *geospatial intelligence* means the exploitation and analysis of imagery and geospatial information to describe, assess, and visually depict physical features and geographically referenced activities on the earth (NGA, 2017). The gathering of geospatial intelligence is accomplished by tasking, whereby imagery is obtained usually by requesting specific images from a variety of agencies and disseminating information to consumer intelligence and tactical agencies.

In many cases, the information collected and processed by NGA is tailored for customer-specific solutions. That is, consumers of intelligence may request specific geospatial information. By giving customers ready access to geospatial intelligence, NGA provides support to civilian and military leaders and contributes to the state of readiness of U.S. military forces. The agency provides other agencies with images and information associated with the images—merging demographic data and information with imagery. NGA also contributes to humanitarian efforts, such as tracking floods and disaster support, and peacekeeping, which requires that the agency maintain a substantial number of images and maps (NGA, 2017). The NGA also has a cadre of analysts, who are tasked with the responsibility of monitoring and analyzing specific problems such as Iran and North Korea's nuclear programs and terrorist training camps.

> **HS Web Link:** To learn more about the NGA, go to https://www.nga.mil/Pages/Default.aspx.

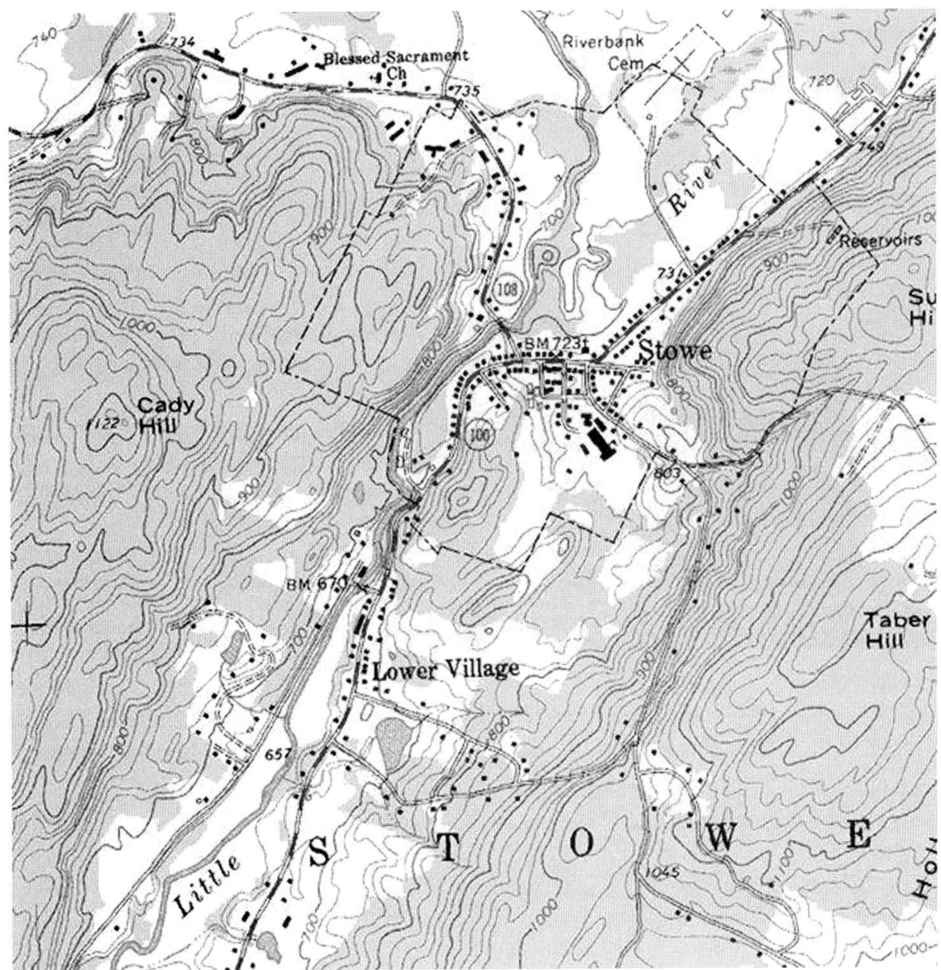

Example of a topographical map produced by the NGA.
Source: https://www1.nga.mil/ProductsServices/TopographicalTerrestrial/Pages/default.aspx.

National Reconnaissance Office

The **National Reconnaissance Office** (NRO) is responsible for maintaining our country's system of satellite surveillance. The director of the NRO reports to the DNI and to the secretary of defense. Satellite imagery plays a key role in military operations, and today, it is important in tracking terrorists and their activities. Moreover, the NRO can provide "real-time" on-the-ground imagery—it allows operatives to actively observe events as they transpire. For example, terrorist training camps can be observed and terrorist movements can be identified. Images also provide a wealth of intelligence about activities throughout the world. The agency provides imagery information to a variety of civilian and defense agencies, and the images are used to make tactical and strategic decisions. For example, the NRO manages satellites and listening posts that are used by the NSA to gather SIGINT. It also provides the NGA with images.

> **HS Web Link:** To learn more about the NRO, go to http://www.nro.gov/.

National Security Agency

The **National Security Agency** is involved in SIGINT. The agency collects SIGINT from a variety of sources, including foreign communications, radar, and electronic communications. The agency uses U.S. embassies, ships, aircrafts, and other locations to monitor

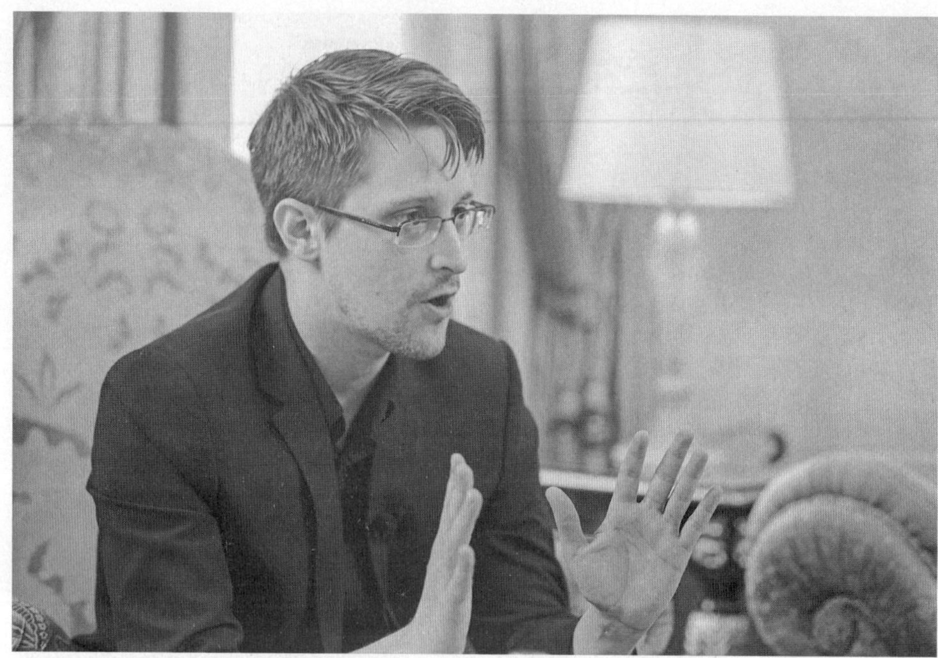

Edward Snowden downloaded NSA documents and fled to Russia. His actions provided the world with secret information about U.S. intelligence operations.
Baikal/Alamy Stock Photo.

communications. Information is collected in other countries in a variety of languages and dialects, necessitating that the NSA have a large number of language interpreters. As an example, many terrorists are forced to use primitive communications methods, face-to-face, notes, and so on because any electronic communications such as via telephones can be intercepted by the NSA. Obviously, the NSA is concerned with intercepting signals relative to terrorist plots that may occur in the United States. Many of the signals collected are coded, requiring the agency to be extensively involved in code breaking. The NSA collects signals information and provides that information to other members of the intelligence community where it is used to make tactical and strategic decisions (NSA, 2017).

The NSA plays a considerable role in the collection of intelligence. For example, Shorrock (2008) noted that about 60 percent of the information contained in the PDBs is derived from intelligence collected by the NSA. The NSA works closely with the NRO in that the NRO operates the nation's satellites and ground stations that intercept signals. A primary consumer of NSA information is the CIA, whose analysts examine signals, telephone calls, and e-mails that are intercepted by the NSA. However, this relationship is not always cordial. For example, the NSA was criticized for not sharing transcripts of cell phone conversations of al Qaeda operatives during the run-up to the 9/11 attacks (see Shorrock, 2008).

The NSA Revealed: The Case of Edward Snowden

In 2013, **Edward Snowden**, a low-level analyst for a NSA subcontractor, released documents detailing some of the NSA's spying activities. It is estimated that he downloaded 1.4 million NSA documents (Dilanian, 2013). The documents revealed that the NSA was collecting information about Americans' telephone and Internet traffic as well as this information on foreigners. In terms of telephone calls, only telephone numbers, originator number and number called, and the duration of the telephone conversation were collected. No conversations were recorded. The NSA was collecting information on most if not all Americans. The NSA was also tapping the phones of heads of state and other world leaders. In some cases, participants in economic, environmental, and other government conferences were tapped. The revelations caused an international furor as well as in the United States. Civil libertarians pointed out that government officials cannot perform this form of spying on Americans without first obtaining a warrant under the Foreign Intelligence Surveillance Act (FISA). However, the NSA and others in government maintained that the NSA was collecting the information, but in the case of Americans, it would only examine the messages or content if there was cause and a FISA warrant was obtained. This requirement does not apply to foreigners. Snowden escaped the United States and received asylum in Russia. He took a substantial amount of downloaded intelligence information with him. There is speculation that he shared this information with the Russian government. Some believed Snowden was a hero by unmasking NSA abuses, while others saw him as a traitor who should be prosecuted.

The justification for collecting this information was that the NSA might identify possible terrorist plots or impending attacks on the United States. However, an analysis of 225 terrorism cases since 9/11 by the New America Foundation found that the collection of phone records had a minimal effect on preventing terrorism. The study found one case in San Diego where a cab driver was convicted of sending money to a terrorist group in Somalia. The report noted that law enforcement and traditional investigative methods provided most of the leads to begin investigations (Kumar, 2014).

Nonetheless, the program ended in December 2015. Rather than collecting the telephone data, the NSA is now required to obtain the data from the telephone companies after obtaining a FISA warrant. The need for the United States to monitor telephone traffic may be increasing. There are several hundred Americans who have traveled to the Middle East and worked with terrorist groups and returned home. There are also large numbers of foreigners who have also done so, and many of these foreigners come from countries that have no visa requirements to travel to the United States. Some of these individuals pose a threat to us as a result of radicalization. More efforts should be made to monitor them.

However, the NSA program may have reaped other benefits. The program obviously makes communications between terrorists more difficult. Before he was killed, Osama bin Laden was forced to use messengers to communicate with al Qaeda operatives because of the NSA and other American clandestine agencies monitoring electronic transmissions. In essence, the NSA program tamps down terrorists' ability to communicate and coordinate their activities. Conducting terrorist activities becomes more difficult.

One negative consequence of the Snowden documents' release was the NSA in 2013 was developing a proposal to begin scanning Internet traffic for cyber-attacks and malicious codes or viruses. The political turmoil over NSA monitoring telephone and Internet traffic made the proposal politically dead in the water and the NSA did not pursue the initiative (Dilanian, 2014). However, given that there are millions of cyber-attacks on government institutions, the banking industry, research centers, corporations, other infrastructure, and citizens every day, it would be beneficial to pursue this initiative. The infrastructure exists for the NSA to monitor all the Internet traffic. If the NSA could intercept and destroy attacks before they reached their targets, it would make the United States much safer. This initiative is critical, given that the greatest threat to homeland security is cyber-attacks on our infrastructure.

HS ANALYSIS BOX 8-3

The Edward Snowden affair created a great deal of controversy. Some thought he was a hero for exposing NSA's electronic spying on American citizens, while others thought he was a traitor. What do you think? As a result of restrictions on the NSA, do you think we are less safe from terrorists?

Armed Services Intelligence

Each branch of the armed services, Army, Navy, Air Force, Marine Corp, and Coast Guard, has intelligence operations that are interconnected with other intelligence agencies, especially the DIA. The U.S. Coast Guard is part of the DHS and collects and provides intelligence to the Departments of Homeland Security and Defense. The U.S. Coast Guard's mission centers on securing our marine borders and our ports. The U.S. Coast Guard is interested in ships and people who are entering the United States via waterways, and it monitors marine activities. For example, all ships approaching the United States must provide a 96-hour notice of arrival. The agency's **Coastwatch Program** analyzes the manifests for prohibited materials and people who may be on watch lists. The Coast Guard sometimes tasks or directs satellites from the NRO or the military to observe marine activities and gather intelligence on arriving vessels (Richelson, 2008). The agency works closely with the CBP agency in securing our ports.

The Army, Navy, Air Force, and Marine Corp have specific intelligence missions that focus on tactical operations. The branches of the military must collect information that assists them when deploying on the battlefield or becoming involved in counterterrorist operations. They are involved in collecting a variety of human, signal, imagery, and technical intelligence. Generally, they are involved in collecting information relative to specific tactical situations. For example, the Army collects information on all sorts of groups in Afghanistan. This information is used to identify enemies, enemy operations, and potential targets, which is especially critical in an asymmetric war. It also collects intelligence on other countries' military operations, since this information is useful in discovering their battlefield strategies and new capabilities. These activities are coordinated with the DIA.

▶ Intersection of Policy Decisions and Intelligence: The Intelligence Cycle

The preceding sections outlined the various intelligence agencies and their operations. As can be seen, the gathering and analysis of intelligence are complicated matters that involve a host of agencies. They involve the collection of homeland security intelligence as well as military and government-related intelligence. They involve civilian agencies as well as military agencies. They center on military and asymmetric threats. Nonetheless, once intelligence is collected, it must be organized into a usable form. This section briefly examines the relationship between policy makers and intelligence. Policy makers are consumers of intelligence, and intelligence is an important ingredient in many of the decisions that are made.

Clarke (2008) and Richelson (2008) have outlined how policy makers intersect with intelligence. It is a five-step process known as the **intelligence cycle** and consists of (1) planning and direction, (2) collection, (3) processing and exploitation, (4) analysis and production, and (5) dissemination, as depicted in Figure 8-3 ■.

First, requirements are identified by the DNI and involve a wide range of actors who have specific intelligence needs such as the White House, congress, or other federal agencies. Specific questions are often the motivation behind intelligence gathering. Intelligence requirements may focus on people, terrorist groups, or countries, depending on what is occurring globally.

Second, planning and direction refers to the management of the intelligence process and is conducted by the White House, the DNI, the National Security Council, agency heads, and other consumers of intelligence. Here, consumers request specific information from the intelligence community about a problem. For example, the Department of State or DOE may request information about nuclear proliferation in Pakistan, Iran, or North Korea.

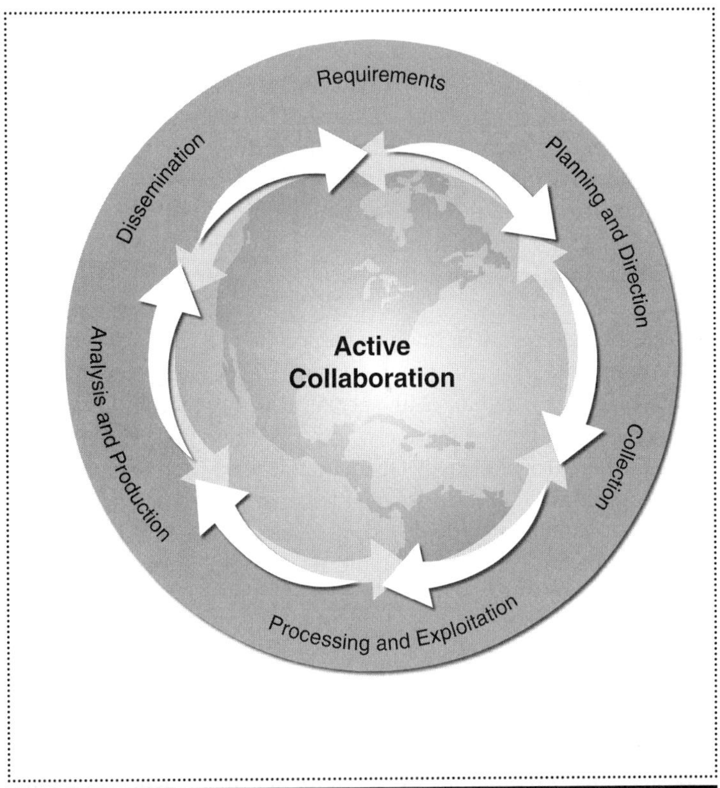

FIGURE 8-3 Intelligence Cycle: A Framework to Ensure an Effective Intelligence Process
Source: http://www.fbi.gov/intelligence/images/active_collaboration.jpg.

In some cases, they collect information about specific national security issues; in other cases, they amass information about persons, places, and activities, keeping in mind that specific information about them may be required or requested in the future.

Third, processing and exploitation occur when information is collated and stored so that it can be easily retrieved and used. It must be processed so that consumers have ready access to it. Moreover, it must address the original questions posed by the requestor.

During the analysis and production phase, analysts pour through the information, connect information, and apply the information to specific problems or issues, which means examining a number of sources in order to get a clear answer to the questions.

Finally, the information must be disseminated to policy makers or intelligence consumers. In some cases, the information is provided as a result of specific requests; in other cases, the analysts identify issues and alert the policy makers. For example, the PDB, produced by the CIA, is an attempt to keep the president abreast of national security issues throughout the world. Policy makers then apply the information when deciding how to proceed relative to planning and actions.

Joint Special Operations Command Specialized Military Antiterrorism Agencies

The **U.S. Northern Command** has a wide range of responsibilities, including coordinating the department of defense's homeland defense and planning and providing military support to civil authorities. For example, Hurricane Katrina in 2005 required that military troops be deployed in New Orleans. The storm and its aftermath overwhelmed civilian resources. A significant terrorist attack likely would require similar military support.

The **U.S. Special Operations Command** (SOCOM) is a unified command including units from the army, marine corps, navy and air force. This allows a flexible response when dealing with a problem. For example, the navy and air force can ferry special units to any location in the world. SOCOM is involved in a variety of operations such as counterterrorism, unconventional warfare, reconnaissance, and direct military action. SOCOM has been involved in Somalia, Iraq, Afghanistan, and a number of other countries. SOCOM coordinates all military antiterrorism activities.

The **Joint Special Operations Command** (JSOC) is a unit that was designed to study, plan, and carryout special operations and is a part of the U.S. SOCOM. It contains several subunits including the delta force, intelligence support, U.S. Navy special warfare development group (SEAL Team 6), and the 24th special tactics squadron. It carries out military and intelligence operations throughout the world. For example, JSOC helped kill Osama bin Laden in 2011. In 2016, President Obama authorized the creation of a new unit in JSOC that was designed to hunt terrorists and terrorist groups across the globe. The unit reports to the pentagon, and when deployed, it reports to regional military commanders. The new unit is designed to be a flexible rapid response to terrorist threats. It is also designed to collect intelligence on groups and possible terrorist attacks (Gibbons-Neff and Lamothe, 2016).

▶ Counterintelligence

The preceding sections provided an overview of the intelligence community and its intelligence gathering activities. In addition to gathering information about various enemies, be they individuals, groups, or countries, our intelligence community is also involved in counterintelligence. Richelson (2008) defined **counterintelligence** as "preventing a foreign government's illicit acquisition of secrets" (p. 394). Within the scope of homeland security, we are not only interested in preventing foreign governments from obtaining critical information but we also want to prevent terrorist groups from acquiring information that may be useful in attacking our critical infrastructure. For example, New York City on several occasions has prohibited photographing mass transit facilities in an effort to prevent terrorist from gaining intelligence that could be used to facilitate an attack. Thus, we are interested in preventing terrorists and sympathetic governments from obtaining information about our counterterrorism activities and potential targets.

The FBI is the primary agency responsible for counterintelligence on American soil. The bureau notes that counterintelligence is the second highest priority, and its importance is derived from protecting the American public from attacks. Counterintelligence is an expansive responsibility. The FBI routinely investigates hundreds of suspected terrorists in the United States and makes a number of terrorist-related cases each year. The FBI's counterintelligence priorities include the following:

1. Keep WMD and other embargoed technologies from falling into the wrong hands—whether terrorists or unstable countries around the globe.
2. Protect the secrets of the U.S. intelligence community. Here, the FBI investigates people and governments that attempt to infiltrate our intelligence and defense communities to obtain tactical and strategic information.
3. Protect the secrets of the U.S. government and contractors—especially in research and development areas. The FBI helps protect our defense and industrial secrets from foreign countries and agents.

4. Protect our nation's critical national assets—such as our weapons systems, advanced technologies, and energy and banking systems. The bureau's role is to identify the source and significance of the threats and work with the "owners" to reduce any vulnerability.
5. Focus on countries that pose the greatest threat to the United States, especially those that want information to further terrorism, economic espionage, proliferation, threats to our infrastructure, and foreign intelligence operations (FBI, 2009).

National Counterterrorism Center

The National Counterterrorism Center (NCTC) was created by President Bush and represents the reforms that was implemented to improve intelligence as a result of the problems identified in the wake of the 9/11 attacks. Although the NCTC is housed in the Office of the Director of National Intelligence, the NCTC is unique in that the director of NCTC reports to the president for executive branch-wide counterterrorism planning as well as the DNI regarding intelligence matters (National Counterterrorism Center, 2015). The NCTC is staffed with personnel from a variety of departments from within the intelligence community. The center is uniquely involved in developing counterterrorism strategies.

The NCTC mission was established by the *Intelligence Reform and Terrorism Prevention Act of 2002*. The NCTC has three primary functions. First, it analyzes threats. It examines domestic and foreign intelligence from all the agencies in the intelligence community and produces assessments to support policymakers in the homeland security arena. These analyses are contained in the President's Daily Briefs (PDBs) and the daily *National Terrorism Bulletin*. The NCTC has several specialized divisions such as the radicalization and extremist messaging groups and groups that focus on chemical, biological, radiological, and nuclear counterterrorism.

Second, the NCTC serves as an information hub for known and suspected terrorists and terrorist groups. The center also provides other agencies with terrorism intelligence analyses. The NCTC maintains restricted websites with intelligence that is available to the other intelligence agencies. This central repository helps ensure that intelligence is shared with other intelligence agencies. The Terrorist Screening Center is supported by the NCTC and the NCTC supports the government's watchlist program.

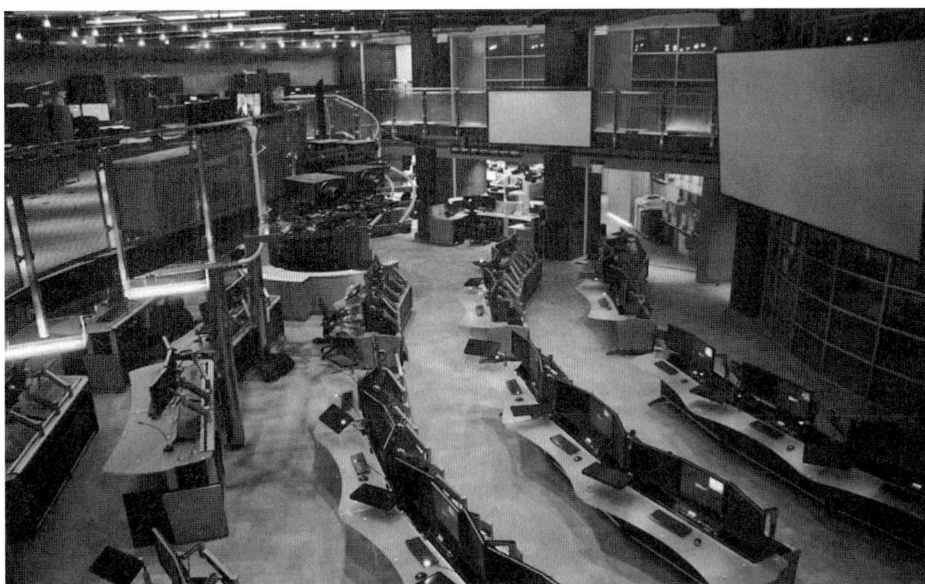

NCTC Operations Center.
Office of the Director of National Intelligence.

Third, the NCTC conducts strategic planning or counterterrorism, and as such it helps coordinate our overall counterterrorism efforts. In some cases, the center assigns analysis responsibilities to other governmental agencies. In essence, the NCTC helps strategically manage all U.S. intelligence activities.

▶ The Globalization of Intelligence

The lack of intelligence sharing became an obvious problem after the 9/11 attacks. The 16 American intelligence agencies were not sharing information that could have pointed to an impending attack. The problem was remedied with the creation of the DNI, whose function was to coordinate the agencies and ensure that intelligence was shared among the various agencies. In addition to being a national problem, it also existed internationally where countries failed to fully inform their allies about terrorist activities. The rationale frequently voiced was the need to ensure that information was secure. However, since the 9/11 attacks, countries have opened communications lines and are more effectively sharing information. It is not known if these efforts have been effective. This movement has consisted of what Svendsen (2008) refers to the "homogenization and international standardization" of intelligence (p. 130). Jensen (2014) found that such efforts must involve full credible intelligence. Less detailed information is not as effective, which means that countries must develop and maintain full-source sharing to combat terrorist plots.

Today, there are many more cooperative relationships, formal and informal, in the intelligence community, spanning a variety of countries. Old foes are now cooperating in the face of terrorist threats. A new enemy necessitated closer working relationships among a variety of countries, which is particularly true since terrorist groups know no boundaries, and globalization has removed a number of borders, geographical and artificial, that previously provided some measure of security.

According to Svendsen (2008), the homogenization and international standardization of intelligence have taken several forms. First, there is increased informational sharing across borders and governments. Countries are more willing to share information reciprocally, and given the terrorist threat based on past attacks, there is ample motivation for cooperation. Second, a number of countries, primarily the United States, are involved in training intelligence officers in other countries in areas such as investigations, surveillance, and counterterrorism. Since terrorist groups or cells can appear anywhere, it is to the advantage of countries that are potential targets to enhance intelligence capabilities across the world in an effort to collect more information and potentially prevent a terrorist attack. This training also engenders closer working relationships as countries cooperatively confront terrorists. Third, countries such as the United States are providing technical assistance, often in the form of liaisons who assist or participate in investigations. Such participation often results in more complete investigations, leading to arrests or the foiling of a terrorist plot.

Western Europe has become a hotbed of terrorist activities with recent attacks in England, Spain, France, and Belgium. Although the European Union has vastly improved its counterterrorism intelligence and operations, individual countries fail to coordinate and cooperate to the fullest extent as a result of legal and bureaucratic entanglements (Mojnar, 2015). Bures (2016) echoed this criticism noting that there is a clear need for borderless counterterrorism efforts in Europe, and even though countries have committed to intelligence sharing, it is unlikely that countries will be able to get their national agencies to comply. Intelligence agencies too often safeguard critical intelligence for fear of the information being compromised. Byman (2014) noted that policy makers and analysts often have fundamental differences regarding intelligence and its dissemination. The walls separating various countries' intelligence agencies must be breached so that intelligence information flows freely across borders.

The globalization of intelligence is to a large degree in its infancy. Given the current world political dynamics, homogenization and international standardization will continue, which will result in more effective intelligence apparatuses and a more effective response to terrorist threats.

Domestic Industrial Espionage

Although the United States is immersed in a war on terror, it should be remembered that terrorism is not the only enemy we face today. Numerous foreign governments compete with us globally and engage in **domestic industrial espionage**, whereby they attempt to obtain our military and industrial secrets. There are also enemy states such as North Korea and Iran that would do us harm and likely would cooperate with terrorist organizations. For example, the Chinese maintain a SIGINT facility in Cuba to spy on the United States. A number of our allies, including Germany, Israel, Japan, and South Korea, have been involved in industrial or defense espionage that was directed against America (Richelson, 2008). The United States spends billions of dollars annually on research and development for defense and industry. When foreign governments obtain this information, they are able to save billions of dollars in research and development; obtain the most sophisticated hardware, software, or equipment; and bring equipment online much quicker. Essentially, industrial espionage undercuts the American economy, posing a critical economic and homeland security threat.

Industrial espionage is a common threat to the United States, with foreign nationals using a variety of tactics to obtain information. Figure 8-4 ■ provides a list of the various tactics used as identified by the Office of National Counterintelligence.

As demonstrated in Figure 8-4 ■, foreign governments use a variety of methodologies in their quest for industrial and defense information and secrets. Moreover, terrorist groups use some of these same techniques when collecting intelligence on American military and civilian operations and personnel. Whereas agents of foreign governments and companies attempt to gain information about industrial or defense technologies, terrorists attempt to obtain tactical information such as troop movements, operations vulnerabilities, and targets.

In addition to a variety of methods of spying on the American industrial and military complexes, a large number of nonimmigrant foreign visitors are involved in this form of espionage. For example, foreign nationals frequently request visits to U.S. military and Department of Defense industries, DOE, and National Nuclear Security Administration facilities (Office of National Counterintelligence, 2006). A number of countries are

- Targeting U.S. firms for technology that would strengthen their foreign defense capabilities
- Posting personnel at U.S. military bases to collect classified information to bolster military modernization efforts
- Employing commercial firms in the United States and in third countries to target and acquire U.S. technology
- Recruiting students, professors, scientists, and researchers to engage in technology collection
- Forming ventures with U.S. firms in hope of placing collector in proximity to sensitive technologies or else establishing foreign research facilities and software development companies outside the United States to work on commercial projects related to protected programs
- Offering technical services to U.S. research facilities or cleared defense contractors in the hope of gaining access to protected technologies
- Exploring foreign visits to the United States and colleting at conventions and expositions
- Relying on cyber tools to collect sensitive U.S. technology and economic information

FIGURE 8-4 Spying Techniques Used to Obtain Defense and Industrial Secrets
Source: Office of National Counterintelligence (2006). *Annual Report to Congress on Foreign Economic Collection and Industrial Expionage-2005.* Washington, D.C.: Author.

HS ANALYSIS BOX 8-4

Domestic industrial espionage is a critical problem, especially considering that so much information is stored on computers and foreign hackers are constantly attempting to break into these computers. Many countries, friend and foe, are engaged in such activities, attempting to steal a wide range of information. What industries do you believe would be the probable targets of industrial espionage? What kinds of information would these agents be seeking?

represented in these requests, including China, India, Russia, Germany, Colombia, and Japan. Many of those requesting access to these facilities are attempting to collect intelligence. Moreover, visits to such facilities represent only one type of intelligence collection with many other methods as listed in Figure 8-4 ■ being used on a regular basis. It is apparent that industrial and economic espionage represents a significant threat to homeland security.

Thus, it can be seen that a variety of individuals use different methods to acquire our military and industrial secrets. As noted earlier, when they are successful, it can have a significant economic impact on our country; therefore, this form of espionage is a real threat to homeland security, and we must take the steps necessary to protect such information.

Dinan (2016) recently reported the no fly list contains about 81,000 names with fewer than 1,000 of those being Americans.

Summary

This chapter provided an overview of our intelligence apparatus and operations and their relationship with homeland security. First, it should be noted that intelligence, especially as it applies to homeland security, is intertwined across numerous governmental agencies as shown in Figure 8-5 ■. Although we are interested in intelligence that assists in protecting the homeland, it is abundantly clear that it is not a simple matter to separate homeland security intelligence from traditional intelligence activities. Homeland security intelligence is a comprehensive effort examining all facets and types of threats whether or not they are confined within the United States or abroad.

The office of DNI, created in the wake of the 9/11 attacks, was established to ensure better cooperation among the intelligence agencies and the sharing of information. The DNI is responsible for coordinating the intelligence operations for 16 different agencies with well over 100,000 employees. These agencies are spread across several federal governmental departments, including Defense, Homeland Security, Justice, State, and Energy. They are involved in several types of intelligence collection, including human, signal, geospatial, scientific, imagery, and open source. The results are a complex myriad of agencies existing in a complex environment that attempt to provide better protection for the homeland.

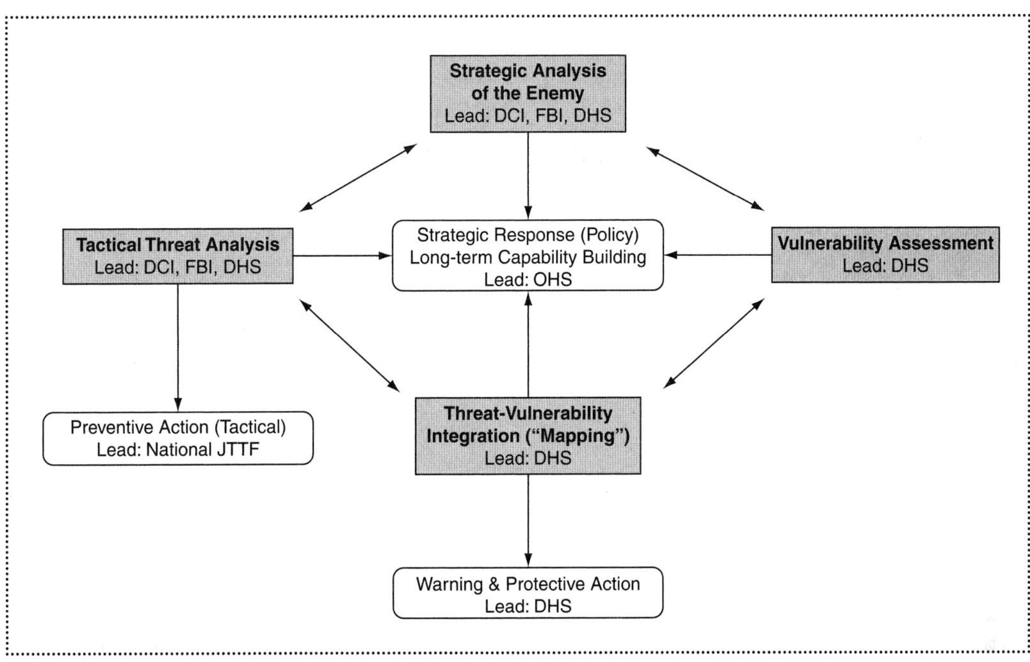

FIGURE 8-5 Roles and Responsibilities of Homeland Security Intelligence and Information Analysis

Source: White House Office of Homeland Security. (2002). *National Strategy for Homeland Security*. Washington, D.C.: Author, p. 16.

Discussion Questions

1. Describe how politicians affect intelligence.
2. What is a National Intelligence Estimate? How are they developed? What are some of the problems associated with them?
3. Explain how human intelligence operates.
4. Compare the various types of intelligence collection methods.
5. Describe the purposes and effectiveness of CIA programs such as rendition and water boarding.
6. What role does the State Department have in intelligence and counterterrorism?
7. Compare and contrast the JTTFs with the intelligence network.
8. Describe the intelligence cycle.

References

Aaronson, T. (2013). *The Terror Factory: Inside the FBI's Manufactured War on Terrorism*. Brooklyn, NY: Ig Publishing.

Baldwin, D. (1995). "Security studies and the end of the cold war." *World Politics*, 48: 117–141.

Bennett, B. (2015). "CIA to create a digital spy division." http://www.latimes.com/nation/nationnow/la-na-nn-cia-cyber-espionage-20150305-story.html (Accessed August 31, 2015).

Betts, R. (2003). "Fixing intelligence." *Terrorism and Counterterrorism: Understanding the New Security Environment,* ed. R. Howard and R. Sawyer, pp. 473–483. New York: McGraw-Hill.

Bures, L. (2016). "Intelligence sharing and the fight against terrorism in the EU: Lessons learned from Europol." *European View*, 15: 57–66.

Byman, D. (2014). "The intelligence war on terrorism." *Intelligence and National Security*, 29: 837–863.

Central Intelligence Agency. (2016). *Website*. https://www.cia.gov/offices-of-cia (Accessed August 10, 2016).

Chertoff, M. (2006). "Remarks." *U.S. Department of Justice and SEARCH Symposium on Justice and Public Safety Information Sharing* (March 14). http://www.dhs.gov/xnews/speeches/speech_0273.shtm (Accessed January 17, 2011).

Clarke, R. (2008). *Your Government Failed You: Breaking the Cycle of National Security Disasters*. New York: Harper Collins.

Clarke, R. M. (2017). *Intelligence Analysis: A Target-Centric Approach.* Thousand Oaks, CA: Sage.

Commission on the Intelligence Capabilities of the United States Regarding Weapons of Mass Destruction. (2015). *Report to the President*. https://fas.org/irp/offdocs/wmd_report.pdf (Accessed August 15, 2017).

Defense Intelligence Agency. (2009). *Website*. http://www.dia.mil/thisisdia/intro/index.htm (Accessed February 17, 2009).

Department of Energy. (2009). *Website*. http://www.energy.gov/nationalsecurity/index.htm (Accessed February 19, 2009).

Department of Homeland Security. (2017). *Website*. http://www.dhs.gov/xabout/structure/gc_1220886590914.shtm (Accessed February 23, 2009).

Department of State. (2017). *Website*. http://www.state.gov/s/inr/(Accessed February 24, 2009).

Department of the Treasury. (2017). *Website*. https://www.treasury.gov/about/organizational-structure/Pages/default.aspx (Accessed August 10, 2016).

Dilanian, K. (2013). "A post-Snowden spying climate: The NSA contractor's leaks mark a turning point in U.S. intelligence, experts say." *Los Angeles Times* (December 22): A3.

Dilanian, K. (2014). "NSA leaks halt defense plans." *Los Angeles Times* (February 2): A15.

Dinan, S. (2016). "FBI no-fly list revealed: 81,000 names, but fewer than 1,000 are Americans. *Washington Times*. http://www.washingtontimes.com/news/2016/jun/20/fbi-no-fly-list-revealed-81k-names-fewer-1k-us/(Accessed August 23, 2016).

Drug Enforcement Administration. (2016). *Website*. https://www.dea.gov/index.shtml (Accessed August 10, 2016).

Federal Bureau of Investigation. (2009). *Website*. http://www.fbi.gov/page2/may05/ciprimer053105.htm (Accessed March 28, 2009).

Fisher, S. (2016). "The fight against terrorism – The need for local police units in the United States' intelligence community." *Journal of Military and Strategic Studies*, 17: 189–208.

Gibbons-Neff, T., and D. Lamothe. (2016). "Obama administration expands elite military unit's powers to hunt foreign fighters globally." *The Washington Post*. https://www.washingtonpost.com/news/checkpoint/wp/2016/11/25/obama-administration-expands-elite-military-units-powers-to-hunt-foreign-fighters-globally/?utm_term=.bd02dfe3fb89 (Accessed November 30, 2016).

House Permanent Select Committee on Intelligence. (1996). *IC21: Intelligence Community in the 21st Century, Staff Study*. Washington, D.C.: Author.

Jensen, T. (2014). "National responses to transnational terrorism." *Journal of Conflict Resolution,* 60: 530–554.

Kumar, A. (2014). "NSA phone collection does not prevent terrorism, according to report." *McClatchyDC*. http://www.mcclatchydc.com/2014/01/13/214297/nsa-phone-collection-does-not.html (Accessed January 15, 2014).

Lumpkin, J. (2002) "Terrorist chatter rises in past week." *Pittsburgh Tribune-Review*. http://www.pittsburghlive.com/x/pittsburghtrib/s_102127.html (Accessed February 9, 2009).

MacGaffin, J. (2005). "Clandestine human intelligence: Spies, counterspies, and covert action. *Transforming US Intelligence*, ed. J. Sims and B. Gerber, pp. 79–95. Washington, D.C.: Georgetown University Press.

Margolis, G. (2013). "The lack of HUMINT: A recurring intelligence Problem." *Global Security Studies*, 4: 43–60.

McKirdy, E., and L. Smith-Spark. (2017). "CIA no longer arming anti-Assad rebels, Washington Post reports." http://www.cnn.com/2017/07/20/politics/cia-syria-anti-assad-rebels/index.html (Accessed August 20, 2017).

Miller, G. (2012). "Pentagon establishes defense clandestine service, new espionage unit." *The Washington Post*. http://www.washingtonpost.com/world/national-security/pentagon-creates-new-espionage-unit/2012/04/23/gIQA9R7DcT_story.html (Accessed April 26, 2012).

Mojnar, J. (2015). "The EU as an international counter-terrorism actor: Progress and constraints." *Intelligence and National Security*, 30: 333–356.

National Commission on Terrorist Attacks. (2004). *The 9/11 Commission Report: Final Report of the National Commission on Terrorist Attacks Upon the United States*. New York: W.W. Norton & Company.

National Counterterrorism Center. (2015). *Overview*. http://www.nctc.gov/overview.html (Accessed December 10, 2015).

National Geospatial-Intelligence Agency. (2009). *Website*. http://www1.nga.mil/Pages/Default.aspx (Accessed March 11, 2009).

National Security Agency. (2017). Signals Intelligence. https://www.nsa.gov/about/faqs/sigint-faqs.shtml.

National Security Council. (2009). *Website*. http://www.whitehouse.gov/administration/eop/nsc/(Accessed February 25, 2009).

Office of the Director of National Intelligence. (2016). *Website*. http://www.dni.gov/who.htm (Accessed August 8, 2016).

Office of National Counterintelligence. (2006). *Annual Report to Congress on Foreign Economic Collection and Industrial Espionage—2005*. Washington, D.C.: Author.

OPSEC. (1996). *Operations Security: Intelligence Threat Handbook*. Alexandria, VA: Author.

Perper, R. (2016). "DEA uncovers major drug trafficking by Hezbollah to fund global terrorism." *The Jerusalem Post*. http://www.jpost.com/Middle-East/DEA-uncovers-major-drug-trafficking-by-Hezbollah-to-fund-global-terrorism-443575 (Accessed August 22, 2017).

Richelson, J. (2008). *The US Intelligence Community*. Boulder, CO: Westview Press.

Shorrock, T. (2008). *Spies for Hire: The Secret World of Intelligence Outsourcing*. New York: Simon & Schuster.

Svendsen, A. (2008). "The globalization of intelligence since 9/11: Frameworks and operational parameters." *Cambridge Review of International Affairs*, 21(1): 129–144.

Weisman, J. (2002). "CIA, Pentagon feuding complicates war effort." *USA Today* (June 17): 11.

Worth, K. (2016). "Lone wolf attacks are becoming more common – And more deadly." *Frontline*. http://www.pbs.org/wgbh/frontline/article/lone-wolf-attacks-are-becoming-more-common-and-more-deadly/ (Accessed August 20, 2017).

9 Homeland Security and Weapons of Mass Destruction

LEARNING OBJECTIVES

1. *Define weapons of mass destruction (WMDs).*
2. *Explain the history of the use of various WMDs.*
3. *Distinguish between types of nuclear threats.*
4. *Explain how biological agents can be used as WMDs.*
5. *Describe the nature of chemicals and their use as WMDs.*
6. *Discuss how the various WMDs can be delivered and their limitations.*

Key Terms

Weapons of mass destruction
Biological WMD
Chemical WMD
Geneva Protocol
Nuclear or radiological attack
Dirty bombs
Bioterrorism
Bacterial organisms
Virus
Toxins
Line source method
Point source method
Blister agents
Blood agents
Choking agents
Nerve agents

▶ Introduction

In terms of homeland security, the greatest threat to public safety is the potential use of a weapon of mass destruction (WMD). WMDs can be biological, chemical, or nuclear. WMDs have the potential to inflict widespread death, injury, and destruction, especially in heavily populated cities. Moreover, depending on the type of weapon used and its method of deployment, use of a WMD could have a significant negative impact on an economy. Use of a WMD would not only affect the local economy but its effects could reverberate throughout the nation. For example, exploding a small nuclear device in a city like Chicago, New York, or Los Angeles could inflict substantial destruction. Not only would it kill and injure large numbers of people, it would essentially shut the city down for a long period of time, possibly decades. It would have other effects. It would overload first responders and hospitals; they would not be able to attend to all the injured and dying. It could have a long-term impact on physical infrastructure. It would substantially affect the economy, having an impact on thousands of persons who were not directly affected by the explosion. Additionally, it would have a lasting negative effect on the ecology, making a city uninhabitable. People surviving an attack would suffer health consequences for decades.

To some extent, the primary purpose of using WMDs is not the initial death and injuries but the residual effects that would be more destructive to a country.

Large-scale terrorist attacks enable and strengthen terrorist organizations. The 9/11 attacks demonstrated that a large-scale, destructive attack could be carried out against the United States. The attacks emboldened terrorists and served as an important recruitment tool. It can be argued that the attacks resulted in the proliferation of terrorist groups and cells willing to attack American interests. Al Qaeda was able to achieve a higher level of respect and esteem in the terrorist world because of the attacks.

Terrorists have long sought access to WMDs because of their destructive capabilities (see Cochran and McKinzie, 2008). The *National Strategy for Homeland Security* (Homeland Security Council, 2007) advises that the desire to inflict catastrophic damage on the United States has fueled a desire to acquire WMDs. There is no doubt that some terrorists and hate groups have a desire to use WMDs against the United States, and it is the mission of homeland security to remove or reduce the opportunity for obtaining and using them in this country. Preventing terrorists and hate groups from using WMDs against the United States is a monumental task requiring substantial resources and planning.

The DHS and other federal agencies have pursued initiatives to prevent attacks; nuclear and radiological attacks represent the greatest threats. Harigel (2000) advised that citizens and military personnel can be protected from chemical and biological attacks. People can be inoculated to protect them from most biological weapons, and individuals can be evacuated or provided protective clothing that reduces or eliminates the effects of chemical attacks. Nuclear attacks, on the other hand, are indiscriminate and have widespread effects. If a nuclear attack were to occur, little short of evacuation could protect people.

Defining Weapons of Mass Destruction

As noted, there are biological, chemical, and nuclear WMDs. Each type of WMD possesses a different set of threats. However, what is a WMD? The federal government has defined **weapons of mass destruction** as

> Any explosive, incendiary, poison gas, bomb, grenade, or rocket having a propellant charge of more than four ounces [113 g], missile having an explosive or incendiary charge of more than one-quarter ounce [7 g], or mine or device similar to the above. (2) Poison gas. (3) Any weapon involving a disease organism. (4) Any weapon that is designed to release radiation at a level dangerous to human life. This definition derives from US law, 18 U.S.C. Section 2332a and the referenced 18 USC 921. Indictments and convictions for possession and use of WMD such as truck bombs, pipe bombs, shoe bombs, cactus needles coated with botulin toxin, etc. have been obtained under 18 USC 2332a.

HS Web Link: To learn more about the definition of WMDs, go to https://www.fbi.gov/investigate/wmd.

This is a legal definition that is promulgated in federal statutes. The law is designed to be all-inclusive. Congressional intent was to allow prosecutors to pursue any case remotely associated with the use of a WMD or terrorism. This definition also includes conventional weaponry. Truck bombs, pipe bombs, and shoe bombs are included, although they generally use conventional explosives as opposed to a biological, chemical, or nuclear agent.

Cameron and Bajema (2009) advised that WMDs simply are weapons that can inflict massive casualties and destruction. They noted that there is debate over the definition of WMDs, as the term originally referred to advanced military weapons, not crude or makeshift weapons most often used by terrorists. Early and his colleagues (2017) argued that conventional weapons should not be included in the definition of WMDs as it confuses

HS ANALYSIS BOX 9-1

Congress has defined WMDs very inclusively, including a number of different weapons that may be prosecuted. The statute covers nuclear devices as well as pipe bombs. Should these less lethal weapons be considered in the same statute as radiological weapons? Should possession by a terrorist group receive more attention as opposed to other criminals possessing such weapons? Why?

two distinct terrorist threats with different risks and consequences. For the most part, this chapter will focus on biological, chemical, and nuclear WMDs.

National Terrorism Advisory System

The NTAS was implemented in January 2011, by DHS Secretary Janet Napolitano. The system serves to alert the American people and homeland security agencies of a possible terrorist attack. It consists of three types of advisories: bulletins, elevated threats, and imminent threats (Figure 9-1 ■).

According to the DHS (2017), "Using available information, the alerts will provide a concise summary of the potential threat, information about actions being taken to ensure public safety, and recommended steps that individuals, communities, businesses and governments can take to help prevent, mitigate or respond to the threat" (p. 1). The alerts are

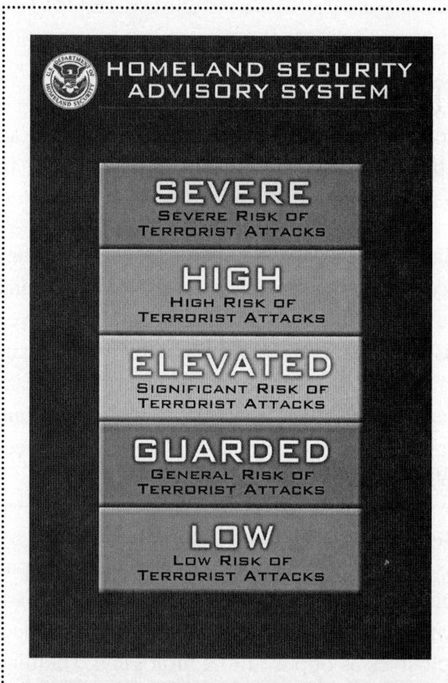

FIGURE 9-1 National Terrorism Advisory System

Source: World History Archive/Alamy Stock Photo.

based on the type and magnitude of the threat, with threat information being sent to law enforcement, affected areas within the private sector, and more broadly to the general public. Such alerts are questionable in terms of their accuracy or effectiveness.

▶ History of the Deployment of WMDs

WMDs present a substantial problem and generate a great deal of fear. The government and populace tend to treat them as a new phenomenon, but WMDs, although very crude ones, have been used for centuries. For example, Iannotti et al. (2016) noted they were used as early as the seventh century. An examination of their historical use provides a foundation to better understanding how they are used and their destructive capacities. This section examines the historical use of biological and chemical WMDs. Nuclear WMDs are not examined here, as they are a relatively new phenomenon with a limited history.

Historical Precedents for Biological WMDs

A **biological WMD** is defined as the use of a bacteria, virus, or other biological pathogen to attack or deliberately infect people, livestock, or crops. Various forms of biological WMDs, often very crude, have been used for centuries. In 184 B.C.E., Hannibal of Carthage hurled pots containing vipers onto the decks of enemy ships, and in 1495, the Spanish attempted to give wine spiked with the blood of leprosy patients to their French enemies near Naples. The Greeks as early as 300 B.C. polluted the drinking water of their enemies by dumping the corpses of animals into the wells. In most cases, these early attempts were ineffective, but they demonstrate that biological weapons have a long history (see DeNoon, 2003; Harigel, 2000).

There is a history of using biological weapons in the United States. In 1763, British officers planned to distribute blankets infected with smallpox to Native Americans at Fort Pitt in Pennsylvania. The American Civil War witnessed numerous attempts to use biological weapons. Luke Blackburn of Kentucky sold blankets contaminated with smallpox and yellow fever to Union troops. General Johnson used the bodies of dead sheep and pigs to pollute water during the siege of Vicksburg. Again, the attempts were crude, but they demonstrate that those engaged in war will use any means to defeat their enemies (see DeNoon, 2003; Harigel, 2000).

Even though there was a substantial increase in the use of chemical weapons during World War I (discussed later), there were some efforts to exploit biological weaponry. The Germans attempted to use glanders (an infectious disease affecting horses, mules, and donkeys) and anthrax in Argentina, Mesopotamia, Norway, Romania, and the United States to infect draft animals, horses, and mules that were destined for use by the Allies in the war effort. The Germans were accused of attempting to start cholera epidemics in Italy and Russia. They also attempted to introduce fungi to Allied wheat crops (see DeNoon, 2003; Harigel, 2000). Again, these efforts were ineffective and had little impact on the intended victims. However, they spurred interest in biological weapons, and many countries including France, England, Canada, Japan, Germany, and the United States began experimenting and developing biological weapons after the war.

HS Web Link: To learn more about the history of biological weapons, go to http://www.aarc.org/resources/biological/history.asp.

More recently, in 1950, the East German government accused the United States of scattering Colorado potato beetles over its crops. From 1962 to 1996, Cuban officials accused the United States 21 times of attempting to use biological weapons against them. Their charges included the use of Newcastle disease against poultry, African swine fever aimed at pigs, tobacco blue mold disease to affect the country's tobacco industry, and sugarcane rust disease against the sugar industry (Zillinskas, 1999). These allegations and attacks demonstrate that biological warfare can be waged against farm crops and livestock, as well as people. Such attacks can cause food shortages and adversely affect a country's or region's economy.

The United States has used chemicals to attack plant life. The United States used herbicides on a limited scale during the last year of the Korean War (Stockholm International Peace

Research Institute, 1971), and the United States extensively used the herbicide Agent Orange in the Vietnam War to clear protective and battle areas around troops. Approximately 77 million liters of the chemical were sprayed across the country (Van-Taun, 2005). The use of Agent Orange in the war resulted in health problems for American troops and the Vietnamese people.

In reality, there is little or no evidence that countries have been successful in using pests and plant diseases to attack food supplies and livestock. It is difficult to mount an effective attack given the geographical dispersion of food and livestock. An attack may be successful in a given area, but it is nearly impossible to have a substantial impact on a country. For the most part, Zillinskas (1999) advised that plant or crop infestations have been the result of newly introduced pests and diseases that arrived in counties as a result of food shipments or commerce, not as a result of a biological attack by an enemy.

The most recent and notable biological weapons attack occurred in the United States in 2001 when several letters laced with anthrax were mailed from Princeton, New Jersey, to several people on the East Coast. Letters were mailed to the editor of a Florida tabloid, the *Sun*; they were mailed to the New York television network offices of ABC, NBC, and CBS. Traces of anthrax were found in the offices of the New York governor, and two such letters were mailed to two U.S. senators. The attacks created a panic as no one initially knew how many anthrax letters ultimately would be mailed. Moreover, the mailings seemed to be indiscriminate, with victims ranging from ordinary citizens to media personnel to politicians. The attacks resulted in the deaths of 5 people and a total of 19 people developed anthrax infections. Approximately 10,000 people were administered antibiotics as a result of the attacks, and the United States produced and stockpiled large quantities of antibiotics to counter anthrax. The attacks also resulted in a wave of "hoax" letters. During October and November following the attacks, more than 550 hoax letters claiming to contain anthrax were mailed in the United States. Most were sent to abortion clinics (Snyder and Pate, 2002). It was not until 2008 that the Federal Bureau of Investigation (FBI) agents were able to identify the perpetrator, who worked in a military bio-weapons laboratory at Ft. Detrick, Maryland.

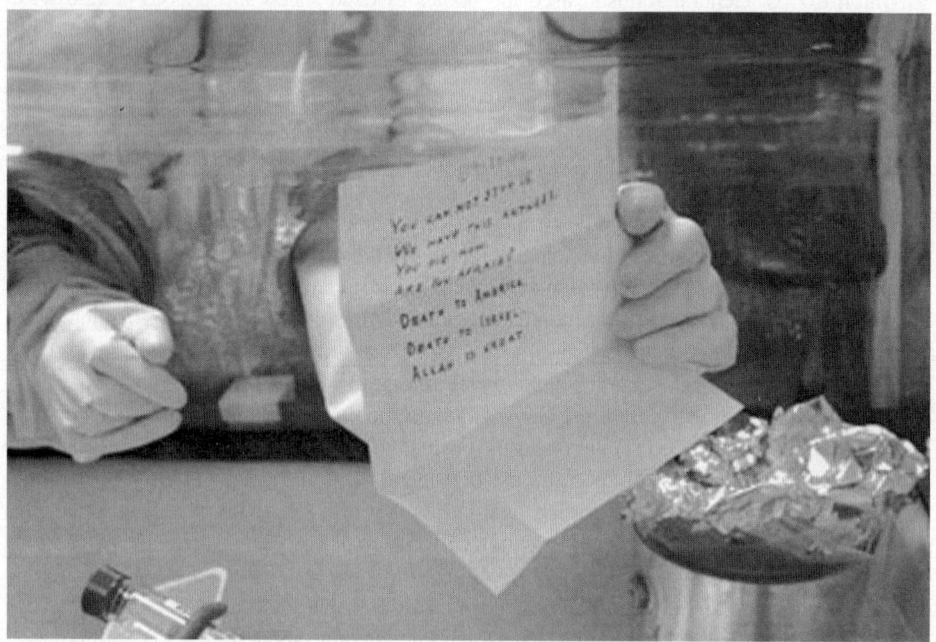

FBI technicians examine a letter tainted with anthrax and sent to Sen. Tom Daschle.
FBI UPI Photo Service/Newscom.

Individuals rather than international groups have committed terrorist attacks using biological weapons. These attacks generally consist of a single and very specific target as opposed to multiple attacks targeting large numbers of people, such as the 2001 anthrax attacks, during which anthrax was mailed to several individuals. Also, citizens, not international terrorist groups, most often commit domestic biological attacks. These attacks usually involve unsophisticated biological agents. For example, in 1984, members of a cult contaminated salad bars in 10 Dalles, Oregon, restaurants with a strain of salmonella. The cult leaders were eventually arrested and jailed. In 1996, someone laced cattle feed with chlordane, a pesticide. In 2003, a supermarket employee deliberately contaminated ground beef with an insecticide. Nearly 100 people became ill as a result of the incident (James Martin Center for Nonproliferation Studies, 2006). It seems that periodically disgruntled people will resort to biological warfare to make a political statement or to obtain revenge for some perceived wrong. But, for the most part, biological attacks are uncommon.

HS Web Link: To learn more about the salmonella attack in The Dalles, Oregon, to go https://www.cdc.gov/phlp/docs/forensic_epidemiology/Additional%20Materials/Articles/Torok%20et%20al.pdf.

Historical Precedents for Chemical WMDs

A **chemical WMD** is a manufactured highly toxic chemical that can sicken or kill humans or animals or destroy plants. Human and animal exposure can occur through inhalation, transdermal or exposure to the skin, or ingestion. Biological warfare dates back more than 2,500 years, but the use of chemical warfare also has a long history. As early as 1000 B.C., the Chinese used arsenic smoke, and in 431 B.C.E. during the Trojan War, the Greeks used a mixture of sulfur and pitch resin to produce suffocating fumes (DeNoon, 2003; Harigel, 2000). The recognition of the devastation that chemical weapons cause resulted in a number of attempts to control their production and use. In 1874, the Brussels Convention made an effort to control them, and these efforts were expounded upon during the First Hague Peace Appeal in 1899 (Harigel, 2000).

These early attempts to control chemical warfare were disregarded, and chemical weapons were used extensively in World War I. In 1915, the Germans used canisters of chlorine gas at the battle of Ypres in Belgium. The gas resulted in the deaths of 5,000 French troops and injured another 15,000. Subsequently, both sides began using poisonous gas and developed more deadly varieties. Ultimately, mustard gas, which burned the skin and lungs, was developed and deployed. Both sides used the gas and it resulted in 91,000 deaths and 1.2 million people injured. Estimates are that 124,000 tons of chemicals were used in the war (Meselson, 1991).

Harigel (2000) advised that even though the use of these weapons resulted in massive casualties, it was generally recognized that they were ineffective as a military weapon. The inhuman consequences on soldiers and civilians resulted in a loss of support for war efforts and retaliation. In 1925, the **Geneva Protocol** was signed; it prohibited the use of asphyxiating poisonous gases and bacteriological methods of warfare. The Geneva Protocol, however, did not prohibit the development and stockpiling of these weapons. Regardless, it is the cornerstone of today's prohibitions preventing biological and chemical warfare.

Although well intended, the Geneva Protocol has not prevented the use of chemical and biological weapons by signatories and non-signatories alike. During World War II, Japan used chemical weapons against China, and Italy used them against Ethiopia. They most likely used these weapons because China and Ethiopia could not retaliate since they did not have chemical weapons. Saddam Hussein used chemical weapons against Kurdish minorities in Iraq and against Iran between 1980 and 1988; it estimated that 5 percent of the Iranian casualties were the result of chemical warfare and that 45,000 soldiers were exposed to mustard gas during the Iraqi-Iranian war (Harigel, 2000). Most recently, the Syrian government indiscriminately used sarin nerve gas as well as chlorine and mustard gas to attack rebel positions during the Syrian Civil War. It is estimated that over 1,000 people were killed as a result of gas attacks (Graham-Harrison, 2016).

HS Web Link: To learn more about the history of chemical warfare, go to https://www.chemheritage.org/distillations/magazine/a-brief-history-of-chemical-war.

Although there were treaties prohibiting the use of biological and chemical agents, countries continued to develop them. The Cold War resulted in new developments in biological and chemical weapons. A number of new toxins were developed, including VX, a nerve gas that can kill if a single drop were applied to the skin. Other toxins including sarin were developed during this period. Chemical agents became more toxic and dangerous. They saw little use, but Soviet troops used them in Afghanistan after their invasion of that country. As a result of the proliferation of state-sponsored weapons programs, the toxicity of these new agents was increased, making it easier to commit a terrorist act with more lethal consequences.

One example of terrorists using chemical weapons involved attacks in Japan. In 1995, the Japanese cult Aum Shinrikyo released containers of sarin gas on several subway trains in Tokyo. The containers were placed in five different bags in plastic containers. The containers were ruptured using an umbrella, and the contents leaked onto the floor of the trains where they evaporated and were inhaled by passengers. The attacks resulted in 12 deaths and several thousand people were injured. This attack was the second deadly attack conducted by Aum Shinrikyo. The group previously drove a truck containing sarin to a residential neighborhood in Matsumoto and remotely released the gas, causing seven deaths and injuries to about 1,000 people (Olson, 1999).

There are several examples of the presence of ricin, a toxin extracted from the castor bean, in the United States, although there are no instances of the chemical's use. In 1995, members of the Minnesota Patriots Council, an extremist antigovernment organization, were arrested for plotting the murder of a U.S. marshal. They had planned to sprinkle ricin on the door handles of the marshal's vehicle as well as on the car heater fan (Center for Defense Information, 2003). In 2008, the police and paramedics were called to a Las Vegas hotel room where a guest had become ill. He later slipped into a coma. A subsequent search of his room resulted in the discovery of vials of ricin. The police also discovered castor beans from which ricin is made and a copy of the *Anarchist's Cookbook* (Thevenot and Mower, 2008).

The Threat of Nuclear Weapons of Mass Destruction: Destructiveness, Potential for Use, and Availability

One of the public's greatest fears is that a terrorist group or rogue nation will use WMDs against the United States. Although there may be groups with the desire to launch a nuclear attack, few have access to these weapons or the logistical support necessary to carry out an attack. Likewise, although there may be a number of "rogue" nations willing to supply these weapons or otherwise assist terrorists with a WMD attack, there are strong deterrents to rendering such assistance.

The world is a much more dangerous place than it was in the past. During the Cold War, enemies were known and well understood. Officials comprehended where attacks might emanate, built defenses, and prepared for attacks. Essentially, nations developed a nuclear and conventional weapons stalemate. All sides understood that a nuclear war could lead to total annihilation. Today, the circumstances have changed. Unlike during the Cold War era, terrorist groups remain hidden in many countries, blending in with populations that do not necessarily desire to instigate war. Terrorists believe this provides them with a modicum of cover and prevents the United States from retaliating should they mount an attack. After the 9/11 attacks, the Taliban provided al Qaeda sanctuary in Afghanistan,

FBI SWAT team member is checking for possible radiological contamination as part of a drill.
Dan Loh/AP Images.

believing the United States would not intercede or violate its national boundaries. Some of today's terrorists are willing to risk total obliteration in order to "defeat" the United States. These circumstances, it is argued, clearly result in a greater level of danger. WMDs present a vexing problem for homeland security.

A **nuclear or radiological attack** can be mounted in several ways. First, an aggressor could obtain a nuclear weapon, smuggle it into the United States, and detonate it. Second, the perpetrator could combine radiological materials with a conventional explosive device and ignite it, hoping to spread radiological materials across a wide area. A third method is to use conventional explosives or attacks on nuclear facilities or materials in the United States, resulting in the spread of radiological debris.

▶ Nuclear and Radiological WMDs

Availability of Nuclear Materials

Nuclear materials are present in most countries whether in the form of nuclear weapons or in the form of peaceful activities such as medicine or nuclear energy. There are nine countries that possess nuclear weapons as listed in Table 9-1 ■.

Iran possesses large quantities of processed uranium and plutonium and likely could construct a nuclear bomb in a relatively short period of time. Together, these countries possess approximately 22,500 nuclear weapons or bombs (Ploughshares, 2011).

TABLE 9-1 Countries with Nuclear Weapons

Countries
United States
Russia
England
France
Pakistan
North Korea
India
China
Israel

Of all the WMDs, nuclear devices raise the most concern. Even a small nuclear weapon detonated in a large city would result in catastrophic destruction and vast casualties. Moreover, the presence of nuclear radiation would result in long-term problems for any country. Examples of the impact of long-term radiation are the meltdown of the Chernobyl nuclear plant in the Ukraine in 1986, and the Fukushima Daiichi nuclear plant in Japan that was damaged by a 9.0 magnitude earthquake in 2011. The Chernobyl disaster resulted in nuclear materials drifting over parts of Europe, Russia, Ukraine, Belarus, and even into the United States. The disaster resulted in more than 300,000 people being evacuated. The amount of radiation released was far greater than the radiation released as a result of the bombing of Hiroshima or Nagasaki (World Nuclear Association, 2008). Thirty years after the disaster, the facility remains closed and parts of the area remain evacuated because of radiation contamination. The Fukushima Daiichi disaster resulted in widespread radiation releases causing evacuations and hundreds of eventual cancer-related deaths.

Nuclear Bombs or Weapons

Essentially, a nuclear device can be constructed from highly enriched uranium or plutonium. There are two ways terrorists could acquire a nuclear weapon. First, they could steal or purchase one that has been constructed by a nuclear power. Second, they could acquire the materials and construct a weapon. The Union of Concerned Scientists (2008) advised that of the two options terrorists are more likely to attempt to acquire the materials and construct a device. If terrorists are able to acquire all the necessary components, it is not difficult to construct a nuclear weapon.

Only a relatively small amount of nuclear material is required to build a bomb. A crude weapon could be constructed from 40 to 50 kilograms of enriched uranium. A more sophisticated device could be constructed from about 12 kilograms of highly enriched uranium or 4 kilograms of plutonium. Many countries have the knowledge and capacity to build nuclear weapons.

The Spread of Nuclear Material and Information

Most notably, North Korea, Pakistan, and Iran pose nuclear challenges. North Korea remains isolated from the rest of the world and is a very poor nation. North Korea does possess nuclear weapons and technology, and it is developing missiles capable of striking the United States. The fear is that it will resort to selling nuclear materials or weapons on the black market to raise currency or to cause problems for the United States. There are many rogue states and groups that seek nuclear weapons.

Today, Pakistan is particularly problematic as it is a nuclear power with 30 to 100 nuclear weapons (Broad and Sanger, 2008). In 2008, Pervez Musharraf (the president of

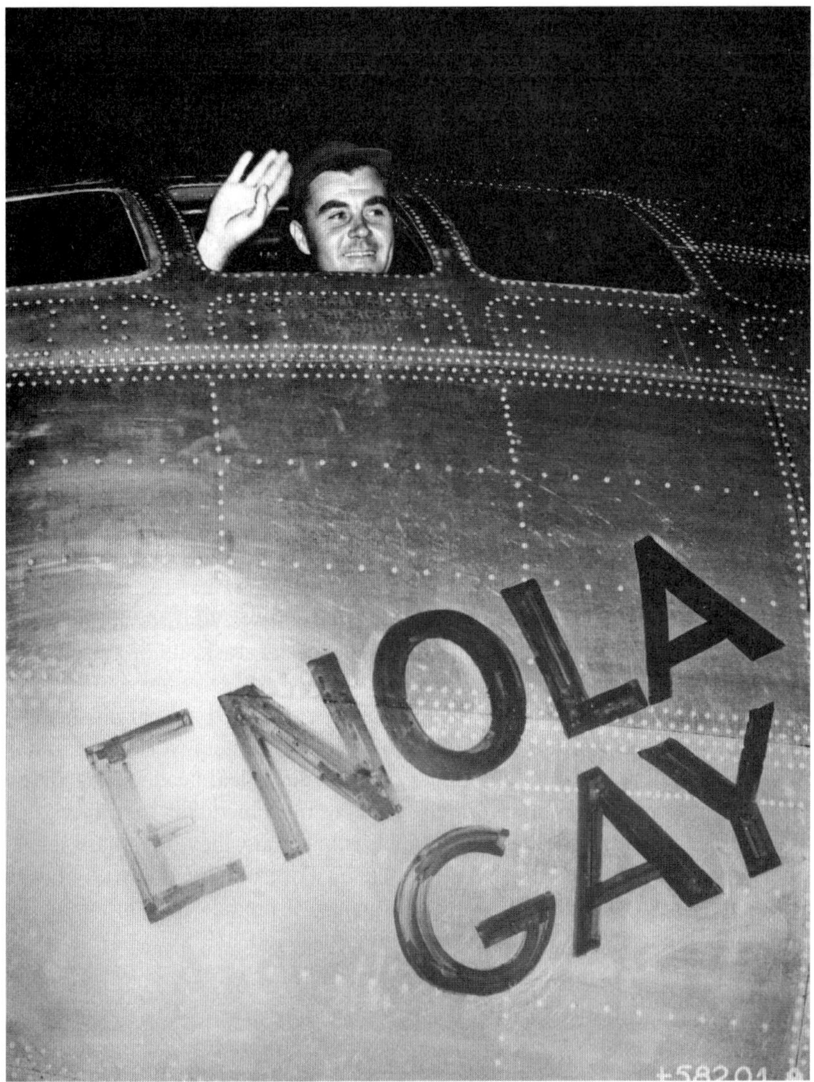

Col. Paul Tibbets piloted the Enola Gay, the plane that dropped the atom bomb on Hiroshima, August 6, 1945.
American Photo Archive/Alamy Stock Photo.

Pakistan and an alleged American ally) was forced to resign, resulting in a degree of instability. During the same time, Islamic terrorists become more active as the government weakened and faced an array of social and economic problems. It is feared that instability in Pakistan increases the probability that radicals within the government might gain control and provide nuclear weapons to terrorists. The Pakistani regions bordering Afghanistan seem ungovernable and are the home to the Taliban and other terrorist groups. These groups have undeterminable numbers of sympathizers in Pakistan, including government officials working in the intelligence apparatus.

Pakistan has a history of sharing nuclear bomb-making information with other countries. In 2004, Abdul Qadeer Khan, an engineer and founder of Pakistan's nuclear program, admitted to sharing nuclear technology and equipment with Libya, Iran, and North Korea. Kahn and his associates developed an international network to smuggle parts and technology out of the country. After his confession, Kahn was convicted in Pakistan but pardoned the next day by President Musharraf. Kahn allegedly sold the technology and materials for

HS ANALYSIS BOX 9-2

Pakistan is a nuclear state, and it is embroiled in a great deal of conflict internally and externally. Of the greatest concern is that the Taliban controls large portions of the country and there are numerous radical Muslims who are sympathetic with jihad in the country. Pakistan represents a place where terrorists may have access to nuclear weapons or materials. Currently, the United States is working with Pakistan to combat the Taliban. How great a threat do you believe Pakistan is in terms of providing terrorists with nuclear weapons? Should the United States conduct more combat operations in Pakistan to defeat the Taliban to reduce the nuclear threat? Why?

several million dollars. After his release, Kahn maintained that Musharraf was aware and involved in all the transactions. It is not entirely clear as to the amount of information and technology that were transferred or the full count of countries that received the assistance (Frantz and Collins, 2007).

In 2015, the United States along with five other countries negotiated a deal with Iran to prevent it from developing nuclear weapons. Although Iran had been enriching uranium for years and maintained that it was not developing nuclear weapons, many world leaders came to the inescapable conclusion that eventually it would develop them. The deal reduced Iran's capacity to enrich uranium and reduced its stockpile of enriched uranium for a decade (BBC, 2016).

The potential for losing nuclear materials is not limited to nation-states. Highly enriched uranium is used to fuel more than 100 research centers worldwide in dozens of countries. These sites include military, industrial, medical, and academic facilities. They are involved in a variety of research projects ranging from medicine to military. Although most of these sites have small quantities of nuclear materials, they often have less security as compared to government-controlled weapon sites. For example, many universities have nuclear research programs, and the security for these materials is at minimum levels at best. These sites represent a potential source of radioactive material.

Smuggling Nuclear Weapons and Materials

Nuclear weapons on American soil are closely guarded by the military, and the Domestic Nuclear Detection Office within the DHS monitors the movement and smuggling of nuclear materials in the United States and worldwide. It would be extremely difficult for terrorists to obtain a weapon in the United States. Given America's security standards for nuclear materials, the most likely scenario is that terrorists will attempt to smuggle a nuclear weapon or weapons' materials into the United States. The United States works with a number of nations to secure nuclear weapons and materials; nonetheless, a substantial amount of radiological materials has been lost, stolen, or otherwise unaccounted for in this country alone. The General Accounting Office found that between 1955 and 1977 several thousand kilograms of nuclear materials had gone "missing." Some of the missing materials likely reflect accounting errors rather than actual losses, but these figures demonstrate at least lax control and accounting (GAO, 1977).

Schmid and Spencer-Smith (2012) performed open source inventory cases of lost, stolen, smuggled, and otherwise missing nuclear materials in the Black Sea region between 1990 and 2011. They found about 100 cases of suspected or illegal movement of nuclear materials. Their research shows that there are large amounts of these materials that are not secured by governments and can appear on the black market. Indeed, Williams and the Associated Press (2015) reported that the FBI working with local authorities had interrupted four attempts by Russian affiliated gangs in Moldova to sell radioactive materials to Middle Eastern extremists over a five-year period.

If terrorists attempt to smuggle nuclear materials into the United States to construct a nuclear device, they will face many challenges beyond security. Terrorists most likely would be forced to make a crude weapon. Such a weapon would be rather large, weighing a ton or more and would require a large amount of highly enriched uranium or plutonium. Transporting the materials would be difficult. Terrorists would have to mask the radioactive materials so that they would not be discovered by radiological detection devices and to protect themselves from radiation exposure. Moreover, they would have to assemble a team with the technical ability and equipment to construct the device. In addition to obtaining the highly enriched uranium or plutonium, they would have to acquire a number of bomb parts. It would be extremely difficult to obtain or manufacture a triggering device and other parts necessary for the weapon. These challenges substantially reduce the likelihood that terrorists will be able to detonate a nuclear device in the United States.

HS Web Link: To learn more about how terrorists may acquire nuclear materials, go to http://www.washingtoninstitute.org/policy-analysis/view/the-potential-for-radiological-terrorism-by-al-qaeda-and-the-islamic-state.

Terrorist Attacks Using Dirty Bombs and Attacks on Nuclear Facilities

Methods other than the detonation of a nuclear weapon could create substantial damage: (1) a dirty bomb and (2) an attack on a nuclear power plant or nuclear facility.

Dirty bombs use conventional explosive materials but are wrapped in or contain radioactive material. The radioactive materials are dispersed as a result of the conventional explosion producing contamination. A dirty bomb does not necessarily have to contain highly enriched uranium or plutonium. It could contain radioactive waste products that are produced at commercial power plants, medical centers, or research facilities. Radioactive waste sites generally have fewer security precautions as compared to locations that house highly enriched uranium or plutonium.

There have been attempts to use a dirty bomb. In 1996, Islamic rebels from Chechnya planted a dirty bomb in a park in Moscow (On, 2016). Although not detonated, it contained dynamite and cesium 137, a by-product of nuclear fission. If the bomb had been detonated, it would have spread radioactive materials into the surrounding area. In 2002, Abdullah Al Muhajir, also known as Jose Padilla, was arrested by federal authorities for plotting to construct and detonate a dirty bomb in the United States. FBI agents arrested Padilla at Chicago's O'Hare Airport. He had a suitcase with $10,000 in cash, and he had undergone dirty-bomb-making training in Lahore, Pakistan. Agents believed he was on a reconnaissance mission for a future dirty bomb attack (Krock and Deusser, 2003). Since terrorists have used dirty bombs in the past, it is plausible that they will resort to them in the future.

Crashing a large aircraft into or using large amounts of explosives at a nuclear power plant could have the same effects as a dirty bomb except the effects would be of a much greater magnitude. Such an explosion could cause the reactor core to melt down (such as occurred at Chernobyl or Fukushima, Japan) or spent fuel waste to be spread across a large geographical area. The effects could be devastating, and the cleanup could take decades.

Security remains a concern for most nuclear plants. There are 99 such facilities in the United States, and they are geographically dispersed throughout the nation. In addition to an air attack, these plants are susceptible to acts of sabotage or ground attack. These plants have security, including electronic monitoring, armed guards, and fencing for perimeter security. But these levels of security may prove inadequate, especially if attacked by a group of motivated, well-armed terrorists. Essentially, terrorists could cause a disaster by using a relatively small amount of conventional explosives to rupture one of the plant's reactors. There have been a number of mock or red team attacks on some of America's nuclear facilities, and although the results are classified, some estimate that the security failed about 50 percent of the time (Project on Government Oversight, 2001).

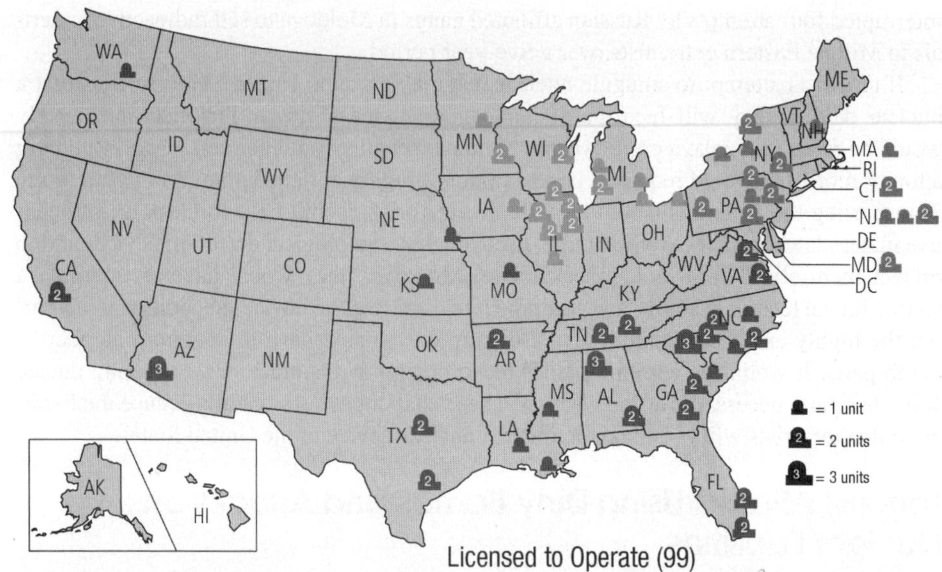

Map of the United States showing locations of operating nuclear power reactors.
Source: https://www.nrc.gov/reactors/operating/map-power-reactors.html.

There is some evidence that power plants have been targeted by terrorists. In August 2003, police in Toronto, Canada, detained 19 Pakistani-born men who had been under surveillance by Canadian authorities. Several had taken flying lessons, been involved in surveillance-like activities, and had filed a flight pattern over a nuclear power plant (Brown, 2003). In March 2003, National Guard troops were dispatched to the Palo Verde Nuclear Power Plant about 50 miles east of Phoenix, Arizona. DHS Secretary Tom Ridge advised that a serious and credible threat had been received. In addition to the troops, a U.S. Customs and Border Protection Black Hawk helicopter was also sent to the scene (Fields, Davis, and Schlesinger, 2003). Although no attacks occurred, these cases demonstrate the serious problem of safeguarding nuclear facilities.

In 2016, after the Paris and Brussels terrorist attacks, the Belgium government began to take precautionary measures in case of a successful attack on one of their nuclear facilities. They began issuing iodine pills to citizens who live within 100 kilometers of a nuclear facility (Dutton, 2016). Given the increase in terror activities across the globe, other countries likely will begin to examine their nuclear security and mitigation operations.

Determining adequate levels of security was discussed in Chapter 3. The first step in critical infrastructure protection is the determination of the required level of security for a given asset. Given that nuclear and radiological attacks present the greatest problems and possibly disastrous outcomes in terms of homeland security, it is imperative that all

HS ANALYSIS BOX 9-3

The United States and the world are facing an energy shortage. It has been advocated that the United States build more nuclear power plants to supply electricity to our growing population. Building additional plants will increase the security risk. Should we build more nuclear plants? Do the advantages outweigh the disadvantages? In this case, does the need for energy outweigh the need for homeland security?

facilities with nuclear and radiological materials have the highest security standards—nuclear facilities have not achieved this standard.

Protection or security is not the only homeland security issue. In 2016, nuclear waste storage tanks at the Hanford nuclear site in Washington leaked radioactive materials sickening 26 workers. The site stores 56 million gallons of radioactive chemicals (RT, 2016). Hansford is not the only nuclear site with problems. Many of our nuclear reactors are decades old, and each year several have problems. Such problems are homeland security issues if they are of significant magnitude.

Palo Verde Nuclear Generating Station, Unit 1.
Larry Lee Photography/Corbis/Getty Images.

▶ Biological Weapons of Mass Destruction

Biological weapons pose a different set of problems for homeland security. Although there are many difficulties in weaponizing biological agents, they are less cumbersome and easier to use than nuclear materials. Also, like radiation, biological weapons do not know borders. The release of biological agents causing disease in one country could easily spread the disease to other countries as a result of animal, plant, and human migration and the winds. The bird flu is a good example. This disease spread from migrating birds and affected animals and people in several Asian countries, and almost a decade later, the virus was responsible for the slaughter of millions of turkeys and chickens in the United States. In 2015, Minnesota declared a state of emergency after more than 7.3 million birds had to be destroyed (Reuters, 2015). Another example is the swine or H1N1 virus that spread across the globe in 2009. It has been estimated that the swine flu killed as many as 203,000 people (Morin, 2013). A recent virus is the Middle East respiratory syndrome (MERS). This virus was first identified in Saudi Arabia, and approximately 35% of those who contract it die (WHO, 2017). Biological WMDs potentially are becoming even more problematic as research advances and information spread across the world. Most of us are familiar with the stockpiling of biological weapons, but perhaps the greatest fear is the development of new organisms.

Biological terrorism represents a threat to the United States and the rest of the world. Currently, more than 100 counties have the capacity to produce biological weapons on a large scale (Sauter and Carafano, 2005). A number of contagions could pose a real health threat to large numbers of people. Given diseases such as smallpox and anthrax, there is the potential to infect large numbers of people over a vast geographical area. Containment perhaps is the greatest issue, along with prevention. There is a great deal of speculation that terrorist groups possess or are attempting to possess biological weapons (Hummel,

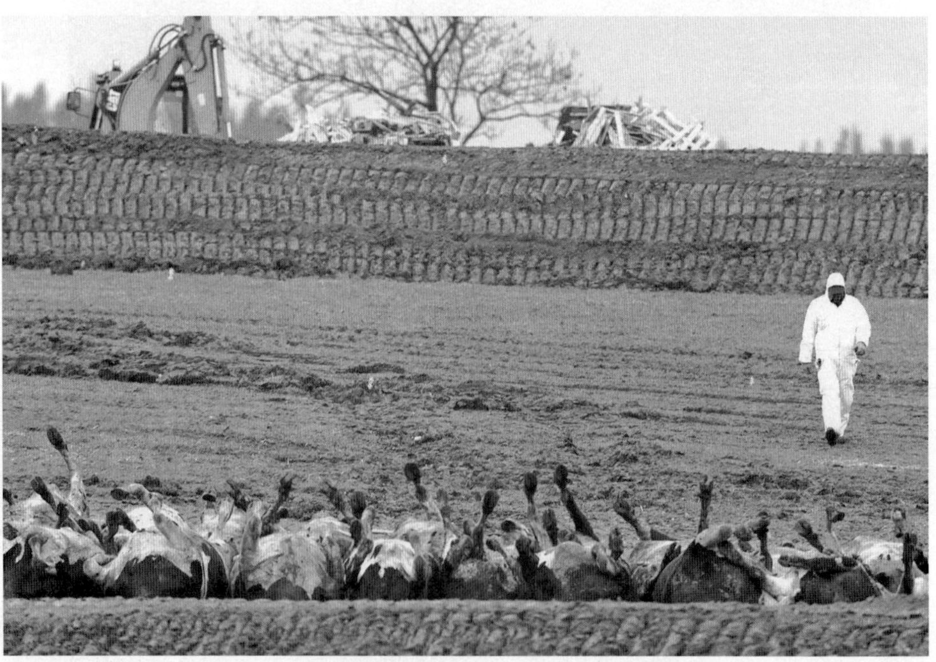

Cattle being destroyed as a result of foot-and-mouth disease.
Owen Humphreys/PA Images/Alamy Stock Photo.

2016). Substantial publicity and public fear resulted in 2001 when anthrax was mailed to several locations causing several deaths and injuries.

There is some confusion over what constitutes bioterrorism. Ackerman and Moran (undated) defined **bioterrorism** as "the use by non-state actors of micro-organisms to inflict harm on a wider population." Cameron and Bajema (2009) advised that biological weapons "employ living micro organisms (pathogens) or toxins produced by living organisms to attack human beings, animals, and/or plants" (p. 271). These definitions include use by terrorist groups and other groups such as organized crime or hate groups. Biological toxins can be used for a variety of rationales with the same outcome—death, panic, fear, and economic devastation. Moreover, the targets for a biological attack may not be humans; there have been instances when toxins were used to destroy crops and livestock. The damages caused by toxins exemplify how biological warfare or acts can have devastating effects on living conditions and local economies.

Types of Biological Weapons

Different biological agents could be used as a WMD. Essentially, there are three general categories of biological agents: bacterial organisms, viruses, and toxins. Figure 9-2 ■ provides a breakdown of the various organisms associated with these three categories. The Centers for Disease Control and Prevention (CDC) has developed a priority system in terms of national risk. Those in the A category are high-priority agents that are rarely seen in the United States, but they can (1) be easily transmitted among people, (2) result in a high mortality rate, (3) result in a public panic or social disruption, and (4) require special action for public health. Category B agents (1) are moderately easily disseminated, (2) result in moderate morbidity and low mortality rates, and (3) require special medical response actions (CDC, 2017). Figure 9-2 ■ contains a listing of the most dangerous and common viruses that can be weaponized.

Bacterial Organisms

Bacterial organisms cause diseases such as anthrax or the plague. Bacteria are a group of usually single-celled organisms that come in many different shapes, sizes, and forms. They live almost anywhere on earth, including on humans. Many forms of bacteria are not dangerous, but some release toxins that can cause diseases. Each year hundreds of people die

Category A Agents	Category B Agents	Category C Agents
Smallpox	Q fever	Nipah virus
Anthrax	Brucellosis	Hantaviruses
Plague	Glanders	Tickborne hemorrhagic fever
Botulism	Typhus fever	Tickborne encephalitis viruses
Tularaemia	Encephalomyelitis	Yellow fever
Filoviruses including Ebola and Marburg hemorrhagic fever	Ricin	Multidrug resistant
Arenaviruses, Lassa and Argentine hemorrhagic fever	Staphylococcus	Tuberculosis

FIGURE 9-2 Biological Agents
Source: http://ocw.jhsph.edu/courses/BiologicalAgentsOfWaterAndFoodborneBioterrorism/PDFs/WaterFoodTerror3.pdf.

HS Web Link: To learn more about biological diseases and agents, go to https://emergency.cdc.gov/agent/agentlist.asp.

from bacteria that grow in body tissue and cause infections. Bacteria-borne diseases are not transmitted from human to human but generally occur as a result of eating contaminated food or the victim consumes the bacteria via inhalation, drinking water, or other liquids. For example, the 2001 anthrax attack in the United States resulted in only eight deaths. The disease did not spread from human to human. To contract the disease, one had to breathe in or otherwise consume the anthrax spores. Animals can also spread bacteria. The Bubonic Plague, which killed one-third of the population in Europe in the Middle Ages, was spread by bites from invested fleas on rats. The bacterium is still present, and in one case in 2013, 20 people in Madagascar died as a result of the bacteria (Beaumont, 2013). For bacteria to be used as a biological weapon, the bacteria would have to be spread over a large area, and victims would have to come into direct contact with the bacteria. Bacteria cannot be used to make an effective WMD.

Viruses

Viruses can cause a host of dangerous diseases, including Ebola, Human Immunodeficiency Virus (HIV), hepatitis, smallpox, avian influenza, and the Severe Acute Respiratory Syndrome (SARS). Viruses are also responsible for a number of less serious medical ailments, such as the common cold, influenza, chickenpox, and cold sores. A **virus** is a microscopic living organism that can grow or reproduce only inside a host cell or living animal. Unlike bacteria, viruses are spread from human to human; a prime example is influenza, with outbreaks occurring each year. Most viruses are eliminated by a person's immune system. Although antibiotics are sometimes given to people infected with a virus, they have no effect on the virus. A number of antiviral drugs have been developed targeting individual viruses. Antiviral vaccines produce immunity to specific or groups of viruses.

In terms of biological WMDs, viruses are the most problematic. Since they can spread across a population, they often are difficult to contain. Each year Americans experience an influenza outbreak, and thousands of people contract the virus with a number of older and younger people dying. Of all the possible biological WMDs, smallpox is the most dangerous. A number of years ago, smallpox was virtually eliminated through vaccinations. Today, there are only a few cases of smallpox and they generally occur in third-world counties. The disease has been absent for so long and Americans no longer receive vaccinations, making many highly susceptible to the disease. One of the homeland security initiatives has been to stockpile smallpox vaccine, should there be an outbreak. It would, however, take a considerable amount of time for the populace to be vaccinated, allowing substantial time for the disease to spread.

An outbreak of smallpox in Yugoslavia perhaps illustrates the problem. In 1972, a number of people contracted smallpox. Prior to the outbreak, no one in Yugoslavia had contracted the disease since 1930. Although a vaccine for the disease had been available for years, people had not received it because smallpox was essentially nonexistent in Yugoslavia and many other countries. Upon learning of the outbreak, the government declared martial law. A number of villages were blockaded to prevent the virus from spreading. The army quarantined thousands of people who had come into contact with those infected with the disease. In about two weeks, most of the population was vaccinated and the epidemic came to an end. A total of 175 people contracted the disease and 35 died (Preston, 1999). The release of smallpox in large population centers would be even more difficult to control, and it would result in larger numbers of casualties.

Nonetheless, viruses remain a significant problem as they mutate creating new ones. For example, scientists have been working with the H5N1 virus, a mutation of H1N1 virus. A moratorium had been placed on H5N1 research for fear it could be accidently escaped or be removed from a research laboratory. The H1N1 has also mutated into the H7N9 virus in China and has killed a number of people. A problem with this virus is that it is resistant to some of the antiviruses that commonly are used to treat viral infections (Rettner, 2013).

HS ANALYSIS BOX 9-4

Numerous viruses and bacteria are dangerous. Currently, the most dangerous is smallpox. It is deadly and it can spread rather quickly. Given its potency, should we begin to inoculate all American citizens? Does the cost of inoculating Americans outweigh the benefit of not having to be concerned with the disease in the future?

A number of these viruses are appearing in the wild, and research is needed to avoid possible pandemics in the future. Other viruses can mutate and pose considerable danger to humans. Some of these viruses are more infectious and may be appealing to terrorists.

Toxins

Although considered biological weapons, **toxins** actually are not biological substances. They are not living organisms like bacteria or viruses, but they are derived from plants and animals. They are biologically derived poisons or toxins and include botulinum toxin, which is derived from a bacterium; ricin, which is derived from the caster bean plant; and saxitoxin, which is derived from marine animals. Toxins are not alive and cannot multiply like bacteria or viruses and therefore have the same effect associated with chemical weapons. They have little value as a WMD. They are difficult to produce in large quantities and numerous chemical weapons are more easily obtained and deployed.

How Biological Weapons Work

Victims of a biological attack can be exposed via three potential routes: (1) contact with the skin, (2) gastrointestinal, and (3) pulmonary. Agents that come in contact with the skin are the least dangerous. The skin provides an excellent barrier against most of these agents except mycotoxins. However, mucous membranes, abrasions, or other lesions may provide a portal of entry for bacteria, viruses, or toxins. Contamination of food or water supplies allows for a potentially significant gastrointestinal exposure. In terms of water contamination, this type of exposure is limited by the direct effects of water dilution and treatment, which inactivate or significantly weaken most microbes and toxins. For this to be a viable method for contamination, the agent must be introduced near the end user in extremely large amounts. Food, on the other hand, is more susceptible to contamination. The agent can be applied directly to the food and later consumed. Exposure via the inhalational route is the most effective mode of delivery for biological agents. Aerosol clouds containing microbes or toxins are not detectable by the senses. Aerosol dispersal mechanisms, however, are limited by the weather (wind, rain, sunlight, and temperature). Nonetheless, aerosol dispersal has the potential for causing widespread illness and death depending on the size of the weapon (Jagminas, 2008).

Biological weapons create a number of problems. The most significant is that they can be deployed, and it may be days or weeks before the deployment becomes evident. A virus must grow and spread within the host population, resulting in a delay before symptoms are evident. Bacteria will affect victims more rapidly, but there likely will be a delay in their discovery. The CDC and other state and federal agencies are constantly monitoring the environment for possible attacks or outbreaks of diseases.

Creating Biological Weapons

Biological weapons are more dangerous than chemical weapons, primarily because they are relatively easy to produce or obtain. Biological agents are not biological weapons. Mere possession of an agent—bacteria, virus, or toxin—does not make it a weapon. The

HS ANALYSIS BOX 9-5

Biological weapons can be used in a variety of locations. Terrorists would likely attempt to use one where there are large numbers of people in order to create the largest number of problems and casualties. Which locations or gatherings in your community would be likely targets if terrorists decided to attack? Does your community have the medical facilities and staff to deal with such an attack?

HS Web Link: To learn more about the dispersing of biological agents, go to https://www.fema.gov/media-library-data/20130726-1549-20490-0802/terrorism.pdf.

agent must be "weaponized." There are four requirements to weaponize a biological agent. First, the payload or agent must be obtained. Moreover, it must be obtained in sufficient quantities, depending on the agent, so that it will have the desired impact. Second, it must have a container or structure that allows delivery. That is, it must be packaged so that it can be effectively delivered to a target. The payload must remain intact and be dispersed when deployed. Third, it must have an adequate delivery system. For example, for anthrax to be used as a WMD, the delivery system must spread the bacteria over a large geographical area. The delivery system cannot destroy the biological payload. If viruses or bacteria were to be deployed using an explosive charge, the subsequent explosion very likely would destroy or kill the agents, limiting the delivery systems that terrorists could use. Finally, the terrorists must have a competent delivery-dispersal system. The system must be functionally capable of delivering the biological agent over a desired area (Jagminas, 2008). Even if terrorists are able to obtain a biological agent, it remains difficult to use it as a WMD.

There are two methods of dispersing a biological weapon: line source and point source. The **line source method** is the most effective dispersal system. An example is a truck or air sprayer that moves perpendicular to the wind during an inversion (when air temperature increases with altitude and holds surface air and pollutants down). Inversions normally occur at dawn, dusk, or night. The line source method results in the biological agent being effectively dispersed over a large geographical area.

The **point source method** uses small packets or containers of the biological agent deployed in a saturation mode in multiple locations. The packets or containers must have a dispersal mechanism as well as the biological agent. Their effectiveness depends on the dispersal mechanism. Agents may be introduced into buildings' heating, ventilation, or air conditioning systems or via food or water contamination. This method requires that a number of packets or containers be strategically located across a large geographical area (similar to the method used by the Japanese cult, Aum Shinrikyo, in the Tokyo subway attack discussed earlier). The point source method is less dependent on weather conditions as compared to the line source method but requires the planting of the agent in multiple locations.

Threat Assessment and Biological Weapons

Threat assessment was discussed in Chapter 3. The level of threat plays a key role in critical infrastructure protection. If a target is desirable to a terrorist group, obviously more resources should be used to protect it. Several variables comprise the threat assessment. This decision-making matrix provides information on how to possibly prevent attacks. If asset vulnerability is reduced, the target is no longer desirable or too difficult to attack. Reducing the means to conduct an attack also impacts the probability of attack. It is a complicated affair to deliver a biological attack of the magnitude that would have a significant impact on the United States. It also assumes that terrorists want to use biological weapons, but this may not be the case. For example, a smallpox outbreak in the United States could easily spread to Middle Eastern countries where there are fewer mechanisms for controlling the outbreak. An attack on the United States could result in far more casualties elsewhere.

Several factors are useful in assessing the threat of bioterrorism. First is the value of the asset to the defender. For example, an agricultural target may not be desirable because of America's immense agriculture infrastructure. An agricultural attack may result in some losses, but in the end it very likely will have little impact on America's economy or food supply. A second impediment to using biological weapons is the potential harm of the biological agent. As noted, it is difficult to develop a biological weapon, even if the terrorists possess the agent. With the exception of viruses such as smallpox, it is difficult to construct a biological weapon that can have widespread effects. The outbreak of smallpox in Yugoslavia discussed earlier highlights this point. Although it was a serious medical problem, authorities were able to contain and eliminate it with only a few fatalities.

A third issue is vulnerability to biological weapons. Threat assessments need to be conducted. Vulnerability to biological weapons is not even. Some countries are more vulnerable to some biological weapons and some areas are more vulnerable than others. Vulnerability analyses may assist in identifying potential targets or areas that require additional protection. The primary method by which to reduce vulnerability is the stockpiling of antivirals and antibiotics, early detection, and rapid response. Fourth is the capability to conduct a bio-terror attack. Acquisition of agents and the construction of an effective delivery device are rather difficult, especially a system that can result in significant casualties. Most experts agree that technology has resulted in it being easier to construct a biological weapon; nonetheless, it remains quite difficult. Even if terrorists have the technology and motivation, it is questionable if they can construct a weapon capable of significant impact.

Perhaps the greatest concern regarding biological WMDs is new strains of viruses that might be created through DNA modification. Although the use of biological weapons is prohibited by treaties, these laws do not apply to all countries and do not ban the possession of these weapons. Many counties continually work to develop more effective biological weapons through cloning and DNA manipulation (Sultan, undated).

▶ Chemical Weapons of Mass Destruction

A chemical weapon contains inorganic substances that can have an effect on living processes and can cause death, temporary loss of performance, or permanent injury to people, animals, and plants. Numerous chemicals are toxic to humans, animals, and plants, but not all of these chemicals can be weaponized. Thus, chemicals can be classified in terms of their potential for use as a weapon. In addition to chemical warfare weapons, industrial toxic chemicals and materials pose a danger and can be used for limited purposes as chemical weapons. Cone (2008) estimated that there are 82,000 chemical compounds that are used in commerce. Many are highly toxic, whereas others present little or no threat. A 2000 Environmental Protection Agency study found that at least 123 American chemical plants contain enough dangerous chemicals that, if released by one plant, could result in millions of deaths (EPA, 2000). A substantial quantity of chemicals at these plants could present a threat.

Numerous chemical releases have caused death and destruction. In 1984, the release of methyl isocyanate at a Union Carbide factory in Bhopal, India, resulted in 2,500 deaths and 200,000 people becoming sick. The release was the result of sabotage by a disgruntled employee (Muller, undated). In 1989, an accidental release of gases at a Phillips 66 chemical plant in Houston, Texas, resulted in an explosion with a force of 2.3 kilotons. The explosion killed 23 and injured 130 people. The explosion deposited debris in adjoining neighborhoods 9.5 kilometers away. Each year, rail accidents, pipeline ruptures, and traffic crashes result in the releases of toxic chemicals. These incidents demonstrate that the chemical industry poses a significant problem that could be exploited by terrorists.

Blister Agents
Chocking Agents
Nerve Agents
Tear Gas
Vomiting Agents
Psychotropic Compounds

FIGURE 9-3 Types of Chemicals That Can Be Used in Chemical Weapons

Chemical weapons have a long history in warfare. Although they have been used by nation-states in times of war; terrorist or political groups seldom use them. Like biological weapons, chemical weapons are difficult to deploy. They must have high levels of toxicity to have an effect, but at the same time, they cannot be too toxic whereby terrorists cannot effectively deploy or handle them. For the most part, terrorists have depended on conventional explosives to carry out attacks. Conventional explosives are easier to obtain, control, and deploy. Nonetheless, chemical weapons must be considered in homeland security planning.

Although literally thousands of chemical compounds are toxic, only about 70 may be useful as a chemical weapon. Today, the most common chemical weapons to be concerned with are sarin and ricin. Figure 9-3 ■ contains a listing of the basic categories of chemical weapons.

Several toxic compounds are contained within each of these categories, which are based on the type of action or impact they have on the victim. For the most part, tear gas, vomiting agents, irritants, and psychotropic compounds are not satisfactory for use as a chemical weapon and are not discussed here. The mortality rate associated with these substances is extremely low. If terrorists desire to use a chemical weapon, they likely will select one that is extremely toxic and has the capability to kill large numbers of people.

Blister Agents

Blister agents are intended to come into contact with the victims' skin. When deployed, blister agents often result in a low mortality rate, but they cause burns and blisters to the skin. Blister agents contain acid-forming compounds that burn the victim. They can be deadly when the agent is breathed by the victim. They cause irritation to the lungs, eyes, and airway. The most common blistering agent is mustard gas, which was used extensively in World War I. Saddam Hussein used mustard gas in the Iraqi-Iranian war, and Syria used it to attack rebels during the Syrian Civil War.

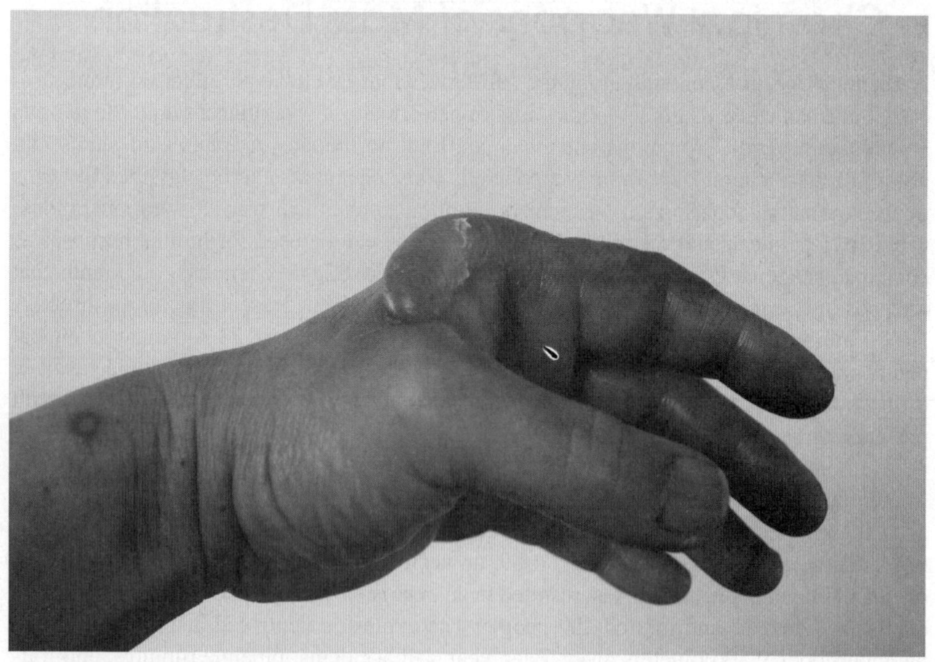

The effects of a blister agent on a victim's arm.
Charcrit boonsom/Alamy Stock Photo.

Blood Agents

Blood agents are chemical weapons that when consumed prevent the body from using oxygen. For example, arsine causes intravascular hemolysis that may lead to renal failure, whereas cyanogen chloride/hydrogen cyanide directly prevents cells from utilizing oxygen. The cells then use anaerobic respiration, creating excess lactic acid and metabolic acidosis. There is speculation that al Qaeda has experimented with cyanide gas. Egan (2001) reported that Ahmed Ressam, an al Qaeda operative, told authorities that the terrorist group experimented with poisonous gases on dogs. It was believed the gases were cyanide.

Choking Agents

Choking agents have similar effects on their victims as do blister agents. Choking agents are acid based and have an effect on the respiratory system, flooding it and often resulting in suffocation. Most choking agents are deadly, depending on the amount of the agent consumed by the victim. The most common choking agent is chlorine, which was first used in World War I by the German army. Chlorine is one of the most commonly used chemicals in manufacturing (Cone, 2008). It is transported throughout the United States by rail and truck, and these tanks could easily be ruptured by conventional explosives. If chlorine were released in a heavily populated area, it could result in substantial casualties. However, any explosion likely would destroy a large portion of the gas, and since it has a distinct odor, it would be quickly identified and the area could be evacuated. This point source dispersion is not an effective method of delivering a chemical weapon.

Nerve Agents

Nerve agents are the most dangerous of chemical agents. **Nerve agents** inactivate certain enzymes affecting neurotransmitters in the brain. They result in the nervous system becoming inactive, which affects all biological systems. Their effects are almost immediate and death can occur in minutes. They can be inhaled or absorbed by the skin, depending on the agent. There are two primary categories of nerve agents: G-series and V-series. The G-series agents were developed shortly after World War II. They include agents such as sarin, tabun, and soman. These agents are deadly and their release would result in high mortality rates. G-agents dissipate fairly quickly, and, therefore, their danger is from inhalation, not contact. Only sarin has been used in a terrorist attack. The Japanese cult Aum Shinrikyo manufactured the agent and deployed it in 1994 and 1995. In the 1995 attack, cult members released the agent on a Tokyo subway, causing 12 deaths and injuring several thousand people (Olson, 1999).

V-agents, relative to G-agents, are more persistent. That is, they remain in the environment for a long period of time, increasing the likelihood that people will be exposed to the agent through contact. Moreover, only a minute amount of the agent is required to kill a victim. The V-agents comprise the most dangerous class of chemical weapons. It is doubtful that terrorist groups will use VX. Its manufacture is extremely complicated and dangerous due to its toxicity, and this toxicity represents a substantial impediment to terrorists.

HS Web Link: To learn more about VX gas, go to https://emergency.cdc.gov/agent/vx/basics/facts.asp.

Advantages of Chemical Weapons

Chemical weapons have distinct advantages. First, they are relatively inexpensive to produce or procure as compared to biological or nuclear weapons. It does not require a highly sophisticated laboratory to construct chemical weapons, and many of the base chemicals required to manufacture these weapons are readily available. Chemical weapons are easier to use than biological weapons because they are more stable and containable. Their delivery systems are more manageable, and to some extent, they can be used for specific geographical targets. Nonetheless, they are difficult to manufacture in large quantities without laboratories.

Weaponizing Chemicals

The American-Israeli Cooperative Enterprise (undated) advises that there are four ways by which a terrorist group could acquire a chemical weapon:

1. Manufacture the weapons
2. Acquire commercially available chemicals that can be used as weapons
3. Theft of chemical munitions from the military
4. Provision of chemical weapons by a state sponsor

As noted, some chemicals are easily manufactured, but they often can be made only in small quantities. Other, more dangerous chemical weapons are extremely difficult to manufacture, making them prohibitive. In terms of the second means in the list, ample amounts of chemicals are manufactured and shipped throughout the United States and the rest of the world that are used in manufacturing and agriculture. In some cases, these chemicals can be used to make chemical weapons; in other cases, they are of sufficient toxicity to serve as a chemical weapon. These chemicals are to some degree monitored by governmental agencies. Thus, attempts to purchase large amounts of them, especially if the purchaser did not have a record of purchasing or using the chemicals, likely would result in suspicion and government investigation. Nonetheless, Parachini (2006) noted that terrorists currently have the capacity to make crude chemical weapons including mustard, sarin, and VX.

The U.S. military has large stockpiles of chemical weapons stored in secure facilities. However, the military also possesses large amounts of aging chemical weapons left over from World War II and the Korean War, and these weapons are stored in numerous locations that have lower levels of security. There also may be large amounts of chemical weapons that could be obtained in other countries. The old Soviet Union had large stockpiles, and some of these weapons are now in the possession of countries less committed to their security. Large quantities of military-grade chemical weapons throughout the world could be purchased on the black market and smuggled into the United States.

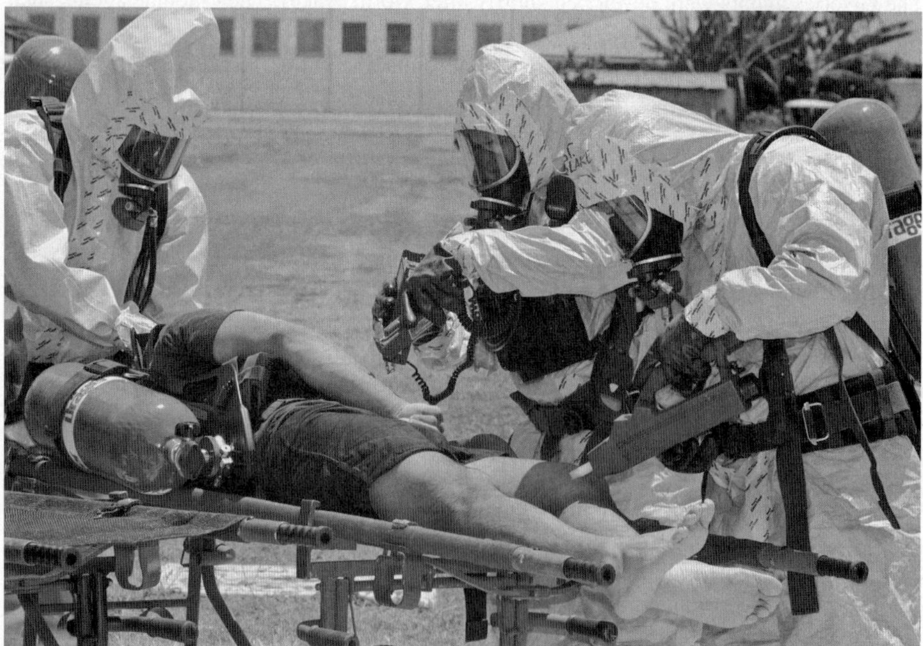

Members of the 93rd Weapons of Mass Destruction Civil Support Team scan a casualty for nerve or blister agents with chemical detection equipment during a drill.
PJF Military Collection/Alamy Stock Photo.

HS ANALYSIS BOX 9-6

Currently, the United States is embroiled in an asymmetric war in Afghanistan. It consists of Taliban insurgents attacking American troops and then fading into the countryside. Our troops are at a significant tactical disadvantage. Do you think we should use chemical weapons to protect our troops? Should we use nonlethal chemical weapons to accomplish this purpose? What are the ramifications if we did use these weapons?

Finally, there is the possibility of a nation-state supplying chemical weapons to a terrorist group. Our primary reason for invading Iraq was the fear that Iraq would supply WMDs to terrorist organizations. The world always has large numbers of conflicts, with various nations having an interest in their outcome. In other words, states have political motivations to supply weapons to terrorist groups, especially when the state believes it is in its best interest. Once the weapons are supplied to the terrorist group, the supplying nation has little or no control over their use.

Means of Delivery

Even though the manufacture or acquisition of chemical weapons may not be difficult, delivering the weapon is quite difficult. First, it would require a large volume of a chemical weapon to have significant effects. Transportation would be highly complicated, given the potential for leaks and other transportation problems. Also, security throughout the world is much more intense than in years past. The potential for discovery is far greater.

Second, dispersal of the agent is problematic. For example, if terrorists intended to produce an event that would result in 5,000 to 10,000 casualties, they would have to deploy large amounts of the agent to achieve the effect. There is a substantial amount of loss during delivery due to weather conditions, windage, humidity, and so on. Most likely a chemical weapon would be used in an area with a high concentration of people, such as a sports arena, shopping mall, or educational facility. It is likely that such an event would not lead to large numbers of casualties. It is interesting to note that Sunnis and Shiites did not use chemical weapons during their sectarian war in Iraq even though such weapons exist in the region. One possible explanation is that chemical weapons do not have the utility or effects as do explosive devices.

In summary, chemical weapons do indeed pose a threat. However, many problems are associated with their use that will be difficult for terrorists to overcome. It appears that if chemical weapons are used, they will be used with small concentrated targets resulting in relatively few casualties.

▶ Factors Constraining Terrorists from Using WMDs

A number of factors determine whether a terrorist group has the capacity to use a WMD, including the following:

1. **Organizational capabilities.** It would require a sophisticated organization (vertically and horizontally) to develop or otherwise obtain WMDs. Most terrorist groups do not possess this capability. They remain fairly small with limited resources. They have a cell structure as opposed to being complex organizations with varying levels of specialization.
2. **Financial resources.** The procurement, development, transportation, and use of a WMD require substantial resources, depending on the WMD. The operation would require substantial resources over an extended period of time, including financial

support from acquisition to deployment. There likely are few, if any, groups that have this level of resources without state sponsorship.

3. **Logistical resources.** Logistics refer to the transportation and storing of materials. The supply chain for WMDs can be a half-world long, potentially crossing a number of countries. As a result of the 9/11 attacks, the United States and other countries have substantially increased their assault on and monitoring of terrorist networks, which increases the likelihood that such a supply chain would be broken.
4. **Knowledge/skill/acquisition.** The use of WMDs requires a high level of knowledge and skill. It is not a simple matter to acquire and deploy a WMD. A terrorist organization can (a) acquire the knowledge and skills via training and education or (b) use personnel with the requisite skills from an outside group. Even though there is a wealth of technical information available, this does not always equate to an ability to acquire the materials, skill, and delivery mechanisms and transport them to a target. In other words, even if technical knowledge is possessed by a terrorist, he or she may not have the experience to transfer that knowledge into a workable WMD (See Hummel, 2016).
5. **Materials and technology acquisition.** There are many examples of biological microorganisms in the world and amounts of chemicals that could be used as a WMD. Obtaining the biological agents, chemicals, or nuclear materials in the quantity necessary to build a WMD is another matter. There always is the possibility of obtaining these materials from the old Soviet Union or another state; it would be difficult to obtain a large enough supply for a devastating attack. Moreover, these materials are highly volatile and there always is the possibility of accidental release or other problems during construction, transportation, and deployment.
6. **Production.** In terms of chemical and biological WMDs, the production of the materials needed for a sizable weapon would be extremely difficult. It requires a fairly large facility with difficult-to-obtain equipment. If a terrorist group uses substandard equipment and expertise, it substantially increases the possibility of leakage, detection, and accidents.

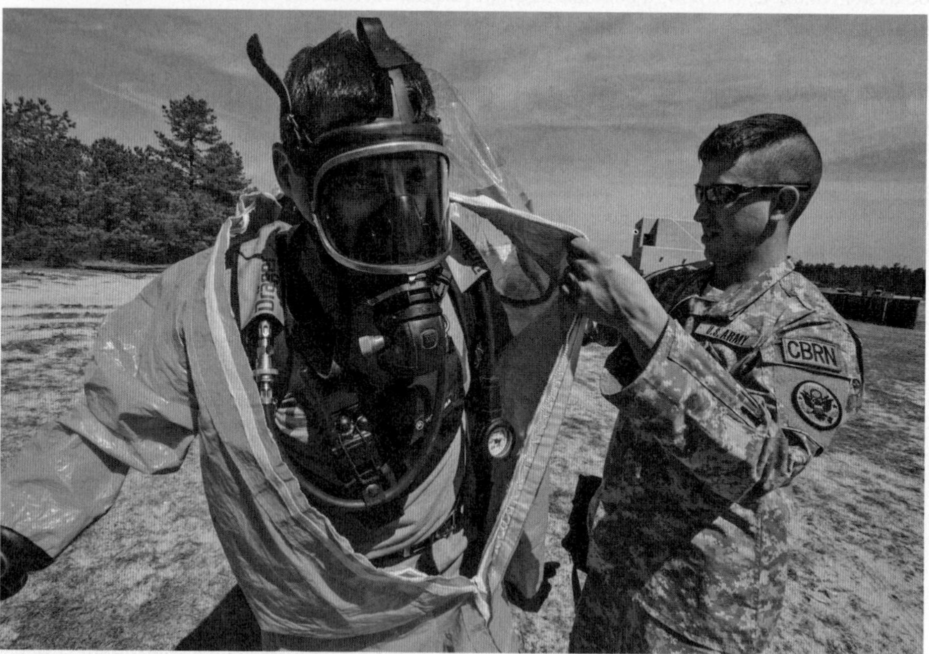

Members of the 21st Weapons of Mass Destruction Civil Support Team New Jersey National Guard prepare for an exercise.
PJF Military Collection/Alamy Stock Photo.

7. **Weaponization and delivery.** The weaponization of chemical and biological agents is difficult, as is the construction of a nuclear device. A biological or chemical weapon can be developed that potentially could destroy a whole city. However, this is an extremely difficult, if not impossible, task. Even if the biological or chemical agents are developed, it is a completely different matter to acquire an effective delivery system. There are many factors that constrict a terrorist group's ability to develop an effective delivery system.
8. **State sponsorship.** A number of countries would consider assisting terrorists in attacking the United States. However, there also are numerous constraints on these countries, particularly retaliation and the possibility that the weapons could be accidentally released in their own country or used against their country. International condemnation is also a key factor.

Relative Destructiveness of WMDs

This chapter examined the three categories of WMDs: nuclear, biological, and chemical. Each type of weapon presents a unique set of problems. Each has the potential to cause mass casualties and disrupt a nation's or region's economy. Each requires a homeland security strategy and countermeasures. However, we find that some WMDs are more deadly and disruptive than others as shown in Figure 9-4 ■.

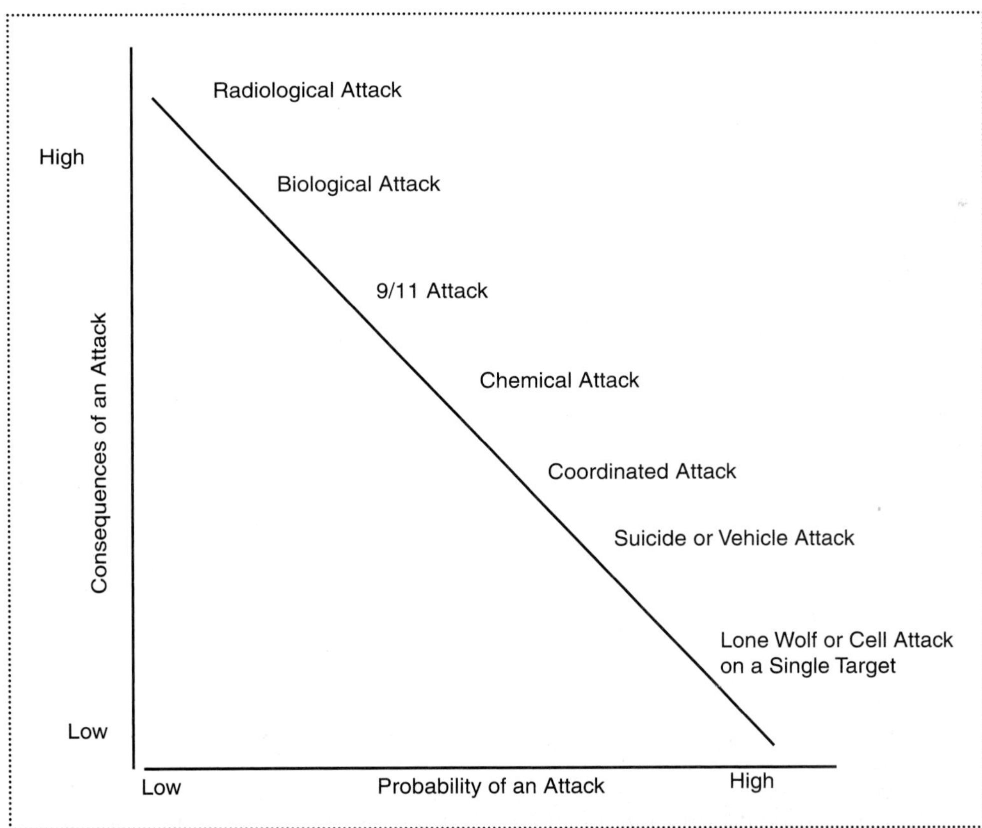

FIGURE 9-4 Degree of Danger Associated with Different Types of Terrorist Attacks
Source: Adopted from Hummel, S. (2016). "The Islamic State and WMD: Assessing the future threat." *CTCSentinel*, 9: 18–21.

A United Nations (1993) study examined the relative impact of hypothetical nuclear, biological, and chemical attacks. Essentially, the study found that a 1-megaton nuclear device if dropped from a bomber might kill 90 percent of unprotected people over an area of 300 square kilometers. A 15-ton chemical weapon might kill 50 percent of the unprotected people in a 60-square-kilometer area. Finally, a 10-ton biological weapon would kill 50 percent of the people in a 60-kilometer area and make 50 percent ill within an area of 100,000 kilometers. These figures demonstrate the potency of the three WMDs.

Examining Which Groups Might Use WMDs

There are hundreds of terrorist groups as well as numerous individuals, lone wolfs, and wolf packs or cells who might possibly use a WMD against the United States or our allies. The preceding sections discussed the types of WMDs and their lethality. We exert a great deal of effort to keep these groups and individuals from obtaining WMDs and WMD materials. We control and monitor the purchase of chemicals and agents, we monitor our ports for radiological materials, and we deploy sensors to identify viruses and bacteria. Finally, we investigate any suspicious activity relating to WMDs.

Ackerman (2005) and Gurr (2005) noted that all terrorists have a desire to use a WMD. However, the overwhelming majority of terrorist attacks have used conventional weapons, guns, and explosives. There has been only a handful of terrorist attacks where a WMD has been used. Gurr noted that rather than concentrating our efforts on all terrorist groups when attempting to intercede in WMDs, we should study these groups to determine if they have the wherewithal and ability to launch a WMD attack. We should profile terrorist groups and set priorities in terms of monitoring their activities relative to WMD acquisition.

Gurr has identified four criteria to judge terrorist groups and their capacity to use a WMD. First is salience of identity. This is where the group is ethnonationalist. Here, the members and leaders all share the same violent extremist views; they have total agreement and devotion to their radical cause. Examples include Sri Lankan Tamil Tiger, Chechen rebels, and certain Sunni militants who attack Shiites and other religious groups in Pakistan. There must be unifying agreement for a group to use extreme violence.

Second is collective incentives where a group feels that it has been ignored, harmed, or denied by others. This sense of loss results in stronger motivations to lash out at their oppressors; they are motivated by self-righteousness. They believe that harming their oppressors is the only avenue by which to resolve their situation. Collective incentives have resulted in genocides and ethnic cleansing.

Third, capacity for collective action refers to groups' cohesion and ability to mobilize. Is there solidarity in their willingness to attack their foes? Such groups require leadership that can not only motivate followers but also control them to the extent that they will abide and resort to extremist behavior.

Finally, in order for a terrorist group to use a WMD, the group must have the opportunity to acquire and use it. The availability of WMDs is very limited, given the monitoring and controls enacted by governments across the globe. For a terrorist organization to acquire one, it requires vast resources and logistical capacity. Few terrorist groups have this capacity.

In sum, we can profile terrorist organizations and identify those that have the most potential for acquiring and using a WMD and concentrate on them. This is not to say that we disregard the others, but the bulk of our efforts should be on those with the capacity.

Summary

This chapter explored the problem of WMDs. WMDs represent a threat to the United States and the world; preventing their use and responding to an incident where WMDs have been deployed are the primary objectives of homeland security. WMDs pose the greatest threat to America in terms of fatalities, health, and economic well-being. The United States must develop strategies that reduce the likelihood of their deployment and be prepared should the fail-safe system prove to be inadequate, and as noted in Chapter 1, our country has been working on a number of WMD countermeasures.

Of the three categories of WMDs, nuclear devices constitute the greatest threat. They potentially can cause the greatest harm in terms of loss of life and economic disruption. They essentially can destroy a whole city or region. Moreover, if deployed, a nuclear attack can devastate an area for many years, having long-term effects. The United States is working with a number of countries to prevent terrorists from obtaining these weapons and materials. Moreover, homeland security is attempting to secure the borders to prevent terrorists from smuggling a device into the United States.

A second nuclear scenario is the destruction of a nuclear facility, such as a nuclear power plant. These facilities could be attacked using a small airplane or by a small group of well-armed terrorists. The destruction of a nuclear power plant could have the same effects as a small nuclear device, as evidenced by the Chernobyl nuclear meltdown in the Ukraine or the Fukushima meltdown in Japan. Finally, terrorists could obtain nuclear waste products, which have little security, and construct a dirty bomb. These three scenarios represent real threats to the United States.

Terrorists can use a host of biological weapons. Most notably, anthrax has already been used in the United States. The attack left eight Americans dead and several injured. Numerous bacteria, viruses, and toxins can be used as biological weapons, and there are research programs worldwide that are possibly developing more toxic and deadly forms of bacteria and viruses. The biological agent that presents the greatest concern is the smallpox virus. A small amount of the virus spread across several locations could create a substantial epidemic. However, one of the homeland security initiatives discussed in Chapter 1 is the stockpiling of vaccines.

Finally, a number of chemicals can be used for WMDs. They range from pesticides to VX gas. Over the years, a number of chemical weapons have been used, most notably during World War I and the Iraqi-Iranian war, and the Iraqis used them against the Kurds in Iraq. Many of the chemical weapons that have been used in the past are not suitable as a WMD. The biggest concern is with newer chemicals such as VX, sarin, and ricin. These are deadly chemicals that have a high kill rate.

Even though terrorists may possess nuclear, biological, or chemical materials, it remains daunting to weaponize the material, and it is a complicated process to deploy such weapons. It requires significant technological knowledge and support system. It also requires a highly developed organization, and most terrorist organizations do not have the ability to deliver a significant WMD, especially since 9/11. The United States and other countries around the world have substantially increased their efforts to prevent terrorists from acquiring and deploying WMDs. This does not mean that they will be unable to do so, but today it is infinitely more difficult.

Perhaps a real example would illustrate the problem. In November 2012, Hamas launched a rocket attack on Israel from the Gaza Strip firing hundreds of rockets, some of which landed near Tel Aviv and Jerusalem. Few of the rockets hit critical infrastructure and many were shot down by Israeli's iron dome anti-missile system. There was speculation that the attacks would continue over time since the rockets which were made in Iran cost only $1,000 to construct. However, Hamilton (2012) noted that the real costs for the Iranian rockets were much greater. The supply line from Iran to Gaza was extremely convoluted crossing a number of countries where the rocket smugglers had to pay bribes, especially Bedouins in the Sinai and Egyptian soldiers in Rafah. Moreover, Israeli armed forces intercept a number of rockets before they reach Gaza and destroy a number on the ground. Hamilton estimated that the cost of the rockets that Hamas launch into Israel end up costing upward to $10,000 per rocket once losses are counted. Even though some of the rockets reach Gaza over time, they may become too expensive given their relative ineffectiveness.

Nonetheless, it is a complicated matter to deploy a WMD, especially in the United States, but it is not insurmountable. Figure 9-5 ■ provides a flowchart of the actions that would be required of terrorists.

This discussion demonstrates that deploying a WMD is a complicated affair. Fortunately, most terrorist groups do not have the capacity to undertake this endeavor. Nonetheless, vigilance must be taken to ensure that the homeland security system maximizes security.

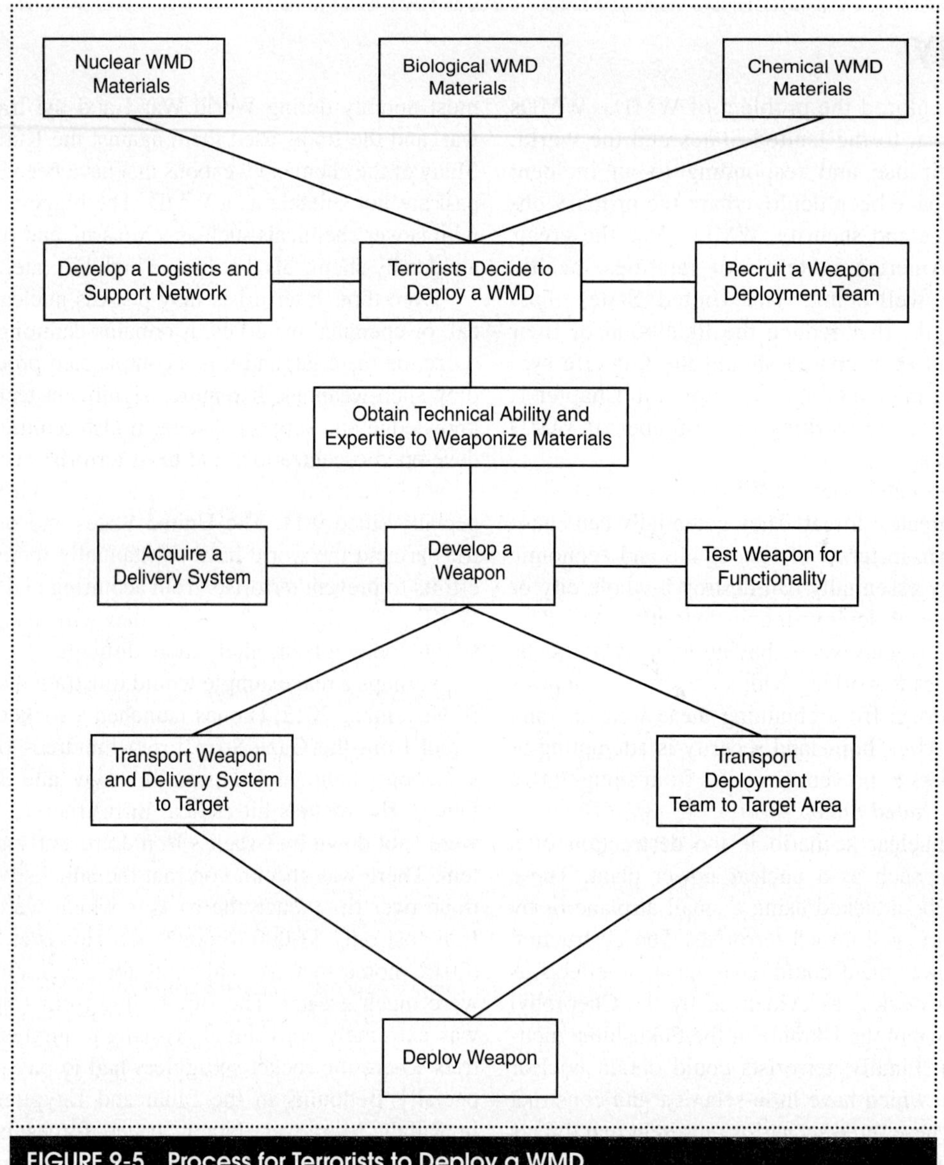

FIGURE 9-5 Process for Terrorists to Deploy a WMD

Discussion Questions

1. What is a WMD? How do public perceptions of WMDs differ from legal definitions of these weapons?
2. Which WMDs are the most dangerous and why?
3. Describe ways in which nuclear or radiological materials can be used as WMD.
4. Describe the historical use of WMDs.
5. Compare bacteria, viruses, and toxins in terms of their use as a WMD.
6. Describe the three types of biological agents that can be weaponized. Which is the most dangerous?
7. Compare point source and line source biological and chemical WMD dispersion.
8. Describe the constraints on terrorist groups preventing them from using WMDs.

References

Ackerman, G. (2005). "WMD terrorism research: Where to from here?" *International Studies Review*, 3: 140–143. http://www.wmdcommission.org/files/No22.pdf (Accessed January 17, 2011).

BBC. (2016). "Iran nuclear deal: Key details." *BBC News*. http://www.bbc.com/news/world-middle-east-33521655 (Accessed August 29, 2016).

Beaumont, P. (2013). "Bubonic plague killed 20 villagers in Madagascar, health experts confirm." *The Guardian*. http://www.theguardian.com/world/2013/dec/11/bubonic-plague-killed-villagers-madagascar (Accessed December 16, 2013).

Broad, W., and D. Sanger. (2008). "In nuclear net's undoing, a web of shadowy deals." *New York Times* (August 25): A1.

Brown, D. (2003). "Canada arrests 19 as security threats." *Washington Post* (August 23): A20.

Cameron, G., and N. Bajema. (2009). "Assessing the post 9/11 threat of CBRN terrorism." *Terrorism and Counterterrorism: Understanding the New Security Environment*, ed. R. Howard, R. Sawyer, and N. Bajema, pp. 267–287. New York: McGraw-Hill.

Center for Defense Information. (2003). *CDI Factsheet: Ricin* (February 7). http://www.cdi.org/terrorism/ricin-factsheet.cfm (Accessed August 5, 2008).

Center of Disease Control. (2017). Bioterrorism Agents/Diseases. https://emergency.cdc.gov/agent/agentlist-category.asp (Accessed December 4, 2017)

Cochran, T., and M. McKinzie. (2008). "Detecting nuclear smuggling." *Scientific American*, 298(4): 98–104.

Cone, M. (2008). "A hazardous dependency: Chemists are hindered in creating safer ingredients for products." *Los Angeles Times* (September 19): A1, A16.

Alan Cowell and Dexter Filkins, "Terror plot foiled; Airports quickly clamp down," *The New York Times*, August 11, 2006, http://www.nytimes.com/2006/08/11/world/europe/11plot.html?pagewanted=all&_r=0 (accessed December 4, 2017).

DeNoon, D. (2003). "Biological and chemical terror history: Lessons learned." http://www.webmd.com/content/article/61/67268.htm (Accessed August 20, 2008).

Department of Homeland Security. (2017). *National Terrorism Advisory System*. https://www.dhs.gov/national-terrorism-advisory-system (Accessed August 28, 2017).

Dutton, N. (2016). *More Belgians Close to Nuclear Facilities Get Iodine Pills*. http://wtvr.com/2016/05/01/belgians-close-to-nuclear-facilities-get-iodine-pills/ (Accessed May 5, 2016).

Early, B., E. Martin, B. Nussbaum, and K. Deloughery. (2017). "Should conventional terrorist bombings be considered weapons of mass destruction terrorism?" *Dynamics of Asymmetric Conflict*, 10: 54–73.

Egan, T. (2001). "A nation challenged: The convicted terrorist; Man caught in 2000 plot is helping investigators." *New York Times* (September 27). http://query.nytimes.com/gst/fullpage.html?res=9403EFD9113AF934A1575AC0A9679C8B63 (Accessed September 4, 2008).

Environmental Protection Agency. (2000). *Chemical Accident Risks in U.S. Industry—A Preliminary Analysis of Accident Risk Data from U.S. Hazardous Chemical Facilities*. Washington, D.C.: Author.

Fields, G., A. Davis, and J. Schlesinger. (2003). "US is pressed to boost role in private-sector security." *Wall Street Journal* (March 21): A4.

Frantz, D., and C. Collins. (2007). "Those nuclear flashpoints are made in Pakistan." *Washington Post* (November 11). http://www.washingtonpost.com/wp-dyn/content/article/2007/11/07/AR2007110702280.html (Accessed August 28, 2009).

Government Accounting Office. (1977). "Commercial nuclear fuel facilities need better security." Cited in J. Stern (2003). "Getting and using the weapons." *Terrorism and Counterterrorism: Understanding the New Security Environment*, ed. R. Howard and R. Sawyer, pp. 158–174. New York: McGraw-Hill.

Graham-Harrison, E. (2016). "Chemical weapons attacks in Syria may normalise war crimes, experts warn." *The Guardian*. https://www.theguardian.com/world/2016/aug/11/syria-suspected-chlorine-gas-attack-in-aleppo-kills-woman-and-two-children (Accessed August 29, 2016).

Gurr, T. (2005). "Which minorities might use weapons of mass destruction?" *International Studies Review*, 7: 143–146.

Hamilton, A. (2012). "Bankrupting terrorism – One interception at a time." *The Jerusalem Post* (November 24). http://www.jpost.com/Opinion/Op-EdContributors/Article.aspx?id=293283 (Accessed November 26, 2012).

Harigel, G. (2000). "The concept of weapons of mass destruction: Chemical and biological weapons, use in warfare, impact on society and environment." Paper presented at the Conference on Biosecurity and Bioterrorism, Rome (September 18–19).

Homeland Security Council. (2007). *Strategy for Homeland Security*. Washington, D.C.: Author.

Hummel, S. (2016). "The Islamic State and WMD: Assessing the future threat." *CTCSentinel*, 9: 18–21.

Iannotti, A., I. Schraffl, C. Bellecci, A. Malizia, Ol Cenciarelli, D. Di Giovanni, L. Palombi, and P. Gaudio. (2016). "Weapons of mass destruction: A review of its use in history to perpetrate chemical offenses." *Defence S&T Technical Bulletin*, 9: 39–52.

Jagmanis, L. (2008). "CBRNE: Evaluation of a biological warfare victim." *EMedicine*. http://www.emedicine.com/emerg/topic891.htm (Accessed September 2, 2008).

James Martin Center for Nonproliferation Studies. (2006). *Chronology of CBW Incidents Targeting Agriculture and Food Systems 1915–2006*. Monterey, CA: James Martin Center for Nonproliferation Studies. http://cns.miis.edu/research/cbw/agchron.htm. (Accessed August 22, 2008).

Krock, L., and R. Deusser. (2003). *Dirty Bomb: Chronology of Events*. Nova. http://www.pbs.org/wgbh/nova/dirtybomb/chrono.html (Accessed August 28, 2008).

Meselson, M. (1991). "The myth of chemical superweapons." *Bulletin of the Atomic Scientists* (April): 12–15.

Morin, M. (2013). "Swine flu may have killed 2013,000, study says." *Los Angeles Times* (November 29): A13.

Muller, R. (undated). *A Significant Toxic Event: The Union Carbide Pesticide Plant Disaster in Bhopal, India, 1984*. http://www.tropmed.org/rreh/vol1_10.htm (Accessed September 21, 2008).

Olson, K. (1999). "Aum Shinrikyo: Once and future threat." *Emerging Infectious Diseases*, 5(4): 513–516.

On, U. (2016). "Radiological terrorism – 'Dirty bombs' and beyond." *The Wire*, https://thewire.in/31457/radiological-terrorism-dirty-bombs-and-beyond/ (Accessed August 25, 2017).

Parachini, J. (2006) "Putting WMD terrorism into perspective." *Homeland Security and Terrorism: Readings and Interpretations,* ed. R. Howard, J. Forest, and J. Moore, pp. 31–42. New York: McGraw-Hill.

Ploughshares. (2011). *World Nuclear Stockpile Report*. http://www.ploughshares.org/news-analysis/world-nuclear-stockpile-report (Accessed January 17, 2011).

Preston, R. (1999). "The demon in the freezer: How smallpox, a disease officially eradicated twenty years ago, became the biggest terrorist threat we now face." *New Yorker* (July 12): 44–61.

Project on Government Oversight. (2001). *U.S. Nuclear Weapons Complex: Security at Risk*. http://www.pogo.org/p/environment/eo-011003-nuclear.html#anchor2 (Accessed August 28, 2008).

Rettner, r. (2013). "H7N9 bird flu may be developing drug resistance." *Livescience*. http://www.livescience.com/38197-h7n9-bird-flu-antiviral-resistance.html (Accessed July 18, 2013).

Reuters. (2015). *Minnesota Declares State of Emergency over Bird Flu*. http://www.nydailynews.com/life-style/health/minnesota-declares-state-emergency-bird-flu-article-1.2197231 (Accessed April 29, 2015).

RT. (2016). *6 More Workers Sickened by Radioactive Fumes at Hanford Nuclear Site*. https://www.rt.com/usa/341742-6-more-workers-sickened-fumes/(Accessed May 5, 2016).

Sauter, M., and J. Carafano. (2005). *Homeland Security*. New York: McGraw-Hill.

Schmid, A., and C. Spencer-Smith. (2012). "Illicit radiological and nuclear trafficking, smuggling and security incidents in the Black Sea region since the fall of the iron curtain – An open source inventory." *Perspectives on Terrorism*. http://www.terrorismanalysts.com/pt/index.php/pot/article/view/schmid-illicit-radiological/html (Accessed August 25, 2017).

Snyder, L., and J. Pate. (2002). *Tracking Anthrax Hoaxes and Attacks*. Monterey, CA: James Martin Center for Nonproliferation Studies. http://cns.miis.edu/pubs/week/020520.htm (Accessed August 23, 2008).

Stockholm International Peace Research Institute. (1971). *The Problem of Chemical and Biological Warfare, Vol. I*. New York: Humanities Press.

Sultan, M. (undated). "Biological terrorism: The threat of the 21st century. *The Institute of Strategic Studies, Islamabad*. http://www.issi.org.pk/journal/2001_files/no_4/article/2a.htm (Accessed September 8, 2008).

Thevenot, C., and L. Mower. (2008). "Guns, anarchy text found in room with ricin: LV police say terrorism not motive despite discovery." *Las Vegas Review-Journal*. http://www.lvrj.com/news/16142962.html (Accessed August 23, 2008).

United Nations. (1993). Disarmament Study Series: No. 25 https://www.un.org/disarmament/publications/studyseries/no-25 (Accessed December 4, 2017).

Union of Concerned Scientists. (2008). Nuclear Terrorism Overview. https://www.ucsusa.org/nuclear-weapons/nuclear-terrorism/overview#.WiWYGktryu4 (Accessed December 4, 2017).

Van-Tuam, N. (2005). *Agent Orange and the War in Vietnam*. New South Wales, Australia: Garvan Institute of Medical Research and University.

Williams, P., and the Associated Press. (2015). "Smugglers tried to sell nuclear material to ISIS." *NBC News*. https://www.nbcnews.com/storyline/isis-terror/smugglers-tried-sell-nuclear-material-isis-ap-investigation-n439851 (Accessed August 25, 2017).

World Health Organization. (2017). *Middle East Respiratory Syndrome Coronavirus (MERS-CoV)*. http://www.who.int/mediacentre/factsheets/mers-cov/en/ (Accessed August 28, 2017).

World Nuclear Association. (2008). *Chernobyl Accident*. http://www.world%20nuclear.org/info/chernobyl/inf07.html (Accessed August 26, 2008).

Zillinskas, R. (1999). "Cuban allegations of biological warfare by the United States: Assessing the evidence." *Critical Reviews in Microbiology*, 25(3): 173–227.

10 Cybercrime and Terrorism

LEARNING OBJECTIVES

1. *Identify the methods of attacking cyber infrastructure.*
2. *Distinguish between cybercrime and cyber terrorism.*
3. *Discuss the various sectors within America that are vulnerable to cyberattacks.*
4. *Identify the types of information that terrorist groups post on their Internet home pages.*
5. *Examine how terrorists use the Internet.*
6. *Describe the federal cyber counterintelligence agencies and their operations.*

Key Terms

Cyberspace
Internet of Things
Physical or conventional attack
Electronic attack
Malicious code
Hacking
Hackers
Cyber terrorism
Cyber warfare
National Cyber Response Coordination Group
Netwar
Cyber squads
Cyber action teams
National Cyber Investigation Task Force
National Cyber Security Protection System
National Cyber Security and Communications Integration Center
U.S. Computer Emergency Readiness Team

▶ Introduction

The topic of cyber terrorism has received a great deal of attention and notoriety (see Clarke, 2008). Agency administrators, politicians, and the media have devoted a substantial amount of discourse to the topic. We have integrated this discussion with other terrorist threats and scenarios, making it a real issue for large numbers of people. There are ample examples of what might happen if cyber terrorist acts occur, and there are examples of hackers attacking a number of computers and databases. However, we must distinguish between the possible, the plausible, and the real. In other words, how real is a cyberattack, what kind of attack could occur, and what are the consequences of such an attack? We must examine these questions rationally, and we must develop realistic policies and countermeasures. It begs the question: how catastrophic can such an attack be relative to our national well-being?

The connection of cyberspace and terrorism is evidenced in several attacks, such as in Mumbai, India, in Paris, France, and in San Bernardino, United States. In all three attacks, the terrorists used the Internet, social media, and smart technologies to carry out the attacks and evade law enforcement for a prolonged period. On November 26, 2008, terrorists affiliated with the Jihadist group Lashkar-e-Taiba (Army of the Pure) attacked six targets in Mumbai, India. Among the targets were a hospital and two famous hotels: the Taj Mahal Palace and the Tower Hotel. Ten gunmen, armed with automatic weapons, suicide bombs, and Internet devices, teamed up in pairs and spread around the city. Some attackers launched their suicide bombs and others started shooting people at the hospital, on the street, inside a train station, and the hotels. What was unique about this attack was that during the attack, the terrorist monitored the social media for tweets and posts about the location of police and the location of victims hiding in the various hotel rooms. They used that information to evade the police and launch their attacks for more than 60 hours. The police eventually made a public announcement and asked the population to stop posting information that could help the terrorists (Express Web Desk, 2016).

The interface between terrorists and social media has also been a growing concern for national security analysts in the United States. The massacre of San Bernardino, California, has shown the detrimental impact of social media on the recruitment of terrorists and terrorist attacks. On December 2, 2015, Syed Rizwan Farok and his wife Tashfeen Malik killed 14 people in the Inland Regional Center in San Bernardino. Following the attack, they posted on Facebook that they belonged to the terrorist group Islamic State (ISIS). Both were killed during a high-speed chase a few hours after the attacks (Winton, 2016).

Cyber terrorism and cyberattacks have been linked to the Islamic State (ISIS), al Qaeda, other terrorists, criminal groups, and nation-states. The U.S. government reported that Iraq had Iraq Net, which was set to attack American computer systems (see Stohl, 2006). When U.S. troops captured al Qaeda computers in Iraq, they often discovered complex information about nuclear plants, water systems, and so on.

It is important to note that terrorist acts can occur across a broad spectrum of targets. In Chapter 3, the *National Infrastructure Protection Plan (NIPP)* (DHS, 2006) was examined. One of the primary categories of infrastructure addressed in the plan was cyberspace and its related technology. The average American does not fully comprehend or appreciate the impact that the Internet and other communications centers have on our society. A substantial amount of our commerce, daily activities, work, and leisure are conducted through the Internet. It touches everyone's life on a daily basis. The Internet and communications systems encompass a substantial amount of telecommunications hardware and software that is vulnerable to attack and hacking. Communications centers located in some of our major cities control the telephone and Internet communications for large portions of states and in some cases several states. Individual servers or communications sites handle large volumes of this traffic. These facilities and activities are likely targets of terrorists and other computer hackers. An attack on our cyber and communications system, depending on the proportion of communications that are affected, could have disastrous effects on American society. The NIPP also applies to all other critical infrastructures including water systems, power plants, and varied organizational structures. To prevent cyberattacks and be better prepared for a security breach, the government and the private sector participants must work closely together. In 2013, President Obama signed the Presidential Policy Directive, establishing a policy for Critical Infrastructure Security and Resilience. The directive outlines the responsibilities, functions, and roles of federal, state, local, tribal, and territorial entities. The directive includes security measures for physical and cyberattacks (Office of the Press Secretary, 2013).

Before proceeding further, it is important to define **cyberspace**. Essentially, it is the world communications domain consisting of vast amounts of hardware, software, and data

HS ANALYSIS BOX 10-1

Cyberspace consists of not only the webpages and browsers widely called the Internet but also the underground world, the so-called darkweb. The darkweb not only provides complete anonymity, but it also works a huge network for criminals and terrorists. The darkweb has its own "amazon" where "customers" can buy weapons, malware kits, and mentoring services. The buyers can rate the quality of the product. Customer support is provided to the buyers and there is even a money back guarantee. For instance, customers of malware kits are guaranteed that the malware works. The opportunities for terrorists are endless on the darkweb. For instance, on July 22, 2016 a German killed nine people at a popular mall in Munich. Weapons are not freely available to purchase in Germany, but the darkweb provides an ample supply of all types of weapons (Hume, 2016). The pistol came via the mail, which is the typical mode of product distribution. Similar to Germany, mail sent within the United States is not typically screened, which makes it the safest way to distribute illegal products.

Terrorists use a variety of methods to attack their enemies, and many are very destructive, including car bombs, armed attacks, and suicide bombers. In many cases, these attacks result in numerous casualties. Do you think a cyberattack would be as destructive? Why?

and information. Some see it as the data and information that freely flow across the globe, but here, cyberspace also includes the equipment that facilitates the flow of information. Barlow (1990) has equated cyberspace to America's Wild West:

> Cyberspace in its present condition has a lot in common with the 19th Century west. It is vast, unmapped, culturally and legally ambiguous... hard to get around in, and up for grabs. Large institutions already claim to own the place, but most of the actual natives are solitary and independent, sometimes to the point of sociopathy. It is, of course, a perfect breeding ground for both outlaws and new ideas about liberty. (p. 1)

Barlow's analogy is correct. Cyberspace is vast, so vast that we have yet to harness or comprehend its potential. We are dependent upon it as it intrudes into every aspect of daily life. He is also correct in noting that there is little or no control over most of this technology in the United States. It is an open system used freely by individuals, businesses, corporations, governments, criminals, and terrorists. It was built to facilitate the free exchange of ideas and data with little thought given to security and the implications of breaches of security. Today, there are already more connected devices, such as computers, tablets, smartphones, and tracking devices than people on this planet. It is estimated that by 2020 there will be 50 billion connected devices, also called the **Internet of Things** (IoTs). Johnson also stated, "as online threats grow, we must secure the Internet and the increasing number of Internet-connected devices and infrastructures. Cyber threats are increasing in their frequency, scale, sophistication, and severity. This affects everyone, across the country and around the globe" (Johnson, 2015). Clarke and Knake (2010) advised that the lack of control and security in cyberspace can result in disasters that are far worse than any other kind of attack—our nation and the world can be brought to their knees as a result of cyberattacks.

▶ Methods of Attacking Cyber Infrastructure

There are three methods for attacking computers and our cyber infrastructure: physical, electronic, and malicious code (Wilson, 2005). First, a **physical or conventional attack** is an attack on a facility with the aim of destroying its infrastructure. At the beginning and during the Iraqi war, the United States often targeted communications facilities to impede

Iraqi army communications and command functions. When al Qaeda attacked the World Trade Center and Pentagon in 2001, the attacks destroyed communications systems that were linked globally (Marlin and Garvin, 2004); the destruction of these communications systems greatly impeded the public safety response. Coordination of the various responding agencies was hampered, and communications among the various responders were substantially limited. Physical attacks can temporarily destroy communications capabilities, disrupting a number of important activities including recovery.

According to Wilson, a second type of physical attack is an **electronic attack** or electromagnetic pulse (EMP), whereby an electrical charge occurs near the computer or server hardware. Essentially, the EMP results in high energy that overloads circuit boards, computer chips, and other electronics. Memory can be erased, software can be disrupted, and hardware can be electronically destroyed. Small, portable electromagnetic devices could be used in a limited fashion to attack cyber infrastructure, but there are no examples of this type of attack. The EMP Task Force on National and Homeland Security, a congressional advisory board, has also described a more significant threat. It would be possible to detonate a nuclear device over the United States that would create a sufficiently large EMP to destroy the U.S. electric grid, causing a long-lasting blackout nationwide. Critics argue that neither of these scenarios is likely, and in fact, no such attack has been carried out across the globe (Burke and Scheider, 2015).

Chinese military hackers wanted by the FBI. Courtesy of the FBI.

Third, the most common form of attacks on cyber infrastructure and systems is **malicious code**. Malicious code can disrupt a computer or network's operation. Moreover, it can spread from one computer to another, resulting in large-scale problems or losses. The first cyber terrorism attack was carried out via the malware "Stuxnet." The Stuxnet worm first emerged in 2010, when it was used to destroy the centrifuges in the Iranian plutonium enrichment plant in Natanz. The worm was planted on a Universal Serial Bus (USB) stick, which was inserted into one of the computers. From there the worm spread quickly and quietly. The workers at the plant did not know that their computer network had been infiltrated and their data were being manipulated. The information displayed on their computers was not real, but a fake version, disguising the fact that the Stuxnet worm had taken control of the computers and systems running the operations.

The Stuxnet worm could spread not only across computers connected to the Internet but also across computers running Windows. Even though it was never officially attributed to the United States, insiders suggest that the United States and Israel were responsible for the attack in an attempt to prevent Iran from building nuclear weapons. Due to the darkweb, the Stuxnet worm is now accessible to terrorists and other criminals, and hackers are likely working on an improved version of the worm that could potentially be used against critical infrastructures in the United States. Our own worm could in the future cause a cyber "Pearl Harbor" that could derail trains, poison water supplies, and cause nationwide blackouts. In the Stuxnet attack, the malware was planted via a USB stick, but several other tools can be used in such attacks.

Tools Used in Hacking and Cyberattacks

Attacking computers and infrastructure using some form of intrusive code or program is referred to as **hacking**. Essentially, it does not matter the mode or intent behind the computer or network intrusions; all attackers will use similar methods of hacking. Furnell and Warren (1999) define **hackers** as, "persons who deliberately gain (or attempt to gain) unauthorized access to computer systems" (p. 29). All instances of hacking result in an array of problems for the victimized computer system and its owners. We must recognize that there are different categories of hackers. They include (1) nation-states such as China, Russia, or North Korea; (2) criminals who attack computers for financial gain; and (3) anarchists, terrorists, and hackers who attempt to gain access to computers to disrupt.

One of the most publicized cyberattacks was the hacking of the Democratic National Committee during the 2016 U.S. Presidential elections, releasing more than 20,000 emails. A report by the National Intelligence Council (NIC) attributed the cyberattack to Russia. The report stated that Russia's intent was to interfere with the election and derail the Clinton campaign. Russia's president Vladimir Putin denied any involvement in the cyberattack, but the evidence presented by the NIC seems reasonably strong to suggest that hackers acting on behalf of the Russian government were responsible. The NIC report stated,

> We assess Russian President Vladimir Putin ordered an influence campaign in 2016 aimed at the US presidential election. Russia's goals were to undermine public faith in the US democratic process, denigrate Secretary Clinton, and harm her electability and potential presidency. We further assess Putin and the Russian Government developed a clear preference for President-elect Trump. We have high confidence in these judgments. (National Intelligence Council, 2017)

Another example of a nation-state cyberattack was the hacking of Sony in 2014, after its announcement to release a movie *The Interview* depicting North Korea's leader Kim Jong-un. North Korea demanded that the movie not be shown, and when Sony refused, hackers broke into Sony's computers and released private information about movie stars and high-ranking executives. The emails released revealed personal and embarrassing exchanges between actors and executives. One high-ranking executive was fired and Sony paid tens of millions of dollars in damage control. North Korea also threatened terror

HS Web Link: To see an example of hacking information on the web, go to https://www.go4expert.com/articles/complete-hacking-information-t16514/.

attacks at movie showings. Sony eventually caved under the pressure and only released the movie on DVD and streaming services. President Obama made a strong statement against Sony's decision to cancel the movie on the big screen as it sends the message that U.S. companies can be intimidated by other nation-states (Borstin, 2015).

Another tool in cyberattacks is the IoTs. In fact, IoTs have become one of the most effective weapons for all different types of hackers. In October 2016, the Mirai botnet attack was the first large-scale botnet attack using IoTs, such as webcams, smartphones, tables, and cameras. The botnet disrupted Internet service across the United States for several hours. Following the attack, the Mirai botnet was up for rent and sale on the darkweb (Fox-Brewster, 2016). A cyberattack by a hostile nation-state using the IoTs could have devastating effects on people's lives. Imagine the effect of an attack on the U.S. Internet or power grid. What would be the consequences if a city like New York would go dark for several days? There would be no lights, no electricity, no alarm systems, no access to computer data or Internet, no elevators, no banking or shopping, no trains, no traffic signals, no air conditioning, and no power for hospitals. Now imagine that simultaneously terrorists would launch an attack similar to 9/11. Police and fire fighters would not be able to respond as quickly because their communications and emergency response systems likely would be effected by the power outage.

Hackers can obtain their hacking tools from a number of sources including the Internet, darkweb, and fellow hackers.

DWD-Comp/Alamy Stock Photo.

In 2011, five million people in San Diego, California, parts of Orange County, and Tijuana, Mexico, were without power for 12 hours due to the unintentional act by an employee of the Arizona Power Service, which provides the electricity for millions of people in California, Arizona, and Mexico (*The Guardian*, 2011). A targeted cyberattack could cause significantly more damage. For instance, a distributed denial of service attack, such as the Mirai attack, could cause a blackout lasting days or even weeks. A cyber security consortium of small utilities based in Nebraska has found nearly four million hacking attacks on their electric grid in one 8-week period. The threat of attacks is growing, as hackers get ever more sophisticated, the number of connected devices increases, and the power grid gets more diverse with the increasing use of renewable energy sources and cloud-linked smart energy-efficiency technology. The sprawling of the grid also has some advantages, however. With more than 300,000 miles of transmission lines and 9,200 generating stations providing power to the United States, attackers would have to successfully launch numerous simultaneous attacks to cause a nationwide blackout. What is more likely is a blackout of a big city or region supplied from one generating station (Begos, 2016).

Vulnerability of critical infrastructures and the national defense platform increases as developments in hardware and software, such as the network of controls, outstrip security mechanisms, although there are continuous efforts to develop security measures. Many companies now use a computerized smart grid, where sensors instead of humans gather data and control the machines based on the data (Begos, 2016). The Internet is increasingly being used in every sector throughout the United States and the world. Deregulation of industries and the need to net greater profits have led to an increased reliance on cyber systems as they add efficiency and effectiveness to the governmental or business enterprise. As an example, many utility companies use computerized systems to control and monitor the flow of electricity, natural gas, and water with substantial information flowing across the Internet. Moreover, many systems use off-the-shelf software, whereby an industry purchases its controlling software from one vender. The off-the-self software creates vulnerability that can be exploited by hackers. If hackers break into one system, they have the knowledge and tools to invade other similar systems. They in essence can have industry-wide access.

One of the most vulnerable industries are hospitals as they keep their equipment for many years. Most hospital technologies still use Windows 2003, which has no security patches and is easy to hack. Hospitals are therefore an easy target for ransomware attacks in which hackers hold the data of the hospital hostage until the hospital pays a certain ransom. Terrorists could also use these vulnerabilities and take hospitals hostage. All patient records are digitized and if the hospital staff cannot access the patient files, they cannot treat the patient effectively. For instance, in 2016, the Hollywood Presbyterian Medical Center paid $17,000 to hackers in exchange to have their systems restored. Neither cyber security experts nor the Federal Bureau of Investigation (FBI) had been able to decrypt the data and the FBI advised the hospital to pay because they were not able to restore the hospital systems (Wagstaff, 2016).

Hackers can also manipulate devices in the surgery room, such as the blood gas analyzer. If the data on the analyzer is incorrect and the medical staff relies on it, people could die. The same is true for Magnetic Resonance Imaging (MRI) devices and other body scanners. Among hackers, an ethical debate has ensued over the hacking of hospitals. Some hackers strongly believe that hospitals should be off limits, others argue that hospitals are one of the best targets because they will always pay (Kremez, 2017).

The Verizon Cyber Breach Report (2016) notes that hackers are more knowledgeable and sophisticated in their hacking, whereas the knowledge and skills required of hackers to break into systems have declined. About 89 percent of all cyberattacks have a financial or espionage motive. The vast majority of attacks stem from outside hackers. There is, however, a significant threat from insiders, that is, people who work in the company and either plant malware or steal data from the company to sell to others. This type of espionage can have substantial negative consequences for companies if their patented products are stolen and reverse engineered by companies in China or elsewhere and sold for much less money. Economic espionage has become one of the greatest threats to the companies as discussed in Chapter 9. In fact, 90 percent of cyber espionage targets proprietary information and trade secrets. Cyber espionage is mainly carried out by state-affiliated hackers (Verizon Enterprise, 2017). An even greater threat stems from terrorist groups hacking computers that hold military secrets or critical infrastructures.

A number of countries have established schools to teach hacking (Clarke and Knake, 2010). These countries want a steady supply of technically savvy people who can attack other countries' computer systems or gather intelligence. For instance, North Korea has an elaborate cyber hacker school and the cyber hackers are part of the military strategy (Park, 2016). The Syrian Electronic Army (SEA) operates on behalf of the Syrian government. In 2016, three Syrian nationals and members of the SEA were charged with multiple accounts of conspiracies related to computer hacking. The charges included "engaging in a hoax regarding a terrorist attack; attempting to cause mutiny of the U.S. armed forces; illicit possession of authentication features; access device fraud; unauthorized access to, and damage of, computers; and unlawful access to stored communications" (Department of Justice, 2016).

There are numerous sources for hackers to learn about hacking methods with a substantial amount of information posted on the World Wide Web. A number of terrorist groups and others including hackers post this information on the darkweb. There is a virtual library for hackers and tutoring and mentoring services from more experienced hackers. Thus, there is a range of sophistication relative to computer hackers from the novice to the expert to the nation-state.

Weimann (2004), Kane (2011), and Clarke and Knake (2010) have identified the primary tools used by hackers to attack computers and data systems. Some tools are designed to infiltrate a computer system, whereas others attempt to gain sensitive financial or personal information from individuals. Figure 10-1 ■ provides a listing and brief description of the various tools and methods.

As noted in Figure 10-1 ■, a number of these tools are used in conjunction, whereas some can operate independently. They can be used by hackers, terrorists, or governments to attack the United States or to steal defense or industrial secrets. The number of attacks is substantial and increasing each year. For example, the Verizon Cyber Attack Report (2017) showed that in 2015 there were about 64,199 cyber incidents across 82 countries. These only include reported incidents. The dark number is likely much higher because many companies

Backdoor	Code inserted in a program that allows someone to gain access to the program or secure computer. Backdoors are commonly inserted in programs to allow programmers access. Criminals and hackers often insert backdoors in programs to obtain data or to control the computer. A backdoor can also be inserted with the introduction of a worm.
Botnet	A group or network of computers that has been commandeered by hackers to attack other computers or systems for illegitimate purposes. The computers operate in unison and are controlled by the hacker.
Denial of Service Attack	Sometimes referred to as blockades or virtual sit-ins, these attacks initiated by a number of computers making multiple requests that cause the targeted computer or system to become overloaded, with the result that it slows down or crashes. Such attacks are usually originated with a botnet.
Phishing and spoofing	Deceptive e-mails and websites are used to entice a user to provide personal or financial information for fraud or identity theft.
Robot or Zombie	This is a computer that has a Trojan or worm inserted that allows someone other than the legitimate owner to control the computer remotely. Botnets are composed of robot computers.
Trojans	These are viruses or worms that appear to be software upgrades, share programs, help files, screen savers, and pictures such as pornography that once opened run in the background causing damage or allowing an illegitimate user to control the computer.
Virus and worms	These are executable programs that are inserted into a computer program via Trojans or hacking. They typically are meant to harm the computer by altering files or data. They often delete, modify, or corrupt data and files.

FIGURE 10-1 Commonly Used Hacking Tools

HS ANALYSIS BOX 10-2

As noted, hackers use a variety of methods to attack computers. They attack individual computers and networks. If you use the Internet, you connect to a network. Botnets and zombie computers seem to be the most troublesome attacks. Has your computer ever been hacked? Do you know if your computer is being used as a zombie? How do you know? Do you have any virus protection software and how effective is it?

do not want to make cyberattacks public as it could have significant negative consequences. There is an increasing number of cyberattacks on every sector of business, industry, defense, government, oil, power, and so on. It is likely that each year hundreds of thousands of attacks are launched. Clarke and Knake (2010) warned that cyberattacks can be just as devastating as conventional weapons or even a weapons of mass destruction (WMD) attack.

▶ What Is Cyber Terrorism?

To some extent, it is difficult to define cyber terrorism, since it encompasses such a wide spectrum of activities, victims, and perpetrators. Weimann (2005) defined it as "the use of computer network tools to harm or shut down critical national infrastructures (such as energy, transportation, government operations)" (p. 130). On the other hand, Pollitt (undated) defined cyber terrorism as, "the premeditated, politically motivated attack against information, computer systems, computer programs, and the data that results in violence against noncombatant targets by subnational groups or clandestine agents." **Cyber terrorism** is the merging of cyberspace, which is a virtual world where computer programs function and data move, and terrorism, the premeditated, politically motivated violence perpetrated against noncombatant targets by subnational or clandestine groups. Although cyber terrorism can be performed by a nation-state, it generally is used by groups that advocate some cause against a perceived or real enemy. It is used to cripple, cause terror, or have an economic impact on a state or group of people.

There is widespread disagreement relative to the threat posed by cyber terrorism. Some homeland security personnel have referred to it as an "impending Pearl Harbor," great danger, or significant threat, whereas others see it more as a minor inconvenience or at least a threat that has been overstated and popularized (see Carafano, 2008; Lewis, 2006; Rattray, 2006; Stohl, 2006; Wilson, 2005). Those who affirm cyber terrorism as a real danger note that our substantial dependence on the Internet and networks and their intrusive relationship with all aspects of society, including commerce, public welfare, finance, and defense leads to considerable vulnerability. There are many avenues for disruption and numerous targets. In 2015, Ardit Ferizi, a citizen of Kosovo, was the first person charged with cyber terrorism in the United States. Ferizi is accused of hacking and disclosing names, email addresses, passwords, locations, and other personal information of military personnel to Junaid Hussain, a member of the Islamic State. Hussain then distributed the data via Twitter endangering the lives of 1,351 U.S. military personnel. Ferizi had obtained the data by hacking a U.S. retail company. Among the 100,000 stolen records were also the 1,351 military personnel records. This case demonstrates the real problem of keeping data safe. The hackers do not need to get into government servers; they can hack any large retail company and get data on military personnel or other government employees (InfoSec Institute, 2016).

On the other hand, those who downplay the threat of cyber terrorism believe that cyberattacks by terrorists do not meet their objectives—large-scale destruction, multiple casualties, or psychological advantage. These results are better achieved with a car or truck bomb! Cyber intrusions by terrorists (although few have been documented) just add to the problem of constant hacking activities, and effective defensive countermeasure systems must be developed to deter hacking and intrusions of all sorts.

▶ Distinguishing Hacking, Cybercrime, Cyber Terrorism, and Cyber Warfare

Hacking, cybercrime, cyber terrorism, and cyber warfare are multidimensional, interconnected problems. A number of crimes and problems are associated with cyberspace. The Internet is used to commit a variety of crimes by nation-states, terrorists, and criminals. Crimes and terrorist acts can emanate from across the globe, including from the United States. They can include the theft of information ranging from financial or personal records to military intelligence and industrial espionage. They can alter or destroy computer systems, adversely affecting our critical infrastructure. Such acts can be conducted by governments, terrorists, professionals, or novice hackers and can target hardware, software, or data files. In essence, cybercrime and terrorism represent a significant challenge to homeland security and law enforcement.

As noted earlier, cyber-related attacks can come from a variety of actors with different motivations. Figure 10-2 ■ provides a breakdown of the different types of cyber criminals, their motivations, and their threat actions.

Type of Cyber Criminal	Motivation	Threat Actions
Hacker	• Challenge • Ego • Rebellion • Curiosity	• Hacking • Systems intrusions • Unauthorized access • Theft
Computer Criminal	• Destruction of Information • Illegal access to information • Monetary gain • Unauthorized data alteration	• Fraud • Cyber stalking • Theft of information • System alteration • Spoofing
Terrorist	• Blackmail • Destruction • Exploitation • Revenge	• Facilitate attacks • Information warfare • System attack • System penetration • System tampering
Industrial Espionage	• Competitive advantage • Economic espionage • Trade secrets	• Economic exploitation • Information theft • Intrusion on personal privacy • Social engineering • Access to proprietary or technology information
Insiders (Employees)	• Curiosity • Ego • Intelligence • Monetary gain • Revenge • Cover up other crimes or errors	• Assault or attacks on employees • Blackmail • Access to proprietary information • Computer abuse • Fraud and theft • Input of false or corrupted information • Interception of information • Destruction of systems or data
Countries	• Intelligence and espionage • Incapacitate systems • Political intervention • Economic destabilization • Cyber warfare	• Hacking • System intrusions • Information losses • Denial of service • Attacks on infrastructure

FIGURE 10-2 Types of Cyber Criminals

Source: Adapted from Stoneburner, G., A. Goguen, and A. Feringa. (2001). *Risk Management Guide for Information Technology Systems.* Special Publication 800-30. Washington, D.C.: National Institute of Standards and Technology.

Figure 10-2 ■ provides a typology of those who would attack computer systems. Hackers are those individuals who attempt to penetrate computers and networks for the challenge. Their attacks essentially are to test their computer skills. In some cases, they will attempt to create damage, but for the most part, their efforts merely are tests of their skills. Computer criminals are motivated by financial reward. They may hack into a computer to steal data such as credit card information or personal information that could be used for gain. In some cases, they may attempt to blackmail a business or group using illegally obtained data or information. Terrorists are more nefarious, and their intentions generally center on creating damage or harm to an enemy. Industrial espionage, as discussed in Chapter 8, involves individuals, companies, and governments with the primary motivation being financial. Theft of trade secrets can reduce product or systems development costs and result in marketing advantages. Countries are involved in industrial espionage as it provides information about another country's infrastructure and defense capabilities and allows for a reduction in weapons and other systems development.

Cybercrime

A variety of crimes are conducted or facilitated via the Internet. Many of these crimes are sophisticated property crimes and others support terrorism. Taylor and his colleagues (2006) provide a number of examples of these crimes as noted in Figure 10-3 ■.

This listing demonstrates that the Internet has become a tool that can be used to facilitate a wide range of criminal acts. Perhaps the most common crime is phishing. Millions of Americans receive countless emails requesting financial information or their involvement in some kind of financial scheme. The perpetrators are attempting to entice the email recipients to provide financial information or to send money so that some large amount of money in a foreign country can be processed or split between the email sender and the victim. They may also attempt to obtain personal information for identity theft purposes. In some cases, the sender may install a worm that sends victims' financial or personal information to the email sender.

Hackers are becoming more sophisticated as a result of the proliferation of computer hardware and their vulnerability. Many computers have firewalls and virus protection, but other devices such as routers, printers, smartphones, and tablets have less or no protection. Hackers are now hacking these devices. Proofpoint Inc., a computer security company, tracked a global attack that sent 750,000 malicious emails from more than 100,000 gadgets including home Wi-Fi, routers, TVs, DVRs, and even a refrigerator (O'Brien, 2014). Essentially, anything with a microprocessor and an operating system can be hacked. As an example, doctors disabled the wireless functionality of former Vice President Dick Chaney's heart implant out of concern that it would be hacked. These vulnerabilities allow

1. Attacks on financial institutions, businesses, and industries, including military installations
2. Cyber stalking
3. Obscenity, including child pornography
4. Child molestation (obtaining contacts)
5. Sex tourism, in which pedophiles seek underage victims
6. Distribution of digital hate (websites and e-mails), especially by hate and terrorist groups
7. Communications among criminal and terrorist groups
8. Gathering of intelligence information on potential targets
9. Identity theft
10. Money laundering

FIGURE 10-3 Criminal Acts Facilitated by the Internet

hackers to use stolen credit cards and order products from a commandeered device. They then have the products delivered to a vacant home. They often identify vacant homes when residents post vacation plans on social medial such as Facebook.

There have been numerous instances in which hackers have accessed retailers' computers and stolen thousands of credit cards' information. For example, in 2013, the retailer Target reported that its system was broached for an undetermined period of time. The number of stolen credit card numbers was approximately 40 million. In another case in 2013, the Credit Reporting Agency Experian reported that 200,000,000 personal files of customers had been stolen. The information stolen goes far beyond credit card numbers (Riley et al., 2014). The biggest hack of all times occurred in 2016 against Yahoo with one billion stolen user accounts (Pham, 2016).

The FBI in conjunction with the National White Collar Crime Center operates an Internet fraud-reporting center. Figure 10-4 ■ shows the distribution of complaints that were received in 2016.

As noted in Figure 10-4 ■, several Internet scams and fraudulent crimes are conducted on the Internet. The most commonly reported complaint is non-payment or non-delivery. In 2016, the Crime Complaint Center registered 82,029 victims for this particular crime. Non-payment refers to a situation in which goods are delivered but the seller does not get paid. Non-delivery refers to a situation where a payment is made, but the goods are not received. Other common cybercrimes are personal data beach, overpayment, phishing, extortion, identity theft, and harassment/threat of violence.

By Victim Count

Crime Type	Victims	Crime Type	Victims
Non-Payment/Non-Delivery	81,029	Lottery/Sweepstakes	4,231
Personal Data Breach	27,573	Corporate Data Breach	3,403
419/Overpayment	25,716	Malware/Scareware	2,783
Phishing/Vishing/Smishing/Pharming	19,465	Ransomware	2,673
Employment	17,387	IPR/Copyright and Counterfeit	2,572
Extortion	17,146	Investment	2,197
Identity Theft	16,878	Virus	1,498
Harassment/Threats of Violence	16,385	Crimes Against Children	1,230
Credit Card Fraud	15,895	Civil Matter	1,070
Advanced Fee	15,075	Denial of Service	979
Confidence Fraud/Romance	14,546	Re-shipping	893
No Lead Value	13,794	Charity	437
Other	12,619	Health Care Related	369
Real Estate/Rental	12,574	Terrorism	295
Government Impersonation	12,344	Gambling	137
BEC/EAC	12,005	Hacktivist	113
Tech Support	10,850		
Misrepresentation	5,436		

FIGURE 10-4 Number of Victims by Type of Crime
Source: https://pdf.ic3.gov/2016_IC3Report.pdf.

Cyber Warfare

Cyber warfare is an attack by one nation-state on another nation-state. It is cyber terrorism conducted by a country. An attack may serve several purposes:

- Gain economic or military intelligence
- Test another country's defenses
- Cripple another country's weapons systems
- Cripple another country's military communications systems
- Cause economic chaos
- Military posturing or political bargaining

In 2015, Russian hackers seized the email system used by the Joint Chiefs of Staff of the U.S. military. Prior Chairman of the Joint Chiefs Martin Dempsey stated that the hackers had infiltrated the unclassified email system within an hour of the attack and had seized the computer credentials of Dempsey and other top officials. The attack started with 30,000 phishing emails, one of which was opened and exposed the U.S. military computer network to the attackers. Even though the information seized was not valuable for intelligence purposes, it exposed the vulnerability of the systems and forced the military to replace their hardware and software. Dempsey also stated that the motive for the attack was likely the economic sanctions imposed by the Obama administration against Russia after Russia's annexation of Crimea (Martin, 2016).

In the past few years, North Korea has emerged as the most pertinent threat to the United States. North Korea has successfully launched a number of rockets and is actively working on nuclear weapons. One of the main strategies of the United States under the Obama and Trump administrations has been cyber and electronic warfare. The Trump administration has warned North Korea that the United States is prepared for an pre-emptive strike should they continue the missile and nuclear testing. These pre-emptive strikes could be a combination of cyber and physical attacks (Tisdall, 2017).

HS Web Link: To learn more about how Russia used cyber warfare in Estonia, go to https://www.theguardian.com/world/2007/may/17/topstories3.russia.

A variant of cyber warfare is cyber intelligence. Countries such as Russia and China are constantly attempting to breach our computer databases to obtain critical information about defense technology and intelligence. In 2014, hackers obtained the personnel records of 22 million federal employees. The files can be cross-listed with other information to possibly determine which employees are employed in the military or intelligence agencies, and the data can be used to identify employees who might be vulnerable as a result of financial difficulties. It may shed light on where employees are located and their travel patterns (Bennett and Hennigan, 2015).

▶ Points of Cyberattacks

In 2016, President Obama signed the new cyber security policy and released the Cybersecurity National Action Plan. The main actions of the proposed plan are:

1. Establish the "Commission on Enhancing National Cybersecurity."
2. Modernize Government IT with a 3.1 billion Information Technology Modernization Fund.
3. Empower Americans to secure their devices with enhanced measures, such as biometrics.
4. Invest more than $19 billion for enhanced cyber security strategies (Office of the Press Secretary, 2016).

Former Secretary of the Department of Homeland Security Tom Ridge stated that these increased cyber security measures are imperative as a cyberattack could cause more damage than a physical attack: "Notwithstanding the pain and horror associated with a physical attack," Ridge said, "the potential for physical, human, and psychic impact with a cyberattack, I think, is far more serious" (Cyber Security Intelligence, 2016).

▶ Cyber Terrorism

Cyber terrorism has been defined as the merging of cyberspace, which is a virtual world where computer programs function and data move, and terrorism, the premeditated, politically motivated violence perpetrated against noncombatant targets by subnational or clandestine groups. However, Denning (2001) advised that for an attack to be considered a cyber terrorist attack, it must "be sufficiently destructive or disruptive to generate fear comparable to that from physical acts of terrorism. Attacks that lead to death or bodily injury, extended power outages, plane crashes, water contamination, or major economic losses would be examples." Much of terrorists' current cyber activities do not meet this benchmark. These activities are more akin to hacking. Indeed, Wilson (2005) advised that there have not been any documented instances of significant cyber terrorism. Nonetheless, it is likely to occur in the immediate future.

HS Web Link: To learn more about terrorists' capacity to launch such attacks, go to http://www.fas.org/sgp/crs/terror/RL33123.pdf.

Cyber terrorism is attractive to terrorists. Weimann (2004) advised that several advantages make cyber terrorism appealing. First, it is relatively inexpensive. The terrorist needs only a computer and expertise. Second, it is anonymous. Given the World Wide Web, it is difficult to determine where a threat originated. Third, the number of targets is enormous and includes governments, industry, universities, public utilities, airlines, and so on. The numerous critical infrastructure targets include utilities and water supplies. Fourth, it does not require physical training, traveling, and the physical risk associated with other types of terrorism. Fifth, it potentially can affect thousands if not millions of people. These advantages mean that terrorists likely will use cyberattacks in the future.

Finally, it should be noted that terrorist organizations will not have the cyber warfare technical skills that governments do. Admittedly, terrorists have a number of highly educated and trained personnel at their disposal. They likely have significant experience with cyberattacks and have conducted some attacks with mixed results. However, governments have two distinct advantages that terrorist organizations cannot overcome. First, governments can allocate billions of dollars to the development of cyber security and warfare—in some cases, resources are virtually unlimited. For example, the National Cyber Security Initiative was originally funded at $6 billion, and the funding has increased to over $19 billion (Office of the Press Secretary, 2016). Other countries that are targets of cyberattacks by terrorists also have a wealth of resources. Terrorists cannot compete in the area of development; they have relatively few resources for cyberattacks.

Second, countries such as the United States have a wealth of expertise. America has the world's strongest engineering and computer science programs within its vast array of universities, and large numbers of cutting-edge research and development companies are located in the United States. For example, Shorrock (2008) noted that approximately half

HS ANALYSIS BOX 10-3

The previous discussion advises that it would be difficult for terrorists to launch a significant cyberattack on the United States, but there are those who believe that terrorist cyberattacks are a credible threat. Do you believe our cyber infrastructure is protected from such attacks? Do you believe the threat of these attacks is credible?

of our intelligence operations (approximately $50 billion annually) are contracted to these private companies, and they have close working relations with government agencies such as the Central Intelligence Agency (CIA), the National Security Agency (NSA), National Reconnaissance Office, and the Defense Intelligence Agency. A large part of their mission is electronic intelligence gathering, but at the same time, they are developing cyber security measures. Gathering electronic intelligence represents a substantial amount of cyber security technical power. No other country or organization can match it. It is questionable as to how much of this technology filters down to nonintelligence government and private entities, but it is likely that these countermeasures ultimately will be integrated into these sectors.

Physical Attacks on Communications Infrastructure

There has been substantial discussion relative to terrorists hacking into computers and stealing information or disabling them with viruses and worms. However, some consideration should be given to the physical destruction of communications infrastructure. As noted earlier, conventional physical and electromagnetic attacks can disable or destroy software and hardware systems. Communications infrastructure that controls communications and the Internet is distributed across the United States. In many cases, these facilities are unprotected or have minimum levels of security. One or more of these facilities may become the targets of terrorist attacks. Again, it appears that there is sufficient engineering overlap and redundancy so that it would be extremely difficult to bring down the complete system or even a major portion of the system. However, the greatest threat would be if terrorists launched a cyberattack in conjunction with a conventional attack.

In 2006, the Business Roundtable commissioned a report examining how to strengthen our cyber terrorism preparedness. The Business Roundtable is an association of Chief Executive Officers (CEOs) from America's largest corporations. They represent companies

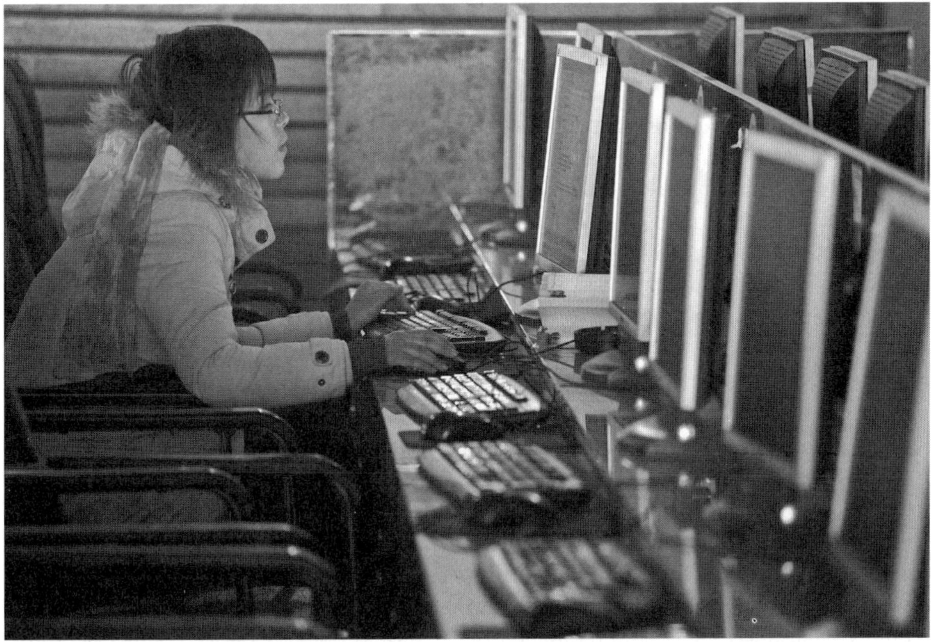

A substantial amount of hacking occurs in Internet cafes.
NIR ELIAS/REUTERS/Newscom.

comprising one-third of the value of the U.S. stock market. They actively pursue technological innovation and have a vested interest in ensuring that the Internet is not breached.

The group advises that the primary problem is that our nation is not prepared to reconstitute the Internet after a massive disruption. The Internet essentially is housed in a number of facilities that could be vulnerable to a coordinated attack. The government is responsible for various aspects of the Internet. However, there is no governmental policy on how and when the government would intervene to reconstitute portions of the Internet as a result of attacks. Although the **National Cyber Response Coordination Group** is responsible for coordinating Internet emergencies, it appears that no action plan is in place should such an emergency arise. For the most part, private companies have plans dealing with emergencies that affect their Internet venues, but this essentially represents piecemeal coverage. In other words, the nation is not prepared to enact a coordinated, comprehensive response to a significant breach in the Internet.

The Internet is the backbone for a number of critical communications functions that affect commerce, banking, public safety, and government in general. A significant breach could have significant long-lasting detrimental effects on our economy, defense, and society in general. We have a vested interest to ensure that it is protected and as secure as possible, and we must ensure that an adequate response to breaches exists and is ready to implement.

▶ Significant Cyber Gaps

The Business Roundtable committee identified several critical gaps. First is a lack of formal trip wires to indicate an attack is underway. We do not have formal mechanisms to quickly identify breaches. Second is a lack of accountability and clarity on which institutions provide reconstitution support. Essentially, there is no workable action plan. Third, there is a lack of resources for institutions to reconstitute the Internet infrastructure should a breach occur. Although Congress allocates funding for the Internet, none of the monies is allocated or kept in abeyance should a significant breach occur.

The primary responsibility for reconstructing the Internet should there be a breach rests with the private sector. The government oversees and to some extent regulates the Internet, but the private sector actually runs and operates it. Companies have responsibilities to ensure that the Internet is reconstituted as seamlessly as possible. Companies must also establish a single point with the authority to reconstitute the Internet should there be a breach. Additionally, companies should have a strategic plan that establishes priorities when reconstituting an Internet breach. Third, companies need to have early warning systems in place that quickly notify managers of problems so that corrective actions can take place as soon as possible. Finally, consistent protocols should be developed so that companies and industries can coordinate their efforts.

In the end, we face a number of possible problems should there be a significant data breach in the Internet. A data breach is problematic given the importance the Internet has relative to American and international life. Nonetheless, our experience shows that this may not be a major problem. Lewis (2006) noted that Hurricane Katrina in 2005 resulted in New Orleans and large portions of the Gulf region being taken off-line. He noted that if the political consequences are managed, there is little impact as a result of such large or massive disruptions.

Lewis (2006) advised that once an attack occurs, systems operators immediately respond with countermeasures. For an attack to have any measure of impact, it must have a high level of redundancy. It must target several computers or servers in the system, and it requires a sustained, successful re-attack to overcome system operators' countermeasures. Relatively speaking, it is fairly easy to have a short-term impact on a system, but it may be exceedingly difficult to have a long-term impact, especially on well-secured systems.

HS ANALYSIS BOX 10-4

The Business Roundtable identified a very important problem. Most of our Internet and cyber infrastructure is controlled by the private sector. Most of the developmental efforts are to expedite the flow of information with little regard for security. A number of cyber experts note that the government should take more control by promulgating more regulations. Do you believe the federal government should force the private sector to install more costly security hardware and protocols?

Nonetheless, we have had a number of successful cyber intrusions. Numerous corporations have been hacked when perpetrators penetrated their systems and stole thousands of credit card numbers and customers' other personal information, for example, Home Depot, eBay, and Target. The most significant hack occurred in 2015. In 2015, hackers obtained the personal data of about four million current and former federal employees by hacking the Office of Personnel Management's system (Beatty, 2015). What makes this problematic is that the hackers can obtain directories of government employees, eliminate them from the list, or alter the information and send it to an intelligence agency or other agency involved in homeland security.

Deterring Cyber Intrusions and Attacks

Given the magnitude of the potential problems associated with cyberattacks, it is obvious that much needs to be done to improve security. Kane (2011) has identified several changes that would improve security. First, remove cyber anonymity. Procedures should be implemented to ensure that email and message senders and sender locations are easily identified and traceable. This would be a substantial deterrent to many hackers. Second, mandate that institutions use and constantly update security software. They too often update their security software after a breach, which is too late. Third, minimize the amount of time that computers are online. This reduces the possibility of malicious code being introduced to computers. At the same time, require Internet providers to scan computers within their user networks for robot or zombie software. Fourth, institutions and Internet providers should periodically check their computers for worms and other malicious code to ensure that it is not transferred to end users. Fifth, centralize reporting of computer breaches and intrusions. Although different institutions and some industries such as defense collect hacking information, there should be a national clearinghouse that could warn end users of potential problems and recommend solutions. Such a clearinghouse could also identify hackers and notify law enforcement to take action. Finally, we need better mechanisms for reporting hacking so that trends and modus operandi can be identified.

Clarke and Knake (2010) advise that the most significant problem in deterring cyberattacks is that there is no agency responsible for combating them. The Department of Defense and the military branches are currently implementing and enhancing security within defense, but there is no coordinating or controlling body over civilian applications. For example, the Department of Homeland Security's National Cyber Defense Division has two primary objectives: (1) build and maintain an effective national cyberspace response system and (2) implement a cyber-risk management program for protection of critical infrastructure (DHS, 2008). Clarke and Knake advocate that the division should do more in terms of enhancing security and protection. The DHS should be given more power to mandate some of the changes advocated by Kane discussed earlier.

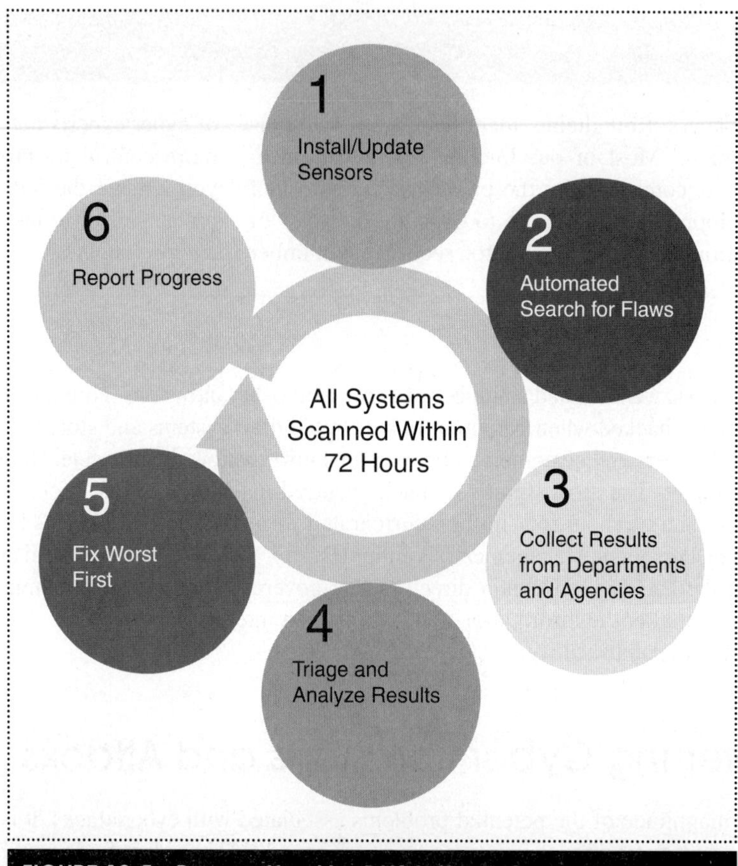

FIGURE 10-5 Process Used by DHS to Scan Computer Systems for Malware
Source: https://www.dhs.gov/cdm.

▶ Terrorists' Use of the Internet

Almost everyone uses the Internet, including terrorists to further their causes. There is little regulation of the Internet, so to some extent, terrorists are free to use it for a variety of purposes. Periodically, different countries will attempt to exert some controls. For example, in the recent past, major companies such as Goggle and Yahoo have cooperated with the Chinese government to limit access to certain materials that the government believes is subversive. In the United States, there have been efforts to limit or control pornography. In most cases, controls have been ineffective. For example, the federal government may attempt to limit pornography in the United States, but these efforts have failed when challenged in court, and pornography can still be accessed from other countries. Thus, we effectively cannot limit groups from using the World Wide Web.

Terrorists increasingly are using the web and engaging in what Arquilla and his colleagues (2003) refer to as **netwar**,

> an emerging mode of conflict and crime at societal levels, involving measures short of traditional war, in which the protagonists use network forms of organization and related doctrines, strategies, and technologies attuned to the information age. (p. 101)

They coined the term *netwar* because many terrorist groups have moved from a hierarchical structure to a network of cells and organizations. Many countries, in the wake of the 9/11 attacks, have stepped up counterterrorism efforts, resulting in terrorist organizations assuming a more covert, dispersed organization. There has been an increase in religious terrorist organizations (see Hoffman, 2006), and these groups or cells are dispersed across countries and continents. Current conditions necessitate a networked communications and coordination system that can best be serviced by the web. Arquilla and his colleagues also noted that netwar best describes how terrorists are able to use the Internet for multiple purposes.

Today, virtually all terrorist organizations maintain a website and use social media, such as Facebook and Twitter, to recruit and spread their cause. There literally are hundreds of websites and Twitter messages spewing hate and propaganda. In the past, policy makers have concentrated their efforts on conventional terrorism methods and largely neglected how terrorist groups are using the web, but this is changing as policy makers and counterterrorism experts see how terrorists are now using the web. Essentially, the Internet is an important tool used by terrorist groups to further their causes and accomplish a number of objectives. Weimann (2004) has identified a number of attributes that are useful to these groups.

Overview of Terrorist Websites

The Internet is used by extremist groups of all stripes and from across the globe. Groups ranging from the Ku Klux Klan on the right to socialist revolutionaries have websites espousing their ideology. The Internet has been used extensively by Muslim extremist and terrorist groups. The following are only a few of the groups that have used the web:

1. Middle Eastern groups include Islamic State, SEA, Hamas, Hezbollah, the al Aqsa Martyrs Brigaes, Fatah Tanzim, the Popular Front for the Liberation of Palestine, the Palestinian Islamic Jihad, and the Kurdish Workers' Party.
2. European groups include the Basque ETA movement and the Armata Corsa (Corsican Army.
3. Latin American groups include Peru's Tupak-Amaru (MRTA), the Shining Path, the Colombian National Liberation Army, and the Armed Revolutionary Forces of Colombia.
4. Asian groups include al Qaeda, the Japanese Supreme Truth (Aum Shinrikyo), the Japanese Red Army, the Liberation Tigers of Tamil Eelam, the Islamic Movement of Uzbekistan, the Moro Islamic Liberation Front in the Philippines, the Lashkar-e-Taiba of Pakistan, and the rebel movement in Chechnya.

A number of these groups will post information using different languages so that a maximum number of viewers can have access to their propaganda. For example, Islamic State, Hamas, and Hezbollah have English versions on their websites. Moreover, the number of terrorist and extremist groups using the web increases exponentially.

HS Web Link: To learn more about the Hamas website, go to http://www.qassam.ps/.

These websites often contain a substantial amount of information and serve a number of purposes. Weimann (2004) researched these websites and identified the following elements as fairly consistently included on extremist and terrorist websites:

1. History of the organization and its activities
2. Review of its social and political background
3. Accounts of its accomplishments and exploits
4. Biographies of its leaders, founders, and heroes
5. Information on political and ideological aims
6. Criticism of its enemies
7. Up-to-date news about the group's activities
8. Maps of territory controlled or areas of conflict with enemies

HS ANALYSIS BOX 10-5

Search the web and find a terrorist website such as the ones operated by Hamas or Hezbollah. Eight different elements are present in terrorist websites. See how many elements are contained in the website that you identify.

Generally, these groups do not discuss their terrorist campaigns on their websites, with the exception of Hamas and Hezbollah. The Islamic State and other terrorist groups also have their own websites on the darkweb. They tend to concentrate on the social and moral bases for their legitimacy. The avoidance of violence and terrorist tactics is an effort to build the organization's image. Hamas and Hezbollah, on the other hand, often provide statistics on the number of their enemies who have been killed and lists of dead martyrs. They appeal to militant individuals in hopes of recruiting them for their cause.

Audiences

Terrorist groups engage in public relations campaigns. They must disseminate information to recruit new members. Information dispensed to the general public is also used to solicit funding and to generate public support. An analysis of the websites' content revealed that the groups were targeting three different audiences (Weimann, 2004).

The first audience is current and potential supporters. Websites allow the group to communicate its message to members and to recruit new members. Providing constant information and propaganda helps maintain a level of commitment. Hats, tee shirts, and other items with the group's slogans and insignias are also marketed to help show a presence in the target area. The website is also used to demonize the group's enemies, helping maintain commitment to the cause. A substantial amount of recruitment and radicalization occur on the Internet (Holt, Freilich, and Chermak, 2016; Weimann, 2016).

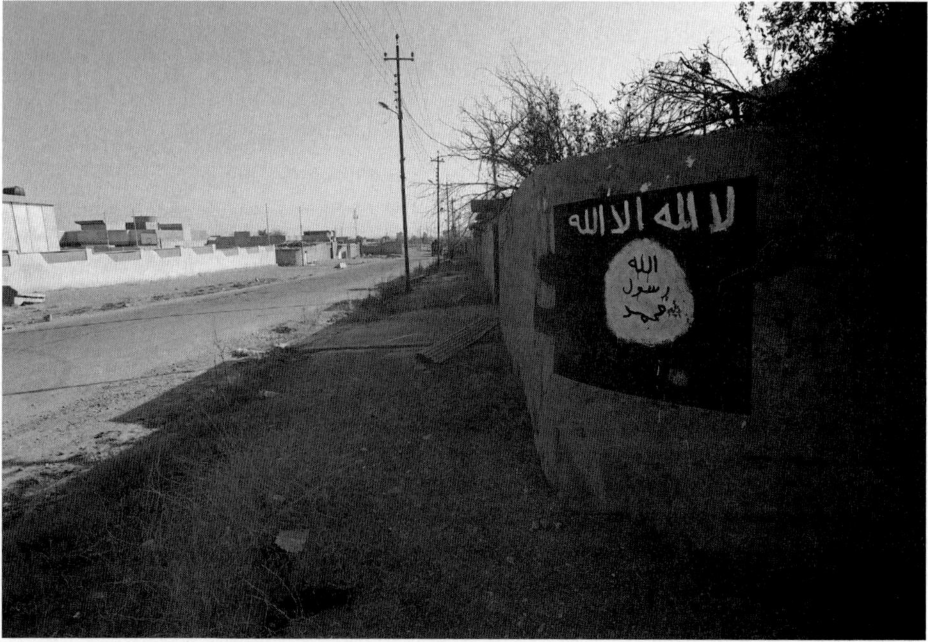

Terrorist groups like ISIS use every opportunity and method to spread their propaganda. Ali Salim/Newzulu/Newscom.

The second audience is international public opinion. Many of the websites are posted in different languages so that they can reach a wider audience. The widespread reach of information via the Internet allows individuals who are not directly involved in the movement, but who have an interest, to gain information about the group's current affairs. These websites are also aimed at journalists. The website can be used to feed positive information about the organization and its activities and to demonize enemies to journalists and the larger population. The groups hope the websites can mediate some of the negative publicity that they receive elsewhere.

Finally, these websites are aimed at their enemies. Information on the sites is used to demoralize the enemy. They attempt to convince citizens who are not directly involved in the conflict but who are aligned with the enemy to morally question their leaders' objectives and tactics. It is an attempt to generate debate or divide constituents in enemy camps. The websites attempt to deconstruct the rationale used by the opposition to create uncertainty.

How Terrorists Use the Internet

Terrorists use the Internet for a variety of purposes, often depending on the targeted audience. For the most part, Weimann (2004) has identified eight distinct uses.

Psychological Warfare

The Internet is a convenient tool for conducting psychological warfare. Terrorists can use the Internet to spread disinformation about their enemies. Spreading disinformation can undermine their efforts to secure support and materials to wage war. It is also used to instill fear. Accounts, pictures, and videos of attacks and deaths are used to develop a sense of hopelessness on the part of the enemy. For example, al Qaeda often releases information about impending massive attacks on the United States. McNeal (2007–2008) found that al Qaeda and other terrorist groups released exaggerated statistics relative to the number of Americans killed in Iraq and Afghanistan and videos depicting executions of Americans. Such information also raises the morale of the group's fighters.

As discussed earlier, in 2015, the Islamic State leaked the names, addresses, and photos of 100 U.S. military members, directing its members to kill those on the list (Brennan and Bleier, 2015). It was a psychological coup for ISIS in that it demonstrated their hacking skills in retrieving the information and it resulted in psychological stress on the part of the soldiers on the list. The web provides opportunities for psychological warfare to target specific audiences. In early 2012, a computer graphic stating "Al Qaeda Coming Soon Again in New York" was posted on a website that had posted terrorist and al Qaeda–related material before. The New York Police Department (NYPD) Intelligence Division described the website as a Category 1 website, meaning that is was heavily used by jihadi and al Qaeda adherents. The posting was investigated by the NYPD and the FBI's Joint Terrorism Task Force (Dienst and Prokupecz, 2012). The posting was an effort to cause panic in the city.

Publicity and Propaganda

The Internet contains a wealth of information. When people read documents from the Internet, they too often believe the information to be correct or true. However, there is no vetting process for information that is posted on the Internet. People essentially can say whatever they desire. Thus, the Internet is ripe with unbridled verbiage of all sorts. Terrorists have direct control over the content of their websites and essentially can target a number of audiences.

Terrorists use three structures to justify their rhetoric. First, they note that they have no choice but to resort to violence. Violence appeals to others who are resigned to the social, political, and economic conditions. Terrorists can argue that governments or other enemies are exacting greater harm on society as compared to the terrorists' violence. Terrorists portray themselves as being persecuted and that their violence is aimed at the persecutors. The objective is to convince others to evaluate how they are being treated, or how they perceive they are being treated, and join with the terrorists overtly or covertly.

Second, they attempt to portray themselves as freedom fighters who were forced into action. They portray the enemy, especially target governments, as ruthless, hostile, and violent. They often point to social injustice and economic ills suffered by the terrorists and their supporters, whereas the government is corrupt and wasting money on its friends. The propaganda is in terms of the "common man against the rich criminals."

Third, they often mix the rhetoric of peace and nonviolence on their websites to insinuate that they desire only a peaceful existence, whereas the other side only makes war against the downtrodden. This posture also is used to solicit support from a variety of quarters, including the international community. As Thomas (2003) noted, the Internet

> empowers small groups and makes them appear much more capable than they might be, even turning bluster into a type of virtual fear. The net allows terrorists to amplify the consequences of their activities with follow-on messages and threats directly to the population at large, even though the terrorist group may be totally impotent. In effect, the Internet allows a person or group to appear to be larger or more important than they really are. (pp. 115–16)

Data Mining

The Internet has exhaustive information on almost everything, and terrorists can use the Internet to collect intelligence on their enemies. In many cases, descriptions and maps of targets can be obtained from the Internet. For example, Goggle now offers satellite images of all locations in the United States and many other countries. In 2006, the Islamic Army in Iraq circulated information on how to aim rockets at U.S. military sites using Google Earth (Eisler, 2008). The Internet provides information about employees, operations, and infrastructure that can be used to develop intelligence for targets.

Fund-raising

The Internet can be used to distribute propaganda to increase the level of sympathy for a cause. It can entice support. The Internet can be used to solicit contributions from a group, region, country, or worldwide. Oftentimes, these sites provide bank codes through which money can be deposited. There are ample examples of where terrorist groups have used this ploy to raise money in the United States.

Recruitment and Mobilization

The Internet is a useful tool in recruitment. Indeed, it is commonly used by governments and business and industry throughout the world for this purpose. Terrorists often post propaganda with religious decrees and anti-American rhetoric. They have chat rooms where they attempt to convince recruits to join their cause. These chat rooms allow for a fairly intimate contact from thousands of miles away. For example, the first trial and guilty verdict of a man who recruited terrorists for the Islamic State took place in 2016/2017 in Arizona. Ahmed Mohammed el-Gammal, 44, of Avondale, Arizona, faces a minimum of 10 and a maximum of 55 years in prison. U.S. District Judge Edgardo Ramos stated that these types of trials will become more common due to the backward-looking social media posts (Riley, 2017).

Networking

The Internet allows for terrorist groups such as Islamic State, Hamas, and al Qaeda to maintain contact with individual cells and individual members. Emails and other information can be sent from any location with Internet access. Since emails can be routed through a number of servers across several countries, it becomes difficult to locate their origin. The Internet also makes it possible for groups to better communicate and coordinate activities with other like-minded groups. This networking is especially critical when these groups coordinate an attack.

Sharing Information

The web has numerous sites that contain information that can assist terrorists. These sites contain information on bomb making, tactics, poisons, assassinations, anti-surveillance methods, and so on. In many cases, the information is very detailed. To some extent, the Internet serves a valuable online training and education function for terrorists. The darkweb has become a common tool for terrorist group to recruit and mentor new members, buy and distribute weapons, and launch cyberattacks.

Planning and Coordination

The Islamic State operatives extensively use the Internet to coordinate terrorist attacks across the globe, including the attack on Paris in 2015 and Munich in 2016. In many cases, terrorists use plain language or unsophisticated codes on open sites. In other cases, the terrorists are using secure websites, making infiltration difficult. Regardless, the Internet serves as an easy, convenient platform for coordinating their activities (Callimachi, 2017).

It is important for us to enhance our monitoring of the Internet. Since it is open, we too may be able to glean valuable intelligence information from it. Anyone can post anything no matter how inflammatory or untrue, and we cannot control the content. We are now fighting information with information—increasing our postings and websites to counter the incorrect information that is being posted by the terrorists.

Terrorists and Social Media

Social media, for many people, has become an integral part of their lives. People spend countless hours on Facebook, Twitter, LinkedIn, and YouTube. Social media is now engrained in culture and is indispensable to many people. Therefore, it goes to reason that terrorists would use social media to assist them in accomplishing their objectives. For example, Anwar al-Awlaki, an American turned Muslim radical associated with al Qaeda, preached that Muslims should attack the United States using YouTube. American Colleen R. LaRose from Philadelphia, who was dubbed G.I. Jane, posted YouTube videos on the Internet under the name Jihad Jane in an effort to recruit jihadist fighters and to help Muslims overseas (Barrett, 2011). She also agreed to kill a Swedish cartoonist after viewing and commenting on YouTube videos.

A number of terrorist organizations are now using social media. For example, Hamas has begun tweeting under the names @hamasinfo and @AlqassamBrigade and others (Torossian, 2012). Similarly, the Islamic State used Facebook and Twitter extensively. Several security experts are warning that terrorist groups such as ISIS and al Qaeda could use digital mercenaries by jihadist groups. Even if terrorist groups do not have cyberattack capabilities, they can easily buy them on the darkweb (Michael, 2017). ISIS also had its own hacker unit, the cybercaliphate, which has shown their ability to hack into companies, such as Newsweek. Social media are a very effective method of communication, planning attacks, impersonation, taking over accounts of innocent users, leaking information, and social engineering. There are more than 3.5 billion social media accounts. About 74 percent of Internet users have active social profiles and 39 percent have accepted friend requests from people they don't know. In addition, there is zero visibility to the traditional enterprise security structure. In other words, terrorists have easy access, the trust of Internet users, and are invisible. It is believed that ISIS held about 50,000 Twitter accounts even though Twitter is actively closing known terrorist accounts. ISIS had six proclaimed goals for which they use social media: (1) recruit to their cause; (2) consolidate local support and increase territorial control; (3) establish a single Islamic State for Syria and Iraq; (4) raise funds; (5) spread propaganda to incite fear, especially in the Western World; and (6) manipulate the military tactics of their adversaries for use toward their own agenda (Foster and Geers, 2017). To counter and monitor terrorist activities in the social media, the Open Source Center in the CIA now monitors social media. The CIA is data mining collecting information about terrorist organizations and their activities. Additionally, there have been calls from congress to shut down terrorist websites and to prevent them from using social media. Twitter has shut down thousands of terrorist accounts in the past year and Facebook actively monitors and shuts down terrorist Facebook accounts.

► Agencies Charged with Combating Cyber Terrorism

The FBI and the Department of Homeland Security are charged with investigating and countering domestic cyber terrorism. The Department of Defense is also involved in cyber security from an international perspective especially as it related to defense.

FBI's Cybercrime Division

The FBI is charged with investigating cybercrimes, including cyber terrorism. The bureau's mission is

> first and foremost, to stop those behind the most serious computer intrusions and the spread of malicious code; second, to identify and thwart online sexual predators who use the Internet to meet and exploit children and to produce, possess, or share child pornography; third, to counteract operations that target U.S. intellectual property, endangering our national security and competitiveness; and fourth, to dismantle national and transnational organized criminal enterprises engaging in Internet fraud. Pursuant to the National Strategy to Secure Cyberspace signed by the President, the Department of Justice and the FBI lead the national effort to investigate and prosecute cybercrime. (FBI, 2008)

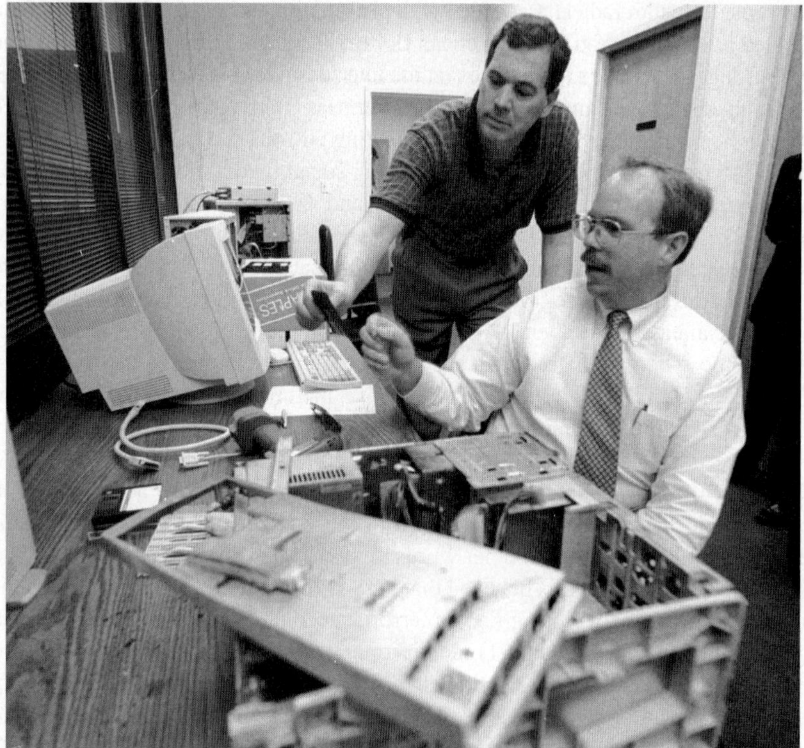

An FBI agent working in the computer forensics lab.
FBI.

In order to accomplish this mission, the FBI has created a cyber division containing three units. Cyber squads are located at headquarters and in the 56 field offices. The cyber squads protect against and investigate computer intrusions and theft of intellectual property and personal information. Cyber action teams (CATs) consist of highly trained computer forensics and malicious code experts. The CATs investigate cyber threats nationally and internationally. As an example of how the CATs operate, in 2006, CATs were sent to Turkey and Morocco to investigate Zotob, a malicious code designed to steal credit card information. The CATs worked with Turkish and Moroccan authorities to arrest the perpetrators. The virus resulted in a large number of computers crashing in several countries. The FBI has also created overseas programs to face the global cyber threat and deploys agents to work directly with foreign partners. The CATs are able to collect intelligence information about different types of computer intrusions because of their international work. Computer Crimes Task Forces are teams of FBI agents who work with other federal and state law enforcement, tracking down sexual predators, scammers, and other criminals by back-tracing emails and posing as online victims.

The FBI also is a member of the national cyber investigative task force. The task force consists of 20 agencies from law enforcement, the intelligence community, and the department of defense. It coordinates and supports cyber threats. It focuses on terrorists, spies, and criminals who attempt to exploit our nation's IT systems (FBI, 2017).

HS Web Link: To learn more about the FBI's cyber investigation activities, go to https://www.fbi.gov/investigate/cyber.

Department of Homeland Security's Cyber Security Systems

The Department of Homeland Security has a number of programs designed to further cyber security in the United States. The national cyber security protection system works with all civilian federal departments to detect intrusions and provide intrusion prevention in an effort to safeguard the federal IT system. It essentially sets IT standards. One of the programs within the national cyber security protection system is EINSTEIN, which provides the federal government with an early warning system for intrusion threats. Another program is the continuous diagnostics and mitigation program, which provides federal departments with cyber security resources. The national cyber security and communications integration center is a 24/7 center, where intrusions are reported and shared with the federal government, intelligence community, and law enforcement. The center contains the U.S. computer emergency readiness team, which analyzes intrusions and provides risk information to governments and the private sector. The industrial control systems cyber emergency response team works to reduce risks with all critical infrastructure sectors in coordination with government agencies and the private sectors. Here, the various infrastructure sector systems are analyzed for possible problems. The DHS's programs focus on identifying cyber intrusions and notifying governments and the private sector so they can be mitigated quickly.

Even though there are areas of duplication in the FBI's and DHS's programming, it appears that the FBI has the primary responsibility of investigating cybercrimes and terrorism, and the DHS is charged with monitoring the cyber infrastructure and providing national and international law enforcement with information about cyberattacks and prevention measures.

HS Web Link: To learn more about the Department of Homeland Security's cyber security, go to https://www.dhs.gov/xlibrary/assets/pso-safeguarding-and-securing-cyberspace.pdf.

Summary

This chapter examined cyber terrorism, and cybercrimes received some attention since they often are intermingled in terms of discussions and investigations. As noted in the *National Infrastructure Protection Plan* (2006), cyber resources are one of the primary infrastructures that require protection. Our cyber and communications system represents a national nervous system by which business, social, and security activities are conducted and coordinated. Our cyber system is crucial to our nation's well-being since we depend so heavily on the Internet communications infrastructure.

Government, technology groups, and others have advocated that our cyber security is lacking substantially. They advise that we are vulnerable to a variety of attacks from across the globe. Numerous studies document cyber intrusions and the potential costs incurred by them. Indeed, there are thousands of attacks on American computers and networks on a daily basis, but these attacks originate primarily from nonterrorist hackers and groups who attempt to gain access to financial information or play a game by planting malicious viruses, codes, and worms. Even though these attacks are not terrorist originated, the outcomes are the same—we must protect our cyber infrastructure. We must continually invest in software and hardware that protects our massive networks from intrusions.

The Internet has become a tool used by terrorists, and all the major terrorist organizations have websites to promote their organization and activities. These websites play a key role in terrorists' recruitment, communications and coordination, and fund-raising. The Internet has substantial appeal to terrorists since it serves many purposes and is an inexpensive tool requiring little training. The Internet and these websites allow terrorist groups to communicate with a variety of audiences, spewing their propaganda unabated. Essentially, it is the most effective communications modality used by terrorists. The United States and other countries engaged in the war on terrorism likely have not devoted enough resources to counter terrorists' use of the Internet.

Finally, the two federal agencies primarily engaged in securing our cyber infrastructure are the Federal Bureau of Investigation and the Department of Homeland Security's National Cyber Security Division. The FBI is responsible for investigating incidents of cyber terrorism, but the bureau is also responsible for investigating a host of other cyber criminal activities. On the other hand, the National Cyber Security Division is responsible for communicating cyber threats to the computing community and coordinating responses should there be a significant breach in our cyber infrastructure.

Discussion Questions

1. Distinguish cybercrime, terrorism, and warfare.
2. Describe the methods of attacking cyber infrastructure.
3. Why would a cyberattack be appealing to terrorists?
4. How do terrorists use the Internet?
5. What kinds of extremist groups have websites and how do they use them?
6. How do terrorists use the Social Media?
7. Compare the FBI and DHS in terms of their mission relative to cybercrime and terrorism.

References

Arquilla, J., D. Ronfeldt, and M Zanini. (2003). "Networks, netwar, and information-age terrorism." *Terrorism and Counterterrorism*, ed. R. Howard and R. Sawyer, pp. 96–119. New York: McGraw-Hill.

Barlow, J. (1990). *Crime and Puzzlement: Desperados of the Data-Sphere*. http://www.sjgames.com/SS/crimpuzz.html (Accessed June 8, 2010).

Barrett, D. (2011). "Jihad Jane, Colleen LaRose, recruited terrorists and plotted murder, prosecutors say." *Huff Post*. http://www.huffingtonpost.com/2010/03/09/jihad-jane-colleen-larose_n_492586.html (Accessed November 27, 2012).

Beatty, A. (2015). "China under suspicion as US admits huge data hack." https://www.yahoo.com/news/us-data-4-million-government-staff-hacked-213714141.html?ref=gs (Accessed May 11, 2016).

Begos, K. (2016). *Protecting the Power Grid. Can Attacks Be Prevented?* CQ Press.

Bennett, B., and W. J. Hennigan. (2015). "China, Russia hacks target spies." *Los Angeles Times* (August 31): A1, A4.

Borstin, J. (2015). "The Sony hack: One year later." CNBC (November 24).

Brennan, C., and E. Bleier. (2015). "Army tells soldiers to get security systems and not meet up with anyone they've met online after ISIS leaks 100 military members' names, photos and addresses." *Daily Mail*. http://www.dailymail.co.uk/news/article-3017220/Army-tells-soldiers-security-systems-not-meet-meet-online-ISIS-leaks-100-military-members-names-photos-addresses.html (Accessed April 15, 2015).

Burke, S. E., and E. Scheider. (2015). Who's afraid of the big bad pulse? *Slate* (July 2).

Callimachi, R. (2017). "Not 'lone wolves' after all: How ISIS guides world's terrorist plots from afar." *The New York Times* (February 4).

Carafano, J. (2008). *When Electrons Attack: Cyber Strikes on Georgia a Wake-up Call for Congress*. Heritage Foundation. http://www.heritage.org/Research/NationalSecurity/wm2022.cfm (Accessed November 28, 2008).

Clarke, R. (2008). *Against All Enemies*. New York: RAC Enterprises.

Clarke, R., and R. Knake. (2010). *Cyber War: The Next Threat to National Security and What to Do about It*. New York: HarperCollins.

Cyber Security Intelligence. (2016). *Cyber Attacks Do More Damage than Physical Attacks*. https://www.cybersecurityintelligence.com/blog/cyber-attacks-do-more-damage-than-physical-attacks-1748.html (Accessed March 2017).

Denning, D. (2001). *Is Cyber Terror Next?* http://essays.ssrc.org/sept11/essays/denning.htm (Accessed June 15, 2010).

Department of Homeland Security. (2008). *National Cyber Security Division*. http://www.dhs.gov/xabout/structure/editorial_0839.shtm (Accessed December 2, 2008).

Department of Homeland Security. (2006). *National Infrastructure Protection Plan*. Washington, D.C.: Author.

Department of Justice. (2016). *Computer Hacking Conspiracy Charges Unsealed against Members of Syrian Electronic Party*. https://www.justice.gov/opa/pr/computer-hacking-conspiracy-charges-unsealed-against-members-syrian-electronic-army (Accessed March 2017).

Dienst, J., and S. Prokupecz. (2012). "FBI, NYPD investigate new terror threat graphic mentioning NYC." *NBC New York*. http://www.nbcnewyork.com/news/local/Al-Qaeda-Coming-Soon-Again-Threat-NYC-Forum-Website-145830735.html (Accessed April 4, 2012).

Eisler, P. (2008). "Google Earth helps yet worries government." *US Today* (November 6).http://www.usatoday.com/tech/news/surveillance/2008-11-06-googleearth_N.htm (Accessed December 5, 2008).

Express Web Desk. (2016). "26/11 Mumbai terror attacks: Here's what happened at Taj Mahal Hotel, Trident Oberoi, Nariman House." *The Indian Express* (November 3).

Federal Bureau of Investigation. (2017). *National Cyber Investigative Joint Task Force*. https://www.fbi.gov/investigate/cyber/national-cyber-investigative-joint-task-force (Accessed August 31, 2017).

Federal Bureau of Investigation. (2008). Webpage. http://www.fbi.gov/cyberinvest/cyberhome.htm (Accessed November 28, 2008).

Foster, J. C., and Geers, K. (2017). *Terror Gone Social: The Islamic State and Social Media*. RSA Conference Presentation.

Fox-Brewster, T. (2016). "Hackers sell $7,500 IoT Cannon to bring down the Internet." *Forbes*.

Furnell, S., and M. Warren. (1999). "Computer hacking and cyber terrorism: The real threats in the new millennium?" *Computers & Society*, 18: 28–34.

Genova, A. (2016). "Your system failed to tackle our attacks. Now we will crush you again: Pro-ISIS hackers post 'kill list' of US government department employees." http://www.dailymail.co.uk/news/article-3558714/Your-failed-tackle-attacks-crush-Pro-ISIS-hackers-post-kill-list-State-Department-employees.html (Accessed May 5, 2016).

Hoffman, B. (2006). *Inside Terrorism*. New York: Columbia University Press.

Holt, T., J. Freilich, and S. Chermak. (2016). "Internet-based radicalization as enculturation to violent deviant subculture." *Deviant Behavior*, 38: 855–869.

Hume, T. (2016). "Munich gunman planned attack for a year, experts say." *CNN News* (July 24).

InfoSec Institute. (2016). *The Ferizi Case: The First Man Charged with Cyber Terrorism*. http://resources.infosecinstitute.com/the-ferizi-case-the-first-man-charged-with-cyber-terrorism/#gref (Accessed March 2017).

Johnson, Jeh C. (2015). *Remarks Made by the Secretary of Homeland Security Jeh C. Johnson at Cybercon 2015*. Office of Homeland Security.

Kane, J. (2011). "Virtual terrain, lethal potential: Toward achieving security in an ungoverned domain." *Toward a Grand Strategy Against Terrorism*, ed. C. Harmon, A. Pratt, and S. Gorka, pp. 252–281. New York: McGraw-Hill.

Kremez, V. (2017). *Psychology of an Eastern European Cybercriminals: Mindset Drives Behavior*. RSA Conference Presentation.

Lewis, J. (2006). "Cybersecurity and critical infrastructure protection." *Homeland Security: Protecting America's Targets (Vol.3)*, ed. J. Forest, pp. 324–328. Westport, CT: Praeger Security International.

Marlin, S., and M. Garvin. (2004). "Disaster-recovery spending on the rise." *Information Week* (August 9): 26.

Martin, D. (2016). *Russian Hack Almost Brought the U.S. Military to Its Knees*. CBS News.

McNeal, G. (2007–2008). "Cyber embargo: Countering the Internet Jihad." *Case Western Reserve*. http://www.usdoj.gov/criminal/cybercrime/cyberstalking.htm (Accessed November 28, 2008).

Michael, T. (2017). "JIHACKERS. Threat of jihadi cyber attack 'very real' as experts warn of dangers of mercenary hackers being employed by ISIS." *The Sun* (January 28).

National Intelligence Council. (2017). *Assessing Russian Activities and Intentions in Recent US Elections*. Office of the Director of National Intelligence.

O'Brien, C. (2014). "Hacker feel right at home: Routers, TVs, DVRs, even refrigerators are being taken over to do Internet dirty work." *The Los Angeles Times* (March 23): A1, A9.

Office of the Press Secretary. (2013). *Presidential Policy Directive – Critical Infrastructure Security and Resilience*. The White House.

Park, D. (2016). *North Korea Cyber Attacks*. The Henry M. Jackson School of Cyberstudies.

Pham, S. (2016). *Got a Hacked Yahoo Account? Here Is What You Should Do*. CNN Tech.

Pollitt, M. (undated). *Cyberterrorism: Fact or Fantasy*. http://www.cs.georgetown.edu/~denning/infosec/pollitt.html (Accessed November 28, 2008).

Rattray, G. (2003). "The cyberterrorism threat." *Terrorism and Counterterrorism: Understanding the New Security Environment*, ed. R. Howard and R. Sawyer, pp. 221–245. Guilford, CT: McGraw-Hill.

Riley, M., B. Elgin, D. Lawrence, and C. Matlack. (2014). *Missed Alarms and 40 Million Stolen Credit Card Numbers. How Target Blew It.* Bloomberg.

Riley, J. (2017). "Man found guilty in Islamic State recruiting trial, faces up to 55 years in prison." *Newsday* (January 30).

Shorrock, T. (2008). *Spies for Hire: The Secret World of Intelligence Outsourcing*. New York: Simon & Schuster.

Stohl, M. (2006). "Cyber terrorism: A clear and present danger, the sum of all fears, breaking point or patriot games." *Crime, Law, and Social Change*, 46: 223–238.

Taylor, R., T. Caeti, D. Loper, E. Tritsch, and J. Liederbach. (2006). *Digital Crime and Digital Terrorism*. Upper Saddle, NJ: Prentice Hall.

The Guardian. (2011). Mass blackout hits California, Arizona, and Mexico. https://www.theguardian.com/world/2011/sep/09/blackout-california-arizona-mexico-san-diego (Accessed March 8, 2017).

Thomas, T. (2003). "Al Qaeda and the internet: The danger of cyberplanning." *Parameters*, 33(1): 112–123.

Tisdall, S. (2017). "North Korea rocket test ups ante with belligerent Trump administration." *The Guardian* (March 19).

Torossian, R. (2012). "Why allow terrorists to use social media? *Frontpagemag.com*. (November 19). http://frontpagemag.com/2012/ronn-torossian/why-allow-terrorists-to-use-social-media/ (Accessed November 27, 2012).

Verizon Enterprise. (2016). 2016 Data Breach Investigations Report. Verizon. http://www.verizonenterprise.com/resources/reports/rp_DBIR_2016_Report_en_xg.pdf (Accessed December 4, 2017).

Verizon Enterprise. (2017). *2016 Data Breach Investigations Report*. Verizon.

Wagstaff, K. (2016). "Big paydays force hospitals to prepare for ransomware attacks." *NBS News*.

Weimann G. (2016) "The emerging role of social media in the recruitment of foreign fighters." *Foreign Fighters under International Law and Beyond*, ed. A. de Guttry, F. Capone, and C. Paulussen. The Hague: T.M.C. Asser Press.

Weimann, G. (2005). "Cyber terrorism: The sum of all fears?" *Studies in Conflict and Terrorism*, 28: 129–149.

Weimann, G. (2004). *Cyberterrorism: How Real Is the Threat.* Special Report. Washington, D.C.: United States Institute of Peace.

Wilson, C. (2005). *Computer Attack and Cyberterrorism: Vulnerabilities and Policy Issues for Congress*. Washington, D.C.: Congressional Research Service.

Winton, R. (2016). "We may never know why the San Bernardino terrorists targeted a Christmas party. Here's what we know." *L.A. Times* (December 2).

11 Terrorist Financing

LEARNING OBJECTIVES

1. *Explain how the terrorists financed the 9/11 attacks.*
2. *Explain the difference between money laundering and terrorist financing.*
3. *Discuss how the United States is attempting to reduce terrorist financing.*
4. *Describe how terrorist organizations raise money.*
5. *Describe how terrorist groups move money.*
6. *Discuss identity fraud and identity theft.*
7. *Explain how breeder documents work.*

Key Terms

Terrorist Finance Tracking Program
Society for Worldwide Interbank Financial Telecommunication
Money Laundering
Terrorist Financing
Due Diligence
Financial Action Task Force on Money Laundering
Zakat
Hawala
Wahhabism
Identity Fraud
Identity Theft
Real ID Act
Breeder Document

Introduction

The United States, as well as other countries, is engaged in an all-out effort to combat terrorism. These efforts are being applied on a number of fronts using a variety of strategies and tactics. Our efforts are not restricted to battlefields such as those in Syria, Iraq, and Afghanistan, but they also involve multiple strategies in the economic arena. Terrorism is a cancer on the world, and one method by which to defeat it is to starve it—deny or eliminate the funding terror organizations require to operate. If terrorist finances can be substantially reduced and in some cases eliminated, it will contribute to our successes on other fronts. Today, the U.S. government is using a variety of means to reduce the amount of funds available to terrorist organizations. It is a difficult task since these organizations have developed a variety of means to raise money for their deplorable acts. Methods used by terrorists to raise money include (1) criminal activities such as bank robbery, kidnapping, extortion, and narcotics trafficking; (2) donations from local and foreign supporters; (3) assistance from supportive nation-states; (4) contributions from wealthy individuals and organizations; (5) white-collar crime; (6) revenues from legitimate businesses; and (7) sale of oil and gas. Nonetheless, we must press on and "drain the swamp" or eliminate as many funding sources as possible.

Globalization has substantially hindered our efforts to reduce terrorist financing. Globalization has led to the free flow of information and money across countries with few limitations. Citibank alone moves $3 trillion on an average day and $9 trillion on peak days in business and international financial flows. These transactions by Citibank constitute more than half of the U.S. Gross Domestic Product (GDP). Almost all of these monies are moved electronically. Banks are also moving toward digital currency, that is, an Internet-based form of currency. The Chief Executive Officer (CEO) of Citibank, Michael Corbat, announced that they are working on becoming the first digital bank. One of the incentives for banks is an increase in customers. Corbat estimates that a 10 percent increase in digital currency would bring about 220 million people into the banking system (Corbat, 2014). This vast amount of money and number of transfers are making it increasingly more difficult to distinguish legitimate transactions from those that are associated with illegal enterprises such as terrorist financing—it is akin to searching for a needle in a haystack. Essentially, there are few international boundaries today, and a number of countries are safe havens for money laundering and illegal finance. Transnational organized crime groups have taken advantage of these conditions, and terrorist organizations have followed. They are adept at hiding their money within this complex of financial transactions.

Prior to the 9/11 attacks, the federal government had done very little to counter global money laundering. Partisan politics held these financial issues in a congressional logjam. For the most part, the Democrats were interested in greater oversight or control with laws aimed at tax evaders and white-collar crime. The Republicans, on the other hand, were opposed to federal laws on the grounds that such laws were intrusive, and they favored the deregulation of the American and world finance systems. They were also opposed to such legislation since it likely would target wealthy individuals and corporations (see Malkin, 2002; Weintraub, 2001). Thus, it was only after the shock of 9/11 that Congress and the president pursued money laundering and terrorist financing in earnest. Even then, there were gaps in policies. Shortly after the 9/11 attacks, President George W. Bush pledged to Congress that his administration would starve terrorist organizations, and in fact, officials had frozen almost $200 million in assets belonging to suspected terrorist groups and fronts. Although all sorts of groups and countries had been targeted by these renewed tactics, the government neglected to take any action against Saudi Arabia's assets, even though a substantial amount of terrorist funding came from the Saudis. The Saudis were seen as allies, and the Bush administration did not want to embarrass them (Armstrong, 2004; Prados and Blanchard, 2004). Indeed, some have questioned governments' willingness and ability to counter money laundering (Naylor, 2006). This late and haphazard attack on terrorist funding created an open window for terrorists to move substantial amounts of money by which to organize and orchestrate attacks.

Limiting terrorist organizations' finances by the United States and other countries represents an important tool in the war against terrorism. The **Terrorist Finance Tracking Program** (TFTP) was established to identify, track, pursue, and disrupt the terrorist network (U.S. Department of Treasury, 2016b). Depriving terrorists of money can contribute to two important outcomes. First, it can directly or indirectly affect a terrorist organization's leadership, morale, and legitimacy. If funding is reduced, it likely will result in a reduction of support from members, other terrorist organizations, and the community at large. Terrorist organizations' wealth or access to money is demonstrable of their relative power. Without this wealth, they are seen as being weaker by their constituents and enemies. It can lead to organizational instability. Second, it may have strategic implications. It may force a group to alter its intentions—the group may not have the resources to carry out a planned attack. Strategically, the group then must abandon its plans or opt to attack a less desirable target. Both of these scenarios are positive in that they result in less destruction (Financial Action Task Force, 2008). One of the greatest assets to the U.S. Treasury Department is a company in Belgium. The U.S. Treasury Department issues subpoenas to the

Society for Worldwide Interbank Financial Telecommunication (SWIFT), which supplies messaging services to thousands of financial institutions worldwide. The United States, in an agreement with the European Union, had to agree that they would only use the information received by SWIFT for counterterrorism measures. The SWIFT data has been imperative in identifying terrorist networks, locate operatives, and restrain the terrorists' access to money (U.S. Department of Treasury, 2016a).

For the most part, we have measured our successes in defeating terrorist financing by the amount of terrorist money that has been seized. Levitt and Jacobson (2008) advised that this is an inadequate strategy:

> Unfortunately, the metrics most often used assess efforts against terrorist financing—the total amount of money seized and the overall designations—are both inadequate and misleading. The Achilles heel of terrorism financiers is not at the fundraising end, but rather at the *choke points* critical to laundering and transferring funds. It is impossible to "dry the swap" of funds available for illicit purposes, but by targeting key nodes in the financing network, we can constrict the operating environment to the point that terrorists will not be able to obtain funds where and when they need them. (p. 3)

This chapter examines these issues in detail. As Levitt and Jacobson noted, the transfer of funds or money laundering is different from raising capital. These activities are distinguished here. This chapter provides information on the financing process and how money is laundered or moved from legitimate sources to terrorist organizations. The various federal agencies involved in countering terrorist financing (attacking choke points) are examined as well as the tools that we currently are using to reduce the flow of money to terrorist organizations. The methods used by terrorist organizations to raise money are examined. For the most part, this chapter focuses on al Qaeda and Islamic State (ISIS) financing since these groups have the most developed systems, they are the most dangerous terrorist organizations, and they have been examined extensively. ISIS emerged in mid-2014 and has reinvented financing their terrorist activities in a variety of ways. First, the money trail for the 9/11 attacks is outlined.

Terrorist Financing of the 9/11 Attacks

The 9/11 Commission (2004) thoroughly investigated the financing of the 9/11 attacks. It is illustrative to examine how the 9/11 attacks were financed since it identifies several of the methods used by terrorists to acquire and move money. It also demonstrates the complexity of money movement and the difficulty for governments to identify and intercept terrorist financial movements. The terrorists and their supporters use the world's enormous global financial system to mask their operations. As a corollary, governments, including that of the United States, must implement procedures that examine even relatively small money transfers. The 9/11 Commission estimated that the attacks cost between $400,000 and $500,000, and the money was moved using several transfers of only several thousand dollars.

Although investigators did not learn where the money originated, it appears that the 9/11 attacks were financed largely through the terrorists' Hamburg cell and coordinated by Khalid Sheikh Muhammad. The Hamburg cell received its funding from al Qaeda. The hijackers, selected from various al Qaeda training camps, were pilots and muscle men. The pilots received additional flight training in the United States, and the muscle men were given training to enable them to physically control passengers and commandeer the airplanes. As they moved from one country to another, they received payments of a few thousand dollars to cover expenses. At one point, several of the hijackers received $10,000 each to purchase forged identity documents and travel from Saudi Arabia to the United States.

HS Web Link: To learn more about the financing of the 9/11 attacks, go to https://govinfo.library.unt.edu/911/staff_statements/911_TerrFin_Monograph.pdf.

According to the 9/11 Commission, approximately $300,000 was deposited in bank accounts in the United States. The money was moved here by (1) bank transfers to U.S. banks, (2) hijackers carrying traveler's checks into the United States, and (3) credit or debit cards used to access foreign bank accounts. The money was used for pilots' lessons and living expenses. A substantial amount of the money came from two financers in the United Arab Emirates. The money was wired to a number of American banks, including banks in California, New York, Florida, and Oklahoma, and in some cases, the money moved through Canadian banks. Money also was wired to the terrorists through Western Union.

After the attacks, there was some speculation that at least some of the funding came from within the United States. However, the 9/11 Commission found that "no credible evidence exists that the hijackers received any substantial funding from any person in the United States" (p. 138). They were funded by al Qaeda and its supporters using an intricate money-laundering scheme and avoiding detection by authorities.

The 9/11 attacks show the intricacy of funding such attacks. Since they were funded with multiple transfers of relatively small amounts of money, terrorist financial operations can be very difficult to detect, so difficult that they were hard to disentangle until after the fact. It appears that terrorists, especially al Qaeda, are adept at using a variety of funding sources to finance their plots. The mechanisms to discover and disrupt terrorist financing before 9/11 did not fail; they essentially were not designed to uncover the type of transactions that financed the 9/11 attacks.

The 9/11 Commission advised that it is unlikely that terrorist financing can be stopped. The Global Economy Survey estimates that 2–5 percent or $1–2 trillion annually are global money laundering transactions and less than 1 percent of these transactions are currently seized by authorities (PWC, 2016). It would require a collaborative, effective response from a number of countries to combat the problem of money laundering and terrorist financing, which is unlikely. Terrorists will always seek out and find loopholes or cracks in these systems, which was the case with the 9/11 attacks. They also will use informal methods outside the financial system to move money.

For instance, the use of digital currency is an emerging strategy by terrorists to evade law enforcement and stay anonymous. The European Commission passed the Fourth Anti-Money Laundering Directive in May 2015 and urged all member states to implement the new regulations by the end of 2017. It is questionable whether all states will comply with the new measures (European Commission, 2016). Globally, an evaluation of different countries shows that a number of them are not taking the actions required to halt terrorist money laundering or transfers. Thus, we continue to negotiate between freezing assets and following the money to collect terrorist intelligence. Gaining international compliance in countering terrorist funding is required if we are to choke their funding and have a measure of success.

HS ANALYSIS BOX 11-1

The 9/11 Commission questioned whether we can stop terrorist funding. It advises that perhaps it is better to follow the money—much like we do in organized crime and drug cases. On the other hand, others advocate that we should make every effort to stop terrorist funding. For instance, the Financial Action Task Force (FATF), which advises the G20 leaders, put forth 40 recommendations to be implemented across diverse legal frameworks and financial systems. The main recommendations center around identifying risks, pursuing money laundering, implementing preventive measures, enhancing transparency, and promoting international cooperation (FATF, 2015). Research by the RAND Corporation suggests that the international efforts have made some strides by causing ISIS, the once richest terrorist organization in the world, considerable money problems (Johnston, 2016). In your opinion, which strategy, stopping the funding or following it, would be the most advantageous? Why?

Pakistani singer and model, Rawalpindi, arrives in court charged with money laundering. She was apprehended at the airport with $500,000 in her luggage.
Newzulu/Alamy Stock Photo.

Distinguishing Terrorist Financing and Money Laundering

Essentially, when attacking terrorist financing, authorities are concentrating on two primary activities: fund-raising and moving or laundering the money. It is important to distinguish these two activities since prevention and enforcement approaches to each, in some cases, are different. Even though terrorist financing and money laundering represent two entirely different activities, they sometimes are interconnected. Money laundering is an activity whereby ill-gotten fruits are cleansed—illegally derived funds are moved through the financial system and returned legitimate. Roberge (2007) noted that money laundering is a three-step process: (1) the illegally derived money is placed into the financial system; (2) it is layered or moved through the financial system, usually internationally, and intermingled with legitimate profits and monies to hide its provenance; and (3) it is returned and reintegrated into the legitimate economy. Historically, money laundering has been used primarily by organized crime and corrupt politicians. Today, terrorist groups have developed extensive financial networks to launder their money. Money laundering from all sources is sizable. For example, Roberge noted that 2–5 percent of the global gross domestic product is laundered annually.

Whereas money laundering is a process whereby illegal monies are moved into the legitimate economy so that they cannot be identified by authorities and used by terrorists, terrorist financing is the mechanisms used by terrorists to raise funds, which are discussed later in this chapter. Organized crime figures and political despots are interested in moving money into the legitimate economy. Terrorists are not interested in doing so; they attempt to raise funds, transfer them without impediment or interception, and spend them for their terrorist activities. The difference is that terrorists are interested only in moving the money from one point to another. They generally are not interested in money laundering or making the money appear legitimate, but in some cases, they must do so to protect the origin of the funds. Nonetheless, this results in increased difficulty in identifying terrorists' funds.

Terrorists must move funds from one country to another to facilitate their global activities. For example, prior to the 9/11 attacks, Osama bin Laden and al Qaeda moved money to banks in several U.S. states to finance the attacks. Once deposited, the hijackers withdrew the money. In this case, the money was laundered in that it did not raise any suspicions on the part of American authorities. The 9/11 Commission found that approximately $300,000 passed through American banks (National Commission on Terrorist Attacks upon the United States, 2004). Prior to the attacks, the money-laundering controls in place at the time focused on drug trafficking and large-scale financial fraud, and the 9/11 terrorists made a number of transfers of relatively small amounts. The money being transferred for the 9/11 attacks essentially arrived under the radar. Afterward, the U.S. government intensified its efforts to restrict the unabated movement of money (implement more effective choke points), especially money that was suspected of being linked with terrorists.

Since 2001, there have been considerable strides made to impede the money laundering by al Qaeda and ISIS, but especially ISIS still controls numerous banks in their occupied territories in Syria, Iraq, and Libya. Moreover, as ISIS is defeated in Iraq and Syria, the terrorist organization is moving into a number of other countries including the Philippines, Yemen, Libya, and North Africa. In addition, traditional money exchanges are filling the void of banks. The operators of these money exchanges may not only tolerate that their services are used by terrorists, but tack on extra charges to profit for terrorist groups to make a greater profit (Fanusie and Heid, 2016).

▶ Federal Mechanisms Used to Counter Terrorist Financing and Money Laundering

After 9/11, the American government endeavored to deprive terrorists of the funding necessary to carry out future attacks. Prior to 9/11, several laws focused on money laundering. For the most part, these laws were enacted to target organized crime and large-scale narcotics trafficking. For example, the Money Laundering Control Act of 1986 created several offenses focusing on money laundering. The Bank Secrecy Act of 1970 (BSA) required an institutional accounting of large currency transfers. The Treasury and the Federal Reserve developed regulations requiring record keeping for financial activities such as wire transfers. The USA PATRIOT Act amended the BSA and required banks and other financial institutions to practice **due diligence**—they were required to determine the sources of financial transactions, creating a paper trail for any subsequent investigations.

Immediately after 9/11, President Bush issued an executive order freezing the U.S. assets of 27 different entities suspected of being terrorist organizations or of collaborating with terrorist organizations. The order also prohibited American financial transactions with these entities and had international implications. The administration believed that terrorists had few assets in U.S. institutions. Thus, President Bush made the order fairly encompassing, giving the United States the power to freeze foreign banks' accounts in the United States when those banks failed to share financial information with U.S. investigative agencies or refused to block terrorists' accounts. The U.S. government is able to enforce this provision, at least to some degree, since foreign banks must conduct business with the American banking and financial system as a result of the global economy. It fell upon the Departments of Treasury and State to enforce the order. This action laid the groundwork for a comprehensive assault on terrorist financing (see Zagaris, 2004).

In 2001, the U.S. Departments of Treasury developed the TFTP with the goal to disrupt terrorist financing and weaken terrorist organizations. The TFTP tracks, identifies, and disrupts terrorist networks by tracking the terrorist money flow. For instance, the TFTP issued subpoenas to the SWIFT and seized data on financial transactions by terrorist

HS ANALYSIS BOX 11-2

An examination of the methods used attempting to stop terrorist financing shows that it is a complicated affair. As noted, some have suggested that a czar be appointed to coordinate these activities, especially in light of the importance of controlling terrorist financing. Should we appoint such a czar? Why? Do you believe that a terrorist financing czar would be more effective than our director of national intelligence?

organizations. SWIFT attempted to avoid providing such information to the United States by moving all data to European servers. Subsequently, the U.S. government reached an agreement with the European Union, which now shares the information with the United States. This information is very valuable and has greatly improved the ability of the United States to locate terrorists and disrupt the money flow (Departments of Treasury, 2017).

To learn more about TFTP, go to https://www.treasury.gov/resource-center/terrorist-illicit-finance/Terrorist-Finance-Tracking/Pages/tftp.aspx.

U.S. Enforcement Actions

A number of changes were made in the financial enforcement landscape as indicated in Figure 11-1 ■. The U.S. Treasury Department created a task force with representatives from the Federal Bureau of Investigation (FBI), the Internal Revenue Service (IRS), Customs, and other agencies to coordinate anti-terrorist financing. The Treasury Department also increased the power and scope of the Financial Crimes Enforcement Network (FinCEN), allowing law enforcement investigators to have readily accessible information on suspect bank accounts. The FBI established the Terrorist Financing Section within its Counterterrorism Division. This section provides investigative support to the FBI's field offices and foreign governments in cases of terrorist financing. The section participated in the disruption of terrorist finance operations in the United Arab Emirates, Pakistan, and Afghanistan, and it was responsible for prosecuting a Hezbollah cigarette-smuggling operation in North Carolina and Michigan (Zagaris, 2004). The Drug Enforcement Agency (DEA) began to give more attention to

1. The Central Intelligence Agency gathers, analyzes, and disseminates intelligence on foreign terrorist organizations and their financing arms.
2. The Bureau of Customs and Border Protection and the Bureau of Immigration and Customs Enforcement are responsible for enforcing financial laws and regulations at the border.
3. The U.S. Secret Service is responsible for investigating terrorist financing involving counterfeiting.
4. The Bureau of Alcohol, Tobacco, Firearms, and Explosives investigates terrorist financing and activities involving alcohol, tobacco, firearms, and explosives.
5. The Drug Enforcement Agency investigates terrorist financing involving drugs.
6. The Federal Bureau of Investigation investigates all aspects of foreign activities and collects intelligence information within the United States.
7. The Bureau of Economic and Business Affairs leads U.S. efforts to develop strategies to obtain international cooperation.
8. The Office of the Coordinator for Counterterrorism coordinates U.S. counterterrorism policy and efforts with foreign governments to deter terrorist financing.
9. The Executive Office for Terrorist Financing and Financial Crime develops and implements the National Money Laundering Strategy as well as other policies and programs to prevent financial crimes.
10. The Financial Crimes Enforcement Network (FinCEN) consists of regional centers that coordinate federal, state, and local financial crime investigations and intelligence.
11. The Internal Revenue Service investigates terrorist financing with an emphasis on charitable organizations.

FIGURE 11-1 Federal Agencies Combating Terrorist Financing

Source: Government Accounting Office. (2003). *Terrorist Financing: U.S. Agencies Should Systematically Assess Terrorists' Use of Alternative Financing Mechanisms.* Washington, D.C.: Author.

narco-terrorism since terrorist organizations are extensively involved in drug trafficking to raise money. Customs and Border Protection and Immigration and Customs Enforcement are responsible for securing our borders. One of their responsibilities is to focus on the transfer of money and valuables coming into and going out of the United States. The Internal Revenue Service was charged with investigating Islamic charities, a primary source of income to terrorist organizations. As demonstrated, several federal agencies concentrate on a number of financial activities that could involve terrorist financing.

HS Web Link: to learn more about the FBI's Terrorist Financing Section, go to https://archives.fbi.gov/archives/news/testimony/countering-terrorist-financing-progress-and-priorities.

In 2016, the U.S. House of Representatives passed the National Strategy for Combating Terrorist, Underground, and Other Illicit Financing Act, which calls for the establishment of a national strategy and an annual evaluation of the strategy and its success (U.S. House of Representatives, 2016).

Financial Action Task Force on Money Laundering

In 1989, the United States in cooperation with the other G-7 nations established the **Financial Action Task Force on Money Laundering** (FATF), which is headquartered in Paris. Originally, FATF was concerned with money laundering and transfers emanating from the narcotics trade. In 2001, FATF's mission was expanded to include attacking terrorist financing. Today, the FATF has 34 members (FATF-GAFI, undated). It attempts to place pressure on nonmember nations to accept FATF's measures that reduce terrorist financing and money laundering. The FATF uses two strategies to gain compliance. First, if nations do not comply with the standards, the organization will name them and attempt to shame or pressure them into compliance. When this does not result in compliance, the FATF can recommend sanctions against noncompliant nations. Although there are about 130 complying nations, some nations have not pursued money laundering and terrorist financing in earnest (FATF-GAFI, undated). Moreover, a number of countries' governments do not have the ability to police their finance and banking systems, which makes enforcement difficult. Nonetheless, a patchwork system currently is in place, and some inroads have been made in thwarting terrorist finance activities.

A total of $207 million was seized in Mexico City—the largest drug cash seizure ever.
U.S. Department of Justice.

▶ Means and Methods of Terrorist Financial Transactions

In the aftermath of the 9/11 attacks, there was speculation that Osama bin Laden was financing the attacks and his terrorist network with his personal fortune. His family has substantial wealth from a well-established construction company in Saudi Arabia. It was estimated that his fortune ranged from $25 million to $300 million (Lee, 2002). However, subsequently it was discovered that his family had not given him large sums of money, and indeed, as result of being cut off by his family, he had only a few million dollars. A few million dollars was not nearly enough money for him to finance his extensive operations. He had to resort to a host of activities to maintain a constant flow of money to maintain his al Qaeda network.

Bin Laden had a vast financial network. He had a number of holdings, including trading firms, construction companies, an agricultural production and export company, and a furniture-making company. He invested $50 million in a Sudanese bank but was forced to sell his stake when the United States and Egypt pressured the Sudanese government to expel him. He had investments in Mauritius, Singapore, Malaysia, the Philippines, and Panama and bank accounts in Hong Kong, London, Dubai, Malaysia, and Vienna. He also had hundreds of millions of dollars secured in real estate and elsewhere (Lee, 2002). Even without his family fortune, he was successful in raising money for his terrorist causes. Bin Laden is an example of how a terrorist and his organization can diversify and finance a terrorist empire.

To some extent, terrorist funding includes a variety of tactics and strategies at the macro and micro levels. At the macro level, large-scale terrorist organizations such as al Qaeda, Hamas, ISIS, and Hezbollah solicit or raise funds for a variety of purposes, including the funding of their extensive networks that span several countries. This funding comes primarily from charities, benefactors, and transnational organized crime activities. The funding of local cells often is intended to finance specific terrorist events. The micro level includes local cells that may or may not be affiliated with a larger terrorist organization. In some cases, local cells, whether affiliated or independent, will engage in fund-raising. They operate legitimate businesses, engage in crime, and have relationships with local charities and supporters. Generally, the local cells will use the money to sustain themselves and fund localized terrorist-related activities. They sometimes will transfer or contribute money to other cells or the terrorist organization with which they are associated. Figure 11-2 ■ shows the funding relationships.

The financial fundraising of ISIS was very different from al Qaeda. ISIS made much money from selling oil from Syria's oil fields. ISIS received about $500 million per year from oil. This stream of money was decimated by about 50 percent when the International Coalition took control of these oil fields. ISIS also stole large sums of much money from banks in occupied countries. For instance, ISIS stole $400 million from the Iraqi Central Bank in Mosul, Iraq in June 2014. The International Coalition seized these funds and stopped the flow of hundreds of millions of dollars to ISIS. ISIS also engaged in looting antiquities, trafficking, extortion, ransomware, and heavy taxation in ISIS-held territories (Johnston, 2016). It is estimated that ISIS had $2 billion at its peak in 2014. Even though the International Coalition has made great progress in restricting the sources of money flow, but ISIS was still able to garner considerable support from or outside sponsors and benefactors (House of Representatives, 2016).

Another significant source of income of terrorist groups stems from nation-states, including Iran, Syria, Sudan, Kuwait, Qatar, and Saudi Arabia. It is likely that other states also sponsor terrorist groups that serve their purpose (House of Representatives, 2016). The state-sponsoring makes it very difficult to stop the flow of money to terrorist groups.

The 2015 FATF report on emerging terrorist financing risks shows that ISIS and other terrorist organizations are increasingly using the Internet for fundraising, extortion, and recruiting. Also the emergence of new untraceable online payment methods, such as Bitcoins, poses significant challenges for law enforcement (FATF, 2015).

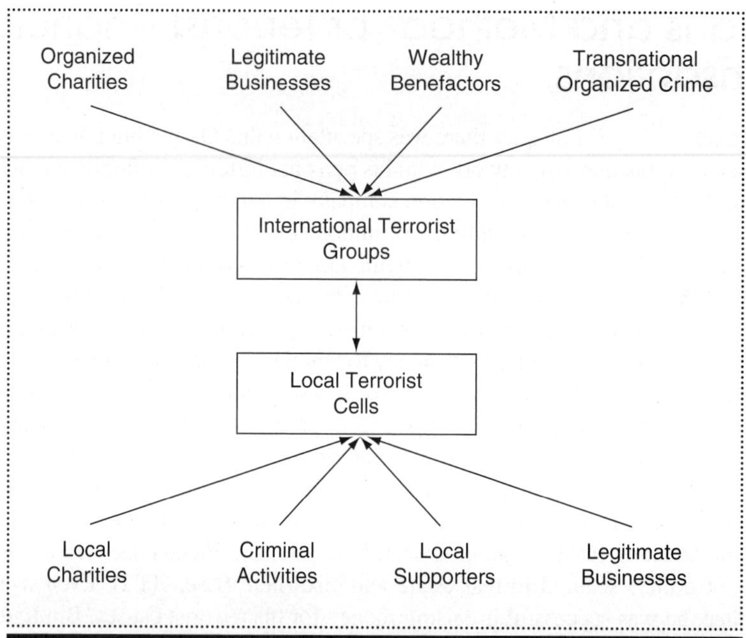

FIGURE 11-2 Sources and Relationships for Terrorist Funding

As shown, terrorist financial transactions are a complicated matter. They are multi-faceted and involve a number of stages and participants. Through intelligence gathering or trial and error, terrorists often identify cracks or loopholes in financing regulations and move their monies accordingly. For the most part, terrorist financing consists of three distinct operations: (1) earning or acquiring resources, (2) moving or laundering the money, and (3) storing or banking the money until it is needed. Figure 11-3 ■ outlines this process and the various mechanisms associated with each operation.

Alternative financing mechanisms	Earning	Moving	Storing
Trade in commodities			
Illicit drugs	X		
Weapons	X		
Cigarettes	X		
Diamonds	X	X	X
Gold		X	X
Systems			
Charities	X	X	
Informal banking		X	
Currency			
Bulk cash		X	X

FIGURE 11-3 Terrorist Alternative Financing Operations and Mechanisms

Source: Government Accounting Office. (2003). *Terrorist Financing: U.S. Agencies Should Systematically Assess Terrorists' Use of Alternative Financing Mechanisms.* Washington, D.C.: Author, p. 10.

▶ Earning and Acquiring Resources

As noted earlier, a variety of methods are used by terrorist organizations to acquire resources. These methods are elaborated on in this section.

Donor Support of Terrorism

Numerous wealthy patrons in the oil-rich Middle East countries and Gulf States support terrorism. For instance, ISIS receives substantial amounts of money from private citizens in Saudi Arabia, Kuwait, and Qatar, often transferred through Kuwait because the government of Kuwait has been very permissive toward terrorist funding. These private donations are only a small fraction of ISIS funding, however. ISIS overall received much less private donation than al Qaeda prior to the 9/11 attacks (Homeland Security Committee, 2016).

Osama bin Laden received some of the financing for the 9/11 attacks from patrons in the United Arab Emirates. In addition to the wealthy supporters, terrorists receive a substantial amount of money from imams at mosques who divert donations to terrorists or their facilitators. There is widespread animosity against America and Israel, and this animosity fuels hatred and support for the terrorists. It is not known exactly how much al Qaeda receives, but the UN Security Council (2002) estimated that individual wealthy donors provide the organization with approximately $16 million annually. Given that al Qaeda's annual budget is approximately $30 million, it appears that donations account for approximately half of its financial needs. Other terrorist groups receive considerable financial support from donors.

Donations from private citizens from the Persian Gulf has been a major source of funding for several Sunni terrorist groups operating in Syria, especially for the Al-Nusrah Front (ANF). ANF has been active against the Assad regime and controls parts of Syria. The group claimed responsibility for the 2012 bombings in Aleppo, al Midan, and Damacus. The group was also responsible for the death of Syria's head of air defense, Lt. Gen. Hussein Ishaq (U.S. Department of State Publication, 2016).

Several countries have been accused of supporting terrorist groups by tolerating donations. The donations are moved via courier, wire transfers, hawalas, and exchange houses to the terrorist groups (U.S. Department of the Treasury, 2016). For instance, Qatar is one of the gulf states accused of not actively combating such donations. In 2017, four gulf states, Saudi Arabia, the United Arab Emirates, Egypt, and Bahrain, stopped all trade with Qatar, ejected Qatar officials and visitors, and banned all travel between their countries and Qatar. The four gulf states gave a list with demands to the government of Qatar. So far, Qatar has denied official support for terrorist financing. Turkey has sided with Qatar and is supplying food and Germany has offered its intelligence service to assist the government of Qatar clear up the allegations of supporting terrorism. U.S. Secretary of State Rex Tillerson met with Qatari foreign minister to find ways to end the crisis (Beaumont, 2017). Insiders believe that this crisis could last for months, however.

HS Web Link: To read more about how the United States is attempting to attack donations to terrorists, go to https://www.treasury.gov/resource-center/terrorist-illicit-finance/Pages/default.aspx.

Criminal Activity

Terrorist groups across the world have a long history of using criminal activities such as robberies, extortion, and kidnapping to fund their activities. In the 1970s, the Symbionese Liberation Army, an American left-wing terrorist group, kidnapped newspaper heiress Patti Hearst; rather than ransoming her, her captors had her become part of the group's crime spree that included bombings and bank robberies. More recently in the United States, a number of right-wing extremist groups have attempted to finance their operations through bank robberies; these groups also plotted terrorist attacks including bombings and murders.

Criminal activities have long been part of terrorist groups' portfolio of activities in South and Central America. Criminals and narco-terrorists in Mexico routinely kill, kidnap, and extort money from citizens, politicians, and businesspeople. The problem stems from Mexico's

U.S. Marines patrol in a poppy field in Afghanistan.
US Army Photo/Alamy Stock Photo.

inability to intervene in wars between the various drug cartels that traffic illegal drugs. The Revolutionary Armed Forces of Colombia (FARC), a terrorist group in Colombia, has a long history of kidnapping, holding, and ransoming people, especially foreigners. It was estimated that in 2008, the group was holding more than 700 people including 40 high-profile victims (BBC America, 2008). The Shining Path, a terrorist group in Peru, also engaged in kidnapping. Terrorist groups and cells worldwide commonly participate in these criminal activities.

In some cases, they participate in large-scale criminal enterprises. In Chapter 7, the relationship between transnational organized crime and terrorist organizations was discussed. As noted there, terroristTerrorist groups' activities often parallel or are similar to transnational organized crime activities, especially in narco-terrorism and weapons smuggling. Terrorism also results in unusual criminal opportunities. For example, after the Khobar Towers bombing in Dharan, Saudi Arabia, in 1996, a number of prominent Saudis met in Paris where they conspired to pay al Qaeda and bin Laden to refrain from mounting attacks in Saudi Arabia. It is alleged that the Saudi royal family has also made such payments (Lee, 2002). Whereas common criminals extort money from businesspersons and individuals, some terrorist groups extort money from countries and multinational conglomerates.

ISIS generates substantial income from taxation, ransomware, extortion, kidnappings, and robberies. It is estimated that in 2014, ISIS received $8 million from taxation and extortion fees in Mosul, Iraq per month. In addition, ISIS raised hundreds of millions of dollars from bank robberies in Iraq and Syria. ISIS basically took the monies transferred to banks in their territory. Iraq has stopped wire transfer to these banks, but Syria continues to donate funds in ISIS controlled banks. Kidnapping for ransom has also been very profitable for ISIS with an estimated $35–45 million per year. Davis S. Cohen, the former Central Intelligence Agency (CIA) director, stated "Kidnapping for ransom is one of the most significant terrorist financing threats" (Homeland Security Committee, 2016).

The narcotics trade represents an important business for terrorist organizations. Numerous significant or powerful narcotics transnational organized crime groups and terrorist organizations are involved in narcotics trafficking in South and Central America. However, it is also prevalent in Asia and Africa. Al Qaeda and the Taliban are involved in the opium trade. When the Taliban came to power in 2000 in Afghanistan, it banned poppy production but became involved in opium production after coalition forces invaded Afghanistan. According to a United Nations' report, as much as 90 percent of the world's heroin comes from Afghanistan opium (UNODC, 2017).

HS Web Link: To read more about the Afghanistan poppy production problem, go to https://www.unodc.org/documents/crop-monitoring/Afghanistan/_Afghan_opium_survey_2015_web.pdf.

Charities

Terrorist organizations use charities to raise money. For example, the Irish Republican Army for decades had charities operating in the United States that raised money to finance its attacks in Northern Ireland and England. Left-wing and right-wing groups worldwide solicit and accept donations to finance their operations. However, in the Muslim world, charities are more institutionalized. **Zakat**, or alms giving, is one of the five pillars of Islam—charity is a religious duty for all Muslims (Comras, 2005). Charity is practiced extensively with numerous Muslim charities worldwide. For example, Saudi Arabia and the United Arab Emirates have no formal income tax system and charities represent the primary mechanism for humanitarian projects. In many third-world countries with dysfunctional governments, charities often are more influential than government entities since they are able to provide scores of citizens with assistance. For example, Hezbollah in Lebanon and Hamas in the Gaza Strip are terrorist organizations that are engaged in providing assistance to the population. This assistance engenders greater levels of support for their activities, including terrorism. It also enables them to seek and receive significant charitable donations.

HS Web Link: To learn more about Zakat and Islamic giving, go to http://www.zpub.com/aaa/zakat-def.html.

Islamic-based charities are numerous and dispersed across the world. About one-fifth of all charitable organizations are Islamic, and they disperse several billion dollars annually (Looney, 2006). These charities gain widespread acceptance in the Muslim world because they not only provide humanitarian aid but also further and cement Islamic religious and cultural philosophies. Charities are a tool by which to counter or reduce foreign influence on Islamic culture. They help solidify xenophobic attitudes.

Regular fundraising events by ISIS supporters have generated hundreds of millions of dollars. These fundraising events are held in mosques or private homes, and also through social media. ISIS has reinvented terrorist financing by extensively using social media pleas. ISIS has also been receiving income by laundering humanitarian aid through charities. These funds not only provide income, but they are also used to support vulnerable populations in an effort to radicalize them. They also fund schools, religious institutions, and hospitals to gain support among the local population (Homeland Security Committee, 2016).

The plight of the Palestinian people has been a rallying point for many charities and givers. It has resulted in substantial donations primarily to Hamas and Hezbollah, two organizations that are recognized as terrorist groups. Other groups are also collecting money on behalf of the Palestinians. The Israeli-Palestinian conflict has resulted in substantial anger in the Muslim world, and this has led to numerous and increased donations from the wealthy and the poor. Most of these charities are legitimate, but some have collected or given money to terrorist organizations. Others serve to collect money solely for terrorist organizations. For example, the 9/11 Commission (2004) found that "entire charities under the control of al Qaeda operatives … may have wittingly participated in funneling money to al Qaeda" (p. 170).

Charities were used extensively by bin Laden to obtain substantial resources for his al Qaeda organization. According to Kohlmann (2006–2007),

> Standing orders were left by bin Laden to keep all transactions involving charitable groups in cash only … these NGOs [non-government organizations] were manipulated as a secret laundry to make al Qaeda's financial network virtually invisible. The charities would then create false documentation for the benefit of unwary donors, purportedly showing that the money had actually been spent on orphans or starving refugees. According to some former employers of these organizations, upwards of 50% of their total funding was secretly diverted to al-Qaeda and Osama bin Laden. (pp. 2–3)

The terrorists then use the money for a variety of purposes including waging war, financing attacks, purchasing arms and explosives, and daily living expenses for terrorists and cells.

Charities have been successful in providing terrorist groups with a substantial amount of untraceable resources. They, to some extent, represent a repository for cash. The charities also serve other functions. Kohlmann (2006–2007) advised that the charities are effective in recruiting new jihadists. As a part of their appeal, the charities emphasize the misery, repression, and injury suffered by Muslims. The charities then solicit donations and "deeds." The deeds often include not only humanitarian assistance but also actions and a jihadist commitment to remove the repressors or enemies and restore Islam to greatness. The charities also allow affiliated terrorists to travel internationally without the usual hindrance; association with a charity facilitates obtaining required travel documents.

As noted, these charities exist throughout the world, including the United States. A good example is the Holy Land Foundation (HLF) of Dallas, Texas, which was shut down by federal authorities. It was estimated that the HLF raised $13 million in the United States in 2000, claiming that the funds were for the care of needy Palestinians. Evidence showed that a portion of this money went to Hamas (see Looney, 2006). Although Hamas is involved in humanitarian activities, particularly in the Gaza Strip, it likely used some of this money for its attacks on Israel. It is interesting that it took a multinational investigation, spanning 11 years, to close the HLF (Henifin, 2004). In a similar case in 2008, former congressman Mark Siljander was indicted in Kansas City for lobbying for an Islamic charity that was funneling money to terrorists. Siljander received $50,000 from the Islamic American Relief Agency to lobby the Senate Finance Committee to have the charity removed from the panel's list of suspected terror fund-raisers. The charity paid Siljander money that was stolen from the U.S. government (Schmidt, 2008). These cases demonstrate the extensive and complicated nature of charity operations. They also show that terrorists are raising money on American soil—money that sometimes is used to attack us.

It was not until after the 9/11 attacks that the United States became serious about dealing with Muslim charities that supported terrorism. Prior to 9/11, they were seen as malevolent but causing little harm. However, the 9/11 attacks resulted in renewed interest in

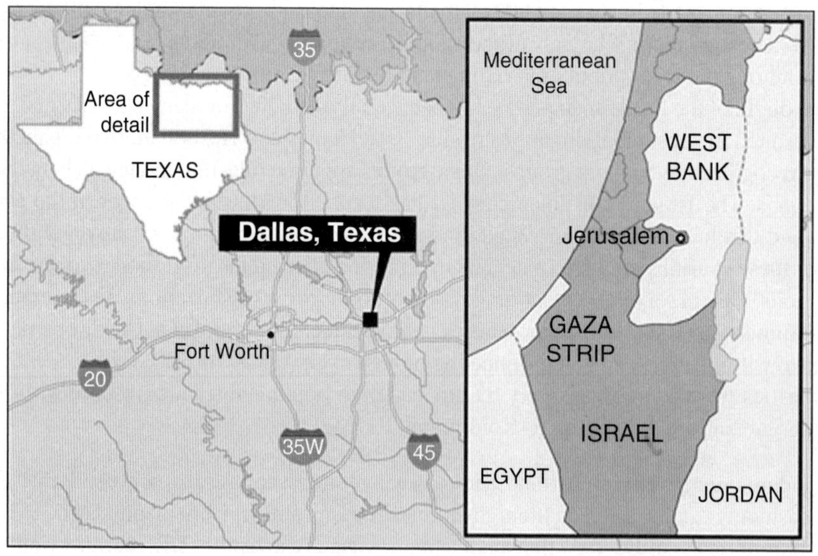

The Holy Land Foundation, based in a Dallas suburb before it was shut down in 2001, provided about $12.4 million in funding to Hamas-controlled organizations in the West Bank and Gaza.
Source: http://www.fbi.gov/headlines/hlf_map112508.jpg

all forms of terrorism funding, and the passage of the Anti-Terrorism Act of 1996 provided the primary mechanism to scrutinize these charities. The act has been used to choke funding to terrorist organizations.

The United States and other countries have received substantial criticism for their efforts to close Islamic charities. Critics maintain that these charities provide a substantial amount of humanitarian service in areas that desperately need assistance. However, the problem remains that many of these charities are intertwined with terrorist organizations and activities, and it is extraordinarily difficult to separate those that are genuinely providing humanitarian services from those that are funding terrorism. Even more problematic is that some of the charities are providing humanitarian aid while funneling some of their resources to terrorist organizations. The U.S. policy is that "it is better to be safe than sorry."

This discussion demonstrates that it is difficult to deal with Islamic charities. They are well organized and extensively involved across the globe. The Soviet Union's invasion of Afghanistan in 1976 resulted in the formation of dozens of Islamic charities to assist the Afghan people. Many of these same charities exist today and are collecting money for the Taliban and other terrorist organizations. Some Islamic charities have decades of experience in developing proficient organizations that provide humanitarian aid and fund wars. They also have uncovered and use procedures to evade government scrutiny.

Legitimate Businesses

Criminal groups have often used the money obtained from criminal enterprises to invest in legitimate businesses. In the United States, youth gangs have invested in car washes and automobile trim businesses using money derived from the drug trade (Decker, Bynum, and Weisel, 2004). Larger and more sophisticated groups often gravitate to large legitimate business since they often have the financing capital. As noted, al Qaeda has been involved in an assortment of legitimate businesses in several countries, including mining, diamonds, trading firms, construction companies, an agricultural production and export company, and a furniture-making company. As another example, al Qaeda has been involved in the honey-trading business. Honey is an important commodity in the Middle East and essentially is part of the culture. However, Miller and Gerth (2001) maintained that in some cases, the honey exportation business was used as a front by terrorist groups for smuggling guns, money, and drugs. Regardless, these examples point out that terrorists can maximize the utility and financial return when operating legitimate businesses, and terrorist organizations readily grasp business opportunities to raise funds. Lee (2002) provided additional examples:

> According to FBI documents, a Madrid al Qaeda cell ran a home repair company that provided masonry, plastering, and electrical services, as well an enterprise that restored and resold dilapidated vehicles. The cell's activities also included a criminal repertoire—credit card and document fraud, as well as street crime such as home burglary and car theft. A Singapore-Malaysia al Qaeda cell sold medical supplies and computer software but also engaged in bank robberies, violent assaults, and kidnappings. (p. 11)

HS ANALYSIS BOX 11-3

Policing charities is a particularly difficult problem given that all sorts of charities exist and operate in the United States as well as other countries. The discussion of the HLF in Dallas shows that it is a slow process. Should the United States enact laws that better control charities? Is it politically feasible to enact such laws since the laws would affect all other charities? What kinds of laws would you favor?

Similar to fundraising, ISIS is using social media extensively to raise funds. One of the emerging strategies is crowdsourcing, where funds are acquired by engaging a group online to raise money and support for ISIS. The money is wired via PayPal, GoFundMe, and CASHU to avoid detection by law enforcement. These online pay systems guarantee anonymity and circumvent formal financial system controls. This type of fundraising makes it very difficult to detect and prevent. Here again, ISIS has reinvented fundraising by using the latest technologies in a very sophisticated manner (Homeland Security Committee, 2016).

▶ Moving or Laundering Money

As noted in Figure 11-2 ■, terrorists move or launder their money in several ways: (1) precious commodities such as gold and diamonds, (2) banking and wire transfers, (3) informal banking or hawaladars, and (4) bulk cash. When engaging in their financial operations, terrorists also work with or interact with other players such as transnational organized crime groups, supporters of terrorist organizations or religious or political causes, and government officials.

Precious Commodities

Precious commodities represent a funding source for terrorist groups. One of the main income sources of ISIS has been the trade of antiquities. ISIS troops have systematically looted archeological sites in Syria, Iraq, and other territories. Satellite images from Syria in 2015 showed that more than 25 percent of Syria's archeological sites had been ransacked. These antiques are highly sought after in Europe and the United States. The most popular antiques are tablets,

The ancient city of Palmyra in Syria. ISIS looted many historical locations and sold antiquities on the black market.
John wreford/Alamy Stock Photo.

manuscripts, and cuneiforms. Any of these artifacts are worth hundreds of thousands of dollars. Not surprisingly, ISIS makes an estimated $100 million per year from the illicit trading of antiquities. Daniel Glaser, the Assistant Secretary for Terrorist Financing, stated "I don't think we've ever seen a terrorist organization that had the ability to command, to draw from its own territory these kinds of resources" (Homeland Security Committee, 2016, p. 10).

Precious commodities can also be a convenient method by which to move large sums of money. For example, Lee (2002) noted,

> Diamonds, it should be noted, are a particularly attractive commodity for smuggling operatives. They don't set off alarms at airports, they can't be sniffed by dogs, they are easy to hide, and are highly convertible to cash. Also, diamonds have a high value-to-weight ratio: a pound of average quality diamonds is valued at approximately $225,000. A pound of $100 dollar bills is worth in the neighborhood of $45,000, and a pound of gold, at $300 an ounce, is worth $4,800. (p 12)

It appears that Osama bin Laden used precious stones (diamonds) to raise money and to move it from one country to another. He supposedly obtained millions of dollars over a three-year period through precious stones. Abdullah Ahmed Abdullah, a top bin Laden advisor, was in contact with diamond dealers who represented Sierra Leone's Revolutionary Front in 1998 and bought uncut diamonds from the group. Al Qaeda operatives then transported the diamonds to Europe and other countries where they were sold for sizable profits (Farah, 2001). In another case, two al Qaeda companies, Tanzanite King and Black Giant, exported large quantities of uncut tanzanite from Kenya to Hong Kong, enabling al Qaeda to make large amounts of money (Block and Pearl, 2001). The FATF advised that precious metals and gemstones are the favored vehicle for moving terrorist funds (Jacinto, 2017).

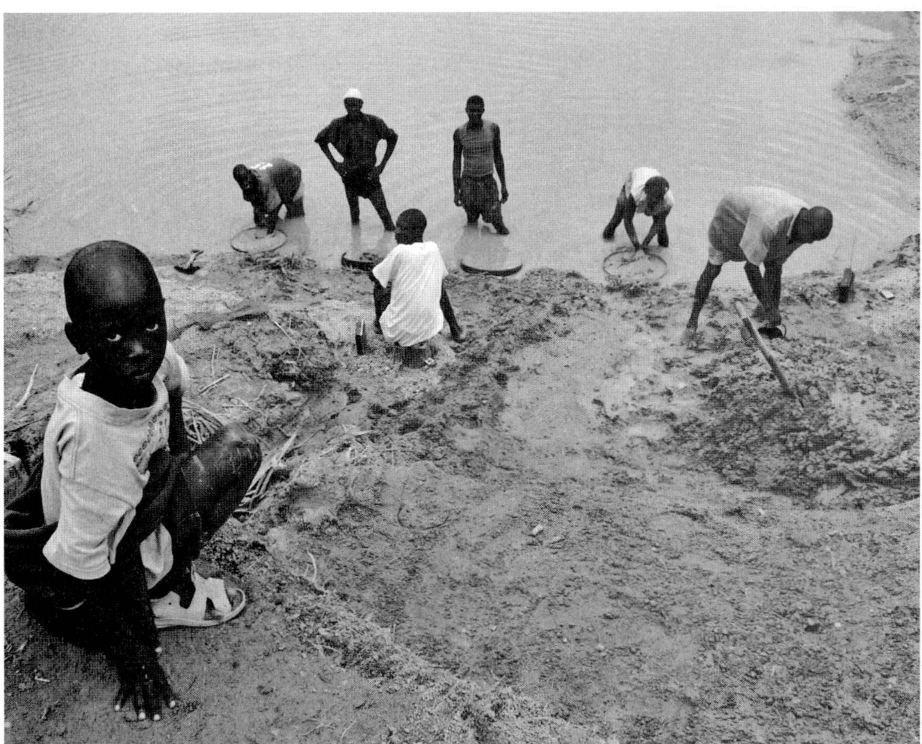

Diamonds being mined in Sierra Leone. Families and children are often forced to mine for diamonds. Diamonds are used by terrorists to move money.
Tommy Trenchard/Alamy Stock Photo.

Banking and Wire Transfers

Terrorists frequently wire money from one bank account to another. American and Western banks have strict controls over such transactions, whereas banks in many third-world and Middle-Eastern countries often have insufficient control mechanisms. Some of these banks willingly facilitate these transfers for ideological reasons or profits. The FBI tracked $90,000 in wire transfers from the United Arab Emirates to New York and Florida bank accounts. The money was accessed by the 9/11 hijackers (FBI, 2002). The U.S. government has been active in pursuing illegitimate funds; for example, the U.S. Treasury Department fined the U.S. arm of a bank in Switzerland, UBS AG, $100 million for funneling $5 billion to countries such as Cuba, Iran, and Libya, and the Riggs Bank was fined $25 million for failing to report unusual transactions. In another case, the Australian government sued the Commonwealth Bank for money laundering. The bank failed to report $77 million in suspicious transactions (Knaus, 2017). The amounts of these fines demonstrate how much illicit money is being transferred or laundered by financial institutions (Weiss, 2005). These actions also demonstrate that numerous legitimate banks have substantially and willingly been involved in terrorists' financial networks in the past. It is unclear to what extent they may still be involved in these activities. The U.S. government continues to monitor and attempt to control these financial transactions.

Banks in Muslim countries operate differently from Western banks. First, there is weak governmental oversight of banks in these countries, as well as in a number of other developing countries. This weak oversight results in many transactions not being scrutinized by any government regulators, facilitating their use by terrorist organizations. The money made by banks generally is used for internal projects or given to charities (Basile, 2009). Many of these banks have Sharia boards that allocate some of these excess funds to charities; it is very likely that some of this money ultimately is transferred to terrorist organizations.

Among one of the emerging fundraising tactics of ISIS is banking and loan fraud. As ISIS has been losing money from oil and gas, they are moving to other income sources (Homeland Security Committee, 2016).

Money Brokers or Hawaladars

There is a time-honored informal, underground banking system within the Muslim world known as **hawalas**. These are alternative remittance systems that involve the transfer of funds or assets from one individual to another using an informal banking system (see FATF, 1999). As noted in Figure 11-4 ■, a simple hawala consists of four steps. Essentially, someone desiring to send money to a person in another country simply contacts the hawala. The hawala then contacts an hawala in the destination country, and the hawala in the destination country delivers the funds without the funds leaving the originating country. This results in a deficit between the two hawalas. The accounts are frequently settled at some future point when someone in the destination country wishes to transfer funds back to the originating country.

The hawalas have a number of advantages for their users. They allow funds to be transferred within a very short time, sometimes in a matter of minutes. There are no written records of the transfers; all actions are made on an informal basis. These informal transfers result in participants not having a tax burden or government scrutiny as a result of the transfers. Those participating in hawala money transfers remain anonymous since the transfers are usually conducted using coded passwords. They are resilient in that they are not affected by economic downturns or war. Finally, hawalas are a less expensive means for people to transfer money as compared to the international banking system, especially when small amounts of money are being transferred.

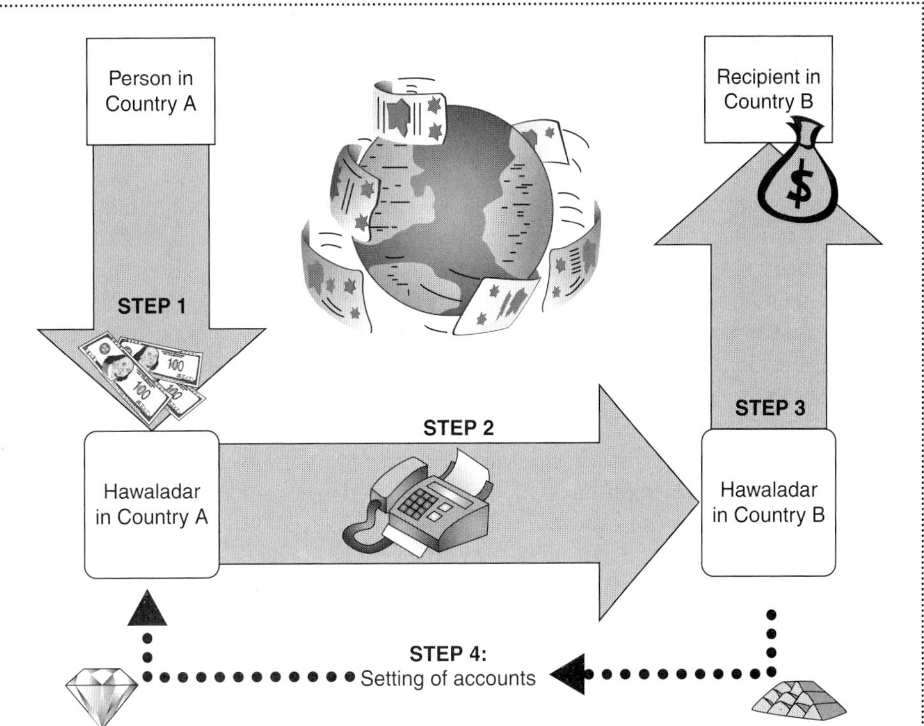

STEP 1. A person in Country A would like to send money to a recipient in Country B. The person in Country A contacts a hawaladar, a hawala operator, in Country A and gives the operator money and instructions to deliver the equivalent value to the recipient in Country B.

STEP 2. The hawaladar in Country A contacts the counterpart hawaladar in Country B via fax, e-mail, telephone. or other method and communicates the instructions.

STEP 3. The hawaladar in Country B then contacts the recipient in Country B and through varification by some code passed from the person in Country A to the recipient in Country B, delivers the equivalent value (in foreign currency of some commodity), less a transaction fee, to the recipient in Country B.

STEP 4. Over time, the accounts between the two hawaladars may become unbalanced and must be settled in some manner. Hawaladars use a variety of methods to settle their accounts, including reciprocal payments to customers, physical movement of money, wire transfer or check, payment for goods to be traded, trade or smuggling of precious stones or metals such as gold and diamonds, and invoice manipulation.

FIGURE 11-4 Interworkings of a Simple Hawala

Source: Government Accounting Office. (2003). Terrorist Financing: U.S. Agencies Should Systematically Assess Terrorists' Use of Alternative Financing Mechanisms. Washington, D.C.: Author, p. 18.

McCusker (2005) and Lee (2002) have identified variations in the hawala system. These variations are sometimes used to even accounts. The first is under-invoicing. Here, a hawalader in one country will send goods to a hawalader in another country, but the goods will be invoiced for less than their value. The hawalader receiving the goods will then sell the goods at market value, recouping what he or she was owed by the hawalader who shipped the goods. The second variation is over-invoicing. Here, the hawalader ships goods to another hawalader who owes him or her money, but the invoice is for a greater amount than the value of the goods. The receiving hawalader pays the bill, which corrects the financial imbalance. On paper these transactions appear to be legitimate business transactions and there is no evidence of the money transfers.

Given the simplicity of the hawala system, one would assume that it is used sparingly. However, it is used extensively in Muslim countries and some Asian countries.

Sander (2003) found that in 2002, $80 billion was remitted through this informal banking system by people living in developing countries. It represented the second-largest flow of capital to these countries behind foreign investment. Officials in Pakistan estimated that at least $7 billion enters that country each year through this alternative remittance system (Lee, 2002).

As noted, the hawala system is used by numerous people for all sorts of transactions. It is used primarily by average people, but the system also is being used to transfer funds for terrorist activities. As discussed earlier, al Qaeda has an extensive network across the globe. The hawala system allows the group to transfer large amounts of money undetected. Other organizations are also using this system. For example, the Colombians are using the hawala system to launder approximately $5 billion annually. U.S. officials note that thus far they have had little luck in tracing the transactions or seizing assets. In another case, in 2002, approximately 390,000 kilograms of U.S. honey were shipped to the United Arab Emirates, Saudi Arabia, and Kuwait. The importers in those countries paid 35 percent over the U.S. price or cost (over-invoicing), yielding funds in excess of $257,000. It could not be determined if the money was used for terrorist activities in the United States, but two of the honey-exporting companies were on a terrorist list (Lee, 2002). According to the FBI, some of the money used to finance the 9/11 attacks was transferred to the United States using hawalas (GAO, 2003). The hawala system presents a significant challenge to U.S. and world authorities who are attempting to reduce terrorist financing.

▶ Storing or Banking Money

The previous sections described the methods by which terrorist organizations acquire and move money. Terrorist organizations accumulate varying amounts of wealth, often in the millions. As noted, these terrorist organizations as a result of these activities accumulate cash and numerous products such as agriculture goods, precious gems and metals, and disposable goods. These goods represent financial resources, but they are not necessarily fluid; they cannot always be converted to cash quickly to finance an operation or sustain a cell. Terrorist organizations develop a business model whereby they estimate their cash flow needs and develop a timely process or method to convert these goods into cash. The hawalas likely are used for some of this conversion. It is also likely that these terrorist organizations retain large amounts of bulk cash since cash is readily accessible and immune from seizure by governments, which might occur if the money were deposited in some banks. They likely concentrate on accumulating goods such as diamonds and precious metals that can be sold fairly quickly.

▶ Black Market Oil and Gas

The ability to exploit the natural resources of captured territories has been unique to ISIS. ISIS has been exceptionally effective in creating a substantial, but shrinking, stream of revenue. Official estimates state that ISIS received about $2–4 million in daily profits. In 2015, ISIS received about $500 million from the sale of oil and gas. In Syria, ISIS oversaw about 1,600 oil workers and they are highly organized in the operation of the facilities efficiently. ISIS operatives conducted audits and flagged accounting discrepancies to maximize profits and prevent corruption. Syria's smuggling routes reached all the way to Europe and oil was smuggled via trucks. There are also reports that Syria's Assad regime also bought oil and gas from ISIS to supply areas surrounded by the terrorist group (Homeland Security Committee, 2016).

▶ Saudi Arabia's Financing of Terrorism: An American Conundrum

Saudi Arabia is perhaps America's closest ally in the Middle East. The United States has maintained close relations with the Saudi Kingdom, which sells large quantities of oil to the United States. There have been cases when the Saudis have increased oil production when other nations that were part of the Organization of Oil Exporting Countries (OPEC) were reducing production in an effort to increase prices. President George W. Bush was friends with members of the royal family. There have been instances when the United States tempered its policies in order to maintain warm relations with the Saudis. Our relations and dependency on the Saudis have become problematic since a significant portion of funding in the Middle East for extremism and terrorism comes from the Arabian Peninsula. Although countries such as Iran, Libya, and Syria outwardly promote terrorism, Saudi Arabia has been responsible for a substantial portion of the covert bankrolling of these movements.

In addition to being America's closest ally in the Middle East, it is also the most conservative and, to some extent, the most radical. This extremism has its roots in **Wahhabism**, Saudi Arabia's brand of Islam. According to the Middle East Media Institute (cited in Gold, 2003),

> Wahhabism leads, as we have seen, to the birth of extremist, closed, and fanatical streams, that accuse others of heresy, abolish them, and destroy them. The extremist religious groups have moved from the stage of *Takfir* [condemning other Muslims as unbelievers] to the stage of "annihilation and destruction," in accordance with the strategy of Al-Qa'ida—which Saudi authorities must admit is a local Saudi organization that drew other organizations into it, and not the other way around. All the organizations emerged from under the robe of Wahhabism.

These radical roots run deep. Not only has Wahhabism spawned Islamic terrorism, it has also made a significant contribution to al Qaeda's beginnings. Indeed, bin Laden is Saudi as were 15 of the 19 attackers in the 9/11 attacks. Bin Laden's ties to Saudi Arabia have resulted in extensive Saudi financial and psychological support for Al Qaeda and other terrorist groups.

> **HS Web Link:** To read more about Saudi Arabia and terrorism, go to http://www.jcpa.org/jl/vp504.htm.

Saudi Arabia, with an abundance of oil money, has been extensively involved in charities with significant amounts of this money going to terrorists in numerous countries, including Afghanistan, Palestine, Bosnia, and Chechnya. The Saudis have operated a number of charities, some of which are rather large, including the International Islamic Relief Organization (IIRO) and the Charitable Foundation of al-Haramain. Bin Laden's brother-in-law ran the Philippine offices of the IIRO and the brother of Ayman al-Zawahiri (second in command in al Qaeda) was employed in IIRO's Albanian office. The Charitable Foundation of al-Haramain funded al Qaeda operations in Southeast Asia. Additionally, it is estimated that more than 50 percent of Hamas's funding comes from Saudi Arabia (Gold, 2003).

In 2003, Saudi Arabia experienced a number of suicide attacks that resulted in the Saudis examining terrorist funding more closely. The government began to crack down on extremists in the kingdom and more closely monitor charitable organizations. However, Gold asserted that officials become concerned only with charitable activities within the kingdom and had little concern for their activities outside the country. Money laundering laws were enacted, but again, they applied primarily to money laundering within the kingdom, and they were not comprehensive enough to stem the flow of money to external terrorist groups and activities. The United States has continued to apply pressure on the Saudi royal family, but the royal family is so

HS ANALYSIS BOX 11-4

Dealing with Saudi Arabia is a difficult problem for American foreign policy. Saudi Arabia is a friend and ally, although a weak one. We must also understand that the actions that the Saudis can take are limited by their political culture. Should the United States forsake Saudi oil and push for more action in countering terrorism? Would the American people understand that higher prices for oil is the price for more effectively fighting terrorism? What policy should the United States adopt?

interdependent with the Wahhabi religious structure that it is questionable if there will be significant results. Indeed, in 2008, Stuart Levey, a treasury undersecretary, reported to a U.S. Senate Committee that Saudi Arabia remains the location where more money is going to terrorism, to Sunni terror groups, and to the Taliban than any other place in the world.

Nonetheless, Saudi Arabia remains a central figure in support for terrorists. Weinstein (2017) noted that of the 61 State Department designated terrorist organizations, the overwhelming majority are Wahhabi-inspired and funded by the Saudi government. Nearly all Sunni terrorist groups receive money from the Saudi government or Saudi citizens. Perhaps the most significant problem is Pakistan. The Wahhabis in the Gulf region have funneled nearly $100 million to radical clerics in Pakistan. The danger is that Pakistan has a number of terrorist groups including the Taliban, and the country has nuclear weapons.

The United States is in a predicament—Saudi Arabia remains the primary source for terrorist funding—but because of our dependence on oil and Saudi support in the Middle East, there is little that can be done. As long as the Saudis fund terrorism, terrorism likely will remain a vibrant destructive force.

There are many other countries that also fund terrorist groups. For instance, Iran provides hundreds of millions of dollars each year to Hizballah (Hamas). This funding source has decreased, however, as Hamas refused to support Iran in its support for Syrian president Bashar al-Asad (U.S. Department of the Treasury, 2016).

▶ Identity Fraud and Theft

A major problem is identity fraud and theft, which are two different but interrelated problems. **Identity fraud** is the process of using a false identity or another person's identity to obtain goods, services, or money. **Identity theft**, on the other hand, is the procuring of this false identity regardless of its use. In most cases, identity theft is used to commit identity fraud, but in some cases, it is used by criminals and terrorists to establish false identities and escape detection. Identity theft and fraud are criminal activities that are closely linked to terrorist financing. In many cases, terrorists will use assumed identities to cover money trails. These assumed identities help reduce the possibility that authorities will discover the money or be able to link the money to a terrorist group or activity. Additionally, terrorists engage in identity theft to provide clandestine cover. In this regard, they use identity theft for three purposes:

1. **Avoid watch lists**—Many terrorists and possible collaborators' names are on terrorist watch lists that serve to monitor their travel and prevent them from traveling. They assume new identities to avoid being discovered or to allow them to travel to other countries.

2. **Obscure their whereabouts**—Terrorists often use one or more different identities, especially when conducting terrorist-related activities, which makes it difficult for law enforcement to trace or apprehend them.
3. **Gain unauthorized access**—Some terrorists or suspected terrorists are barred from entry into certain countries or from using mass transportation such as air travel, and false identities allow them to frustrate such limitations.

Identity theft, not only in terms of terrorism but also in terms of other financial crimes, has resulted in numerous governmental and private actions to prevent it from occurring. Identity fraud has grown exponentially primarily as a result of the Internet. A substantial amount of commerce is being conducted via the Internet, which has led to the fraudulent acquisition of personal data or information. Moreover, numerous personal identifier databases that are linked to the web are not adequately protected with fire walls. For example, many state and local governments post databases with personal information on the Internet as a part of their open records programs (most notable is real estate information). This open records program has resulted in large numbers of nefarious individuals attempting to commit some form of identity theft using information gathered from the Internet.

HS Web Link: To learn more about identity theft and fraud, go to http://www.justice.gov/criminal/fraud/websites/idtheft.html.

The theft of personal data is used not only to create false identities but also to target U.S. citizens. In 2015, a hacker from Malaysia was arrested for passing on personal data of military personnel to ISIS. ISIS created a "kill list" (Perez, Soichet, and Bruer, 2015).

Real ID Act

Perhaps the best-known effort to counter identity fraud and theft is the **Real ID Act**, which was passed in 2005. It establishes national standards for driver's licenses. In the past, there has been no uniformity in driver's licenses, and consequently, border security officers and other law enforcement officials would not necessarily know if a driver's license was a forgery, especially if it came from another state and the officers were not familiar with that state's license format. At a minimum, drivers' licenses must contain,

1. A photo identity document (except that a non-photo identity document is acceptable if it includes both the person's full legal name and date of birth)
2. Documentation showing the person's date of birth
3. Proof of the person's Social Security account number (SSN) or verification that the person is not eligible for an SSN
4. Documentation showing the person's name and address of principal residence

Additionally, before issuing a driver's license, the states must verify the information. Congress passed the Real ID Act in an effort to reduce the amount of identity theft and fraud.

In the United States, a driver's license is the primary form of identification. It is used to process all sorts of transactions. One of the reasons for passing the Real ID Act was to make it more difficult for terrorists to obtain identification. The 9/11 Commission found that the terrorists involved in the attacks had obtained more than 30 driver's licenses even though many of them had overstayed their visas (Dinam, 2012). Controlling driver's licenses is important because they often serve as a breeder document that can be used to obtain other forms of fraudulent identification, and as of the beginning of 2013, only 13 states had enacted the Real ID requirements. The Real ID Act must be implemented. Beginning in January 2018, individuals not possessing a driver's license or state ID that does not comply with the real ID requirements will not be able to fly within the United States unless the state has received an exemption from the DHS. By 2020, all states must be in compliance (TSA, 2017).

HS ANALYSIS BOX 11-5

A driver's license is an important identification document in the United States, and the states have different standards, making it difficult for police officers and other officials to identify valid and counterfeit licenses. Many states have not enacted Real ID because of the costs to issue the new licenses. Should Congress require the states to implement Real ID? Given the federal budget deficits, should Congress fund the states to implement the act? Should American citizens be required to carry some type of national identification card? Why?

Breeder Documents and the Mechanics of Identity Fraud

Gordon and Willox (2003) have identified the mechanics or process by which terrorists and criminals attempt to develop a false identity. They begin by creating a new identity, often by providing fictitious personal information or assuming the identity of another person. The fraudulent identity is then used to obtain a **breeder document**, usually a Social Security card, driver's license, passport, or birth certificate. Fraudulent identities allow the individual to obtain other fraudulent documents. When this occurs, there often is no victim and the identity theft is not reported to authorities.

The documents allow access financial systems. There are cases in which charlatans have assumed a homeowner's identity and sold the home or property, thereby committing bank fraud. The documents are often used to obtain government benefits such as unemployment (when a false nonexisting employer is used), welfare, and other governmental benefits. In some cases, terrorist groups have raised large amounts of money in this manner by using multiple fictitious identities. Since most of the information on entitlement

The FBI recovers dozens of fake identification documents, including Social Security cards, UN ID cards, and birth certificates from three states.
ZUMA Press, Inc./Alamy Stock Photo.

programs is confidential, there are few investigations unless the investigation is initiated as a result of other wrong-doing. In other cases, fraudulent documents have been used to obtain visas and green cards.

Once an individual has created an identity, he or she can more easily become involved in a variety of criminal activities. Most important, since the identity is false, it becomes more difficult to apprehend the perpetrator. Terrorists can use these identities to obtain money, launder money, export money, fund terrorist activities within the United States, purchase arms, and move across borders. The identities can be used in smuggling and trafficking drugs and weapons, which are lucrative financial endeavors for terrorists. In some cases, the fraudulent identities are passed on to illegal aliens who are smuggled into the United States.

▶ Terrorists' Financial Needs

Terrorism requires a substantial amount of funding. The CIA estimated that al Qaeda raised approximately $30 million a year (Looney, 2006; Naylor, 2002), which resulted in a substantial budget for the organization. The leading terrorist organization is without doubt ISIS, raising about $1 billion dollars per year (Homeland Security Committee, 2016). This would appear to be insurmountable in terms of the number and types of terrorist activities that could be financed, especially considering that the 9/11 attacks cost al Qaeda less than $500,000 (9/11 Commission, 2004). Levitt and Jacobson (2008) note that the London subway and bus attacks that killed 52 people cost an estimated $15,000. The Madrid subway attack and the attack on the USS *Cole* in Yemen each cost approximately $10,000. The Paris attacks on November 13, 2015 only cost $8,000 (Goulet, 2015). The amount of destruction possible with very little money is of great concern for national security experts. It seems that terrorist attacks are inexpensive relative to al Qaeda's and ISIS's overall operating budget.

However, al Qaeda, ISIS, and other terrorist organizations, depending on their size and scope, have a significant operational or maintenance budget. Documents seized by the U.S. military show that one branch of al Qaeda in Iraq spent more than $175,000 in a four-month period with only about half the expenditures for weapons. Documents also show that al Qaeda is very bureaucratic, requiring receipts for almost all of subordinates' expenditures, which is dangerous since such records can be discovered by the group's enemies, providing important intelligence information (see Jackson, B. 2004). In fact, parts of this paper trail were uncovered by investigators, and they provided some insights into the organization's financing. What is important is that al Qaeda is "tight fisted" with its money. Even though the organization has a budget of approximately $30 million per annum, it has massive expenses. Reportedly in 1995, when Ramzi Ahmed Yousef was arrested for the first bombing of the World Trade Center, an FBI agent reminded him that his attack was unsuccessful. Yousef retorted that if he had enough money and explosives, the World Trade Center would have been leveled (Levitt and Jacobson, 2008). This statement by Yousef that he lacked money demonstrated that he did not have the resources necessary to successfully carry out the attack.

Terrorist organizations have substantial expenses. They generally spread thin across a number of fronts. The group has numerous expenses and overhead. It must pay its fighters and in many cases provide sustenance for their families. It must train fighters in its camps, resulting in considerable expenditures. In many cases, it must pay local officials and corrupt politicians; for example, the Taliban and al Qaeda has been able to maintain bases in Pakistan by bribing or paying a number of the tribal chiefs. It has been estimated that bin Laden paid as much as $20 million to tribal chiefs before his death (Lee, 2002).

ISIS spent most of its operating budget on salaries to ministries that govern the captured territories, repairing and maintaining facilities and infrastructures, and services to civilians, including social welfare. ISIS also paid each fighter a monthly salary of $400–600. Married fighters received an extra stipend to support their families. It was estimated that the actual expenditures were actually higher than the income of ISIS (Humud, Pirog, and Rosen, 2015).

In reality, al Qaeda, ISIS, and other terrorist groups have tremendous expenditures, requiring a significant cash flow. It appears that eliminating at least some of this flow of money would have significant repercussions on terrorists' activities.

Summary

This chapter examined terrorist funding. To a large extent, this chapter focused on al Qaeda and ISIS. The focus on ISIS and Al Qaeda does not mean that other terrorist organizations are not involved in raising funds; indeed, there are numerous such networks across the globe, perhaps several hundred such organizations. However, al Qaeda and ISIS were examined more closely here because they represent the largest and most sophisticated and problematic terrorist networks in the world. Through its various enterprises, they raise approximately millions of dollars year (Looney, 2006; Naylor, 2002). ISIS receives about $1 billion per year from its various income sources (Homeland Security Committee, 2016). A number of narco-terrorist organizations in South and Central America have more substantial revenues, but the fruits of their activities relate more to greed than terrorism; they often use terrorist acts to facilitate their ability to realize financial gains. Terrorist organizations such as al Qaeda and ISIS raise money to directly support terrorism.

Terrorist funding is a process with three distinct phases: (1) earning or acquiring resources, (2) moving or laundering the money, and (3) storing or banking the money until it is needed. Al Qaeda, ISIS, and other terrorist groups have developed extremely complex and effective financial networks. Terrorist organizations and ISIS are akin to multinational conglomerates. They use a variety of techniques to raise money, including criminal enterprises, common crimes, legitimate businesses, charities, black market commodities, oil and gas, taxation, and donations from wealthy patrons.

The existence of these multiple funding sources makes it difficult to reduce terrorist funding. When authorities are able to intervene in one area, it appears that other sources are available to take up the financial slack. Moreover, Looney (2006) noted that when countries enact tougher anti-terrorist funding initiatives, the terrorists move their operations to countries that are less restrictive. Indeed, the 9/11 Commission (2004) suggested that it is impossible to eliminate terrorist funding and that a better strategy might be to follow the money. Terrorist groups and activities might be identified by following funding sources—the money trail can provide significant intelligence information.

On the other hand, Levitt and Jacobson (2008) advised that terrorist groups have extremely large organizational maintenance costs and that eliminating a portion of their finances likely would cause the groups operational problems. The U.S. government stated that there are three important lessons about terrorist financing. First, terrorist organizations across the globe draw on the wealth and resources of the United States to fund their terrorist activities. Second, every terrorist group has unique fundraising methods and thus strategies of reducing the money stream must be specific to different terrorist groups. Third, terrorist organizations are very creative in exploiting vulnerabilities in the U.S. financial system. It is important that the United States and other countries continue to reduce terrorist funding.

Discussion Questions

1. Terrorist financing consists of two distinct activities. What are they and how do they operate?
2. Terrorists have alternative financing mechanisms. Distinguish among earning, moving, and storing resources.
3. How does a hawala operate?
4. Describe the relationship between the United States and Saudi Arabia and how Wahhabism affects Saudi Arabia and that relationship.

5. What are breeder documents and how do they function?
6. Describe how the terrorists funded the 9/11 attacks.
7. What is the Real ID Act? How effectively has it been implemented?

References

Armstrong, D. (2004). "Charity cases." *Harper's Magazine*, 308(1846): 81–83.

Basile, M. (2009). "Going to the source: Why al Qaeda's financial network is likely to withstand the current war on terrorism financing." *Terrorism and Counterterrorism*, ed. R. Howard, R. Sawyer, and N. Bajema, pp. 530–547. New York: McGraw-Hill.

BBC America. (2008). *New Kidnappings in Colombia*. http://news.bbc.co.uk/2/hi/americas/7188509.stm (Accessed December 13, 2008).

Beaumont, P. (2017). Qatar: Rex Tillerson to fly to Kuwait in efforts to diffuse crisis. *The Guardian* (July 7). https://www.theguardian.com/world/2017/jul/07/qatar-crisis-four-arab-states-vow-fresh-economic-and-political-sanctions (Accessed July 14, 2017).

Block, R., and D. Pearl. (2001). "Underground trade: Much smuggled gem called tanzanite helps bin Laden supporters—Bought and sold by militants near mine, stones often end up at Mideast souks—Deal making at the mosque." *The Wall Street Journal* (November 18): A1.

Comras, V. (2005). "Al Qaeda finances and funding to affiliated groups." *Strategic Insights*, 6(1), 1–17.

Corbat, M. (2014). "CEO Michael Corbat's keynote at the Mobile World Congress." Citibank. http://www.citigroup.com/citi/news/executive/140225Ea.htm (Accessed March 21, 2017).

Decker, S., T. Bynum, and D. Weisel. (2004). "A tale of two cities: Gangs as organized crime groups." *American Youth Gangs at the Millennium*, ed. F. Esbensen, S. Tibbetts, and L. Gaines, pp. 247–274. Long Grove, IL: Waveland.

Departments of Treasury. (2017). Terrorist Finance Tracking Program (TFTP). https://www.treasury.gov/resource-center/terrorist-illicit-finance/Terrorist-Finance-Tracking/Pages/tftp.aspx (Accessed December 4, 2017).

Dinan, S. (2012). "Homeland security postpones stricter driver's license rules." *The Washington Times* (December 20). www.washingontimes.com/news/2012/dec/20/dhs-postpones-stricter-drivers-license-rules/ (Accessed December 22, 2012).

European Commission. (2016). *Commission Presents Action Plan to Strengthen the Fight against Terrorist Financing*." Press Release, February 2.

Fanusie, Y., and L. Heid. (2016). "What ISIS is banking on." *Forbes* (June 17). https://www.forbes.com/sites/realspin/2016/06/17/what-isis-is-banking-on/#175ad3b61651 (Accessed April 17, 2017).

Farah, D. (2001). "Al Qaeda cash tied to diamond trade, sale of gems from Sierra Leone; rebels raised millions." *The Washington Post* (November 2): A1.

Federal Bureau of Investigation. (2002). "Financing of terrorism and terrorist acts and related money laundering." *Briefing* (September 30).

Financial Action Task Force. (undated). Homepage. http://www.fatf-gafi.org/pages/0,3417,en_32250379_32235720_1_1_1_1_1,00.html (Accessed December 11, 2008).

Financial Action Task Force. (1999). *1998–1999 Report on Money Laundering Typologies*. Paris: Author.

Financial Action Task Force. (2008). *Terrorist Financing*. http://www.fatf-gafi.org/media/fatf/documents/reports/FATF%20Terrorist%20Financing%20Typologies%20Report.pdf (Accessed December 10, 2008).

Financial Action Task Force. (2015). *Emerging Terrorist Financing Risks*. Paris: Author. http://www.fatf-gafi.org/media/fatf/documents/reports/Emerging-Terrorist-Financing-Risks.pdf (Accessed April 17, 2017).

Gold, D. (2003). *Saudi Arabia's Dubious Denials of Involvement in International Terrorism* (Number 504, October 1). Jerusalem: Jerusalem Center for Public Affairs. http://www.jcpa.org/jl/vp504.htm (Accessed January 1, 2009).

Gordon, G., and N. Willox. (2003). *Identity Fraud: A Critical National and Global Threat*. Utica, NY: Economic Crime Institute.

Goulet, N. (2015). *Following the Money: How to Prevent Terrorist Financing*. AlMonitor. http://www.al-monitor.com/pulse/originals/2015/12/prevent-terror-financing.html (Accessed April 25, 2017).

Government Accounting Office. (2003). *Terrorist Financing: U.S. Agencies Should Systematically Assess Terrorists' Use of Alternative Financing Mechanisms*. Washington, D.C.: Author.

Henifin, D. (2004). "What took so long? Closing the Holy Land Foundation: A case study in counterterrorism." A paper presented at the National War College.

Homeland Security Committee. (2016). *Cash to Chaos: Dismantling ISIS' Financial Infrastructure*. House Homeland Security Committee Majority Staff Report. https://homeland.housc.gov/wp-content/uploads/2016/10/Dismantling-ISIS-Financial-Infrastructure.pdf (Accessed April 17, 2017).

House of Representatives. (2016). *Stopping Terror Finance: Securing the U.S. Financial Sector*. 114th Congress, Second Session. http://financialservices.house.gov/uploadedfiles/terror_financing_report_12-20-2016.pdf (Accessed April 16, 2017).

Humud, C. E., R. Pirog, and L. Rosen. (2015). *Islamic State Financing and U.S. Policy Approaches*. Congressional Research Service. https://fas.org/sgp/crs/terror/R43980.pdf (Accessed April 25, 2017).

Jacinto, L. (2017). "Are diamonds the terrorists' best friends?" *ABC News*. http://abcnews.go.com/Business/story?id=86326 (Accessed September 1, 2017).

Jackson, B. (2004). Organizational Learning and Terrorist Groups. *RAND*. https://www.rand.org/content/dam/rand/pubs/working_papers/2004/RAND_WR133.pdf.

Johnston, P. (2016). *The Islamic State's Money Problems*. RAND Corporation. http://www.rand.org/blog/2016/03/the-islamic-states-money-problems.html (Accessed April 16, 2017).

Kean, T. and L. H. Hamilton. (2004). 9/11 Commission Report. https://www.9-11commission.gov/report/911Report.pdf.

Knaus, C. (2017). "Commonwealth Bank accused of money laundering and terrorism-financing breaches." *The Guardian*. https://www.theguardian.com/australia-news/2017/aug/03/commonwealth-bank-accused-of-money-laundering-and-terrorism-financing-breaches (Accessed September 1, 2017).

Kohlmann, E. (2006–2007). *The Role of Islamic Charities in International Terrorist Recruitment and Financing*. Copenhagen: Danish Institute for International Studies.

Lee, R. (2002). *Terrorist Financing: The U.S. and International Response*. Washington, D.C.: Congressional Research Service.

Levitt, M., and M. Jacobson. (2008). *The Money Trail: Finding, Following, and Freezing Terrorist Finances*. Washington, D.C.: The Washington Institute for Near East Policy. http://www.washingtoninstitute.org/templateC04.php?CID=302 (Accessed December 23, 2008).

Looney, R. (2006). "The mirage of terrorist financing: The case of Islamic charities." *Strategic Insights*, 5(3), 1–14.

Malkin, L. (2002). "Terrorism's money trail." *World Policy Journal*, 19(1): 60–71.

McCusker, R. (2005). "Underground banking: Legitimate remittance network or money laundering system?" *Trends & Issues in Crime and Criminal Justice* (No. 300). Sydney: Australian Institute of Criminology.

Miller, J., and J. Gerth. (2001). "Trade in honey is said to provide money and cover for bin Laden." *The New York Times* (October 11): A1.

National Commission on Terrorist Attacks upon the United States. (2004). *Monograph on Terrorist Financing* (Staff Report). http://govinfo.library.unt.edu/911/staff_statements/911_TerrFin_Monograph.pdf (Accessed December 11, 2008).

Naylor, R. (2002). *Wages of Crime: Black Markets, Illegal Finance, and the Underworld Economy*. Ithaca: Cornell University Press.

Naylor, R. (2006). *Satanic Purses: Money, Myth and Misinformation in the War on Terror*. Montreal: McGill-Queen's University Press.

Perez, E., C. E. Soichet, and W. Bruer. (2015). "Hacker who allegedly passed U.S. military data to ISIS arrested in Malaysia." *CNN News*. http://www.cnn.com/2015/10/15/politics/malaysian-hacker-isis-military-data/ (Accessed April 25, 2017).

Prados, A., and C. Blanchard. (2004). *Saudi Arabia: Terrorist Financing Issues*. Washington, D.C.: Congressional Research Service.

PWC. (2016). *Money Laundering Destroys Value*. http://www.pwc.com/gx/en/services/advisory/forensics/economic-crime-survey/anti-money-laundering.html (Accessed March 22, 2017).

Roberge, I. (2007). "Misguided policies in the war on terror? The case for disentangling terrorist financing from money laundering." *Politics*, 27(3): 196–203.

Sander, C. (2003). *Migrant Remittances to Developing Countries*. London: Bannrock Consulting. http://www.dai.com/pdf/Migrant_Remittances_to_Developing_Countries.pdf (Accessed December 16, 2008).

Schmidt, R. (2008). "Ex-Rep Rick Siljander indicted." *The Los Angeles Times* (January 17). http://www.latimes.com/news/nationworld/nation/la-na-indict-17jan17,1,1025865.story?track=rss (Accessed December 18, 2008).

TSA. (2017). "Real ID and air travel." *Department of Homeland Security*. https://www.tsa.gov/sites/default/files/resources/realid_factsheet.pdf (Accessed September 2, 2017).

United Nations Office on Drugs and Crime. (2017). *Afghanistan: Opium Survey 2016*. https://www.unodc.org/documents/wdr/WDR_2010/1.2_The_global_heroin_market.pdf (Accessed August 31, 2017).

United Nations Security Council. (2002). *Second Report of the Monitoring Group Established Pursuant to Security Council Resolution 1363 (2001) and Extended by Resolution 1390 (2002)*. United Nations Security Council Committee

U.S. Department of State Publication. (2016). *Country Reports on Terrorism 2015*. https://www.state.gov/documents/organization/258249.pdf (Accessed April 28, 2017).

U.S. Department of Treasury. (2016a). *National Terrorist Financing Risk Assessment 2015*. https://www.treasury.gov/resource-center/terrorist-illicit-finance/Documents/National%20Terrorist%20Financing%20Risk%20Assessment%20%E2%80%93%2006-12-2015.pdf (Accessed April 28, 2017).

U.S. Department of Treasury. (2016b). *Terrorist Finance Tracking Program (TFTP)*. https://www.treasury.gov/resource-center/terrorist-illicit-finance/Terrorist-Finance-Tracking/Pages/tftp.aspx (Accessed March 21, 2017).

U.S. House of Representatives. (2016). *National Strategy for Combating Terrorist, Underground, and Other Illicit Financing Act*. https://www.congress.gov/bill/114th-congress/house-bill/5594/text (Accessed April 16, 2017).

Weinstein, A. (2017). "The real largest state sponsor of terrorism." *The Huffington Post*. http://www.huffingtonpost.com/entry/the-real-largest-state-sponsor-of-terrorism_us_58cafc26e4b00705db4da8aa (Accessed September 2, 2017).

Weintraub, S. (2001). "Disrupting the financing of terrorism." *The Washington Quarterly*, 25(1): 53–60.

Weiss, M. (2005). "Terrorist financing: The 9/11 Commission recommendation." *CRS Report for Congress*. Washington, D.C.: Congressional Research Service.

Zagaris, B. (2004). "The merging of the anti-money laundering and counter-terrorism financial enforcement regimes after September 11 2001." *Berkeley Journal of International Law*, 22: 123–158.

12 Border Security and Immigration

LEARNING OBJECTIVES

1. *Explain the relationship between immigration and border security.*
2. *Describe the patterns of illegal immigration to the United States.*
3. *Discuss philosophies and methods of border protection.*
4. *Describe the responsibilities and actions of DHS agencies involved in protecting our border and interior.*
5. *Explain how we control or monitor the flow of goods and people across our borders.*

Key Terms

Countries of special interest
Prevention
North American Complementary Immigration Policies
Interdiction
Deterrence
Secure Border Initiative
Border security and immigration enforcement improvements executive order
Workplace Enforcement Unit
United States Citizenship and Immigration Service
US-VISIT
Nonimmigrant visas and immigrant visas
Non-Visa or Visa Waiver Program
Secure Electronic Network for Travelers Rapid Inspection
NEXUS program
Maritime Transportation Act of 2002
Transportation Workers Identification Credential program
Customs-Trade Partnership Against Terrorism program
Container Security Initiative

Introduction

This chapter examines U.S. border security and immigration. Border security has become a critical component of homeland security. It is essential to secure the borders to ensure that terrorists do not enter the country and that weapons of mass destruction (WMDs) are not smuggled across. In the past, the U.S. borders have been rather permeable with scores of illegal immigrants entering the United States annually with little effort. They have come from all points on the globe, and they arrive by land, sea, and air. The majority of illegal immigrants seek employment, a better life, or escape from tyrannical conditions in their home country. They have not wished to do the United States any harm; they simply wish to participate in the American dream. However, as a result of terrorism and the conditions in the Middle East and elsewhere, today there are numerous terrorists who would come to the United States to cause our citizens and infrastructure harm. They wish to repeat the attacks of 9/11. They possibly will use the same routes that are used by good-intentioned migrants.

Border Patrol agent pats down an illegal alien before returning him to Mexico.
Source: http://www.cbp.gov/xp/cgov/newsroom/multimedia/photo_gallery/afc/bp/37.xml.

There are numerous estimates. The federal government estimated that in 2012, between 11 and 12 million illegal immigrants were living in the United States. The number of illegal immigrants has increased substantially over the last three decades. In 1980, the number of illegal immigrants increased from 2 to 4 million. By 2000, about 8.5 million people were residing illegally in the United States, and by 2010 the number of illegal immigrants exceeded 11 million. It has remained stable around 11million since (Department of Homeland Security, 2013). These are estimates, however. It is not possible to accurately identify the number of illegal immigrants currently living in the country, which vividly demonstrates the lack of control over the borders. If there is little control over who enters or leaves the country, the United States may be exposed to terrorist attacks. This realization has resulted in a number of homeland security initiatives. Principally, there is concern over border control, immigration, and the false documentation that is used to illegally gain entrance into the country.

▶ Immigration

A number of cities and counties have experienced large increases in the number of legal and illegal immigrants settling in their communities. Many of these communities heretofore were fairly homogeneous with little ethnic diversity. The immigration of Mexican nationals into the United States has resulted in a substantial amount of xenophobia and anger toward immigrants. Congress has been considering a number of bills to restrict or otherwise control illegal immigration, particularly along our southern border with Mexico. In 2010, Arizona passed SB1070, which gave the police authority to investigate and detain suspected illegal immigrants. Moreover, five states enacted similar legislation: Alabama, Georgia, Indiana, South Carolina, and Utah. Since 2010, much of the enacted laws have been rolled back by courts. Arizona's original bill SB1070 aimed to limit immigration through attrition. But several of the bill's provisions have been ruled unconstitutional by the Supreme

Court in 2012. Only one provision remained; that is, police officers are required to request proof of legal status papers from suspected illegal immigrants they encounter. However, the enforcement of this provision became difficult when the courts warned Arizona not to extend or prolong police stops. In 2016, Arizona announced an end to this provision of the bill also, rendering the bill toothless. The question is whether Arizona and other states will revive their bills under the Trump presidency (Duara, 2016).

Illegal immigration and bills implemented to decrease illegal immigration have become a heated political topic. Anxiety and angst revolve around the two issues surrounding illegal immigration and border reform: (1) securing the borders from would-be terrorists who may illegally enter the United States and (2) dealing with about 11 million undocumented immigrants who currently reside in the United States.

One side proposes that the United States must secure its borders and expel the illegal immigrants. They believe that the country cannot develop and implement an effective immigration policy until it has achieved this level of security. President Trump promised during his election campaign, and has been confirming his plans since, to build a wall along the Mexican border. According to house leader Republican Mitch McConnell, the building of a wall would cost about $15 billion. Trump promised that Mexico would pay for the wall, but that seems rather unrealistic as Mexico has refused to pay for the wall. Opponents advise that the building of a wall does not prevent illegal immigrants from crossing over if they have already traveled for several days over mountains and through desert. Being held up for a few minutes by a fence is not a major hurdle. John Kelly, former chief of the Department of Homeland Security (DHS), stated, "physical barriers will not do the job. When you build a wall, you would still have to back that wall with patrolling of human beings, by sensors, by observation devices" (Drew, 2017). In addition, opponents also argue that many of these illegal immigrants are productive, having jobs and paying taxes. They further advocate that several sectors of the economy, particularly agriculture, construction, and unskilled labor, require this illegal workforce—Americans cannot be recruited to perform many of these tasks due to low pay, lack of benefits, long work hours, and harsh conditions.

Although securing the borders is an important task, it is questionable if all the illegal immigrants can be deported. Would it be realistically possible to identify and deport the 11 million illegal immigrants who currently reside in the United States? Such a task would be insurmountable and cost prohibitive. Immigration policy is an issue that is separate from border control, and both policy issues should be approached simultaneously, but separately.

The dispute in Congress has stalled immigration reform, but Congress has funded border security on a piecemeal basis. The DHS is currently implementing additional security measures at various locations on the border. Implementation of security measures has been conducted on a cost-benefit basis. Those areas where the largest number of illegal entries occur have been receiving enhanced security measures, although it is currently envisioned that the United States, ultimately, will obtain total border security. Security is provided with a combination of physical and electronic barriers. Even though today homeland security focuses on border control, it should be remembered that immigration policy is intertwined with border security, and immigration policy cannot be neglected if the United States is to achieve security.

HS ANALYSIS BOX 12-1

Immigration is a thorny issue eliciting emotion from both sides. There are those who want to shut down the country's borders and remove all illegal immigrants. On the other side, there are those who say the United States needs them for a number of jobs that Americans will not do. It is a real conundrum. What should be done? Many advise that the country should not tackle immigration before it secures the borders. Is this possible? How should the United States proceed?

▶ Originating Countries of American Immigrants

When discussing immigration, most people refer to those illegal immigrants coming from Mexico. Such discussions make it appear that Mexican immigration is the country's only border problem. However, even though a large number of Mexican nationals are illegally immigrating to the United States, large numbers of people are coming from other countries. Figure 12-1 ■ shows the origin of legal permanent residents immigrating to the United States from 2012 to 2014.

Figure 12-1 ■ shows the country of birth of the legal immigrant population. The vast majority of immigrants (42.4%) come from Asia. With regard to countries, in 2014, the

(Countries Ranked by 2014 LPR Flow)

Region and Country of Birth	2014		2013		2012	
	Number	Percent	Number	Percent	Number	Percent
REGION						
Total	1,016,518	100.0	990.553	100.0	1,031,631	100.0
Africa	98,413	9.7	98,304	9.9	107,241	10.4
Asia	430,508	42.4	400,548	40.4	429.599	41.6
Europe	83,266	8.2	86,556	8.7	81.671	7.9
North America	324,354	31.9	315,660	31.9	327,771	31.8
Caribbean	133,952	13.2	122,406	12.4	127,477	12.4
Central America	44,403	4.4	44,724	4.5	40,675	3.9
Other North America	145,999	14.4	148,530	15.0	159,619	15.5
Oceania	5,112	0.5	5,277	0.5	4,742	0.5
South America	73,715	7.3	80,945	8.2	79,401	7.7
Unknown	1,150	0.1	3,263	0.3	1,206	0.1
COUNTRY						
Total	1,016,518	100.0	990,553	100.0	1,031,631	100.0
Mexico	134,052	13.2	135,028	13.6	146,406	14.2
India	77,908	7.7	68,458	6.9	66,434	6.4
China, People's Republic	76,089	7.5	71,798	7.2	81,784	7.9
Philippines	49,996	4.9	54,446	5.5	57,327	5.6
Cuba	46,679	4.6	32,219	3.3	32,820	3.2
Dominican Republic	44,577	4.4	41,311	4.2	41,566	4.0
Vietnam	30,283	3.0	27,101	2.7	28,304	2.7
Korea, South	20,423	2.0	23,166	2.3	20,846	2.0
El Salvador	19,273	1.9	18,260	1.8	16,256	1.6
Iraq	19,153	1.9	9,552	1.0	20,369	2.0
Jamaica	19,026	1.9	19,400	2.0	20,705	2.0
Pakistan	18,612	1.8	13,251	1.3	14,740	1.4
Colombia	18,175	1.8	21,131	2.1	20,931	2.0
Haiti	15,274	1.5	20,351	2.1	22,818	2.2
Bangladesh	14,645	1.4	12,099	1.2	14,705	1.4
Nigeria	12,828	1.3	13,840	1.4	13,575	1.3
Nepal	12,357	1.2	13,046	1.3	11,312	1.1
Ethiopia	12,300	1.2	13,097	1.4	14,544	1.4
United Kingdom	12,225	1.2	12,984	1.3	12,014	1.3
Iran	11,615	1.1	12,863	1.3	12,916	1.3
All other countries	351,028	34.5	357,152	36.1	361,259	35.0

Source: U.S. Department of Homeland Security.

FIGURE 12-1 Lawful Permanent Resident Flow by Region and Country of Birth
Source: https://www.dhs.gov/sites/default/files/publications/Lawful_Permanent_Residents_2014.pdf.

HS ANALYSIS BOX 12-2

Although most of the illegal immigrants flowing into the country are from Mexico, large numbers are coming from other countries. Many of them are dangerous—for example, gangs from Central America and Asia and organized crime from Russia and Europe. Yet these groups are not considered in the discussion of illegal immigration. Should the discussion include these groups? Would this change the focus of the debate? How should the discussion on this aspect proceed in the future?

vast majority of legal immigrants were from Mexico (13.2%). It is also noteworthy that California has the largest authorized immigrant population with 19.5% of all legal immigrants (2013).

Additionally, the DHS (2013) reports that close to 32 million, or approximately 10 percent of the U.S. population, are foreign-born, with about 40 percent naturalized as citizens. These statistics demonstrate that America has a long history of immigration, with a substantial number of people coming to the country each year, and they are being integrated into the society. It will be difficult to curb this trend.

HS Web Link: To learn more about globalization and immigration, go to http://www.globalissues.org/article/537/immigration.

Figure 12-2 ■ provides estimates for illegal immigration from 2000 until 2012. As evident in Figure 12-2 ■, illegal immigration increased from 8.5 million in 2000 to 11.4 million in 2012. The majority of illegal immigrants come from Mexico, estimated to be about 6.7 million, followed by El Salvador, estimated at 690,000. Most of the unauthorized immigrants reside in California (2.8 million) and Texas (1.8 million) (Baker and Rytina, 2013).

Indeed, it is likely that the United States will experience increased immigration. Several factors will contribute to this trend. The National Intelligence Council (2017) examined a number of world problems, one of which was migration. Shortages in

	Estimated population in January		Percent of total	
Country of birth	2012	2010	2012	2010
All countries	11,430,000	11,590,000	100	100
Mexico	6,720,000	6,830,000	59	59
El Salvador	690,000	670,000	6	6
Guatemala	560,000	520,000	5	4
Honduras	360,000	380,000	3	3
Philippines	310,000	290,000	3	2
India	260,000	270,000	2	2
Korea	230,000	220,000	2	2
China	210,000	300,000	2	3
Ecuador	170,000	210,000	2	2
Vietnam	160,000	190,000	1	2
Other countries	1,760,000	1,720,000	15	15

FIGURE 12-2 Country of Birth for Unauthorized Immigrant Population

Source: https://www.dhs.gov/sites/default/files/publications/Unauthorized%20Immigrant%20Population%20Estimates%20in%20the%20US%20January%202012_0.pdf

food, energy, and water will result in increased world migration. The Council estimated that climate change and human demand would drastically affect food production and the availability of water, resulting in shortages in numerous countries. In 2015, there were about 244 million migrants, globally, moving due to economic reasons, to flee conflict and worsening environmental conditions, and forcible displacement. These migrants could still be moving to a number of countries, including the United States. It is questionable if walls will be able to keep them out. The Council did, however, note that world economic power of Western Europe and the United States will be struggling for the next 5 years. China will continue its efforts to move toward an investment-centered and consumption-based economy, which may threaten the growth of trade with countries around the globe, including the United States. The changing economic and political climate nonetheless is a major factor that will contribute to instability in countries that have weak governments, poverty, and poor infrastructure (White House, 2015).

Illegal immigration is not the only rationale for securing the country's borders. There remains a possibility that WMDs or WMD material will be smuggled into the country. A substantial portion of the drugs coming into the United States enters through Mexico. Drugs such as cocaine, heroin, methamphetamine, and marijuana come overland from Mexico. Thousands of pounds of drugs enter the United States each year from across the southern border. Obviously, if such large quantities of drugs can be smuggled across the border, it would not be difficult to smuggle WMD material into the country. The smuggling routes and mechanisms are already in place.

In addition to illegal immigration, there is substantial human trafficking in which women and children are sold as prostitutes or forced to work in sweatshops. They are smuggled into the United States where they become virtual slaves to their handlers or owners with little hope of having a normal life. Their living conditions often are worse than that in their former countries. They are deprived of liberty and rights. This is morally repugnant and maximum efforts should be exerted to curtail this crime problem; increased border security is one method of accomplishing this objective.

Finally, as a result of competing drug and crime cartels, Mexico has witnessed a substantial increase in the level of violence, violence that literally is out of control with several thousand homicides annually. Walsh (2009) reported that there were 5,367 narco-homicides in 2008. Multiple homicide victims are discovered almost on a daily basis. Politicians, police and military officials, and reporters have been murdered almost indiscriminately. Kidnapping has become a common occurrence. In a number of cases, this violence has spilled over into the United States with U.S. citizens being killed on both sides of the border. Since Mexican drug operations are tied to drug traffickers in the United States, it is likely that this problem will worsen in the future. Enhanced border security might aid in keeping these problems from affecting the United States. Moreover, enhanced border security might reduce the volume of drugs coming into the country; tighter border security certainly would make it more difficult to smuggle drugs across the border. A reduction in the flow of drugs might lead to a reduction of violence in Mexico, a collateral benefit.

Border Security Issues

It is a considerable task for the United States to control its borders—they are rather extensive. The United States shares a border with Mexico that is approximately 2,000 miles in length, and the border with Canada is about 5,500 miles long. Additionally, Forest (2006) advises that the United States has 26,000 miles of navigable rivers and waterways and 12,383 miles of coastline. The country also has hundreds of major airports that serve approximately 120 million passengers leaving and entering the United States each year and approximately 4,000 marine ports and terminals. Given the sheer magnitude of the borders, it is a considerable task to secure them. In fact, it is questionable if the United States has the personnel and resources to do so. Nonetheless, the United States has implemented a number of programs to accomplish this task, and it must implement programs that at a minimum provide a large measure of security.

As noted, there is considerable controversy over the number of illegal immigrants coming into the United States. The problem from a homeland security perspective is that there is evidence that potential terrorists are illegally entering the United States from Mexico and Canada. Generally, these people travel to a third country such as Brazil and then travel to Mexico or Canada. Mexico is particularly problematic because of the number of illegal immigrants entering the United States and the number of human smuggling rings that exist in Mexico and stretch well into South America. As noted in Figure 12-3 ■ presented in a later section, more than 1.1 million illegal immigrants are apprehended each year on the U.S. southern border. Once in Mexico, they will contact a human smuggling operation to secure passage into the United States.

The border with Canada is also problematic. Although there are only about 7,300 apprehensions each year, the border is extremely long and often desolate and unprotected. Terrorists and illegal immigrants entering from Canada often attempt to obtain documentation, often forged, and simply cross into the United States. Once in the United States, they often travel to some predetermined location and possibly link up with other potential terrorists or become integrated into immigrant communities. Another problem is that Canada historically has had less stringent immigration policies as compared to the United States. For example, hundreds of Haitians crossed illegally into Canada from the United States in 2017 as a result of President Trump's proposed immigration policies (Stevenson, 2017).

Border Protection agent watches for illegal aliens attempting to cross the border.
Department of Homeland Security.

Such migration may result in terrorists immigrating to Canada, obtaining documentation, and then traveling to the United States.

> HS Web Link: To learn more about illegal immigration, go to http://www.pewresearch.org/fact-tank/2017/04/27/5-facts-about-illegal-immigration-in-the-u-s/

Illegal Border Migration: A Case Study in Tucson

Substantial numbers of illegal immigrants enter the United States from Mexico; more than 1.1 million were apprehended in 2006. Figure 12-3 ■ shows the various routes used by illegal immigrants to enter the Tucson, Arizona, area from Mexico. Notice that within this fairly limited geographical boundary, numerous entry points are used by hundreds of illegal immigrants. The number of entry points in the Tucson area indicates that there are thousands of entry points between our ports of entry.

> HS Web Link: To learn more about the Tucson area border patrol, go to https://www.cbp.gov/border-security/along-us-borders/border-patrol-sectors/tucson-sector-arizona

The Tucson example shows that the U.S. border is extremely porous. There are numerous entry points across the border with most of the entry points close to towns and cities. Entering the United States in a populated area like Tucson makes detection much more difficult since the illegal immigrants often blend in with the indigenous population.

Border Apprehensions

According to the DHS, in 2016, the U.S. Customs and Border Protection agency apprehended 415,816 immigrants. The vast majority of apprehensions—331,333 apprehensions—occurred on the country's southwest border (U.S. Customs and Border Protection, 2016). There were relatively few apprehensions on the Canadian border; indeed, there were more apprehensions along the U.S. coastline. The statistics also show that the overwhelming majority of apprehensions were of Mexicans, followed by people

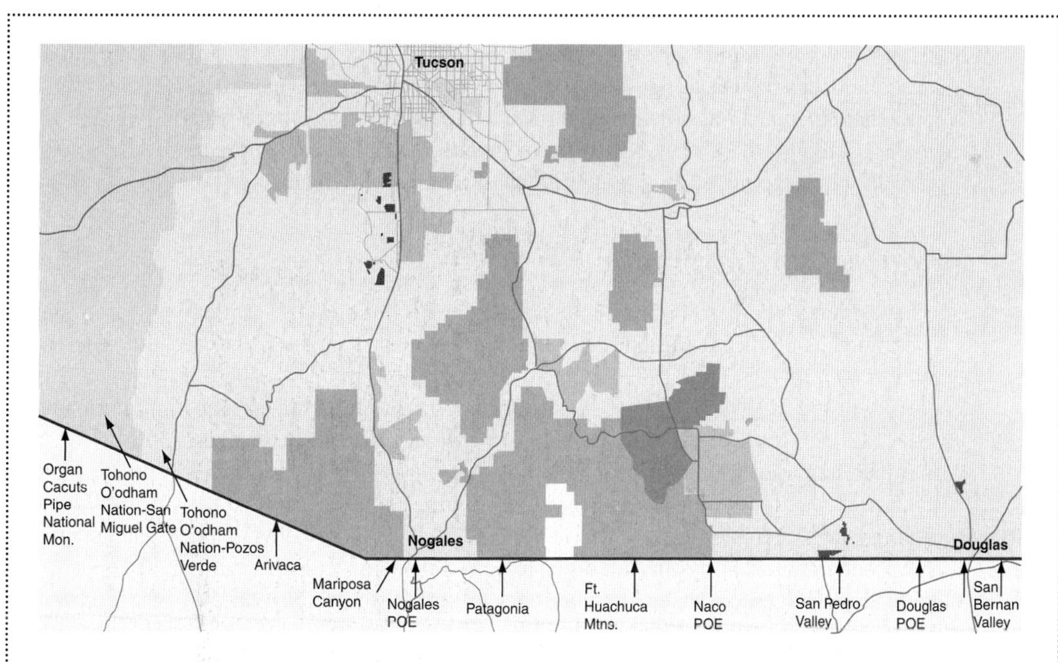

FIGURE 12-3 Tucson, Arizona, Area Illegal Border Crossing Points

Source: Adapted from Ordonez, K.J. (2006). "Modeling the U.S. Border Patrol Tucson Section for the Deployment and Operations of Border Security Forces." Masters Thesis, Naval Post-Graduate School, Monterey, CA.

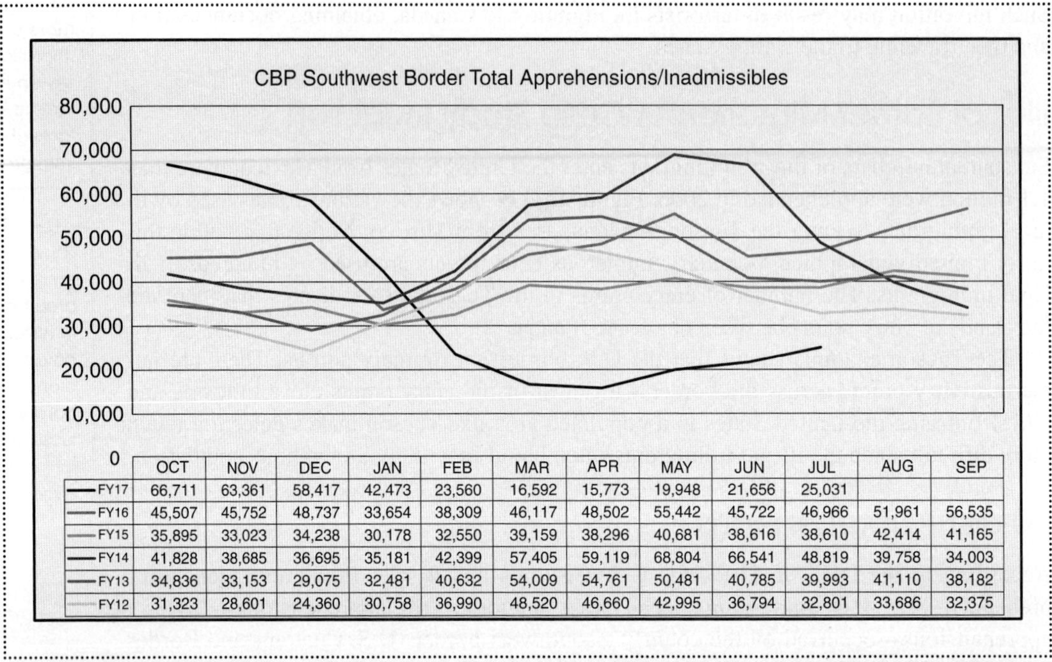

	OCT	NOV	DEC	JAN	FEB	MAR	APR	MAY	JUN	JUL	AUG	SEP
FY17	66,711	63,361	58,417	42,473	23,560	16,592	15,773	19,948	21,656	25,031		
FY16	45,507	45,752	48,737	33,654	38,309	46,117	48,502	55,442	45,722	46,966	51,961	56,535
FY15	35,895	33,023	34,238	30,178	32,550	39,159	38,296	40,681	38,616	38,610	42,414	41,165
FY14	41,828	38,685	36,695	35,181	42,399	57,405	59,119	68,804	66,541	48,819	39,758	34,003
FY13	34,836	33,153	29,075	32,481	40,632	54,009	54,761	50,481	40,785	39,993	41,110	38,182
FY12	31,323	28,601	24,360	30,758	36,990	48,520	46,660	42,995	36,794	32,801	33,686	32,375

FIGURE 12-4 Mexican Border Apprehensions

Source: https://www.cbp.gov/newsroom/stats/sw-border-migration

from other South and Central American countries. Figure 12-4 ■ shows the change in apprehensions between 2012 and 2017. There appears to be a substantial decrease in apprehensions in 2017 as compared to prior years. Most of the apprehensions were of adult males, although there were a number of juveniles and females apprehended. Many were most likely traveling to the United States to seek employment.

Terrorist Infiltration via Illegal Immigration

There is a fear that terrorists are intermingling with immigrants to enter the United States. The number of illegal immigrants other than Mexican in origin has steadily decreased over the past several years. The number of illegal immigrants peaked in 2000 to 1.8 million and decreased to 462,388 in 2015. The vast majority of illegal immigrants—that is, 267,885—came from Mexico (Department of Homeland Security, 2016c). Of that number, very few came from countries of special interest. There are 35 special interest countries, including Iran, Jordan, Lebanon, Syria, Egypt, Saudi Arabia, Kuwait, Pakistan, Cuba, Brazil, Ecuador, China, Russia, Yemen, Albania, Yugoslavia, and Afghanistan, that have been identified by the intelligence community as countries that could export individuals to the United States to commit acts of terrorism (Majority Staff of the Committee on Homeland Security, 2006).

The Committee on Homeland Security further reported that each year hundreds of illegal immigrants from countries known to harbor terrorists or promote terrorism are routinely encountered or apprehended attempting to enter the United States via smuggling routes. For example, Mahmound Youssef Kourani pleaded guilty to providing material support to Hezbollah. He had paid Mexican coyotes (human smugglers) to smuggle him into the United States. He then established residency in the Lebanese community in Dearborn, Michigan. The committee (2017) further found,

> Just recently, intelligence officials report that seven Iraqis were found in Brownsville, Texas in June 2006. In August 2006, an Afghani man was found swimming across the Rio Grande River in Hidalgo, Texas; as recently as October 2006, seven Chinese were apprehended in the Rio Grande Valley area of Texas. (p. 29)

The director of the FBI has confirmed that there are individuals from countries with an al Qaeda presence who are changing their surnames to Hispanic-sounding names and obtaining false Hispanic identities. They are learning Spanish and attempting to immigrate to the United States as Hispanics (Mueller, 2005). In 2011, three Pakistani citizens plead guilty to conspiracy to provide material support to the terrorist organization Tehrik-i-Taliban Pakistan (TTP), the Pakistani Taliban (U.S. Department of Justice, 2011). The three Pakistanis had attempted to smuggle a person associated with the TTP into the United States. More recently, the Texas Department of Public Safety reported that between November 2013 and July 2014, 143 individuals on the U.S. terror watch list were apprehended trying to cross the Mexican border and enter the United States illegally (Richey, 2017).

Many of the questionable individuals who are slipping across the border are being assisted by human smuggling organizations in Mexico. Salim Boughader Mucharrafille, a businessman in Tijuana, Mexico, was convicted of illegally smuggling more than 200 Lebanese into the United States, some of whom had ties to Hezbollah (Office of the Federal Register, 2015). In 2004, Immigration Customs Enforcement apprehended Neeran Zaia, who smuggled Iraqi, Jordanian, and Syrian nationals. The immigrants would be smuggled from the Middle East to staging areas in Central and South America. From there they would be smuggled into the United States (Schoch, 2006).

According to the Bureau of Counterterrorism and Countering Violent Extremism (2016), Venezuela has been providing support to radical Islamic groups. The government has provided thousands of cedulas (equivalent to the U.S. Social Security cards) to people

Syrian refugees arriving in Europe. There is a fear that terrorists are intermingled with those trying to escape the violence.
MARKA/Alamy Stock Photo.

HS ANALYSIS BOX 12-3

The previous discussion demonstrates that there is potential for terrorists to slip into the United States across the southern border. It demonstrates that the United States must implement more effective controls on the borders. Given the complexity of the problem, what actions should the United States take? How can the United States effectively keep terrorists from slipping across the borders? Do you believe that the United States can solve this problem?

from places such as Cuba, Colombia, and Middle Eastern countries that host terrorist organizations. These documents allow them to obtain Venezuelan passports and in some cases visas to the United States. Many terrorist organizations are currently operating in Paraguay; their members can travel to Venezuela, obtain documentation, and then attempt to enter the United States.

The civil war in Syria has created a refugee crisis, with refugees fleeing mainly to Europe, but also to the United States. Among the refugees were also ISIS terrorists. Due to the lack of identification procedures it has been very challenging for law enforcement to determine who is a true refugee and who is a terrorist. Neither Europe nor the United States can say with any certainty how many terrorists have entered Europe and the United States by taking advantage of the flood of refugees from the region. However, several terror attacks have been carried out in France, Belgium, and Germany during 2015 and 2016. For instance, on March 22, 2015, terrorists attacked the Brussels International Airport and the Maelbeek Metro Station and killed 32 people and injured 340. The three suicide bombers who were associated with ISIS and had come as part of the refugees also died (BBC News, 2016). What is significant about these attacks is the fact that the attackers did not buy any plane or metro tickets and never had to pass through any security measures. Departure halls in airports and metro stations are open to the public and crowded, which provides easy targets for terrorists. The United States and other countries have stepped up security measures. The Transportation Security Agency (TSA) has increased security by increasing the presence of their Visible Intermodal Prevention and Response teams (VIPR) in airports and metro stations. The VIPR teams consist of Federal Air Marshals, Behavior Detection Officers, Transportation Security Specialists–Explosives, Transportation Security Inspectors, and Canine Teams (Department of Homeland Security, 2016a).

There is no estimate of the number of terrorists or persons from terrorist-friendly countries who are entering the United States. However, terrorists generally have access to large amounts of cash, allowing them to hire the best or most efficient smuggling services in Mexico and South and Central America. Consequently, a greater percentage likely succeeds in entering the United States as compared to others who attempt to improperly enter the United States.

► Border Protection Philosophy after 9/11

According to Riley (2006), the 9/11 attacks and the magnitude of the country's extensive borders have resulted in a new philosophy regarding border protection. This new philosophy has two components. First, the United States has pushed the borders out and away from its shores. Border or security measures were implemented in countries where people and material originated, to prevent entry into the United States. For example, checking the identities of U.S.-bound passengers in the originating countries can likely intercept terrorists, undesirable or suspicious persons, and illegal immigrants before entry into the United

States. This can be accomplished by checking the watch lists. The same philosophy applies to goods and material being shipped to the United States. Inspecting them at their origination point reduces contraband, drugs, and possibly WMDs from entering the country. These measures are intended to remove threats before they reach U.S. shores. They also reduce the bottleneck of goods and people awaiting inspection at the borders. They are discussed in more detail in this section.

The second component of the philosophy of border protection is the profiling of people and goods at their originating point. Profiling was seen as a method of reducing the workload and the distractions from inspecting large numbers of people and material at ports of entry. The United States has identified safe originating points and those points that are suspect or lack required levels of security. For example, some countries, such as England, have more effective intelligence and security. People traveling from more secure countries require less scrutiny as compared to travelers from other countries. Some countries control cargo shipments more effectively, resulting in a measure of safety for the cargo when it reaches the United States. U.S. officials can become more efficient by concentrating efforts on insecure areas. This does not mean that safe points are neglected since security programs have been implemented in those areas. Profiling also allows the United States to identify those people and material that should receive more consideration.

Since his inception, President Trump has issued an executive order banning travel of people from six Muslim-majority countries to the United States: Syria, Iran, Yemen, Libya, Somalia, and Sudan. The travel ban has been challenged repeatedly in various courts, which held that the travel ban, as written, was unconstitutional. In the Spring of 2017, the travel ban reached the U.S. Supreme Court, which ruled that parts of the travel ban were constitutional. The latest revision of the executive order was challenged in the Ninth Circuit Court in *Hawaii v. Trump* based on religious discrimination. The judges have not made their decision yet, but the travel ban seems to be heading toward the Supreme Court (Liptak, 2017). However, it was only a temporary travel ban, and it remains to be seen if it is extended.

The new philosophy outlined by Riley focuses on prevention. **Prevention** is the most important part of any strategy to subjugate aggression or terrorism. A critical part of military strategy is to deploy resources to prevent an enemy from attacking—defense and protecting critical assets are of paramount importance. The country's national drug control strategy deploys personnel in foreign countries to interdict drugs and prevent them from coming into the United States. The U.S. Department of State works with countries to prevent terrorist groups from succeeding in those countries. Prevention should be an important and integral part of U.S. border protection strategy. The USA PATRIOT Act gives law enforcement more investigative powers to intercede in terrorists' operations to prevent such acts. Even though prevention is routinely recognized as an important strategy, prevention in border security strategies historically has not been predominant.

In 2001, new immigration policies were implemented. A part of these policies was to deny entry, detain, prosecute, and deport immigrants associated with or suspected of engaging in terrorist activities. Foreign students were barred from taking courses that contained sensitive material. Databases were used to locate and apprehend suspected terrorists or supporters of terrorism inside the United States. The **North American Complementary Immigration Policies** called for the United States to work with Mexico and Canada to develop compatible screening protocols at the borders. These protocols facilitate the identification of persons coming from Mexico or Canada who would do harm to the United States. This goal was not accomplished, as the DHS focused on border hardening (Smart Border Initiative), which did little to assist in monitoring persons coming across the borders.

HS Web Link: To learn more about immigration policies and terrorism, go to http://www.fas.org/irp/offdocs/nspd/hspd-2.htm.

Patrolling Border Patrol agent scans for illegal aliens.
Department of Homeland Security.

Part of the problem in developing effective protocols for the identification of persons who could harm the United States was defining prevention. Prevention became operationalized as interdiction or physically preventing people, especially terrorists, from entering the country. Prevention also includes interdiction and deterrence. **Interdiction** is an attempt to stop a plot once it has begun. **Deterrence**, on the other hand, occurs when potential terrorists believe that defenses are insurmountable and therefore do not attempt intrusion. Deterrence cannot be easily measured, as discussed in Chapter 3; consequently, agencies become less interested in it. Although elements of prevention, interdiction, and deterrence are contained in the current policies, they are piecemeal and no comprehensive system currently is in place.

Secure Border Initiative

During the 1990s, the U.S. Border Patrol changed tactics. The agency began to emphasize deterrence over apprehension. Several programs were implemented, including Operation Hold the Line, Gatekeeper, and Safeguard. These programs placed personnel and equipment as close to the border as possible, and their primary objectives were to deter or prevent illegal crossings and to break up smuggling rings as opposed to apprehending illegal immigrants after they crossed the border, which previously had been the policy. The deterrence strategy resulted in a reduction in illegal border crossings as measured by apprehensions. The programming resulted in higher levels of public support on the part of American border residents.

The shift in strategy brought criticism from conservatives who believed that the programs were too weak as they resulted in fewer apprehensions. They mistakenly viewed apprehensions as the best measure of security. Liberals criticized the programs because they were too intrusive into community affairs. Others believed that the programs went beyond the Border Patrol's mandate. As a result of the criticisms and politics, programming became less vigorous. The United States' policies again began to emphasize apprehension as opposed to prevention and deterrence. Disbanded smuggling operations again became operational, and there was an increase in the number of illegal immigrants crossing the border (Bach, 2005).

The 9/11 attacks resulted in renewed interest in border security. However, interdiction and apprehension, not deterrence or prevention, were emphasized; organizational effectiveness was measured by apprehensions. Immigration and Customs Enforcement concentrated on locating illegal immigrants and removing them once they were prosecuted. It is without doubt that interdiction leads to substantial public attention and media recognition, but it is not as efficient as prevention. Also, the costs associated with identifying, tracking, prosecuting, and deporting illegal immigrants are quite substantial, costs that are not associated with an effective prevention program. A comprehensive prevention program including cooperation with the Mexican and Canadian governments is by far the most promising strategy. Unfortunately, such a strategy has not come to full fruition.

Border security became an explosive political issue as thousands of illegal migrants streamed across the southern border. As an example, in 2005, Governor Bill Richardson of New Mexico and Governor Janet Napolitano of Arizona declared a state of emergency as a result of the number of illegal immigrants crossing state borders. Arizona, in 2010, passed a strict immigration law designed to control illegal immigrants. Duncan Hunter, chair of the House Armed Services Committee, proposed building two parallel walls stretching from the Pacific Ocean to the Gulf of Mexico, although Michael Chertoff, then secretary of the DHS, advised that such a fence would be cost prohibitive (Global Security, undated-a). Some have referred to this idea as the "great wall of Mexico" (Global Security, undated-b). The cost and debate resulted in a compromise whereby physical barriers and Customs and Border Protection agents were increased, and other forms of border monitoring were deployed.

A program implemented by the DHS to secure the country's borders was the **Secure Border Initiative** (SBI), which was a multiyear project that attempted to secure the northern and southern borders. The SBI was intended to be comprehensive, addressing a number of deficiencies that led to increased illegal immigration. According to the DHS, the primary components of the SBI included the following:

- More agents to patrol the U.S. borders, secure ports of entry, and enforce immigration laws;
- Expanded detention and removal capabilities to eliminate "catch and release" once and for all;
- A comprehensive and systemic upgrading of the technology used in controlling the border, including increased manned aerial assets, expanded use of UAVs, and next-generation detection technology;
- Increased investment in infrastructure improvements at the border—providing additional physical security to sharply reduce illegal border crossings; and
- Greatly increased interior enforcement of our immigration laws—including more robust worksite enforcement. (DHS, 2005)

In 2011, Janet Napolitano, then secretary of Homeland Security, canceled the program after spending $1 billion due to the high costs and lack of viability (Preston, 2011).

The Border Security and Immigration Enforcement Improvements Executive Order

With the election of Donald Trump as president, talks about building a wall along the southern border were revived and much discussion has focused on the logistics of building the wall, and especially the costs. President Trump promised during the election campaign that he would build the wall and that Mexico would pay for it. Lately, there has been little discussion about Mexico paying for the wall. President Trump has reportedly backed off his threat to shut down the government if a funding bill would not include money for the border wall (CNBC, 2017). It is all speculation at this point and it is doubtful that the entire U.S. border could be protected by a wall. Nonetheless, in 2017, President Trump signed the **Border Security and Immigration Enforcement Improvements Executive Order**, which directed all departments to deploy all lawful means to secure the nation's southern border through the construction of a fence (Office of Inspector General, 2017).

HS Web Link: To learn more about the SBI, go to http://www.gao.gov/products/GAO-10-651T.

Increase in Customs and Border Protection Agents

Prior to the 9/11 attacks, the Border Patrol was woefully understaffed, given that the agency was responsible for securing about 7,500 miles of border. In 2005, the Customs and Border Protection agency received funding to increase the number of agents to about 3,000. Additionally, the Immigration and Customs Enforcement (ICE) agency received funding to increase the number of investigators by approximately 250 agents. The funding increase also resulted in the hiring of 400 new Immigration Enforcement agents and 400 detention officers.

In January 2017, President Trump issued an executive order to hire another 5,000 agents. The agency estimates that it will take 5 to 10 years to hire that many agents. The agency is also considering loosening the hiring standards to achieve the hiring goal. Many applicants are not eligible because they don't pass the entrance exam, polygraph test, or fitness test. In 2010, Congress passed an anti-corruption bill, which requires all applicants to pass the polygraph test. Congress was mainly concerned about agents being bribed and corrupted by gangs and cartels operating at the U.S. borders. The estimated costs of the hiring plan are $328 million in fiscal year 2017 and $1.9 billion for 2018 (CNN Wire, 2017). These agents and officers are involved in investigating illegal immigrants within the United States. The ICE fugitive teams collect apprehended illegal immigrants for deportation. Even with these increases, it remains questionable if there are ample agents to adequately secure our borders given the vastness of the problem.

Expanded Detention and Removal Capabilities

In the past, ICE has not had the personnel or facilities to hold and process all the illegal immigrants who were apprehended. The agency had a policy of catch and release as a result of the inadequate resources. This resulted in few apprehended illegal immigrants returning to their home countries. Funding was provided to increase the bed space in detention facilities. In 2016, ICE placed 352,882 illegal immigrants in civil detention facilities and deported 240,255. About 92 percent of the deported immigrants were previously convicted of a crime (ICE, 2016). The DHS has been working with other federal, state, and local agencies to develop innovative strategies to increase holding or bed space, for example, holding detainees in local jails. The increased capacity prevents detainees from being released before deportation. Basically, when detainees are released before deportation, many blend into society, fail to appear at their deportation hearings, and remain illegally in the United States.

HS Web Link: To learn more about the detention of illegal immigrants go to http://trac.syr.edu/immigration/library/P737.pdf.

HS ANALYSIS BOX 12-4

There are legal processes that must be followed when deporting illegal immigrants. The country has bestowed certain rights on them. Consequently, some deportation proceedings take a considerable amount of time, requiring that the illegal immigrants be detained. There are those who believe they should not be given these due process rights but should be deported immediately without lengthy hearings. On the other side, civil rights advocates maintain that the United States should recognize the rights of everyone in the country. Should the United States expedite the removal of illegal immigrants? Should the United States disregard their rights?

Another impediment to controlling illegal immigration has been the length of time it has taken to deport or remove illegal immigrants. Deportation has taken months and even years in some cases. Extended detentions result in occupied bed spaces at holding facilities, reducing the number of detainees that can be held. The SBI gave the DHS legislative authority to expedite the deportation of some illegal immigrants. For example, anyone apprehended within the previous 2 years is subject to expedited removal. The DHS has implemented this policy at all ports of entry and between ports of entry only along the southwest border for immigrants apprehended within 100 miles of the border. The program was applied to the southwest border because this area has the highest levels of illegal immigration. Expedited deportation has resulted in less strain on the system.

Improved Technology

It is impossible to protect the nation's borders solely with personnel, given that the United States has about 7,500 miles of border. The DHS has implemented two strategies to improve border security: Prevent illegal immigrants from entering the United States and

Drones are playing a more important role in border security.
CBP Photos/Alamy Stock Photo.

apprehending and removing aliens who have violated U.S. immigration laws. In 2014, DHS announced a new strategy to improve the effectiveness of their operations. They are focusing mainly on illegal immigrants with criminal convictions and felonies and significant misdemeanors rather than arrests and minor violations.

Increased Infrastructure Protection (Fencing)

Customs and Border Protection has been constructing and maintaining barriers along the Mexican border since 1991. These barriers, for the most part, have been limited to urban areas. Two types of fencing have been used. One is primary pedestrian fencing that is located directly on the border in a number of urban areas and meant to prevent pedestrians from crossing the border. Secondary or triple fencing has been constructed in the San Diego area. The presence of two or three layers of fencing is more daunting to those who would attempt to cross the border. In addition to the fencing, vehicle barriers have been constructed in some areas (see Nunez-Neto and Vina, 2006). As of December 2015, DHS had completed a total of 353 miles of primary pedestrian fencing, 36 miles of secondary fencing, 14 miles of triple pedestrian fencing, and 300 miles of vehicle fencing (Federation for American Immigration Reform, 2017).

There has been considerable criticism of building walls and fences along the nation's borders. If a 20-foot fence is built, illegal immigrants attempting to enter the United States will build a 21-foot ladder. In addition to climbing these fences, illegal immigrants can

High-tech equipment used to see and hear approaching illegal aliens.
Department of Homeland Security.

dig tunnels under them. It is highly questionable if a fence, especially one several miles or several hundred miles long, can be constructed in such a fashion that it cannot be breached. Moreover, the costs of such a fence have been estimated to be approximately $15 billion (Drew, 2017). Currently, it appears that they are somewhat effective in fairly short spans in urban areas where they are supplemented with patrol personnel.

Customs and Border Protection continues to expand the types of technology used to secure the borders. In 2012, the DHS requested the purchase of 14 Predator drones for an estimated cost of $443 million. These new drones would supplement the 10 drones currently used by Customs and Border Protection to patrol the nation's borders with Mexico and Canada (Becker, 2012). However, the DHS Office of the Inspector General criticized the request because Customs and Border Protection had failed to develop an operational plan that ensured program effectiveness. Nonetheless, drones are becoming a new tool in border security and law enforcement. Sasso, (2012) reports that at least 13 state and local police agencies have used drones in the field or in training. Departments in Houston, Seattle, Miami-Dade, and North Little Rock are using drone technology. It is also predicted that by the end of the decade, as many as 3,000 government commercial drones could be operational in the United States. Drones are appealing to police departments because they are less expensive to operate as compared to helicopters.

The application of technology and physical barriers attempts to seal the nation's borders. Past programs have used physical barriers and increased border patrols in high-traffic areas. Operation Gatekeeper was implemented in San Diego, Operation Hold-the-Line along the border in El Paso, and Operation Safeguard in Arizona. The number of illegal immigrants crossing the border in these areas was substantially reduced as a result of these concentrated resources. However, there is some evidence that the numbers were "cooked" by Border Patrol officials. In 1996, members of the Border Patrol union in the San Diego area filed a lawsuit alleging that officials had ordered agents to not make arrests so as to give the impression that the programs had reduced the number of illegal immigrants (Global Security, undated-b). Keeping illegal immigrants out of the country still remains a conundrum. In March 2003, in response to the terrorist attacks on September 1, 2001, the DHS was established and Border Patrol became part of DHS. Since then Border Patrol has also established cooperation with neighboring countries to enhance their effectiveness in preventing illegal border crossings (Customs and Border Protection, 2014).

Enhanced Enforcement of Immigration Laws: Interior Enforcement as Deterrence

Another area of border security is deterrence through enforcement. The USA PATRIOT Act allows the use of immigration laws by various authorities when investigating terror suspects. Consequently, the majority of terrorist investigations have not led to convictions on terrorism charges, but for immigration violations. Oftentimes, it is easier for authorities to make an immigration case than a terrorism case. Terrorism investigations have morphed into immigration enforcement. For example, in 2005, Wagdy Mohamed Ghoneim voluntarily left the United States for an undisclosed Middle Eastern country. Ghoneim was an influential Islamic cleric in Orange County, California, who was suspected of giving speeches and raising money for groups with terrorist connections. He was not charged with any crime associated with terrorism, such as providing material support for terrorist groups. Rather, ICE officials charged him with immigration violations. Ghoneim left the country rather than fight the immigration charges (Reyes, 2005).

Such actions have resulted in immigrant communities in the United States becoming less cooperative with federal authorities when investigating terror suspects and activities. They also fear deportation as federal agencies cast a wider net in terror-related investigations. On February 21, 2017, President Trump issued an executive order that aims to increase border patrol to prevent illegal border crossings and a faster apprehension and removal of illegal immigrants. President Trump ordered the hiring of an additional 5,00 agents, increase of physical barriers, detaining illegal immigrants near the border, an end of the "catch and release" practice, and removing illegal immigrants more quickly (Office of the Press Secretary, 2017).

Traditional immigration enforcement has hinged on three principles: (1) workplace enforcement whereby illegal immigrants are removed and deported, (2) lengthy detention to convince immigrants to not enter the United States illegally, and (3) mass removal of illegal immigrants to eliminate incentives for them to find work. This strategy has not worked. Too often when illegal immigrants are removed from the workplace, there are others to replace them. Detention and removal have become cumbersome and expensive processes, making them ineffective. Moreover, many of those deported often return within a short time. Some illegal immigrants have been removed multiple times. A California study showed that more than half of illegal immigrants arrested and incarcerated for felonies often returned to the same city and committed new felonies. It is obvious that traditional tactics have been unreliable.

More effective prevention strategies include focusing on smuggling or human trafficking operations and programs that thwart illegal immigrants from gaining employment. Smuggling operations account for large numbers of illegal immigrants entering the United States. Interdicting these operations can have an exponential impact on the number of illegal immigrants entering the country. We also must develop effective systems that allow employers to determine if potential employees are here legally. However, critics argue that strategies should focus on apprehension and deportation—a strategy that provides media publicity but is ineffective in terms of reducing the overall numbers of illegal immigrants in the country. Deterring illegal immigration became less important than apprehension and "bean counting."

ICE has stepped up its enforcement of illegal immigration. In 2014, ICE established Operation Coyote, focusing on human smuggling at the Rio Grande Valley area in Texas. Within the first 90 days, agents made 676 criminal arrests, issued 403 indictments, and had 240 convictions. ICE also dismantled eight smuggling organizations and seized $1.5 million plus properties worth about $1 million.

Another project, called Project Southbound, focuses on the arresting and removing gang members who immigrated illegally. In 2014, ICE arrested 638 gang members. ICE also works with international organizations to dismantle human trafficking organizations and assist victims of human trafficking. For instance, ICE identified and assisted 446 human trafficking victims and 1,036 child exploitation victims (Department of Homeland Security, 2016c). Since the beginning of 2017 ICE has increased operational activity in "sanctuary cities"; that is, cities or jurisdictions that refuse to honor ICE immigration detainers. Immigration detainers are 48-hour hold requests for illegal immigrants during which the immigrants are held in jail until federal agents can take over their case. Several cities have declared themselves as "sanctuary cities." These sanctuary cities are increasingly targeted by ICE, raising criticism from the communities and civil rights advocates. Many sanctuary cities have remained steadfast and some, such as Los Angeles and New York, have implemented additional measures to protect undocumented immigrants, but ICE will likely target these cities with more raids (Santana, 2017).

The accelerated deportation of criminal illegal immigrants has resulted in cost savings for several states. Early deportation results in fewer days in jail. It costs a jail or prison about $95 per day to house an inmate. The state of Arizona is holding over 1,300 inmates for deportation. The state claimed that this policy had saved approximately $17 million. New York State had turned over about 2,000 inmates who were deported for a savings of $141 million (Bazer, 2008). Other sources state that the costs for apprehension and deportation are very high and have actually increased. In 2016, ICE spent $3.2 billion on

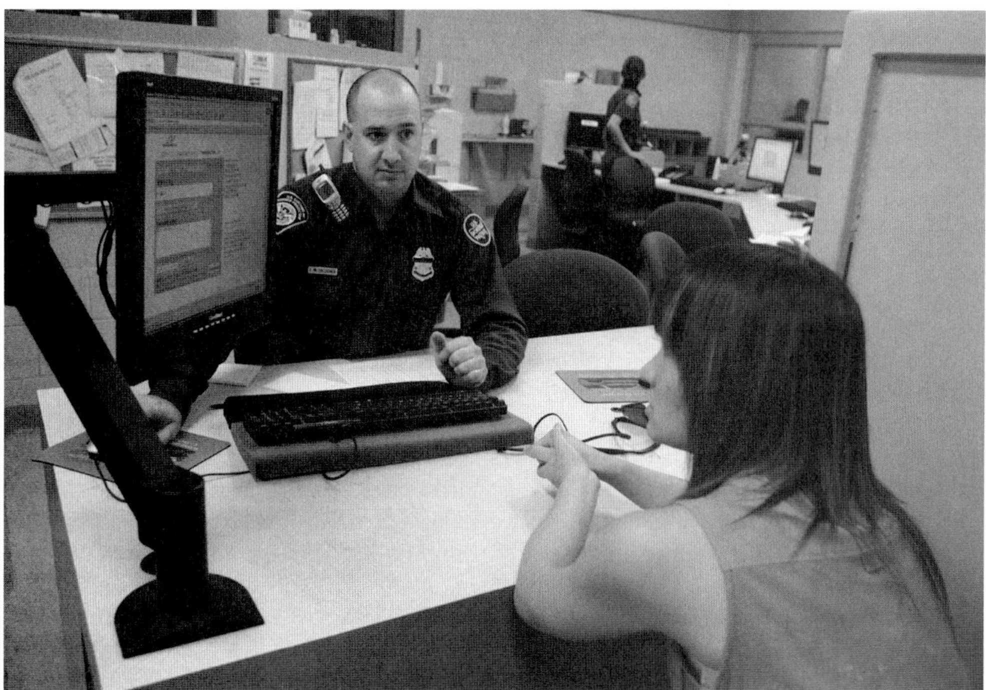

A Border Patrol agent uses a computer word translator to assist in determining the needs of this illegal immigrant.
Department of Homeland Security.

arrest, detention, and deportation of illegal immigrants. About $129.4 million was spent on apprehension. Apprehending illegal immigrants is costly because agents first have to investigate, prepare, and stakeout the residence and then ICE sends a team of 6 to 12 agents to the residence who wait there all day until the resident shows up. Even more expensive than apprehension is the detention of illegal immigrants, which costs an average of $5,663 per person with an average stay of 31 days. Cases that go to court (about 15%) cost another $1,200 to $1,500. Finally, transporting the deportees back to the home country costs another $1,978 on average. Some transportations cost significantly more. For instance, ICE must send two Marshalls with any deportee returned to China and they must travel on a U.S. airline. Immigrants from countries that don't cooperate with the United States can end up in detention for years. Since 2015, some costs have been rising as more families with children are crossing the southern border. In 2016, this cost ICE an addition $345 million (Blanco, 2017).

In 2016, the total budget of ICE was $6.3 billion and had a total of 19,791 fulltime employees (Department of Homeland Security, 2016b). In comparison, in 2012 the total budget was $5.8 billion (U.S. Immigration and Customs Enforcement, 2011).

ICE has stepped up enforcement of the prohibition from hiring undocumented immigrants. ICE has visited and reviewed employment records at a number of businesses and employers. This is being accomplished primarily by its **Worksite Enforcement Unit**. This unit focuses on

> Egregious employers involved in criminal activity or worker exploitation. This type of employer violation will often involve alien smuggling, document fraud, human rights abuses and/or other criminal or substantive administrative immigration or customs violations having a direct nexus to the employment of unauthorized workers. Worksite investigations also encompass employers who are subjecting unauthorized alien workers to substandard or abusive working conditions. Also included in these types of investigations are employers

who utilize force, threat, or coercion, such as threats to have employees deported in order to keep the unauthorized alien workers from reporting the substandard wage or working conditions. (ICE, 2008)

ICE enforces immigration laws by conducting raids on various employers. Here, ICE officers conduct checks of employees to determine if they are legally authorized to work in the United States. For the most part, these raids have focused on employers who hire unskilled and semiskilled employees, for example, the agriculture, food services, manufacturing, and meat-processing industries. There are numerous examples. Since 2017 ICE has increasingly targeted farmworkers. In March 2017, ICE arrested several apple pickers in Western New York and several dairy workers were arrested in Vermont (Woodie, 2017). Generally, those arrested do not have documentation or have forged or false documentation. Most of them do not have criminal records. The raids have received a substantial amount of criticism as they often separate families. For example, a mother and father may be detained and no arrangements are made for any children in the family. In some cases, family members become destitute since the wage earner is incarcerated. It is also problematic when children are U.S. citizens and their parents are illegal immigrants. In addition, critics argue that the raids hurt U.S. farms by depriving them of workers. For instance, a large percent of dairy workers in Vermont are undocumented (Woodie, 2017). According to researchers from the University of California, Davis, about 70 percent of farmworkers are undocumented. Deporting large numbers would have significant negative consequences for the economy. Farmers who had supported Donald Trump during the elections are now very concerned about their ability to harvest and sell their products (Dickerson and Medina, 2017).

HS Web Link: To learn more about ICE's Worksite Enforcement program, go to https://www.ice.gov/worksite.

The **United States Citizenship and Immigration Service** (USCIS) is responsible for providing visas to immigrants who desire to work in the United States. Those individuals possessing student visas, guest worker visas, and permanent resident or green cards are allowed to be employed on a limited basis. Also, employers can initiate proceedings to employ a foreign national by completing paper work with the USCIS. Additionally, USCIS has developed a computerized system to check the employment status of foreign nationals. The system E-Verify requires that employers and foreign employees be registered with USCIS. Currently, approximately 65,000 employers participate in the program. Since 2006, 12 states have begun requiring employers to use the system when hiring. A major problem confronting E-Verify is its accuracy rate, which is approximately 94 percent (Marks, 2008). A number of employers and verified employees have complained about the problem—it has resulted in employers not being able to hire verified employees on a timely basis. For example, between January and July 2008, Intel, one of the nation's largest employers, had 12 percent of its 1,360 new hires rejected by the system. Intel appealed 143 of the rejections and all were found to be legal U.S. residents (Frank, 2009).

HS ANALYSIS BOX 12-5

The previous sections discussed the various means that are used to secure the southern border, including personnel, electronic surveillance, and fencing methods. Additionally, the enforcement of immigration laws in the workforce is being increased. There are problems associated with each of these methods. How should the southern border be secured? Which methods do you believe have the greatest potential to be effective? Can the border really be secure?

Formulating a Coherent Policy for Border Security

Several elements of the border security system have been implemented. However, it appears that each element is being implemented independently of the others. Wermuth and Riley (2007) observe that this uncoordinated, patchwork effort has led to a number of problems. Moreover, it is rather expensive and very likely not cost effective. In some cases, when technology is involved, there is no guarantee that it will operate at expected levels of effectiveness. Wermuth and Riley point out that improvements must be made. It must be remembered that border risk is being managed, not eliminated. It is virtually impossible to totally seal the borders, and decisions must be made relative to the level of effectiveness required and the expense that can be endured.

Evaluative matrices need to be developed to measure the level of program effectiveness. For example, what impact have the current arrangements had on illegal immigration? Are they working? Funds may go toward implementing programs that in the end do not achieve the required goals. To this end, what are the goals? Politicians discuss border security in terms of totally sealing them from illegal immigrants, but this is impossible. What levels of security does the United States want to achieve in the end? Do current and planned programs achieve this level of security? To answer these questions meaningful outcome or evaluative measures must be developed.

Wermuth and Riley advise that a comprehensive and well-thought-out roadmap is needed for achieving the stated goals. This essentially means that current and planned efforts must be examined to ensure that they are integrated into a cohesive border security effort. Security measures must be installed at insecure points that effectively deal with the problems that may be encountered. It also means that all the security measures must be integrated into a working system, and any inadequacies in the system must be understood and considered. This applies not only to physical and electronic barriers but also to human security measures. When there are limitations on physical and electronic security systems, it might be necessary to use Customs and Border Protection and ICE personnel to fill the gaps. Regardless, there must be an understanding of how all these programs or pieces fit into a logical and working secure border system.

US-Visit Program

A major problem with immigration and foreigners visiting the United States is ensuring their correct identification. As discussed earlier, there are ample examples of possible terrorists obtaining false documents to enter the country. Statistics indicate that identity fraud is a prevalent problem, especially at the borders. The U.S. General Accounting Office, in a report to several committees of the House of Representatives, detailed the problem (Stana, 2002).

The total number of people with such documentation is not known, since it must be assumed that officials are not able to intercept everyone carrying a fraudulent entry document. There is a significant problem and measures need to be taken to ensure the integrity of documents as people leave and enter the United States.

The 9/11 Commission recommended that better controls over identification procedures are needed to make it more difficult for terrorists and others to enter the United States.

One program addressing this problem is the US-VISIT program. The United States has deployed the US-VISIT program to collect biometric data (all 10 fingerprints) on persons entering and leaving the United States. The program can help identify those individuals who overstay their visas. It can identify persons who are using someone else's identification. Such a program serves first to verify one's identity. It is also used for identity discovery: to learn the identity of people who are posing as someone else (Morgan and Krouse, 2005).

One of the main problems encountered by border agents is that of illegal immigrants who use stolen identities to enter the United States. In 2009, the ICE started Operation Genesius, which aimed to combat document fraud. ICE collaborates with the printing industry by sharing information and investigating organized document fraud rings (U.S. Immigration and Customs Enforcement, 2015).

► Types of Visas

According to the Bureau of Consular Affairs, there are two types of visas—**nonimmigrant visas and immigrant visas**. Visas for nonimmigrants are for diplomats, business people, temporary workers, and students. Immigrant visas are for spouses and fiancés of citizens, family members, and certain workers (Bureau of Consular Affairs, 2015). A number of people enter the United States each year using these visas.

Non-Visa or Visa Waiver Program

Additionally, travelers to the United States come from visa and non-visa countries. There are 38 non-visa countries, and travelers from those countries are not required to obtain a visa. They must possess a passport that contains machine-readable biometric data, which

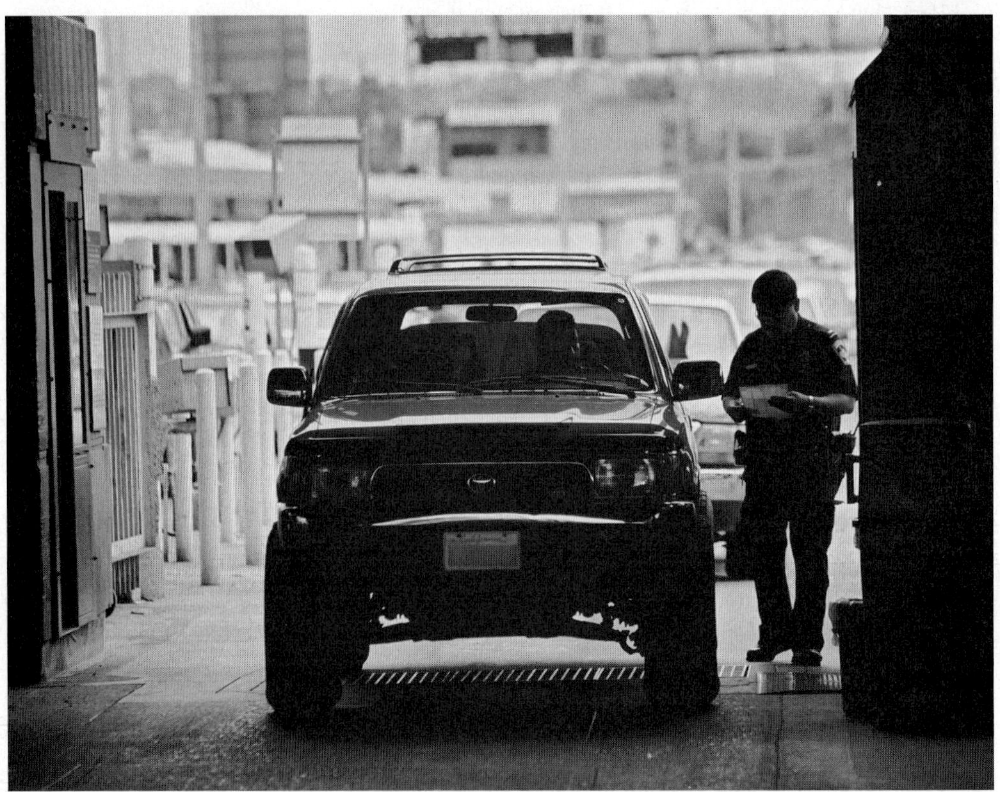

Border Protection agent checks vehicles coming into the United States.
Department of Homeland Security.

can be accessed at ports of entry to assure identity. In visa countries, travelers are required to visit an American consulate or other visa-issuing point to obtain a visa. Applicants are photographed and their fingerprints are scanned as part of the visa-issuing process. At that point, the information is checked against a watch list of known criminals and suspected terrorists. Visas are denied to individuals who are on this watch list or who have suspect documentation. Upon arrival to the United States, their fingerprints are again scanned to assure proper identification; this reduces the probability that terrorists or other undesirables will obtain another person's visa. Non-visa travelers are scanned when they enter the United States, and their biometric data are examined.

In 2015, in the aftermath of the San Bernardino terrorist attack, Congress and the president moved to tighten the restrictions on non-visa travelers to the United States. One of the San Bernardino terrorists, Tashfeen Malik, traveled to the United States on an immigrant visa. Previously, Richard Reid, the "shoe bomber" traveled from Paris to Miami without a visa and, Zacarias Moussaoui, the "20th hijacker from 9/11 flew from London to Chicago with a French passport and no visa." Approximately 5,000 people from non-visa countries have traveled to Iraq and Syria and are eligible to travel to the United States without a visa. There are about 20 million people who travel to the United States each year from non-visa countries. Legislation would require these countries to check these travelers' backgrounds with INTERPOL databases, place visa requirements on citizens from Iraq and Syria, and place restrictions on anyone who had traveled to Iraq or Syria in the previous five years. It also requires countries to share counterterror information with the United States (Werner, 2015).

HS Web Link: To learn more about the US-Visit program, go to https://epic.org/privacy/surveillance/spotlight/0705/editorial.html

Vehicular Screening at Border Crossings

The previous sections examined securing the nation's borders with a focus on people. However, as a result of the North American Free Trade Agreement (NAFTA), trade barriers between the United States, Mexico, and Canada were virtually dissolved, resulting in a tremendous amount of cargo entering the United States at the borders. Canada and Mexico are the two largest trading partners of the United States. According to Ackleson (2005), 11.6 million trucks and 16 million cargo containers cross the land borders each year. Additionally, millions of passenger vehicles cross the border each year. This traffic results in a substantial workload for Customs and Border Protection personnel when attempting to screen vehicles. Delays at borders can substantially affect commerce and the costs of goods coming into or leaving the United States.

Customs and Border Protection has implemented several programs designed to expedite the flow of vehicular traffic. First, the **Secure Electronic Network for Travelers Rapid Inspection** (SENTRI) has been implemented on the border with Mexico. SENTRI users are allowed to use special traffic lanes and generally bypass the inspection process. Participants must enroll in the program and pass a criminal background check. SENTRI participants are low risk and generally cross the border repeatedly. The program allows Customs and Border Protection personnel to concentrate their inspection efforts on vehicles that are not verified.

The **NEXUS program** is similar to SENTRI, but it has been implemented along the Canadian border. These programs are evolving as technology enhancements become available. For example, in some instances automatic vehicle identifiers are being used. The identifier information is electronically scanned, and the resultant information is checked with a database. This same technology is being applied to trucks carrying cargo, which has substantially reduced the delay in crossings for these vehicles.

Within the next few years, there likely will be widespread use of facial recognition programs to check people as they cross the borders. Facial recognition programs are

HS Web Link: To learn more about the SENTRI program, go to https://www.cbp.gov/travel/trusted-traveler-programs/sentri.

currently being tested at several airports, including Dulles, TX, New York, JFK, and London Heathrow. President Trump has fast-tracked facial recognition technology. Customs and border protection is currently experimenting with it at several U.S. airports as are Canadian and British officials. Travelers' photos can be compared with their passport and visa photos and to photos in the DHS biometric database (Brandom, 2017). The DHS is also experimenting with biometric recognition at the Otay Mesa Port of Entry in California (U.S. Customs and Border Protection, 2015).

▶ Port and Marine Security

The nation's 77 ports are vast complexes with extremely large numbers of personnel and machinery primarily engaged in the loading and unloading of materials from cargo ships. Two billion tons of freight move in and out of the ports annually, representing 99 percent of the international trade (Bentzel, 2006; Bullock et al., 2005). In 2000, the Interagency Commission on Crime and Security in U.S. Ports reported substantial levels of crime, trade fraud, alien smuggling, importation of drugs and other contraband, environmental crimes, and cargo theft occurring at the ports. The commission also concluded that vulnerability to terrorist attacks was high, and there were no standard security procedures in place. The report resulted in the passage of the **Maritime Transportation Security Act of 2002**.

A number of maritime security measures have been enacted as a result of the act. The Coast Guard conducts assessments of the ports for security problems and potential vulnerabilities. Further, the **Transportation Workers Identification Credential program** has been enacted. The program mandates that all persons in a port area must have an identification card that is only issued after a background investigation. This program is similar to

One of many container ships coming to the United States each day.
Department of Homeland Security.

the one used for employees at the nation's airports. The Maritime Transportation Security Act mandated the merger of the intelligence functions of the Coast Guard, Navy, TSA, and the Customs and Border Protection to form a centralized maritime intelligence center. The act also mandated that all ships passing through U.S. waters must carry transponders so that high-interest and suspect vessels can be tracked. Finally, the act mandated high levels of security for cargo coming into the United States. This is carried out by the TSA and Customs and Border Protection, both within the DHS. Containers coming into the United States are subject to X-ray or gamma imaging to identify WMDs or WMD material. Two programs have been implemented to enhance cargo security prior to its arrival in the United States: Customs Trade Partnership Against Terrorism (CTPAT) program and the Container Security Initiative (CSI).

CTPAT and CSI

The **Customs Trade Partnership Against Terrorism program** (CTPAT) is a program that attempts to guarantee the security of cargo at the originating country. Foreign companies verify their supply chain for security and are allowed to ship material with minimum inspections or fast tracking. Shippers, importers, brokers, manufacturers, and warehouses adhere to security protocols as established by the Customs and Border Protection, and they allow periodic inspections of facilities. These inspections ensure that procedures are being followed.

The **Container Security Initiative** (CSI) is a program whereby Customs and Border Protection agents are positioned at major ports throughout the world and inspect cargo destined for the United States. These two programs result in less congestion at U.S. ports of entry. They effectively distribute the workload over a larger geographical area, thus reducing bottlenecks.

HS Web Link: To learn more about the Customs Trade Partnership Against Terrorism program, go to https://www.cbp.gov/border-security/ports-entry/cargo-security/ctpat.

Summary

This chapter explored a number of issues relative to securing the borders of the United States and its immigration controls. As noted, immigration control and border security are two different problems, but they are intertwined politically and operationally. Compounding the problem is the impact of various programs on the flow of commerce—economic interests lobby for programs that do not impede the flow of goods and criticize programs that negatively affect this flow. This intermingling of policy perspectives has resulted in a hodgepodge of programs that theoretically operate seamlessly. Nonetheless, the United States must concentrate its efforts on border security to keep potential terrorists and WMD materials out of the country. This goal certainly is most important, and it should trump immigration and economic concerns.

In terms of immigration, an immense volume of people enters and leaves the United States each year by land, air, and sea. The vast majority of these travelers adhere to laws and procedures. However, a number of people attempt to sneak into the United States, especially across the southern border. Most are seeking employment or a better life, but there are some who are potential terrorists, criminals, or other undesirables. The United States is bolstering immigration policies through border security, deploying electronic monitoring and fences, in an effort to control migration and force migrants to use legal procedures to enter. The United States also has increased the number of Customs and Border Protection agents to secure the borders.

It is virtually impossible to secure the borders and keep illegal immigrants out of the country. Some suggest that a more effective program is to deny illegal migrants employment, thus removing the incentive for their coming to the United States. The Immigration and Customs Enforcement agency has stepped up its enforcement of the employment of illegal immigrants and has made numerous raids on businesses across the country. If the United States is able to prevent illegal immigrants from entering the country through employment enforcement, it will reduce the number of aliens crossing the borders, making control more manageable.

Discussion Questions

1. Describe the patterns of immigration into the United States.
2. Distinguish between border security and immigration.
3. Riley describes a new border protection policy consisting of two components. Explain how they operate and complement each other.
4. Discuss the issues for programs such as Operation Hold the Line.
5. Discuss the elements contained in the Secure Border Initiative.
6. One of the methods of enhancing border security has been the construction of fences and other types of barriers. Describe these efforts and their effectiveness.
7. According to Wermuth and Riley, what improvements need to be made relative to border security?

References

Ackleson, J. (2005). "Border security technologies: Local and regional implications." *Review of Policy Research*, 22(2): 137–55.

Bach, R. (2005). "Transforming border security: Prevention first." *Homeland Security Affairs*, 1(1): 1–15.

Baker, B., and Rytina, N. (2013). *Estimates of Unauthorized Immigrant Population Residing in the United States: January 2012*. Office of Immigration Studies. Department of Homeland Security. https://www.dhs.gov/sites/default/files/publications/Unauthorized%20Immigrant%20Population%20Estimates%20in%20the%20US%20January%202012_0.pdf (Accessed July 19, 2017).

BBC News. (2016). *Brussels explosions: What we know about airport and metro attacks*. http://www.bbc.com/news/world-europe-35869985 (Accessed May 17, 2017).

Becker, A. (2012). "U.S. border drones deal with General Atomics Aeronautical Systems Inc. draws criticism." *Huff Post*, (November 19). http://www.huffingtonpost.com/2012/11/19/us-border-drones-deal-wit_n_2159255.html (Accessed November 26, 2012).

Bentzel, C. (2006). "Port and maritime security." *The McGraw-Hil Homeland Security Handbook*, ed. G. Kamien, pp. 631–48. New York: McGraw-Hill.

Blanco, O. (2017). *How much it costs ICE to deport an illegal immigrant*. CNN Money. http://money.cnn.com/2017/04/13/news/economy/deportation-costs-undocumented-immigrant/ (Accessed May 21, 2017).

Brandom, R. (2017). "Facial recognition is coming to US airports, fast-tracked by Trump." *The Verge*. https://www.theverge.com/2017/4/18/15332742/us-border-biometric-exit-facial-recognition-scanning-homeland-security (Accessed September 4, 2017).

Bullock, J., G. Haddow, D. Coppola, E. Ergin, L. Westerman, and S. Yeletaysi. (2005). *Introduction to Homeland Security*. Burlington, MA: Elsevier.

Bureau of Consular Affairs. (2015). Directory of Visa Categories. http://travel.state.gov/content/visas/en/general/all-visa-categories.html (Accessed December 14, 2015).

Bureau of Counterterrorism and Countering Violent Extremism. (2016). Chapter 2. Country Reports. Western Hemisphere. Department of State. https://www.state.gov/j/ct/rls/crt/2016/272234.htm (Accessed December 6, 2017).

CNBC. (2017). Trump reportedly backs off government shutdown threat over border wall funding. September, 1. https://www.cnbc.com/2017/09/01/trump-reportedly-changes-stance-on-shutt.html.

CNN Wire. (2017). *Customs and border protection estimates show hiring could take a decade: Report*. http://ktla.com/2017/03/07/customs-and-border-protection-estimates-show-hiring-could-take-a-decade-report/ (Accessed May 19, 2017).

Customs and Border Protection. (2014). *Border Patrol History*. https://www.cbp.gov/border-security/along-us-borders/history (Accessed May 20, 2017).

Customs and Border Protection. (2016). CBP Border Security Report FY2016. https://www.cbp.gov/sites/default/files/assets/documents/2016-Dec/CBP-fy2016-border-security-report.pdf.

Department of Homeland Security. (2005). *DHS Fact Sheet: Secure Border Initiative*. Washington, D.C.: Author. https://www.hsdl.org/?abstract&did=457390 (Accessed December 26, 2008).

Department of Homeland Security. (2013). 2013 Yearbook of Immigration Statistics. Office of Immigration Statistics. https://www.dhs.gov/sites/default/files/publications/Yearbook_Immigration_Statistics_2013_0.pdf.

Department of Homeland Security. (2016a). *Terrorism cases: TSA's VIPR teams deter Brussels-type attacks here at home*. https://www.dhs.gov/terrorism-cases (Accessed May 17, 2017).

Department of Homeland Security. (2016b). *Budget-in-Brief. Fiscal Year 2016*. https://www.dhs.gov/sites/default/files/publications/FY_2016_DHS_Budget_in_Brief.pdf (Accessed May 21, 2017).

Department of Homeland Security. (2016c). *DHS Immigration Enforcement 2016. Annual Flow Report*. Office of Immigration

Studies. https://www.dhs.gov/sites/default/files/publications/DHS%20Immigration%20Enforcement%202016.pdf (Accessed July 13, 2017).

Dickerson, C., and Medina, J. (2017). California farmers backed Trump, but now fear losing field workers. *The New York Times* (February 9). https://www.nytimes.com/2017/02/09/us/california-farmers-backed-trump-but-now-fear-losing-field-workers.html (Accessed May 21, 2017).

Duara, N. (2016). "Arizona's once feared immigration law, SB1070, loses most of it's power in settlement." *Los Angeles Times* (September 15). http://www.latimes.com/nation/la-na-arizona-law-20160915-snap-story.html (Retrieved April 30, 2017).

Drew, K. (2017). "This is what Trumps border wall would cost." http://www.cnbc.com/2015/10/09/this-is-what-trumps-border-wall-could-cost-us.html (Accessed April 30, 2017).

Federation for American Immigration Reform. (2017). *The Current State of the Border Fence*. http://www.fairus.org/issue/the-current-state-of-the-border-fence (Accessed May 20, 2017).

Forest, J. (2006). "Protecting America's borders and points of entry: An introduction." *Homeland Security Protecting America's Targets, Volume 1*, pp. 1–18. Westport, CT: Praeger.

Frank, T. (2009). "Trying to verify employee IDs: Opponents cite flaws in use of federal database." *USA Today* (February 6), p. 3A.

Global Security. (undated-a). *US-Mexico Border Fence: Great Wall of Mexico Secure Fence*. http://www.globalsecurity.org/security/systems/mexico-wall.htm (Accessed December 27, 2008).

Global Security. (undated-b). *Operation Gatekeeper Operation Hold-the-Line Operation Safeguard*. http://www.globalsecurity.org/military/ops/gatekeeper.htm (Accessed December 27, 2008).

Liptak, A. (2017). "3 judges weigh Trumps revised travel ban, but keep their poker faces." *The New York Times*, May 15. https://www.nytimes.com/2017/05/15/us/politics/trump-travel-ban-appeals-court.html?_r=0 (Accessed May 17, 2017).

Majority Staff of the Committee on Homeland Security, Subcommittee on Investigations. (2012). *A Line in the Sand: Countering Crime, Violence and Terror at the Southwest Border*. Washington, D.C.: Author. https://homeland.house.gov/files/11-15-12-Line-in-the-Sand.pdf.

Marks, A. (2008). "With E-Verify, too many errors to expand its use." *Christian Science Monitor* (July 7). http://www.csmonitor.com/2008/0707/p02s01-usgn.html (Accessed December 28, 2008).

Morgan, D., and W. Krouse. (2005). *Biometric Identifiers and Border Security: 9/11 Commission Recommendations and Related Issues*. Washington, D.C.: Congressional Research Service. https://www.dhs.gov/sites/default/files/publications/Lawful_Permanent_Residents_2014.pdf (Accessed July 13, 2017).

Mueller, R. (2005). *FBI FY 2006 Budget Request: Hearing before the House Committee on Appropriations*. Written Statement (March 8).

National Intelligence Council. (2017). *Global Trends 2035: Paradox of Progress*. Washington, D.C.: Author.

Nunez-Neto, B., and S. Vina. (2006). *Border Security: Barriers Along the U.S. International Border*. Washington, D.C.: Congressional Research Service.

Office of the Federal Register. (2015). *Test To Collect Biometric Information at Up to Ten U.S. Airports ("Be-Mobile Air Test")*. https://www.federalregister.gov/documents/2015/07/28/2015-18418/test-to-collect-biometric-information-at-up-to-ten-us-airports-be-mobile-air-test.

Office of Inspector General. (2017). *Special Report: Lessons Learned from Prior Reports on CBP's SBI and Acquisitions Related to Securing Our Border*. https://www.oig.dhs.gov/sites/default/files/assets/2017/OIG-17-70-SR-Jun17.pdf (Accessed September 3, 2017).

Office of the Press Secretary. (2017). *Fact sheet: Executive Order: Border security and immigration enforcement improvements*. Department of Homeland Security. https://www.dhs.gov/news/2017/02/21/fact-sheet-executive-order-border-security-and-immigration-enforcement-improvements (Accessed May 20, 2017).

Preston, J. (2011). "Homeland security cancels 'Virtual Fence" after $1 Billion is spent." *The New York Times* (January 14). http://www.nytimes.com/2011/01/15/us/politics/15fence.html (Accessed May 17, 2017).

Reyes, D. (2005). "Islamic cleric leaves country after lockup." *The Los Angeles Times* (January 4), p. B7.

Richey, W. (2017). "Terror and the Mexico border: How big a threat?" *The Christian Science Monitor*, https://www.csmonitor.com/USA/Justice/2017/0115/Terror-and-the-Mexico-border-How-big-a-threat (Accessed September 3, 2017).

Riley, J. (2006). "Border control." In *The McGraw-Hill Homeland Security Handbook*, ed. D. Kamien, pp. 587–612. New York: McGraw-Hill.

Santana, M. (2017). *Source: ICE is targeting "sanctuary cities" with raids*. http://www.cnn.com/2017/03/23/politics/sanctuary-city-ice-raids/ (Accessed May 21, 2017).

Sasso, B. (2012). "Police drones prompt privacy concerns." *The Hill*, (Nov. 3). http://thehill.com/blogs/hillicon-valley/technology/265693-police-drone-use-prompts-privacy-concerns. (Accessed November 26, 2012).

Schoch, R. (2006). "Setting post 9/11 priorities at the Bureau of Immigration and Customs Enforcement." Hearing before the Subcommittee on National Security, Emerging Threats and International Relations of the House Committee on Government Reform (March 28).

Stana, R. (2002). *Identity Fraud: Relevance and Links to Alien Illegal Activities*. Washington, D.C.: Government Accounting Office.

Stevenson, V. (2017). "Why are thousands of Haitians streaming into Canada from the U.S.?" *CBCNEWS*. http://www.

cbc.ca/news/canada/montreal/haitians-may-lose-protected-status-in-us-1.4233797 (Accessed September 3, 2017).

United States Attorney's Office. (2017). Bronx man and Michigan man arrested for terrorist activities on behalf of Hizballah's Islamic Jihad Organization. Southern District of New York. https://www.justice.gov/usao-sdny/pr/bronx-man-and-michigan-man-arrested-terrorist-activities-behalf-hizballah-s-islamic. (Accessed December 6, 2017)

U.S. Customs and Border Protection. (2015). CBP to Begin Biometric Entry/Exit Testing at Otay Mesa Port of Entry. https://www.cbp.gov/newsroom/local-media-release/cbp-begin-biometric-entryexit-testing-otay-mesa-port-entry.

U.S. Department of Justice. (2011). *Three plead guilty to conspiracy to provide material support to the Pakistani Taliban*. Federal Bureau of Investigation. https://archives.fbi.gov/archives/miami/press-releases/2011/three-plead-guilty-to-conspiracy-to-provide-material-support-to-the-pakistani-taliban (Accessed May 18, 2017).

U.S. Immigration and Customs Enforcement. (2008). *Worksite Enforcement*. http://www.ice.gov/pi/worksite/index.htm (Accessed December 28, 2008).

U.S. Immigration and Customs Enforcement. (2011). *ICE Fiscal Year (FY) 2012 Enacted Budget*. https://www.ice.gov/factsheets/budget2012.

U.S. Immigration and Customs Enforcement. (2015). *Operation Genesius. Working Together to Combat Document Fraud*. https://www.ice.gov/sites/default/files/documents/Document/2016/operation-genesius.pdf (Accessed July 13, 2017).

U.S. Immigration and Customs Enforcement. (2016). *FY 2016 ICE immigration removals*. https://www.ice.gov/removal-statistics/2016#wcm-survey-target-id (Accessed May 20, 2017).

Walsh, M. (2009). "Mexico murders soar as drug violence spirals out of control." *Telegraph*. http://www.telegraph.co.uk/news/worldnews/centralamericaandthecaribbean/mexico/4217538/Mexico-murders-soar-as-drug-violence-spirals-out-of-control.html (Accessed August 18, 2010).

Wermuth, M., and J. Riley (2007). *The Strategic Challenge of Border Security*. Santa Monica, CA: RAND

Werner, E. (2015). "House tightens controls on visa-free travel to US." https://www.apnews.com/aac031b66700473cbe9231da8a1a92c5 (Accessed December 14, 2015).

White House. (2015). *Findings from Select Federal Reports: The National Security Implications of a Changing Climate*. Washington, D.C.: Author.

Woodie, C. (2017). *Trump's immigration crackdown is hurting US farms with its unintended consequences. Business Insider*. http://www.businessinsider.com/trump-ice-immigration-crackdown-arresting-migrant-farmworkers-2017-3 (Accessed May 21, 2017).

13 The Response to Homeland Security Incidents

LEARNING OBJECTIVES

1. *Explain the significance of Hurricane Katrina in terms of emergency response.*
2. *Describe how the National Response Framework operates.*
3. *Discuss how the Stafford Act affects the federal response to emergencies and events.*
4. *Specify the workings of the National Incident Management System.*
5. *Discuss how incident command operates in an emergency situation.*
6. *Explain medical response to disasters and other emergencies.*

Key Terms

Federal Emergency Management Agency
Mitigation
Risk management
National Response Framework
Layered response
State homeland security director
Prevention stage
Protection mission
Public information and warning
Operational coordination
Response
Emergency support function annexes
Recovery
Surge Capacity Force
Stafford Act
National Incident Management System
Preparedness
Common operating picture
Resource management
Incident command system
National Disaster Medical System
National strike teams

▶ Introduction

In Chapter 1, we noted that one of the primary responsibilities of homeland security was to "respond to and recover from significant homeland security incidents." Obviously, our first priority is to prevent incidents that result in significant damage and loss of life. However, we must recognize that this objective may not always be met. We are likely to suffer from future terrorist attacks, and numerous natural and human-made disasters result in significant destruction. An important part of homeland security is to prepare an orderly and effective response to all such events.

To a large extent, when we consider homeland security, we focus on terrorist threats and attacks. However, as Department of Homeland Security (DHS, 2016a) and Bellavita

Debris clean up in Key West, Florida after Hurricane Irma in 2017.
FEMA Photo Library.

(2008) advised, numerous types of destructive events must be considered or responded to using our homeland security response mechanisms. These events include terrorist attacks, fires, floods, earthquakes, tornados, hurricanes, and human-made events such as explosions at chemical or nuclear facilities. For example, the Arkema chemical factory in Houston exploded and burned as a result of Hurricane Harvey in 2017 (Kaufman, 2017). In essence, we need to have effective response mechanisms that are capable of mitigating the impact of all sorts of large-scale disasters. Although the DHS was created and a number of response mechanisms were implemented because of the potential for future terrorist attacks, it has become important response mechanisms for all disasters that may befall us.

When considering response, we must include these other potential problems, and in actuality, at some level, the response to a natural disaster will contain many of the same operational elements as does a response to a terrorist attack, for example, Hurricanes Irma and Harvey in 2017. Moreover, there is a greater likelihood of disasters occurring relative to terrorist attacks. A number of major disasters require a federal response. On average, the United States faces 10 severe weather events per year, which cost about $85 billion every year for emergency response, recovery, and relief efforts. Effective disaster management has become increasingly important as the number of yearly natural disasters has grown from two such events during the 1980s to 10 in 2013. This number could continue to rise as the result of environmental factors (Kostro, Nichols, and Temoshchuk, 2013). These events have become much more disastrous as exemplified by hurricanes Katrina, Sandy, Harvey, and Irma.

FEMA: The Primary Response Agency When Disasters Occurs

The federal agency with primary responsibility for response is the **Federal Emergency Management Agency** (FEMA), which is a part of the DHS. In addition to FEMA, a number of other local, state, federal, and private agencies respond to disasters and terrorist attacks, including National Guard troops and active military personnel. The 9/11 attacks had lessened the importance of FEMA—the DHS was concentrating on preventing and responding to terrorist attacks. As a consequence of this organizational perspective, FEMA was pushed down into the bowels of the department's bureaucracy. There, it received little support and a substantial level of neglect—it was operating in a top-heavy bureaucracy that was unprepared for major disasters or problems. This problem was exemplified by Hurricane Katrina in 2005.

FEMA's response was deficient across the board with numerous failures and few successes. For example, Sobel and Leeson (2006) highlighted several problems. The Red Cross attempted to go into New Orleans to deliver much needed relief supplies but was prevented from doing so, FEMA confiscated emergency hospital supplies that were destined for a New Orleans hospital that had more than 100 critical care patients, and a Florida emergency response team was able to assist in Mississippi long before FEMA could effectively respond. Cable News Network (CNN) (2005) reported on similar problems. While fires raged in New Orleans, fire equipment was delayed because FEMA required firefighters to attend training sessions on community relations and sexual harassment. Water trucks were not allowed in the devastated area because they did not have the proper paperwork. Not only was the initial response botched, but numerous scandalous reports surfaced for months later with criticism of the temporary trailers FEMA bought for displaced residents and the ineffective distribution of food, water, and vouchers. Without a doubt, FEMA and the DHS's responses to Katrina were disastrous. They raised serious questions as to whether FEMA could adequately respond to a Weapons of Mass Destruction (WMD) attack on one of our cities. The critics pointed out the necessity to improve our emergency response mechanisms at all levels.

FEMA received a substantial amount of blame for the less than adequate response to Katrina. However, it should be noted that the city of New Orleans and the state of Louisiana shared a measure of the fault. Officials in New Orleans refused to evaluate the city on a timely basis, and the governor largely remained out-of-play until the situation had become a significant disaster. Essentially, the city and state did little until it was too late. The lack of response by the officials demonstrates that state and local governments must be more actively involved in planning responses prior to a disaster.

HS Web Link: To learn more about FEMA's response to Katrina, go to https://www.weather.gov/mob/katrina.

FEMA's response to Katrina was a wakeup call. Washington politicians began to comprehend the agency's importance. The agency's response to Sandy in 2012 and Harvey and Irma in 2017 was significantly improved. FEMA began dispatching resources to the troubled areas before the storms hit land. The agency worked closely with state and local disaster response agencies prior to the storms landing and continued to coordinate mitigation activities. President Trump and congress immediately provided FEMA with billions of dollars to ensure the agency had an adequate operational budget. The failures of Katrina resulted in lessons learned.

▶ Response Goals and Objectives

In 2016, the DHS elaborated the objectives for ensuring resilience to disasters:

- Mitigate hazards
- Enhance preparedness
- Ensure effective emergency response
- Rapidly recover (pp. 59–64)

Since 2005, the DHS has attempted to develop plans that would result in emergency response operations that would be more coordinated and effective in meeting these objectives. Today, the foundation for our emergency responses is the *National Response Framework* and the *National Incident Management System*. These plans in combination

HS ANALYSIS BOX 13-1

Risk management includes making decisions about actions that should be taken. Decisions are often limited by the amount of resources and the magnitude of the disaster. In terms of responding to a disaster such as a hurricane, what should be the priorities? How would you establish priorities if you had limited resources—that is, not enough resources to address every priority?

provide a framework from which to respond to significant national emergencies. Our planning and response mechanisms focus on "all hazards," including terrorist attacks.

The *National Response Framework* provides guidance on responding to terrorist attacks and catastrophes. It focuses on the relationships among the federal, state, and local governments and their obligations. However, before discussing the *National Response Framework*, it is instructive to discuss mitigation. **Mitigation** is a process whereby we attempt to reduce the impact of hazards, terrorist attacks, natural disasters, or human-made disasters before they occur. Mitigation often includes **risk management**, a process of hardening or increasing the safety features associated with critical infrastructure as discussed in Chapter 3. We can reduce the impact of an event if mitigation actions are taken previously. For example, if we had attended to flood protection measures in New Orleans, the impact of Hurricane Katrina might have been mitigated or reduced. Mitigation measures are often legislated or mandated by executive orders, building codes, safety requirements, and so on. For example, California now has strict building standards that reduce the amount of damage when earthquakes occur, and other building codes that reduce the likelihood of fires and their ensuing damage. Florida has codes to reduce the amount of damage in the event of a hurricane. As discussed in Chapter 3, we should deploy target hardening and other mitigation measures as part of our efforts to protect infrastructure.

Scorched earth after a wild fire in Mountain Ranch, California likely will contribute to flash flooding.
FEMA Photo Library.

National Response Framework

The **National Response Framework** was an effort by DHS to clarify the roles and responsibilities of those who are involved in responding to a significant catastrophe. Schneider (2008) advised that the mismatch between expected roles and responsibilities and actual performance has resulted in gaps when responding to critical incidents. That is, citizens and units of government have different expectations, especially those who are the victims of a disaster or who are responding to these victims, as compared to how governmental units sometimes see their responsibilities. Perhaps the greatest disconnect is between federal authorities and local citizens. The *National Response Framework* attempts to clarify responsibilities and ensure that we have coherent responses to events.

The federal government sees any response to a catastrophe, whether it is a terrorist attack or a natural disaster, in terms of a **layered response**. Although stated obtusely, this essentially means that local governments are responsible first and state governments second for responding to some catastrophe. This is exemplified by language commonly used in response plans—the federal government will respond to catastrophes and disasters that are of a "significant national emergency." This language and perspective serve to prevent the federal government from assuming responsibility for every mishap, especially those that are minor in nature. Units of local and state governments must take responsibility and control lesser disasters.

At the same time, this language allows the federal government to delegate a large measure of responsibility to local and state governments even for major incidents. Here, the federal government sees itself in a supplemental or supportive role. Local and state governments seldom have the resources or capacity to adequately respond even to a catastrophe of medium magnitude. The *National Response Framework* clarifies the relationship and duties of governments at all levels for disaster response.

The *National Response Framework* was developed as a result of political reaction to its predecessor, the *National Response Plan*. Lindsay (2008) and Birkland and Waterman (2008) identified a number of deficiencies with the original plan. First, there was confusion over the federal role in catastrophes relative to state and local responsibilities. The federal role, especially considering that the DHS sees itself in a supporting role, was not clearly articulated. The confusion over responsibilities resulted in response voids when the plan was set in motion. Second, it was overly bureaucratic and difficult to apply in operational terms. Finally, it was not a true operational plan as it identified relationships among various agencies but failed to provide specific operational guidance.

National Response Framework: An Analysis

The *National Response Framework* was designed to improve on the *National Response Plan*, and it addressed the *Plan*'s shortcomings. Primarily, the *Framework* has a national, rather than a federal government, focus; it attempts to integrate federal, state, and local

HS ANALYSIS BOX 13-2

Response to disasters and other events consists of a layered response with local authorities being responsible for minor events, state governments intervening in medium-sized events, and the federal government responding to major disasters and events. What types of events should remain under the purview of local authorities? What types of events should include a state response? Finally, what types of events require federal assistance? Can these events be easily distinguished?

1. Describe scalable, flexible, and adaptable coordinating structures, as well as key roles and responsibilities for integrating capabilities across the whole community, to support the efforts of local, state, tribal, territorial, insular area, and Federal governments in responding to actual and potential incidents.
2. Describe, across the whole community, the steps needed to prepare for delivering the response core capabilities.
3. Foster integration and coordination of activities within the Response mission area.
4. Outline how the response mission area relates to the other mission areas, as well as the relationship between the response core capabilities and the core capabilities in other mission areas.
5. Provide guidance through doctrine and establish the foundation for the development of the Response Federal Interagency Operational Plan (FIOP).
6. Incorporate continuity operations and planning to facilitate the performance of response core capabilities during all hazards emergencies or other situations that may disrupt normal operations.

FIGURE 13-1 National Response Framework Principles

Source: DHS. (2016). *National Response Framework* (3rd ed.) Washington, D.C.: Author.

HS Web Link: To view the *National Response Framework*, go to https://www.fema.gov/media-library-data/1466014682982-9bcf8245ba4c60c120aa915abe74e15d/National_Response_Framework3rd.pdf.

activities rather than focus exclusively on federal responsibilities. It serves as an outline of activities and does not provide specific policy and operational directives, which can be a shortcoming if agencies do not develop procedures and enact them. The *National Response Framework* was revised in 2016 (DHS, 2016b). Lindsay (2008, p. 5) provided an overview of the *Framework*'s doctrine, which is provided in Figure 13-1 ■. The doctrine consists of five principles that provide the boundaries of the federal response.

Local Responsibilities under the National Response Framework

When an incident occurs, local authorities are the first responders. They have the immediate responsibility for controlling and responding to the event to reduce the loss of life and property. A response to a catastrophe is a complex endeavor for large or small jurisdictions because all the elements in an effective response must be present. They must have a multitude of resources at their disposal including governmental and private agencies, for example, public health, law enforcement, disaster relief, utilities, waste management, fire, American Red Cross, and so on, as depicted in Figure 13-2 ■. Even though local authorities may receive support from state and federal officials, depending on the magnitude of the incident, it may be several days before this support arrives. That support may be fragmented and in some cases deficient as exemplified by past disasters. Consequently, responsibility falls squarely on local officials and their immediate response.

Local elected officials must ensure that a functioning plan of action is in place. Jurisdictional chief executives are responsible for providing strategic guidance and resources. They obtain aid from other governmental agencies, provide direction for response activities, and ensure that the public receives the appropriate information. Every jurisdiction should have an emergency manager who coordinates the local emergency response. Their role includes advising officials, coordinating agencies, assessing damage, coordinating resource requests, and conducting exercises to test response plans, determining shortcomings of such response plans, and improving them (DHS, 2016b).

The implementation of a functional plan of action in an emergency situation has not occurred or has occurred haphazardly in many jurisdictions. Local leaders are more concerned and consumed by the daily operations of government—delivering services to citizens. When a plan exists, it often is outdated or untested (Donahue and Tuohy, 2006). For example, the city of New Orleans had emergency response plans for storm and

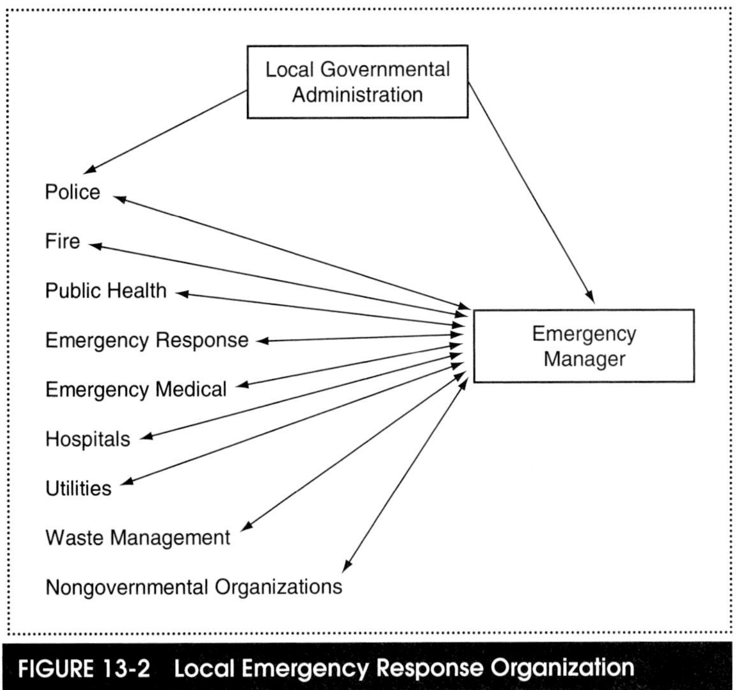

FIGURE 13-2 Local Emergency Response Organization

hurricane events, but they were of little value or were disregarded when Katrina struck. The plan's shelf life had expired through neglect and inattention. Hurricane Katrina was of such magnitude that plans were of little use. Nonetheless, a jurisdiction should have an emergency manager who is responsible for coordinating and controlling the jurisdiction's response to an emergency. A major part of this coordination and control is ensuring that a workable response plan is in place. This response plan must *be scalable*, that is, applicable to any event regardless of size or magnitude. It must be *flexible* so that it applies to a range of situations.

The test of the new response framework came in 2012, when Hurricane Sandy struck the U.S. East Coast. Hurricane Sandy's landfall winds were somewhat lower with 80 mph as compared to 100+ mph of Hurricane Katrina. Both hurricanes were over land for a similar duration: Sandy for 32 hours and Katrina for 33 hours. However, the death toll of Sandy was much lower with 109 people than Katrina, which took the life of 1,800 people. In addition, Katrina displaced about 1 million people, whereas Sandy displaced about 100,000. This is interesting as the population affected by Sandy was much greater with 17.5 million as compared to Katrina with 15 million (Kaleem and Wallace, 2012). The response to Sandy suggests that the changes made after Hurricane Katrina had positive effects and disaster management has become more efficient.

> **HS Web Link:** To view the variety of resources available to state and local governments in the event of a disaster, go to https://www.fema.gov/plan-prepare.

State Responsibilities under the *National Response Framework*

The governor is the chief executive officer for the state. He or she is directly responsible for ensuring that a state has an organizational framework and capacity to respond to a terrorist attack or disaster. Overall state command and coordination for such events are usually delegated to a state emergency management agency, state homeland security director, or commander of the state police or highway patrol. Large states will have all three operational entities, whereas smaller states may have only one of these offices.

The state has several responsibilities in terms of preparing for and responding to disasters. First, the state must effectively communicate event information to the public. This communication serves to assist in coordinating and controlling people in the disaster area. People need guidance and information in a disaster. These efforts reduce panic in the affected area and especially in unaffected areas. People generally want to know what is happening and what they should do when such events occur. As an example, Texas Governor Abbott and Florida Governor Scott both held frequent press conferences when hurricanes hit their states. Their messages focused on moving people out of harm's way.

Second, the governor can activate the National Guard, state police, and other resources. (The National Guard is a state's primary emergency resource in large catastrophes.) For example, Governors Abbott and Scott activated members of the National Guard to assist in mitigating the effects of the hurricanes. These resources are required in all but the most minor events. Third, the state coordinates mutual assistance plans with other states. For example, a number of Western states have mutual aid compacts to provide assistance in large fires. These compacts should be in place should a state experience other types of disasters. Finally, the governor is responsible for communicating requests for federal assistance. Generally, federal assistance is not provided until such a request is made, usually through the FEMA.

The state machinery often includes a state director of homeland security and a director of state emergency management. The **state homeland security director** is responsible for developing a statewide homeland security plan. The plan is fairly broad, focusing on both

National Guard personnel stack sandbags next to a levee in Winfield, Missouri in anticipation of the levee breaching.
FEMA Photo Library.

HS ANALYSIS BOX 13-3

As noted, a significant event, depending on its nature, can require the services of a large number of agencies and community-based organizations. If a large chemical spill occurred at an industrial area in your hometown, what agencies would be required to respond? Would outside assistance be required? Who would be in charge of the response?

prevention and response. It generally details different programs and relationships among state and local agencies. The director of state emergency management, on the other hand, is concerned with responding to incidents. This office maintains a network of local emergency response managers and capabilities. This office will coordinate state emergency management activities at an incident site, coordinating with the local emergency management personnel.

Federal Responsibilities under the National Response Framework

As noted in the *Framework*, the president is responsible for leading federal response efforts when a terrorist attack or disaster occurs. The president's National Security Council provides national strategic policy advice on incident response preparation and how the federal government should proceed during incidents. For example, the White House Office of Homeland Security developed the *National Strategy for Homeland Security*, which is discussed in detail in Chapter 1.

The secretary of DHS is the federal officer responsible for incident management. He or she is responsible for prevention, preparation, response, and recovery operational preparedness. The secretary is responsible for developing and maintaining the overall homeland security architecture using policies that are developed by the president's various advisors. FEMA coordinates federal disaster relief when incidents occur. Depending on the nature of the incident, a variety of other federal agencies may become involved in the federal response. If the incident is the result of a terrorist attack, the Federal Bureau of Investigation (FBI) will conduct a criminal investigation. Large-scale or incidents of significant magnitude may result in the military being activated. The secretary of defense authorizes the use of military assets in domestic catastrophes at the direction of the president. The military would play a key role in WMD attacks in terms of decontamination, evacuation, quarantine, and logistical support.

As noted earlier, the *National Response Framework* uses a layered response, whereby federal resources are deployed only when local and state resources are unable to adequately deal with an incident. In some cases, the federal government may take control of an incident. The DHS (2008a) in the *Framework* identifies four scenarios when the federal government assumes command and control:

1. A federal department or agency acting under its own authority has requested DHS assistance.
2. The resources of the State and local authorities are overwhelmed and Federal assistance is requested.
3. More than one federal agency has become substantially involved in responding to the incident.
4. The Secretary has been directed by the President to assume incident management responsibilities. (p. 25)

► Response as Dictated by the National Response Framework

According to the *Framework*, response is a multistage process consisting of (1) prevention, (2) protection, (3) mitigation, (4) response, and (5) recovery. Continuous planning and development must occur across all stages if an adequate response is to occur.

<table>
<tr><th>Prevention</th><th>Protection</th><th>Mitigation</th><th>Response</th><th>Recovery</th></tr>
<tr><td colspan="5">Planning</td></tr>
<tr><td colspan="5">Public Information and Warning</td></tr>
<tr><td colspan="5">Operational Coordination</td></tr>
<tr><td colspan="2">Intelligence and Information Sharing</td><td rowspan="4">Community Resilience
Long-term Vulnerability Reduction
Risk and Disaster Resilience Assessment
Threats and Hazards Identification</td><td colspan="2">Infrastructure Systems</td></tr>
<tr><td colspan="2">Interdiction and Disruption</td><td rowspan="3">Critical Transportation
Environmental Response/ Health and Safety
Fatality Management Services
Fire Management and Suppression
Logistics and Supply Chain Management
Mass Care Services
Mass Search and Rescue Operations
On-scene Security, Protection, and Law Enforcement
Operational Communications
Public Health, Healthcare, and Emergency Medical Services
Situational Assessment</td><td rowspan="3">Economic Recovery
Health and Social Services
Housing
Natural and Cultural Resources</td></tr>
<tr><td colspan="2">Screening, Search, and Detection</td></tr>
<tr><td>Forensics and Attribution</td><td>Access Control and Identity Verification
Cybersecurity
Physical Protective Measures
Risk Management for Protection Programs and Activities
Supply Chain Integrity and Security</td></tr>
</table>

FIGURE 13-3 Core Capabilities by Mission Area
Source: DHS (2016), *National Response Framework*. Washington, D.C.: Author, p. 21.

Prevention

The **prevention stage** consists of developing the capabilities to avoid, stop, or prevent terrorist acts and other imminent threats to national security. Prevention includes intelligence and information sharing; interdiction and disruption; screening, search, and detection; and forensics and attribution. Figure 13-3 ■ demonstrates this cycle.

Protection

The **protection mission** includes access control and identity verification, cybersecurity and physical protection measures, risk management, and supply chain security and integrity. The protection mission includes 11 core capabilities. Three of the core capabilities span all mission areas: planning, public information and warning, and operational coordination.

First, planning must occur at all levels: local, state, and federal. This planning must be a continuous process. As Schermerhorn (2008) noted, "When planning is done well, it creates a solid platform for the other management functions" (p. 184). One cannot manage, lead, organize, or control a situation without foundational planning. Planning allows organizations to respond effectively across the life cycle of a potential crisis. This planning must be inclusive, detailing the roles and responsibilities of various agencies, including nongovernmental agencies; the collection and use of intelligence information; mutual aid compacts; policy and procedure requirements; and so on. Planning should be flexible, addressing a variety of events, and it should be scalable to meet the requirements of events of varying magnitude. Planning should be comprehensive and include tactics addressing preparation to recovery. Since planning encompasses responses from a number of agencies and organizations, it must be ongoing since structural arrangements in some of these organizations will change and evolve over time. The plan must be contemporaneous, reflecting current organizational arrangements, capabilities, and commitments. Figure 13-4 ■ shows the decision processes involved in planning.

Protection requires considerable pre-event planning. The DHS has developed a number of action or operational plans that are implemented when an event of national significance occurs. However, successful implementation requires that all the possible scenarios be considered. Preoperational planning must be comprehensive.

There are eight critical tasks that need to be accomplished during the planning stage:

1. Flexible planning process.
2. Build community partnerships for information sharing.
3. Identify and prioritize critical infrastructures and determine how best to protect them.
4. Assess vulnerabilities, risks, and coordinate protective measures.
5. Determine joint protective measures within and across mission areas.
6. Develop plans for security, resilience, and continuity plans and programs.
7. Create protection plans for the community as a whole, including communities with animals and ensure that essential functions are performed under all circumstances.
8. Develop protection plans that are mutually supportive and do not conflict with each other or mission goals (DHS, 2016a).

An effective response is well organized, and this organization must occur at two strategic levels. First, agencies and organizations that are involved in response should have the organizational capacity to maximally respond. An effective response necessitates that each organization has its organization, procedures, and action plans in place. As the saying goes, a chain is only as strong as its weakest link. Second, substantial planning must be conducted to ensure that all involved agencies' responses are coordinated. Any response to an incident will include a number of federal, state, local, and nongovernmental agencies. They must have specific roles and objectives that in combination represent a comprehensive, effective response. In some cases, the federal government and the states use pre-scripted operational assignments to ensure that their response is adequate. Incident management organization is addressed in the *National Incident Management System*.

Public Information and Warning

In order to provide an effective response to an emergency and contain the number of victims, the public must be informed quickly and correctly. The DHS has developed a plan that ensures that prompt, reliable, and actionable information is delivered to the community. All communications must be accessible and culturally and linguistically appropriate.

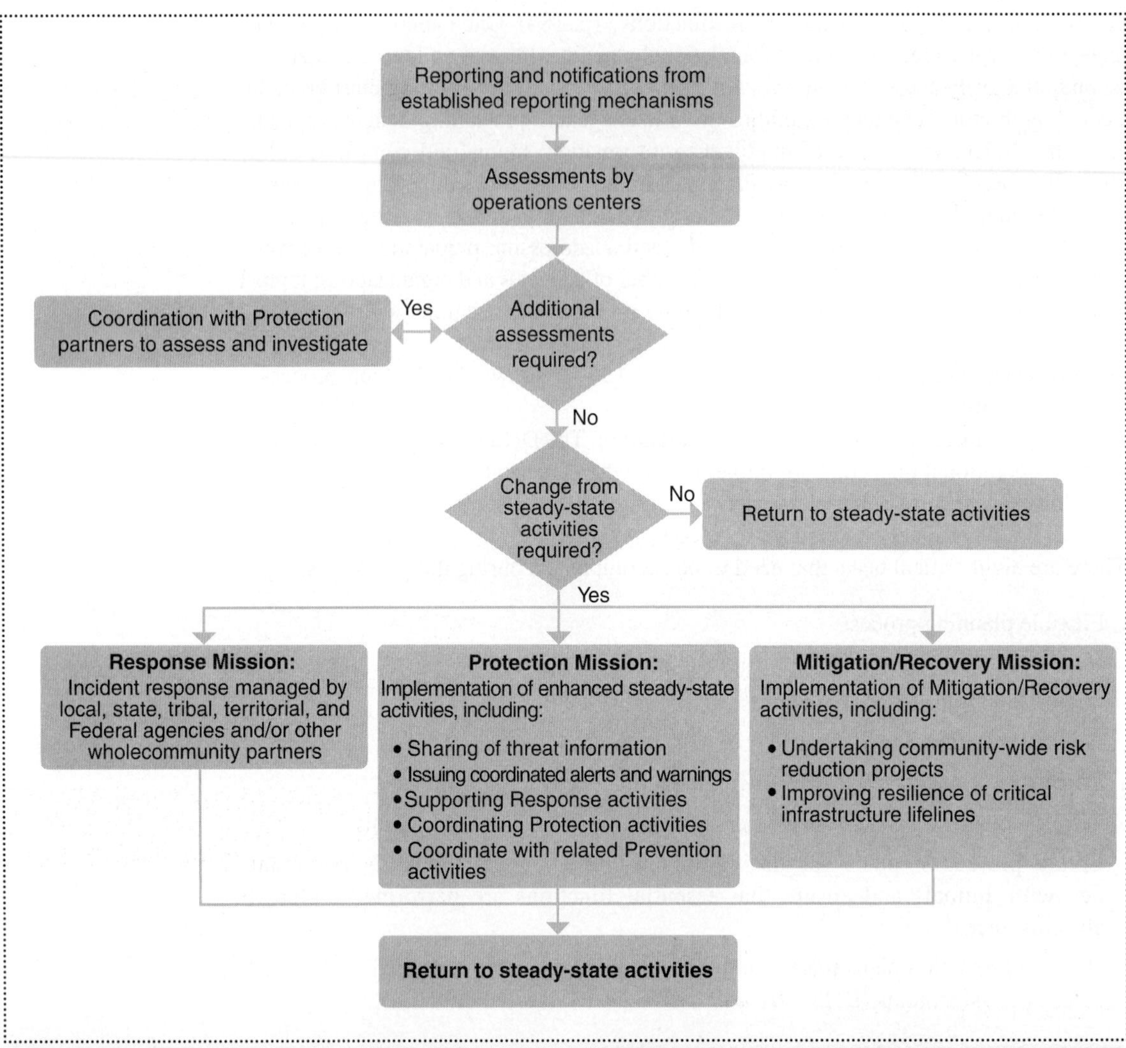

FIGURE 13-4 Protection Escalation Decision Process

Source: DHS (2016). *National Protection Framework.* Washington, D.C.: Author, p. 25.

There are seven critical tasks that need to be accomplished for **public information and warning**.

1. Increase public awareness.
2. Determine what information stakeholders need and how the information can be shared.
3. Develop information sharing requirements and processes for the community.
4. Information shared must be accessible.
5. Promptly share important information with the public, government agencies, private companies, and nonprofit companies.
6. Employ all available communication means, including social media, Integrated Public Alerts, Warning Systems, and the National Terrorism Advisory System.
7. Counter all violent extremist messages using social media and other communication outlets (DHS, 2016a).

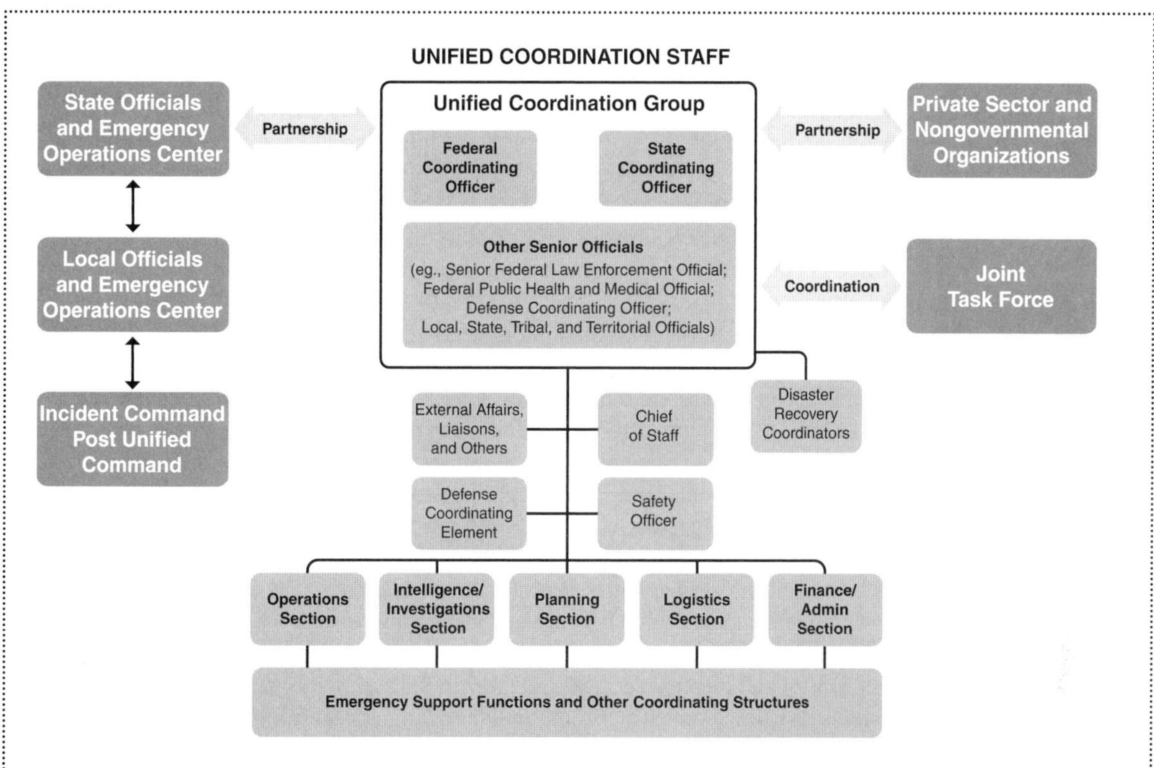

FIGURE 13-5 Unified Coordination Staff and the Prevention Cycle
Source: DHS (2016), *National Response Framework*. Washington, D.C.: Author, p. 43.

Operational Coordination

The third component is **operational coordination**, which aims to provide an operational structure and process that ensures the execution of core capabilities. The operational coordination also integrates all stakeholders and supports networking, planning, and coordination between protection partners. The operational coordination includes nine critical tasks:

1. Develop joint concepts of operation for delivering protection capabilities.
2. Collaborate with all appropriate protection partners.
3. Establish jurisdictional priorities and determine how resources will be allocated.
4. Develop efficient communication pathways for participating organizations and jurisdictions.
5. Establish and communicate roles and responsibilities to courses of action.
6. Ensure unity in effort by all participating organizations and jurisdictions.
7. Engage all levels of government, private and nonprofit sectors to protect against terrorist threats, investigate threats, and other tasks.
8. Develop interoperable communications.
9. Coordinate between mission areas to ensure the use of the most effective protection capabilities (DHS, 2016a).

Protection and Prevention Core Capabilities

There are three core capabilities that span the mission area of protection and prevention: (1) intelligence and information sharing; (2) interdiction and disruption; and (3) screening, search, and detection. First, intelligence and information must be shared timely and with all appropriate partners, government agencies, and private and nonprofit sectors to ensure that terrorist threats can be counteracted and to ensure that there is a prompt and effective response to emergency situations. The ability to share intelligence and information effectively depends on developing the technical and analytical capabilities, including networks and procedures.

Second, interdiction and disruption refers to delaying, diverting, or securing a threat. These threats include domestic and international terrorism and the movement of biological and nuclear materials and technologies. One of the main goals with regard to terrorist organizations is to disrupt terrorist financing and prevent terrorists from entering the country. Critical tasks also include preventing the spread of violent extremism in the United States, securing special events, and increasing the visibility of law enforcement.

Finally, screening, search, and detection refers to identifying and locating threats or hazards through surveillance and search procedures. Technologies used to detect threats or hazards are biosurveillance technologies, sensors, and physical examination. Critical tasks include the screening of cargo, mail, and baggage and identifying persons and networks that pose a threat.

There are five additional core capabilities, which are unique to Protection. First, access control and identity verification refers to the control of access to critical locations and systems. It is imperative to prevent unauthorized persons from entering critical infrastructures, such as nuclear power plants, because an attack on these critical infrastructures could have devastating consequences.

Second, cybersecurity measures are employed to protect electronic communication systems and information from being accessed and exploited. For instance, a distributed denial of service attack (DDoS) could incapacitate the Internet and telephone services. If there was a terrorist attack and a simultaneous DDoS attack, emergency personnel and police would not be able to communicate the threat to the community or would not even know about the attack and may not respond. If you cannot call the police, they cannot stop the terrorists.

Third, physical protective measures aim to reduce and mitigate the risk of a threat by controlling movement and protecting borders, critical infrastructures, and the homeland. Critical tasks include identifying and prioritizing assets, implementing security plans and trainings, implementing biosecurity and biosafety programs, and protecting critical lifeline functions. For instance, in case of a terrorist threat, it is imperative to have functioning power supply, communication systems, transportation systems, and water supply.

Fourth, risk management activities assess the likelihood that a threat will endanger critical infrastructure. Critical tasks include gathering data to identify risks, updating risk assessments, and investing in secure and resilient infrastructure to help communities withstand the effects of a terrorist attack or disaster. Communities need to understand what their vulnerabilities are and what to do if they get exploited to minimize the damage of an attack.

Finally, supply chain and security aims to protect key nodes, methods of transport between nodes, and materials in transit. The global supply chain is very expansive, which makes it vulnerable to disruption by terrorists and natural causes.

Mitigation/Recovery

The main purpose of mitigation is to reduce the loss of life and property by reducing the effect of the disaster or emergency. Effective mitigation depends on a good assessment of the vulnerabilities and consequences of a disaster. If you understand the risk, you can make plans to manage these risks and respond effectively to reduce the impact. The assessment of the risk must be based on science, technology, and intelligence—and validated by experience. Mitigation plans must also consider the impact on the economy, health, social services, infrastructure, and resources.

Mitigation consists of seven core capabilities:

1. Threats and hazards identification
2. Risk and disaster resilience assessment
3. Planning
4. Community resilience
5. Public information and warning
6. Long-term vulnerability reduction
7. Operational coordination

Roles and Responsibilities of Community Entities

In states with a high risk of earthquakes, hurricanes, tornadoes, or floods, communities should prepare for natural disasters by updating and enforcing building codes and implementing effective evacuation procedures. For example, a number of experts noted that the damage to Houston from Hurricane Harvey would have been less if the city had building codes that considered flooding problems and incorporated potential flooding in city planning. Individuals should also familiarize themselves with public information and warning systems.

Communities have the unique ability to bring private, nonprofit, and governmental organizations together and create partnerships that assist in sharing information and disaster preparation. Communities are often in the best position to reduce risks and manage emergencies because they are the most familiar with the risks and understand the needs of the residents. For instance, during a flood, communities have the most specific knowledge of the most endangered areas and evacuation routes.

Nongovernment entities are also an important factor in mitigation as they can help residents understand risks, be prepared for emergency situations, and provide assistance during a disaster. Examples of these organizations are voluntary organizations, faith-based organizations, national and professional organizations such as the Red Cross and the Salvation Army, and educational institutions. These organizations are also uniquely equipped to assist individuals with disabilities and special needs, children, individuals with animals, and individuals with limited English proficiency.

Response

The response to incidents is the fourth part of the *National Preparedness System.* **Response** refers to the building of the necessary capabilities to save lives, protect property and the environment, and ensure that basic human needs are met. These basic needs include shelter, food, and water, as well as personal safety. During Hurricane Katrina, the basic needs were not met for many residents in New Orleans for several days. The failure to meet the basic needs led to general chaos, looting, and violence, exacerbating the negative consequences of the hurricane. FEMA learned its lessons and the response to Hurricanes Sandy, Harvey, and Irma was much improved.

When an incident occurs, it triggers a number of processes and procedures on the part of a number of agencies. It requires substantial communication across a variety of agencies at all levels of government. It requires that efforts be comprehensive and coordinated. A comprehensive and coordinated response means that support needs must be identified, and requests for support must be made expeditiously. Local officials must immediately notify state officials, and when a situation is of sufficient magnitude, federal authorities must be notified. Any delays in requests for assistance result in exaggerated problems.

Some immediate actions at the scene that must occur are:

- Those injured must be evacuated.
- People in convalescent homes and hospitals must also be evacuated.
- Safe shelters for victims and those who are evacuated from the affected area must be identified and made ready.
- Arrangements for food and water must be made.
- Search and rescue operations must commence immediately to reduce the incidence of injuries and fatalities.
- Treatment facilities for the injured must be established.
- Hazards such as fires or contamination must be contained.
- In some cases, quarantines must be established and maintained.
- Arrangements must be made to ensure the safety and health of the first responders.
- Provide information to the public.

All of these activities must occur in short order, which requires substantial coordination and a lucid command operation. It also requires that workable procedures be in place ready for activation.

Emergency Support Functions

The ***emergency support function annexes*** (ESFs) were developed to provide a structure for coordinating support for a federal response to a disaster. They coordinate assistance to the states when responding to an incident. Each of the ESFs has a coordinating agency. They organize support within their functional area and coordinate with other support agencies, state officials, and other stakeholders to maximize the use of all available resources. They also make plans for incident management and short-term and long-term recovery. The ESFs and the coordinating agencies are found in Table 13-1 ■.

Perhaps the best way to examine these resources is to explore one of the annexes. For example, the public works and engineering ESF coordinator is located in the U.S. Army Corps of Engineers. Activities conducted as a result of this ESF includes assessment of damage to public works and infrastructure, contracting for support for life-saving and life-sustaining services, providing technical assistance, providing emergency repair of damaged public infrastructure, and implementing FEMA Public Assistance and other programs (DHS, 2008b, p. 17). Even though the U.S. Corps of Engineers has overall coordination responsibility, other federal agencies are available to assist, depending on the nature of the disaster and the scope of damage.

The guide advises that federal, state, and local officials should identify priorities, cooperatively identify support needs, and track the status of response and recovery activities.

Recovery

For the most part, **recovery** is the responsibility of FEMA. The types of assistance required for the recovery stage vary from community to community—community attributes dictate needs as well as the type of disaster. Flooding will require a different recovery assistance matrix as compared to an earthquake or WMD attack. Moreover, there are short-term recovery considerations and long-term recovery considerations. Short-term needs refer to the restoration of services such as transportation, utilities,

TABLE 13-1 Emergency Support Functions and ESF Coordinators

ESF #1—Transportation

ESF Coordinator: Department of Transportation

Key Response Core Capability: Critical Transportation

Coordinates the support and management of transportation systems and infrastructure, the regulation of transportation, and management of the Nation's airspace and ensures the safety and security of the national transportation system. Functions include but are not limited to:

- Transportation modes management and control
- Transportation safety
- Stabilization and reestablishment of transportation infrastructure
- Movement restrictions
- Damage and impact assessment.

ESF #2—Communications

ESF Coordinator: DHS/National Communications System

Key Response Core Capability: Operational Communications

Coordinates the reestablishment of the critical communications infrastructure, facilitates the stabilization of systems and applications from cyber attacks, and coordinates communications support to response efforts. Functions include but are not limited to:

- Coordination with telecommunications and information technology industries
- Reestablishment and repair of telecommunications infrastructure
- Protection, reestablishment, and sustainment of national cyber and information technology resources
- Oversight of communications within the Federal response structures.

ESF #3—Public Works and Engineering

ESF Coordinator: DOD/U.S. Army Corps of Engineers

Key Response Core Capabilities: Infrastructure Systems, Critical Transportation, Public and Private Services and Resources, Environmental Response/Health and Safety, Fatality Management, Mass Care Services, Mass Search and Rescue Operations

Coordinates the capabilities and resources to facilitate the delivery of services, technical assistance, engineering expertise, construction management, and other support to prepare for, respond to, and/or recover from a disaster or an incident. Functions include but are not limited to:

- Infrastructure protection and emergency repair
- Critical infrastructure reestablishment
- Engineering services and construction management
- Emergency contracting support for lifesaving and life-sustaining services.

ESF #4—Firefighting

ESF Coordinator: USDA/U.S. Forest Service and DHS/FEMA/U.S. Fire Administration

Key Response Core Capabilities: Critical Transportation, Operational Communications, Public and Private Services and Resources, Infrastructure Systems, Mass Care Services, Mass Search and Rescue Operations, On-scene Security and Protection, Public Health and Medical Services

Coordinates the support for the detection and suppression of fires. Functions include but are not limited to:

- Support to wildland, rural, and urban firefighting operations.

ESF #5—Information and Planning

ESF Coordinator: DHIS/FEMA

Key Response Core Capabilities: Situational Assessment, Planning, Public Information and Warning

Supports and facilitates multiagency planning and coordination for operations involving incidents requiring Federal coordination. Functions include but are not limited to:

- Incident action planning
- Information collection, analysis, and dissemination.

ESF #6—Mass Care, Emergency Assistance, Temporary Housing, and Human Services

ESF Coordinator: DHS/TEMA

Key Response Core Capabilities: Mass Care Services, Logistics and Supply Chain Management, Public Health, Healthcare, and Emergency Medical Services, Critical Transportation, Fatality Management Services

(continued)

TABLE 13-1 Emergency Support Functions and ESF Coordinators (continued)

Coordinates the delivery of mass care and emergency assistance. Functions include but are not limited to:

- Mass care
- Emergency assistance
- Temporary housing
- Human services.

ESF #7—Logistics

ESF Coordinator: General Services Administration and DHS/FEMA

Key Response Core Capabilities: Logistics and Supply Chain Management, Mass Care Services Critical Transportation, Infrastructure Systems, Operational Communications

Coordinates comprehensive incident resource planning, management, and sustainment capability to meet the needs of disaster survivors and responders. Functions include but are not limited to:

- Comprehensive, national incident logistics planning, management, and sustainment capability
- Resource support (e.g., facility space, office equipment and supplies, contracting services).

ESF #8—Public Health and Medical Services

ESF Coordinator: Department of Health and Human Services

Key Response Core Capabilities: Public Health, Healthcare, and Emergency Medical Services, Fatality Management Services. Mass Care Services, Critical Transportation, Public Information and Warning, Environmental Response/Health and Safety, Logistics and Supply Chain Management

Coordinates the mechanisms for assistance in response to an actual or potential public health and medical disaster or incident. Functions include but are not limited to:

- Public health
- Medical surge support including patient movement
- Behavioral health services
- Mass fatality management.

ESF #9—Search and Rescue

ESF Coordinator: DHS/FEMA

Key Response Core Capability: Mass Search and Rescue Operations

Coordinates the rapid deployment of search and rescue resources to provide specialized lifesaving assistance. Functions include but are not limited to:

- Structural collapse (urban) search and rescue
- Maritime/coastal/waterborne search and rescue
- Land search and rescue.

ESF #10—Oil and Hazardous Materials Response

ESF Coordinator: Environmental Protection Agency

Key Response Core Capabilities: Environmental Response/Health and Safety, Critical Transportation, Infrastructure Systems, Public Information and Warning

Coordinates support in response to an actual or potential discharge and/or release of oil or hazardous materials. Functions include but are not limited to:

- Environmental assessment of the nature and extent of oil and hazardous materials contamination
- Environmental decontamination and cleanup, including buildings/structures and management of contaminated waste.

ESF #11—Agriculture and Natural Resources

ESF Coordinator: Department of Agriculture

Key Response Core Capabilities: Mass Care Services, Critical Transportation, Logistics and Supply Chain Management

Coordinates a variety of functions designed to protect the Nation's food supply, respond to plant and animal pest and disease outbreaks, and protect natural and cultural resources. Functions include but are not limited to:

- Nutrition assistance
- Animal and agricultural health issue response
- Technical expertise, coordination, and support of animal and agricultural emergency management
- Meat, poultry, and processed egg products safety and defense
- Natural and cultural resources and historic properties protection.

TABLE 13-1 Emergency Support Functions and ESF Coordinators (continued)

ESF #12—Energy **ESF Coordinator: Department of Energy** Key Response Core Capabilities: Infrastructure Systems, Logistics and Supply Chain Management, Situational Assessment Facilitates the reestablishment of damaged energy systems and components and provides technical expertise during an incident involving radiological/nuclear materials. Functions include but are not limited to: • Energy infrastructure assessment, repair, and reestablishment • Energy industry utilities coordination • Energy forecast.
ESF #13—Public Safety and Security **ESF Coordinator: Department of Justice/Bureau of Alcohol, Tobacco, Firearms, and Explosives** Key Response Core Capability: On-Scene Security, Protection, and Law Enforcement Coordinates the integration of public safety and security capabilities and resources to support the full range of incident management activities. Functions include but are not limited to: • Facility and resource security • Security planning and technical resource assistance • Public safety and security support • Support to access, traffic, and crowd control.
ESF #14—Superseded by National Disaster Recovery Framework
ESF #15—External Affairs **ESF Coordinator: DHS** Key Response Core Capability: Public Information and Warning Coordinates the release of accurate, coordinated, timely, and accessible public information to affected audiences, including the government, media, NGOs, and the private sector. Works closely with state and local officials to ensure outreach to the whole community. Functions include, but are not limited to: • Public affairs and the Joint Information Center • Intergovernmental (local, state, tribal, and territorial) affairs • Congressional affairs • Private sector outreach • All Hazards Emergency Response Operations Tribal.

Source: DHS (2106). *National Response Framework.* Washington, D.C.: Author, pp. 34–37.

food, shelter, and government programs. Long-term needs, on the other hand, may take months or even years to meet and refer to the redevelopment of affected areas. Figure 13-6 ■ shows the recovery continuum depicting the interaction between short, intermediate, and long-term recovery.

FEMA provides a range of federal assistance. Depending on the type of incident, roads must be reconstructed; permanent housing must be built; schools, government buildings, and medical facilities must be established; and so on. In some cases, funding comes in the form of grants and loans; in other cases, individual citizens receive payments to assist them in recovery. FEMA has several programs, including the Disaster Housing Program that provides housing, reimbursement of expenses for temporary shelter, and repair of homes; Individual and Family Grants that address victim housing needs; Small Business Administration Disaster Loans that are made to affected businesses; Disaster Unemployment Assistance, a program that expedites unemployment benefits and legal services; and FEMA's Public Assistance Grant Program, which provides funds to local and state governments to assist in the resumption of services (Bullock et al., 2005). Recovery, depending on the magnitude of the incident, can cost millions or even billions of dollars. Table 13-2 ■ shows the different recovery capabilities that a community must have to effectively mitigate and recover from a disaster.

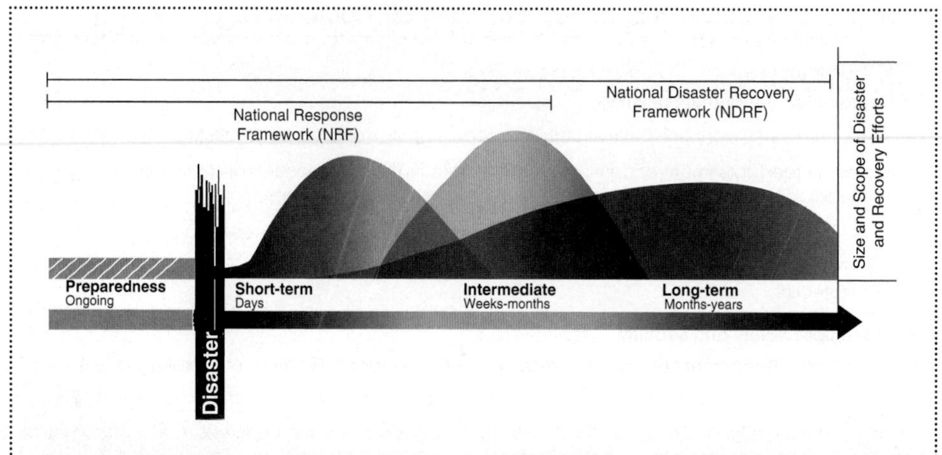

FIGURE 13-6 Recovery Progression for Disasters

Source: DHS (2016). *National Disaster Recovery Framework.* Washington, D.C.: Author, p. 5.

TABLE 13-2 Recovery Capabilities Necessary for Disasters

Planning

Conduct a systematic process engaging the whole community as appropriate in the development of executable strategic, operational, and/or tactical-level approaches to meet defined objectives.

Public Information and Warning

Deliver coordinated, prompt, reliable, and actionable information to the whole community through the use of clear, consistent, accessible, and culturally and linguistically appropriate methods to effectively relay information regarding any threat or hazard and, as appropriate, the actions being taken and the assistance being made available.

Operational Coordination

Establish and maintain a unified and coordinated operational structure and process that appropriately integrates all critical stakeholders and supports the execution of core capabilities.

Economic Recovery

Return economic and business activities (including food and agriculture) to a healthy state and develop new business and employment opportunities that result in an economically viable community.

Health and Social Services

Restore and improve health and social services capabilities and networks to promote the resilience, independence, health (including behavioral health), and well-being of the whole community.

Housing

Implement housing solutions that effectively support the needs of the whole community and contribute to its sustainability and resilience.

Infrastructure Systems

Stabilize critical infrastructure functions, minimize health and safety threats, and efficiently restore and revitalize systems and services to support a viable, resilient community.

Natural and Cultural Resources

Protect natural and cultural resources and historic properties through appropriate planning, mitigation, response, and recovery actions to preserve, conserve, rehabilitate, and restore them consistent with post-disaster community priorities and best practices and in compliance with applicable environmental and historic preservation laws and executive orders.

Source: DHS (2016). *National Disaster Recovery Framwork.* Washington, D.C.: Author, p. 25.

▶ Critique of Past Responses and the *National Response Framework*

Generally, there are weak or virtually no lines of communication between the department decision makers and operatives in the field. Even in the gravest situations, this often leads to disconnect and less than satisfactory solutions. Similar problems often exist in the relationships between state and local governments. In the past, the *Framework* received mixed reviews. Lindsay (2008) noted that in the past it was used sparingly. But, discussions with emergency response personnel note that federal involvement in disaster relief has improved. Officials in Texas, reporting on the federal efforts with Hurricanes Gustav and Ike, indicated that the federal effort was "good."

One of the biggest improvements since the *Post Katrina Reform Act* is that states can declare a state of emergency before the storm hits. Being able to declare a state of emergency prior to the catastrophe helps prepare people and start the supply chain, such as storing food, water, and equipment. This allowed New Jersey to be prepared for Hurricane Sandy. Altogether there were 34 points of distribution for water, food, blankets, and other supplies. Three days after Hurricane Sandy made landfall, FEMA had supplied 1.9 million meals and 1.3 million liters of water. Also, due to the early preparation, within 48 hours of landfall, New Jersey had 1,200 people in the field to assist the community.

FEMA also deployed its **Surge Capacity Force** consisting of volunteers from various homeland security departments. A variety of other federal agencies deployed their agents promptly, such as the Coast Guard, Army Corps of Engineers, the Department of Defense, and the Marines. In addition, hospitals were placed on high alert and the Department of Health and Human Services deployed Disaster Medical Assistance Teams to set up field hospitals.

A major problem with many disasters is the lack of electrical power. FEMA established the National Power Restoration Task Force, which supplied personnel and equipment to restore power as quickly as possible in affected areas. The U.S. Air Force transported vehicles, equipment, and supplies for power restoration to disaster-affected areas.

Another significant problem was the immense amount of water in the tunnels and subways that needed to be pumped out. The Army Corps of Engineers due to early preparation was able to pump 474 million gallons of water within two weeks. Finally, most vehicles and other equipment run on fuel. Due to the damage to the streets, it was impossible to supply enough fuel to the gas stations for the residents and supply all of the first responders. The Defense Logistics Agency delivered 2.3 million gallons of fuel to New York and New Jersey, making it possible to residents to resume their lives (Byrne, 2013).

All of the above examples demonstrate that FEMA has learned from prior disasters. FEMA was also well funded at the time. Currently, President Trump has proposed cuts to several FEMA programs. For instance, he has proposed a cut of $1 billion (or 16.3% of the budget) to the Army Corps of Engineers, who had pumped millions of gallons of water out of the tunnels and subways. In addition, the budget proposal includes cuts of $667 million from FEMA state and local grant funding, including the Pre-Disaster Mitigation Grant Program and the Homeland Security Grant Program. The totality of these cuts would likely have a negative impact on the effectiveness of FEMA during a disaster (Kopan, 2017).

► Procedures for Activating Federal Assistance in an Emergency

The federal government and its many departments and agencies possess a multitude of resources that can be deployed to assist local and state governments in the event of a terrorist attack or other disaster. These resources are not deployed automatically but are activated as a result of a state request and federal deployment procedures as described in the Stafford Act (DHS, 2016c). The Stafford Act outlines and coordinates disaster response efforts. When an incident occurs that exhausts local and state resources, the state can request assistance from the federal government. The **Stafford Act** essentially authorizes the president to provide support to the states in such emergencies. Figure 13-7 ■ charts this process.

> **HS Web Link:** To learn more about the Stafford Act, go to https://www.fema.gov/media-library-data/1490360363533-a531e65a3e1e63b8b2cfb7d3da7a785c/Stafford_ActselectHSA2016.pdf.

If a situation of substantial magnitude occurs, federal resources may be deployed prior to a request from the state. Generally, however, the governor will make a request for assistance to the regional FEMA administrator. Prior to any such request, however, the governor must have activated the state's emergency response apparatus. Once the request is made to the regional FEMA administrator, the administrator and the governor survey the damage to determine its extent and the types of aid that are required to mitigate the problem. The request is then forwarded to the president through the FEMA administrator, and then the president issues a declaration. The declaration allows various federal agencies to provide assistance to the disaster area.

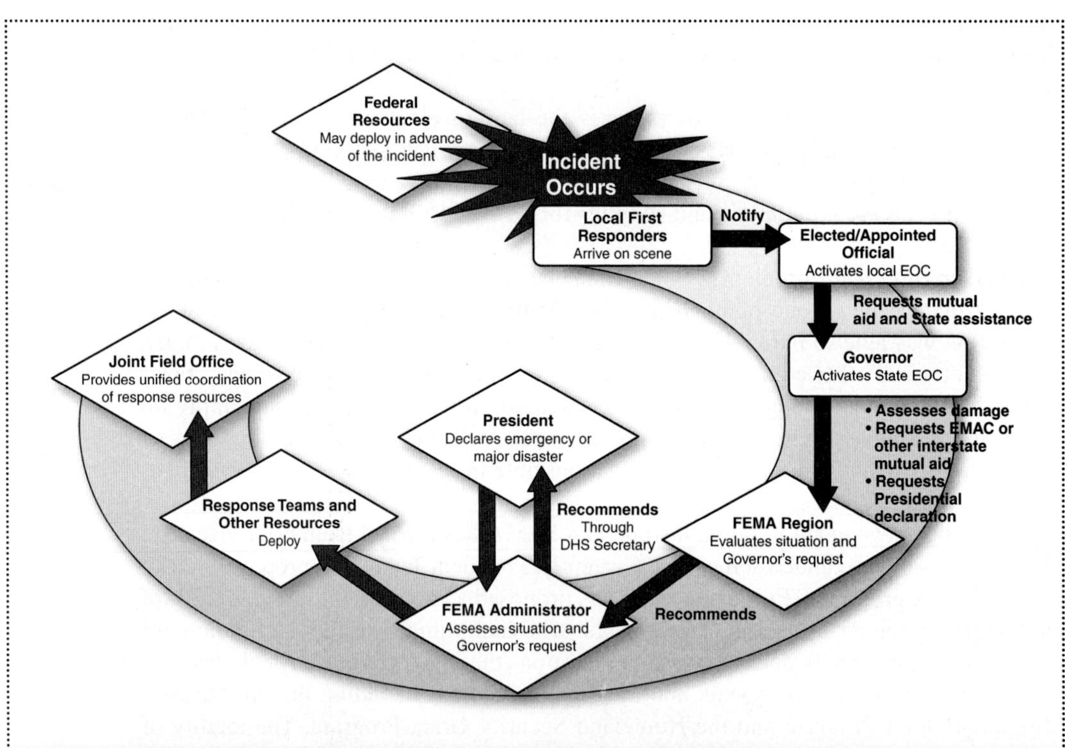

FIGURE 13-7 Process for Obtaining Federal Support in Emergencies

Source: Department of Homeland Security. (2008b). *Overview: ESF and Support Annexes Coordinating Federal Assistance in Support of the National Response Framework.* Washington, D.C.: Author, p. 5.

HS ANALYSIS BOX 13-4

In order to secure a federal response to a disaster, the president has to declare a national emergency. Generally, a request is made by the governor of the affected state to the regional FEMA administrator. Do you believe this request process as dictated by the Stafford Act is too cumbersome? How do you think FEMA and the president determine if an event is of significant magnitude to warrant federal assistance? Do states attempt to obtain assistance in less significant events?

In some cases, federal authorities will begin moving emergency resources in place prior to a request. When a large-scale disaster such as a hurricane, earthquake, or flood occurs, FEMA recognizes the level of severity and mobilizes resources so that relief efforts can begin as quickly as possible. A terrorist attack, especially one involving weapons of mass destruction, would result in the immediate mobilization of resources. FEMA monitors incidents and attempts to react as quickly as possible.

Even though the Stafford Act has made disaster response more efficient, it has its shortcomings. The main criticisms relate to the speed and size of disaster efforts provided to communities. First, the Stafford Act has two major classifications: "emergencies" and "major disasters." The level of funding and resources provided to the impacted community depends on the classification, but the aid provided is insufficient even if an event is categorized as a major disaster. A quick recovery is inhibited by slow and inefficient bureaucratic process, such as providing federal loans. Some scholars and politicians have suggested the creation of a third category called "catastrophic disaster" under which the federal aid provided would be greater and distribution of the aid would be faster by eliminating some of the procedures typically applied in emergency situations (Kostro, Nichols, and Temoshchuk, 2013).

▶ National Incident Management System

HS Web Link: To learn more about the National Incident Management System, go to https://www.fema.gov/media-library-data/1405716454795-3abe60aec989ec-ce518c4cdba67722b8/July18FEMAStratPlanDigital508HiResFINALh.pdf.

Thus far, the emergency response programming, particularly the *National Response Framework*, has been addressed. An effective and coherent response requires an efficient command and control system. Heretofore, such systems have been somewhat haphazard with little consistency across disaster responses. The DHS (2008c) developed the **National Incident Management System** (NIMS) in an effort to ensure some measure of consistency and a more effective response. The system provides guidelines on how incidents are managed. The DHS envisions that the *National Response Framework* and the *National Incident Management System* would interface and provide a cohesive approach to an emergency response.

As noted, the DHS attempted to develop a system that had continuity. The department identified six attributes for the NIMS, which are listed in Figure 13-8 ■.

The NIMS contains five primary components: (1) preparedness, (2) communications and information management, (3) resource management, (4) command and management, and (5) ongoing management and maintenance. Each of these components is addressed next.

Preparedness

Preparedness centers on a unified approach whereby the NIMS structure is integrated into agencies' emergency operations. Agencies should achieve some level of preparedness relative to communications, resource management, and command. It also requires that agencies are capable of providing varying or scalable levels of service, depending

- A comprehensive, nationwide, systematic approach to incident management, including the Incident Command System, Multiagency Coordination Systems, and public information
- A set of preparedness concepts and principles for all hazards
- Essential principles for a common operating picture and interoperability of communications and information management
- Standardized resource management procedures that enable coordination among different jurisdictions or organizations
- Scalable, so it can be used for all incidents (from day-to-day to large scale)
- A dynamic system that promotes ongoing management and maintenance

FIGURE 13-8 Attributes of the NIMS

Source: Department of Homeland Security. (2008c). National Incident Management System. Washington, D.C.: Author, p. 6.

on the magnitude of the incident. Agencies should take stock of their resources, human resources, supplies, command structure, and interoperable relationships among agencies and ensure that they have the capacity to respond to an incident. It also includes the development of plans and procedures, ensuring that first responders are trained and properly equipped, and the development and maintenance of mutual aid agreements for all governmental and nongovernmental agencies. It is most important that all parties potentially involved in an emergency response understand their roles and responsibilities. Essentially, preparedness is a matter of coordinating the various components prior to an incident.

Communications and Information Management

Communication is critical to a well-coordinated and effective response. The DHS (2008a) advises that agencies should have a **common operating picture**:

> A common operating picture is established and maintained by gathering, collating, synthesizing, and disseminating incident information to all appropriate parties. Achieving a common operating picture allows on-scene and off-scene personnel—such as those at the Incident Command Post, Emergency Operations Center, or within a Multiagency Coordination Group—to have the same information about the incident, including the availability and location of resources and the status of assistance requests. (p. 23)

An emergency response communications system should have several qualities. First, it must have interoperability—various agencies must be able to communicate with one another. One of the primary impediments in the response to the 9/11 World Trade Center attack was that various first responders could not communicate—fire, police, National Guard, and other responders used different radio channels or frequencies, which prevented them from communicating with other first responder organizations. The problem was exacerbated when the city's communication center was destroyed; it was located in one of the World Trade Center towers (Simon and Teperman, 2001). The failure of communication to first responders was a primary obstruction in recovery efforts. Second, the communications system must be reliable and flexible so that first responders and managers can communicate in all sorts of conditions. Third, communications systems should be resilient and reliable under different conditions, and there should be some level of redundancy so that communications could be maintained if one section or system becomes inoperable.

Resource Management

It is important to realize that the response to a disaster incident, especially a large-scale incident, requires immense amounts of resources requiring effective **resource management**. Resource management includes resources needed for the initial response through recovery. Moreover, these resources must be made available almost immediately. For example, first responders, victims, and the displaced must be fed, housed, and otherwise cared for. In some cases, supplies must be shipped from locations that are hundreds if not thousands of miles from the site. Logistics are complicated but, nonetheless, must be effectively managed. Figure 13-9 ■ graphically shows this process in action.

As shown in Figure 13-7 ■, resource management for an incident is complicated. Once an incident occurs, requirements must be identified, and there is a wide array of requirements or materials that may be needed to mitigate the situation. How many and what types of personnel are needed—military, law enforcement, fire, paramedics, medical, search and rescue, heavy equipment operators, and so on? What types of equipment will be needed—heavy equipment to move debris, communications, temporary shelter for victims and rescue personnel, electric generators, vehicles to evacuate the displaced and injured, and so on? A substantial volume of supplies will be required—water, food, temporary shelter, medical supplies, gasoline for equipment

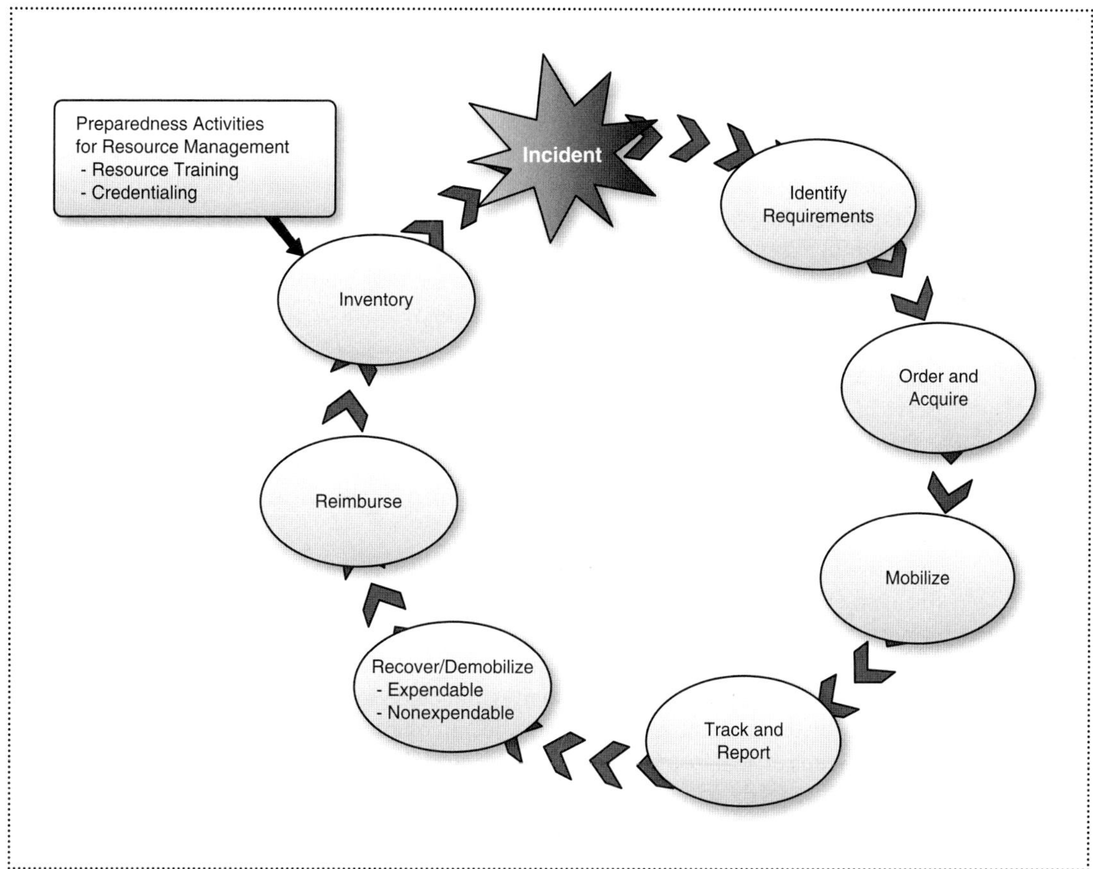

FIGURE 13-9 Resource Management during a Disaster or Attack

Source: Department of Homeland Security. (2008c). National Incident Management System. Washington, D.C.: Author, p. 35.

HS ANALYSIS BOX 13-5

It is important for those responding to a disaster that they have adequate resources to respond and mitigate the conditions. Disaster response usually requires large amounts of supplies. Agencies often are criticized when they order too many supplies because of the costs or too little supplies resulting in an inadequate response. How can responding agencies determine how many supplies to order? Should they err on the side of too many or too little given today's environment of limited resources?

and evacuation vehicles, and so on. Obviously, the type and size of the incident will dictate the resource requirements. Nonetheless, resources must be made available at the scene as quickly as possible to effectively mediate or attend to the situation.

Once an inventory of resources has been determined, resources must be acquired. Some resources will be available locally, whereas others may have to travel from hundreds or thousands of miles from the site. They must be tracked to ensure that they arrive on a timely basis. Once resources are ordered and acquired, they must be mobilized. That is, there must be an action plan that describes activities, responsibilities, and personnel who are involved in the recovery. Personnel must be matched with equipment and supplies in a deployable manner. The action plan should be of sufficient detail to ensure that all issues and problems are addressed. The plan must be comprehensive and address every detail; omissions often result in problems and in some cases injuries or the loss of life. Moreover, activities must be monitored to ensure that they are consistent with the plan. In some cases, as new problems are identified, the plan and activities will be adjusted. Once the incident has been mitigated, there will be an accounting to determine levels and types of expenditures. It is therefore important to track and report on costs and activities. For example, FEMA was severely criticized in the wake of Hurricane Katrina for a number of wasteful expenditures that likely amounted to more than a billion dollars (Hall, 2006).

Once the incident has been controlled and the damage mitigated, demobilization occurs. Excess stocks of resources are returned to vendors or stored for the next incident. Emergency response agencies must restock emergency supplies that are used during the initial response to the emergency. Personnel are returned home or sent back to regular service. Finally, government agencies, primarily the federal government, must pay for the expenses associated with the recovery effort.

Mechanisms for Requesting and Receiving Assistance during a Major Incident

As noted, Figure 13-9 ■ provides the resource management process during an emergency incident. However, it is important to examine the response processes when a disaster occurs. Figure 13-10 ■ shows the flow of assistance and requests for help in a large-scale event. First, note that requests for assistance originate from the local emergency command center. The first response to any incident will include local first responder units and organizations. If the incident is significant, a local command structure will be established to evaluate, control, and respond. A judgment will be made if external assistance is required, whereupon requests will be made to the state and other jurisdictions that have mutual aid compacts with the affected jurisdiction. If state resources are not adequate, the governor will make a request to the regional FEMA director for assistance. FEMA representatives will evaluate the situation, and if warranted, request that the president declare a state of emergency. The federal response often includes assistance from several federal agencies. A joint field office is established to coordinate the federal response, which as noted includes a wide range of activities and services.

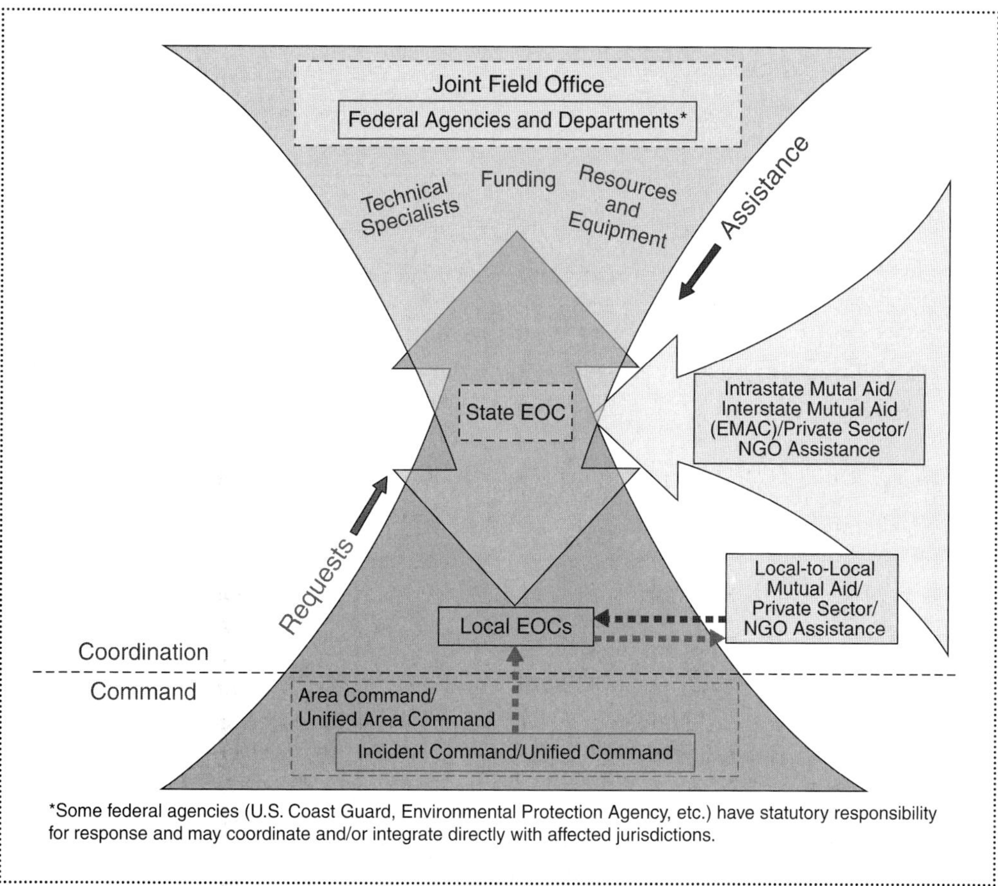

FIGURE 13-10 Flow of Requests and Assistance during Large-Scale Incidents

Source: Department of Homeland Security. (2008c). National Incident Management System. Washington, D.C.: Author, p. 36.

As noted in Figure 13-6 ■, once the assistance begins to flow to the incident, activities can be categorized as coordination and command. From a coordination standpoint, there is an increase in the number of agencies involved in the response as the size of the incident increases. Moreover, the agencies include local, state, federal, and private entities, and they are involved in a range of activities that comprehensively mitigate the problem at hand. Their efforts and responsibilities should fit together like pieces in a puzzle, and if there is a piece missing or services are not delivered as projected or needed, the response will be less than effective. In some cases, agencies do not operate as expected or there are significant delays in their response or initiation of operations.

Command and Management at an Incident

The *National Incident Management System* attempts to standardize incident management for all hazards and incidents across governments. A standardized format results in enhanced operational effectiveness since agencies' roles are predetermined and understood. The primary on-the-ground control mechanism is the **incident command system** (ICS). The ICS is the command center where all efforts to respond to and mitigate an incident are coordinated. Fire and police departments have used such structures for decades when responding

HS Web Link: To learn more about the ICS, go to http://training.fema.gov/EMIWeb/IS/ICSResource/index.htm.

to a critical incident. It encompasses agencies, personnel, communications, equipment, procedures, and a unified command structure. When operated correctly, an ICS reduces the probability of errors and affords better coordination of effort. It results in the establishment of overall and agency goals and objectives and results in a cohesive management and operational plan.

The ICS results in unity of command, whereby one individual is identified as being responsible for overall command and coordination. In the past, this has not always occurred; there would be squabbling among the various agency heads or representatives as to which agency was the lead agency. In some cases, it became extremely complicated when local, state, and federal agencies became involved. Implementation of the ICS requires that an incident commander be identified, and the incident commander is responsible for commanding and coordinating all response activities. Even though the ICS is part of the NIMS, questions remain as to whether command will be assumed smoothly and effectively. For example, in most responses, FEMA is charged with coordinating the federal effort, a position assumed by FEMA managers during hundreds of incident responses. However, if the incident involves weapons of mass destruction requiring a response from the military and federal law enforcement officers, it remains to be seen if command will be ideally coordinated or assumed. In major incidents, the ICS system consists of a number of sections. Figure 13-11 ■ provides a schematic of the workings of a large ICS.

Ongoing Management and Maintenance

In large incidents, the incident commander will have a command staff generally consisting of public information, safety, and liaison officers. The public information officer is responsible for communicating with the public. It is important for response personnel to communicate and advise citizens who are affected by the incident about what is happening, especially in volatile or changing conditions. People need to be informed of evacuation plans and routes, shelter, where to obtain food and water, and how medical care is being

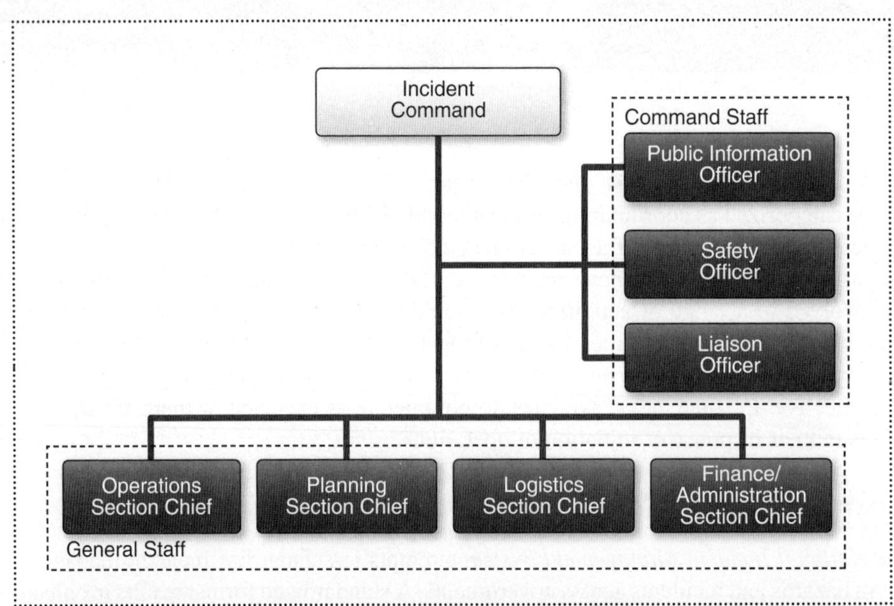

FIGURE 13-11 Incident Command Center Staffing and Organization

Source: Department of Homeland Security. (2008c). National Incident Management System. Washington, D.C.: Author, p. 53.

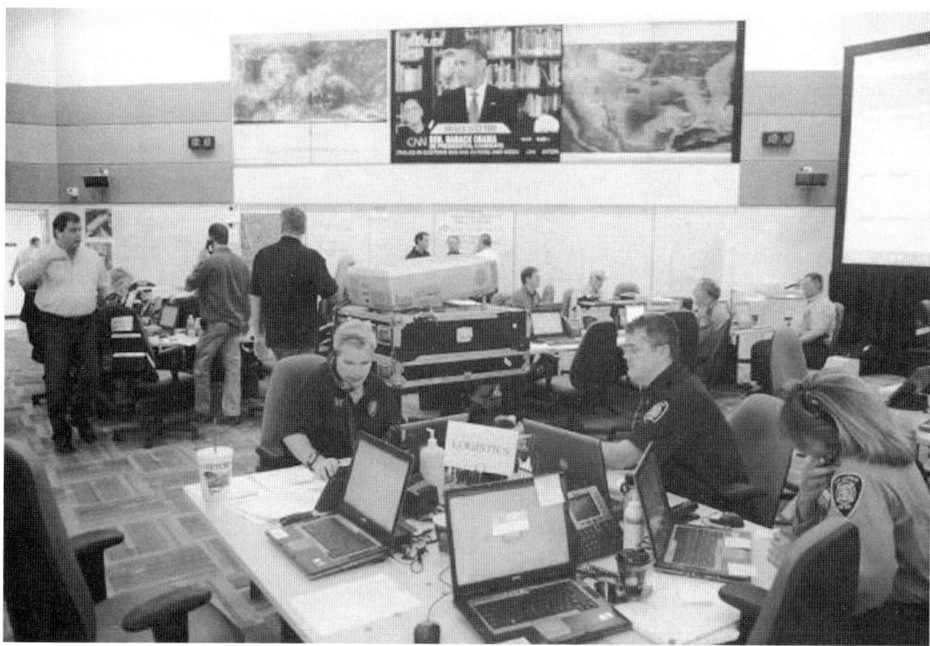

Emergency operations center in San Antonio, Texas, after Hurricane Ike.
FEMA Photo Library.

provided. One of the early mistakes in Hurricane Katrina was that citizens in affected areas were not given this information in a timely fashion. The public information officer is able to gain citizens' compliance and cooperation in the recovery effort.

The safety officer is responsible for advising the incident commander about safety issues, especially concerning response procedures and personnel. There are always dangers when personnel are working in devastated areas. The safety officer ensures that emergency workers do not take chances or endanger themselves or others. The liaison officer is responsible for maintaining contact with the various agencies involved in the response to ensure that coordination is maintained. The liaison officer is constantly communicating with the various agencies and relaying problems and information to the incident commander.

In addition to these officers, there generally are four section chiefs: (1) operations, (2) planning, (3) logistics, and (4) finance and administration. The operations chief is responsible for the tactical operations. This individual actually coordinates recovery efforts. The planning section chief collects, evaluates, and disseminates information about the incident. This is especially critical in a biological or chemical incident. Also, as an example, when floods occur, the flooding may continue and even increase for several days. It is important to map and plan for changes with the continued flooding. The planning section chief is responsible for keeping other responders updated on such situational changes. The planning chief also is responsible for ensuring that all the necessary equipment is acquired. Finally, this individual must plan for demobilization.

The logistics section chief is responsible for ensuring that necessities such as food, water, shelter, and support are available for emergency workers and victims and those who are evacuated or without adequate supplies and services. The logistics chief is also responsible for ensuring that there are working communications to coordinate relief efforts.

Finally, the finance and administration section chief is responsible for a number of financial activities. First, this chief is responsible for procuring food, water, and other expendables and items such as temporary shelter. Orders for material must be placed with

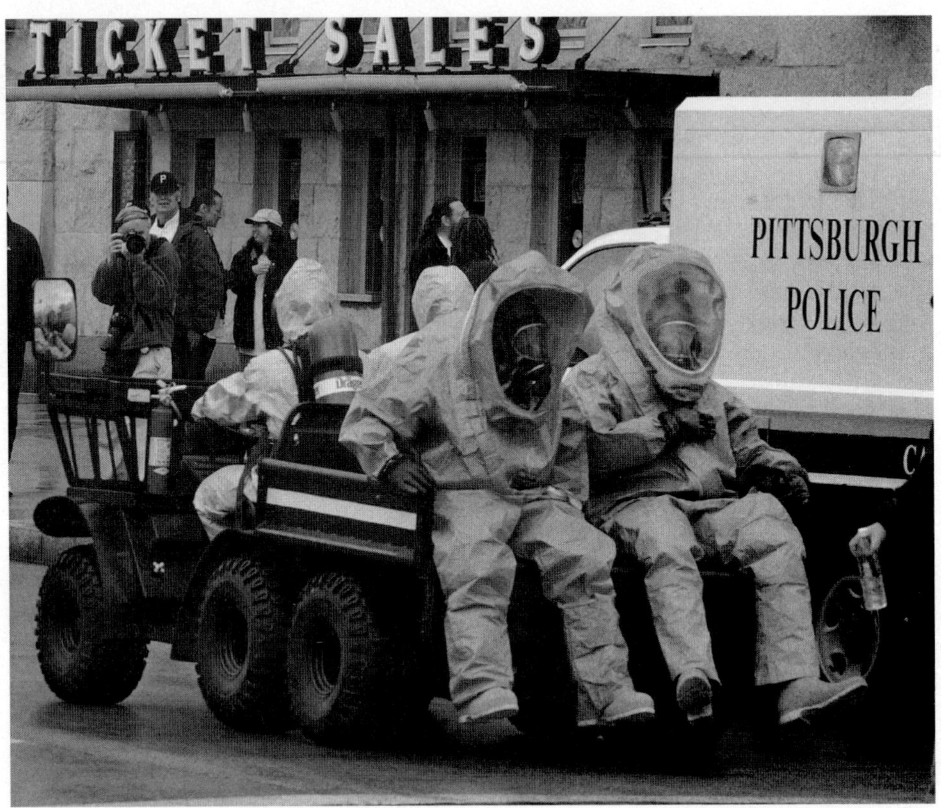

First responder teams participate in emergency drill.
Keith Srakocic/AP Images.

a variety of geographically dispersed vendors. If adequate supplies are not acquired, the recovery effort will be hampered. This individual is responsible, at least initially, for processing victims' claims for food, shelter, and other necessities. The financial section chief has a significant pecuniary responsibility, which includes accounting to ensure that funds are spent properly and within legal guidelines.

▶ Medical Response to Critical Incidents

Hospitals, like police and fire departments, are open and available 24 hours a day. As such, they have come to be seen as an indispensable resource for the public in terms of receiving care in the event of a medical emergency. Hospitals operate to handle a constant flow of traffic or patients. In some cases, staffing will change during certain periods of the year or even days of the week, such as Fridays and Saturdays, when minor spikes occur in demand for services. However, should there be a major incident such as a WMD attack, hospital resources would quickly be overwhelmed. Moreover, unlike other emergencies, the demand for exaggerated levels of medical care would continue for a longer period of time. Medical resources would very quickly be exhausted.

In one study, Treat et al. (2001) surveyed a number of hospitals to determine their readiness should there be an incident such as a WMD attack. The survey showed that 73 percent of the hospital respondents believed that they were not prepared for a nuclear or chemical incident. None of the hospitals reported being prepared to respond to a biological attack. Only one hospital had stockpiled medicines for a WMD attack. Approximately 80

HS ANALYSIS BOX 13-6

It appears that hospitals and medical services throughout the United States are not prepared to respond to a major event such as a radiological or biological attack. Primary care facilities would be quickly overrun with casualties. Given that such events have a low probability of occurring, what should we as a nation do, given that the development of medical services and facilities is a very expense proposition?

percent of the hospitals reported that their emergency rooms would be able to handle between 10 and 50 victims at a time. The research demonstrated that hospitals in the sample were aware of the potential WMD problems and had taken some actions, but overall, they were not prepared to handle a major event. A significant biological, chemical, or nuclear attack could result in hundreds of casualties that would require immediate treatment. The general lack of preparedness for such emergency has not changed. In a 2005 study, Jasper et al. (2005) found similar results.

Steps have been taken to at least partially solve this problem. The Office of Emergency Preparedness in the Department of Health and Human Services has established a **National Disaster Medical System**. The system consists of a number of teams that would respond to medical disasters. Several thousand volunteers comprise various types of teams: disaster medical assistance teams, national medical response teams, burn teams, pediatric teams, crush medicine teams, international medical-surgical teams, mental health teams, veterinary medical assistance teams, and disaster mortuary teams. The teams comprise a national network with some of the teams able to respond within 12 to 24 hours (Knouss, 2001). Even with the availability of these teams and medical support from other governmental and private entities, a large incident could result in a number of medical care problems.

HS Web Link: To learn more about the National Disaster Medical System, go to http://www.phe.gov/Preparedness/responders/ndms/Pages/default.aspx.

National Response Teams

As discussed earlier, the *National Response Framework* and the *National Incident Management System* were developed by the DHS to provide for a more uniform coordinated response to hazards or incidents. Implementation of these two systems, especially during an event, requires a substantial level of coordination and cooperation among a potentially large number of agencies that may not be immediately available. Past experiences demonstrate that achieving the desired and necessary levels of cooperation likely will fall short of expectations (Donahue and Tuohy, 2006; Sauter and Carafano, 2005). Although the two systems represent a comprehensive, rational approach to hazard response, they remain cumbersome and at least to some degree, bureaucratic (see Sobel and Leeson, 2006). The systems likely will operate more effectively when small- or medium-sized hazards occur, but it is questionable if they can sustain the level of required services in the event of a large-scale hazard.

Crowe (2008) has suggested an alternative strategy, one that could be used as a supplement in the event of a large-scale event. He advocates the creation of **national strike teams**, especially for low-probability, high-consequence events. Since such events occur so infrequently, it is difficult for localities and states to prepare and maintain preparedness for them. Moreover, there is such a wide range of possible occurrences, including floods, earthquakes, hurricanes, tornadoes, chemical attacks, biological attacks, and nuclear attacks, that it is difficult for jurisdictions to maintain a constant state of readiness since

Emergency medical team prepares for disaster.
US Department of Defense.

each type of hazard will require, at least to some degree, a different set of response tactics. Crowe provides an excellent example:

> Rather than spending an estimated ten billion dollars nationally to achieve basic bioterrorism preparedness, national mass prophylaxis strike teams could be created and mobilized in association with activation of the Strategic National Stockpile. Each team would be comprised of individual experts who receive training, support, and equipment to establish regional and national teams. The national mass prophylaxis teams would be moved into areas impacted by a bioterrorism attack to provide life-saving medications within the necessary window of twenty-four to forty-eight hours. This would eliminate the possibility that local jurisdictions are unable to provide the equipment and personnel to execute mass prophylaxis in the timeframe required to be life-saving. (p. 3)

Strike teams could be created for different kinds of hazards and dispersed regionally across the nation. By concentrating on the development of these teams as opposed to preparedness in every locale, we likely would have a less expensive but more effective response to potential events or hazards. Strike teams would result in a paradigm shift. Heretofore, the policy has been that emergency management and response to events were a local responsibility with the state and federal governments providing assistance in the event of major catastrophes. Thus far, the federal government has been reluctant to assume this responsibility. Nonetheless, strike teams appear to have a number of advantages over current policies, particularly a more effective response to low-probability, high-consequence incidents.

Summary

This chapter examined the response to catastrophic events, including natural, human-made, and terrorist originated. In recent years, our country has witnessed a number of such events, particularly the New York City and Washington, D.C., terrorist attacks and Hurricane Katrina on the Gulf Coast and Hurricane Sandy on the East Coast. Each year numerous natural disasters result in emergency declarations, but most are not of the magnitude of the 9/11 attacks or a category 5 hurricane. Nonetheless, we must be prepared to respond to all sorts of hazards of various magnitude, especially considering that our country has been attacked, and terrorists likely will attack us again in the future.

All disasters or catastrophes occur in a local community, and as such, local personnel are the first to respond. Today, federal policy places the brunt of responsibility for mediating these occurrences with local and state governments; the federal government sees its role as one of assistance. Obviously, some of these occurrences quickly overwhelm local responders' capabilities, necessitating state and federal assistance. In the past, unified responses—the combined efforts of the many agencies involved in a response—to some degree have been haphazard. In an effort to rectify this situation, the DHS developed the *National Response Framework* and the *National Incident Management System.*

The *National Response Framework* attempts to provide a framework for responding to hazards. It essentially identifies the numerous agencies across levels of governments that are involved in a response. The *Framework* advises that it is important for roles and responsibilities to be identified and the various responding agencies' efforts to be coordinated. The *Framework* attempts to identify the pre-event actions such as training, equipping, and organizing that must occur if there is to be an effective response to a hazard. The response to Hurricane Sandy demonstrated the improved response capabilities by FEMA.

The *National Incident Management System* attempts to ensure consistency in the strategies and tactics used in a response. Whenever a catastrophe occurs, responders must be organized and tactically prepared to respond. The National Incident Management System provides a framework that contributes to consistency and effectiveness in terms of on-the-ground tactics. It enumerates the functions that must occur and where responsibilities are vested. The baseline for a response is the ICS, and the implementation of the ICS entails a variety of functions. The system does provide an operating structure that can contribute to the successful response to an event. We must continue to scrutinize our capabilities and their effectiveness in future responses.

Discussion Questions

1. Critique our response to Hurricane Katrina.
2. Describe the functions of the *National Response Framework.*
3. When a major disaster occurs, the federal government will use a layered response. What is a layered response and how does it work?
4. Explain the preparedness cycle that is part of the *National Response Framework.*
5. Exercising is a part of preparation for a catastrophe. What is it and what are the limitations associated with exercising?
6. Describe the components and function of the incident command system.

References

Bellavita, C. (2008). "Changing homeland security: What is homeland security?" *Homeland Security Affairs*, 4(2): 1–30.

Birkland, T., and S. Waterman. (2008). "Is federalism the reason for failure in Hurricane Katrina?" *Publius*, 38(4): 692–714.

Bullock, J., G. Haddow, D. Coppola, E. Ergin, L. Westerman, and S. Yeletaysi. (2005). *Introduction to Homeland Security.* Burlington, MA: Elsevier.

Byrne, M. (2013). *Sandy Response in New York Shows How FEMA Has Changed.* Emergency Management. http://www.govtech.com/em/disaster/Sandy-Response-Shows-How-FEMA-has-Changed.html (Accessed May 27, 2017).

CNN. (2005). *Leadership Vacuum Stymied Aid Offers.* http://www.cnn.com/2005/US/09/15/katrina.response/(Accessed January 6, 2009).

Crowe, A. (2008). "National strike teams: An alternative approach to low probability, high consequence events." *Homeland Security Affairs*, 4(2): 1–5.

Department of Homeland Security. (2008a). *National Response Framework*. Washington, D.C.: Author.

Department of Homeland Security. (2008b). *Overview: ESF and Support Annexes Coordinating Federal Assistance in Support of the National Response Framework*. Washington, D.C.: Author.

Department of Homeland Security. (2008c). *National Incident Management System*. Washington, D.C.: Author.

Department of Homeland Security. (2016). *National Response Framework* (3rd ed.). https://www.fema.gov/media-library-data/1466014682982-9bcf8245ba4c60c120aa915abe74e15d/National_Response_Framework3rd.pdf (Accessed May 22, 2017).

Department of Homeland Security. (2016). *National Protection Framework*. Washington, D.C.: Author.

Department of Homeland Security. (2016a). *National Disaster Recovery Framwork*. Washington, D.C.: Author.

Department of Homeland Security. (2016b). *The Stafford Act, as Amended and Emergency Management-Related Provisions of the Homeland Security Act, as Amended*. FEMA. https://www.fema.gov/media-library-data/1490360363533-a531e65a3e1e63b8b2cfb7d3da7a785c/Stafford_ActselectHSA2016.pdf (Accessed May 28, 2017).

Donahue, A., and R. Tuohy. (2006). "Lessons we don't learn: A study of the lessons of disasters, why we repeat them, and how we can learn them." *Homeland Security Affairs*, 2(2): 1–28.

Hall, M. (2006). "Senators hear 'shocking examples' of FEMA waste." *USA Today* (February 13). http://www.usatoday.com/news/nation/2006-02-13-katrina-report_x.htm (Accessed January 29, 2009).

Jasper, E., M. Miller, B. Sweeney, D. Berg, E. Feuer, and D. Reganato. (2005). "Preparedness of hospitals to respond to a radiological terrorism event as assessed by a full-scale exercise." *Public Health Management & Practice*, 11: S11–S16.

Kaleem, J., and Wallace, T. (2012). Hurricane Sandy v. Katrina infographic examines destruction from both storms. *Huffington Post* (November 4). http://www.huffingtonpost.com/2012/11/04/hurricane-sandy-vs-katrina-infographic_n_2072432.html (Accessed May 23, 2017).

Kaufman, A. (2017). "Houston chemical plant fire highlights dangers of deregulation," *Huffington Post*. http://www.huffingtonpost.com/entry/arkema-deregulation_us_59a9ab48e4b0dfaafcf05c5e (Accessed September 4, 2017).

Knouss, R. (2001). "National disaster medical system." *Public Health Reports*, 116: 49–52.

Kopan, T. (2017). *Here's What Trumps Budget Cut Proposes to Cut*. CNN. http://www.cnn.com/2017/03/16/politics/trump-budget-cuts/ (Accessed May 27, 2017).

Kostro, S. S., A. Nichols, and A. Temoshchuk. (2013). *White Paper on Disaster Preparedness and Resilience: Recommendations for Reform*. Center for Strategic and International Studies. https://csis-prod.s3.amazonaws.com/s3fs-public/legacy_files/files/publication/130828_CSIS_Pennington_Disaster%20Reform_%20FINAL.pdf (Accessed May 22, 2017).

Lindsay, B. (2008). *The National Response Framework: Overview and Possible Issues for Congress*. Washington, D.C.: Congressional Research Service.

Sauter, M., and J. Carafano. (2005). *Homeland Security: A Complete Guide to Understanding, Preventing, and Surviving Terrorism*. New York: McGraw-Hill.

Schermerhorn, J. (2008). *Management* (9th ed.). New York: Wiley.

Schneider, S. (2008). "Who's to blame? (Mis)perceptions of the intergovernmental response to disasters." *Publius: The Journal of Federalism*, 38(4): 715–738.

Simon, R., and S. Teperman. (2001). "The World Trade Center attack: Lessons for disaster management." *Critical Care*, 5: 318–320.

Sobel, R., and P. Leeson. (2006). *Flirting with Disaster: The Inherent Problems with FEMA* (Policy Analysis No. 573). Washington, D.C.: Cato Institute.

Treat, K., J. Williams, P. Furbee, W. Manley, F. Russell, and C. Stamper. (2001). "Hospital preparedness for weapons of mass destruction incidents: An initial assessment." *Annals of Emergency Medicine*, 38: 562–565.

14 Homeland Security and Policing

LEARNING OBJECTIVES

1. *Describe the role of law enforcement in combating terrorism.*
2. *Explain why community policing is an important part of the police response to terrorists.*
3. *Describe how terrorism and homeland security have affected police organization.*
4. *Explain intelligence-led policing.*
5. *Discuss how police tactics are affected by the threat of terrorism.*

Key Terms

Community policing
Community partnerships
Police liaison officer
Multiculturalism
Public education
Fusion center
Citizen academies
Inventory of the critical infrastructure
Intelligence-led policing
Tactical intelligence
Strategic intelligence

▶ Introduction

Homeland security represents a major operational area for state and local governments. In the event of a terrorist attack or major disaster, state and local officials are the first to respond—they represent the "boots on the ground." During this initial response, officials must control the situation and mitigate damage. It may take days or even weeks for the necessary federal assets to arrive on the scene. The delay in getting the necessary assets for the initial response places a substantial burden on local and state resources, which are limited and often inadequate, especially if there is a substantial event like Hurricane Irma or Harvey in 2017. Local law enforcement must be considered in the decision-making matrix when a homeland security event occurs; local police are first to arrive. Response planning must be integrated across political subdivisions, whereby federal agencies work closely with local law enforcement as exemplified in the *National Incident Management System* and the *National Response Framework* as discussed in Chapter 13.

Police departments and their relationship to homeland security are addressed in this book because the police play several key roles in homeland security. First, they are the first responders whether it is a terrorist attack or a disaster. Police officers are omnipresent in every community 24 hours a day, 365 days a year. Response to a disaster is one of their primary duties. Second, police departments play a key role in preventing terrorist attacks. Police officers as the result of their duties come to know their patrol beats and the people residing in their communities. They are in a position to identify suspicious people and activities. Fisher (2016) advised that the police must play a key role in intelligence gathering; they fill in intelligence gaps and supplement the work of federal agencies. Third, the police mitigate the impact of a disaster. Officers inform people of impending conditions, move them to safe areas, summon other first responders, and so on. Fourth, the police play an important role in identifying and safeguarding critical infrastructure. Here, departments develop response plans and work with private entities such as private security to better protect infrastructure. Fifth, when a terrorist attack occurs, the police are charged with its investigation. The Federal Bureau of Investigation (FBI); the bureau of alcohol, tobacco, firearms, and explosives; and other federal agencies will be involved in the investigation. However, if local officers do not play a primary role, they certainly will have a secondary role and be intimately involved in any investigation. Initially, local officers will identify witnesses, protect the crime scene, and collect evidence.

Substantial confusion exists over the role local agencies play in protecting local assets from terrorist attacks. However, we must "think globally and act locally" (Carter, 2004). Essentially, attacks on a local asset can come from anywhere in the world. Even though many think that terrorist groups that would do harm to America are located mostly in the Middle East, groups across the globe might attack the United States, and groups within our country could mount terrorist attacks against our infrastructure and citizens, as discussed in Chapter 6. Local authorities will assume a large amount of the responsibility to prevent an attack and mitigate its effects should an attack occur.

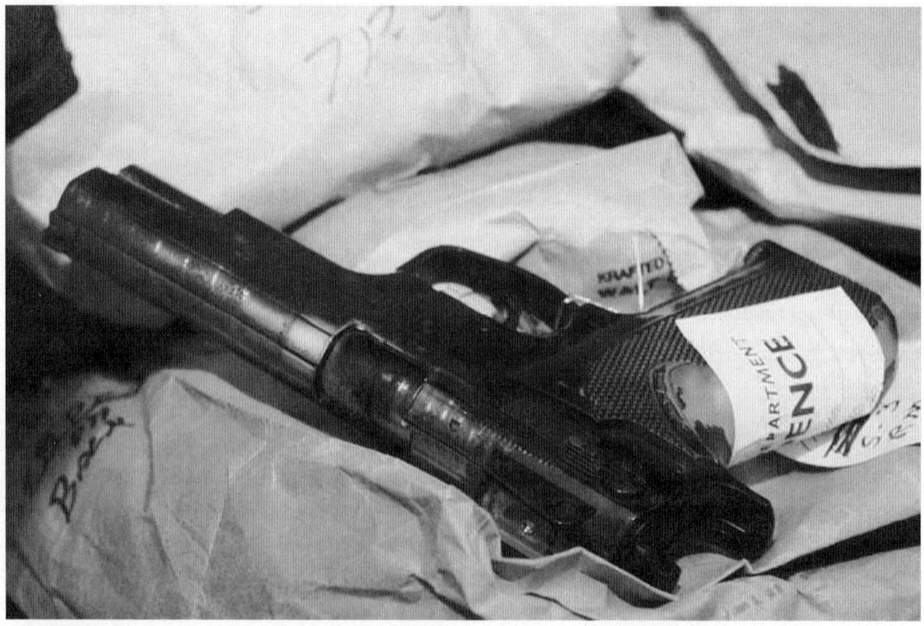

Evidence must be collected at the scene of a terrorist attack.
National Criminal Justice Reference Service.

Community Policing and Homeland Security

Community policing, according to research, is the dominant modality by which police departments deliver services. Most major police departments have community policing as part of their mission statement; officers are assigned community policing duties; and departments have policies governing community policing activities. Police departments throughout the country have committed to community policing. It is more effective as compared to traditional policing when dealing with issues and providing services to citizens.

HS Web Link: To learn more about community policing and terrorism, go to http://www.homelandsecurity.org/journal/articles/Scheider-Chapman.html.

Kappeler and Gaines (2015) advised that the two key ingredients in community policing are problem solving and community partnerships. Problem solving means that the police will not only respond to calls for service, crime, and disorder but will also actively attempt to resolve the conditions that cause the problems. Thus, problem solving results in a safer community. When a disaster or terrorist attack occurs, the police have many problems that must be solved.

The second ingredient in community policing, **community partnerships**, can play a key role in fighting terrorism at the local level. Community partnerships suggest a positive relationship between the police and the public. Here, the police must foster close, positive relations with all neighborhoods and groups in the community. In some cases, relations must be repaired if problems existed in the past. It means that the police need to listen to people and solicit their input regarding police problems and priorities. There are ample examples of where positive community relations have assisted the police when dealing with problems. When police officers are viewed positively, citizens are more likely to report suspicious activities and persons.

Brown (2007) provided the example of John Allen Muhammad and John Lee Malvo. In the fall of 2002, Muhammad and Malvo terrorized the Washington, D.C., area by randomly shooting and killing several people. The situation was so grave that the government applied all sorts of resources to apprehend them, including roadblocks and surveillance by military aircraft. They were apprehended only after the suspects' vehicle was identified and the information made public; two cooperative community members heard the information and called 911 to report the suspects' whereabouts. Many criminal cases are solved as a result of community cooperation, which has long been recognized as an important ingredient in successful law enforcement. It also applies to countering terrorism.

Police Departments and Homeland Security: Where Are We?

Some have advocated that the 9/11 attacks thrust American policing into a new era that mades homeland security the dominant organizational initiative (Oliver, 2007). Police departments' efforts have been mixed relative to adopting homeland security initiatives. In

HS ANALYSIS BOX 14-1

It appears that community partnerships are an important part of policing and homeland security. Most communities in America are heterogeneous, with numerous racial, ethnic, and religious groups. Are there any groups in your community with whom the police should attempt to develop better relations? How do they differ from the majority in the community? What actions should the police take to develop better relations?

their survey of departments, Haynes and Giblin (2014) found that most departments have identified potential terrorist targets by essentially making educated guesses about potential targets; they have not attempted a rational examination as discussed in Chapter 3. Ortiz and his colleagues (2007) found that police departments have made only marginal changes to adopt homeland security as a dominant theme. Morreale and Lambert (2009) found similar results when they sampled New England police chiefs. Homeland security is not a high priority in many departments. It appears that the potential for terrorism is taken more seriously by our largest city police chiefs.

Only after the 9/11 attacks, many advocated that the police should abandon community policing. It was suggested that traditional police tactics such as investigation, surveillance, and interrogations should be emphasized to root out terrorists. On its face, it might appear that preventing terrorism at the local level is the antithesis of community policing. That is, a "war on terrorism" requires that police officers use intrusive, aggressive, and militaristic tactics to ferret out terrorists and terrorist plots. Such tactics often alienate people who are the subject of them. Some police officials may equate the war on terrorism with a military exercise requiring such tactics. However, we find that preventing terrorism is actually complementary with community policing (Murray, 2005; Pelfrey, 2007; Chappell and Gibson, 2009). The police, to a large extent, must depend on the public to supply terrorist-related information to effectively thwart local terrorist plots. When a police department fosters good relations with the community, citizens are more likely to report suspicious people and activities. Thus, community policing is an important part of homeland security.

▶ Policing Muslim Communities

Historically, the United Sates is the world's melting pot where immigrants from all over the world have embarked on new lives. Many came to America to escape political or religious persecution, whereas others came to make a better life for their families and themselves. Although it may be comforting to think of our nation as a melting pot, America is more like a patchwork of people and places. Immigrants coming to America often cleave together for economic and social support. Any large city in America has dozens of ethnic groups oftentimes living in enclaves, which are named after the dominant group living there—"China Town," "Little Italy," or "German Town." These enclaves are an essential part of the country's landscape. Even today, as the nation grapples with protecting the borders, one must remember that for most of us, our ancestors immigrated to this country.

The United States has a history of ethnic tensions, particularly with the African American and Latino populations. Ethnic tensions substantially worsened for Muslims after the 9/11 attacks. There have been numerous incidents in which Muslims were attacked and assaulted. In fact, Levin (2016) in a national study found that hate crimes against Muslims have been increasing. This criminal behavior was not limited to one area but occurred across the country. Moreover, many non-Muslims have been attacked. A number of Asians and people of other nationalities have been mistaken for Muslims and attacked by people with racist views. For example, in 2012, a gunman killed six Sikhs at a Milwaukee Temple (Yaccino, Schwirtz, and Santora, 2012).

Prior to the 9/11 attacks, a controversy in American law enforcement was racial profiling. Numerous studies showed that African Americans and Latinos were stopped and investigated by police at greater rates than white citizens (Gaines, 2006). After 9/11, the controversy subsided and public opinion shifted to substantial approval for racial profiling for Arab and Muslim people. There was tacit approval for violating civil rights. The rule of law was replaced by hysteria clamoring for security from terrorists or to derive revenge for the 9/11 attacks.

Comparatively speaking, the United States does not have a large Muslim population. The Pew Research Center estimates that there are 3.3 million Muslims living in the United States, or 3.3 percent of the population is Muslim (Mohamed, 2016). Many Muslims are concentrated in cities. For example, the Detroit area has the largest concentration of Muslims and Arabs outside the Middle East.

Arabs and Muslims often feel they are under siege. American citizens see that they commit a majority of the terrorist activities across the globe. They often dress differently. Many people do not understand their religion. They often are culturally different. After the 9/11 attacks, federal law enforcement cracked down on them making many high-profile arrests and deportations. Arabs and Muslims oftentimes face a number of challenges as a result of discrimination and suspicion. These individuals and communities often come to distrust the police and are not willing to work with officers.

HS Web Link: To learn more about policing Arab communities, go to http://www.ncjrs.gov/pdffiles1/nij/221706.pdf.

Henderson, Ortiz, Sugie, and Miller (2008) examined policing in Arab and Muslim communities. They found four obstacles to positive relations between the police and these communities: (1) distrust between Arab and Muslim American communities and the police, (2) lack of cultural awareness, (3) language barriers, and (4) concerns about immigration status and fear of deportation. It is important for the police to have positive relations with all segments of a community. Given the levels of anger and racism after the 9/11 attacks, it is important for the police to work more closely with these communities to foster better relations and to ensure adequate levels of protection for Arab and Muslim people.

The police must bridge the gap between themselves and Arab and Muslim communities and reduce distrust. The primary mechanism for accomplishing this is community policing, which can lead to an improvement in communication. Individual officers, commanders, and administrators should informally reach out and attempt to establish communications with individuals and the community. Police officials should also attempt to establish formal contacts and relations. Establishing contacts can be accomplished by implementing community forums and advisory committees such as those formed in cities such as Portland, Oregon; Los Angeles; and Seattle. These meetings should be held in the community as opposed to police or governmental facilities. Meeting in the community instills a higher level of trust. It also engenders greater participation from the community. It is also important for line-level officers to be involved, since they have the most contact with Arab and Muslim people. Distrust can be reduced when police officials have an open-door policy that allows people to voice their concerns; when concerns are voiced, it is important for the police to address them. Hollow responses only antagonize people and contribute to increased distrust.

The appointment of a **police liaison officer** from the community can help reduce distrust. A liaison officer in effect becomes the advocate for the community. As an advocate, the officer can work closely with community groups, generate support, and identify problems that otherwise may not have been identified. The liaison officer can also help in recruiting Arab and Muslim Americans for the police department and other governmental positions. Inclusion is one of the most effective means of reducing distrust.

A good example of creating a vehicle for improving relations occurred in 2016. The FBI established partnerships with communities in New Jersey. These Shared Responsibility Committees were formed consisting of community leaders, clergy members, and mental health professionals. The committees' goal was to identify people who might support terrorist activities or have mental health issues. It was hoped that the committees could help prevent terrorism before it occurred through intervention and mental health counseling (CBS, 2016). The committees also delegated some responsibility for combating terrorism to citizens within the communities.

The police have a long history of being accused of lacking cultural awareness. In the 1990s and early 2000s, many police departments developed cultural awareness training programs in the wake of the accusations of racial profiling or "driving while black"

HS ANALYSIS BOX 14-2

The immigration debate in the United States has become rather heated with President Trump vowing to build a wall on our southern border. Some areas, such as Arizona, are strictly enforcing immigration laws; other communities have left such enforcement to the ICE. Those who are not enforcing laws are seen as an impediment to law enforcement. Which position do you think is better for American law enforcement? Can these two perspectives be balanced so that both objectives can be met?

controversies. **Multiculturalism**, "the embracing of cultural diversity, a willingness to coexist with people from different backgrounds and cultures, and the celebration of difference, centers on whether [it] divides a society or unifies it" (McNamara and Burns, 2009, p. 7). When a department polices an ethnic community, it must attempt to embrace cultural differences and unite the community. Policing an ethnic community is best accomplished by understanding cultural differences and understanding how to treat and interact with people. Police officers must understand that many Arabs and Muslims do not embrace many aspects of American culture, and in some cases, police behavior is an affront to their beliefs or way of life. Proper training can minimize cultural conflict.

Language barriers abound. For example, people in Los Angeles speak more than 80 languages. When there is a significant ethnic population, police departments must ensure that they can communicate with people. In cities with large Arab populations, the department should take steps to provide language training for some of its officers. A number of cities with large Latino populations have developed training programs to teach officers Spanish. Learning the language or at least critical phrases and words can be a significant factor in communicating and developing relations in minority communities. Departments with large Arabic-speaking populations certainly must have enough translators so that the department can effectively communicate with people, and the departments should produce their critical literature in Arabic. Police effectiveness depends on good communications, so the police often must bridge this communications gap if they are to be effective public servants.

Another major barrier to effectively serving some ethnic communities is that many people fear that the police will have them deported or otherwise alter their immigration status. Because of this fear and the wedge it creates between the police and the community, a number of police departments have not cooperated with Immigration and Customs Enforcement (ICE) programs requiring police officers to check the immigration status of people. The primary reason for this reluctance is that when the police cooperate with immigration officials, people are less likely to cooperate with the police. As noted earlier, cooperation between the community and the police is essential for effective law enforcement. The police are placed in an awkward position as they attempt to balance immigration laws and gain community cooperation.

▶ Homeland Security Public Education Programming

For a police department to have an effective homeland security program, it must involve members of the community. Terrorist attacks are preceded by unobtrusive activities that include surveillance, dry runs, and the acquisition of the materials with which to conduct the attack. In one study, Smith (2008) found that, on average, terrorists perform 44 such activities prior to an attack. These activities blend into usual daily activities, making it difficult to discern terrorist activities from normal activities. Nonetheless, law enforcement must implement measures that attempt to identify possible terrorists during these pre-attack activities. Identifying potential terrorists requires substantial public cooperation and participation. To gain this community participation, the police must educate the public and provide guidance. Public education is paramount in preventing crime and terrorist attacks.

Public education in the realm of homeland security serves a number of functions, including (1) fear reduction, (2) reduction of community tensions, and (3) encouragement of people to provide the police with valuable information. Police departments must devise several public education programs and plans since every community consists of different ethnic groups, neighborhoods, and population groups. Public education programming must target these groups. One type of program may work with one group, but not with others. Therefore, it is important to ensure that everyone is exposed to this programming and reports suspicious activities to law enforcement. Care, however, must be taken that these programs do not advance discriminatory sentiments or needless fear.

Public education programs should have specific goals. The primary goal is to elicit support and information from the public regarding crime and terrorism matters or intelligence. Not only must the police prepare the public to report suspicious activities, they must also educate it about terrorism. When people are informed, they are more likely to report credible information and are less prone to panic or engage in behavior that results in community problems. Such training should have a component that reduces senseless fear of terrorist attacks. The probability of terrorists attacking any city is close to zero. The police need people to take a rational approach when soliciting their cooperation. Carter (2004: 48) advised that these programs should encourage people to engage in the following behaviors:

1. Know how to observe
2. Know what is suspicious
3. Know how to report
4. Know what to report
5. Know what happens next

Some departments have established **citizen academies** to help educate people (Bumphus, Gaines, and Blakely, 1999). These academies are open to the public and can serve as an excellent tool for informing the public and gaining trust and support. However, not every neighborhood or group may be represented in these academies and the department must devise several different modes for educating the complete spectrum of groups in the community. Other public education modalities include disseminating pamphlets describing what community members can do to assist the police. All public outreach and education programming should include realistic and factual information about the terrorist threat and governmental responses. Finally, community forums and speakers bureaus can provide information to the public. Police departments should approach public education comprehensively. The primary objective of these programs is to get people to report suspicious persons and activities. The police have long used similar programs in the war on drugs and to solicit assistance in apprehending wanted criminals.

Lyon (2002) advised that the police especially should develop programs in communities or neighborhoods that are likely to harbor terrorists. For example, Arab terrorists most likely will attempt to live in a community that contains many people from their native home; it allows them to blend in and be less conspicuous. In addition to obtaining information, cooperation from these communities could assist in developing an intelligence network in close proximity to possible problems.

A prime example of how public education programs can produce positive results occurred in New Jersey. On May 9, 2007, the FBI arrested six suspects who had planned to attack and kill soldiers at Fort Dix. The initial investigative lead was supplied by an alert clerk who was asked to copy a videocassette onto a DVD. The cassette contained footage of the suspects training for their attack. The alert store clerk notified the police, which resulted in an extended FBI investigation and subsequent arrests. This incident exemplifies how law enforcement can obtain valuable intelligence information from the public.

One of the problems with these types of programs is that in some cases police departments receive many more calls or tips than can be processed. The failure of police to respond to calls results in lowered evaluations of police performance and a reluctance to call the police in the future. Additionally, only a relatively few number of calls result in an investigation. The reporting of "suspicious" persons or possible terrorists becomes even more problematic because some people will make reports based on race and not on actual suspicious activities.

▶ Examining Police Calls for Service for Terrorist Leads

As noted, the police should be interested in suspicious activities. When people observe and report these behaviors, they generally do so using the police department's 911 emergency telephone number. Large cities receive thousands of calls each year. It is important for police departments to begin examining these calls for possible terrorist activities. For the most part, this has not been occurring. When a department receives a call about a suspicious activity, the dispatcher will send an officer to investigate. If a crime is not occurring, the officer generally will not do anything. Moreover, these types of calls often receive a low priority so it may be some time before an officer investigates. These suspicious activities generally fall below the radar.

There is a need to develop a mechanism to examine these calls. Hollywood, Strom, and Pope (2008) conducted a preliminary study using Washington, D.C., Metropolitan Police data. They examined 1.3 million calls for service. First, they isolated all calls that included a suspicious person, suspicious vehicle, suspicious package, bomb threat, and other similar calls. Isolating calls using these criteria resulted in identifying 100,000 calls. These calls were then examined for other identifiers. They looked for key words such as surveillance, video, photography, taking notes, and using binoculars when examining the suspicious persons and vehicle calls. For the suspicious package calls, they looked to see if explosive ordnance demolition teams were called or if area traffic was restricted. This second round of examinations resulted in the identification of 1,200 calls. A more detailed examination resulted in the number being reduced to 850. The other 350 were eliminated as the suspicious activities were explained, as normal work, tourism, misplaced luggage, and so on. The remaining calls were considered possible terrorist activities.

Next, the researchers examined the time of day for the calls and their locations. The calls were also examined to determine if they clustered in a particular area. The researchers then developed a scale to evaluate the calls: (1) atypicality of reported activities, (2) attractiveness of target, (3) whether the call was part of a cluster (multiple surveillance activities), and (4) whether a police report was taken. Applying the calls to the scale resulted in six calls being considered highly probable and several other calls that were highly suspicious. The locations where suspicious activities occurred included bridges, the train station, hospitals, hotels, a military base, and a public safety center.

Although the research did not identify any targets that were ultimately attacked by terrorists, it demonstrated that data mining of police calls for service could produce investigative leads. Future research should focus on automating and refining these techniques. Data

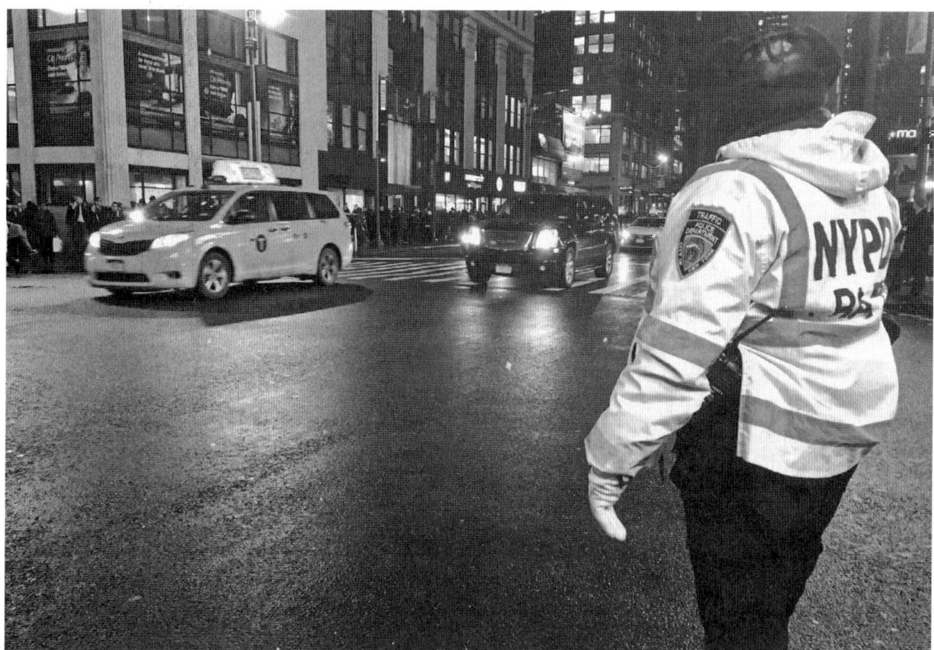

Police officers should constantly observe for suspicious people and activities.
BravoKiloVideo/Shutterstock.

produced from such analyses could provide pre- and post-attack information. The research also demonstrates that the police department's computer-aided dispatch and automated records systems should collect more information than they currently do.

Police Efforts to Safeguard Local Critical Infrastructure

Numerous potential infrastructure targets exist in a given location. At some point, local police departments will take **inventory of the critical infrastructure** within their communities. As noted in Chapter 3, the DHS has attempted to develop a national database, but thus far, the efforts have fallen short largely due to a failure to identify workable criteria for the inclusion of specific infrastructure assets as well as political considerations. Communities will need to identify assets and develop response plans, especially given the numerous potential targets that may exist in a given jurisdiction and that attacks on different types of targets present dissimilar challenges to the police and other first responders. Thus, it is important for local police departments to create a catalog or database of all possible terrorist targets in the jurisdiction, especially those that would result in significant damage, loss of life, or economic losses if attacked.

The identification of these critical infrastructure assets serves two primary purposes. First, the database allows the department to develop response plans. A police department should have a response plan in place for each of the infrastructure locations. These plans should include the roles and responsibilities of all first responders, including police, hospitals, emergency medical services, utilities, fire, public works, and so on. Second, it results in focusing attention on areas that are of interest to possible terrorists. Once assets are identified, the police department should focus intelligence operations near and around the locations. It is very likely that if a terrorist plans to attack an asset, he or she will conduct reconnaissance. As discussed earlier, reports of suspicious behavior around these locations should be thoroughly investigated. Due vigilance may result in the terrorist being identified before the attack is consummated.

HS ANALYSIS BOX 14-3

There are likely terrorist targets in most communities in the United States. They can be population gatherings, key industries, large businesses, shopping malls, and so on. If you were given the task of identifying possible targets in your community, what would you include on your list? What criteria would you use to include them on the list?

Critical Incident Response Plans

Police departments should have critical incident response plans for responding to natural disasters, airplane crashes, and many major crimes such as hostage situations. These plans include information about command and control, tactical responses, and use of other support agencies such as disaster, medical, fire, and chemical and radiological personnel. It is important that these plans are consistent with the National Incident Management System as discussed in Chapter 13. These plans are flexible in that they can be used to deploy resources for a host of problems anywhere within a jurisdiction.

Donahue and Tuohy (2006) noted that these plans often fail for a variety of reasons, including uncoordinated leadership among the various responding agencies; failed communications, including inoperability of communications systems and a lack of desire for agencies to communicate with one another; weak planning, whereby plans are developed in a vacuum without the benefit of "real-life" experiences; and resource constraints since most emergencies of any magnitude quickly strip a jurisdiction's resources to maintain a maximum response. Donahue and Tuohy noted that some of these problems can be overcome through tabletop exercises or drills. However, when these drills occur, critiques are generally conducted piecemeal, with each agency examining its response as opposed to the total response, and the critiques generally focus on what went right as opposed to identifying and documenting failures and problems. Police agencies must examine their critical incident response plans and ensure that they are comprehensive and applicable to terrorist threats or attacks. Pelfrey (2005) advised that planning is the most critical aspect of homeland security. Many departments often are well equipped but do not have adequate plans in place.

HS Web Link: To learn more about private security and policing, go to http://www.policechiefmagazine.org/private-police-coming-to-a-neighborhood/.

Nonetheless, police agencies will begin to catalog the critical infrastructure assets in their communities. Although appearing to be a straightforward process, it likely will be a taxing endeavor. Not only must officials identify these assets, they must also examine vulnerabilities. For example, what impact would a bombing of a natural gas transmission line or a petrochemical plant have on a given city? As previously noted, much of this critical infrastructure is privately controlled, and police departments often do not have access to information and the facilities or the technical expertise to evaluate different terrorist scenarios.

Partnerships between Law Enforcement and Critical Infrastructure Security Personnel

Private security is mentioned here because it is a significant force in public security and safety. Each year more is spent on private security than on public police departments, and the private sector employs larger numbers of personnel than do public police departments (Morabito and Greenberg, 2005). Policing and private security are not necessarily mutually exclusive domains. For example, Green (1981: 25) has defined the role of private security as, "those individuals, organizations, and services other than public law enforcement and regulatory agencies that are engaged primarily in the prevention and investigation of crime, loss, or harm to specific individuals, organizations, or facilities." This definition shows that there is substantial overlap between private security and the police. Private security continues to grow, and its role in public safety is enhanced as a result of homeland security and terrorism threats.

Many of these private security personnel are assigned to guard much of the critical infrastructure in this country, and this critical infrastructure would likely be a terrorist's target. Historically, there has been little cooperation or communication between the police and private security personnel even though they, to some extent, have parallel responsibilities. However, the threat of terrorism and the need to secure critical infrastructure are beginning to change this perspective. Now, police departments are encouraged to develop formal working relationships with private security firms. Such relations would (1) improve joint responses to critical incidents, (2) coordinate infrastructure protection, (3) improve communications and data interoperability, (4) bolster information and intelligence sharing, (5) prevent and investigate high-tech crime, and (6) devise responses to workplace violence (Ohlhausen Research Inc., 2004).

It is logical for the police to develop and formalize these relationships. The police and private security personnel have common goals, and to a great extent, the private security personnel are more informed about problems, critical points, and vulnerabilities for particular facilities as compared to the police. Many of these facilities have controlled access and activities; therefore, security personnel are more likely to observe people and actions that are out of the ordinary or suspicious and, independently or in cooperation with the police, investigate them. At a minimum, the police need to be aware of those facilities that are target hardened through private security and have procedures that include private security personnel when responding to those installations.

Partnerships with the police are critical. Some of the activities that must occur are:

1. cooperative training on the development and implementation of potential terrorist profiles;
2. mapping potential targets in a jurisdiction to include security assets;

Private security represents an important resource in preventing terrorist attacks.
Brian Jackson/Alamy Stock Photo.

3. development and coordination of critical incident plans outlining responses to acts of terror and disasters;
4. better communication between law enforcement and the private security industry;
5. ensuring that the police and private security share intelligence information as it relates to a specific critical infrastructure;
6. identifying security assets in the private sector that can be used by police to combat possible terrorists;
7. identifying the ramifications (destructive, human, and economic) of an attack on specific critical infrastructure assets.

A number of departments now have cooperative relationships with private security. The Dallas Police Department has training workshops for police officers and security personnel. In Las Vegas, police officials meet monthly with hotel security personnel to discuss training, crime, and security problems (Morabito and Greenberg, 2005). To date, most of the partnerships between the police and private security have focused on business districts and retail outlets. Not enough has been done to develop programming with high-value targets such as communications centers, manufacturing facilities, petrochemical plants, and so on. Many of these targets have security operations that are quite sophisticated and elaborate, but the police often know little of their operations. Moreover, many of these facilities have closed-circuit television monitoring that could provide the police with valuable information about possible terrorist operations. The police must do a better job of integrating their operations with area security operations.

Although everyone in law enforcement is well aware of domestic terrorism, few departments have initiated comprehensive planning and programming. Threats of terrorism likely will remain for the next several decades, and the police must enhance their capabilities to respond to them. Private security will play a key role in this new priority.

Local agencies must develop strategies and policies to deal with homeland security and counterterrorism. As noted, it is the local agencies that at least initially will be responsible

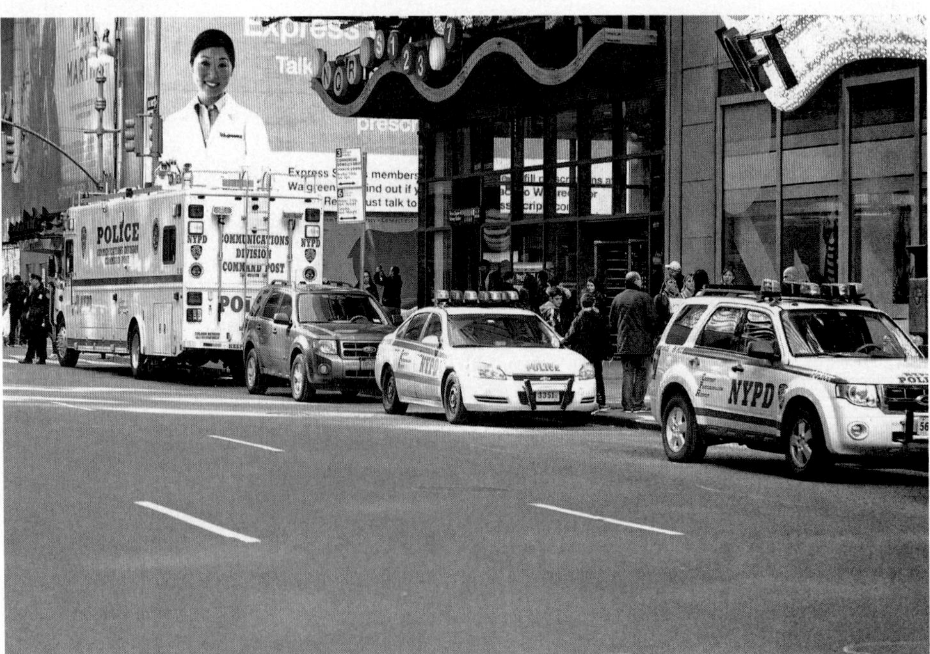

New York City police officers flood Times Square after a bomb threat.
Splash News/Alamy Stock Photo.

for response and protection. Police departments will be the first agency to respond to a terrorist attack. If police departments are to effectively deal with terrorist attacks and homeland security issues, they first must have organizational mechanisms in place that facilitate an effective response.

▶ Police Organization and Terrorism

Police departments are complex organizations, and they are structured to facilitate the accomplishment of goals. They have high levels of specialization, and specialized units are created to perform specific functions associated with groups of tasks (Gaines and Kappeler, 2008; Gaines and Worrall, 2011). Given the critical nature of homeland security, it is incumbent on police departments to establish a homeland security unit or in smaller departments, ensure that these tasks are assigned to a multitask unit. The department's structure must be reengineered to ensure that homeland security becomes an embedded activity. Certain homeland security activities must be accomplished. Police departments must be organized so that they can prevent terrorist attacks, or when they are unable to prevent them, they are in a position to mitigate their impact. Given today's climate, the public expects the police to be prepared if an attack occurs.

There is some question as to how rapidly police departments are incorporating homeland security and the war against terrorism in their organizational mantra. For example, DeLone (2007) examined the mission statements for a number of large police departments and found only one department had added this important mission. Marks and Sun (2007) examined references to organizational change and discovered similar findings. Only the larger departments were changing their organization to better incorporate homeland security and terrorism within the organization. Ortiz (2007) examined a number of departments' adaptation of homeland security and found that they incorporated homeland security mechanisms in varying degrees. For the most part, they conducted business as usual. The most significant change was that they exhibited more cooperation with federal agencies such as the FBI and DHS on homeland security issues. The research indicates that police departments have been slow to incorporate homeland security, and it appears that they remain preoccupied with traditional policing responsibilities.

The specific responsibilities for the homeland security unit and its commander should be clearly enumerated. Enumeration of responsibilities is accomplished by the promulgation of policies and procedures. The policies will list the responsibilities of the commander and the organizational resources that are available to complete required tasks. Moreover, these policies should enumerate the working relationships with other units in the police department. They should enable the homeland security commander to directly contact other units to obtain information and assistance. A clear chain of command should be established.

As noted, the homeland security unit will have a number of specific responsibilities, including the following:

- Manage terrorist and homeland security information, including intelligence
- Maintain a database of critical infrastructures and their vulnerabilities
- Maintain working relations with critical infrastructure owners, managers, and security personnel
- Maintain liaison with state homeland security officials
- Maintain liaison with federal intelligence agencies such as the FBI and the Joint Terrorism Task Forces

- Coordinate department responses to terrorist events
- Coordinate police activities with those of other first responder agencies
- Identify homeland security training needs for the department
- Conduct or coordinate homeland security–related investigations
- Monitor the readiness of the police department and other first responders in the event of a terrorist attack
- Investigate terrorist attacks or activities

A number of police departments have integrated homeland security into their organization. Departments have approached it differently. For example, the Chicago Police Department has an intelligence section with the bureau of organized crime that focuses on terrorism. The joint terrorism task force and the FBI human intelligence task force are located in the bureau. Units including the Special Weapons and Tactics (SWAT) team, bomb squad, airport law enforcement, and marine/helicopter are located in the patrol bureau. The department does not have a formalized homeland security unit. The Houston Police Department has a *homeland security command* headed by an assistant chief. The command contains several units: air support, airport security, gang, special operations, and tactical operations.

The Washington, D.C., Metropolitan Police Department has a more sophisticated organization. Its *homeland security bureau* is commanded by an assistant chief and contains three divisions: special operations, intelligence, and joint strategic and tactical analysis command center. The *Special Operations Division* contains units that would directly respond to a terrorist attack. The division contains specialized patrol and tactical, rescue, and security services.

The *Intelligence Division* contains several units that are involved in collecting and analyzing intelligence. Some units are involved in intelligence within the jurisdiction, whereas other units collaborate with other federal agencies, for example, the Joint Terrorism Task Force (as discussed in Chapter 8) and the D.C. Fusion Center (fusion centers are addressed in more detail later in this chapter).

The *Joint Strategic and Tactical Analysis Command Center* keeps command staff and the community informed about crime in neighborhoods and works with the Washington regional threat analysis center and the capitol police. The division provides research services to support police operations.

The homeland security organization for the Chicago, Houston, and Washington, D.C., police departments demonstrate that departments have used a variety of organizational structures. A common problem is that units assigned to homeland security often have other daily responsibilities, which sometimes results in homeland security preparedness being neglected. Homeland security events are infrequent, but efforts must be made to ensure that the units remain prepared to respond.

When establishing a homeland security unit, it is important that the commander have the rank and authority required to not only command the unit but also enable him or her to bridge the rank structure to gain cooperation with other units on homeland security activities. Officers assigned to a variety of units should be actively involved in some homeland security activities: (1) patrol, (2) criminal investigation, (3) crime analysis, (4) intelligence, (5) specialized tactical units (SWAT) including hostage negotiators, and (5) community relations and community policing. Members of these units must have a shared vision of the terrorist threat and the department's preventive responses. It is also important that the unit have close working relations with other community service organizations such as paramedics and emergency response, fire, street and road department, and social services. These agencies can provide primary and support services should there be a terrorist attack. Finally, the homeland security unit will be the agency's and jurisdiction's point of contact

SWAT team members approach a suspect after using a non-lethal round to take him into custody.
Chester Brown/Alamy Stock Photo.

with state and federal agencies. These state agencies are the conduits for making requests for federal assistance from the DHS. A working relationship must be in place to facilitate any such requests. Having a police department homeland security unit allows for more immediate state and federal responses, should an event occur.

One of the functions of a homeland security unit is to identify and investigate suspicious persons, places, and activities that may be associated with terrorists. Patrol essentially is the "eyes and ears" of the police department. Patrol covers all parts of the jurisdiction 24 hours a day. Patrol officers have the most information about what is occurring on their beats. A working relationship with patrol officers results in more intelligence information being submitted to homeland security analysts. In the same vein, detectives investigating crimes may uncover suspicious activities and forward relevant information to homeland security officials. Crime analysis is a support function within police departments, and essentially, officers assigned to this unit examine crime trends temporally and spatially. They attempt to identify patterns of crime and behavior.

The intelligence unit should work closely with the homeland security unit; the intelligence unit or some of its activities could be incorporated into the homeland security unit. Intelligence units historically collected information about criminals and criminal groups. Notably, these units collected information about organized crime, gang activities, and white-collar crime. Today, these units must devote resources to collecting information about possible terrorists and their activities. It is also critical to understand that, today, terrorist organizations have become intertwined with transnational organized crime, making the investigation of organized criminal syndicates even more important.

Specialized tactical units are deployed when there is a dangerous criminal event such as a hostage taking, barricaded person, or drug or gang raid. These units possibly would be deployed should there be terrorist activities. They can collect valuable information during such a deployment that can be used by the homeland security unit to analyze the situation. Finally, community relations or community policing personnel have a substantial amount of direct contact with citizens and community groups. Such contacts can be useful in attempting to identifying terrorists in a community.

HS ANALYSIS BOX 14-4

Not all police departments have homeland security organizational units. Reasons for this might include the size of the department, the department's budget, and significant crime problems that must be addressed. What factors should a police chief consider when he or she is deciding on developing a homeland security unit within the department? Even if a department does not have such a unit, which of the functions should be added to other units in the department?

In addition to establishing the internal workings of the intelligence unit, decisions must be made in terms of relationships with outside agencies, especially other local, state, and federal agencies that are involved in homeland security and antiterrorism investigations. There should be formal agreements specifying the types of information that can be shared. Generally, such relations are set out in contracts or memoranda of understanding (MOUs) or in mutual aid pacts. A number of legal requirements must be fulfilled for these MOUs to be finalized with most of the regulation centering on maintaining the privacy of records. Federal requirements can be found in 28 CFR Part 23. Should an agency violate these requirements, it opens the agency and the intelligence function to civil litigation and public disclosure. In addition to a possible monetary loss, civil suits often result in the subpoenaing of all sorts of records that likely would jeopardize the unit's operations and intelligence.

As can be seen, the homeland security unit not only has primary functions, but it also serves to coordinate other police resources in protecting a community. This unit is an important addition to a police department in that it will help ensure that the department is ready to respond to a terrorist attack. Its primary responsibility is the collection and analysis of intelligence. Today, intelligence-led policing is the primary operational platform used by homeland security units to accomplish this task.

Police departments must collect and analyze crime and terror intelligence in order to better respond to problems.
RosalreneBetancourt 14/Alamy Stock Photo.

▶ Intelligence-Led Policing

The 9/11 attacks on New York City and the Pentagon, as well as the attack in San Bernardino, California, demonstrate that any location could be attacked. Even though the probability of an attack on a specific city is extremely low, all jurisdictions must be prepared for the possibility. Threat assessment at the local level implies that local police departments must become involved in identifying potential terrorists and suspect activities, although there is some debate as to whether terror intelligence gathering should be a federal function or should involve state and local agencies (Thatcher, 2005). Fisher (2016) noted that local police departments can collect a substantial amount of intelligence that otherwise might not be available.

Local police departments should be involved in collecting terror-related intelligence. Smith and his colleagues (2006) examined 65 right-wing terrorist incidents. First, they found that on average the terrorists took two to three months to plan their attacks. Second, half of the terrorists attacked a target within 30 miles of where they resided. Based on their research, it appears that terrorists likely will be present in the target area for a period of time and given that they live in close proximity, they will likely leave a footprint prior to their attacks. Active intelligence efforts by local police departments increases the probability that the suspects are discovered before they attack.

Currently, police departments are improving their intelligence capacity through intelligence-led policing (Carter and Phillips, 2013). **Intelligence-led policing** essentially is the enhancement of police intelligence-gathering capability. Most major police departments already have some form of intelligence-gathering capabilities, narcotics, gangs, or organized crime. The emergence of intelligence-led policing is closely related to homeland security. Many researchers have merged the two concepts. Intelligence-led policing was a response to the 9/11 attacks, as a strategy to enhance policing (Carter and Carter, 2009). Intelligence-led policing dictates that departments not only begin collecting information about possible terrorists and possible targets, but that they should also enhance their intelligence-gathering and intelligence-using skills. It is logical to include possible terrorists and terrorist activities, especially considering that narcotics trafficking and other forms of organized crime are used to finance terrorism (Kleiman, 2004; McCaffrey and Basso, 2003).

One of the major difficulties for local departments in collecting terrorist intelligence is that unlike other organized crime groups, little is known about who might be a terrorist and his or her potential activities. For the most part, there is an absence of baseline data or information to guide intelligence and investigative activities. It is too late to gather information about possible terrorists once they have committed a terrorist act. Nonetheless, departments are encouraged to begin gathering information on "persons of interest" who fit some profile of terrorists. As witnessed with the 9/11 attacks, one undiscovered attack can result in the loss of thousands of lives. Local agencies cannot solely depend on the federal government to identify and prevent attacks.

Intelligence-led policing is compatible and complementary with community policing (McGarrell, Freilich, and Chermak, 2007). Police officers across the country are now working more closely with citizens and communities. These relationships represent a vast reservoir of "eyes and ears" for the police. Relationships with the community not only enhance problem solving but also represent a method to collect intelligence about suspicious persons and activities in a community. Intelligence gathered in the community can be collated and compared to other intelligence to provide a clearer picture of the activities in a jurisdiction. It is important for police managers and supervisors to reinforce this new mandate.

HS Web Link: To learn more about intelligence-led policing, go to http://www.ncjrs.gov/pdffiles1/bja/210681.pdf.

The Intelligence Process

Essentially, intelligence is "the combination of credible information with quality analysis—information that has been evaluated and from which conclusions have been drawn" (IACP, 2002: v). Carter (2004) provided more depth to the definition:

In the purest sense, intelligence is the product of an analytic process that evaluates information collected from diverse sources, integrates the relevant information into a cohesive package, and produces a conclusion or estimate about a criminal phenomenon by using the scientific approach to problem solving (i.e. analysis). Intelligence, therefore, is a synergistic product to law enforcement decision makers about complex criminality, criminal enterprises, criminal extremists, and terrorists. (p. 7)

Carter (2004) advised that intelligence analysis should focus on four important questions:

1. Who poses threats?
2. What are the relationships among possible actors?
3. What is the modus operandi of the threat?
4. What is needed to catch the offenders and prevent the incident?

These questions guide investigations and the intelligence process. It is a process that results in the identification of suspects and their collaborators, information about how they commit their crimes, and evidence required to make an arrest or prevent a crime or terrorist event. It is critical to homeland security. Although federal agencies such as the FBI are investigating conspiracies, local authorities must be attentive to suspicious activities in their communities, and intelligence-led policing best serves this purpose. The FBI and other federal agencies perform top-down investigations, whereas local authorities conduct bottom-up investigations.

Intelligence is a process; it is not merely the accumulation of information and data. Information is collected from a variety of sources and used to produce useful reports. Essentially, the intelligence process consists of four steps:

1. Collecting information from a variety of sources.
2. Collating and analyzing the information. That is, it must be organized in a usable format and then analyzed in an effort to garner intelligence or intelligence-related information.
3. Disseminating the information. It is not enough to develop intelligence information; it must also be provided to those who can use it to defeat a terrorist attack or develop policies.
4. Using intelligence and other information. In some cases, agencies may be provided intelligence information, but fail to use it. In the end, intelligence must be integrated into strategic and tactical operations. The use of intelligence into strategic and tactical operations is why it is collected in the first place.

Intelligence-led policing implies that it be more data driven. Although law enforcement has always been involved in crime prevention, the prevention of terrorist acts is much more critical. Not preventing a burglary is one thing, whereas failure to prevent a WMD attack is another matter altogether. This essentially means that the law enforcement community, at all levels, must be involved in gathering intelligence and using that intelligence to prevent terrorist acts.

Sources of Intelligence Raw Data

It is important to remember that intelligence information can come from a variety of sources. In some cases, a substantial amount of intelligence can be obtained from official agencies such as other law enforcement agencies. For example, the FBI and the Department of Homeland Security maintain terrorist watch lists. A great deal of information can come from a variety of the sources, including

- Travel agents
- Department of Motor Vehicle records
- Property ownership records

- Financial records, including withdrawals and deposits, especially the source of deposits
- Credit card information in terms of what is being purchased and name and address of card holders
- Known associates
- Travel patterns—locally, regionally, and internationally
- Telephone and cell phone records
- Daily or routine activities
- Wiretaps

These activities or sources of information can produce large amounts of raw data. The intelligence officer attempts to collate the information, looking for suspicious patterns that might indicate that an individual is involved in terrorist or suspicious activity. *Link analysis* is one of the most useful methods of analyzing raw intelligence. Basically, a flow chart is constructed showing everyone that a suspect has contact with, and those individuals' contacts are also shown on the flow chart. In some cases, it shows that a suspect is in contact with other people who have relationships with still other suspicious individuals. There may be several degrees of separation, but ultimately the link analysis can identify a number of people who have relationships or who may be involved in a criminal or terrorist conspiracy. Link analysis, more or less, connects the dots and often can provide a wealth of investigative leads.

The old adage "follow the money" has driven a number of criminal investigations, especially those involving organized crime and drug trafficking. The adage is also true for terrorism. In some cases, terrorist or associates of terrorists are engaged in activities to raise money to finance terrorist plots. As discussed in Chapter 11, it is important to stop terrorist-financed operations; in some cases, the investigation of terrorist finances leads to information about terrorist plots and activities. It is just as important from an intelligence perspective to focus on ancillary activities as actual terrorist plots and activities.

There are important rules to follow in the intelligence process. First, it is important to ensure that security is maintained. Obviously, terrorists or those supporting terrorist activities want to know if they have come to the attention of authorities, and they likely will take efforts to discover if they have been identified. If they believe that they have been compromised, they very likely will alter their activities, thus negatively affecting the ongoing investigations. Along these lines, the media is constantly attempting to collect news information about continuing police investigations. There are those who would reveal information if given the opportunity, regardless of intentions or motivation. Intelligence information should be maintained on secure servers, and strict security should be maintained on any electronic or paper reports that are generated.

Second, one must consider intelligence information for what it is. In many cases, it is unconfirmed information. There may be instances when intelligence information will prove to be reliable; in other cases, it may not. In still other cases, the intelligence may point to a possible crime when indeed no crime has been, or is about to be, committed. The point is that the police should not base accusations on unconfirmed intelligence information. Before proceeding with charges or invoking criminal justice procedures, the police must establish probable cause. Without meeting this legal standard, the police may accuse an innocent person or reveal an investigation to a suspect before enough evidence has been gathered.

Third, intelligence units often collect any information possible. The homeland security unit commander should enumerate the kinds of intelligence information needed. Too often, these units collect everything, which equates to little more than nothing. Priorities must be established. Priorities should be based on leads and other information that point to an individual, activity, or location. This is not to say that other information should not be collected, but that there must be priorities and intelligence officers and analysts should pursue these priorities.

HS Web Link: To learn more about police intelligence operations, go to http://www.it.ojp.gov/documents/LEIU_audit_checklist.pdf.

Intelligence Products

Once intelligence is collected, it must be disseminated to those who can use the intelligence to thwart a crime or terrorist activity. Such reports generally are written for a specific audience—patrol officers, detectives, private security personnel, or the general public. They should be written using the terminology that is commonly used by the group in clear language. If the information is to be useful, it must be understandable. The information should include a time line. That is, when is the event supposed to occur? In order to react, responders must have concrete information. Finally, there should be some follow-up. Intelligence officers or other management personnel should investigate what actions occurred as a result of the intelligence and its dissemination.

Three different products may be needed or used by intelligence officers:

1. Reports that aid in the investigation and apprehension of offenders or terrorists
2. Reports that provide threat advisories in order to harden targets
3. Strategic analysis reports to aid in planning and resource allocation

Crime analysis and intelligence units must have products that are distributed on a regular basis. Regular distribution of products ensures a steady flow of information to operational units, and it assists in maintaining contact with the operational units. In addition to the regular products, these units will produce special reports addressing specific individuals, geographical locations, and crime problems.

Tactical and Strategic Intelligence

Intelligence should be used at all levels of the police organization. **Tactical intelligence** is intelligence that is used to guide police operations. That is, if the intelligence unit acquires information about a specific crime or event, then that information will be used to guide officers or detectives to either intercede in the event or apprehend the perpetrators. The use of tactical intelligence is a central part of police problem solving, whereby officers attempt to predict criminal occurrences or patterns and respond to them. McGarrell and his colleagues (2007) and Smith and his colleagues (2006) advised that diligent police investigation and intelligence collection can uncover and prevent terrorist plots. Thus, intelligence can lead to tactical successes.

A relatively new form of tactical intelligence for police agencies is cell-tracking technology. Gillum (2014) reported that police departments across the country are using Stingray, a suitcase-size devise that pretends to be a cell tower. It intercepts phone calls and text messages and tricks cellphones into disclosing location and information to the device. The police see it as a useful way to track criminals and potential terrorists.

Strategic intelligence, on the other hand, is used by police managers. **Strategic intelligence** often provides a "big picture." It provides information on how resources should be allocated. It is important when a problem or series of problems occur that there are enough police resources to counter the problems. Strategic intelligence entails examining all potential problems related to crime and potential terrorism and ensuring that resources match the problems. Strategic intelligence is used to determine the number of patrol officers and detectives needed across time. It is also informative about whether the department needs specialized units—is there an adequate workload to justify the unit?

▶ Fusion Centers

The FBI has developed cooperative relationships with state and local agencies across the country by establishing fusion centers. These centers act as multi-agency task forces that gather and analyze intelligence information. The benefit of fusion centers is that they generally are under the direction of the FBI, and the FBI can help ensure that the center's operations are safeguarded and can operate within legal restrictions.

Fusion centers are a new innovation in intelligence collection. The **fusion center** is designed to facilitate the sharing and flow of information. The Department of Justice and the Department of Homeland Security (DOJ/DHS) (undated) note that fusion centers are part of a "process [that] supports the implementation of risk-based, information-driven prevention, response, and consequences management programs" (p. 2). Essentially, they are an overarching network of public and private entities that are engaged in planning and implementing homeland security programming.

HS Web Link: To learn more about fusion centers, go to http://www.it.ojp.gov/default.aspx?area=nationalInitiatives&page=1181.

The fusion center provides coordination of all response and counterterrorism elements within a community or metropolitan area. As information or intelligence gathered by local and federal agencies is fed into the fusion center, it is analyzed using the intelligence management model discussed earlier. The fusion center is a comprehensive approach in that it allows for the analysis of information from a variety of sources. It is the most comprehensive manner by which to collect and analyze data for a particular geographical area. Once analyzed, terrorist threat or activity information is generated and supplied to affected constituents. The fusion center also allows for more comprehensive planning and a better coordinated response should a terrorist event occur.

Of critical importance is that the centers include a variety of police, public safety, government, and infrastructure representation. A fusion center can have members from a variety of public and private sectors, and a fusion center's constituency generally is based primarily on the public and private institutions that comprise a jurisdiction or metropolitan area. To this end, the DOJ/DHS (undated: 3) has identified the possible participants in a fusion center:

- Agriculture, food, water, and the environment
- Banking and finance
- Chemical industry and hazardous materials
- Criminal justice
- Education
- Emergency services
- Energy
- Government
- Health and public safety
- Hospitality and lodging
- Information and telecommunications
- Military facilities and defense industrial base
- Postal and shipping
- Private security
- Public works
- Real estate
- Social services
- Transportation

The goal is to include all the parties that may have information about a terrorist attack and to gain information from all the sources by which to develop strategies and response plans. For example, fusion centers generally include medical and fire department personnel as well as law enforcement personnel. The medical personnel can provide the fusion center with information about suspicious diseases or illnesses—an early warning system for a biological attack—and firefighter personnel can provide information about suspicious fires or chemical problems.

A number of fusion centers have been constituted. Some are confined to a single city or metropolitan area; some are regional or provide services to a state. Cities and counties have partnered with the FBI to form terrorism early warning groups or fusion centers (Sullivan, 2006). In some cases, they are part of a Joint Terrorism Task Force, which is operated by the FBI. It is critical that the FBI be involved in the fusion center or have some formal relationship with law enforcement personnel, since one of its primary responsibilities is to collect terrorist intelligence and investigate terrorist activities.

▶ Police Tactical Considerations

Previous sections in this chapter addressed some of the administrative and strategic considerations when attempting to implement an effective local homeland security program. A number of tactical considerations should also be mentioned. They focus on responding to a terrorist attack and officer safety. Since police officers are on the front line, they could become terrorists' targets. Even if they are not the primary targets, they often become victims while responding to terrorist attacks. Indeed, a number of police officers and firefighters lost their lives in the 9/11 attack on the World Trade Center. The threat of terrorism brings new dangers to police officers and firefighters.

Over the past several years, a new trend has developed in terrorism worldwide: a transition from numerous low-level incidents to more destructive attacks. Today, terrorists think in terms of attacks that receive worldwide attention. They seek to show their followers that they can inflict significant harm on their enemies. Their goals are simple: produce mass casualties, attract intense media coverage, cause social unrest, and inflict economic and political harm.

Police officers confronting terrorists in the United States now find themselves vulnerable in six types of situations (Garrett, 2002):

1. ***Traffic stops:*** Law enforcement lacks prior knowledge of the individual being stopped; the officer may be isolated and the potential terrorist may be in a heightened state of suspicion or anger as a result of the stop.
2. ***Residence visits:*** Officers are on the extremists' home turf, putting them at a disadvantage; the visit may be routine, but the extremist may not view it as such, and the home may be armed and fortified.

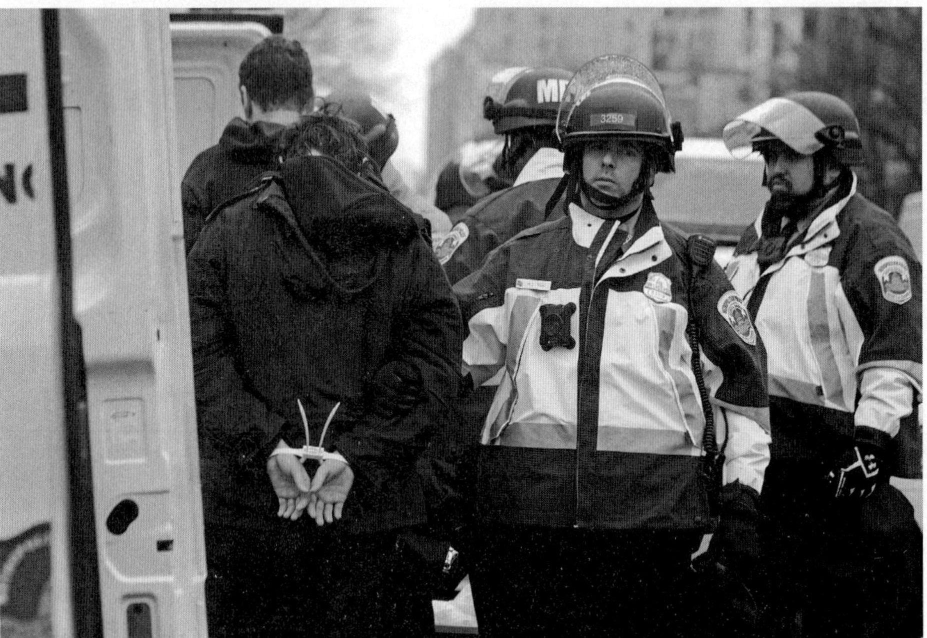

Washington Metropolitan police officers arrest protesters at an anti-Trump rally.
B Christopher/Alamy Stock Photo.

3. ***Rallies/marches:*** The risk to police usually comes not from the group holding the event, but from protestors, often anarchists who hate the police and believe that the best way to confront the demonstrators is through physical violence.
4. ***Confrontations/standoffs:*** All such incidents can arise from the three previous situations.
5. ***Revenge and retaliation:*** A terrorist may be motivated by personal benefit or revenge, such as one who attempts to blow up an Internal Revenue Service office because he or she was audited.
6. ***Incident responses:*** These can take many forms, ranging from activities of terrorists to acts of nature.

Police departments must ensure that responses to these threats are incorporated into training. Officers must understand and be able to respond safely to any threat. Since terrorist attacks are very infrequent and have occurred in only a few American cities, most police officers likely are complacent.

Immediate Police Response to an Act of Terrorism

As noted, a number of weapons can be used in a terrorist attack, and the police must be prepared for all of them. The police must coordinate their response with that of other first responders such as fire, emergency medical, hospitals, and disaster agencies at the local, state, and federal levels. Obviously, the type of attack will influence the response. For example, a biological attack will necessitate a response that is different from a conventional explosives attack. Nonetheless, there are some guidelines that should be followed. Figure 14-1 ■ provides the general guidelines that law enforcement should follow when responding to a terrorist attack.

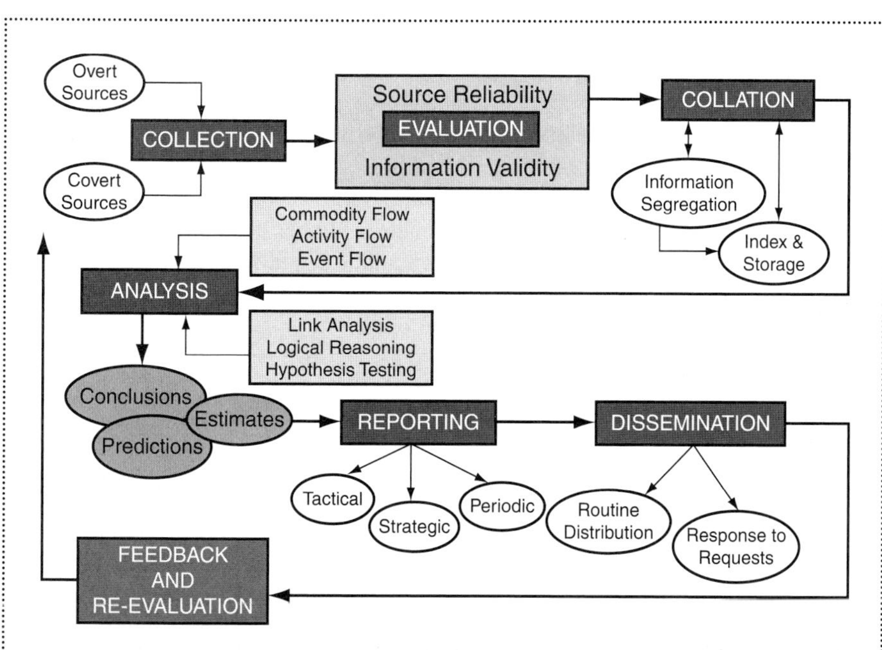

FIGURE 14-1 The Intelligence Process

Source: Carter, D. (2004). *Law Enforcement Intelligence: A Guide for State, Local, and Tribal Law Enforcement Agencies.* Washington, D.C.: Office of Community Oriented Policing Services.

Officer with a bomb-sniffing dog patrols Union Station in Washington, D.C.
Xinhua/Alamy Stock Photo.

► New York City: A Case Study in Local Homeland Security

A terrorist event in the United States is likely to take place in a major city such as New York, Chicago, Los Angeles, or San Francisco. The 9/11 attacks that occurred in New York City raised that city's awareness. City and police officials are acutely aware that their city remains a high-priority potential target for terrorists, with numerous potential targets, including Wall Street; city, state, and federal buildings; sporting events; high-density housing; a mass transit system that carries more than 6.5 million passengers daily; and petrochemical facilities. Consequently, the city has made a number of changes to prevent future attacks or to enable it to respond should a future attack occur. It is illustrative to examine some of the actions New York City has taken, especially considering that the city likely has instituted more safeguards as compared to other cities.

First and perhaps foremost, the New York Police Department (NYPD) has reorganized to include several homeland security elements within the department. The department has more than 37,000 police officers with approximately 1,000 assigned to terrorist duties. One of the tactics used by these officers is the "surge." Essentially, each day about 200 officers are sent to a specific location, usually a potential terrorist target. They surge in the area as a show of strength and deterrence. Officers observe and investigate suspicious persons and activities. Along these same lines, the department has increased the number of bomb-sniffing canines and routinely deploys them throughout the city. The canines serve as a deterrent as well as could possibly locate explosive materials.

The city is proactively using counterterrorism tactics in its mass transit system. Each week, NYPD officers conduct more than 300 explosive-screening deployments. Here, officers physically check bags, briefcases, and other containers or conduct external swabs of containers that could hold explosives. NYPD transit bureau supervisors are provided with radiation sensors and random radiological screening occurs on facilities. Various mass transit facilities are inspected daily to ensure that all alarms and access control systems are operational. Canine units are often used to detect explosives in mass transit facilities (Fralkenrath, 2007). Essentially, the department has substantially increased its efforts to deter attacks and to detect potential attackers. Deterring attacks and detecting potential attackers is important, since some terrorist attacks involved mass transit.

The NYPD is actively involved in gathering intelligence about terrorists and terrorist operations. The department created a counterterrorism bureau that has analysts and detectives examine terrorist organizations, potential terrorists, and bomb-making technology. The department has dispatched officers to a number of foreign countries to work with counterterrorism personnel in those countries. For example, when the Madrid bombing occurred, the NYPD officer in Israel was immediately dispatched to Madrid, who collected intelligence information and forwarded it to the counterterrorism bureau. The information collected overseas may likely be helpful in detecting and preventing attacks in New York City. The NYPD Counterterrorism Bureau cooperates with federal agencies but is not dependent on them.

The responsibilities of the counterterrorism division have wide-ranging responsibilities. For instance, the unit is responsible for designing and implementing large-scale counterterrorism projects, including the Lower Manhattan Security Initiative and Project Sentinel, which encircle Manhattan with thousands of security cameras. Essentially, security cameras are being installed throughout portions of the City. Eventually, there will be about 3,000 cameras with approximately 2,000 owned by private businesses. The London Metropolitan Police Department used similar cameras to identify suspects after the subway bombings in 2005. New York City is also considering movable roadblocks that can be activated remotely should a terrorist or other crime problem occur. In the future, the NYPD may install facial recognition programming to enhance the identification of suspected terrorists or criminals. The city is also installing radiation detection devices around its ports of entry to screen cargo for nuclear materials.

The counterterrorism division also develops and implements training for patrol officers, other law enforcement agencies, and private security companies. One of the greatest concerns in New York City or any city is the protection of critical infrastructures, including electricity, water, and public transportation. The Threat Reduction Infrastructure Protection Section (TRIPS) identifies critical infrastructures and develops strategies on how to protect them against terrorist attacks. Another great threat to people arises from biological, chemical, and nuclear weapons that may be used by terrorists. The NYPD has established a Chemical, Biological, Radiological, Nuclear, and Explosives (CBRNE) Section that researches and tests emerging technologies used to detect and combat chemical, biological, and nuclear explosives. Imagine, the Boston Marathon bomber would have detonated a dirty bomb. The damage would have been much greater, possibly making the city of Boston and surrounding areas uninhabitable. The NYPD also has a special unit, the Maritime Team, protecting the harbor with the help of the Tactical Radiological Acquisition Characterization System (TRACS). TRACS scans for background radiation in the port of New York/New Jersey. Finally, the NYPD SHIELD Unit coordinates the relationship between the departments and private security agencies (NYPD, 2017).

HS ANALYSIS BOX 14-5

A number of civil rights groups have been critical of New York City and other cities because they believe that cameras are a violation of privacy. Further, they believe that the purported benefits do not outweigh the disadvantages. They question if the camera will provide useable information. Should cities install camera systems to observe what is occurring on the streets? How effective are such camera systems in your estimation?

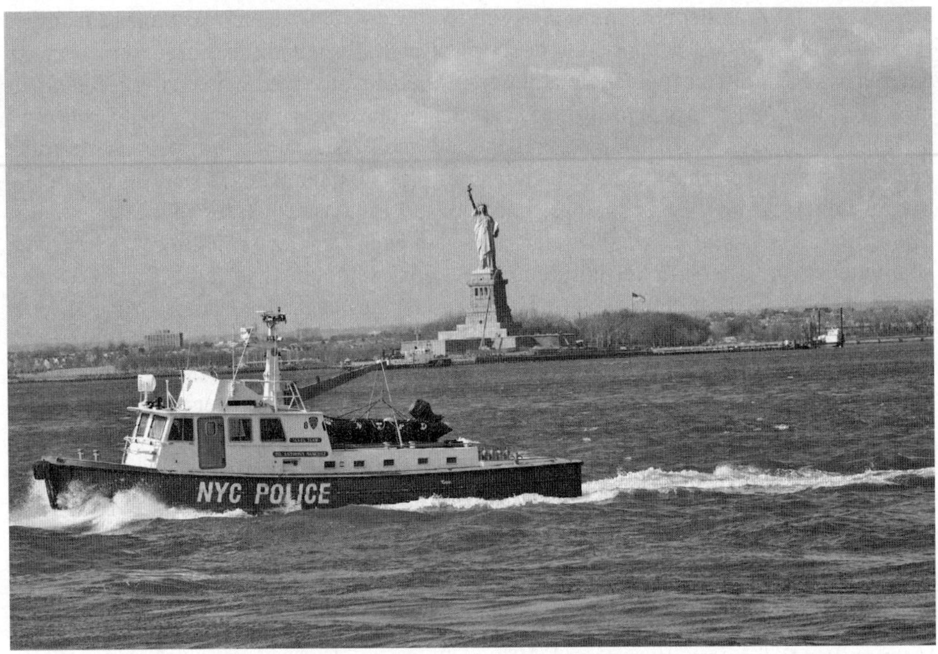

Since 9/11 NYPD has enhanced the department's surveillance on a number of fronts.
Len Holsborg/Alamy Stock Photo.

New York is ahead of other major cities in the United States, in terms of homeland security. It has essentially overtaken the Department of Homeland Security in setting up counterterrorism measures. City officials see New York City as a possible target and are attempting to prevent terrorist attacks. This move has resulted in a different NYPD. Counterterrorism is now one of its primary objectives. It is likely that other major cities will follow New York's lead. Most major cities are creating homeland security units but few are as advanced as New York City.

Summary

This chapter examined the role of the local police in homeland security. First response to terrorist attacks was addressed in Chapter 13. As noted, homeland security creates new demands on the police. The police must often balance aggressive police tactics when implementing homeland security tactics with maintaining positive community relations. Community policing is not antagonistic to homeland security. Community policing helps build police–community relationships that can result in the provision of intelligence about possible terrorists and their activities.

In order to effectuate homeland security, the police must involve the community. Involvement of the community is accomplished through education programs. The police must provide accurate and useful education. The intent of these programs is not to generate fear but to provide the public with the tools and understanding by which to assist the police. The public can provide valuable assistance to the police when they identify individuals who may be conducting surveillance on a possible target. Obtaining assistance from the public means that the police must educate citizens on observation methods and how to distinguish suspicious activities.

Police departments must be organized in such a fashion that the homeland security function is conducted properly. Effective organization generally means establishing a specialized unit within the department or having someone in charge of homeland security operations. Homeland security personnel must have effective working relationships with other units since officers assigned to other units can provide valuable intelligence information. Policies should enumerate the unit's responsibilities and authority. These policies should address all aspects of homeland security, thus ensuring that all important functions are conducted.

Intelligence will play an important role in localized homeland security. Localized homeland security means that the homeland security personnel should be collecting, collating, analyzing, and disseminating intelligence to officers in the department. This function is not foreign to police departments. Many departments have intelligence and crime analysis units that collect information about organized crime, gangs, and drug trafficking. Terrorism intelligence should be integrated into this process. Many departments now are joining the FBI and other regional agencies to form fusion centers. These fusion centers operate as regional terrorism intelligence centers. They provide an interface among federal agencies, local law enforcement, and other first responder agencies. This holistic approach results in superior coordination in intelligence and response operations.

Discussion Questions

1. Discuss how community policing can help arrest potential terrorists.
2. Explain the importance of educating citizens about police efforts to find potential terrorists.
3. Discuss how terrorism has affected police organization and policing.
4. Discuss what intelligence-led policing means and how it is used to prevent terrorist attacks.

References

Brown, B. (2007). "Community policing in post-September 11 America: A comment on the concept of community-oriented counterterrorism." *Police Practice and Research*, 8(3): 239–251.

Bumphus, V., L. Gaines, and C. Blakely. (1999). "Citizen police academies: Observing goals, objectives, and recent trends." *American Journal of Criminal Justice*, 24(1): 67–80.

Carter, D. (2004). *Law Enforcement Intelligence: A Guide for State, Local, and Tribal Law Enforcement Agencies.* Washington, D.C.: Office of Community Oriented Policing Services.

Carter, D. L., and J. G. Carter. (2009). "The intelligence fusion process for state, local and tribal law enforcement." *Criminal Justice and Behavior*, 3612: 1323–1339.

Carter, J. G., and S. W. Phillips. (2013). "Intelligence-led policing and forces of organizational change in the United States." *Policing & Society*. https://scholarworks.iupui.edu/bitstream/handle/1805/4003/Carter_2013_Intelligence-Led.pdf?sequence=1&isAllowed=n (Accessed May 30, 2017).

CBS. (2016). *FBI Setting Up Shared Responsibility Communities in New Jersey to Stop Home-Grown Terrorism.* http://newyork.cbslocal.com/2016/05/01/fbi-new-jersey-terrorism/ (Accessed May 5, 2016).

Chappell, A. T., and Gibson, S. A. (2009). Community policing and homeland security policing. Friend or Foe? *Criminal Justice Policy Review*, 20(3), 326–343.

DeLone, G. (2007). "Law enforcement mission statements post September 11." *Police Quarterly*, 10(2): 218–235.

Department of Justice/Department of Homeland Security. (undated). *Fusion Center Guidelines: Developing and Sharing Information and Intelligence in a New Era.* Washington, D.C.: Bureau of Justice Assistance.

Donahue, A., and R. Tuohy. (2206). "Lessons we don't learn: A study of the lessons of disaster, why we repeat them, and how we can learn from them." *Homeland Security Affairs*, 2(2): 1–28.

Fisher, S. (2016). "The fight against terrorism – The need for local police units in the United States' intelligence community." *Journal of Military and Strategic Studies*, 17: 189–208.

Gaines, L. (2006). "An analysis of traffic stop data in Riverside, California." *Police Quarterly*, 9: 210–233.

Gaines, L., and J. Worrall. (2011). *Police Administration*. Belmont, CA: Delmar.

Gaines, L. K., and V. Kappeler. (2008). *Policing in America* (6th ed.). Cincinnati, OH: Lexis-Nexis.

Garrett, K. (2002). "Terrorism on the homefront." *Law Enforcement Technology* (July): 22–26.

Gillum, J. (2014). "Police keep quiet about cell-tracking technology." *ABC News*. http://abcnews.go.com/Technology/wireStory/police-quiet-cell-tracking-technology-23016515 (Accessed March 27, 2014).

Green, G. (1981). *Introduction to Security*. Stoneham, MA: Butterworth.

Haynes, R., and Giblin, M. (2014). "Homeland security risk and preparedness in police agencies: The insignificance of actual risk factors. *Police Quarterly*, 17(1): 30–53.

Henderson, N., C. Ortiz, N. Sugie, and J. Miller. (2008). "Policing Arab-American communities after September 11." *Research for Practice*. Washington, D.C.: National Institute of Justice.

Hollywood, J., K. Strom, and M. Pope. (2008). *Developing and Testing a Method for Using 911 Calls for Identifying Potential Pre-Planning Terrorist Surveillance Activities*. Washington, D.C.: National Institute of Justice.

IACP. (2002). Criminal intelligence sharing: A national plan for intelligence-led policing at the local, state, and federal levels. Office of Community Oriented Policing. https://ric-zai-inc.com/Publications/cops-w0418-pub.pdf.

Kappeler, V., and L. Gaines. (2015. *Community Policing: A Contemporary Perspective* (5th ed.). Cincinnati, OH: LexisNexis.

Kleiman, M. (2004). *Illicit Drugs and the Terrorist Threat: Causal Links and Implications for Domestic Drug Control Policy.* Washington, D.C.: Congressional Research Service.

Levin, B. (2016). *Special Status Report: Hate Crime in the United States, 20 States Compilation.* San Bernardino, CA: Center for the Study of Hate and Extremism.

Lyon, W. (2002). "Partnerships, information, and public safety." *Policing*, 25: 530–543.

Marks, D., and I. Sun. (2007). "Organizational development among state and local law enforcement agencies." *Journal of Contemporary Criminal Justice*, 23(2): 159–173.

McCaffrey, B., and J. Basso. (2003). "Narcotics, terrorism, and international crime: The convergence phenomenon." *Terrorism and Counterterrorism: Understanding the New Security Environment*, ed. R. Howard and R. Sawyer, pp. 206–221. Guilford, CT: Dushkin.

McGarrell, E., J. Freilich, and S. Chermak. (2007). "Intelligence-led policing as a framework for responding to terrorism." *Journal of Contemporary Criminal Justice,* 23(2): 142–158.

McNamara, R., and R. Burns. (2009). *Multiculturalism in the Criminal Justice System.* New York: McGraw-Hill.

Mohamed, B. (2016). "A new estimate of the U.S. Muslim population." *Pew Research Center.* http://www.pewresearch.org/fact-tank/2016/01/06/a-new-estimate-of-the-u-s-muslim-population/ (Accessed September 27, 2017).

Morabito, A., and S. Greenberg. (2005). *Engaging the Private Sector to Promote Homeland Security: Law Enforcement–Private Security Partnerships.* Washington, D.C.: Bureau of Justice Assistance.

Morreale, S. A., and Lambert, D. E. (2009). Homeland security and the police mission. *Journal of Homeland Security and Emergency Management*, 6(1), 1-19.

Murray, J. (2005). "Policing terrorism: A threat to community policing or just a shift in priorities?" *Police Practice and Research*, 6(4): 347–361.

New York City Police Department. (2017). *Counterterrorism.* http://www1.nyc.gov/site/nypd/bureaus/investigative/counterterrorism.page (Accessed May 31, 2017).

Ohlhausen Research Inc. (2004). *Private Security/Public Policing: Vital Issues and Policy Recommendations.* Alexandria, VA: IACP.

Oliver, W. M. (2007). The fourth era of policing: Homeland security. *International Review of Law, Computers, & Technology*, 20, 1–2, 49–62. .

Ortiz, W., Hendricks, N.J., and Sugie, N.F. (2007). "Policing terrorism: The response of local police agencies to homeland security concerns." *Criminal Justice Studies*, 20(2): 91–109.

Pelfrey, W. (2007). "Local law enforcement terrorism prevention efforts: A state level case study." *Journal of Criminal Justice*, 35: 313–321.

Schaible, L. M., and J. Sheffer. (2012). "Intelligence-led policing and change in state law enforcement agencies." *Policing: An International Journal of Police Strategies and Management*, 354: 761–784.

Smith, B. (2008). *A Look at Terrorist Behavior: How They Prepare and How They Attack.* National Institute of Justice. http://www.ojp.usdoj.gov/nij/journals/260/terrorist-behavior.htm (Accessed August 24, 2010).

Smith, B., K. Damphousse, and P. Roberts. (2006). *Pre-Incident Indicators of Terrorist Incidents: The Identification of Behavioral, Geographic, and Temporal Patterns of Preparatory Conduct.* Washington, D.C.: National Institute of Justice.

Sullivan, J. (2006). "Terrorism early warning groups: Regional intelligence to combat terrorism." *Homeland Security and Terrorism*, ed. R. Howard, J. Forest, and J. Moore, pp. 235–245. New York: McGraw-Hill.

Thatcher, D. (2005). "The local role in homeland security." *Law & Society Review*, 39(3): 635–676.

Yaccino, S., M. Schwirtz, and M. Santora (2012). "Gunman kills 6 at a Sikh temple near Milwaukee." *New York Times.* http://www.nytimes.com/2012/08/06/us/shooting-reported-at-temple-in-wisconsin.html (Accessed September 27, 2017).

Index